Movies and Mental Illness

Dedication

For Lester R. Bryant, MD, ScD
Mentor, model, scholar, friend.
DW

For the outstanding mental health nursing staff at the St. Louis VAMC
MAB

For my humble Sister, valorous Brother, grateful Mother, and fair-minded Father.
RMN

About the authors

Danny Wedding, PhD, MPH, directs the Missouri Institute of Mental Health, a policy, research, and training center associated with the University of Missouri-Columbia School of Medicine. He is the editor of *PsycCRITIQUES: Contemporary Psychology – APA Review of Books*, the series editor for *Advances in Psychotherapy: Evidence-Based Practice*, and 2009 President of the APA Division of Media Psychology.

Mary Ann Boyd, PhD, DNS, PMHCNS-BC, is Professor Emeritus at Southern Illinois University Edwardsville and Director of Mental Health Consultants, LLC. She serves on the Editorial Board for *Archives in Psychiatric Nursing* and is an internationally recognized expert in the care of persons with schizophrenia and dementia.

Ryan M. Niemiec, PsyD, is a licensed psychologist in Cincinnati. He is Education Director of VIA Institute on Character, a certified coach with Hummingbird Coaching Services, and a frequent lecturer and workshop leader. He is co-author of *Positive Psychology at the Movies: Using Films to Build Virtues and Character Strengths,* and a number of articles and book chapters. He is film editor of *PsycCRITIQUES* and received a specialization in film studies from Michigan State University.

Movies and Mental Illness

Using Films to Understand Psychopathology

3rd revised edition

Danny Wedding
Missouri Institute of Mental Health
School of Medicine
University of Missouri-Columbia, Saint Louis, MO

Mary Ann Boyd
School of Nursing
Southern Illinois University Edwardsville, IL

Ryan M. Niemiec
VIA Institute on Character, and
Hummingbird Coaching Services
Cincinnati, OH

HOGREFE

Library of Congress Cataloguing-in-Publication Data
is available via the Library of CongressMarc Database
under the LC Control Number 2009932963

National Library of Canada Cataloguing in Publication
Wedding, Danny
    Movies and mental illness : using films to understand
psychopathology / Danny Wedding, Mary Ann Boyd, Ryan M.
Niemiec. -- 3rd rev. ed.

Includes bibliographical references and index.
ISBN 978-0-88937-371-6

    1. Psychology, Pathological--Study and teaching--Audio-
visual aids. 2. Mental illness in motion pictures. I. Boyd, Mary Ann
II. Niemiec, Ryan M III. Title.

RC459.W43 2009   616.89   C2009-904539-7

PUBLISHING OFFICES
USA: Hogrefe Publishing, 875 Massachusetts Avenue, 7th Floor, Cambridge, MA 02139
               Phone (866) 823-4726, Fax (617) 354-6875; E-mail info@hogrefe.com
EUROPE: Hogrefe Publishing, Rohnsweg 25, 37085 Göttingen, Germany
               Phone +49 551 49609-0, Fax +49 551 49609-88, E-mail publishing@hogrefe.com

SALES & DISTRIBUTION
USA: Hogrefe Publishing, Customer Services Department,
               30 Amberwood Parkway, Ashland, OH 44805
               Phone (800) 228-3749, Fax (419) 281-6883, E-mail custserv@hogrefe.com
EUROPE: Hogrefe Publishing, Rohnsweg 25, 37085 Göttingen, Germany
               Phone +49 551 49609-0, Fax +49 551 49609-88, E-mail publishing@hogrefe.com

OTHER OFFICES
CANADA: Hogrefe Publishing, 660 Eglinton Ave. East, Suite 119-514, Toronto, Ontario M4G 2K2
SWITZERLAND: Hogrefe Publishing, Länggass-Strasse 76, CH-3000 Bern 99

Hogrefe Publishing
Incorporated and registered in the Commonwealth of Massachusetts, USA, and in Göttingen, Lower Saxony,
Germany

Printed and bound in the USA
ISBN 978-0-88937-371-6

Foreword to the Third Edition

You know a book is valuable when it enters multiple editions in tumultuous economic times. Such is certainly the case for *Movies and Mental Illness,* now entering its third edition as a classic resource and an authoritative guide.

Movies play a powerful and pervasive role in our culture and, increasingly, in our classrooms. Psychologist Ken Gergen (*The Saturated Self,* 1991, pp. 56–57) opined that movies have become one of the most influential rhetorical devices in the world: "Films can catapult us rapidly and effectively into states of fear, anger, sadness, romance, lust, and aesthetic ecstasy – often within the same two-hour period. It is undoubtedly true that for many people film relationships provide the most emotionally wrenching experiences of the average week."

If a picture is worth a thousand words, then a movie is worth tens of thousands of words in even the most engaging of textbooks. My students – all students – clamor for immediate, personal, and riveting examples of mental disorders and their treatment.

Movies can easily be integrated into education to illustrate psychopathology, but can also be used for clinical purposes. The use of films for treatment can be traced back to the 1930s, but more professionals are recommending or prescribing specific films. Whether it's called cinematherapy, movie treatment, or reel therapy, the goal is to enhance health and happiness.

Many of the movies featured in these pages portray healing stories. The best of them typically increase awareness about a disorder or treatment; *As Good as It Gets* springs to mind for its accurate and humorous depiction of obsessive-compulsive disorder. The best movies also show flawed, yet effective role models struggling realistically with problems and ultimately triumphing; a case in point is the inspiring film *The Soloist* about living well with psychosis. Such films literally stir the soul as they generate hope and offer a fresh perspective on ourselves and our relationships.

Like the very movies it recommends, *Movies and Mental Illness* is a powerful medium for teaching students, engaging patients, and educating the public. Wedding, Boyd, and Niemiec have produced an invaluable guide for all those committed to understanding the human experience.

John C. Norcross, PhD
University of Scranton
Editor, *Journal of Clinical Psychology*
2009 President of the Society of Clinical
Psychology

Foreword to the Second Edition

John Milton, in *Paradise Lost*, tells us that we must "strike the visual nerve, for we have much to see." So, too, in this present work, do Wedding, Boyd, and Niemiec admonish us that there is much to learn by seeing with the mind's eye what these well-chosen films, by turns sad and silly, offer us in illuminating the psychopathologies set forth in the *Diagnostic and Statistical Manual* of the American Psychiatric Association.

Ranging from such classics as the depiction of alcoholism in *The Lost Weekend*, to relatively obscure films perhaps known only to the aficionado of foreign films, Wedding, Boyd, and Niemiec have achieved a work which may itself become a classic in this genre, particularly with respect to its intended purpose of teaching how the various psychopathologies might play themselves out in an approximation of real-life, real-world situations of which these films are a simulacrum.

Wedding, Boyd, and Niemiec provide a brief synopsis of the particular film in relation to the major category of psychopathology being covered in a chapter, and they relate the manifest and latent content of the film to the various diagnostic symptoms within a category, such as childhood disorders, and further provide an illustrative case study to assist in the process of generalizing from the film to actual diagnostic work.

As a didactic tool, the work by Wedding, Boyd, and Niemiec should have a salutary effect in engaging the attention of the student, as well as in engaging the affective response of the student to the vicarious identification with the film characters portrayed and, hopefully, enhancing the learning process of what otherwise tends to be a rather tedious pedagogical adventure for most students.

The authors provide a lively expository style, and the use of epigraphs for each chapter is a particularly happy device for setting a tone for each chapter and for capturing a pithy bit of dialogue that may cause the reader to engage in some cognitive restructuring, as when one of the characters says, "I recall every fall, every hook, every jab" in the chapter on the dementias, a quote which instantly evokes an image of the prizefighter with organic brain damage. Other such examples abound and contribute significantly to the teaching potential of the work.

On balance, this is a work that is likely to become a classic of its type and a particularly useful teaching tool for the diagnosis and understanding of the various psychopathologies for students of the helping professions. I commend it to the reader, be the reader student or professor.

Allan Barclay, PhD
St. Louis, Missouri

Table of Contents

Preface

> *"Mental health movies are often like going to the zoo. They can be wonderful but you go with the normal person surrogate and together you view the person with mental illness. You see the disease from the outside in, and it does a disservice to our ability to empathize and understand. If we saw the world the way the people who suffer see it, we would understand them differently. The hope being that if one person came home from the movie theater, just one, and saw somebody screaming at empty air on the street corner and related to them differently with understanding, then we would have done our job."*
> Akiva Goldsman, screenwriter of *A Beautiful Mind*, in the DVD's section titled "Development of a Screenplay"

We wrote *Movies and Mental Illness* because of our conviction that films are a powerful medium for teaching students (in psychology, social work, medicine, nursing, and counseling), engaging patients, and educating the public about the fascinating world of psychopathology. In addition, we wrote the book because we genuinely love watching and talking about movies. It is important to understand that while this book's title is *Movies and Mental Illness*, we also discuss serious problems that do not reflect mental illness per se, including mental retardation, physical or sexual abuse, and violence.

We have made numerous changes in this third edition. We have added hundreds of recent films to Appendix F, expanding this resource to well over 1,000 films that illustrate psychopathology. Although it is impossible to list every film depicting every disorder, we feel we have seen and critiqued the majority of important films that illustrate psychopathology. The reader will find a significant number of these new films discussed in relevant chapters. We have added a number of rarely depicted psychological disorders in films such as representations of shared psychotic disorder (*Folie a Deux*), compulsive hoarding, Asperger's disorder, trichotillomania, body dysmorphic disorder, factitious disorder by proxy, and seasonal affective disorder.

We've added a new appendix containing a sample course syllabus with film examples, and we've shifted many of the "headliner films" to offer new perspectives on the various disorders (e.g., reading the patient evaluation of Anton Chigurh from *No Country for Old Men* can help students better appreciate and understand the absence of remorse that characterizes antisocial personality disorder).

This new edition contains several other changes that we believe will enhance the book. Now there is a comprehensive index that will allow the reader to quickly identify those sections of the book that discuss particular films of interest. One way to approach *Movies and Mental Illness* is to simply start with Appendix F and a highlighter, identifying interesting films and then seeing what we have to say about them in the book.

We have also added a list of our ten favorite films in each category (Authors' Picks). The authors did not always agree about which films were most important for readers to see, but we negotiated and debated each list and eventually selected ten films that balanced artistic merit and pedagogical utility. This addition is in response to the frequent request for our recommendations for movies that are relevant to the training of psychologists, nurses, and other health professionals.

Finally, we have taken the audacious step of recommending a single book and a single article for "Future Exploration" at the end of each chapter. We envision that these additional readings will be used in honors courses or perhaps as supplemental readings to compensate for a missed class, exam or assignment. All students will benefit from taking time to read the recommended books and especially the key articles we identify.

We plan to maintain and expand our *Movies and Mental Illness* blog (*moviesandmentalillness. blogspot.com*); many of the films from Appendix F have been and will be discussed on this blog. We hope the blog continues to be a useful resource for students, teachers, lecturers, consumers, mental health professionals, and people simply interested in psychology and mental illness.

Due to numerous requests from readers, we have either expanded or added a section on international films to each chapter. Often these films are more powerful and accurate than anything the United States has produced. We hope this will entice readers to watch more foreign films; we have found this an especially interesting and rewarding way to learn about other cultures.

In discussing psychopathology, we occasionally reveal endings or surprise twists to films, and we realize this may spoil these films for some readers. We apologize in advance if this occurs.

The book was originally designed to supplement core texts in abnormal psychology; if the book is being used in this way, the relevant core chapters in the primary text should be read before reviewing the corresponding chapter in *Movies and Mental Illness*. (However, it is usually helpful to review the "Questions to Consider" section that introduces each chapter on psychopathology before seeing the recommended film.) We will occasionally present detailed and specific information about mental illness, but these facts are almost incidental to the discussion of the films themselves, and we have tried to avoid redundancy with the many fine textbooks that already explain psychopathology in considerable detail. We assume the reader will look up unfamiliar terms or discuss them in class, and we have not always defined each new term.

Each chapter is introduced with a fabricated case history and Mini-Mental State Examination. We have developed composite presentations linked as closely as possible to the character being portrayed in the film being discussed. In every case, the diagnoses we present reflect hypotheses, not facts; the case studies are designed to generate ideas, enliven discussion, and stimulate learning. Our diagnoses and character descriptions are always derived from our own judgment and clinical experience, and our fabricated evaluations are anchored in the events portrayed on screen, even when films are based on actual figures (e.g., the characters of John Nash in *A Beautiful Mind*, Ray Charles in *Ray*, and Teena Brandon in *Boys Don't Cry*).

Although educated and trained in different disciplines (Clinical Psychology, DW and RMN; Nursing, MAB), we are all clinicians and educators who have found that the judicious use of films dramatically increases students' and patients' understanding of abnormal behavior. For example, when lecturing about alcoholism, we might supplement our lectures with a "demonstration" of delirium tremens using *The Lost Weekend*. Before a lecture on bipolar disorder, we'll ask our students to watch *Michael Clayton* or *Mr. Jones*. All three films offer a richness and an intensity that simply cannot be captured by a classroom lecture or the printed page. Likewise, when working with a patient going through a divorce who becomes incensed over the

behavior of his or her spouse, we might recommend watching *Kramer vs. Kramer* or a more recent film, *The Squid and the Whale*. We have found that the discussion of relevant films offers a wonderful way to open clinically relevant areas that have not previously been explored.

We discuss a variety of films throughout the book; however, we usually use one or two films as primary illustrations of each disorder. These "headliner" films are movies we have watched repeatedly. In many cases, they are popular movies that students are likely to have already seen (e.g., *A Beautiful Mind*).

Usually the connection between the films being discussed and the chapter is immediate and direct, but we occasionally include obscure films when a small section relates in a meaningful way to the points made in the chapter. There are also some classic films such as *Psycho*, *A Clockwork Orange*, and *One Flew Over the Cuckoo's Nest* that have tremendous pedagogical value, and we take great pleasure in introducing a new generation of students to these movies. In addition, films such as *Pelle the Conqueror* are occasionally included, even when there is no direct connection to psychopathology, because the films are provocative and moving and are good illustrations of various psychological phenomena, even when they do not address psychopathology per se.

Films can be integrated into courses in abnormal psychology and psychopathology in a variety of ways. The particular approach selected will vary from course to course, depending on the needs of the instructor and the interests of students.

First, students can be asked to take responsibility for seeing many of these films on their own. Because we have selected popular films as the exemplars for each clinical chapter, students can easily rent them from any number of commercial sources. Costs are minimized if students choose to see the films in small groups. This promotes the intellectual camaraderie, discussion, and debate that characterize effective learning. We recommend that whenever possible students see the films before coming to class to discuss the corresponding topic.

Second, we have used films in classes that meet twice weekly. The first class meeting is devoted to seeing the film; the second is spent discussing the content of the related textbook chapter and determining whether or not the film accurately represents the disorder being discussed. It is ideal when such courses can be team taught by a mental health professional and a literature/drama professor. Danny used this approach in the abnormal psychology course he taught at Yonsei University in Seoul, Korea where he spent the 2008–2009 academic year as the Fulbright-Yonsei Distinguished Scholar.

Finally, most professors choose to use class time to show selected vignettes from pedagogically powerful films, and they encourage students to view the entire film and other related films on their own time. The goal with this approach is to augment lectures with relevant in-class discussion while minimizing the total amount of class time spent watching films. Using a film vignette that vividly depicts a psychiatric disorder circumvents the ethical issues (confidentiality, securing releases and permission, etc.) associated with using real cases and clients as illustrations in the classroom.

When films are used in the classroom, it may be necessary for the educational institution (or the professor teaching the class) to pay a fee for public usage. Most colleges and universities have audiovisual departments well equipped to handle such administrative details.

Many readers will disagree about the ratings we have assigned films included in Appendix F. However, it is important to remember that our ratings are based *primarily* on the utility of the film as a teaching tool and only secondarily on the film's artistic merit.

We are including our e-mail addresses below so we can get feedback about the book. We hope those readers who share our enthusiasm about movies as a teaching tool will recommend additional films that we can include in the next edition of *Movies and Mental Illness*.

Danny Wedding, PhD, MPH
danny.wedding@mimh.edu

Mary Ann Boyd, PhD, DNS, APRN, BC
mboyd@siue.edu

Ryan M. Niemiec, PsyD
ryan@viacharacter.org

Acknowledgments

We are constantly writing about and discussing movies, and there are numerous friends and colleagues to acknowledge. Many of our ideas and the selections of films to be included in *Movies and Mental Illness* over each edition grew out of discussions with these individuals, especially those who are mental health professionals interested in the fascinating ways in which psychopathology is portrayed in film.

Rob Dimbleby at Hogrefe Publishing is an extraordinary publisher, a true visionary, and a valued friend. We appreciate his enthusiasm for publishing an expanded and enhanced edition of this book.

Vicki Eichhorn worked almost daily with us over the months we devoted to preparation of the third edition of *Movies and Mental Illness*. She has worked with Danny for almost 18 years, and he appreciates her good work more than she will ever know.

Many people gave us specific feedback or suggestions relating to the psychopathology or movie portions of the book. We believe these have helped us make solid improvements throughout this particular edition. Thanks go to Arash Javenbakht, Sunil Kiran, Kris Copeland, Jeanne Richart, Ann Weber, and Todd Kashdan. Some of the suggestions came in the form of book reviews: We feel humbled by and grateful to Sherry Lynn Hatcher (*PsycCRITIQUES*), Roy C. Fitzgerald (*Journal of Clinical Psychiatry*), Yvonne Hall (*Bulletin of the Menninger Clinic*), and Lt. Col. N. K. Cooper (*Journal of the Royal Army Medical Corp*) for their enthusiastic reviews of the last edition.

Danny benefited from hundreds of discussions about films with colleagues in the American Psychological Association's Division of Media Psychology (Division 46). He especially appreciates the strong support and numerous helpful suggestions he received from Judy Kuriansky, Frank Farley, Lenore Walker, David Shapiro, Mary Gregerson, Helen Friedman, and Florence Kaslow.

Colleagues at the Missouri Institute of Mental Health (especially Joel Epstein and Kelly Gregory) and the American University of the Caribbean (especially Lockie Johnson, Kim Kirkland, and Hiroko Yoshida) also made dozens of important recommendations, as did Ken Freedland, Sara Serot, Todd Susman, Millard Susman, Ron Margolis, Maggie Ulione, Karl Wilson, Barbara Bennett, Ray Fowler, Tony Marsella, Bradley Daniels, Natalie Clapp, Carla Leeson, Sue Beachem, Joshua Wedding, and Jeremiah Wedding (whose decision to major in film studies was no doubt influenced by his father's habit of watching two or three movies each week).

Danny is the editor of *PsycCRITIQUES: Contemporary Psychology – APA Review of Books*, and Ryan is the Associate Editor for Films for this American Psychological Association publication. When Danny became editor, he reinstated the practice of reviewing psychologically relevant films in the journal, a practice first introduced by the journal's founding editor, E. G. Boring. Reading weekly film reviews written by psychologists has both sharpened and deepened our appreciation for the psychological relevance of films. Although the journal itself requires a subscription, interested readers can read and comment on selected film reviews at no cost by visiting *psyccritiquesblog. apa.org*.

Special thanks goes to Ryan's wife, Rachelle Plummer, who continues to support Ryan's compulsive need to watch movies; this often entails light-up pens in movie theaters, tolerating the ubiquitous laptop he keeps by his side while watching movies at home, and frequent interruptions from new alerts on recent movies on his i-Phone.

We want to thank Dr. Antonio Díez Herranz who translated *Movies and Mental Illness* into Spanish, and especially Professor Seung-hwa Beack, a world-class scholar from Myong-Ji University, who translated the first edition of our book into Korean.

We also appreciate the feedback from our colleagues, friends, family, and the many readers who have taken the time to share suggestions, opinions, and support for our work. We hope you will contribute to our blog at *moviesandmentalillness.blogspot.com* and let us know when you come across a great film that should be discussed in the next edition.

Chapter 1

Films and Psychopathology

Introduction

In all of human perceptual experience, nothing conveys information or evokes emotion quite as clearly as our visual sense. Filmmakers capture the richness of this visual sense, combine it with auditory stimuli, and create the ultimate waking dream experience: the movie. The viewer enters a trance, a state of absorption, concentration, and attention, engrossed by the story and the plight of the characters. When someone is watching a movie, an immediate bond is set up between the viewer and the film, and all the technical apparatus involved with the projection of the film becomes invisible as the images from the film pass into the viewer's consciousness. The viewer experiences a sort of dissociative state in which ordinary existence is temporarily suspended, serving as a "psychological clutch" (Butler & Palesh, 2004) in which the individual escapes from the stressors, conflicts, and worries of the day. This trance state is further enhanced in movie theaters where the viewer is fully enveloped in sight and sound, and in some instances experiences the sense of touch through vibration effects. No other art form pervades the consciousness of the individual to the same extent and with such power as cinema. Many consider movies to be the most influential form of mass communication (Cape, 2003).

Hollywood took the original invention of the cinematic camera and invented a new art form in which the viewer becomes enveloped in the work of art. The camera carries the viewer into each scene, and the viewer perceives events from the inside as if surrounded by the characters in the film. The actors do not have to describe their feelings, as in a play, because the viewer directly experiences what they see and feel.

In order to produce an emotional response to a film, the director carefully develops both plot and character through precise camera work. Editing creates a visual and acoustic **gestalt**, to which the viewer responds. The more effective the technique, the more involved the viewer. In effect, the director *constructs* the film's (and the viewer's) reality. The selection of locations, sets, actors, costumes, and lighting contributes to the film's organization and shot-by-shot **mise-en-scene** (the physical arrangement of the visual image).

The Pervasive Influence of Films

Film has become such an integral part of our culture that it seems to be the mirror in which we see ourselves reflected every day. Indeed, the social impact of film extends around the globe. The widespread popularity of online movies, DVDs by mail (e.g., Netflix), $1 Redbox rentals at the street corner, the use of unlimited rentals for a monthly fee (e.g., Blockbuster), and in-home, cable features like On-Demand make hundreds of thousands of movies available and accessible to virtually anyone in the world (and certainly anyone who has Internet access). No longer are individuals limited solely to the film selection and discretion of the corner video store. People now have wide access to films beyond Hollywood, including access to films from independent filmmakers, even those from developing countries. Moreover, with the affordability of digital video, neophyte and/or low-budget filmmakers can now tell their stories within the constraints of a much more reasonable budget without sacrificing quality (Taylor & Hsu, 2003);

this increases the range of topics and themes that can be covered. Award-winning films such as *Dancer in the Dark* (2000), *The Celebration* (1998), and *The Fast Runner* (2001) were all shot on digital video.

We believe films have a greater influence than any other art form. Their influence is felt across age, gender, nationality, culture, and even across time. Films have become a pervasive and omnipresent part of our society, and yet people often have little conscious awareness of the profound influence the medium exerts.

Films are especially important in influencing the public perception of mental illness because many people are relatively uninformed about the problems of people with mental disorders, and the media tend to be especially effective in shaping opinion in those situations in which strong opinions are not already held. Although some films present sympathetic portrayals of people with mental illness and those professionals who work in the field of mental health (e.g., *The Three Faces of Eve*, *David and Lisa*, *Ordinary People*, and *A Beautiful Mind*), many more do not. Individuals with mental illness are often portrayed as aggressive, dangerous, and unpredictable; psychiatrists, psychologists, nurses, and other health professionals who work with these patients are often portrayed as "arrogant and ineffectual," "cold-hearted and authoritarian," "passive and apathetic," or "shrewd and manipulative" (Niemiec & Wedding, 2006; Wedding & Niemiec, 2003).

Films such as *Psycho* (1960) perpetuate the continuing confusion about the relationship between schizophrenia and dissociative identity disorder (multiple personality disorder); *Friday the 13th* (1980) and *Nightmare on Elm Street* (1984) both perpetuate the misconception that people who leave psychiatric hospitals are violent and dangerous; movies such as *The Exorcist* (1973) suggest to the public that mental illness is the equivalent of possession by the devil; and movies such as *One Flew Over the Cuckoo's Nest* (1975) make the case that psychiatric hospitals are simply prisons in which there is little or no regard for patient rights or welfare. These films in part account for the continuing stigma of mental illness.

Stigma is one of the reasons that so few people with mental problems actually receive help (Mann & Himelein, 2004). The National Institute of Mental Health (NIMH) estimates that only 20% of those with mental disorders actually reach out for help with their problems, despite the fact that many current treatments for these disorders are inexpensive and effective. In addition, there is still a strong tendency to see patients with mental disorders as the cause of their own disorders – for example, the National Alliance for the Mentally Ill (NAMI) has polling data that indicate that about one in three U.S. citizens still conceptualizes mental illness in terms of evil and punishment for misbehavior.

Cinematic Elements

A film director must consider countless technical elements in the making of a film, often orchestrating hundreds of people, many of whom monitor and pass down orders to hundreds or thousands of other collaborators. There are three general phases involved in making a film.

The time spent prior to filming in the **pre-production phase** is often seen as the most important. Many directors "storyboard" (draw out) every shot and choreograph every movement for each scene to be filmed. Countless meetings with each technical supervisor (e.g., cinematographer, costume designer, set designer, electrician) are held to facilitate preparation, coordination and integration. The director will also scout out locations, work with casting appropriate actors and actresses for the various roles, and may re-work the screenplay.

In the **production phase**, the director attempts to film his or her vision, working closely with the actors and actresses to encourage, stimulate, guide, or alter their work, while carefully monitoring camera angles, lighting, sound, and other technical areas.

In the **post-production phase**, editing and laying out the musical score and background sounds are major areas of focus. The director integrates each of these elements while working to honor the original purpose, message, and underlying themes of the film.

Some of the most important cinematic elements are summarized with film examples in Table 1.1. Of course, these three phases exclude countless other tasks involving financing, budgeting, marketing, and other business, administrative, consulting, and legal aspects. A mental health consultant may be used with certain films and may play an important role in any phase, particularly involving fine tuning the screenplay and helping the director and actors understand psychological and related phenomena; we believe mental health consultants should be sought out for *every* film portraying a psychological condition or a therapeutic encounter. Unfortunately, such consultants are sorely underutilized in cinema.

Table 1.1. Film elements with movie examples

Film Element	Explanation	Classic Example	Recent Example
Themes	Overall meaning, messages, motifs	*It's a Wonderful Life* (1946)	*Slumdog Millionaire* (2008)
Cinematography	Visual appeal, framing, camera-work, lighting	*Lawrence of Arabia* (1962)	*Pan's Labyrinth* (2006)
Pacing	Movement, fluidity	*M*A*S*H* (1970)	*The Departed* (2006)
Sound	Music, score, sound effects	*Ben-Hur* (1959)	*The Dark Knight* (2008)
Mood	Tone, atmosphere	*M* (1931)	*No Country for Old Men* (2007)
Art	Set design, costumes	*Star Wars* (1977)	*The Curious Case of Benjamin Button* (2008)
Dialogue	Conversation, modes of communication	*Annie Hall* (1977)	*Lost in Translation* (2003)
Acting	Character portrayal, depth and quality, casting	*The Philadelphia Story* (1940)	*Doubt* (2008)
Editing	Continuity, transitions	*Citizen Kane* (1941)	*Crash* (2005)
Screenplay	Story-line, plot; original or adapted to the screen	*One Flew Over the Cuckoo's Nest* (1975)	*Little Miss Sunshine* (2006)
Direction	All elements together, quality of film overall	*A Clockwork Orange* (1971)	*Amelie* (2001)

Directors attempt to artfully integrate the technical elements of sound, camera, and lighting fluidly with the plot, themes, pacing, and tone of the film while ascertaining quality acting performances. Danis Tanovic, director of an Academy Award winner for Best Foreign Film, *No Man's Land* (2001), about the Bosnian-Serbian war, speaks to many of these elements as he describes the shock and disharmony of the war that he attempted to depict in his film:

"This shock is something I have reproduced through my film. On one side, a long summer day – perfect nature, strong colors – and on the other, human beings and their black madness. And this long, hot summer day reflects the atmosphere of the film itself. Movements are heavy, thoughts are hard to grasp, time is slow and tension is hiding – hiding but present. When it finally explodes, it is like fireworks – sudden, loud, and quick. Panoramic shots of landscape become unexpectedly mixed with nervous details of action. It all lasts for a moment or two, and then tension hides again, waiting for the next opportunity to surprise. Time slows down again." (Danis Tanovic, quoted in the DVD insert).

Changes in color and sound have a significant impact on the viewer's experience of a film. Butler and Palesh (2004) offer the example of Steven Spielberg's manipulation of these cinematic elements in *Saving Private Ryan* (1998). In addition to screams turned slowly into sobs or mumbles, colors are subdued to an almost black-and-white appearance so that when the color of red is introduced at the battle scenes amidst the muted background, the depiction of the reality of war becomes even more vivid for the viewer.

For the most skilled directors, virtually everything that the camera "sees" and records is meaningful. The sense of subjective experience produced by a sequence of **point-of-view** shots facilitates the viewer's identification with the film's characters, their perceptions, and their circumstances. Extreme **close-up shots** and a variety of **panning techniques** facilitate the importance of an emotional expression or inner conflict, or develop pacing for the film. High-angle and low-angle shots give emphasis to character control, power, strength, weakness, and a variety of other dynamics. For example, in *American Beauty* (1999), high-angle shots are used at the beginning of the film on Lester Burnham (Kevin Spacey) to indicate a passiveness and submission to authority prior to his transformation to a strong-willed, commanding character.

Each viewer possesses unique perceptual preferences, prior knowledge about the film's content, and preconceptions about the images the film contains that mediate his or her perceptions and experience. Rarely, if ever, do any two viewers have an identical experience when viewing the same film. Each viewer subjectively selects, attends to, and translates the visual and acoustic images projected in a theater into his or her own version of the story. Often viewers are affected by or identify with the film's characters so strongly that it appears clear that the defense mechanism of **projection** is present. This process is facilitated when the viewer can anticipate the story line, the plot, or the outcome. The avid moviegoer quickly realizes familiar themes, similar settings, and "formulas" for plots and endings across a variety of films.

The Close-Up

When we see an isolated face on the screen, our consciousness of space is suspended and we become vividly aware of all the nuances of emotion that can be expressed by a grimace or a glance. We form beliefs about a character's emotions, moods, intentions, and thoughts as we look directly into his or her face. Indeed, many of the most profound emotional experiences (such as grief) are expressed much more powerfully through the human face than through words. Consider the dynamic film, *Amelie* (2001), in which director Jean-Pierre Jeunet purposefully chooses characters (as he does for all of his films) that have very expressive faces. There are numerous close-ups on several of the characters' faces throughout the film. He explains that he wants to have characters that are interesting for the viewer to look at. In turn, this enhances viewer interest and character development.

This ability to share and comprehend subjective experiences through empathic interpretation of the language of the face is clearly evident in early **silent films**, and these films still have the power to evoke strong emotions. In fact, many early directors of silent films, confronted with the development of "talkies," feared that the addition of sound would place a barrier between the spectator and the film and restore the external and internal distance and dualism present in other works of art. The principles of observing emotional nuances can be extended from the human face to the background and surroundings in which the character moves, and a character's subjective vision can be reproduced by a film as objective reality. For example, film can show the frightened, paranoid individual, but also the distorted, menacing houses and trees which the protagonist views. This technique was used in the expressionist film *The Cabinet of Dr. Caligari* (1919).

What we see in a facial expression is immediately apparent to the spectator without the distraction of words, and a good actor can convey multiple emotions simultaneously. It has been shown repeatedly that real people playing themselves are less convincing than actors. This is true with instructional films, advertisements, and docudramas, as well as feature films. In *Ordinary People* (1980), director Robert Redford attempted to cast an actual psychiatrist in the role of the therapist, but the effect was unconvincing. Redford finally decided to cast actor Judd Hirsch in the role and the film ended up winning an Academy Award for Best Picture and Hirsch received a nomination for Best Actor. The one notable exception was *One Flew Over the Cuckoos Nest* (1975), where a psychiatrist actually played a psychiatrist.

Identification

As a film is being projected onto a theater screen, we project ourselves into the action and identify with its protagonists. At one time it was thought that in order to maintain the attention of viewers, a film had to have a central character and theme. At times this central figure has been an "anti-hero." However, directors such as Robert Altman and Quentin Tarantino have experimented with techniques in which they rapidly shift among short vignettes that may be only loosely linked with a story line or central character. Altman's *Short Cuts* (1994) and Tarantino's *Pulp Fiction* (1994) are two examples of this approach. A more recent film, *Crash* (2005), directed by Paul Haggis, was so masterful at interweaving stories to enhance meaning and viewer engagement that it won an Academy Award for Best Picture, among many other awards.

Filmmakers have also experimented with other means of maintaining the psychological continuity, such as making an inanimate object or an animal the center of the story. Most films, however, use a single character to maintain the integrity of the film as a psychological whole.

The classic question posed to students regarding films in introduction to cinema classes – "Are movies merely art imitating real life?" – is perhaps unanswerable. For some viewers, seeing movies becomes so important that it seems that films and film characters have supplanted their lives.

Suture

Viewers integrate separate, disjointed photographic images into coherent scenes and weave different scenes into the whole film experience without conscious effort or appreciation of the complicated psychological processes involved. "**Suture**," to use a medical metaphor, occurs when cutting or editing occurs and the resulting cinematic gaps are "sewn" shut by viewers.

According to suture theory, instead of asking, "Who is watching this?" and "How could this be happening?" viewers tacitly accept what is seen on the screen as natural and "real," even when the camera's gaze shifts abruptly from one scene, location, or character to another. Suture works because cinematic coding makes each shot appear to be the object of the gaze of whoever appears in the shot that follows. The most commonly cited example of suturing is the **shot/reverse shot**, in which each of two characters is alternately viewed over the other's shoulder.

The Representation of Psychological Phenomena in Film

Film is particularly well suited to depicting psychological states of mind and altered mental states. The combination of images, dialogue, sound effects, and music in a movie mimics and parallels the thoughts and feelings that occur in our stream of consciousness. Lights, colors, and sounds emanate from the screen in such a way that we readily find ourselves believing that we are actually experiencing what is happening on the screen.

In *Secrets of a Soul* (1926), German director G. Pabst dramatized psychoanalytic theory with the help of two of Freud's assistants, Karl Abraham and Hanns Sachs, and depicted dream sequences with multi-layered superimposition (achieved through rewinding and multiple exposures). Freud himself did not want his name connected with the project and had misgivings about the film's ability to convey the nuances of psychoanalytic process. In a letter to Abraham, Freud wrote, "My chief objection is still that I do not believe satisfactory plastic representation of our abstractions is at all possible." This perspective is in direct contrast to Stanley Kubrick's quote that opens this chapter asserting that any abstraction can be filmed. Freud himself remained skeptical about the cinema all his life.

Film is frequently used to objectively portray subjective states such as dreams. Perhaps the best example of this is Hitchcock's collaboration with Salvador Dali on the dream sequence in *Spellbound* (1944). Hitchcock wanted to "turn out the first picture on psychoanalysis." He was determined to break the traditional way of handling dream sequences through a blurred and hazy screen. Hitchcock wanted dreams with great visual sharpness and clarity, and images sharper than those in the film itself. He chose Salvador Dali as a collaborator because of the architectural precision of the artist's work. Hitchcock originally wanted to shoot *Spellbound* in the open air and in natural light, but he wound up shooting the film in the studio to cut costs. *Spellbound* depicts the cathartic recovery of repressed memories, and an emotional experience intense enough to eliminate the hero's amnesia. This is a psychological process that has been depicted in film since its early days.

Films can also be used to interweave fantasy and reality, and a director may intentionally set up situations in which the viewer cannot tell if the film portrays reality or the unconscious fantasies of a character. Examples of this technique include Ingmar Bergman's *Persona* (1966), Federico Fellini's *Juliet of the Spirits* (1965), Luis Buñuel's *Belle de Jour* (1966), and Robert Altman's *Images* (1972) (Fleming & Manvell, 1985). Director David Lynch has made this approach his trademark with such films as *Mulholland Drive* (2001), *Lost Highway* (1997), *Blue Velvet* (1986), and *Eraserhead* (1977).

Processes such as thinking, recalling, imagining, and feeling are not visible, but the language of the **montage** and camera techniques such as **slow fades** can suggest these invisible processes. Also, the film can be edited in such a way that the viewer is forced to think about psychological phenomena. The inclusion of images with symbolic meaning, such as a hearse passing by or the well-known chess game with Death in *The*

Seventh Seal (1957), can evoke certain moods or prepare the viewer for events that are about to occur. Symbolic sounds, such as a baby crying, can have a similar effect.

Another symbol often used in film is the mirror. When a character is filmed looking in the mirror, it often represents self-reflection, insight, a new identity emerging or changing, or even a narcissistic preoccupation with oneself. *Monster's Ball* (2001) uses mirrors and other reflective objects to symbolize self-distortion and negative self-perception in the two lead characters who are numb to their own lives. Mirrored images depict Marlon Brando's broken and distorted character in *Last Tango in Paris* (1972), self-deprecation in *American Splendor* (2003), self-criticism in *Soldier's Girl* (2003), deterioration in *Focus* (2001), and externalization of blame in a dramatic, comical scene in *25th Hour* (2002).

"Beyond all physical and palpable reality another dimension defined only in painting, a mirror which deforms life... an instant reflected... a magical reality where all is possible."

Goya in Bordeaux (1999)

Films offer numerous examples of unconscious motivation and **defense mechanisms**, involuntary patterns of thinking, feeling, or acting that arise in response to the subjective experience of anxiety. **Acting out** in reaction to stress or inner conflict is present in *Intimacy* (2000), *You Can Count On Me* (2000), *Lantana* (2001), and in Michael Douglas' response to the stress in his life in *Falling Down* (1993). **Altruism** can be seen in *Patch Adams* (1998), and the character of the doctor who devotes himself to the indigent people of India in *Streets of Joy* (1994). **Denial** is dramatically illustrated in Katharine Hepburn and Ellen Burstyn's gripping roles as drug addicts in *Long Day's Journey into Night* (1962) and *Requiem for a Dream* (2000), respectively, as well as most townspeople in both *The Village* (2004) and *Dogville* (2003). **Intellectualization** is present in *Lorenzo's Oil* (1992) and **suppression** is apparent in *The United States of Leland* (2003) as well as *Kill Bill, Vol. 2* (2004), and is commonplace in *Gone with the Wind* (1939).

"I'll think about it tomorrow. Tara! Home. I'll go home, and I'll think of some way to get him back! After all, tomorrow is another day!"

Gone with the Wind (1939)

The Depiction of Psychological Disorders in Films

This book organizes categories of psychological disorders with appropriate film examples. Table 1.2 presents an overview of well-recognized and accepted disorders and some of the best representations of them in cinema. Watching any of these films will provide the viewer with insights about the presentation of the particular disorder portrayed.

Psychopathology in Different Film Genres

The depiction of mental illness in films most commonly appears in three popular genres: the drama, the horror film, and the suspense film. Often the most effective portrayals of mental illness are those that infuse surreal and expressionistic images into a montage that is realistic and plausible, powerfully conveying the "interior" of a character's psyche.

The popular genre of **drama** is perhaps the most fertile ground for psychopathology to be portrayed in movies in a very realistic, engaging way. Every chapter in this book has numerous examples of dramatic films depicting psychological disorders. The range is vast and it extends from the slow-moving drama of *The Human Stain* (2003) and the disjointed, complex drama of *21 Grams* (2003) to the affectively engaging dramas of *Love Liza* (2002) and *Mystic River* (2003).

An early film that served as a prototype for **horror** films, Wiene's *The Cabinet of Dr. Caligari* (1919), is highly expressionistic and established a precedent for setting macabre murders in mental institutions. Like dozens of films that followed, it linked insanity and the personal lives of psychiatrists and implied that mental health professionals are all "a little odd." Evidence of the enduring

Table 1.2. Psychological disorders and movies that portray them

Category	Classic Film Examples	Recent Film Examples
Disorders of Childhood and Adolescence	*Kids* (1995)	*The Chorus* (2004); *Thirteen* (2003)
Mental Retardation	*Sling Blade* (1996)	*Pauline and Paulette* (2000); *I Am Sam* (2001)
Autism and Pervasive Developmental Disorders	*David and Lisa* (1962); *Rain Man* (1988)	*Breaking and Entering* (2006); *American Splendor* (2003)
Neuropsychological Disorders	*On Golden Pond* (1981)	*Away From Her* (2006); *Memento* (2000)
Substance-Related Disorders	*The Lost Weekend* (1945)	*Half Nelson* (2006); *Love Liza* (2002)
Schizophrenia	*Clean, Shaven* (1994)	*Proof* (2005); *A Beautiful Mind* (2001)
Mood Disorders	*Ordinary People* (1980)	*Shopgirl* (2005); *The Hours* (2002)
Anxiety Disorders	*Vertigo* (1958)	*Batman Begins* (2005); *Matchstick Men* (2003)
Somatoform Disorders	*Persona* (1966)	*Therese* (2004); *Hollywood Ending* (2002)
Dissociative Disorders	*Psycho* (1960)	*Unknown White Male* (2005); *Identity* (2003)
Sexual Disorders	*Lolita* (1962)	*The Woodsman* (2004); *Secretary* (2002)
Gender Identity Disorders	*Boys Don't Cry* (1999)	*Transamerica* (2005); *Normal* (2003)
Eating Disorders	*The Best Little Girl in the World* (1982)	*Primo Amore* (2004); *Center Stage* (2000)
Sleep Disorders	*My Own Private Idaho* (1991)	*The Machinist* (2004); *Insomnia* (2002)
Impulse-Control Disorders	*Marnie* (1964)	*Klepto* (2003); *Owning Mahowny* (2002)
Adjustment Disorders	*The Wrong Man* (1957)	*The Upside of Anger* (2005); *Best in Show* (2000)
Personality Disorders	*Compulsion* (1959); *Fatal Attraction* (1987)	*Notes on a Scandal* (2006); *One Hour Photo* (2002)

effects of these themes is found in the successful and highly acclaimed film *The Silence of the Lambs* (1991), in which Anthony Hopkins plays a mentally deranged and cannibalistic psychiatrist. The various *Saw* (2004; 2005; 2006; 2007; 2008) movies and *House of 1000 Corpses* (2003) portray psychopathic villains who are clearly out of touch with reality.

The seminal films of Alfred Hitchcock provide the best examples of the **suspense** genre. They are unique in the way they engage the viewer and pander to his or her anxieties in subtle, unrelenting, and convincing ways. The majority of Hitchcock's films, noted for their stylized realism, invariably evoke a sensation of vicariously pulling the viewer "in" to the plight of the characters as a not-so-innocent bystander, through a carefully edited montage

of a variety of objective and subjective camera shots. Hitchcock's filmography reflects not only a fascination with pronounced and extreme psychopathology (e.g., *Psycho*, 1960), but more importantly, an appreciation of more subtle psychological phenomena such as acting out, reaction formation, idealization, repression, and undoing. These defense mechanisms are depicted in Hitchcock's films *Shadow of a Doubt* (1943), *Spellbound* (1945), and *Marnie* (1964). Hitchcock's style is immensely popular and has been imitated frequently by other directors such as Brian De Palma and Roman Polanski.

Mental illness is also depicted, although less often, in the genre of **documentary** films. Frederick Wiseman's *Titicut Follies* (1967) and *Capturing the Friedmans* (2003) illustrate clear cases of psychopathology. It is interesting to contrast the former movie with the horror film *Bedlam* (1945) or "docudramatic" films such as *The Snake Pit* (1948), *Pressure Point* (1962), and *One Flew Over the Cuckoo's Nest* (1975), all dealing with mental institutions and the treatment of people with mental illness. At least two heralded films, *The Three Faces of Eve* (1957) and *Sybil* (1976), provide viewers with full-scale case histories and the struggles between patient and psychiatrist.

The **comedy** genre has its share of films portraying psychopathology. *Drop Dead Fred* (1991), *What About Bob?* (1991), *High Anxiety* (1977), and *Scotland, PA* (2001) portray psychological aberrations with quirky humor that is used to defuse the sense of anxiety that is produced by the behavior of the lead characters in each of the films. Director Woody Allen has made a career out of portraying anxiety, neuroticism, and somatization in various films such as *Hannah and Her Sisters* (1988) and *Hollywood Ending* (2002), but more recently has turned to subtle, dark, and complex psychopathology as seen in the portrayal of personality disorders in *Match Point* (2005) and *Vicky Cristina Barcelona* (2008).

Misconceptions and Stereotypic Themes in Films

Otto Wahl, an authority in media psychology, summarizes the media's portrayal of mental illness in *Media Madness* (1995): "Overall, the mass media do a poor job of depicting mental illness, with misinformation frequently communicated, unfavorable stereotypes of people with mental illness predominating, and psychiatric terms used in inaccurate and offensive ways" (pp. 12–13). This is largely due to **media framing**, a concept that refers to the way a form of media presents and organizes information that leads to interpretations by the public. In the case of mental illness in films, media framing is overwhelmingly negative and usually inaccurate (Goffman, 1986; Sieff, 2003). The media frames for mental illness are typically narrow and distorted, frequently presenting those with mental illness as violent, dangerous, simplistic, disillusioned, and/or innocent. This is troubling for at least two reasons: (1) Mental health literacy levels for the general public are low (Orchowski, Spickard, & McNamara, 2006); (2) Research has shown that people's primary source of information about mental illness is the mass media (Wahl, 1995).

Steven Hyler (Hyler, Gabbard, & Schneider, 1991) has provided a compelling analysis of the portrayal of mental illness in films. Hyler and his colleagues describe six common stereotypes that perpetuate stigma. The first of these is that of the mental patient as **rebellious free spirit**. Examples of this portrayal can be found in films such as *Francis* (1982), *Nuts* (1987), *The Dream Team* (1989), *The Couch Trip* (1989), *An Angel At My Table* (1990), *Shine* (1996), *K-Pax* (2001), *Asylum* (2005), and perhaps most clearly in *One Flew Over the Cuckoo's Nest* (1975). The stereotype of the **homicidal maniac** is present in many of the slasher/horror films described earlier. However, the authors point out that this stereotype can also be traced back as far as D. W. Griffith's 1909 film *The Maniac Cook*, in which a psychotic employee attempts to kill an infant by cooking the child in an oven. *Sling Blade* (1996), a well-intentioned and sympathetic film about a man with mental retardation who commits a second murder after leaving a psychiatric hospital 25 years after murdering his mother and her lover, perpetuates the misconception that people with mental illness and mental retardation are dangerous.

The patient as **seductress** is seen in films such as *The Caretakers* (1963) and *Dressed to Kill* (1980), and most clearly in the 1964 film *Lilith*, which stars Warren Beatty as a hospital therapist who is seduced by a psychiatric patient played by Jean Seberg. The stereotype of the **enlightened member of society** is linked to the work of writers such as R. D. Laing and Thomas Szasz and is illustrated in films such as *King of Hearts* (1966) and *A Fine Madness* (1966). The **narcissistic parasite** stereotype presents people with mental disorders as self-centered, attention-seeking, and demanding. It is reflected in films such as *What About Bob?* (1991), *Annie Hall* (1977), *High Anxiety* (1977), and *Lovesick* (1983). Finally, the stereotype of **zoo specimen** is perpetuated by films that degrade people with mental illness by treating them as objects of derision or a source of amusement or entertainment for those who are "normal." Films that exemplify this stereotype include *Bedlam* (1948) and *Marat/Sade* (1966). A variation on this theme occurs in Brian De Palma's *Dressed to Kill* (1980), in which a psychotic and homicidal psychiatrist murders a nurse in a surrealistic amphitheater-like setting, with dozens of other patients sitting in the gallery and watching in silent approval.

Hyler (1988) describes three dominant themes in film that contribute to stereotypes about the etiology manifestation of mental disorders. The first is the **presumption of traumatic etiology**. This theme reinforces the belief that a single traumatic event is the cause of mental illness. Examples include the amnesia experienced by Gregory Peck that was eventually shown to be related to his role in the childhood death of his brother (revealed by Hitchcock in a dramatic and unforgettable flashback scene) in *Spellbound* (1945), and the dissociative identity disorder that resulted when a child was required to kiss the corpse of her dead grandmother in *The Three Faces of Eve* (1957). Other examples of this theme are found in films such as *Suddenly, Last Summer* (1959), *Home of the Brave* (1949), *Nuts* (1987), and Robin Williams' character in *The Fisher King* (1991).

Hyler's second theme is that of the **schizophrenogenic parent**. This is a widely held misconception that holds parents (most often, the mother) accountable for serious mental illness in their children. The National Alliance for the Mentally Ill (NAMI) has worked hard to dispel this unfounded but pervasive belief, but it is deeply rooted in popular culture and commonplace in films. Examples include *Agnes of God* (1985), *Face to Face* (1976), *Sybil* (1980), *Carrie* (1976), *Frances* (1982), *Fear Strikes Out* (1957), and *Shine* (1995).

"Insanity runs in my family. It practically gallops."

Mortimer Brewster (Cary Grant) in
Arsenic and Old Lace (1944)

The third misconception discussed by Hyler is that **harmless eccentricity is frequently labeled as mental illness and inappropriately treated**. We see this theme most vividly presented in the film *One Flew Over the Cuckoo's Nest* (1975). Jack Nicholson's character, Randle P. McMurphy, is charismatic, flamboyant, and colorful. The only diagnosis that seems at all appropriate is that of antisocial personality disorder, although it is not even clear that this is justified. However, once in the system he cannot get out, and he is eventually treated with electroconvulsive therapy and lobotomy, presumably as a way of punishing his misbehavior in the name of treatment. The same theme is found in two films released in 1966, *King of Hearts* and *A Fine Madness*, and in the film *Chattahoochee* (1990). A related theme, that treatment in mental health facilities is actually a form of social control, is reflected in the work of Thomas Szasz (e.g., in books such as *The Myth of Mental Illness* and *Psychiatric Slavery*). It is

also reflected in films depicting excesses in treatment, such as the aversion therapies portrayed in *A Clockwork Orange* (1971). For a full list of misconceptions perpetrated in movies accompanied by film examples see Appendix D. Appendix E looks specifically at the mental health profession and delineates a list of both "balanced" and "unbalanced" portrayals of psychotherapists.

Psychopathology and its representation in films will be discussed in some detail in the chapters that follow. In general, we will follow the nosology of the American Psychiatric Association's *Diagnostic and Statistical Manual*, Fourth Edition – Text Revision (*DSM-IV-TR*). Appendix F includes a filmography broken down by diagnostic category. Readers who take time to review even a few of the films included in Appendix F will find that the experience will supplement and enhance their understanding of psychopathology.

Mental Illness, Mental Health, and the Human Condition

No doubt mental illness is one of the most fascinating phenomena a filmmaker can depict on screen. There is, of course, much more to the human condition than psychopathology and that which is going wrong with individuals. In another book, *Positive Psychology at the Movies: Using Films to Build Virtues and Character Strengths*, Niemiec & Wedding (2008) focus on what is right with people, and they review numerous cinematic portrayals of triumph, virtue, and positive influence. They take the classification system from *Character Strengths and Virtues* (Peterson & Seligman, 2004) of 24 universal character strengths, and discuss important cinematic examples of each (e.g., creativity, curiosity, kindness, fairness, etc.). Indeed, there is overlap with the discussion here as individuals with mental illness have character strengths and virtues (like all other human beings) and often use their strengths to overcome mental adversity. Such films are often more true to the human condition, as they are less likely to offer one-dimensional portrayals or shock-value sensationalism and more likely to reveal the complexity and intrigue of what it means to be human. Films like *A Beautiful Mind* (2001) offer a compelling portrayal of schizophrenia, but this film also illustrates the character strengths of love, bravery, and persistence. See Table 1.3 for examples of films that speak clearly to both dimensions of the human condition.

Table 1.3. Films portraying psychopathology as well as character strengths and virtues

Film	Psychopathology	Virtue	Character Strength(s)
Elling (2001)	Anxiety disorder	Courage	Bravery and Persistence
Away from Her (2006)	Dementia	Humanity	Love
Mishima: A Life in Four Chapters (1985)	Suicide	Temperance	Self-regulation
Canvas (2006)	Schizophrenia	Wisdom and Transcendence	Creativity and Hope
K-Pax (2001)	Delusional or dissociative disorder	Wisdom	Perspective and Creativity
Insomnia (2002)	Sleep disorder	Courage	Bravery and Persistence
American Beauty (1999)	Mood disorder	Transcendence	Appreciation of Beauty
It's a Wonderful Life (1946)	Adjustment disorder	Transcendence	Gratitude and Hope
A Clockwork Orange (1971)	Personality disorder	Wisdom and Transcendence	Curiosity and Appreciation of excellence

Critical Thinking Questions

- What cinematic element do you believe is most crucial to the portrayal of psychopathology in movies (e.g., musical score, lighting, etc.)?
- Consider a film character that has had an impact on your understanding of a psychological disorder. How did the cinematic elements of the film accentuate or contribute to your understanding?
- Do you believe that a purist approach to filmmaking (e.g., the Dogme 95 films that avoid special effects, sound external to the film, etc.) does more justice to psychological phenomena than an approach that emphasizes special effects?
- Describe some examples of how a film's music has enhanced the portrayal of depression, schizophrenia, and anxiety disorders. In what way was the music different for each? Was this dependent on the genre?
- Do most films that portray a dynamic, complex character with mental illness also portray the character's strengths and virtues? For those that don't, can this still be an accurate, full depiction of the individual?
- How much time do you spend watching movies or other activities in which you automatically enter a state of trance-like absorption and concentration? What is the function of this state of mind for you in terms of your everyday life?

The mental health community comes together each year to present the Voice Awards; these awards recognize films that promote awareness of mental health issues and the power of recovery. The recipients are writers and producers of entertainment programming (film and television) who have given voice to individuals with mental health problems by building in dignified, respectful, and accurate portrayals in their scripts and productions. While each of the feature film winners can be found in this book, we give particular attention to *Canvas* (2006), *Reign Over Me* (2007), and *The Aviator* (2004). The Voice Awards are sponsored by the Center for Mental Health Services (CMHS), a division of the Substance Abuse and Mental Health Services Administration (SAMHSA).

Further Exploration

If you have time to read just one book relevant to the medium of film, make it:

Dick, B. F. (2009). *Anatomy of film* (6th ed.). Boston: Bedford/St. Martin's.

If you only have time for one article, read:

Hyler, S. E., Gabbard, G. O., & Schneider, I. (1991). Homicidal maniacs and narcissistic parasites: Stigmatization of mentally ill persons in the movies. *Hospital & Community Psychiatry, 42*, 1044-1048.

Films and Psychopathology

All Time Favorites

- *A Beautiful Mind* (2001)
- *Persona* (1966)
- *Memento* (2000)
- *Rain Man* (1988)
- *Fatal Attraction* (2002)
- *One Flew Over the Cuckoo's Nest* (1975)
- *Psycho* (1960)
- *The Lost Weekend* (1945)
- *Vertigo* (1958)
- *A Clockwork Orange* (1971)

Chapter 2

Anxiety Disorders

*Sometimes I truly fear that I...am losing my mind.
And if I did it.. .it would be like flying blind..."*
Howard Hughes in *The Aviator* (2004)

Questions to Consider While Watching *The Aviator*

- Howard Hughes experiences symptoms of several anxiety disorders. How common do other anxiety disorders co-occur with obsessive-compulsive disorder (OCD)?
- How are Howard Hughes' obsessions related to his compulsions? Are there any compulsions that appear to be illogical and unrelated to his obsessions?
- What other psychiatric disorders are clearly present throughout the film, but are not addressed?
- What is the treatment of choice for OCD? What comorbid symptoms compromise this treatment?
- Is it possible to separate Howard Hughes' personality from his disorder?
- Would Howard Hughes have been as successful in aviation and entertainment industries without having OCD?
- Can people with OCD experience hallucinations? Is the episode of a germ-free environment realistic for someone with OCD?
- When would have been the optimal time to begin treatment for Howard Hughes? What treatment would have produced the best results?
- Hughes didn't have a will at the time of his death, and his fortune was divided between 22 cousins. Do you think Hughes would have been competent to write a will during the last years of his life? Why or why not?

Patient Evaluation[1]

Patient's stated reason for coming: "There is no safe place; there is no safe place."

History of the present illness: Mr. Howard Hughes, a 42-year-old Caucasian male, was brought to the clinic by his accountant who reports that the patient has been living in one room of his mansion which he has turned into a "germ-free environment." All entrances to his room are covered with masking tape, he uses tissue to pick up items, and he refuses to use dishes or glassware. He has numerous obsessions and compulsions that have been present for several years, but are becoming increasingly debilitating. The most troubling obsession is his fear of germs, which has developed into a severe phobia. He burns his complete wardrobe when he is exposed to anyone who is sick. He also requires his friends and employees to follow very strict hygiene practices. Recently, he has begun to experience severe panic attacks caused by extreme fear of dirt, messiness, or any perceived disorder in his life. He once reported "seeing things" that others cannot see. He has panic attacks daily and is very afraid that he will have an attack in public.

Past psychiatric illness, treatment, and outcomes: There is no reported history of mental health treatment, but symptoms have been present for years. He adamantly denies having a mental illness, but is aware that some of his behavior might make him appear mentally disturbed.

Medical history: Mr. Hughes has a long history of minor physical illnesses beginning in childhood. Driven by fear of developing life-threatening diseases, his mother frequently sought treatment for young Howard for colds and

---

1   This fictitious interview is based on the character portrayed in the film *The Aviator*. It is not intended in any way to represent an interview with the real Howard Hughes.

somatic complaints. At age 13, Mr. Hughes developed a medically unexplained paralysis that confined him to a wheelchair for 2 months. His parents believed that he had contracted polio, but the diagnosis was never confirmed. He has chronic pain from a series of plane accidents which resulted in serious facial, leg, and internal injuries. He currently takes pain medication from multiple prescribers.

Psychosocial history: Mr. Hughes, an only child, enjoyed a close relationship with his parents, Howard Sr. and Allene Hughes. His mother died unexpectedly when he was 16. Two years later, his father died of a heart attack. During childhood, his mother is reported to have been overly protective of her only child and was preoccupied with his physical and emotional condition. Mr. Hughes noted he learned early in life that he could attract attention or avoid unpleasant situations by complaining of an illness. His father was rather flamboyant and well known for his gregarious lifestyle. Devastated and lonely following his wife's death, Mr. Hughes Sr. removed his son from a private school and brought him back home. Until his father's death, he lived in California, where he engaged in a glamorous Hollywood lifestyle, often meeting with celebrities from the film industry. His paternal uncle was a noted film producer. Even though he never earned a high school diploma, his influential father managed to have him admitted to Rice University. He later quit college (after his father's death) and became the sole beneficiary of a very successful family-owned business.

Mr. Hughes married at age 19 and divorced 5 years later. There were no children. He continues to oversee the family business and is a well-known movie producer. He is also a celebrated aviator who started a successful airline. He never re-married, but has had multiple short-term, romantic relationships including several with teenage girls. His accountant is his closest friend.

Drug and alcohol history: Mr. Hughes uses legally prescribed narcotics for pain control. He uses ETOH daily and in combination with the narcotics. There is strong evidence suggesting addiction.

Behavioral observations: Mr. Hughes is a disheveled, tall, emaciated, white male appearing older than his stated age. He arrived with his accountant. He entered the room hesitantly and refused to shake hands. He brushed off his chair before sitting down and answered most questions with anger and impatience. He avoided eye contact. During the interview, he frequently covered his mouth with a tissue making his words unintelligible. His shoulder-length hair was uncombed and his fingernails were dirty and unusually long. His clothes were dirty and wrinkled. He was agitated and restless throughout the interview and answered most questions with a one-word response, usually a mere "yes" or "no."

Mental status examination: Mr. Hughes was alert and oriented to time and place, but did not know the day or date. He denied suicidal or homicidal thoughts, but stated he would like to go to sleep and not wake up. He admitted to occasionally seeing things (bugs, germs, images) that others do not see. While these events are disturbing to him, he explained them as his mind playing tricks on him. He also admitted that these events usually occur following use of alcohol and codeine substances. He completed serial sevens to 65 until he became distracted with an outside noise. When asked the meaning of "why does a rolling stone gather no moss?" he sat in silence and then said "that's me." When anxious, he repeated phrases over and over. It is unclear whether the repetition of phrases is truly a compulsive behavior or a memory problem.

Functional assessment: Within a very short period of time, Mr. Hughes has become a successful filmmaker, aviator, airplane designer, and airline executive. He is independently wealthy, living on profits from his manufacturing company. He has not worked for the last 6 months, following a break-up with a girlfriend and a collapse of a business venture. His food is prepared by a personal chef who follows very specific directions including disinfecting all cooking utensils. Even though he is very concerned about transmission of disease, he bathes infrequently and does not attend to personal hygiene. He lives like a hermit, rarely seeking outside contact.

Strengths: Mr. Hughes is clearly a creative, ingenuous, and innovative man. He has had periods of successful functioning in which he established new businesses and engaged in friendships and romantic relationships. He recognizes that his psychosis may be related to substance use. He easily discusses his childhood experiences. He is motivated to manage his panic attacks.

Diagnosis: Obsessive-compulsive disorder; panic disorder with agoraphobia; substance abuse disorder. Rule out: bipolar disorder.

Treatment plan: (1) Consider an intensive outpatient/inpatient anxiety management program that employs the evidence-based treatment of *in vivo* exposure and response prevention; (2) Psychiatric consultation to initiate pharmacotherapy for managing OCD symptoms; (3) Weekly cognitive-behavioral therapy to identify and manage obsessions, compulsions, and panic attacks; (4) As anxiety management improves, target residual substance abuse problems via psychotherapy, support groups, and other adjunctive sources; (5) Psychoeducation for lifestyle changes, nutrition, and general self-care/hygiene.

Prognosis: Fair, if Mr. Hughes adheres to the treatment plan. However, he is likely to resist and it will be challenging to engage him fully in treatment.

The Aviator and OCD

The Aviator (2004), an award-winning film directed by Martin Scorsese and starring Leonardo DiCaprio, illustrates many factors that may contribute to the development of OCD – overprotective parents, fear of germs, impulsivity, need for immediate gratification, and the untimely death of both parents. Based upon the real life of tycoon Howard Hughes, Jr. (1905–1976) from age 24 to 42, the film depicts his psychosocial and physical deterioration. The underlying effect of his addiction to codeine is not as clearly portrayed, but the use of alcohol can be clearly seen. Like symptoms of many people with OCD, the obsessions and compulsions develop over time. The film also shows how stress can exacerbate one's symptoms. Leonardo DiCaprio prepared for his marvelous portrayal of Hughes by spending time interacting with patients with OCD.

"I want ten chocolate chip cookies. Medium chips. None too close to the outside."

Howard Hughes (Leonardo DiCaprio) in *The Aviator* (2004), displaying OCD behavior

---

Anxiety Disorders

Anxiety, a normal reaction to a situation or stressor, is a motivator for performance and can be a healthy warning signal of danger or something that needs attention. Existential writers and mental health specialists agree that anxiety is an expected part of the human condition. There are a variety of theoretical explanations for anxiety. Richard Lazarus, a well-known psychologist, described anxiety as a negative emotion that occurs when facing an uncertain, existential threat (Lazarus, 1999). Psychoanalysts view anxiety as a warning signal that danger is present and that overwhelming emotions are imminent, giving rise to unmanageable helplessness. Cognitive-behaviorists associate persistent anxiety with a negative self-view, along with a strong sense of desperation and vulnerability.

When anxiety significantly interferes with school, work, or social interactions, an underlying psychiatric disorder may be present. The *DSM-IV-TR* categorizes anxiety disorders as obsessive-compulsive disorder, panic disorders, phobias, and stress/anxiety disorders (i.e., posttraumatic, acute, generalized). The forthcoming diagnostic manual will most likely re-categorize these disorders. The commonality of all of these disorders is an abnormal or exaggerated anxiety response which negatively affects physical health, psychological well-being and cognitive and social functioning. Stress exacerbates the symptoms. Untreated, anxiety disorders can result in physical deterioration, despair, extreme fear, broken relationships, and unemployment. Suicide may be the ultimate outcome.

There is no one single etiology of the anxiety disorders. Instead, there are multiple factors that are responsible for the development of these disorders. Genetic predisposition, environmental changes, and psychosocial events all contribute to their development. As these disorders develop, changes occur in the brain that set into motion the abnormal response characteristic of anxiety disorders. Treatment focuses on changing thoughts and behaviors, as well as establishing new brain interaction patterns, with cognitive behavioral therapy and medication.

Obsessive-Compulsive Disorder

People with **obsessive-compulsive disorder** (OCD) are distressed by recurring thoughts and/or irrational behaviors that can be so time consuming that they interfere with work and social relationships. In severe cases of OCD, these thoughts and behaviors dominate virtually every minute of every day.

Obsessions are "intrusive, inappropriate, recurrent and persistent thoughts, impulses, or images that cause marked anxiety or distress" (*DSM-IV-TR*). Obsessions are of greater magnitude than the everyday worry that is part of almost all our lives. Those with OCD repeatedly try to suppress these thoughts, but the very act of suppression serves to increase their intensity. These recurrent thoughts are disagreeable and alien to the sense of self (i.e., ego-dystonic). Common obsessional themes include harming others (especially children or helpless individuals), contamination with germs or feces, exposure to toxins or infectious diseases such as AIDS, blasphemous thoughts and sexual misbehavior. Obsessions can also coexist with other disorders such as posttraumatic stress disorders.

Compulsions are repetitive behaviors or mental acts that are carried out to reduce the discomfort associated with the obsessions. Sometimes there is a logical connection between the compulsion and the obsession (e.g., repeated hand washing *may* help prevent contamination from germs). However, in other cases there is no logical connection between the two (e.g., the patient who feels a compulsive need to sing the first few lines of a popular commercial before pulling away from every stoplight knows there is no meaningful connection between the behavior and the likelihood of an accident).

Matchstick Men (2003) does an outstanding job of highlighting the psychological consequences of OCD. Roy Waller, played by Nicholas Cage, is a successful con man who is able to use his attention to detail to execute complicated bait-and-switch schemes. When his life is disrupted by the appearance of his estranged teenage daughter (whom he has never seen), he is no longer able to maintain control over his illness or his life. His symptoms erupt and he deteriorates. The viewer is able to not only observe the numerous odd, incapacitating behaviors of a patient with OCD, but also his therapy sessions in which he vividly explains internal conflicts typical of OCD.

In another popular film, *As Good As It Gets* (1997), Melvin Udall, a misogynist and a homophobe played by Jack Nicholson, has a pronounced obsession with cleanliness. He eats at the same restaurant every day, sits at the same table, insists on the same waitress (Helen Hunt), and always orders the same meal. Melvin always brings his own paper-wrapped plastic utensils to this restaurant, so he does not have to "risk" contamination from dirty silverware. Whenever anything disrupts this well-established routine, Melvin becomes anxious and belligerent. He wipes off door handles before opening doors, and he carefully avoids stepping on cracks as he walks to his therapist's office. Melvin's obsessions are his repetitive thoughts about germs and disease; his compulsions are the ritualistic behaviors he engages in as a consequence of his thoughts. Patients with OCD frequently have multiple obsessions, and the film *As Good As It Gets* provides a realistic presentation of the disorder (with the possible exception that a patient with an obsession about cleanliness as severe as that present in Nicholson's character would be unlikely to be willing to touch a small dog). Some clinicians argue that Melvin also would meet the *DSM-IV-TR* criteria for a dual-diagnosis of OCD and OCPD (obsessive-compulsive personality disorder) due to his pervasive rigidity, interpersonal control, and inflexibility.

It is rare to find a film that depicts OCD patients who are compulsive hand-washers. One exception is a short film called *Waiting for Ronald* (2003). It is a simple film about a man, Ronald, leaving a supervised residence to take a bus to live in the community with his friend, Edgar. Both men have developmental disabilities. Edgar has OCD and he is a compulsive hand-washer. He is very precise in the way he places his hat, fixes the folds in the hat, and places objects in his bag. He arrives early at the bus stop, and since Ronald misses the first bus, Edgar has to wait longer than he anticipated. Edgar has a strong need to use the restroom, which he finally does, knowing he might miss Ronald's arrival. Edgar begins to wash his hands and continues, even though he has heard the bus arrive. He wants to stop washing but cannot; his anguish is palpable. He winces and struggles, moaning in mental pain. He washes his hands harder, crying, trying to push himself away from the sink. The viewer can clearly see the pain and suffering the hand-washing causes him. Edgar coaches himself over and over (using the words and name of his therapist), "You can do it. Joe says you can do it… just breathe." Eventually, he slowly pulls his hands away from the sink one hand at a time.

The comedy *What About Bob?* (1991) stars Bill Murray as a patient with multiple problems, including overwhelming anxiety when he cannot be close to his therapist, played by Richard Dreyfuss.

Compulsive hoarding, while not an official *DSM-IV-TR* diagnosis, is commonly associated with OCD and shares many of the OCD criteria. Hoarding refers to the collecting and saving of excessive quantities of possessions (e.g., newspapers, pets, sticks) that are of little use or value in large quantities; in severe cases, safety and health can be at risk. Hoarding is portrayed briefly in Juliette Binoche's character in *Bee Season* (2005) and in the character of Harvey Pekar, the comic strip artist portrayed in *American Splendor* (2003). In *Winter Passing* (2005), Ed Harris portrays an alcoholic who is a disheveled mess, perhaps partly as a reaction to his wife's recent suicide. He lives in a home filled with trash. He is a compulsive hoarder, and the numerous stacks of books in his home serve as a symbolic boundary outlining the entire house, including the stairs and each room, making it challenging to maneuver around.

For details about the treatment of OCD (and other anxiety disorders) as depicted in films used to treat OCD via the strategy of *in vivo* exposure and response prevention, see Chapter 15: Treatment.

Disorders of Fear: Panic, Phobias, Social Anxiety, and PTSD

Panic Attacks

Intense, irrational fears and very distressing physical reactions are the primary symptoms of a **panic attack**. Some persons fear losing control, while many others fear dying. Even though these fears are recognized as illogical, they *feel* very real. Generated by the fear, the physical symptoms include palpitations, accelerated heart rate, sweating, trembling, shortness of breath, a feeling of choking or smothering, chest pain, nausea, dizziness, lightheadedness, numbness or tingling sensations, and/or chills or hot flushes and they only reinforce these irrational beliefs. Panic attack symptoms are similar to those of an impending heart attack. The first panic attack usually begins after contact with a potentially dangerous or repulsive external object such as a knife or a snake, which later becomes the focus of the fear. Events associated with loss of control such as being in an enclosed space or being raped or abused can also be the first antecedent to the attack. Patients usually vividly recall their first panic attack. In *Dirty Filthy Love* (2004), Mark's anxiety often leads to panic attacks. In *Matchstick Men* (2003), Roy has several panic attacks throughout the film. In *Something's Gotta Give* (2003), Jack Nicholson's character Harry Sanborn experiences panic attacks on two separate occasions. This film makes the point that panic can often present with symptoms very similar to those accompanying a heart attack; the cause of Harry's panic appears to be relational stress with the main female character, Erica Barry, played by Diane Keaton. In the film *The Departed* (2006), Billy Costigan (Leonardo DiCaprio), experiences panic attacks which contribute to the suspense of the movie; his medication (lorazepam) is discussed as an anxiety treatment.

In *Broken English* (2007), Parker Posey portrays an event planner who sits around much of the day bored at her computer. When she begins to date and moves toward a relationship commitment, she begins to experience panic attacks in public. She immediately escapes from the situation back to the comfort of her home. She later faces her anxiety directly, symbolized in her traveling to another country where the man lives whom she had begun to avoid; she initially travels with a supportive friend, but when the friend leaves, she is forced to confront her anxiety on her own.

Panic Disorders

A **panic disorder** is diagnosed when panic attacks become regular, but still unpredictable, events. These episodes seem to come out of nowhere. The fact that they seemingly occur anywhere and at any time is one of the reasons that a panic disorder is such a debilitating condition. Some people will have daily panic episodes, while others may be able to go for weeks or months without experiencing panic. Misdiagnosis often leads to delays in treating panic disorder, which in turn exacerbates the anxiety disorder. In the true story *Nobody's Child* (1986), patient rights' advocate Marie Balter (Marlo Thomas) is misdiagnosed as having schizophrenia and spends more than 15 years in a state mental hospital. In reality, she suffered from depression and panic disorder. Following her release she earns a baccalaureate and master's degree and returns to the state hospital as an administrator.

Robert De Niro plays a mob boss with panic disorder who meets with a psychiatrist, played by Billy Crystal, in both *Analyze This* (1999) and *Analyze That* (2002). Paul Vitti (De Niro) believes he is suffering a heart attack, but Dr. Ben Sobel (Crystal) explains the important difference between a panic attack and a heart attack and eventually helps Vitti get in touch with the deep pain and suffering that trigger his attacks. Though Vitti resolves some important issues in his life, this therapeutic approach risks misleading the viewer into believing this is the typical treatment for panic disorder; in fact, empirically validated treatments such as medications, cognitive-behavioral therapy and exposure therapy are much less dramatic, and require much more work on the part of the patient. Another hit man who suffers from panic attacks without agoraphobia is Pierce Brosnan's character in *The Matador* (2005).

In *Panic Room* (2002), Meg (Jody Foster) and her young daughter, Sarah, move into an extravagant mansion on the Upper West side of Manhattan, and while spending their first night in their new home, three thieves, expecting an empty house, break in hoping to steal millions of dollars. Meg and Sarah find refuge in the steel-plated, impervious "panic room" which holds both the money and their safety. The viewer sees Meg experiencing symptoms of a panic disorder as she experiences difficulty breathing and her face expresses fear when she becomes enclosed in the panic room for the first time in a non-threatening situation and her daughter asks, "Mom you're not gonna wig out, are you?" When confronted with a dangerous situation, Meg shows resiliency and her panic is justified. It is interesting to note that the stress of the situation triggers Sarah's anxiety and causes a hypoglycemic response so severe her face changes color.

In *Lady in a Cage* (1964), Olivia de Havilland stars as Mrs. Hilyard, an upper class woman who is trapped inside her home elevator when the electricity in her house goes out. In making a call for help, she attracts thieves who rob her and try to hurt her. The film melodramatically and metaphorically illustrates claustrophobia and panic attacks. Panic attacks are also frequently depicted in a realistic way but with only a minor role in the overall story, as in *Das Experiment* (2001), *My First Mister* (2001), *Monster's Ball* (2001), and *Hannah and Her Sisters* (1986).

Panic Disorder with Agoraphobia

When there is a feeling of vulnerability and fear of experiencing a panic attack, **panic disorder with agoraphobia** is diagnosed. The individual suffering from this type of panic disorder is afraid of the perceived consequences of a panic attack (e.g., losing control, going crazy or dying) and finds ways to limit his or her life to avoid subsequent panic episodes. The avoidance can be quite subtle (e.g., these individuals may be able to leave the home comfortably if they leave with a person perceived to be "safe" and whose presence would somehow magically protect them from the catastrophic consequences of a panic attack). Although the word agoraphobia comes from the Greek word for fear of the marketplace, the idea that people with agoraphobia fear all "open places" is incorrect; the person may associate any number of situations or places with fear of panic attacks. In the film *Matchstick Men* (2003), it is unclear if Roy has fear of panic or fear of situations and places. If the latter criterion is met, it is more likely he is experiencing *situational* panic due to his fear of contamination and this is what causes him to avoid public places – nevertheless, these symptoms are not sufficient to justify a diagnosis of agoraphobia.

It is important to differentiate between true agoraphobia (which is driven by a strong desire to avoid the perceived catastrophic consequences associated with symptoms of anxiety that occur whenever one leaves a safe area) and the isolation, withdrawal, and seclusion that result from thought disorders such as paranoid schizophrenia. For example, an announcement of a support group for agoraphobia was advertised in the local paper, one person called and requested an opportunity to participate. However, during a brief telephone interview, the woman disclosed that she was genuinely concerned about being eaten by aliens if she ventured far from her home. Clearly, she had a thought disorder and would not be an appropriate candidate for the group.

Panic disorder with agoraphobia should also be differentiated from the diagnosis given to an individual with **agoraphobia without panic** who may experience catastrophic fears related to other physiological experiences such as fainting, vomiting, headaches, etc. These individuals are not afraid of panic attacks; however, the avoidance seen in these situations can be identical to the avoidance in those who are attempting to avoid panic attacks. With both disorders, the individual is literally housebound and cannot leave the perceived safety of their home. In extreme cases, people with agoraphobia are unable to leave their bedrooms.

Sean Connery's character William Forrester in *Finding Forrester* (2000) could probably be diagnosed with panic disorder with agoraphobia (he also has characteristics of avoidant personality, a clinical problem with features that overlap with anxiety disorders). Forrester does not leave his apartment (in part out of a fear he will have a panic attack in public), is socially awkward, and experiences panic when he is required to go into a public place. He does what many people with agoraphobia do – he has his groceries delivered so he does not have to leave his apartment. The film captures the subjective experience associated with Forrester's panic attacks when the camera shows his "spinning" feeling, and sound is blurred. In the throes of his anxiety, Forrester wanders off and gets lost. At the end of the film, the viewer sees the potential for successful treatment of agoraphobia when Forrester is shown riding his bike on busy and crowded streets.

One of the most interesting cinematic portrayals of agoraphobia is found in Robert Taicher's movie *Inside Out* (1986). In this film, Elliott Gould plays Jimmy Morgan, a New York businessman with marked agoraphobia who has not left his house for ten years. He has food delivered to him, arranges for call girls to come to his apartment for anonymous sex, places bets over the phone, and almost never ventures out of his house until forced to by circumstances beyond his control.

Phobias

Fears are labeled as **phobias** only when specific conditions are met. Marked anxiety must be present in the presence of the phobic stimulus and must routinely occur with exposure to the stimulus. In addition, the phobic individual must generally be aware that the magnitude of the fear response is excessive. Most people with specific phobias will avoid the stimulus situations that leave them fearful to avoid the extreme distress they experience in these situations. Successful treatment of phobia involves exposing the person to the phobic object in a safe and controlled environment. Over time and with continual exposure, the person becomes comfortable with the object. However, the fear never truly leaves, and at times of extreme stress, the original fear and anxiety around the object can reappear.

Tom Hanks' character Dr. Robert Langdon in *The Da Vinci Code* (2006) is afraid to go into small, enclosed spaces such as an elevator or the back of a locked truck. He experiences shortness of breath and becomes hyperfocused (intense mental concentration focusing on a narrow subject). Mel Brooks' character in *High Anxiety* (1977) suffers from severe acrophobia which generalizes to a fear of planes, escalators, elevators, higher numbered floors in hotels, and any high places where he can look down. He experiences dizziness, nausea, and vertigo in these situations. Specific fears are sometimes justified. Spiders can bite us; people do fall from high spaces; and even small cats can scratch us. Specific phobia occurs when there are excessive or unreasonable fear of an object or situation and the anxiety-provoking stimulus is avoided. Various subtypes of this disorder include animals (i.e., dogs, insects), natural environment (i.e., storms, water), blood-injection/injury (i.e., medical procedures), situational (i.e., bridges, elevators), or other miscellaneous stimuli (i.e., situations that might lead to choking). Specific phobias will occasionally remit spontaneously in the absence of treatment, but this is relatively rare. A fear of flying is depicted in Rachel McAdams' character in the Wes Craven thriller *Red Eye* (2005).

Many phobias are triggered by a specific traumatic event (at least traumatic to the individual experiencing the event). This was clearly the situation in *Vertigo* (1958), a classic Alfred Hitchcock film that stars Jimmy Stewart as John Ferguson, a San Francisco police detective, who is paralyzed by his fear of heights. The phobia has a traumatic etiology: While chasing a criminal across a rooftop, John almost falls to his death. A fellow officer, trying to aid John, is killed when he plunges to the street below. John, overcome with guilt, develops **acrophobia**, a debilitating fear of heights. The term *vertigo* refers to either marked dizziness or a confused, disoriented state of mind. Both meanings apply in this complex and the engrossing film. At one point in the film, John designs his own behavior modification program, stating, "I have a theory that I can work up to heights a little bit at a time." He puts a stepladder near the window, stands on the first step, waits, gets down, stands on the second step, waits, goes to the third step, becomes frightened and dizzy, and then falls to the floor.

In *Batman Begins* (2005), eight-year old Bruce Wayne (Christian Bale) develops a bat phobia after falling into a cave and encountering a swarm of bats. After Bruce urges his parents to leave an opera featuring actors dressed as bat-like creatures, his parents are murdered in front of him. He blames himself for his parents' murder by reasoning that they would not have left the theatre if he had not been afraid of bats. In response to these traumatic events, he gradually exposes himself to the feared stimulus and eventually transforms into a superhero with a bat-like appearance. By becoming "batman," he further reduces his anxiety and conquers his fear.

Claustrophobia is evident in Dakota Fanning's character in *War of the Worlds* (2005). Her father repeatedly teaches her to use coping skills involving an integration of safety reminders, closing her eyes, positioning her arms in a self-soothing way, imagination, and self-talk.

Social Phobia

Intense and persistent fears of criticism and rejection characterize social phobias. People with social phobias experience anxiety in response to the possibility of or perception of thoughts of negative evaluation or scrutiny, and consequently they avoid situations in which they are likely to be observed by others. The disorder can take many different forms and occurs in situations that require public speaking, public performance, test taking, or social skills. Some male patients with social phobias are unable to urinate in public places (also called **paruresis**), as shown briefly in *Roger Dodger* (2002); other patients are unable to eat in public for fear they will make a mistake and be ridiculed. The disorder is related to common phenomena such as performance anxiety, stage fright, and shyness. When fears relate to almost *every* social situation, the social phobia is considered "generalized."

The onset of social phobias typically occurs in childhood or adolescence and the clinical course, if left untreated, is usually chronic, unremitting, and associated with significant impairment. Few people with social anxiety seek professional help. The symptoms of social phobia include tachycardia, trembling, sweating, blushing, dizziness, and hyperventilation and occur in anticipation of or during a social interaction. Even more distressing is the sensation of impending doom that frequently occurs. Finally, patients feel an overwhelming need to escape from the social situation that is causing their distress. In the *40 Year Old Virgin* (2005), Andy Stitzer (Steve Carrell) avoids dating and sexual relationships due to anxiety. The film's premise is that Andy is a virgin due to intense fear of criticism or rejection.

Woody Allen's character in *Play It Again, Sam* (1972) is an exaggerated portrayal of someone with social anxiety (related to dating) and other neuroses. His portrayal personifies the "worst-case-scenario thinking" that individuals may engage prior to and even during a date. His character bumbles about and knocks things over, all in chaotic, comical movements. Any person nervous about an upcoming date can watch this portrayal and think, "At least I won't be that bad!" It is important to remember that shyness, performance anxiety, stage fright, and anticipatory anxiety are *normal* anxiety experiences to stressful and/or social situations.

Anticipatory anxiety about social situations often sets up a self-fulfilling prophecy. The phobic individual worries excessively about the performance demands of an upcoming event, loses sleep worrying about the situation, becomes tremendously anxious just before the event, and in fact performs poorly in the actual situation because of the high levels of anxiety. This poor performance then confirms people's beliefs about their inability to perform adequately in these situations, and their fear is exacerbated, causing them to perform even more poorly in similar situations in the future.

Social phobias are portrayed or implied in numerous films. In *Coyote Ugly* (2000), a young woman, Violet, moves to New York City to try to make it as a songwriter. Her social anxiety disorder keeps her from reaching her full potential so she takes a job as a "coyote" bartender at a wild nightclub. At this bar she begins to perform in front of large groups, deliberately "exposing" herself to those situations that she fears; moreover, her boyfriend helps to desensitize her by having her sing in the dark. It is this exposure that helps her manage and work through her anxiety symptoms. In the film's climax, she begins to get stage fright while performing and attempts to leave the stage; however, when the lights are turned off she is able to perform and she continues performing when the lights come back on. Violet believes the etiology of her social phobia is genetic; her mother also went to New York City to be a singer but left because of her own social phobia, and Violet believes she is carrying a "gene" for her inability to sing in front of others and her other avoidance symptoms. After she is able to perform, Violet learns it was her

father who encouraged her mother to move home, and her mother never had a social phobia.

The painfully shy woman is a common film motif found in *Amelie* (2001), *Lonely Hearts* (1981), *Rocky* (1976), *The Fisher King* (1991), and *I've Heard the Mermaids Singing* (1987). Shy and socially unskilled men are portrayed in *Bubble* (2005), *The Shape of Things* (2003), *Dummy* (2002), *Marty* (1955), *Untamed Heart* (1993), *Awakenings* (1990), *Goodbye, Mr. Chips* (1939), *Howard's End* (1992), *The Remains of the Day* (1993), and all of the Charlie Chaplin films in which he played the Little Tramp. The ways in which two shy adolescents come to grips with their emerging sexuality and a racist society are portrayed in a wonderful Australian film, *Flirting* (1990).

Posttraumatic Stress Disorder

Posttraumatic stress disorders (PTSD) occur after exposure to traumatic events. The individual with a posttraumatic stress disorder must have personally witnessed or experienced some event that involved actual or threatened death or serious injury and must have responded with "intense fear, helplessness, or horror" (*DSM-IV-TR*). The traumatic event is then re-experienced by the individual in the form of nightmares, recurrent recollections, and flashbacks or as physiological distress. The PTSD victim works hard to avoid these recurrent experiences. In addition, the individual usually experiences sleep disturbance, irritability, difficulty concentrating, hypervigilance or an exaggerated startle response.

Military combat is a common cause of posttraumatic stress disorder, but the disorder can also occur in response to earthquakes, fires or floods, mugging, rape, the witnessing of violence, or any of a variety of other traumatic situations. Often, seemingly innocuous stimuli will cause an individual to relive the anxiety-producing experience; for example, hearing a car backfire may trigger a terrifying war memory of combat for a war veteran. In war films such as the award-winning *Saving Private Ryan* (1998), even though PTSD is not portrayed *per se*, it would be easy to understand how one could develop PTSD as the viewer observes the ubiquitous trauma the soldiers experience. The award-winning film, *In the Valley of Elah* (2007) is based on the July 13, 2003, murder of Richard Davis, a 23-year-old army soldier who had just returned to Fort Benning, GA., when he was declared AWOL. The young veteran's charred remains were discovered in the woods four months later. Hank Deerfield (Tommy Lee Jones), father of the murdered soldier and a retired army investigator, uncovers the events surrounding his son's murder.

"Every man I kill, the farther away from home I feel."

Capt. John H. Miller (Tom Hanks)
in *Saving Private Ryan* (1998)

Many victims of combat or natural disasters experience what is sometimes referred to as **survivor guilt**. Some might feel guilty when they realize that their lives were spared while those of more "worthy" individuals (e.g., children, young parents) were taken. Consider Tom Cruise's character Ron Kovic, who would meet the criteria for PTSD, in *Born on the Fourth of July* (1989). Kovic's guilt about the death of his buddy "Wilson" is an example of survivor guilt.

In the fictitious film *Reign Over Me* (2007), Adam Sandler plays the role of a dentist coping with PTSD and survivor guilt after the death of his wife and three daughters who were passengers on one of the planes involved in the 9/11 destruction of the World Trade Center. Refusing to acknowledge his past or the tragedy, Charlie Fineman enters extreme isolation regressing to a child-like existence in which he spends his time playing video games, listening to loud music, riding around on a scooter, watching movies, and pounding on his drums. He gets considerable emotional support as a results of the efforts of an old friend, another dentist played by Don Cheadle. However, the film is somewhat clumsy in dealing with this delicate subject, and teaches the viewer very little about the sequelae associated with something as traumatic as loss of one's entire family.

Suicide and suicide attempts are somewhat common in patients with PTSD. In addition, it is essential to assess for comorbidity (especially substance abuse) in cases of PTSD. Nearly all PTSD patients who are suicidal will be found to have a concomitant psychiatric condition.

The movie *Fearless* (1993) provides an interesting picture of an unusual reaction to trauma. Max Klein (Jeff Bridges) is one of a small group of survivors of a devastating plane crash. He assists a number of other passengers and is celebrated as a hero and a saint. He becomes convinced he is invulnerable and grows increasingly impatient

with the banal concerns of his wife and child. After a near-death experience precipitated by an allergic reaction to strawberries, he returns to normal and reestablishes a loving relationship with his wife and son. The movie includes a very interesting segment in which a psychiatrist (who is employed by the airlines because he has written a best-selling book about PTSD) leads a discussion group for survivors of the crash.

Kevin Spacey's portrayal of Prot, a man who claims to be from another planet, presents a diagnostic enigma in *K-Pax* (2001). One way to view the film (another way is discussed in Chapter 3) is to assume that this character has PTSD. The viewer learns through flashbacks that Prot is Robert Porter, a man who experiences trauma when he returns home to find his wife and daughter murdered and the killer still in the home. Prot/Porter re-experiences the trauma under hypnosis and displays significant physiological arousal (e.g., a racing heart rate, elevated blood pressure) when his psychiatrist (Jeff Bridges) forces him to recall the traumatic incident. Porter engaged in extensive avoidance following the trauma – denial, estrangement from his home town, inability to recall information, and a restricted range of affect.

In *The Fisher King* (1991), Robin Williams plays a former college professor who becomes homeless and psychotic after witnessing his wife being gunned down in a restaurant. However, the active, well-formed, and specific hallucinations Williams experiences (e.g., a red knight riding a horse in Central Park with flames shooting out of his head) would be very unlikely to occur as a result of a traumatic experience. The character Jeff Bridges plays in the same film, a disc jockey who withdraws from life and abuses alcohol and drugs after a traumatic event, presents a far more realistic portrayal of PTSD. Although *The Fisher King* is imprecise and confusing in the way it links trauma to psychosis, PTSD is not uncommon among people who are homeless.

The stressors experienced by homeless people are illustrated in the films *Ironweed* (1987) and *The Saint of Fort Washington* (1993). *Ironweed* (1987) is a compelling film in which Jack Nicholson plays an alcoholic whose drinking is apparently related to his guilt about dropping and killing his infant son. Many of the symptoms of PTSD have become obliterated by Nicholson's alcoholism, which has become the dominant theme in his life. *Ironweed* illustrates the way in which alcohol abuse can develop as a secondary problem in response to trauma and can then become the primary psychological problem as abuse progresses to addiction.

Dozens of movies have been made about the Vietnam War, and many of these (as well as other war movies) illustrate either acute stress disorders or, more commonly in those that follow the hero home after the war, PTSD. Some of the most powerful of these films are *Born on the Fourth of July* (1989), *Coming Home* (1978), *The Deer Hunter* (1978), *Apocalypse Now* (1979), *The Killing Fields* (1984), *Platoon* (1986), *Good Morning, Vietnam* (1987), *Hamburger Hill* (1987), and *Full Metal Jacket* (1987).

In the original version of *The Manchurian Candidate* (1962), Frank Sinatra plays a brainwashed trauma victim who has recurring nightmares. He wakes up screaming with extensive sweating and a recollection of traumatic dreams that seem real. In a recent remake of *The Manchurian Candidate* (2004), director Jonathan Demme updates the film by including contemporary politics and more recent wartime experiences. Denzel Washington plays a Major who returns from the Gulf War with PTSD, paranoia, nightmares, and memories he cannot understand. He displays flat affect when he describes events surrounding the war, and he experiences intrusive memories. He becomes obsessed with trying to uncover the truth about what happened to him and his men. He hallucinates blood oozing from the forehead of a woman and has a flashback to a time when he was seeing a hypnotist; this symbolizes a real memory coming back and triggers a panic attack. He slowly begins to put together the sinister pieces of a political plot that involved extensive trauma and torture as well as physical and psychological abuse and brain-washing. PTSD symptoms are also displayed by Nicole Kidman's character in *The Human Stain* (2003) as well as by characters in *Open Hearts* (2002), *The Princess and the Warrior* (2000), and *The Pawnbroker* (1965). The latter film portrays a defeated concentration camp survivor who has become numb and indifferent in response to wartime experiences that included seeing his wife raped and his children killed.

Acute Stress Disorder

Acute stress disorder is in many ways similar to PTSD. However, acute stress disorder occurs relatively quickly after the traumatic event (within no more than four weeks) and may resolve quickly or develop into PTSD. In contrast, the symptoms of PTSD by definition have to last more than a month, and the onset of symptoms may occur months or even years after exposure to trauma. In the small, but powerful movie, *Grace is Gone* (2008), Stanley Philips (John Cusack) is unable

to accept and process his wife's death in Iraq. Instead, he drives his daughters from the upper Midwest to a Disneyland-like Park for a brief vacation. Marisa Tomei's character in *In the Bedroom* (2001) experiences a traumatic event when her boyfriend is murdered by her estranged husband. In a subsequent scene, she is shown as depressed and expressionless.

Generalized Anxiety Disorder

Some people are characterologically anxious; they walk around with a sense of apprehension and experience physiological arousal in a variety of different situations. They display what is sometimes called **free-floating anxiety**. Their condition can be quite debilitating. These individuals frequently receive a diagnosis of **generalized anxiety disorder**; the diagnosis requires that worry and anxiety be present more days than not.

Anxiety symptoms associated with generalized anxiety disorder include the same physiological, cognitive, and behavioral symptoms associated with other anxiety disorders, but the symptoms are chronic. The individual with this disorder may have multiple somatic complaints such as tachycardia, a dry mouth, and gastrointestinal distress. He or she will worry constantly about the multiple things that can go wrong in life and may be irritable and short-tempered because of anxiety. The lifetime prevalence of generalized anxiety disorder in the general population is about 5%, but relatively few of these patients actively seek out treatment. Onset of symptoms typically occurs in childhood or adolescence.

Nicholas Cage plays two twin brothers, Charlie and Donald, in *Adaptation* (2002). Both brothers are screenwriters, but one is much more neurotic than the other. No make-up or artistic tricks are used to differentiate the two twins; instead, Cage's talent alone is sufficient to portray both the worried and neurotic Charlie and the easy-going Donald. This provides a nice contrast for people studying anxiety. Charlie anxiously struggles with writer's block and he is plagued with self-doubt and preoccupation with himself, both hallmark symptoms of generalized anxiety disorder. In another scene, Charlie is too anxious to approach an attractive woman played by Meryl Streep. The viewer learns about Charlie's anxiety, worry, and rumination not only through cinematic close-ups displaying his anxiety symptoms (e.g., sweating), but also through the voice-over indicating his thought processes. A major theme of this film speaks to how people try to "adapt" to circumstance, problems, and, in this case, anxiety.

Kissing Jessica Stein (2002) explores sexuality and relationships through the character of a New York journalist, Jessica Stein, who is tired of the dating scene and its limited offerings. She places an ad for "women seeking women" and meets a woman who turns out to be a great match. As their relationship develops, Jessica must battle her own neuroses about a lesbian relationship as well as her feelings for an ex-boyfriend who is still in love with her. Jessica experiences generalized anxiety as a worrier and classic neurotic. She is uptight and rigid, and very anxious about anything new or different. She does not have the self-confidence necessary to defend herself when she is criticized in public. She rarely stands up for herself and is unable to be honest to family or friends about her female lover. Jessica describes her experiences with panic attacks and mentions various other anxiety symptoms. She stumbles over her words and tries to control situations in which she becomes nervous. After reading a book about lesbians she realizes she is afraid of both sexuality and sensuality. Her anxiety is particularly noticeable at the dinner table prior to a family member's wedding; she is preoccupied with what people think of her and is unable to be honest, covering up the truth with repeated lies. This film emphasizes honesty, individuality, and the potential for change.

"I check my answering machine nine times every day and I can't sleep at night because I feel that there is so much to do and fix and change in the world, and I wonder every day if I am making a difference and if I will ever express the greatness within me, or if I will remain forever paralyzed by muddled madness inside my head. I've wept on every birthday . . . and I feel that life is terribly unfair and sometimes beautiful and wonderful and extraordinary but also numbing and horrifying and insurmountable and I hate myself a lot of the time. The rest of the time I adore myself and I adore my life in this city and in this world we live in. This huge and wondrous, bewildering, brilliant, horrible world."

Jessica Stein describing the ways her anxiety disorder has limited her life

---

Most Woody Allen comedies will include at least one character with an anxiety disorder, and many depict characters with generalized anxiety disorder (usually played by Woody Allen himself). Indeed, neurotic, insecure, and self-absorbed characters and the existential anxiety produced by the need to cope with a complex and impersonal world form the basis for much of Allen's humor. *Annie Hall* (1977) and *Manhattan* (1979) are the Woody Allen films that best illustrate generalized anxiety disorder.

Mel Brooks' now classic film *High Anxiety* (1977) makes fun of numerous movies with Hitchcock-like psychological motifs. Mel Brooks plays Dr. Richard H. Thorndyke, an anxiety-ridden psychiatrist, who takes over a prestigious mental institution, "The Psycho-Neurotic Institute for the Very Very Nervous." Thorndyke must battle an unethical and murderous staff in order to save his patients and himself. Meanwhile he struggles with his own generalized anxiety and phobias.

International Films: Anxiety Disorders

An excellent portrayal of obsessive-compulsive disorder is seen in *Dirty, Filthy, Love* (2004, UK). This short but powerful film begins with a successful architect, Mark Furness (Michael Sheen), taking a leave of absence from work due to his OCD. His wife leaves him because she can no longer deal with his odd behaviors. During periods of stress, his OCD symptoms are exacerbated and his tics (from Tourette's syndrome) worsen. This film depicts a warm and sensitive person who is trying to cope with the challenges and consequences of mental illness. Many typical compulsions are displayed such as climbing the stairs by walking up four stairs and down two, flicking lights on and off, and touching walls going up and down the stairs. Throughout the film, rituals dominate every aspect of Mark's life. Seeing Mark find acceptance in a "support group" allows the viewer to glimpse the variety of behaviors associated with OCD and the spectrum of behavioral interventions used in treating anxiety disorders. As Mark becomes increasingly ill, the destructive nature of mental illness is portrayed.

In the comedy, *Nothing* (2003, Canada), two roommates, Dave and Andrew, struggle with the stress and struggles of everyday life. Andrew has an anxiety disorder, most likely panic disorder with agoraphobia. He refuses to leave the house and has avoided going outside since his teen years. He has arranged to work as a travel agent so he can stay at home. He reacts to situations with anxiety and distress, always thinks the worst in any situations, catastrophizes, jumps to conclusions, and is exceedingly fearful. Dave and Andrew discover that they are able to make things disappear by hating whatever they want to make disappear. The problem is if they go too far with this ability they are unable to make things reappear again.

Andrew: "Oh my God, we are going to die."
Dave: "For once I don't think you're overreacting"
Andrew: "For as long as I can remember I've been afraid of going outside and now it's not there. But I'm not going to be around to enjoy it not being there"

Two best friends in *Nothing* (2003)

The Norwegian film *Elling* (2001) presents an honest and fair portrayal of what it is like to cope with the debilitating effects of mental illness. A small, feeble man named Elling is taken to a psychiatric hospital after his mother, who was his caregiver for 40 years, dies. It is there Elling meets another eccentric, Kjell, who has sexual obsessions about women and problems with anger management. The two men are discharged together and placed in supportive housing under the guidance of a social worker. The film is about their return to the reality of everyday living. Each man must prove he can live on his own.

Elling states he has two enemies: dizziness and anxiety; "they follow me everywhere." He refuses to leave his house and believes he is unable to answer the phone (even when it is only the social worker checking in). He has learned to be completely dependent on his mother and the hospital staff, so it is a great achievement when he is able to walk to the end of the block to go to a store. Further challenges are met when Elling begins to talk on the phone, eat at a restaurant, and go on vacation. Elling takes another big risk in battling his anxiety by going to a public poetry reading; arriving several hours early, he befriends an isolated, famous poet. Elling is rigid in his behavior, worries constantly, and is terrified of losing his only friend Kjell to Kjell's new girlfriend. Elling

expresses this fear in jealous passive-aggressiveness whenever he feels he has been left out or abandoned. His friendship with Kjell develops and deepens as they sacrifice for one another and stick together through the difficult times. "Hard work pays off" is a theme applied to the psychological challenges Elling and Kjell face. Rather than avoiding their fears, they face them and in turn, find freedom – freedom from dependency, from the hospital, and from isolation.

The interaction between the social worker, Frank, and Elling is noteworthy and inspirational. Frank sets firm boundaries and gives clear directives to Elling, taking a "tough love" approach that emphasizes that Elling must take chances to challenge himself or he will lose his new residence. Frank is accepting and understanding of Elling's eccentric ideas, and tolerant at the film's end when he walks into the home and finds Elling lying on the couch, drunk, and having thrown up on himself. Elling awakens and believes he is sure to lose his house and his freedom; instead, the opposite happens because this all too human behavior confirms in Frank's mind Elling's readiness to live on his own in the outside world.

Enduring Love (2004, UK) is a film about a freak hot air balloon accident in which several men attempt to save a young boy by grabbing onto a hot air balloon that is out of control. As the balloon rises higher and higher, each man saves himself by letting go soon enough, except for one who eventually dies. This traumatic incident leads the protagonist to develop symptoms of acute stress disorder and to vacillate from avoidance to rumination and from detachment to agitation in his relationships. His emotional distress is palpable as he displays inappropriate affect and struggles with guilt and anger.

In the Australian film *Walking on Water* (2002), an assisted-suicide plan for a man dying of AIDS goes awry and a friend forcefully suffocates the dying man. The friend is plagued by intrusive images and memories of the suffocation; he tries hard to avoid his memories, acts out in self-destructive ways, and displays considerable irritability and interpersonal conflict. He appears to be suffering from acute stress disorder.

The protagonist in *She's One of Us* (2003, France) clearly struggles with social anxiety. She is socially awkward, frequently displays inappropriate affect, and misperceives social situations. In interactions, she pauses, looks away, hesitates and shakes; heavy breathing can be heard off-camera to simulate her anxiety. She is eager to please and to seek reassurance.

Critical Thinking Questions

- How does anxiety play a role in OCD and how does this differ in panic disorder?
- Compare and contrast the symptoms of Howard Hughes in *The Aviator* (2004), Mark Furness in *Dirty Filthy Love* (2004), and Roy Waller in *Matchstick Men* (2003).
- How might the cinematic characters who have returned from the Iraq war with PTSD differ from those who return from Vietnam with PTSD?
- Some existential therapists such as Irvin Yalom and Rollo May have argued that anxiety is an essential part of the human condition, and that it needs to be confronted rather than avoided (e.g., they discourage the use of benzodiazepines after the experience of intense trauma). Do you agree?
- Are there some occupations in which it might be adaptive to have OCD?
- Compare the dysfunction associated with the specific phobia of John Ferguson (*Vertigo*, 1958) with that experienced by Dr. Robert Langdon (*The Da Vinci Code*, 2006).

Anxiety Disorders

Obsessive Compulsive Disorders

- *The Aviator* (2004)
- *Matchstick Men* (2003)
- *Dirty, Filthy Love* (2004)
- *As Good As It Gets* (1997)

PTSD

- *Born on the Fourth of July* (1989)

Panic Disorder

- *Finding Forrester* (2000)

Phobias

- *Vertigo* (1958)
- *Elling* (2001)
- *Batman Begins* (2005)
- *Play It Again, Sam* (1972)

Further Exploration

If you have time to read just one book relevant to this chapter, make it:

Antony, M. M., & Rowa, K. (2008). *Social anxiety disorder*. Cambridge, MA: Hogrefe & Huber Publishers.

If you only have time for one article, read:

Bouton, M. E., Mineka, S., & Barlow, D. H. (2001). A modern learning theory perspective on the etiology of panic disorder. *Psychological Review, 108*, 4–32.

Chapter 3

Dissociative and Somatoform Disorders

Matricide is probably the most unbearable crime of all...
so he had to erase the crime, at least in his own mind.
A police psychiatrist attempts to explain
Norman Bates' behavior in *Psycho* (1960)

Questions to Consider While Watching *Psycho*

- Alfred Hitchcock's *Psycho* (1960) is regarded as one of the greatest films ever made. Is it an accurate presentation of mental illness?
- Do films like *Psycho* do a disservice to people with mental disorders by perpetuating the myth of the homicidal psychopath?
- Bates' voyeurism seems almost innocuous compared with his other behaviors. How often are paraphilias (such as voyeurism) linked with violence?
- Bates has trouble saying the word "bathroom" when he shows the hotel room to Marion (Janet Leigh). Is it common for people who commit sexual crimes to be uncomfortable with mature discussions of sexuality or elimination?
- How often in a lifetime of clinical experience would a therapist treat a patient with a dissociative disorder? How often would a Norman Bates come along?
- Marion has stolen $40,000. How does Hitchcock manage to make her a sympathetic character with whom we can all identify?
- How does a patient with a dissociative disorder suppress the evidence presented by everyday experience (e.g., the nonresponsiveness of the dead Mrs. Bates)?
- How does Hitchcock's storyline fit with the psychological zeitgeist of the 1960s?
- Would you feel comfortable working with a patient like Norman Bates? Would you insist that security officers be present during your evaluation?

Patient Evaluation

Patient's stated reason for coming: "I had to come. They made me. Of course, I'm eager to get any help you can offer. I truly do suspect you can be helpful."

History of the present illness: Norman Bates is a 27-year-old white male who has been referred for psychological evaluation by the Madison county court. Mr. Bates is awaiting sentencing on four counts of murder. The alleged murder of his mother and stepfather occurred more than a decade ago; the two recent killings are reported to have occurred within the past 30 days.

Past psychiatric illness, treatment, and outcomes: Mr. Bates has a long history of eccentric and odd behavior, including isolation, withdrawal, seclusiveness, and secrecy. These behaviors have been noted by local authorities; however, there has never been any evidence of danger to self or others, and Mr. Bates has never received treatment in the mental health system.

Medical history: There is a history of the usual childhood diseases, such as mumps and chicken pox. Aside from these childhood experiences, Mr. Bates has never seen a physician. He has never been hospitalized.

Psychosocial history: Mr. Norman Bates reports that he walked and talked at about the normal times. He has a long history of self-imposed isolation. He is reported to have been lonely and withdrawn in school, and he cannot identify anyone he regarded as a friend when he was growing up. He obtained passing grades, although he dropped out of school at the age of 16 to help run a family motel. When the expressway bypassed the motel, business dwindled to almost nothing. His mother and stepfather died approximately 10 years ago; since that time, Mr. Bates has managed the motel and the family home on his own. He manages the books for the motel, and he performs routine maintenance on both the motel and the family home. He has no brothers or sisters, and there are no living relatives. He reports devoting almost all of his leisure time to his hobby of taxidermy. Mr. Bates has never been married or involved in a significant romantic relationship. He does not date, and he has no regular or routine social activities.

Drug and alcohol history: Mr. Bates denies any history of drug or alcohol use. He believes drunkenness is a sin, and he prefers not to be tempted by social drinking. He does not smoke.

Behavioral observations: Mr. Bates arrived on time for the evaluation, accompanied by a deputy sheriff. He was appropriately groomed and dressed. He was polite to the point of being obsequious. He cooperated fully with all tasks, except for those instances in which his identity would be questioned or challenged. At these points, the patient became resentful and stopped cooperating with the evaluation.

Mental status examination: Mr. Bates was alert and oriented to place and time. He was disoriented to person, however, and steadfastly maintained that he was actually his mother. He became agitated and threatened to leave the room when the obvious was pointed out (e.g., he had male features, she had been buried some years ago, etc.). After the evaluator stopped challenging his assertion that he was in fact his mother, he cooperated with the evaluation and was able to answer all other questions on the Mini Mental State Exam, obtaining an overall score of 29.

Functional assessment: The patient appears to be of average intellectual ability. He has not completed high school, and he has no significant occupational abilities other than minimal bookkeeping skills. However, he appears to have been able to manage on his own for the past 10 years. He has no living family, and there are no friends to provide social support. (Mr. Bates appears comfortable in his isolation and does not appear to be distressed by the solitary nature of his existence.) Mr. Bates' social skills are limited, and he tends to be quite awkward and uncomfortable in social situations. However, his entrenched and well-defended delusional disorder appears to be his most limiting feature, and he is unlikely to function successfully in either occupational or social settings as long as he continues to maintain he is his mother.

Strengths: Mr. Bates is of at least average intelligence and he possesses the skills necessary to manage on his own. He is usually friendly and he has many years of experience as a hotel manager.

Diagnosis: Dissociative identity disorder

Treatment plan: Mr. Bates was referred by the court for a forensic evaluation, and therefore no systematic treatment plan has been developed. Given his legal problems, it is likely that Mr. Bates will be imprisoned for life, and it is unlikely he will be offered the benefits of active psychological treatment in the correctional system. Even if treatment is available, it will require years of daily work before Mr. Bates begins to understand himself or his problems.

Prognosis: Mr. Bates lacks insight into the nature of his problems or their causes. He resists efforts to change his belief system. He has maintained these fallacious beliefs for the past decade, and they are likely to prove intractable. If he is acquitted by reason of insanity, he will be remanded to the state hospital for intensive treatment. However, even then his prognosis is poor.

Psycho and Psychopathology

In the latter half of the 1900s, films began depicting the psychological complexities of the human personality. *Psycho*, Alfred Hitchcock's 1960 film, describes a young man who assumed the personality of his mother after he murdered her and her lover. This film is regarded by many as Hitchcock's finest film. It is a superb movie; unfortunately, it also contributes to the negative stereotype of persons with mental illnesses.

The film begins in a hotel room in Phoenix, with Marion Crane, played by Janet Leigh, who is scantily dressed. She is discussing her future with her lover, Sam Loomis, played by John Gavin. Marion wants to get married, but Sam is unable to make a commitment because of previous financial commitments to his ex-wife. After the afternoon rendezvous, she returns to work, where she steals $40,000. The next morning she heads toward Sam's hometown with the money.

During a rainstorm, she seeks shelter at the Bates Motel, only 15 miles from Sam's home. Norman Bates, played by Anthony Perkins, invites her to dinner at his home behind the motel. Marion hears Norman's mother yelling at him for wanting to bring a girl to dinner. Norman fixes sandwiches for Marion and apologizes for his mother's behavior. They talk in a room adjacent to the office, and Norman shows off his taxidermy collection. Norman later watches her undress through a peephole separating her room from the office. That night Marion is brutally murdered by someone who appears to be Norman's mother. The murder scene occurs in a shower, and this scene (with its non-diegetic dramatic music) is one of the most famous scenes in film history.

Norman cleans up the blood from the shower room and puts Marion's body in the trunk of her new car (and unknowingly hides the stolen $40,000 there as well). He then drives the car to an isolated area, where he is able to sink the car and its contents into a swamp.

Instead of telling the police about the stolen money, Marion's boss hires a private detective, Milton Arbogast, to track Marion and recover the money. He traces her to the Bates Motel after following Marion's sister, Lila, to Sam's. Neither Lila nor Sam know anything about the stolen money. Mr. Arbogast is killed when he visits the Bates home to investigate his hunch that Norman Bates is somehow involved in the disappearance of Marion.

"I'll just sit here and be quiet, just in case they do suspect me. They're probably watching me. Well, let them. Let them see what kind of a person I am. I'm not even going to swat that fly. I hope they are watching. They'll see. They'll see and they'll know and they'll say, 'Why, she wouldn't even harm a fly.'"

Norman Bates sits in his (her) cell, smiling and thinking to himself (herself)

Lila and Sam then contact the local sheriff, who is willing to investigate Marion's disappearance if an official missing persons report is made. He also informs Sam and Lila that Norman's mother has been dead for 10 years and that she killed herself after poisoning her lover.

Lila and Sam return to the motel to solve the case. In a very suspenseful ending, they find that Norman Bates had exhumed his mother's grave, mummified her corpse, and kept her body with him in the house for the past 10 years. Bates had always been a disturbed child, and, after he killed his mother and her lover, he coped with his guilt by assum-

ing her identity. By the end of the movie, Norman has totally assumed the alter ego of his mother.

Gus van Sant remade *Psycho* in 1998, this time in color. Van Sant's version is faithful to the original script and pays homage to Hitchcock, but the remake lacks the power and fascination of the original.

Dissociation, Trauma, and Films

Alteration in consciousness can occur under many different conditions. With alcohol intoxication, there is a clouding of consciousness with attenuated awareness of sensory stimuli and diminished attention to the environment and self. Some drugs produce a dream-like state in which the individual is conscious but inattentive. Heightened states of attention, concentration, and absorption brought about through hypnosis, meditation, or relaxation are further examples of alterations in consciousness.

Dissociation involves a separation of consciousness with closely connected feelings, behaviors, thoughts, or memories of events (APA, 2000). In dissociation, events and information that would ordinarily be connected or integrated are divided from one another. Dissociation is often viewed as a normal defense mechanism that can be used in frightening, stressful, or painful situations to cope with stress. It allows an individual to detach from overwhelming fear, pain, and helplessness generated by trauma.

Dissociation can be viewed on a continuum from minor dissociative experiences of everyday life (i.e., daydreaming) to major forms of psychopathology, such as multiple personality disorder (Allen & Smith, 1993; Bernstein & Putnam, 1986). Most people have minor dissociative experiences, such as driving a car over a familiar route and suddenly realizing that they do not remember what happened during all or part of the trip. In some cultures, dissociative states, such as trances, are common and accepted cultural activities or a routine part of religious experience. The development of extreme dissociative behavior patterns has been linked to trauma. For example, in *Sybil* (1976), the lead character's development of 16 different personalities was found to be the result of repeated physical and psychological abuse she experienced at the hands of a deranged and delusional mother.

Numerous films depict characters experiencing a traumatic event and many depict the lead character dissociating from the traumatic experience in order to cope. However, it is unlikely that any of the characters in the following five examples would be given a dissociative disorder diagnosis as there is not enough evidence in the film to meet all of the diagnostic criteria. In *Lilya 4-Ever* (2002), a young girl is prostituted against her will in a foreign country and she is neglected and abused; she dissociates during sexual intercourse with a paying customer. In *The Princess and the Warrior* (2001), a man is trapped in a bathroom stall while his wife is killed; his various traumatic reactions include "freezing," dissociating from reality, feeling tense and shaky and experiencing flashbacks. In *Natural Born Killers* (1994), Woody Harrelson and Juliette Lewis play characters who are both victims and perpetrators of various violent and traumatic events; in the film, dissociative pain numbing, dissociative perceptual distortion, dissociative time distortion, and dissociative derealization are depicted. *Swimming Pool* (2002) portrays a young woman exhibiting dissociative amnesia in her inability to remember killing a man. One particular dissociative episode occurs when she thinks she is seeing her mother; she screams when she is told her mother is not there, and then she faints. In the independent film *Searching for Paradise* (2002), a woman, in the middle of sex with a "fantasy-come-true" man, suddenly stops and states she feels betrayed by her partner; this seems to be a dissociative experience in which she is confusing her father who had left her and this "fantasy" man who has become real.

Another dissociative experience often experienced in traumatic situations is **derealization**. In derealization, the person feels detached from familiar people or places that seem unreal and non-recognizable. The size or shape of objects may be perceived as altered or strange, and people may seem mechanical. During the 1989 San Francisco Bay Area earthquake, 40% of the 101 persons interviewed afterward reported feeling as though their surroundings were unreal (Cardea & Spiegel, 1993). Filmmaker David Lynch's films seem to induce a derealization state for both his characters and his viewers, and his characters' identities are often confused and locations seem unreal. The films *Lost Highway* (1997) and *Mulholland Drive* (2001) are particularly good examples of this kind of derealization.

Dissociative Disorders in Films

There is controversy in the mental health community about the categorization of dissociative experiences as psychiatric disorders. Dissociation, by itself, does not necessarily lead to impairment and is not clear evidence of psychopathology. However, if dissociative states lead to distress and impairment in psychological, interpersonal, social, or vocational functioning, then they should be evaluated as psychiatric problems. Because dissociative symptoms such as amnesia and depersonalization can be present in other psychiatric disorders such as posttraumatic stress disorder and schizophrenia, no other psychiatric disorders can be present if a person's symptoms are diagnosed as a dissociative disorder. In addition, the disorder cannot be caused by a traumatic brain injury; this is the reason why films such as *Memento* (2000) are discussed in the "Neuropsychological Disorders" chapter.

There are four primary dissociative disorders: dissociative amnesia, dissociative fugue, dissociative identity disorder, and depersonalization disorder.

Dissociative Amnesia

Dissociative amnesias are characterized by an inability to recall important personal information, usually of a traumatic or stressful nature (e.g., the death of a child). Affected individuals can usually remember events up to the time of the trauma but have memory loss for events that occur after the event. Even though significant personal information is lost with dissociative amnesias, cognitive abilities and the ability to remember new information remain intact. This memory impairment is reversible. In the classic disorder, the person is quickly brought to a mental health provider because of the overt, dramatic change in memory. Persons with amnesia may have intense emotional reactions to stimuli without knowing the reasons for the reaction or the significance of it.

Even though filmmakers do not typically focus on the psychological etiology of amnesia, they have often used amnesia as a central theme. One example is the 1940 Academy Award-winning satire, *The Great Dictator*, starring Charles Chaplin, Paulette Goddard, and Jack Oakie. Chaplin plays a dual role as a Jewish barber and Adenoid Hynkel, dictator of Tomania. This spoof of Adolf Hitler begins when Chaplin plays a Jewish barber in a "Tomanian" ghetto who is recovering from amnesia and wakes up to find himself living under the thumb of Hynkel (also played by Chaplin). He escapes to Austria with a Jewish laundress, Paulette Goddard, who is in love with him. In Austria, he is mistaken for Hynkel, who had recently assumed control of the country. Chaplin then assumes the role of the dictator.

Amnesia is also portrayed in the excellent film *Sullivan's Travels* (1941) starring Joel McCrea and Veronica Lake and directed by Preston Sturges. The main character becomes amnestic when he is hit over the head and ends up being sentenced to six years on a chain gang. An example of traumatic amnesia triggered by a murder can be found in the film *Dead Again* (1991).

Amnesia allows a spoiled, self-centered, rich woman to experience life at the other end of the social ladder in the comedy *Overboard* (1987), directed by Garry Marshall. Dissociative amnesia is also illustrated in the classic films *Spellbound* (1945) and *Suddenly, Last Summer* (1959).

It would appear that the Jim Carrey and Kate Winslet characters in *Eternal Sunshine of the Spotless Mind* (2004) have some form of dissociative amnesia, as they are unable to remember certain events and people, particularly those related to a former significant other. However, because the memories are intentionally erased through the help of a specialist who erases traumatic memories with sophisticated technology, the diagnosis would not apply.

Hollywood movies have reaped some financial gain with action films using amnesia as a plot device, such as the successful *The Bourne Identity* (2002), and the unsuccessful *Paycheck* (2003). In the former, Jason Bourne, a CIA assassin, loses his memory after a failed spy mission and he is left to try to uncover who he is before he is killed.

The Forgotten (2004) stars Julianne Moore as Telly Paretta, a mother grieving over the loss of her nine-year-old son who was killed in an airplane accident. The plot thickens when Telly's husband and her therapist tell her that she never had a son, and that she created all the memories she has of her son as a response to a miscarriage. The movie is spoiled by a silly ending that negates the value of what could otherwise be a meaningful psychological exploration.

Mirage

In the film *Mirage* (1965), David Stillwell, played by Gregory Peck, develops amnesia after witnessing the accidental death of his boss and mentor, Calvin Clark. Stillwell, a scientist, has just discovered a method for neutralizing the effects of nuclear fallout. Believing that his mentor was working for world peace, Stillwell shares the information with him. When Stillwell realizes that his formula would end up being used to "produce" nuclear weapons, he sets the formula on fire in front of an open window. In an attempt to save the piece of paper, Calvin lunges toward Stillwell and falls to his death from the 27th floor. Stillwell observes the fall, is horrified, and then calmly picks up his empty briefcase and leaves the office. He has developed amnesia. The lights in the office building go out.

The audience has none of this information until the end of the film. The film actually opens during a blackout in an office building in New York City. David Stillwell appears to be a very calm, rational individual who leads a woman, Sheila, played by Diane Baker, down the darkened stairs. He does not recognize Sheila, but she recognizes him. Upon returning to his apartment, he is greeted by a man who attempts to kill him. Stillwell overpowers the intruder and leaves him unconscious in the service quarters. Gradually, Stillwell begins to realize that he has lost his memory, but he becomes convinced that he has been in an amnestic state for two years instead of two days. He seeks help from a psychiatrist, who questions his amnesia and throws him out of the office.

In this Hitchcock-style thriller, Stillwell's belief that he had been a cost accountant in New York is reinforced by his enemy, the Major, who hires thugs to follow Stillwell and get the formula. Stillwell next employs Detective Ted Caselle, played by Walter Matthau, to discover his identity and figure out who is trying to kill him. Caselle attempts to fit the pieces together but is killed in the process. A romance is rekindled between Sheila and Stillwell, who had previously been lovers.

Following the detective's death, Stillwell desperately contacts the same psychiatrist, who is again skeptical of Stillwell's amnesia. By now, Stillwell's memory is beginning to return and he realizes that his memory loss has been present for only two days. The psychiatrist asks some questions that provoke the retrieval of more memories. Gradually, the amnesia for his mentor's death lifts, and he is able to face the horror of the event.

Dissociative Fugue

Dissociative fugues are characterized by sudden, unexpected travel away from home or one's customary place of work, an inability to recall one's past, and confusion about personal identity or the assumption of a partial or completely new identity (e.g., a person whose business is failing may show up in a new city with a new identity and no memory of previous problems). With the onset of fugue, a person begins a new autobiographical memory that replaces the original one. These individuals appear normal and will not reveal any evidence of dissociative symptoms unless asked. When the fugue resolves, the original memories are recovered, but the fugue memories are lost. The individual then has a permanent void in personality history. Even though the prevalence of dissociative fugue has been reported as only 0.2% of the general population, it may be more common in times of war, natural disaster, and dislocation (Fullerton, Ursano & Wang, 2004).

Some patients with dissociative fugue disorders will travel short distances over brief periods; others may travel far and remain in a fugue state for months or years. The acclaimed and thought-provoking, Wim Wenders film, *Paris, Texas* (1984) introduces the character of Travis Clay Henderson, an individual suffering from dissociative fugue. He has been lost for four years and is found wandering in the desert. Eventually, he (partially) puts the pieces of his shattered life back together.

Renee Zellweger's character in *Nurse Betty* (2000) witnesses her husband's murder and shortly thereafter becomes convinced she is the former fiancée of her soap opera idol, and she travels across the country to find him. This character provides a fascinating springboard for a discussion of the differentiation between delusional disorder and other potential diagnoses. Jim Carrey's lead role in *The Majestic* (2001) would be another example of dissociative fugue had the experience not been caused by a head injury from an automobile accident; Carrey's character has amnesia, has traveled away from home, and readily takes on the identity of a "missing in action" soldier in a small town.

Amnesia and identity are central themes in *Identity Unknown* (1945), starring Richard Arlen and Cheryl Walker. In this film, a soldier develops amnesia during World War II and tries to recover his identity.

Unknown White Male

Perhaps the best film to date to examine the life of someone experiencing a fugue state is *Unknown White Male* (2005). This documentary, directed by Rupert Murray, is based on the real-life experience of Doug Bruce, a man who seemingly without reason developed a profound retrograde amnesia for everything that happened to him before July 3, 2003. Bruce is disoriented when he discovers himself on a subway bound for Coney Island with no recollection of any of the previous 37 years of his life. He is taken to a Coney Island hospital where he is examined for neurological injuries and then taken to a psychiatric ward where he is given a wristband that reads "Unknown White Male."

"There are aspects of his experience I do envy. Everything is new to him. To eat chocolate mousse for the first time and to have the language to describe it... that is an experience we won't have. To wipe the slate clean is desirable in a way. The first film he saw at the cinema was a restored print of *Taxi Driver*. Someone gave him a list of 50 films he had to see, and he's become a real movie buff [because] he's never seen a bad one."

Unknown White Male
Director Rupert Murray

The film underscores the fascinating complexity of what we unthinkingly call memory. Bruce can't remember his own name, but he remembers how to *sign* his name (although the signature is illegible). He goes to the beach and remembers how to swim – but he doesn't *know* that he remembers until he is actually in the water. He is unable to recall the names of his parents, but he can still speak French. He doesn't remember that he once liked the Rolling Stones, but he enjoys their music when it is played for him. Signing his name, swimming, typing, playing a musical instrument and riding a bike are all examples of **procedural memory**.

"A bunch of flowers shining with their own inner light. Those folds – what a labyrinth of endlessly significant complexity! I was seeing what Adam had seen on the morning of his own creation – the miracle, moment by moment, of naked existence."

Aldous Huxley describing his experiences with mescaline and the phenomenon of beginner's mind in *The Doors of Perception*

Unlike many individuals who experience fugue states, Bruce is frustrated and deeply troubled by his loss of memory. He has a girlfriend's phone number in his pocket, and she agrees to take him from the hospital and help him reestablish his past life. The cause of Bruce's memory loss was never determined.

The film underscores the intimate and profound link between memory and one's sense of self, and illustrates what it is like for someone to genuinely experience what Buddhists call "beginner's mind."

K-Pax

Kevin Spacey as both Robert Porter and Prot in *K-Pax* (2001) is a diagnostic quandary. In addition to hypothetical diagnoses of schizophrenia and PTSD, a valid and highly arguable case can be made for dissociative fugue.

From this vantage point, a man named Robert Porter experiences a highly traumatic event. Upon returning from work one day, he finds his wife and child murdered with the perpetrator still in his house; Porter quickly kills the man, cleans up, and jumps in a nearby river. He then travels from his home in New Mexico to New York City under a completely new identity as Prot, a highly spiritual person with great knowledge of planetary rotations. Porter interacts with other people comfortably with this new identity and claims no knowledge of any other past history. Under clinical hypnosis (age regression), the amnesia is lifted and he painfully faces his past trauma.

Dissociative Identity Disorder

Dissociative identity disorder (DID), formerly called multiple personality disorder, is an extremely rare condition characterized by disturbances in memory and identity. The essential feature is the presence of two or more distinct identities, or alters (personality states), that assume control over behavior. Amnesia is present in one or more of the personalities. Usually, the more passive the personality, the greater the amnesia. Dissociative identity disorder is usually believed to be a posttraumatic condition that emerges after overwhelming traumatic childhood experiences (APA, 2000).

The symptoms of DID are associated with many other psychiatric states such as anxiety symptoms (phobia, panic attacks, obsessive-compulsive behaviors), mood symptoms (manic and depressive), other dissociative symptoms (amnesias, fugues, depersonalization), somatoform symptoms (conversion), sexual dysfunctions, suicide attempts, self-mutilations, substance abuse, eating disorders, sleep disturbance, symptoms of schizophrenia, symptoms of posttraumatic stress disorder, and borderline personality disorder. Since many symptoms of PTSD occur in dissociative identity disorder, some argue that these two are variants of the same disorder (Piper & Merskey, 2004).

There is no evidence of spontaneous remission or integration of personality alters without mental health treatment. Therapy is long-term and requires the establishment of a strong therapeutic relationship with the individual. Hypnosis may be used at varying stages of treatment. Through the support of the relationship, the original traumas are accessed and examined and the psychological pain is soothed and viewed from an adult perspective. At this point in therapy, internal conflict can be addressed and resolved.

Fight Club, Identity, and Secret Window

None of these three popular, contemporary film examples of DID is especially helpful in portraying important and accurate psychopathology information of this disorder, and they are not as educational as *The Three Faces of Eve* (1957) and *Sybil* (1976) (to be discussed later). In their defense, these films don't pretend to educate viewers about DID; instead, the condition is used as an important plot device to enhance excitement, intrigue, fascination, and entertainment. Each of the three films is unique in its cinematic approach and has something to offer the viewer interested in dissociative disorders, therefore each is worth seeing.

David Fincher's fast-paced, visceral *Fight Club* (1999) begins with the narrator, Jack (brilliantly played by Edward Norton), struggling with insomnia and perhaps depression. Jack begins to deteriorate as he is entrenched in an unsatisfying consumerist lifestyle, feels apathetic at work, and becomes addicted to attending different support group meetings each day just for emotional release. The culmination of his deterioration happens early on in the film when he meets Tyler Durden (Brad Pitt), although he (and the viewer) do not realize Tyler is Jack's alter ego for much of the film. Tyler is everything Jack is not: flamboyant, exciting, seductive, unconventional, and self-empowering. The two (really just Jack) fight one another (he fights himself) and begin a "fight club" that attracts other disenfranchised men wanting a release. It is interesting to note that there are many clues to Jack's DID given in the film, including one-frame cinematic flashes of Tyler Durden until the full alter develops, illustrating Jack's full dissociation. Some mental health professionals argue that the identities of DID typically are not aware of one another; this argument suggests a diagnosis of schizophrenia is most appropriate for Jack.

Identity (2003) takes a different approach to DID. The viewer sees two stories: one story depicts ten characters stranded at an isolated motel trying to hide and elude from a mysterious serial killer on the loose in the area; the other story portrays a convicted serial killer, Malcolm Rivers, on the night of his final hearing before having the death penalty carried out. The viewer later learns these two stories are integrated in that Malcolm has DID and that the ten characters represent Malcolm's alters whom he is trying to kill off to achieve integration.

Secret Window (2004) manipulates the viewer and it is not until the conclusion of the film that the protagonist's dissociative identity disorder is revealed. Johnny Depp plays Mort, a man who experiences the trauma of seeing his wife cheating on him in a motel room. Mort confines and isolates himself in the woods to write his next novel and subsequently begins to deteriorate (this is a direct parallel with Jack Nicholson's famous and more dramatic character in *The Shining* (1980)). Coinciding with his deterioration (which takes the form of angst about his deteriorating marriage, anger toward his wife's boyfriend, an inability to quit smoking, alcohol abuse, and writer's block), are Mort's provocative encounters with Shooter (John Turturro) who wants amends claiming Mort has stolen his story. These interactions become more dangerous and threatening and Shooter kills various people and Mort's dog. Toward the end, a frustrated Mort throws an ashtray against the wall – the wall and house begin to crack and he hallucinates the crack spreading around the house; this scene is a metaphor for his own fragility and continuing decompensation. We then see Mort talking to himself and begin to hear his inner voice, which then shows up visually and multiplies. According to the film's themes, Mort had been so afraid of the Shooter part of his personality that he developed it as an alter and suppressed it from his conscious awareness.

The Three Faces of Eve

In *The Three Faces of Eve* (1957), narrator Alistair Cooke prepares the viewer for a documentary of a true story about a woman with multiple personality disorder (DID). This black-and-white film takes place in 1951 in a small Georgia town. Joanne Woodward introduces the viewer to Eve White, a quiet, passive, modest homemaker who begins having severe headaches, followed by "spells." She cannot remember what she does during these spells. Mrs. White is married to a rigid, dull, unimaginative man named Ralph, who is frustrated with the changes in his wife's behavior. Their unhappy marriage is even more stressed by these unexplained events.

During these spells, Eve Black, the second personality, "comes out." Eve Black is a seduc-tive, sexually promiscuous single woman, who buys flashy and provocative clothes, smokes, drinks, and frequents nightclubs. Eve White, who is unaware of Eve Black's existence, is afraid she is going crazy because of her unexplained periods of amnesia and hearing voices. Eve Black, on the other hand, knows of Eve White, dislikes her husband and their child, Bonnie, and delights in having Eve White feel the hangover following Eve Black's night of carousing. Eve White and her husband seek psychiatric treatment from Dr. Curtis Luther, played by Lee J. Cobb, for her headaches and spells.

It is well over a year before Dr. Luther is able to identify the existence of Eve Black. Following an incident in which Eve Black attempts to strangle Bonnie, Eve White is admitted to the hospital. She vows not to be reunited with her daughter until she is well. While Eve is in the hospital, Dr. Luther is able to establish a therapeutic relationship with both personalities and attempts to integrate them into one. The diagnosis of multiple personality disorder is explained to Eve White and her spouse, who both attempt to understand the problem. Ralph is never able to understand the disorder and eventually divorces Eve.

As Eve White struggles to work during the day, Eve Black parties at night. They both continue to be treated by Dr. Luther. Eventually, a third personality, Jane, emerges who is aware of both Eve White and Eve Black, even though neither is aware of her. Following a visit with her daughter, Bonnie, at her parents' home, Jane begins to have memories of playing under the porch as a child. Gradually, through the use of hypnosis, Dr. Luther is able to help Eve recall the trauma that precipitated her personalities splitting (being forced to kiss her dead grandmother's corpse). After reliving the memory, only Jane remains.

Sybil

The film *Sybil* (1976), based upon a true story, stars Sally Field as Sybil and Joanne Woodward as Dr. Cornelia Wilbur. It is interesting to note that Woodward, who received an Academy Award in 1957 for her lead role in *The Three Faces of Eve,* returned almost two decades later to play the psychiatrist treating *Sybil.* The viewer is introduced to Sybil, a distressed young woman who is working as a preschool teacher while attending art school. As Sybil is talking with the children, the creaking sound of a swing stirs traumatic childhood memories. Sybil unsuccessfully attempts to attend to her assigned task of organizing the children into a game of follow-the-leader. In the next scene,

Sybil is standing in the middle of a fountain, obviously confused. Her supervisor is scolding her for leading the children the wrong way. Sybil returns to her apartment, where she curls into a fetal position, trying to escape her tormenting memories. In desperation, she breaks her apartment window, which seems to give her some psychological relief. Because of her cut wrist, she ends up in an emergency room. Due to her confusion, she is referred to a psychiatrist, Dr. Wilbur, who evaluates her and begins treatment that lasts for 11 years.

This episode represents one of many in which Sybil is initially overwhelmed with flashbacks of traumatic childhood events that lead to periods of irrational behavior followed by a climactic event, such as breaking a window and injuring herself. The viewer gradually realizes that, as Sybil recalls traumatic memories, one of her 16 other personalities, or "alters," gains control and triggers the irrational behavior. Each of the other alters represents a part of Sybil and serves a particular purpose. For example, Vanessa is musical and enjoys playing the music Sybil once played. Vicki is very much in charge of life and is fearless. Peggy is a child who feels the terror and anger of childhood trauma. Marsha represents her despair and is often suicidal.

Through interaction with the different personalities and the use of hypnosis, Dr. Wilbur gradually pieces together Sybil's traumatic past. The goal of therapy is to integrate the personalities by helping the alters remember the past, experience the emotions associated with the traumatic events, and develop an adult perspective on the trauma. Patiently, Dr. Wilbur develops a warm, therapeutic relationship with all of the alters who are able to share their experiences. Dr. Wilbur, in turn, is able to help Sybil remember parts of her life that were previously shut off. Gradually, as the repeated abuse of her childhood is relived, Sybil is able to remember her childhood experiences and integrate them into her whole personality.

Other DID Films

The film *Primal Fear* (1996) should be seen to provide a certain degree of skeptical balance as it portrays a man (Edward Norton) who feigns DID in an attempt to evade murder charges. This film reminds clinicians of the potential for malingering in suspected cases of multiple personality disorder.

In *X-Men: The Last Stand* (2006), superheroine mutant Jean Grey is portrayed as someone with a dissociative personality disorder. She quickly becomes a danger to herself and others and as is painfully common in most films depicting "split personalities," the alter becomes dangerous, murderous, out-of-control, and perpetrates the misconception that people with mental illness are violent. Actress Famke Janssen, who researched DID to make her character more realistic, plays the part. The movie is an allegory in which society's need to control and limit the mutant's powers parallels society's inevitable attempts to make "them" more like "us."

Dissociative identity disorders are also illustrated in *Raising Cain* (1992) and *Voices Within: The Lives of Truddi Chase* (1990), a made-for-television movie based on the best-selling book *When Rabbit Howls*.

Depersonalization Disorder

Depersonalization disorder is diagnosed when there is evidence of persistent or recurrent feelings of detachment from one's mental processes or body. There is an alteration in the perception of self and often a sense that one is living out a dream. The person feels like an outsider looking in but continues to be connected with reality during the experience. Transient experiences of depersonalization are common in adolescents and decline with age in normal individuals (Putnam, 1985). During a traumatic event such as rape, depersonalization is sometimes experienced by women who report they were floating above their own bodies during the assault (Classen, Koopman, & Spiegel, 1993). Closely related to depersonalization experiences are **out-of-body** experiences in which the individual has the experience of leaving his or her body. Often these individuals are able to describe scenes as if viewed from above and report a sense of being isolated and detached from their bodies.

Since depersonalization occurs as a symptom in a variety of disorders, some authorities have questioned whether depersonalization is a distinct disorder. The cause of depersonalization is unknown. Some authorities speculate that the phenomenon is related to a neurobiological disturbance produced by temporal lobe dysfunction. Others claim that depersonalization is an adaptation to overwhelming trauma. Still other authorities argue that depersonalization is a defense against painful and conflictual stimuli, or that it is a split between the observing and participating selves that allows the person to become detached from self (Steinberg, 1991).

Numb (2007) is one of the few films in which a leading character is explicitly diagnosed with depersonalization disorder (a term likely to be very unfamiliar to most viewers). The movie stars Matthew Perry (from *Friends*) as Hudson, a screenwriter who apparently developed his profound sense of detachment as a result of taking 12 hits from a bong in 12 minutes (it is important to note that if depersonalization symptoms occur exclusively as a direct effect of a substance, then the diagnosis of depersonalization disorder would not be given). He feels chronically detached, much as though he were watching himself in a film. He has no interest in himself, others or anything that is happening around him. He spends his days and most of his nights watching the golf channel or very long-running movies (e.g., *Star Wars*). His neurological exam is normal, but he tells the doctor "stab me with a fork and I wouldn't feel it." He is treated with clonazepam but finds the medication dramatically diminishes his libido (a genuine potential side effect of the drug). He engages in extensive "doctor shopping," seeing one therapist after another. One psychiatrist is only interested in pharmacological management of Matthew's problems ("Fuck talking…take drugs!"). Matthew is able to overcome his malady only when he becomes genuinely interested in a new woman in his life, Sara (Lynn Collins). The film perpetuates the myth that love is sufficient to conquer mental illness. While it is questionable whether Hudson actually has depression or this disorder (since depersonalization is being used as a convenient plot device), it makes for interesting discussions on differential diagnosis.

"I just wanted to let you know that if you lost all your limbs, we'd still be together forever. I mean I really hope that doesn't happen because I think your limbs are pretty great. And when I said your name, it would always sound safe. I'm not sure about the perfume and the cologne thing but I could try… And if you like this shirt, I wouldn't take it off for a month. And I would be more than willing to paint your grandmother's toenails so your grandfather doesn't have to do it anymore. You don't have to save me Sara. But I am going to love you for the rest of my life, so things would be a lot better for me if you were around."

Matthew admits his love for Sara
in *Numb* (2007)

The Butterfly Effect

It might be a stretch to place the film *The Butterfly Effect* (2004) under this diagnostic category; however, while it does not seem to fit any category neatly, it can inform us about depersonalization. Evan, a 20-year-old, college student experiences frequent blackouts during highly emotional or stressful times. When he reflects on his amnestic blackouts and reads his copious journal entry of a given memory, he is transported to the actual past memory. He is then able to change the memory with various ensuing consequences on his and others' lives in the present.

Each of the memories he engages can be seen as his detachment from his body; he enters the memory, relives it, and changes it while maintaining reality testing to his world and the new world (due to the changed memory) around him. This process causes him significant personal and social distress as he realizes each of these "detachment" episodes has a profound effect on his own life and on the lives of those around him.

Other Examples of Dissociative Disorders in Films

Dissociative disorders are among the most fascinating forms of mental illness, and it is not surprising that they are portrayed fairly often in films. In addition to the clinical examples cited, film history is replete with examples of quasi-dissociative conditions in which one character exchanges personalities (or sometimes even bodies) with another. The classic example is Bergman's *Persona* (1966), in which two characters gradually exchange personalities. A similar theme is found in the Robert Altman film, *3 Women* (1977), in which two of the women appear to exchange personalities.

In the mock-documentary/comedy, *Zelig* (1983), Woody Allen plays a human chameleon whose personality changes to match whatever situation he is in – if he is around black musicians, he talks and acts like black musicians; if he's around politicians, he becomes a politician. Ronald Coleman finds himself merging his own personality with that of Othello in *A Double Life* (1947). The comedy *Prelude to a Kiss* (1992) is about an old man and a young bride who mysteriously exchange bodies after kissing on the bride's wedding day. The film raises interesting questions about what it is that one person loves in another: is it a physical body or a set of personality characteristics, such as wit, charm, and grace? The means through which the transformation is effected is never specified in *Prelude*. In contrast, it is very clear in *Black Friday*, a 1940 horror film in which Boris Karloff transplants the brain of a criminal into the body of a college professor.

The theme of contrasting personalities in the same person is seen in those films in which someone presumed to be dead returns to his or her old social roles, usually as a vastly improved human being. We see this in *Sommersby* (1993) and *The Return of Martin Guerre* (1982). The dramatic force of both films is heightened by the sexual excitement both women feel as they go to bed with a man who may or may not be the husband who left them years earlier.

Dissociation is also used in a plethora of films that contrast the forces of good and evil inherent in all of us. Oftentimes, the evil is inherent in a twin. For example, the personalities of good and evil twins are juxtaposed in *The Dark Mirror* (1946) and in Brian De Palma's *Sisters* (1973). The latter film adds an interesting twist by making the two women Siamese twins who were separated as children.

Films have often presented the duality of the human personality, usually depicting a struggle between good and evil. In 1920, *Dr. Jekyll and Mr. Hyde* was first introduced as a silent film, starring John Barrymore and Martha Robinson. The 1931 remake, directed by Rouben Mamoulian, was the first sound version of this Robert Louis Stevenson classic. In this film, Dr. Harry Jekyll (played by Fredric March, who won an Academy Award for his performance) represents all that is good and kind. He is a well-respected physician who devotes endless hours to hospital charity work. His innate curiosity, as well as his own socially unacceptable feelings, have led him to speculate about good and evil within human beings. He believes that the evil of humans can be captured and isolated. As the film opens, he is engaged to Muriel, played by Miriam Hopkins, with whom he is deeply in love. According to the custom of the time, Muriel's father has set a marriage date that is too far in the future to suit Harry. The audience gets a glimpse of Dr. Jekyll's underlying impulsiveness, his impatience, and the sexuality that he is trying hard to repress.

When Muriel's father takes her away for an extended trip, Dr. Jekyll tests his theory about inherent evils. He mixes and swallows a potion that he believes can isolate the evils of human beings. He then becomes the evil Mr. Hyde, who seduces, abuses, and finally kills a woman who is his social inferior. Eventually, he can no longer control the "coming out" of the alter personality (Mr. Hyde), and he confides his mistake to his future father-in-

Critical Thinking Questions (Dissociative Disorders)

- How can an understanding of the phenomenon of hypnosis help us understand dissociative disorders?
- Movies such as *Primal Fear* (1996) suggest it is relatively easy to fool lawyers and therapists into believing you have a multiple personality disorder. How would you assess the likelihood of malingering if you were a clinician evaluating a patient with an alleged dissociative disorder?
- Many reputable psychologists believe DID does not exist. What evidence do you find for and against this claim?
- Are there instances where dissociation occurs, but not amnesia?
- Compare dissociative experiences that are culturally acceptable with those that are considered abnormal.
- What are some other causes of dissociative disorders aside from trauma?
- Name a few of the inaccuracies and misconceptions perpetrated in the DID depiction in the film *Identity* (2003).
- Compare and contrast Edward Norton's character in the modern-day film *Fight Club* (1999) with Joanne Woodward's character in the classic, *The Three Faces of Eve* (1957).

law. After attacking his fiancée, Dr. Jekyll is caught and killed.

Dr. Jekyll and Mr. Hyde was remade in 1941, this time starring Spencer Tracy and Ingrid Bergman. It was filmed again in 1968, with Jack Palance, and given the full title *The Strange Case of Dr. Jekyll and Mr. Hyde*. One of the best adaptations of the Dr. Jekyll and Mr. Hyde story is in the more recent *Mary Reilly* (1996), starring John Malkovich and Julia Roberts. A somewhat different twist on the same theme is found in *Steppenwolf* (1974), an adaptation of the Hermann Hesse novel, illustrating the problem of a single individual grappling with these two competing aspects of self.

Additional film examples of depersonalization disorder are found in the fascinating movie *Tarnation* (2003), *Dead of Night* (1945), *Altered States* (1980), and Martin Scorsese's *The Last Temptation of Christ* (1988).

Somatoform Disorders

While 80% of healthy individuals experience somatic symptoms in any one week, the following disorders go beyond transient bodily complaints: somatization disorder, undifferentiated somatoform disorder, conversion disorder, pain disorder, hypochondriasis, and body dysmorphic disorder.

Somatization disorder is diagnosed when there is a pattern of recurrent and multiple somatic complaints that require medical treatment or that limit the effectiveness of an individual, but for which no clear organic etiology can be identified. In addition, multiple organ systems must be involved. Specifically, there must be at least four pain symptoms, two gastrointestinal symptoms, one sexual symptom, and one pseudoneurological symptom for the diagnosis to be made. The enormous economic impact of the medical treatment of the unexplained symptoms has gained international attention. Rarely is mental health treatment sought (Hiller & Fichter, 2004).

Patients with somatization disorder are poor historians, and their complaints may vary from session to session. This problem is complicated by the fact that they easily become dissatisfied with their health care provider and may constantly be changing providers, sharing different parts of their story with each new provider. In addition, since most visits result in a prescription of some sort, these patients are often taking multiple medications, some of which produce side effects that result in general somatic distress. This pattern sets up a vicious cycle and makes diagnosis of the patient with a somatization disorder a challenging dilemma. Diagnosis is further complicated by the fact that some genuine medical conditions, such as multiple sclerosis, hyperparathyroidism, and systematic lupus erythematosus, can have vague symptoms that affect multiple organ systems. Occasionally, patients have multiple physical complaints that appear to be somatoform-like but are not sufficiently varied or of sufficient duration to meet the full criteria for somatization disorder. In these cases, the residual diagnosis of **undifferentiated somatoform disorder** is used. The common diagnoses of irritable bowel syndrome and chronic fatigue syndrome often fall under the undifferentiated somatoform disorder category as they do not meet the full criteria for somatization disorder yet the individual is experiencing bodily symptoms not fully explained by medical tests.

Safe

The Todd Haynes film *Safe* (1995) almost exclusively focuses on a woman with a somatoform disorder. Carol White (Julianne Moore) slowly begins to deteriorate with unexplained symptoms related to chemical sensitivity, allergy, and somatic com-

plaints. Doctors tell her stress is the cause of her problem, and advise her to learn to relax. However, it is difficult to see what is stressful in her life – she has a loving husband, beautiful home, good social life, and servants to do the cooking and cleaning. Her bodily system becomes overloaded and overwhelmed by fumes, toxins, fragrances, and other "pollutants" – these come from traffic, her shampoo, her husband's cologne, or a new sofa. It is as if she is being attacked by plastics, ozone, chemicals, high-energy wires, pollution, additives, preservatives, and hamburger fumes. Carol continues to get physically sicker and sicker, leaving her physicians baffled. At one point, she is hospitalized due to extensive bleeding.

Carol makes the decision to travel to another part of the country to a specialized clinic that offers group therapy, seminars, and social activities for people suffering from similar anomalous problems. During a casual group session, the therapist asks probing questions of the patients (and metaphorically to society and the viewer): "Why did you get sick" and "What's behind your sickness?" One character speaks of abuse experienced as a child, how she made herself sick to remember, and how she had not forgiven the perpetrator and took it out on herself. For other characters, what they believed was behind their sickness is self-blame or anger, and in one man's case, a drug addiction. Upon hearing other characters speak of coming to terms with their inner self-hatred, Moore's character admits to also having a deep sense of self-hatred. However, despite all of her treatment, she seems to just get worse. The treatment emphasizes simplistic themes of a need to love oneself more, that we all make ourselves sick, and the role of the mind; while these ideas can play an important role, particularly the impact of the thoughts and feelings on the immune system, the approach comes across as trite and misleading.

Ultimately, the film is a dark comedy and a satirical social commentary. Todd Haynes cleverly uses the cinematic element of a background hum to suggest to the viewer that we can never fully escape the impact of the environment.

Agnes of God

The complex film *Agnes of God* (1985), stars Meg Tilly as a young nun (Sister Agnes), Anne Bancroft as the Mother Superior of the convent, and Jane Fonda as the psychiatrist sent to investigate the apparent murder of a newborn baby who was found wrapped in bloody sheets and stuffed in a wastebasket at the convent. The film juxtaposes reason and faith and quickly convinces the viewer that, although Sister Agnes is surely one of "God's innocents," she is just as surely the mother and the murderer of the child.

Fonda uses hypnosis in treating Sister Agnes, and it turns out that she was sexually molested by her mother as a child. It also turns out that the mother was the sister of the Mother Superior. At the end of the film, the court finds Sister Agnes not guilty by reason of insanity, and she returns to the convent, where she will continue to receive psychiatric care.

Sister Agnes' confusion seems very real and the label of insanity seems justified. It appears that a dissociative amnesia may have been present, and the viewer becomes convinced that Sister Agnes had repressed the memories of her rape and was genuinely amnestic for the incident in which she strangled the child with his umbilical cord. Agnes begins to experience stigmata once in a convent room and once in a chapel while praying. **Stigmata** is the name given to bleeding in the hands and feet, presumably from the sites that nails were driven into when Christ was crucified. It is a relatively rare but well-documented phenomenon that is found in people with deep religious convictions. In the case of *Agnes of God*, the blood of Christ, the blood of the murdered infant, and the blood of Agnes all seem to comingle. The somatic element of the stigmata in this film is much more complex, powerful, and integrated into the story and personal life of Agnes than the stigmata depicted in the suspense film titled *Stigmata* (1999).

Conversion Disorder

A conversion disorder exists when (1) patients experience significant distress or impairment from motor or sensory symptoms that appear to be neurological but for which no adequate neurological explanation can be determined and (2) it appears that psychological factors have played a significant role in the etiology or maintenance of the disorder. In addition, the clinician must rule out malingering before the diagnosis is made.

The very name conversion disorder is linked to a psychological theory that maintains that unconscious psychological distress can be "converted" into physical manifestations. Interestingly, symptoms are far more likely to occur on the left side of the body (presumably because most people are right-handed).

Conversion disorders are fascinating, in part because the underlying dynamics seem so transparent to an external observer. The soldier who can't fire a rifle because his arm is paralyzed has found a convenient way of avoiding battle; the woman who becomes functionally blind after witnessing a car wreck in which her son was killed can never see anything this awful happen again. In actual practice, few cases of conversion disorder are this tidy.

Woody Allen's character, Val Wawman, in *Hollywood Ending* (2002) develops a clear example of hysterical blindness, a previously frequent but currently rare conversion disorder. Just prior to the first day of directing a new film (in which there is the added stress of his ex-wife being the co-producer with her new fiancé), he loses his sight. This would suggest a neurological condition but an extensive medical examination fails to produce medical or physiological reasons for Wawman's blindness. He goes to see a psychologist who explains this is psychological in origin and supports this comment with individualized interpretations – Val's fears of failure, internal conflicts, and poor relationship with his son. Val also exhibits numerous hypochondriacal symptoms including his extreme fear of getting an illness and preoccupation with illness. He previously thought he had experienced many outlandish diseases (e.g., diseases that only trees can get, the plague, etc.), all due to his misinterpretation of bodily symptoms. Another case of hysterical blindness is portrayed in the 1939 film *The Secret of Dr. Kildare*. In this film, Dr. Kildare performs a sham operation in order to restore his patient's sight, raising interesting ethical questions that probably wouldn't have been debated in the 1930s.

The film *Sorry, Wrong Number* (1948) stars Barbara Stanwyck as a bedridden heiress who is partially paralyzed, although her doctors cannot determine any neurological reason for her inability to walk. One evening, she happens to overhear two men planning a murder; later she realizes that she is the intended victim. Much of the suspense of the film revolves around the realization that she must get out of bed in order to save herself.

Thérèse: The Story of Saint Thérèse of Lisieux (2004), tells the story of Saint Thérèse who became a Carmelite nun at age 15 and died from tuberculosis when she was 24. Thérèse's mother died when Thérèse was only four years old, and she experienced marked periods of depression. She also appears to have multiple psychosomatic complaints including stomach pains when she thinks about minor sins, and pounding headaches. One evening she faints at the dinner table. She experiences restless sleep, and at one point she is shown as delirious for two weeks. During the period of delirium, she doesn't eat, loses weight, cries out, and hallucinates. She coughs repeatedly and spits up blood when her father's health deteriorates. Her influence on the Catholic Church has been tremendous; her memoir, *Story of a Soul*, has been translated into over 60 languages and has sold over 100 million copies.

Pain Disorder

Patients with somatoform disorders often present with pain as a symptom; in fact, the presentation is a necessary condition for the diagnosis of somatization disorder. However, some patients will be preoccupied with the experience of pain, and their activities will be dramatically limited by the presence of pain, even when there is no lesion, history of trauma, or other objective medical data that could account for their suffering. According to the American Pain Foundation, back pain is the leading cause of disability in Americans under the age of 45. Over 26 million Americans between the ages of 20 and 64 experience frequent back pain and two-thirds of American adults will have back pain during their lifetime. In many of these cases, psychological factors play an important role in the cause, exacerbation, and/or maintenance of the pain experience.

A large number of associated disorders can be comorbid with pain disorder. In addition, it is common for patients with chronic pain, whether due to medical or psychological reasons or both, to become depressed, anxious, or angry in response to their pain. Psychological tests such as the **Minnesota Multiphasic Personality Inventory** (MMPI) and questionnaires such as the **McGill Pain Questionnaire** may be helpful in determining the extent to which psychological "overlay" is present in a patient's report of pain.

In the black and white thriller *Pi* (1998), the lead character is a computer wizard and mathematician who suffers from excruciating migraine headaches. His pain becomes so debilitating he bangs his head on a sink and eventually drills into his head. If seen in a psychology clinic, one of this character's diagnoses would be pain disorder associated with both psychological factors and a general medical condition.

Hypochondriasis

The hypochondriac is preoccupied with thoughts of disease, infirmity, and death. This person worries that simple, benign body sensations or symptoms may be indicative of a serious disease. In the extreme, a hypochondriac might interpret routine stomach pain as cancer of the bowel, headaches as a consequence of a brain tumor, and/or misplaced keys or glasses as an undeniable early indication of Alzheimer's. The preoccupations persist despite physical exams, lab tests, X-rays, and other examinations suggesting there is no illness present.

Some patients who have been labeled as hypochondriacs are later found to have bona fide medical disorders. This is especially common with disorders that have vague symptoms and a slow progression (e.g., multiple sclerosis). In addition, patients who are initially believed to have hypochondriasis are sometimes later found to have somatic concerns related to anxiety, depression, or another psychiatric disorder.

Hypochondriasis is easy to ridicule, and there is something comical about the person who goes through an "organ recital" when describing his or her health. However, the concerns of these patients are very real and deserve sympathetic attention and empathic understanding.

In *Dogville* (2003), one character is a hypochondriacal doctor who misinterprets lumps and various other physical complaints; he is someone who needs the reassurance of others to tell him he is not dying. In *Something's Gotta Give* (2005), Jack Nicholson plays a 63-year-old man obsessed with dating younger women who becomes hypochondriacal after suffering his first heart attack; all subsequent episodes turn out to be panic attacks.

Bandits

In *Bandits* (2001), Billy Bob Thornton plays Terry Collins, a bank robber with hypochondriasis. Terry is convinced he has various illnesses despite his physician assuring him there is nothing wrong. While in prison, he ruminates about how helpful garlic is and becomes upset when it is banned from the prison cafeteria; in a later scene, he incessantly screams in the prison yard about ringing in his ears. In his leisure time, he reads a medical dictionary and while driving listens to *Merck Manual* cassette tapes alphabetically defining diseases.

After escaping from prison and robbing a bank with his cohort in crime, Joe Blake (Bruce Willis), Terry's arm becomes numb, he complains of seeing spots, and makes weird noises with his throat. When challenged by his partner, he exclaims, "I have sanitation issues, Joe."

When stressed, Terry experiences a sneezing attack and a tic in his left eye. He then begins to talk fast and speak in medical jargon. He also becomes preoccupied about one pupil being larger than the other. Each of his senses is affected in some way throughout the film. In addition, he suffers from food allergy, lactose intolerance, and various obscure phobias such as a fear of getting smaller, a fear of antique furniture (Billy Bob Thornton is reported to have this fear), a fear of historic figures, and a fear of black and white movies. He experiences numbness in his arm, lips, and legs that leads him to collapse and flail about on the floor in one scene.

Hannah and Her Sisters

Hannah and Her Sisters (1986) is one of Woody Allen's funniest and most gratifying films. Allen plays Mickey, the role of a neurotic television executive, who is a classic hypochondriac. He is on his way to get a blood test when the film opens, and we soon realize that he is preoccupied with doctors, hospitals, and his own fragile mortality. He works in a high-stress job and early on in the film he remarks, "Has anybody got a Tagamet? My ulcer is starting to kill me." (Director Woody Allen has a remarkable sense for the prevailing concerns and habits of the American public. A decade earlier, he had amused his viewers with a similar line about Valium.)

"This time I think I really have something... It's not like that adenoidal thing, where I didn't realize I had them out."

Mickey Sachs (Woody Allen) discussing his hearing loss with his physician in
Hannah and Her Sisters (1986)

Mickey has experienced some hearing loss and is convinced that he has a brain tumor. He suspects that his doctors have known this all along but "they don't tell you [these things] because sometimes the weaker ones will panic." He awakens in the middle of the night, terrified, crying out "There's a tumor in my head the size of a basketball." With each new test, he grows more apprehensive. When his computerized tomography scan turns out to be completely negative, he is at first elated and then plunges into despair as he realizes that this is just a temporary reprieve and that eventually he must die.

Questions to Consider While Watching *Bandits* and *Hannah and Her Sisters*

- How can nonmedical therapists rule out organic pathology?
- Does *every* client with a psychological problem have to be worked up medically to ensure that there is no medical disease present?
- How common is it for a patient who has headaches actually to have a brain tumor?
- Should patients be able to insist on expensive tests (such as CAT scans and MRIs), or is this decision ultimately up to the physician? Should it matter if a patient has insurance?
- Is the percentage of clients who visit psychologists for what are eventually determined to be medical problems about equivalent to the number of patients who visit physicians for treatment of what are ultimately determined to be psychological problems?
- Do the symptoms of hypochondriacs worsen under stress?
- Is the reassurance typically offered hypochondriacal patients possible in a world of managed care? Will these changes in policy exacerbate or ameliorate the patients' concerns and symptoms?
- What is the optimal approach for a physician or medical professional to take in working with a person with suspected hypochondriasis?

Body Dysmorphic Disorder

When somebody becomes so obsessed with a perceived physical imperfection that he or she is unable to function successfully interpersonally or on the job, a diagnosis of body dysmorphic disorder may be appropriate. Individuals with this problem may spend hours each day looking into a mirror and brooding about their perceived inadequacy.

In 1987, Steve Martin played the role of a modern-day Cyrano de Bergerac in the film *Roxanne*. However, in this film his nose is truly of grotesque proportions and he would not qualify for the diagnosis of body dysmorphic disorder (which requires an *imagined* defect in appearance). In the French film, Depardieu's nose is elongated but not grotesque, and one suspects that his concerns are at least as much psychological as real.

The artistically eccentric Peter Greenaway directed the film *The Belly of an Architect* (1987) in which the viewer is introduced to Stourley Kracklite (Brian Dennehy) who is a prominent American architect putting on an exhibition in Rome. Kracklite is too preoccupied with himself to care much about his wife's flirtations with a younger man. In particular, Kracklite becomes obsessed with his stomach. This begins to occupy all of his attention. His doctor states it is nothing more than gas and egotism. Kracklite examines other options – dyspepsia, fatigue, over-excitement, lack of exercise, too much coffee, too much constipation – but his stomach obsession continues. He makes photocopies of a statue of Augustus, obsesses over the statue's stomach region, and compares it with his own. In a memorable scene, Kracklite's obsession with his stomach extends to his covering his entire room including the floor with photographs of bellies. The film presents interesting differential diagnosis challenges involving other somatoform disorders, OCD, and delusional disorder. Support for a diagnosis of hypochondriasis is found in his unshakable belief that his body is being consumed by a tumor. There are other psychological elements contributing to his disorder: fear of being embarrassed, fear of death, isolation, psychological stress, and narcissistic factors of grandiosity and self-preoccupation.

Differential Diagnosis

Patients with somatoform disorders will often experience some amount of **secondary gain** as a result of their medical problems, such as extra care and attention from others, worker's compensation benefits, reduced expectations from family, or avoidance of difficult activities. It is important to be cognizant of normal secondary gain factors while separating a given somatoform disorder from both malingering and factitious disorder. In **malingering**, a person deliberately "fakes" his or her symptoms in order to achieve a clearly understood goal (e.g., one character in *Memento* (2000)). A death row inmate may feign symptoms of mental illness – for example, believing that the state cannot execute someone who is not mentally competent. Likewise, a small child may complain of stomach pain, remembering that the last time this occurred he or she was allowed to stay home from school and eat ice cream.

In contrast, **factitious disorders**, a completely separate diagnostic category, involve feigning illness with the specific intent of assuming the sick role. Some patients with factitious disorders will present with predominantly psychological symptoms while others will have predominantly physical symptoms. **Factitious disorder by proxy** (also called Munchausen syndrome by proxy)

occurs when symptoms are intentionally produced in another person, the classic example being the mother who makes her child sick to assume the "sick role." We see an example of factitious disorder by proxy in Kevin Bacon's film *Loverboy* (2004), which stars Bacon's wife, Kyra Sedgwick, playing an enmeshed and overly protective mother (Emily), and the couple's real life daughter, Sosie Bacon, who plays the role of Emily seen as a ten-year-old child in a series of flashbacks.

The term **psychosomatic** is often used as a derogatory term for people suffering with the disorders mentioned in this chapter. The term usually refers to physical disorders in which emotional processes play a role indicating a mutual influence of physical and psychological factors; the generality of this concept can be applied to not only somatoform disorders but most medical and psychological conditions as well.

International Films: Dissociative and Somatoform Disorders

A rare, compelling example of body dysmorphic syndrome is found in Gerard Depardieu's portrayal of *Cyrano de Bergerac* in the 1990 French film by the same name. Cyrano is deeply in love with his cousin Roxane but cannot profess his love because he is too ashamed of his long (and to him) deformed nose. Instead, he writes long love letters for his friend Perez. The letters are successful, and Roxane falls deeply in love with the romantic Perez. Perez is killed in battle and Roxane enters a convent, where Cyrano continues to visit her. Fifteen years later, as he is dying, Cyrano recites one of the last letters from Perez by memory and Roxane realizes that he has been the one whom she has really loved all this time.

Gerard Depardieu also stars in another French film, *The Pact of Silence* (2003), in which he plays a Jesuit priest who is also a physician trying to make sense out of a nun's "spells" during which she falls to the floor, experiences tremendous pain, and speaks incoherently. The psychosomatic episodes coincide with occasions when her twin sister, who is incarcerated, is in danger (e.g., when her prison cell is set afire by other inmates).

Georgette in *Amelie* (2001, France) would probably meet all the criteria for somatization disorder if she were to appear at a doctor's office. While operating a cigarette counter, she complains of various symptoms from sciatica to the discomfort of smoke getting in her eyes. One interesting quote used in the film describes Georgette precisely: "A woman without love wilts like a flower without the sun." When Georgette's mind is not occupied with love, she is preoccupied with enough symptoms to meet the criteria for somatization disorder, but when she has a love interest, she feels perfectly healthy and happy.

The Spanish film *Inconscientes* (*Unconscious*, 2004) is set in Barcelona in 1913 and satirizes psychoanalysis and psychoanalysts; for example, in one scene, a psychiatrist tries to hypnotize a patient using a swinging pocket watch, only to become hypnotized himself, eventually revealing his deepest secret (he is a transvestite). The film shows multiple examples of hypochondriasis and conversion disorder, and a character playing Sigmund Freud makes a brief appearance to promote his new book, *Totem and Taboo*.

Persona (1966), the complex Ingmar Bergman film regarded as one of the greatest films ever made, deals with a famous actress, Elisabeth Vogler (Liv Ullmann), who suddenly, and seemingly without reason, stops talking. Her doctor can find nothing wrong with her and is at a loss to explain her patient's symptom. However, she prescribes rest and constant attention, and Elisabeth spends the summer at a house on the coast in the care of a full-time nurse, Alma (Bibi Andersson). Although Elisabeth almost never speaks, we know that she retains the capacity for speech. At one point, when Alma appears to be about to throw boiling water on Elisabeth, the actress shouts, "Don't."

Although the conversion disorder portrayed in the film is fascinating, the more interesting element is the merging of the personalities of the two women. There are a number of interesting dream sequences, and one scene presents a face on the screen that is a composite of Elisabeth and Alma (one-half of each woman's face is shown). In selecting the title for the film, Bergman was likely thinking both about the masks worn by Greek actors in classical theater and of Carl Jung who used the term to refer to those parts of our personality that we show to the outer world. Perhaps Elisabeth quit speaking because she had resolved to stop acting and wear no more masks. The ending of the film is somewhat unclear, but it appears that Elisabeth returns to acting, Alma returns to nursing, and the personalities of the two women do not remain merged.

Further Exploration

If you have time to read just one book relevant to this chapter, make it:

Vermetten, E., Dorahy, M., & Spiegel, D. (Eds.) (2007). *Traumatic dissociation: Neurobiology and treatment.* Arlington, VA: American Psychiatric Publishing.

If you only have time for one article, read:

Lilienfeld, S. O., Kirsch, I., Sarbin, T. R., Lynn, S. J., Chaves, J. F., Ganaway, G. K., & Powell, R. A. (1999). Dissociative identity disorder and the sociocognitive model: Recalling the lessons of the past. *Psychological Bulletin, 125*, 507–523.

Authors' Picks

Dissociative and Somatoform Disorders

Dissociative Disorders

- *Psycho* (1960)
- *Unknown White Male* (2005)
- *Paris, Texas* (1984)
- *Sybil* (1976)
- *Primal Fear* (1996)

Somatoform Disorders

- *Persona* (1966)
- *Agnes of God* (1985)
- *Hannah and Her Sisters* (1986)
- *Safe* (1995)
- *The Belly of an Architect* (1987)

Critical Thinking Questions (Somatoform Disorders)

- How do somatoform disorders affect the national health care budget?
- How are people with somatoform disorders affected by the adoption of managed care practices?
- What percentage of major medical illnesses are missed when they are being mislabeled as psychosomatic?
- What particular mind-body treatment strategies are most useful with these disorders?
- What personality characteristics are most closely associated with somatization disorder and hypochondriasis?
- Why is pain one of the most common and least understood problems facing the medical profession?
- How does the film *Safe* (1995) both add to and detract from the understanding of somatoform disorders?

Chapter 4

Psychological Stress and Physical Disorders

A lot of people told me that I'd never wrestle again, they said "he's washed up,"
"he's finished," "he's a loser," "he's all through." You know what?
The only ones gonna tell me when I'm through doing my thing, is you people here.
You people here... you people here. You're my family.
Randy "the Ram" speaking to a crowd of fans in *The Wrestler* (2008)

Questions to Consider While Watching *The Wrestler*

- Does Randy have a mental illness?
- How would you describe Randy's identity or definition of himself?
- Is stress a significant risk factor for cardiovascular problems?
- Does Randy have good stress management skills? What are his healthy and unhealthy coping mechanisms?
- What is the connection between Randy's physical and psychological status?
- Does steroid use contribute to cardiovascular disease?
- How significant is Randy's social isolation in terms of his physical and mental well-being?
- Should Randy give up wrestling completely? If not, under what conditions should he perform?
- How does someone recreate his or her life when the one thing they were fully committed to is eliminated?
- What is the best way to help a person who is committed to a behavior that seems likely to lead to self-destruction?
- What is the first-line treatment for someone like Randy?

Patient Evaluation

Patient's stated reason for coming: "My doc thinks I need to see you for stress. Yeah, I got plenty of stress but that's just something I gotta deal with. I don't need to see no shrink about it, no offense."

History of the present illness: Randy Robinson, who goes by the nickname, "the Ram," was referred to counseling by both his primary care physician and his cardiologist. He recently suffered a heart attack and has struggled with depression and alcohol abuse following his treatment.

Past psychiatric illness, treatment, and outcomes: Randy denied any previous treatment for psychiatric illness and substance abuse. He stated he has never previously met with a counselor of any kind.

Medical history: Randy's health has deteriorated significantly. He recently had open-heart surgery following a collapse in which he lost consciousness after a particularly rigorous wrestling match. Prior to this, Randy had frequently experienced chest pains, however, he had assumed it was just indigestion or pain that resulted from wrestling. Randy stated he had not gone to a physician for a physical checkup since his childhood and was surprised to see how much his health had deteriorated. He was also diagnosed with hypertension. In addition, he suffers from lower back pain. While Randy was in the hospital, an MRI was performed and the results were negative. Other medical tests were normal.

This patient's work as a professional wrestler is both intense and dangerous. He fights with chairs, glass, staple guns, and barbs, and many of his wounds are self-inflicted to entertain wrestling fans. He has had several broken bones over the years and his doctors have recommended he give up wrestling.

Psychosocial history: Randy is a 47-year-old Caucasian male who lives alone and has never been married. He stated he has burned a lot of bridges in his life and his only friends are some children nearby his trailor who play video games with him, a handful of adoring wrestling fans, and his fellow wrestlers who seem to genuinely respect him. Otherwise, Randy reports being quite lonely. He has recently attempted to reach out to his daughter, Stephanie, as well as a stripper named Cassidy with whom he has had some meaningful conversation. Randy says these relationships have had their "ups and downs." He has an interest in renewing his relationship with Stephanie and marrying Cassidy. He says he has no idea what a healthy relationship looks like. In addition to working as a professional wrestler on the weekend, Randy has recently taken up work in the deli department of a grocery store doing customer service and stocking. He reports that he has not wrestled for the past three months.

Drug and alcohol history: Randy has a history of alcohol and drug abuse. He uses steroids regularly to enhance his wrestling physique and performance.

Behavioral observations: Randy's physical appearance showed the results of recent steroid abuse – he has a sunken face, puffy lips, and enlarged muscles in the chest, arms, shoulders, and neck. He was pleasant and polite, but distant and somewhat guarded in his responses. Affect and mood were depressed with some anxiety, perhaps the result of the fact that this was his first psychological evaluation. Hallucinations, delusions, and paranoia were denied and not evident. He denied homicidal and suicidal ideation.

Mental status examination: Randy earned a score of 25/30 on the Mini Mental State Examination. The MMSE was low but still in the normal range. His recent memory is spotty. He lost points on a question that required recalling 3 objects, the figure drawing, and serial sevens.

Functional assessment: Randy's self-care has been steadily declining over the years; however, it apparently has never been strong. Since his surgery, his sleep and eating habits have improved.

Strengths: Randy desires more connections in his life. He exhibits the virtue of courage, and the specific character strengths of bravery and integrity. He is honest when asked direct questions.

Diagnosis: Anabolic steroid dependence; adjustment disorder with mixed disturbance of emotions and conduct; rule out major depression

Treatment plan: Individual psychotherapy is highly recommended. It does not appear Randy is prepared to fully give up wrestling, despite his physician's orders. As stopping wrestling is critical to his health and livelihood it should be given priority focus in treatment. Motivational interviewing techniques, such as cost-benefit analysis, should be implemented as early as possible. Treatment should also emphasize adherence to both his medication regimen and his biweekly visits to his cardiologist.

His steroid abuse puts him at greater risk of physical (e.g., liver disease) and psychological (e.g., depression) problems. Treatment should focus on education, namely, the impact of steroid use and strategies for decreasing and eventually stopping use. He would also benefit from stress management, relationship building skills, and general life coaching.

Prognosis: Fair. This patient's prognosis is guarded; however, he will improve if he follows his physician's orders and commits to regular psychotherapy.

Stress, Physical Illness, and *The Wrestler*

The Wrestler (2008) was directed and produced by Darren Aronofsky. This young director (age 40) has already made a number of poignant stories about the struggles of humanity – he depicted the horrors of migraine headache in *Pi* (1998), drug abuse in *Requiem for a Dream* (2000), and the denial in facing the realities of someone with a terminal illness in *The Fountain* (2006); each film is marked by its intensity and deep psychological exploration of character. *The Wrestler* is no exception.

Mickey Rourke portrays a professional wrestler named Randy "the Ram" Robinson. Randy is unable to live in the real world so he lives under the persona of "Ram," someone who is popular and successful in the world of choreographed wres-

tling (although the graphic depictions of wrestling matches are gripping and believable, suggesting that not everything about wrestling is staged and exaggerated). The crowds and his fellow wrestlers have great respect for Ram, who has continued to wrestle ever since his glory days ended 20 years ago. Ironically, Ram's introduction theme music for most of his matches is "Metal Health (Bang Your Head)" by Quiet Riot. After collapsing from a heart attack and receiving surgery, Randy begins to realize he is aging fast, his body is no longer holding up, and that he has lived his life in this persona of Ram and consequently not sustained any long-term relationships. The toll that wrestling and steroid abuse have taken on his body is substantial. The stress of these on his cardiovascular health has been significant. He notes that things don't "feel right," and he is referring to more than just his physical health (his mental, emotional, and social health as well).

Randy decides to make some genuine efforts to re-formulate his life – to start anew – and accepts a non-demanding and steady job at a deli department. He also makes progress in connecting with his daughter, Stephanie, whom he had abandoned and neglected, and a new romantic interest, Cassidy (Marisa Tomei). He begins to question where he belongs and which world he fits in better, eventually deciding to give up wrestling and connect with others. There are several touching scenes revealing Randy's innocence and genuine efforts to connect. One occurs when he dances with Cassidy in a bar; another is seen when he and his daughter revisit places she had liked as a child and he acknowledges his bad decisions, indicates his willingness to accept the consequences of his actions ("I deserve to be alone"), and states his desire to change. Nevertheless life presents challenges and problems, and Randy, unskilled in coping, makes bad decisions that lead to unfortunate consequences. He eventually abandons his new life and returns to what is most familiar to him – his persona of Ram. The film vacillates between hope and despair and portrays the struggles and joys of the human condition.

It is interesting to note that while the themes in this film speak to the comeback of Randy "the Ram," it also marks the comeback of actor Mickey Rourke, who had fallen from stardom and grace and who was honored with a Golden Globe award and a nomination for an Academy Award for his work in this film. His career has re-surged as noted in the Internet Movie Database's records of Rourke planning to be involved with over 10 films in just a one-year time span. Partial credit for selecting Rourke goes to director Aronofsky who lobbied hard for Rourke as his top choice to play Ram. The studio's choice was Nicholas Cage (who had already begun doing research for the role).

The Dynamic Nature of Stress

Stress, a universal experience, affects the body and mind in a multitude of ways. A normal part of everyday life, stress responses are expressed at physiological, cognitive, emotional, behavioral, social, and spiritual levels. In *The Wrestler*, Randy "the Ram" experiences the impact of each of these stress levels, including the spiritual level (e.g.,

his quest for meaning and purpose in his life). Acute stress is easily recognized by the "fight or flight response" characterized by rapid heart beat, increased blood pressure, and psychological intensity. The effects of chronic stress are more subtle and, ultimately, more severe. Over time, chronic stress can precipitate or contribute to the development of a mental disorder such as depression. Even though stress is not a mental illness, it plays a role in the development of most mental disorders.

The study of stress can be approached from several theoretical perspectives. The **Psychoneuroimmunologists** focus on changes that occur in the brain and immune system as a result of stressful life experiences. During stressful periods, illness symptoms can get worse in chronic diseases that are sensitive to the immune system (McEwen, 2005). The **behavioral** perspective views stress as a consequence of rewarding illness behaviors. How one copes with an illness is determined by whether illness behaviors are rewarded. For example, if a person receives attention while experiencing the stress of adapting to a wheelchair, the attention is rewarding. The individual then may be more likely to seek out situations in which a wheelchair can be used in order to receive attention.

Cognitive theorists emphasize thoughts and their intimate relationship with behavior. This approach relates stress to the meaning of the illness or the person's control over it. The more severe the illness, the greater the stress. An example of the cognitive approach is found in the work of Richard Lazarus and his colleagues (2001). Lazarus argues that stress depends on the relationship between a person and the environment that is "appraised" by the person as taxing – the more threatening the environment, the greater the stress. **Psychodynamic** theorists focus on interpersonal relationships and family interactions. They believe that the greater the dysfunction in interpersonal relationships, the greater the stress. The **sociocultural** perspective maintains that stress is a result of the society in which the person lives. Social disruption, such as a divorce or the death of a family member, precipitates stress in an individual.

Stress in Everyday Life

The stress associated with everyday life is convincingly portrayed by Michael Douglas in *Falling Down* (1993), while the stress of the business world is apparent in films such as *Jerry Maguire*

(1996), *Glengarry Glen Ross* (1992), and *Death of a Salesman* (1951/1985). The stressors involved with being threatened and alone in a foreign country can be seen in the remarkable movie *Transsiberian* (2008) starring Woody Harrelson, Kate Mara, and Ben Kingsley. In this film, Harrelson and Mara are seen coping admirably with stressors that include attempted rape, commiting a murder, being imprisoned, and having to witness another prisoner being mercilessly tortured.

Characters experiencing stress can be seen in numerous films. Almost any film dealing with war will address the physical and psychological consequences of prolonged exposure to combat stress. Two classic movies that give the viewer a sense of the horrors of war are *Paths of Glory* (1957) and *Apocalypse Now* (1979). Films like *The Caine Mutiny* (1954), starring Humphrey Bogart as Captain Queeg, illustrate the stress of confronting and challenging inept leadership, while other classic films like *Twelve O'Clock High* (1949) document the stressors associated with military life.

Stress and Coping

There are a variety of different styles of coping, and how a person copes with and manages stress depends upon several factors such as the meaning of stressful situations and available coping skills. In the movie *Noise* (2007), David Owen (Tim Robbins) copes with the stressful noises of the city, specifically car alarms, by becoming aggressive and destructive. At first the noise is an irritant to him. Later, David interprets the noise as an assault on everyone. He becomes a crusader, protecting those who cannot stand up to the nonresponsive authorities. As his grandiosity increases, he becomes more and more driven to damage automobiles with active car alarms. Once arrested, he describes his feelings as "calm" now that his behavior is controlled. However, his dysfunctional coping behaviors are reinforced by others who treat David as a hero.

Some people cope by internalizing their stress. For example, Woody Allen's characters in many of his films somaticize stress and develop bodily complaints. In *Hollywood Ending* (2002), film director Val Waxman (Woody Allen), goes temporarily blind when he is hired to direct his ex-wife who is dating the studio boss. Others deny stress; for example, all three lead characters reject offers of help from others in *The Station Agent* (2003); still others remain stoic and hardened in the face

of stress, e.g., Western hero John Wayne; and some people externalize or blame others, e.g., Annette Bening in *American Beauty* (1999). *The Station Agent* explores the various coping strategies the film's characters use to handle their stress and suffering. These coping approaches range from dangerously maladaptive methods to positive and healing approaches. Alcohol abuse, isolation, denial of help, and suicide attempts exemplify the destructive approaches, while friendship, developing a hobby (train watching), communal dinners, and painting are some of the healthy coping strategies.

Stress of Physical Disorders

Stress is compounded when a person has a physical illness. Internal stress (anxiety about the future, self-blame, regret over behavior, depression), external stressors (work, school, family environment), and the stress of illness (limited mobility, decreased work hours, loss of relationships) all interact and increase the burden of coping.

Stress and Cancer

A number of films portray coping with the diagnosis and realities of cancer. A particularly interesting and unique form of coping is displayed by Ann, a 23-year-old woman dying of ovarian cancer in *My Life Without Me* (2003). She decides not to tell her husband or children she is dying and lies to them when they ask about her doctor's appointment. Despite feeling alone where "lies are your only company," Ann decides to live her life more fully and prepare her family for when she is gone. She creates a "to-do list" which includes making tapes for both of her children's future birthdays, making a man fall in love with her, and picking out a future mate for her husband. In many ways her coping is maladaptive, manipulative, selfish, and dishonest (i.e., she creates a double-life); in other ways, it is inspirational, thoughtful, and transformative.

In *The Bucket List* (2008), two terminally ill hospital roommates, Edward Cole (Jack Nicholson) and Carter Chambers (Morgan Freeman) cope with their impending deaths by doing things that they have always wanted to do. Edward is a caustic, bitter billionaire who is twice divorced and estranged from his only daughter. Carter is a quiet man who has been successfully married for 45 years and has two successful children. Edward is self-centered; Carter has always put his family's needs before his own. Shortly after both men receive information regarding their terminal illnesses, they make a list of things they want to do before they "kick the bucket." Both learn from each other as they face their final months. *Rails and Ties* (2007) portrays a patient coping with recurrent cancer and chronic pain. When an emotionally vacant man (Kevin Bacon) and his wife who is dying of cancer (Marcia Gay Harden) informally adopt a young boy, they begin to face the reality of the cancer and build intimacy, empathy, and joy.

A terminally ill child diagnosed with brain cancer is told he has 3–6 months to live in *Blue Butterfly* (2004). The boy's symptoms include paleness, vomiting, fatigue, and dizziness, and he is confined to a wheelchair because the tumor throws him off balance. His mother, desperate to find a way to lift his spirits, convinces an entomologist to take the boy with him to the jungle in search of a rare, blue butterfly.

Stress and HIV/AIDS

The film *In America* (2003) is loosely based on director Jim Sheridan's personal life. It is a story about a family that emigrates from Ireland to the United States following the death of their two-year-old child. Each member of the family grieves in his or her own way, with the father having the most difficulty in letting go. After finding a home in a dilapidated Hell's Kitchen apartment in a drug-invested area of New York City, they befriend the downstairs tenant, Mateo, (Djimon Hounsou) a Nigerian artist dying from AIDS.

Mateo is known by the apartment tenants as "the man who screams," and he displays intermittent episodes of rage where he intensely cries out in anguish, throws objects in his apartment, and violently slashes his paintings with a knife. The family's introduction to Matteo is frightening: He is depicted as stern, with a tense appearance and periodic tortured screams. "Keep Away" is painted on his door, and he bellows a threatening "Go away!" to two little girls when they come trick-or-treating. However, Mateo soon softens to the girls and is very kind to them. The girls see Mateo's entire refrigerator is stocked with medications and no food; it is then the viewer learns there is a good reason for Mateo to scream. The girls tell Mateo the story of their younger brother, Frankie, who had died of a brain tumor. Mateo cries upon hear-

ing this story – the child's story seems to parallel his own disease.

Every physical illness has a psychological impact. In addition to anger and rage, Mateo is isolated and depressed. It is apparent that his emotional stress interacts with his physical illness and complicates his coping abilities. Mateo's condition further deteriorates as the chronic fatigue of having an immune disease leads him to pass out and experience shortness of breath. In the latter stages of AIDS, Mateo develops blistering lips, facial sores, temperature sensitivity, and exhaustion, leading him to fall asleep when talking to others. Underneath Mateo's rage and hatred toward life is a gentle softness and wisdom. The Irish family, particularly the two young energetic girls, help Mateo rediscover his ability to love and connect with others. His screaming and anguish subside. He begins to accept the reality of his disease and embraces death and suffering in a magnanimous way, continuing to reach out and influence the lives of others until the day he dies.

"I'm in love with you. And I'm in love with your beautiful woman. And I'm in love with your kids. And I'm in love with your unborn child. I'm even in love with your anger! I'm in love with anything that lives."

Mateo, *In America* (2003)

Behind the Red Door (2001) is another recent film about a man suffering and dying of AIDS who responds to his disease by vacillating between intermittent, explosive anger and depression. This film stars Keifer Sutherland as Roy, a person with AIDS; unlike Mateo, Roy does not write "Stay Away" on his door, but Roy's narcissism pushes people away just as effectively. As with Mateo, Roy is connected with others (in this case, previously estranged sister), and this helps Roy to cope psychologically, which brings him to accept his illness in a deeper way. Both men make the transition from fighting to embracing death.

Perhaps the most powerful film illustrating the stress associated with a diagnosis like AIDS, especially in an environment that is hostile and unnurturing, is *Philadelphia* (1993). Tom Hanks won an Academy Award as Best Actor in a Leading Role for his portrayal of Andrew Beckett, a young gay attorney with HIV. Denzel Washington had a memorable role as Beckett's attorney.

Stress and Other Degenerative Diseases

Successful adaptation to a degenerative disease such as amyotrophic lateral sclerosis is documented in films such as *Pride of the Yankees* (1942), the life story of Lou Gehrig, *Tuesdays with Morrie* (1999), and *A Brief History of Time* (1992), an examination of the life and ideas of cosmologist Stephen Hawking. Another film depicting remarkable coping with a chronic illness is *Darius Goes West* (2007), a film in which the protagonist, Darius, suffers from Duchenne's, a type of muscular dystrophy.

In the film *Duet for One* (1986), multiple sclerosis is the major stressor in the life of Stephanie Anderson (Julie Andrews), a famous concert violinist whose life changes dramatically in a few short months. Her loss of tactile sensations in her hands and unpredictable falling result in her giving up the stage and being confined to a wheelchair. Her struggle with her illness becomes an identity crisis as her career and marriage to well-known, glamorous husband-composer David Cornwallis (Alan Bates) ends. Throughout the movie, Stephanie vacillates between very good feelings (euphoria through denial) to extreme depression and suicidal thoughts. Part of her mood swings can be explained by the loss of her career and her lifestyle. Some of her mood changes can be attributed to her illness.

"I'm healthy and I'm normal and I'll be alive after you die!"

David Cornwallis confronting Stephanie Anderson with the reality of her illness in *Duet for One* (1986)

Rory O'Shea Was Here (2005; released in the UK as *Inside I'm Dancing*, 2004) portrays the extreme dependence and loss of freedom that can result from physical disabilities. In this film, two young men attempt to find their own independence and freedom despite their physical conditions of muscular dystrophy and cerebral palsy. They support one another as roommates and hire a support person to help them in their daily life.

"Independent living helps me to grow and mature as a person. It helps me to fulfill the potential I have within myself. It's not always realized by institutional living. It opens the way for me to make a real contribution [and] to live a fuller life."

Michael, a young man with cerebral palsy whose words run together, being interpreted by his friend and roommate, Rory, who has muscular dystrophy

---

Music Within (2007) also portrays cerebral palsy, however, the film focuses on the discrimination experienced by individuals with disabilities. There is a particularly brutal, memorable scene in which a waitress at a pancake house denies a man service because of his "disgusting" appearance (i.e., because he has cerebral palsy). Much of the film, however, is inspirational as it depicts the story and background of Richard Pimentel, the man behind the creation of the landmark 1990 Americans with Disabilities Act, who had become deaf as a result of injuries sustained during the Vietnam war. He advocates for the deaf and his friends, who have various disabilities, using charisma, ingenuity, and principles of fairness.

The stress of being susceptible to illness is highlighted in M. Night Shyamalan's thought-provoking film *Unbreakable* (2000). In this movie, Elijah (Samuel L. Jackson) has a rare genetic bone disease and is highly vulnerable to breaking a bone with any action or movement he makes. His character is directly contrasted with David Dunne (Bruce Willis), who is a "superhero" archetype – he is practically invulnerable as he has never been sick, and he is the only survivor (seemingly untouched) after a deadly train crash. This character contrast sets up interesting questions regarding a continuum of low susceptibility to disease or injury versus high susceptibility to disease/injury and the role that stress plays with this continuum. A very similar bone disease is depicted in the character of "The Glass Man" in *Amelie* (2001), who is unable to leave his home because he could easily shatter his bones.

Stress and Gastrointestinal Disorders and Pain

Irritable bowel syndrome (IBS) is often used as comic relief in films, which does a disservice to the countless individuals who suffer from this malady. For example, IBS is depicted in a Coen Brothers' film, *The Ladykillers* (2004). The man with IBS is depicted mostly for comic relief, but some of his suffering is shown and it exemplifies how symptoms can strike at inopportune moments. The late lead singer of Nirvana, Kurt Cobain, apparently suffered from severe stomach problems (perhaps similar to IBS) as shown in the documentary *Kurt Cobain About a Son* (2006). The film emphasizes the significant psychological impact that the chronic pain had on Cobain's life, and how it contributed to his suicidal ideation.

The stress of migraine headaches is dramatically and skillfully portrayed in Darren Aronofsky's *Pi* (1998). The protagonist does whatever he can to try to stop or prevent his pain, including drilling into his head. Aronofsky skillfully uses the cinematic element of sound – piercing, screeching, and droning during the headache episodes to enhance the experience of suffering. The film, *Chrystal* (2004) portrays a character who suffers from chronic pain that significantly affects her life.

Stress and Physical Limitations

Triumph over a physical limitation (a deformed leg) can be found in *Emmanuel's Gift* (2005), in which Emmanuel, a man living in the poor country of Ghana, receives a prosthesis and within two weeks begins riding a bike and within one year completes a triathalon. His example helps eliminate many of the negative perceptions of the disabled and reduces the stigma associated with disability.

The film *The Waterdance* (1992), starring Eric Stoltz, Wesley Snipes, and Helen Hunt, offers a convincing portrayal of what life is like for someone confined to a wheelchair after a biking accident. The film deals convincingly and sympathetically with the sexual concerns that accident victims often face after their injuries. At one point, one of the hospitalized patients clearly articulates a question the new patient, Joel Garcia (played by Eric Stoltz), has been asking himself: "How long is it going to take before that pretty little girl leaves you for someone who can tune her engine?" The patients in the hospital are divided by race, values, and social class; however, they are united in a profound way by the devastating reality of their injuries and the resulting physical limitations, and ultimately these similarities prove to be far more significant than the trivial differences that separate them. Many of the same themes had

been effectively portrayed by a wheelchair-bound Marlon Brando in *The Men* (1950), a film cast with real paralyzed veterans from a California Veterans Administration Hospital.

Jimmy Stewart is confined to a wheelchair and subsequently develops an interest in voyeurism in Hitchcock's *Rear Window* (1954). The psychological adaptation required to adjust to life in a wheelchair is portrayed in *Born on the Fourth of July* (1989) and *Coming Home* (1978), and somewhat less convincingly in *Crash* (1996). Pathological adaptation to paralysis is presented in *Bitter Moon* (1992), *The People vs. Larry Flynt* (1996), and *Breaking the Waves* (1996). The stress associated with caring for someone who is wheelchair-bound is presented in *Passion Fish* (1992); the stress parents experience with a chronically ill or dying child is poignantly illustrated by the film *Lorenzo's Oil* (1992). *The Accidental Tourist* (1988) is a film in which William Hurt plays a man struggling to cope with the death of his son. Samuel Goldwyn's film *The Best Years of Our Lives* (1946) depicts the changes that occur in the life of a sailor who comes home from the war missing both hands.

Stress Contributing to Physical Disorders

Seyle's early work (1956; 1974) identified the relationship between physiological changes and stress. He suggested chronic stress caused endocrine changes that resulted in physical illnesses. There is an interesting illustration of the psychosomatic consequences of stress in *The Secret Lives of Dentists* (2002). One child experiences a high degree of family stress; some is overt stress (the parents yelling, blaming and cursing) and some is covert stress (the parents keep secrets from one another, become isolated, and spend less time with each other). This child begins to develop physical symptoms with no known origin and eventually gets the flu; as a result, the entire family gets sick. This example speaks to the body becoming more vulnerable due to stress (i.e., resulting in lowered immune system responses) with sickness following.

61 (2001), directed by Billy Crystal, is the story of the 1961 baseball race between Mickey Mantle and Roger Maris to beat Babe Ruth's single-season home run record. The film depicts the physical impact of the stress and pressure on Maris in that he loses his hair, develops a skin rash, and has a number of psychological and behavioral difficulties.

International Films: Psychological Stress and Physical Disorders

*The Diving Bell and the Butterfly (*2007) is an excellent film based on the life of Jean-Dominique Bauby (Matthieu Amatric), who in 1995, at the age of 43, suffered a stroke that paralyzed his entire body with the exception of his left eye. Suffering psychologically from a **locked-in syndrome**, Bauby's mental faculties were left totally intact, and he learned to communicate with the outside world by blinking his left eyelid. Bauby was able to compose his memoirs by blinking his one good eye; unfortunately, he died two days after his memoirs were published. The physical limitation of Bauby is reminiscent of the limitation experienced by Ramon, a quadriplegic, in *The Sea Inside* (2004, Spain).

Yesterday (2004, South Africa) portrays the realities of coping with HIV/AIDS in an area where treatment is scarce. A mother who is very ill, named Yesterday, and her young daughter, Beauty, repeatedly walk several miles in the hot African sun to the village doctor only to be turned away as the doctor has reached the limit of people to be seen for the day. Yesterday moves forward – not letting her illness or lack of access to treatment discourage her or distract her from her goal of watching the day her daughter will go to school – and prepares to come back the next day. At times, she falls over coughing with fatigue while working, and at other times completely collapses. She is the caretaker for both her dying husband and her healthy child. The film also portrays how many people have misconceptions about AIDS as a result of ignorance about HIV is transmitted and what constitutes a genuine risk for infection.

An Academy Award winning film from Canada, *The Barbarian Invasions* (2003), is about living with a terminal illness. A narcissistic man, Remy, is dying of cancer and his family and friends gather around to show their support. Remy is a university professor who has been separated from his wife for 15 years because he insisted on having sex with students and mistresses, and he has previously taken great pride in his sexual prowess. He has a poor relationship with his son, Sebastian, and he is overly critical of Sebastian's highly successful work with video games. Remy stubbornly argues and criticizes Sebastian, as well as society, while lying in his hospital bed. Nevertheless, Sebastian does whatever he can to help his father cope; he makes various accommodations for his father, including arranging for an entire vacant floor in

the hospital for just his father, bribing his father's students to show support and care, and purchasing heroin for pain management. Remy begins to smoke the heroin in the hospital to cope with his pain, and he experiences serious withdrawal when he goes one day without it.

"Only idiots refuse to change."

Sebastian arguing with his dying father in *The Barbarian Invasions* (2003)

The Eye (2002), filmed in Hong Kong, is a suspense-filled thriller about a young woman who undergoes a cornea-transplant and regains her sight. She immediately begins to see and experience ghosts, identified as the souls of the dead, who are forced to relive their death and die each and every day until resolution or forgiveness takes place. The woman comes to realize she has been given the eyes of one of these ghosts and must go on a journey to achieve resolution and healing. The film addresses the interesting theme of vision recovery and speaks not only to the patience needed but equally to the fear involved in such a process. It also addresses the challenges these transplant patients face, such as shifting from a well-developed kinesthetic memory to visual memory, even when interacting with simple objects. *The Eye* illustrates this challenge in a scene in which the woman tries to use a stapler. Regrettably, this film, like so many others, features a psychologist who crosses professional boundaries in the name of love.

The Danish film *Open Hearts* (2003) depicts a random accident in which a man, Joachim, is getting out of his car and is hit by another speeding car, leaving him paralyzed from the neck down. Joachim's reaction is anger and resentment toward his girlfriend, nurse, and society. The girlfriend, Cecilie, is stricken with confusion, hurt, and grief, as is the female driver who hit Joachim. Cecilie, feeling rejected, turns to support from the driver's husband, and an affair develops. The movie forcefully conveys the powerful emotions that result from physical injury and explores the impact of such an injury upon loved ones. It also shows what happens when coping is compromised and the emotional confusion, loneliness, and pain that can result.

Italian for Beginners (2000, Denmark/Sweden) is a story about a woman in extraordinary pain who is dying from pancreatic cancer. She copes through externalizing blame onto others, is mean-spirited, and insists upon morphine injections for her pain. *Cinema Paradiso* (1988, Italy) portrays the friendship between a projectionist and a young boy; the projectionist becomes blind as a result of a fire, but must continue to live his life as fully as he can. The powerful role of stress is emphasized in *Son of the Bride* (2002, Argentina), a film about a man whose heart attack seems directly related to the amount of pressure he is under as well as the denial of the importance of his family. He uses his heart attack as an opportunity to change the areas of his life he has neglected. Another character who faces life head on despite a cardiovascular diagnosis is the character of Burt Munro, played by Anthony Hopkins, in *The World's Fastest Indian* (2005, New Zealand). He has an angina attack and is diagnosed with arteriosclerosis, yet goes on to compete with his Indian motorcycle.

An extraordinary Australian film, Rolf de Heer's *Dance Me to My Song* (1998), tells the story of Julia (Heather Rose), a young woman who is constrained in a wheelchair by cerebral palsy and trapped psychologically by a cruel, manipulative caregiver, Madelaine (Joey Kennedy). In this sensitive and entertaining story, Julia, who communicates through a computer and a speaking machine, finds love and companionship in Eddie (John Brupton), only to have Madelaine determined to have him for herself. The film shows the stress of living with a crippling disease and the strength needed to engage in meaningful relationships. *My Left Foot* (1989, Ireland/UK) is based on the true story of Christy Brown, a successful artist/author who triumphs over cerebral palsy by learning to paint with just his left foot. Brown accepted and overcame his physical disorder at a time when no effort was made to assist or treat those with cerebral palsy. *Oasis* (2002, South Korea), a film touted as being about a misfit who falls in love with an outcast, does a good job at portraying a woman with severe cerebral palsy. Intense facial expressions, grunting noises, jerking movements, and muscular rigidity characterize her body language, and it is clear that there is significant functional impact of her condition as she is severely isolated and not given any opportunity to contribute to society. Her condition gets worse under stress and in stressful situations she loses all ability to communicate. The portrayal (i.e., behaviors, sounds, mannerisms) is so striking that the viewer becomes certain the actress herself must have cerebral palsy; however, filmmaker Chang-dong Lee does something remarkable and creates scenes of sur-

realism throughout the film. For example, in one scene the two characters spontaneously become symptom-free and gracefully dance around for a short time until returning to character. The film directly speaks to common viewer preconceptions of disability.

Critical Thinking Questions

- If you were working with someone like Randy "the Ram" as a patient, and he asked you to come attend a wrestling match sometime, would you go? If "yes," what conditions would you set forth? If not, would there be any circumstances under which you would say "yes"?
- How can environmental stress (noise, pollution, excessive wind, traffic) be managed successfully in order to avoid dysfunctional coping? Was David Owen justified in his destructive episodes in *Noise* (2007)
- Is the role of stress even more significant for people with immune system diseases?
- What are the most successful medical and psychological approaches in slowing down the progression of AIDS?
- What is the best explanation for Stephanie Anderson's reaction to her illness in *Duet for One* (1986) – behavioral, cognitive, psychodynamic, or biological?
- How common is it for someone to react to a devastating diagnosis (such as multiple sclerosis or cancer) by making significant changes in their personality? Compare the coping skills of Edward and Carter in *The Bucket List* (2008) with those of Elijah in *Unbreakable* (2000).
- Is there stress with *every* illness, disease, and disorder?
- What advice or level of support would you give to a woman like Ann in *My Life Without Me* (2003) who has decided not to share with her family the fact that she is dying?
- Are films such as *Falling Down* (1993) accurate in their suggestion that contemporary American life is becoming more stressful? Support your answer with evidence.
- When a person like Michael Douglas' character in *Falling Down* "snaps," is this indicative of mental illness? Can this occur without an underlying or unaddressed psychological problem?
- *The Diving Bell and the Butterfly* (2007) depicts the enormous patience of a stroke victim. What life lessons are taught in this film?

In *Dancer in the Dark* (2000, Denmark), singer Björk Guðmundsdóttir portrays Selma, an immigrant gradually losing her sight. Her loss of vision affects her work, her relationships, and her interests such as dancing.

Further Exploration

If you have time to read just one book relevant to this chapter, make it:
Wicks, R. J. (2008). *The resilient clinician.* New York: Oxford University Press.

If you only have time for one article, read:
Miller, T. W. (2007). Trauma, change, and psychological health in the 21st century. *American Psychologist, 62,* 889–898.

Psychological Stress and Physical Disorders

The Diving Bell and the Butterfly (2007)
In America (2003)
The Waterdance (1992)
Duet for One (1986)
Son of the Bride (2002)
Philadelphia (1993)
Transsiberian (2008)
Music Within (2007)
The Station Agent (2003)
Oasis (2002)

Chapter 5

Mood Disorders

The first time I ever saw a box jellyfish, I was twelve. Our father took us to the Monterey Bay Aquarium.
I never forgot what he said... That it was the most deadly creature on earth.
To me it was just the most beautiful thing I'd ever seen.
Ben Thomas in *Seven Pounds* (2008)

Questions to Consider While Watching *Seven Pounds*

- Does *Seven Pounds* glamorize suicide?
- Does Ben Thomas meet the criteria for a diagnosis of mood disorder?
- Is there evidence for a "contagion effect" when films (and other media) portray suicide in a positive way? Does this film do that?
- What other films suggest suicide is a rational way to solve life's difficult problems?
- Would the symptoms of PTSD be more likely than depression in someone who survived a terrible car crash?
- Ben Thomas chooses a very unusual way of commiting suicide. What ways are the most common? The most lethal?
- Is it ethical for Ben's friend Dan Morris to collude in Ben's suicide? What would you do in a similar situation?
- Would a character like Ben be likely to admit to a mental health professional that he was planning to kill himself?
- Ben gives away his beach home to a woman who has been repeatedly abused by her boyfriend, and giving away prized possessions is a classic warning sign for suicide. What are some other warning signs?
- Does the movie *Seven Pounds* accurately portray the way in which organ donation works?
- What is the significance of Ezra Turner's name? What about Ben's repair of the printing press?
- Is there a relationship between cell phone use (texting, e-mailing, or calling) and automobile accidents?
- What is the significance of the number seven in the title and throughout the film?
- Is it possible to use psychological tests and methods to identify suicidal risk in an individual who is determined to keep you from knowing his or her suicidal plans?
- Why have critics and the general public responded so strongly to this film? Why does it elicit such visceral reactions in the viewer?

Patient Evaluation

Patient's stated reason for coming: "I'm only here because of my brother... however, I did do something really bad once and I'm never gonna be the same."

History of the present illness: Mr. Ben Thomas came in at this brother's insistence. Although Mr. Thomas denies being depressed, he has lost approximately ten pounds and acknowledges difficulty sleeping. He has diminished libido and is not currently sexually active. He acknowledges some difficulty with concentration and moderate irritability. He described a recent incident in which he ridiculed and derided a blind telemarketer without reason. Mr. Thomas denies suicidal ideation.

Past psychiatric illness, treatment, and outcome: There is no significant psychiatric history. Mr. Thomas has a brother with whom he communicates on a regular basis, and he has a wide range of friends, some of whom he has known since high school. Both of his parents are deceased. This patient was involved in a serious automobile accident approximately one year ago in which his fiancé and six other people were killed; despite the magnitude of this traumatic event, Mr. Thomas neither sought out nor received mental health services.

Medical history: Unremarkable.

Psychosocial history: Mr. Thomas is a well educated (MIT), successful, and affluent engineer. He reports a normal childhood. He has made a great deal of money from successful inventions, and he is no longer required to work. He now devotes most of his time to philanthropy. He acknowledges being involved in a romantic relationship with a woman he recently met; however, he maintains that the relationship is currently platonic and "likely to remain that way."

Drug and alcohol history: Mr. Thomas denies any past or recent history of alcohol or drug use.

Behavioral observations: This patient arrived on time for the evaluation. He was well dressed, poised, and articulate. He maintains that he only scheduled the appointment to placate his brother and sister-in-law, both of whom are convinced he is depressed and still grieving over the loss of his fiancé in the automobile accident mentioned above.

Mental status examination: Mr. Thomas was oriented to person, place, time, and situation. The Mini Mental State Examination was administered and he scored 30 out of 30. This patient is exceptionally intelligent, and appeared to be amused by the simple questions he was asked as part of the mental status examination.

Functional assessment: Mr. Thomas shows some signs of moderate depression; however, he currently does not meet the *DSM-IV-TR* criteria for depression or posttraumatic stress disorder.

Strengths: This is a gifted patient with multiple strengths. He is handsome, educated, articulate, and socially skilled. He possesses a wry sense of humor and appeared to be at ease throughout the evaluation.

Diagnosis: None.

Treatment plan: Mr. Thomas apparently is only interested in placating the concern of his relatives. He is not interested in receiving additional services at this time. He was offered supportive psychotherapy but declined.

Prognosis: Fair.

Seven Pounds

Will Smith initially worked with Italian director Gabriele Muccino to produce the movie *The Pursuit of Happyness* (2006), a moving portrayal of a man and his son who triumph over economic difficulties and homelessness. The actor and the director teamed up again to produce *Seven Pounds* (2008), a provocative and controversial movie in which the protagonist, Ben Thomas, attempts to attone for a single tragic mistake in an otherwise charmed life by committing suicide and giving away his home, his wealth, and various body parts (including his eyes and his heart) to seven decent and deserving individuals. In some obscure way, this allows Thomas to "undo" his responsibility for the death of his fiancé and the six other individuals killed in an accident that he clearly caused after attempting to read a Blackberry message while driving a vintage Corvette far too fast. Thomas becomes romantically (but not sexually) involved with Emily Posa (Rosario Dawson), a woman who will die unless a suitable doner can be found and she receives a heart transplant. Thomas works with a childhood friend to ensure that his heart goes to Emily, his eyes go to Ezra Turner (a blind, vegan telemarketer played by Woody Harrelson), and other needy individuals receive other body parts. The movie is overtly sentimental and there is not clear evidence of psychopathology in Will Smith's character; however, we do believe the film raises interesting questions about the movie industry's tendency to glamorize suicide, and it suggests that suicide can sometimes be an altruistic act. The patient evaluation (above) is designed to make the point that mental health professionals are hard pressed to identify suicidal thinking in any patient who denies it, and we hope the film will provide a springboard for lively class discussions about depression, suicide, and the societal responsibilities of directors and producers.

Mood Disorders

Periods of depression are normal in most persons' lives. For example, failing an examination or the ending of a relationship often precipitates a predictable period of sadness. In addition, the feelings of high energy that accompany major events such as a graduation or marriage are also common in everyday life. However, some illnesses involve affective states that resemble these normal periods of depression or elation, but in fact they are very different. The individual experiencing a mood disorder is consumed by negative emotions and is unable to alleviate them through normal coping mechanisms. These illnesses are characterized by emotions that are so intense they begin to dominate a person's life. Mood disorders include many different cognitive, emotional, and behavioral manifestations, but the overriding symptoms of all mood disorders are *emotional* in nature. The *DSM-IV-TR* categorizes types of mood disorders as **depressive** and **bipolar**.

Depressive Disorders

Depressive disorders, one of the most common types of mental disorders, occur in an estimated 16 million people in the United States. Most surveys show that depression is twice as common in women. There is a relationship between depressive disorders and social class, and depressive symptoms are more prevalent in individuals with fewer economic advantages.

A **major depressive episode** is associated with depressed mood and a loss of interest or pleasure in daily activities. Sleep, eating habits, appetite, concentration, motivation, self-esteem, and energy level are areas most often affected. An episode can range from mild (few symptoms) to severe, and in some instances major depressive episodes can be accompanied by delusions and hallucinations. Some people experience a **masked depression** in which they unconsciously mask their depression and experience physical aches and pains rather than traditional depressive symptoms. These physical manifestations of depression are often misdiagnosed as physical illnesses. Others experience an **agitated depression** where frustration and anger seem to dominate and cover up depressive symptoms. If chronically depressed moods, low self-esteem, and feelings of pessimism, despair, or hopelessness are present for two years without suicidal thoughts or limitations in functioning, the diagnosis of **dysthymic disorder** is made (APA, 2000).

Two quality portrayals of depression can be found in *Mind the Gap* (2004) and *Shopgirl* (2005). The first film interweaves several vignettes of characters honestly and earnestly struggling to change their lives. In one vignette, an African American man is clearly depressed with considerable evidence of suppressed anger. He sits around watching television all day in his lonely apartment. He is riddled with guilt for having cheated on his wife and abandoned his son. He purchases a shotgun at the store and writes a suicide note telling his son that the son is not to blame. However, before pulling the trigger, he consults a priest who gives him some wise advice on the distinction between

saying "I'm sorry" and asking someone for their forgiveness; the man then travels to speak face-to-face with both his ex-wife and his son to ask for their forgiveness in two powerful scenes. *Shopgirl*, based on screenwriter/actor Steve Martin's novella, is another film that offers a realistic, non-stereotyped portrayal of depression. In this film, a young, isolated, depressed woman, Mirabelle, falls in love with an older man; the film uses muted colors and positions Mirabelle's work station in a way that highlights her isolation from the other workers.

In *American Splendor* (2003), comic strip writer, Harvey Pekar displays the symptoms and behaviors associated with dysthymia. His depression is expressed through agitation and negativity, and he kicks and breaks objects and sees life through a very pessimistic filter, frequently describing himself as "a nobody." He has a chronically furrowed brow that emphasizes his agitated affect and frustrated view of the world.

Harvey has few social skills; he is socially distant, unfriendly, awkward, inappropriate, and has poor eye contact. Despite success with his comic books, he remains cynical and pessimistic; this theme is emphasized when he repeatedly appears on the David Letterman show and comes across as a defensive misanthrope, Harvey denies having any sense of spirituality. He is lonely and makes a quick decision to marry after one meeting with a woman who travels from out of state to visit him; to the viewer, it seems obvious that these are two lonely people covering up their pain. Nevertheless, Harvey seems to have found a good match in his wife (Hope Davis) who also has a dysthymic quality; she is easily agitated, highly somatic, pessimistic, and suffers from hypersomnia.

Various coping strategies are exhibited in the film. When diagnosed with cancer, Harvey explores creative expression of the disease through comics. On a less healthy note, Harvey has some characteristics of hoarding: His home is dirty and cluttered; there are stacks of comic books everywhere; and he regularly goes to thrift stores and garage sales to acquire more "stuff."

In the emotionally intense *Monster's Ball* (2001), Hank (Billy Bob Thornton) and Leticia (Academy Award winner Halle Berry) are two lost, self-hating people who become even more lonely and raw after each loses an only child – Hank's son commits suicide in front of him, and Leticia's son is hit by a car. Both parents had been physically and verbally abusive to their sons as they attempted to work through their inner turmoil and struggles. The film emphasizes how both characters are trying to escape from their internal hell;

in some ways, the prison in which Hank works is a metaphor for their inner pain, loneliness, isolation, and futility. Hank quits his job at the prison, where he works with death row inmates, realizing the emotional toll his job has taken on his personal life. The relationship of the racist Hank and the beautiful Black woman Leticia begins following an act of kindness by Hank when he aids a screaming Leticia he finds on the side of the road; he explains that he just felt like "doing the right thing" and that he is trying to get outside of his "insides." After becoming drunk, they engage in raw, uninhibited sex "just to feel." Both are emotionally numb and overwhelmed by their personal pain; scenes of the two lovers interacting are juxtaposed with flashes of human hands reaching into a "cage" to release a bird desperately flapping its wings. Through their connection, which becomes more intimate and genuine over time, both characters find meaningful, expressive outlets for their depression for the first time.

The Cooler (2003) is about Bernie (William H. Macy), an "unlucky" man, who works for a traditional, antisocial casino boss (Alec Baldwin). Bernie's job is walking around successful casino patrons to bring them bad luck. Bernie is "the cooler" because he turns winners into losers; his appearance at a table is enough to make a winning patron quickly go bankrupt. He claims he can do this easily; "I just be myself." He is stuck in the past and trapped by it, unable to move on since he is forced to use his "bad luck" to pay off his extensive gambling debt or be killed by the casino boss. When we look deeper beyond the plot, the viewers see that Bernie's personality is very self-critical, self-defeating, and negativistic. His "unlucky" quality is a self-fulfilling prophecy. He is isolated, lives alone, and is too passive to take action to change his life.

This film presents a classic depressive triad: The protagonist is hapless (unlucky), hopeless, and helpless. A cognitive therapy approach emphasizing the impact of one's thoughts, beliefs, and attitudes as affecting mood states is highlighted. Upon falling in love, Bernie's luck changes, he becomes assertive, and his presence at casino tables enhances the success of others. The power of attitude is an overriding theme in the film and we see Bernie's negative attitudes keeping him from love and luck, while positive attitudes bring him good luck and success.

In many ways, the story is clichéd – the fight for love to the death, escape from a tyrannical boss, and tremendous luck in the end saves the heroes from their seemingly inevitable demise.

In *Scent of a Woman* (1992), Lieutenant Colonel Frank Slade exhibits many of the classic symptoms of a major depressive episode and would probably qualify for the diagnosis. He has both a depressed mood and a loss of interest and pleasure in everyday activities (**anhedonia**). Slade's angry comment "I have no life, I'm in the dark" clearly suggests his depression is related to his blindness, and the sentence captures the lack of meaning and purpose in his life. His daily activities, sitting alone and drinking himself into oblivion when he is not tormenting his four-year-old niece, are clear indications of his loss of interest in life.

People who are depressed are typically not pleasant, and they can be quite difficult to be around. They are often agitated and easily angered. This serves to hide their underlying need for help. Colonel Slade is irritable, intimidating, and verbally abusive to anyone who approaches him. Expression of this type of anger and abuse has a distancing effect on others, who naturally withdraw from unpleasant situations. Charles Simms, a college student hired to accompany the Colonel on a trip, does not want to stay with Slade after meeting him, and Simms dreads the weekend he is forced to spend with the Colonel.

Another interesting film depicting depression is the 1971 Academy Award winner *The Hospital* starring George C. Scott as Herbert Bock, a middle-aged, depressed, suicidal physician who is trying to cope with the mayhem of a crowded and disorganized institution, where negligence and confusion result in a series of deaths. Bock's personal life is as chaotic as the hospital he runs.

 Additional Questions for Discussion (*Scent of a Woman*)

- Will the use of alcohol alleviate depression?
- The Colonel decides to shoot himself while in uniform. Would his previous military experience increase the likelihood that Slade would actually kill himself?
- Does the true likelihood of suicide increase because Slade is blind?
- Who should determine if a decision about suicide reflects an accurate appraisal of life and its likely rewards?
- Who is qualified to determine if a decision to commit suicide is the consequence of a disease such as depression?
- Should people who are believed to be at risk for suicide be involuntarily hospitalized?

He is recently divorced, alienated from his children, and suffering from both personal and sexual impotence. He had been believed to be a medical genius in his early career; however, at the point we are introduced to him in the film, he is washed up and discouraged. At one point in the film, Bock is seen sitting in his office, preparing to inject a fatal dose of potassium.

Bock demonstrates the classical symptoms of a depressive episode. His depressed mood is expressed through his explosive angry episodes and chronic irritability. He is anhedonic and expresses no interest in his patients, his profession, or any of the activities of daily living through which most of us find meaning and purpose. Bock cannot sleep, he feels worthless, and he is plagued by recurrent thoughts of suicide. Dr. Bock's behavior is remarkably similar to that of Lt. Colonel Slade – it is similar because both men are clinically depressed.

Marlon Brando plays a depressed man trying to come to grips with the meaning of his wife's suicide in Bernado Bertolucci's powerful film *Last Tango in Paris* (1972). The character of the coach's wife in Peter Bogdanovich's *The Last Picture Show* (1971) is clearly depressed, and her affect and behavior offer good teaching examples of depressed affect for students learning how to give a mental status examination. The despair that overcomes a man when he is abandoned by his wife is presented in the Australian film *My First Wife* (1984). Finally, Joanne Woodward gives a memorable performance as a depressed housewife in *Summer Wishes, Winter Dreams* (1973).

We highly recommend *Prozac Nation* (2001) as a film that illustates the devastation caused by depression in a gifted but deeply troubled Harvard freshman (Lizzi) played by Christina Ricci. The film presents a compelling portrayal of Lizzi's slow descent into depression, and Lizzi provides an insightful description of her illness: "Hemingway has this classic moment in *The Sun Also Rises* when someone asks Mike Campbell how he went bankrupt. All he can say is, 'gradually, then suddenly.' That's how depression hits. You wake up one morning afraid that you're going to live." Lizzi knows she needs medication, but she also knows that it is not sufficient to solve her myriad personal problems. At one point she states "I call this the crack-house where I come to score. Dr. Sterling is my dealer. Seems like everyone's doctor is dealing this stuff now. Sometimes it feels like we're all living in a Prozac nation."

The Visitor (2007), directed by Tom McCarthy, is a sensitive portrayal of the human suffering associated with social isolation and with the restrictive immigration policies in the United States. The film stars Richard Jenkins as a depressed and ineffectual college professor who has never recovered from the death of his wife. Jenkins' character, Professor Walter Vale, makes a half-hearted attempt to learn to play the piano, but lacks the energy, passion, and talent necessary to succeed at this task. Watching Vale interact with his colleagues and students reminds the viewer of Hamlet's lament, "O God, O God, how weary, stale, flat, and unprofitable seem to me all the uses of this world!" Vale's life has become weary, stale, flat, and unprofitable, and he finds meaning, purpose and some degree of contentment only when he stops contemplating his own unhappiness and becomes invested in helping a pair of undocumented workers he finds living in his infrequently used New York City apartment. Walter's transition from a staid, discouraged, and unhappy college professor to someone genuinely interested in life and others is symbolized by the transition from his desultory attempt to learn to play classical music on the piano to his enthusiasm for the *djembe* (an African drum that he passionately plays in the subway in the film's final moments). The film illustrates both depression and burnout, and it is a convincing demonstration of the therapeutic truism that one helps oneself most by learning to reach out and help others.

Hyler (1988) has pointed out that many of the characters who appear depressed in films would meet the *DSM-IV-TR* criteria for **adjustment disorder with depressed mood** rather than major depression. The examples Hyler cites include Jimmy Stewart's character in Frank Capra's *It's a Wonderful Life* (1946) and Henry Fonda's character in *The Wrong Man* (1956). In the latter film, Fonda develops a reactive depression after he is unjustly accused of murder.

Bipolar Disorders

Bipolar disorder occurs less frequently than depressive disorders but affects approximately 0.5–1% of the population. Unlike depression, bipolar disorders occur equally often among males and females. Like most mental disorders, the prevalence is greater in lower socioeconomic groups, in part because these illnesses interfere with a person's ability to work and in part because the cost of the illnesses quickly depletes the economic resources of all but the very wealthy. Even wealthy clients can quickly become impoverished, however, because of the poor judgment associated with manic episodes.

A **manic episode** is a distinct period of an abnormally and persistently elevated, expansive, or irritable mood, lasting at least one week, during which the mood disturbance causes marked impairment of work or functioning. The manic episode may range from mild to severe and may be accompanied by psychotic features. A **hypomanic episode** results in a period of sustained elevated mood, lasting at least four days. This change is obvious to others and alters a person's level of functioning. However, by definition, a hypomanic episode is *not* severe enough to impair work or social functioning.

People with bipolar illnesses are often very likable. Their basic personality is usually outgoing, and they often work in people-intensive occupations such as sales. During a manic episode, they feel good about themselves and their moods are contagious. They are often very generous and may buy strangers expensive gifts. During a manic episode, judgment is typically very poor. Individuals may gamble away their life savings or spend money they can't afford to lose on an expensive vacation. They often have multiple sexual partners within a short period. They also seem to have endless physical energy, appear to function perfectly well without sleep, usually eat very little, and may lose 30 or 40 pounds within a few weeks. The potential for physical exhaustion during a manic episode is very real, and the long-term consequences of a manic episode can be devastating for families. For example, it may take years to pay back a debt or forgive infidelities.

Bipolar I illnesses are diagnosed when a person has both manic and depressive episodes and cycles from one to another. The depressive episode may last 3–6 months before the person swings to a manic phase. The diagnosis of **bipolar II** disorder is reserved for those who have primarily depressive episodes, with occasional hypomania. These patients do not have full-blown manic episodes. **Cyclothymic** disorders are found in individuals who never experience a major depressive or manic episode but who have hypomanic and depressive symptoms.

Mr. Jones

Alan Greisman and Debra Greenfield's 1993 film *Mr. Jones* is about a musician, Mr. Jones, played by Richard Gere, and his psychiatrist, Dr. Libbie Bowen, played by Lena Olin. *Mr. Jones* is a clearcut illustration of bipolar I disorder. The film portrays Jones as elated, seductive, and euphoric. He is a charismatic man with tremendous personal charm. He persuades a contractor to hire him,

proceeds to the roof, and prepares to fly after rhythmically pounding a few nails into the roof. Before climbing to the front of the roof, he insists that Howard, his newfound friend, accept a $100 bill. After realizing that Jones really believes that he can fly, Howard persuades him to move away from the beam where he was teetering. The ambulance arrives and takes Jones to a local psychiatric emergency unit, where he is released after a few hours. At the hospital, he is misdiagnosed and given inappropriate medications.

Next, Jones goes to a bank and withdraws $12,000; he seduces the teller in the process, and then goes on a spending spree. He purchases a baby grand piano, checks into an expensive hotel, and then attends a concert. He is arrested and returned to the hospital after he disrupts the symphony by attempting to take over for the conductor as the orchestra is playing Beethoven's "Ode to Joy" – Jones is convinced that Beethoven would have wanted the piece played at a much faster tempo. Jones is once again hospitalized in a state of manic exhaustion, and this time he is accurately diagnosed and treated by psychiatrist Elizabeth (Libbie) Bowen.

Jones knows he has manic-depressive illness. He was first diagnosed in late adolescence and had several hospitalizations. However, he refuses to take his medication, which makes his hands shake. It is during the "highs" or the manic phases that he feels best about himself. The rest of the time Jones is lonely and depressed. His lows are life threatening and result in suicide attempts. The viewers are able to gain some insight into the impact of a mental illness on the promising career of a classical musician. In addition, the film illustrates the ways in which interpersonal relationships are affected by a condition such as bipolar disorder. Jones' one important prior relationship ended when a woman he loved could no longer deal with his mood swings.

Unfortunately, the rest of the movie involves the romantic relationship that develops between Dr. Bowen and Jones. Even though Dr. Bowen resigns from the hospital, underscoring the unethical nature of this doctor-patient relationship, the true impact of the psychiatrist's behavior is never addressed in the movie.

Other Films Depicting Bipolar Disorder

Some films describe characters with bipolar disorder and do not show them as symptomatic. In *The Last Days of Disco* (1998), for example, one character is stereotyped as "looney" and "crazy"; however, he is also depicted as compliant with lith-

Additional Questions for Discussion (Mr. Jones)

- Why does Dr. Elizabeth Bowen question the resident's admitting diagnosis of paranoid schizophrenia?
- At what point is the doctor/patient relationship first compromised? Are there early warning signs that should have alerted the psychiatrist to her countertransference to this patient?
- Does Jones' history of a previous suicide attempt increase the likelihood of another attempt?
- Is an affair between a doctor and a patient more serious than one between an orderly and a patient?
- Would it have mattered if the patient had been discharged? Why?
- Is it ethical for a psychiatrist to visit a university to get historical information that may be relevant to a patient she is treating?
- Should patients with illnesses such as bipolar disorder be required by the courts to take medication, even if they dislike the effects of the medication and find it dampens their creativity?

ium, and shown to be stable, kind, and balanced. *Garden State* (2004) also depicts a patient diagnosed with bipolar disorder. However, this patient becomes noncompliant with his medication and finds that his life improves dramatically without exacerbation of his bipolar symptoms. While **drug holidays** might be recommended by physicians on occasion, films of this sort mislead the public and suggest that these important decisions can be made without medical consultation.

One of the best films depicting a bipolar illness is *Call Me Anna*, a 1990 made-for-TV movie starring Patty Duke, who plays herself in this adaptation of her best-selling autobiography. The film traces her career and her battle with a bipolar disorder and vividly portrays her mood swings and the accompanying personality changes she experienced. In real life, Patty Duke has become a vocal advocate for persons with mental illness.

Gena Rowlands plays a woman who appears to have a bipolar disorder in the John Cassavetes film *A Woman Under the Influence* (1974). She is quite convincing during a manic episode, and there is a memorable scene in which a neighbor stops by to drop off his children and then decides that it is not safe to leave them with Rowlands. He does not know exactly what's wrong, but it is clear to him that *something* is not right. Unlike *Mr. Jones*, the actual diagnosis is never specified in *A Woman*

Under the Influence, despite the fact that Rowlands spends six months in a psychiatric hospital.

Another example of an apparent bipolar disorder is found in the Harrison Ford character in *Mosquito Coast* (1986), although Ford's eccentric habits and obsessional style are probably adequate to support multiple diagnoses. The biographical film *Mommie Dearest* (1981) suggests that Joan Crawford had a bipolar disorder.

Examples of the type of rapid speech, quick thinking, and impulsive behavior associated with a hypomanic episode can be seen in the college president character played by Groucho Marx in *Horse Feathers* (1932) and in *Good Morning, Vietnam* (1987), in which Robin Williams plays an Air Force disc jockey with a rapid and clever repartee that endears him to his military audience.

One of our favorite films portraying bipolar disorder is *Blue Sky* (1994) starring Jessica Lange and Tommy Lee Jones. Lange, who won an Academy Award for her role in this film, plays the role of Carly Marshall, a woman whose bipolar disorder (diagnosed with the then appropriate term manic-depressive disorder) gets her family in considerable trouble. She sunbathes topless and acts out sexually, and the film illustrates the effects of a disease like bipolar disorder on families.

"You take water, for example. Sometimes it's water, sometimes it's ice. Sometimes it's steam, vapor. It's always the same old H$_2$O. It only changes its properties. Your mother's like that. She's like water."

Henry Marshall (Tommy Lee Jones) tries to explain their mother's erratic behavior to his children in *Blue Sky* (1994)

Two recent films have presented fairly accurate portrayals of bipolar disorder. These are *Running with Scissors* (2006) and *Michael Clayton* (2007). In the first film, Annette Bening plays the role of a bipolar mother who turns over her son's life to her psychiatrist; in the second film, Tom Wilkinson portrays a senior attorney in a large law firm who becomes manic. Wilkinson's character displays inappropriate behavior (e.g., stripping in court), pressured speech, and grandiose thinking. His illness is controlled by medication, but he becomes quite ill when he stops taking his lithium, and the film illustrates the critical importance of adherence to medication regimens for anyone with this disorder.

Theories of Mood Disorders

There are three main theoretical explanations associated with mood disorders: The **genetic**, which is useful in understanding familial tendencies; the **biological**, which explains the physiological changes and the rationale for pharmacotherapy and electroconvulsive therapy; and the **psychological**, which gives direction for understanding behavior and psychotherapy treatment for the impact of the illness. The environment and external events are an extremely important factor in the manifestation of mood disorders, i.e., loss of a job or a recent divorce.

Genetic Theories

Twin and adoption studies have documented that there is a genetic vulnerability to mood disorders. Bipolar disorder, in particular, has been shown to have a very high heritability estimate of 93% in identical twins (Kieseppa, Partonen, Haukka, Kaprio, & Lonnqvist, 2004).

When researchers compared the incidence of mood disorders in identical twins (who share the same genetic code) with that of fraternal twins (who have different genetic material), the concordance rate was 67% for the identical twins and 15% for fraternal twins. The high concordance for identical twins has also been found in twins who were raised in different environments. Clearly, there is a significant genetic component in mood disorders.

Biological Theories

The biological approach to mood disorders focuses on the activity of the neurotransmitters in the limbic system. The neurotransmitters involved include **dopamine**, **serotonin**, **acetylcholine**, and **norepinephrine**. In depression, it is believed that there are fewer available neurotransmitters in the synaptic junction; in mania, there is an excess.

The limbic system also regulates the pituitary hormone, a key element in the highly complex endocrine system. Changes in the endocrine system also influence mood. There have been many studies documenting the changes in the function-

ing of the pituitary gland and thyroid that occur with mood disorders. Some depressed persons have been found to secrete an excessive amount of cortisol, a hormone produced by the pituitary gland. Additionally, persistently low thyroid hormone levels have been noted in some cases of depression, and an elevated thyroid hormone level is present in some rapid cycling bipolar disorders.

Psychological Theories

Psychological theories have always played an important role in the understanding and treatment of mood disorders. While the depressive and bipolar disorders clearly have a biological basis, the psychodynamic conceptualization of these disorders provides a different way of understanding the behavioral and emotional problems associated with these conditions. Many of the psychological features of depression are readily apparent in films.

The early psychoanalysts (e.g., Freud, Abraham) noticed that people with depression experienced **ambivalence** toward significant persons in their lives. That is, they often acted as if they loved and hated the same person. In *Scent of a Woman* (1992), Lt. Col. Slade is both affectionate and antagonistic toward his niece, brother, and other family members. He also becomes antagonistic and aggressive when Charlie Simms tries to help him.

Introjection, the unconscious "taking in" of qualities and values of another person or a group with whom emotional ties exist, was also identified as a characteristic feature of depression. In *Scent of a Woman*, Slade introjected the values of the military and continued to treat everyone as if he or she reported to him. Interestingly, Slade had been discharged from the military because of his overbearing behavior. Colonel Slade's difficulties in the Army were likely related to a long-standing history of untreated depression.

Regression, another characteristic of depression, refers to a return to an earlier pattern of behavior. During a depression, childhood behavioral patterns may appear, and a person may act less mature. In *Scent of a Woman*, Slade's ongoing battle with a four-year-old is not acceptable adult behavior for a retired Colonel.

Denial, ignoring the existence of reality, is characteristic of persons experiencing a manic episode. These patients often stop taking their medication because they believe that there is nothing wrong with them. They reject any advice from family members and may become belligerent at any suggestion that they are ill. Jones had been hospitalized multiple times after he discontinued his medication in *Mr. Jones*, and he is smart enough to know it will happen again. However, each time he convinces himself that this time will be different. This is a classic example of denial.

Cognitive-behavioral theorists have contributed significantly to the understanding of the experience of depression. Aaron Beck has described a **cognitive triad** that is common in these patients. The triad consists of (1) perceiving oneself as defective and inadequate, (2) perceiving the world as demanding and punishing, and (3) expecting failure, defeat, and hardship. These "automatic thoughts" are readily apparent in *American Splendor* (2003), *The Cooler* (2003), *Scent of a Woman* (1992), *The Hospital* (1971), and Julianne Moore's character in *The Hours* (2002).

Mood Disorders and Creativity

There is compelling evidence that mood disorders may be related to the creative process, and numerous artists, poets, and composers have been diagnosed as depressed or bipolar, or have biographies that suggest that these disorders were present. Dean Simonton, a researcher on creativity and creative genius for over 35 years, notes that artists and those in professions involving skills that are subjective, intuitive, and emotive are more likely to have mental illness than those who are scientists or in professions using skills that are rational, logical, and formal (Ludwig, 1998; Simonton, 2009). Simonton adds that some creators are able to control their bizarre thoughts and use them productively. Similarly, Kay Redfield Jamison, a psychologist with bipolar disorder, notes that the periods of creativity in many individuals with this disorder typically happen during healthy periods in which the person draws upon the experiences that occurred in their manic, hypomanic or depressed phase (Jamison, 1993). Two recent short documentaries discuss this link between psychopathology and artists – *Between Madness and Art* (2007), which tells the story of Dr. Hans Prinzhorn, a man who collected hundreds of artistic creations by patients with mental illness from various institutions, and *Hidden Gifts: The Story of Angus MacPhee* (2005), the story of a mute man with schizophrenia who made incredibly creative objects and clothes out of twigs and sticks.

Several actors and actresses have reported or been rumored to have struggled with bipolar disorder, including Richard Dreyfuss, Patty Duke, Carrie Fisher, Linda Hamilton, Jean-Claude Van Damme, and Vivien Leigh. Examples of poets believed to have experienced mood disorders include William Blake, Ralph Waldo Emerson, Edgar Allan Poe, Lord Byron, Alfred Lord Tennyson, John Berryman, Sylvia Plath, Theodore Roethke, and Anne Sexton; examples of painters and composers with mood disorders include Vincent van Gogh, Georgia O'Keefe, and Robert Shuman (Jamison, 1993). Sylvia Plath's difficulties with depression are detailed in the film adaptation of her semi-autobiographical novel *The Bell Jar* (1979), in which Gwyneth Paltrow plays the title role as *Sylvia* (2003). Novelist Virginia Woolf's mood disorder is portrayed in the highly recommended movie *The Hours* (2002). The troubled life of Beethoven is portrayed in the 1995 film *Immortal Beloved*. Vincent van Gogh's life, work, and mental illness (which may have been bipolar disorder) have been documented in the films *Vincent* (1987), *Vincent & Theo* (1990), and *Van Gogh* (1991). However, none of these match the artistic achievement established by the 1956 film *Lust for Life*, in which Kirk Douglas plays van Gogh and Anthony Quinn plays the supporting role of Paul Gauguin. The final days of influential Nirvana lead singer/guitarist, Kurt Cobain, are portrayed in Gus van Sant's *Last Days* (2005) and *Kurt Cobain: About a Son* (2006); Cobain had been diagnosed with bipolar disorder and committed suicide in 1994. Wedding (2000) provides examples of the cognitive distortions found in the poems of Anne Sexton; these particular distortions are common in depressed and suicidal people.

 Additional Questions About Creativity

- Are people with certain mental illnesses more creative than people without such disorders?
- How do you make sense of such a significant split between dramatic creativity and complete chaos and disorder that often mark such individuals' lives?
- What are your own views on van Gogh? What behaviors support a diagnosis of mood disorder? What evidence suggests a seizure disorder may have been present? Are there any other competing hypotheses?
- If you had the power to cure someone like van Gogh, but you knew that the treatment would destroy his creativity, would you proceed?
- What other artists and writers have experienced mood disorders?
- Can you name other artists, writers, and poets who have committed suicide?

Shakespeare was fascinated by people who took their own lives, and his plays and their film adaptations provide a useful and fascinating way to approach the study of suicide. Major Shakespearean plays in which suicide is a prominent theme include *Romeo and Juliet*, *Julius Caesar*, *Hamlet*, *Anthony and Cleopatra*, *Macbeth*, *Othello*, and *King Lear*. There have been multiple film adaptations of each of these plays.

Suicide

Suicide and Depression

Suicide is the eighth most frequent cause of death throughout the world, but suicide rates vary widely among different countries. Generally, the suicide rate is low in the less prosperous countries and highest in the more affluent ones, such as Germany, Switzerland, and Sweden. However, the suicide rate is also high in all Eastern European nations. The suicide rates in the United States and Canada are in the middle range. Among adolescents, suicide is the third most frequent cause of death. While men are more likely to commit suicide, women attempt suicide more frequently than men. Men are more successful in their attempts because they are more likely to choose a more lethal means (e.g., guns).

Mortality rates for suicide are generally higher in urban areas, and prevalence rates for suicide have been shown to be positively correlated with the size of cities. Although suicide has a low incidence in closely-knit rural communities, the problem is more common among the elderly, in areas where agriculture is in decline, and among workers who are immigrating to the cities. The incidence of suicide increases with age, with the elderly at greatest risk for killing themselves (NIMH, 2003).

One of the best predictors of who will attempt suicide is a history of a psychiatric disorder. Those who are at the highest risk for suicide are those who have no hope. People who express hopelessness are more likely to commit suicide than those who have some hope for the future. The association between suicidality and hopelessness is stronger and more stable than the association of suicidality with the presence of depression and substance use disorders (Kuo, Gallo, & Eaton, 2004). The lead characters in two films discussed earlier, *Scent of a Woman* (1992) and *The Hospital* (1971), each have a strong sense of hopelessness.

House of Sand and Fog

House of Sand and Fog (2003) offers a compelling illustration of the ways in which depression can present. The movie stars Jennifer Connelly as Kathy, a depressed, recovering alcoholic, Ben Kingsley as Behrani, a former high-ranking Iranian colonel working hard at two menial jobs to create success for his family, and Ron Eldard as Lester, a married police officer who protects Kathy and wants to start a new life with her. Director Vadim Perelman succinctly describes the dynamics of each character's psyche as follows: "Behrani wants up, Kathy wants in, and Lester wants out. Those are their motivations." Kathy's house is seized due to tax payment delinquency and Behrani wins the house in an auction, thus beginning a complex web of morality, conflict, individual needs, and pursuit of one's dreams.

"The woman has come here and tried to take her own life. We must help her. She's a bird, a broken one. Your grandfather used to say the bird which flies into your house is an angel. You must look upon its presence like a blessing."

Behrani giving advice regarding Kathy's first suicide attempt in
House of Sand and Fog (2003)

Kathy lives alone in a house she and her brother inherited from their father. In one of the opening scenes, Kathy is sleeping when she is awakened by her advice-giving mother on the phone; after discussing the need for her to attend support group meetings, Kathy ends the conversation with a single tear streaming down her cheek and hangs up the phone. She then rises from her shaking waterbed (an early symbol of her instability) and begins to walk around her dirty house that includes a dripping faucet and a large stack of unopened mail blocking her front door. The opening scenes set up a depiction of an unsteady woman with a history of alcoholism who lives a sedentary, isolated, and unmotivated life. These scenes set the stage for Kathy's battles with alcoholism and depression.

Kathy seems to have an underlying depression quality marked by agitation, numbed and blunted affect, and social isolation. Early on, she alludes to her struggle with depression and remarks "I'm trying not to harp on the negative." Kathy also has financial problems, and because she is unable to afford a motel for two days, she begins to live and sleep in her car, turning the engine on for heat. She finds some comfort and escape from her loneliness through an affair with a married man. As stress increases, she begins to smoke cigarettes again. There is a clear link between alcohol and depression, yet this begins with denial. Kathy says, "See, when I think of my sobriety I don't think about wine, alcohol was never a problem." She then begins to drink wine with a subtle smile. This is a break in her two years of sobriety and it rapidly results in physical and emotional deterioration. This is a serious and severe relapse for Kathy, clearly triggered by the stress and chaos in her life.

Kathy's overt "cry for help" comes when she calls her brother, pleading with him to visit and support her: "I just feel lost, Frankie, I just feel lost." Her brother, a typical busy American, claims there are new things needing attention at his job and quickly gets off the phone. Kathy's despair continues to escalate. With tearfulness and blood-shot eyes from crying, Kathy purchases several miniature bottles of whiskey and some gasoline. She drinks the whiskey while driving and crying. Her depression and helplessness then lead to two suicide attempts. While despairing over the house she lost, she tries to kill herself with a gun, pulling the trigger several times; however, the gun is not loaded. She is found, taken in and cared for by her rival Behrani and his family, and she attempts suicide a second time, swallowing several bottles of unnamed prescription medicine. She is saved again, this time because she is found early and forced to throw up most of the medicine.

Metaphors for depression abound in this film. The emergence of the moon and the setting or rising of the sun represent character transitions and shifts into different mood and mental states. As the title suggests, sand and fog are important elements in the film; one possible interpretation is that both represent the symptoms of depression. Sand is a naturally unsteady element representing the sinking nature of suicide. As Kathy sinks deeper into depression, fog is seen in many scenes, becomes thicker and more concealing until in one scene it completely surrounds the house. There are several camera shots of "moving fog" in which the fog quickly covers trees, mountains, water, and homes. This is similar to the rapid clouding associated with the negative thoughts, helplessness, and self-destructive behaviors one finds in depression. The film opens with life being cut down (trees) and concludes

Additional Questions for Discussion (*House of Sand and Fog*)

- Based solely on the film, does Kathy meet the criteria for a diagnosis of mood disorder?
- At what point would hospitalization be recommended for Kathy?
- What are the negative automatic thoughts likely to occur in Kathy?
- What is the relationship between alcohol and depression in this film? How commonly does alcohol and drug abuse co-occur with mood disorders?
- How much more likely is a depressed drinker to commit suicide than a depressed non-drinker?
- Describe the ways characters react to Kathy's suicide attempts. Are these reactions typical?
- What suicide signs are evident for Kathy? Compare and contrast the suicide risk factors for Kathy and Behrani?
- What is the purpose of the film's title? Does it relate to depression or addiction?
- Some reviewers have described Kathy as a weak person. Do you agree?
- What are Kathy's healthy and unhealthy coping strategies?

with a shot of a tree surrounded and protected by a fence.

The viewer is particularly challenged with this film, as he or she can empathize with both characters and can see the needs of both sides. As tension rises and conflict continues, this challenge becomes more complex, even to the point where a state of helplessness is induced in the viewer which mirrors the helplessness portrayed on screen.

The Hours

The Hours (2002) is a film of enormous psychological, emotional, and cinematic proportions. The film was nominated for Academy Awards as Best Picture, Best Director, and Best Adapted Screenplay. The all-star cast includes Nicole Kidman, Meryl Streep, Julianne Moore, Ed Harris, Claire Danes, Jeff Daniels, Toni Collette, John C. Reilly, and Miranda Richardson. Music was brilliantly composed by the renowned Philip Glass, and the script was adapted by David Hare. Ironically, one of the least known figures in this film is perhaps the most important – the director. This was director Stephen Daldry's second feature film, though his extensive work and awards in the London theater show he was more than equal to the challenge of directing a movie.

> "If I were thinking clearly, Leonard, I would tell you that I wrestle alone in the dark, in the deep dark and that only I can know, only I can understand my own condition."
>
> Virginia Woolf (Nicole Kidman) talking to her husband in *The Hours* (2002)

The film depicts three stories about three women who are closely connected although they live in different periods. Each struggles with both serious depressive symptoms and suicide issues.

Kidman plays the now celebrated novelist Virginia Woolf, struggling to write her soon-to-be-famous novel *Mrs. Dalloway* in the early 1900s while suffering with what would be identified today as bipolar disorder. The film dramatically begins and ends with the suicide of Virginia Woolf, who drowns herself in a quickly flowing river with heavy rocks in her pockets to weigh her down. Woolf's depression is emphasized in the film, though some mania symptoms are depicted, including her agitation, decreased need for sleep, poor judgment, and indecisiveness, such as when she decides to leave her house against doctor's orders with the intention to move to and live in London. She has a history of "fits," problems with mood, she hears voices, and she has made two suicide attempts. Though her life has been set up to protect her, the inner turmoil she experiences is simply too painful for her to continue to live. She smokes marijuana to calm herself, focus her thoughts, and numb the pain.

The character of Laura (Julianne Moore) is living in a quaint neighborhood home in the 1950s. She reads *Mrs. Dalloway* with interest and passion, finding comfort and inspiration in the lead character. Laura's character is an enigma, but she is clearly depressed and overwhelmed by life and its demands. She is socially awkward and skittish, at times unsure of how to respond socially and at other times standing near the door (after the doorbell rings) but not answering it. She is overwhelmed by easy tasks (e.g., baking a cake) and is self-critical of her mistakes. Laura, like Woolf, feels alone and craves connections though does not seem to know how to make them. She kisses her visiting neighbor, Kitty (Toni Collette), on the lips, clearly trying to connect with another life. She spends a lot of time alone and experiences frequent crying spells. At one point, she decides to commit suicide, leaves her son with a baby-sitter and checks into a hotel – a suicidal dream seems to be the catalyst that changes her mind. Ultimately, life is too much for her to cope with and rather than committing suicide, she travels to Canada to restart her life, abandoning her husband and children.

> "There are times when you don't belong and you think you're going to kill yourself. Once I went to a hotel. Later that night I made a plan. The plan was I would leave my family when my second child was born. That's what I did. I got up one morning, made breakfast, went to the bus stop, got on a bus, left a note... What does it mean to regret when you have no choice? It's what you can bear. There it is. No one's going to forgive me. It was death. I chose life."
>
> Laura (Julianne Moore) explaining herself in *The Hours* (2002)

The third interweaved story is set in New York City in 2001 and involves Clarissa (Meryl Streep), a woman trying to impress others and cover up her pain by throwing a party (just as in *Mrs. Dalloway*) for Richard (Ed Harris), her former lover, a prize-winning poet dying of AIDS. Clarissa is a strong woman who is socially confident and appears sure of herself. Her vulnerability is slowly disclosed through her struggles to help Richard, through her distant relationship with her partner of several years, and in her emotions that rush to the surface when she confronts a former lover (Jeff Daniels).

> "I still have to face the hours, don't I?... I mean the hours after the party and the hours after that."
>
> Richard (Ed Harris) alluding to his suicidal thoughts when speaking to Clarissa in *The Hours* (2002)

Clarissa covers her inner pain through self-sacrifice, trying to help Richard cope with his

Additional Questions for Discussion (The Hours)

- Compare and contrast Virginia Woolf's decision to commit suicide and Laura's decision to live but abandon her family. Is one decision healthier? More just?
- Is suicide the right decision for a person such as Woolf who feels trapped in life and consumed by intense inner turmoil, or is suicide a selfish attempt to escape one's pain?
- How might a therapist approach a predicament and character such as Woolf's?
- What is the prognosis for Clarissa at the film's conclusion?
- What depression elements are paralleled in each woman across the generations?
- Can someone painfully dying of AIDS (e.g., Richard) still have a life worth living? What can be said to a patient who would answer "no" to this question?

hallucinations, noncompliance with medication, depression, and cynicism. Ultimately, Richard commits suicide by jumping out of the apartment window in front of Clarissa.

Other Films Dealing with Depression and Suicide

A number of recent films portray protagonists who end their life, indicating there is no trend to decrease the frequency of the portrayal of suicide in films; consider *Revolutionary Road* (2008), *The Reader* (2008), *Boy A* (2007), and the sacrificial suicide in *Gran Torino* (2008).

Hopelessness and suicidal intent are well depicted in the film *Night, Mother* (1986), starring Sissy Spacek as Jesse and Anne Bancroft as the mother, Thelma. This film is a thought-provoking and gripping film adaptation of a Pulitzer Prize-winning stage play about suicide. The entire film takes place in the mother's home, where Jesse has lived since her divorce. As the play begins it is 6:05 p.m., and Jesse has just informed her mother that she plans to kill herself that night. The two women examine their lives as Thelma tries to protect her daughter from her decision. Ultimately, Jesse explains that she has no hope and ends her life at 7:45 p.m.

Suicide makes for high drama, and it is a common theme in films. Some examples include the unforgettable Russian roulette death of the soldier who remained in Vietnam in *The Deer Hunter* (1978); the suicide by drowning of a young man who feels he cannot please his critical father in

The Field (1990); the murder/suicide by a Marine recruit in *Full Metal Jacket* (1987); the lead character in the Roman Polanski film *The Tenant* (1976), who becomes suicidal after renting the apartment of a woman who in fact had recently committed suicide; the female protagonist (played by Greta Garbo) committing suicide by stepping in front of an oncoming train in *Anna Karenina* (1935); and the suicide staged to look like a hunting accident in *Mountains of the Moon* (1990). Japanese novelist Yukio Mishima, one of the most fascinating characters in contemporary literature, committed *seppuku* (ritualistic suicide), and his life and death are portrayed in the film *Mishima: A Life in Four Chapters* (1985). Peter Finch, playing Howard Beale, the mad prophet of the evening news, announces to the world that he will commit suicide on the air in two weeks and sees his ratings soar in the film *Network* (1976). In the independent film, *Eye of God* (1997), a young boy views his mother's suicide. He is left in acute stress, confusion, and terror, unable to speak and catatonic. Shortly after, he kills himself at the age of 14.

Often a failed suicide attempt is a means by which a director can heighten tension or set the stage for future character development. After Olivia (Patricia Clarkson) attempts suicide in *The Station Agent* (2003), her relationship with two other lonely characters deepens and the three complete a close bond of support and friendship. When Pu Yi, the last emperor of China, attempts to commit suicide by slashing his wrists in a railroad station restroom in Bernardo Bertolucci's *The Last Emperor* (1987), we get some insight into his character and a better sense of the despair he is experiencing. Alex Forrest (Glenn Close) attempts suicide by slashing her wrists in *Fatal Attraction* (1987), and the attempt is necessary to establish the extent to which she is willing to go to manipulate and control her lover. After Emmett Foley (Gary Oldman) shoots himself in the chest in the opening scenes of *Chattahoochee* (1989), we learn that he is afraid to die and not genuinely psychotic.

Suicide is sometimes romanticized in film, such as in the hauntingly beautiful *Elvira Madigan* (1967), in which two lovers decide on a double suicide. In *The Hairdresser's Husband* (1992), the female protagonist jumps to her death by drowning in order not to lose the happiness she has found with her new husband.

Finally, suicide is often treated as a humorous topic. Examples include Burt Reynolds' character in *The End* (1978), the multiple suicide attempts of Harold in the black comedy *Harold and Maude* (1972), the Italian judge who tries to get his sister to commit suicide in *Leap into the Void* (1979), the elaborate last supper for the impotent and suicidal camp dentist in *M*A*S*H* (1970), and the inadvertent death by hanging in *The Ruling Class* (1972).

The Virgin Suicides (1999) was Sofia Coppola's directorial debut. The story involves a repressed family with five daughters who commit suicide in response to their mother's overbearing control and repression. Unfortunately, this film supports the public misconception that suicide is caused by over-controlling parents when in fact it is the opposite that occurs.

Dead Poets Society

Dead Poets Society (1989) stars Robin Williams as John Keating, an unconventional English teacher at a strict boys' preparatory school. This film was nominated for several Academy Awards. Set in 1959, this drama contrasts institutional values and individual creativity. By fostering "critical thinking" in his classroom, Keating broadens students' educational experience and their ability to think independently. The students also discover that when Keating was a student at the school, he started a secret society, the Dead Poets Society, dedicated to intellectual creativity. These students reactivate the society.

One important conflict in the film is between Neil, a student who wants to be an actor, and his father, a domineering businessman who wants his son to be a doctor. Neil's father will not allow him to try out for a campus production of *A Midsummer Night's Dream*. Neil disregards his father's demands, goes to the audition, and is selected for the lead role. Keating encourages Neil to explore the relationship with his father and to enlist his father's support. Neil's father is enraged when he views his son's successful performance. Neil is immediately brought home and, in an act of desperation, believing that his father will never "allow" him to become an actor, Neil shoots himself with his father's gun. Keating becomes the scapegoat for Neil's suicide, and the school's administration uses the suicide as an excuse to fire the unconventional teacher. The film ends with the other students protesting against Keating's dismissal.

Wristcutters: A Love Story (2006) opens with Zia, the lead character, slashing his wrists. He then finds himself in a kind of purgatory, populated by other people who have committed suicide. He considers killing himself again, but suspects he'll only wind up in a still worse setting. The film will teach you very little about depression and suicide, and it insults the viewer's intelligence by making use of a cheap "it was all just a dream" plot device that explains everything away.

Harold and Maude (1971) is a cult classic that opens with Harold, a troubled teenager, pretending to hang himself. He routinely fakes suicide attempts, primarily to annoy his intrusive mother, and amuses himself by attending funerals of people he has never met. At one of these funerals he meets Maude, a 79-year-old woman who also enjoys attending funerals. These two unlikely companions become fast friends, and Harold professes his love for Maude shortly before she dies.

There is a memorable suicide by hanging in *The Shawshank Redemption* (1994), and few viewers are able to forget the Russian Roulette games that prisoners of war are forced to play in *The Deer Hunter* (1978).

Risk Factors and Antecedents

There are many risk factors associated with suicide. The demographic risk factors include being adolescent or elderly, male, white, separated, divorced or widowed, isolated, and unemployed. Other risk factors include depression, alcoholism, bipolar disorders, and neurological disorders.

Unfortunately, even though risk factors and the antecedents of suicide have been well established, accurately predicting who will commit suicide is extraordinarily difficult. Most clinicians include a suicide assessment in their initial interaction with any client who has an emotional problem or a mental illness. An assessment for suicide focuses on three areas: intent, plan, and lethality.

Intent, or thinking about suicide, is a specific indicator of an impending suicide and probably the single most important predictor. Those people most intent on suicide have worse insomnia, are more pessimistic, and are less able to concentrate than

Additional Questions for Discussion (*Dead Poets Society*)

- Would Neil qualify for a psychiatric diagnosis under *DSM-IV-TR*? If so, which one?
- How common is it for someone to commit suicide as a way of punishing someone else?
- Does the presence of a handgun in a house increase the likelihood of suicide?
- Would a daughter have been as likely to shoot herself?
- What else could John Keating have done to reduce the conflict between Neil and his father?

those with less intent. In the film *Night, Mother* (1986), the total story focuses on Jesse's plan to kill herself. Those individuals most intent on killing themselves are more often males, older, single or separated, and living alone. However, experts also know that intent is episodic, and that even if there is no intent today, there may be tomorrow. In *Dead Poets Society* (1989), there is no mention of Neil's intent and the viewer is led to believe that he does not intend to kill himself until he returns home, feels helpless, and convinces himself there is no way out of an untenable situation. If someone had recognized his intent or if he had reached out for help (e.g., by calling a suicide hotline), Neil might have been able to identify creative alternatives to suicide.

Most experts believe that even though a person is intent on suicide, there is almost always an underlying wish to be rescued. Thus, a person who is very intent upon killing himself or herself may consciously or unconsciously send out signals of distress, evidence of helplessness, or pleas for help. Some of the verbal cues may be "I am going away" or "You won't be seeing much of me from now on." There may also be unusual behaviors such as putting one's affairs in order, giving away prized possessions, engaging in atypical acts, or becoming socially isolated. These behaviors are all present in *Scent of a Woman* (1992). Lt. Colonel Slade puts his financial affairs in order, visits his family, says good-bye, and has his "last fling."

People who have a **plan** for committing suicide are more likely to actually kill themselves than those who have vague thoughts about not wanting to live. Clinicians are trained to determine whether their patients have a plan to kill themselves and how specific their plans are. An individual who does not have a plan is considered to be at lower risk than someone who knows how he or she can commit suicide, and who has access to the planned method. In *The Hospital* (1971), Dr. Herbert Bock plans to kill himself by injecting a lethal dose of potassium. He demonstrates both plan and intent, and, because of his easy access to potassium, he is clearly at high risk.

The **lethality** of the method is also an indicator of the risk of suicide. The more lethal the chosen means, the more likely it is that the person will commit suicide, especially if there is easy access to the method selected (e.g., guns in the home). The most lethal suicide methods are using guns, jumping off buildings and bridges, and hanging. Slashing one's wrists and ingesting 15 or fewer aspirin are common methods of attempting suicide, but they are seldom lethal. Other methods

that carry a moderate to high risk of lethality are drowning, carbon monoxide suffocation, and deep cuts to the throat. In both *Scent of a Woman* (1992) and *Dead Poets Society* (1989), the lethality was high because guns were the means selected for the suicidal act.

Prevention of Suicide

Since there are no clear predictors of suicide, there are no foolproof prevention strategies. Treatment of an acutely suicidal individual involves protecting him or her and connecting with that part in each person that wants to be rescued. Usually, a person who is suicidal is hospitalized and not allowed to be alone. Even in those instances, if a person wants to commit suicide, a hospital environment cannot prevent it, and many suicides have been completed in a protected environment. In the film *Crossover* (1983), a psychiatric nurse is plagued by self-doubt after one of the patients he works with commits suicide.

Ordinary People

Ordinary People (1980), an Academy Award-winning film based on Judith Guest's novel by the same name, depicts the aftermath of a suicide attempt. Conrad Jarret, played by Timothy Hutton, is a sensitive teenager who has attempted suicide following a boating accident that killed his brother, Buck. Conrad could not overcome his feelings of guilt, attempted suicide, and was hospitalized for four months. The film begins following Conrad's return home and traces his struggle for personal redemption and his futile attempts to communicate with his parents. His father, Calvin, played by Donald Sutherland, is a successful tax attorney who tries to respond to Conrad's needs. His mother, Beth, played by Mary Tyler Moore, is well intentioned but ultimately unable to meet the needs of her son. Beth is the nucleus of a family in a crisis.

Upon his return from the hospital, Conrad is inattentive in class and distant with classmates. He is also ill at ease with his parents. His father encourages Conrad to contact a psychiatrist, and eventually he begins therapy with Dr. Tyrone Berger, played by Judd Hirsch. In therapy, Conrad explores his relationship with his parents. When Dr. Berger suggests that the entire family meet together, Beth refuses. Throughout the movie, Beth's feelings toward her living son become obvious. Calvin begins to question his relationship with Beth and unsuccessfully attempts to re-engage his wife in their relationship. Beth eventually leaves her husband and son, who come to terms with Beth's limitations and begin to rebuild their lives around their love for each other.

Other characters play an important role in the movie. Conrad's swimming coach quizzes him about his hospitalization, asks him whether he received shock treatment, and is demanding during training sessions. Conrad finally decides to quit the swimming team.

Another important character is Karen, a girl Conrad met at the hospital. While hospitalized, Conrad and Karen had a completely "open and honest" relationship. When Conrad contacts her at home, she is distant but appears to be in control. She is involved in school activities and maintains she no longer thinks about the problems that resulted in her suicide attempt. She also decides not to see a therapist. Karen's newfound confidence is startling to Conrad, who begins to question his own fragile condition. When he tries to get in touch with her later, however, Conrad learns that she has committed suicide.

Karen's death forces Conrad to relive the boating accident that took Buck's life. At last, he is able to explain his guilt – he lived and Buck did not. Conrad realizes that he was angry with Buck because he did not hang on to the boat. With the help of Dr. Berger, he experiences the intense pain of his loss and resolves his guilt.

If a suicide attempt is survived, the meaning of the attempt should be examined. Even though the viewer is not told whether Conrad has symptoms of depression, it is safe to assume that they were present prior to the suicide attempt. Conrad's suicide attempt was both an attempt to kill himself and a cry for help. His family fails to appreciate or respond to his distress over his brother's death. His mother is unable to relate to anyone, and his father is withdrawn from family interaction. Through a suicide attempt, Conrad got his family and friends to acknowledge his desperate situation.

Every suicide threat should be taken seriously. While attempting suicide is often an impulsive act,

it is also an act of communication. If Conrad had possessed the necessary communication skills, he could have discussed his feelings and explored their meaning.

International Films: Mood Disorders and Suicide

Respiro (2002) is a highly recommended Italian film about a woman who would meet *DSM-IV-TR* criteria for the diagnosis of bipolar disorder. Her behavior is erratic, unpredictable, and frequently inappropriate (e.g., she invites her sons to go swimming with her in the nude). The people in her small Mediterranean fishing village insist that she be sent to Milan for psychiatric hospitalization after she releases a pack of caged dogs that have to be shot from the rooftops. She avoids psychiatric hospitalization when her oldest son helps her find refuge in a cave, and her husband and the villagers eventually come to miss her eccentric but life-affirming behavior.

The slow-moving but powerful Iranian film *Taste of Cherry* (1997) won the Palme d'Or at the Cannes Film Festival. The movie illustrates the grim determination of a man who has decided to take his own life, but who cannot find anyone to help him. He has dug a hole in the ground and plans to lie in the hole and die after taking a handful of pills; however, it is important to him that he find someone to fill up the hole after he has died. One person he attempts to persuade to take on this task asks a poignant question that leads to the suicidal man questioning his decision: "Do you want to give up the taste of cherries?"

Turtles Can Fly (2004, Iran/France/Iraq), filmed on the Iraqi/Turkish border, depicts an adolescent with severe PTSD who is depressed, homicidal, and suicidal, clearly in reaction to the horrors and atrocities of war; the film does not hold back in its messages of what happens to children in war-torn countries.

The Japanese film *Maboroshi No Hikari* (*Maborosi*; 1995) shows how a young woman is affected after the seemingly senseless and random suicide of her husband who chooses, without any apparent reason, to deliberately walk in the path of an oncoming train.

Suicide Club (2002) is a Japanese film that explores the phenomenon of suicide and raises more questions than it answers. It assesses possible links between suicide and crime, music, violence,

Additional Questions for Discussion (*Ordinary People*)

- How would you describe Conrad's family in *Ordinary People*?
- If you were a therapist working with this family, how would you proceed?
- Do any of the characters in the film meet *DSM-IV-TR* criteria for depression?

group contagion, internal compulsions, consumerism, evil forces, and various external factors. After 54 young girls mysteriously and collectively commit suicide by jumping in front of an oncoming subway train, mass hysteria and confusion develop and several individuals and groups around the country take their lives. One scene depicts a group of students joking about creating a suicide club, and they gather at the edge of a building's roof and chant for each other to "jump." One by one, they watch each other plummet to their death. The film illustrates the phenomenon of suicide **contagion** (de Leo & Heller, 2008; Hacker et al., 2008), a serious problem that is compounded by new media such as the internet (Mehlum, 2000).

Rain (2001) is a New Zealand film about a young girl coming of age as she interacts with family and neighbors on a beach. The film is included in this chapter because of the girl's depressed mother, an alcoholic who acts out sexually and only seems to be happy when she is drinking. The drinking clearly helps her escape from her depression.

The Scottish film *Wilbur Wants to Kill Himself* (2002) is helpful only insofar as it allows the viewer to witness the various stereotypes and misconceptions possible in a movie. Wilbur is a depressed and angry man who curses children, rejects women, and cheats with his brother's wife even though his brother is the person who repeatedly keeps Wilbur from killing himself. The brother is depicted in the role of protector, frequently checking up on Wilbur, supporting him, and removing sharp objects from his home. Wilbur's persistence in his suicide attempts include pills, gas from the oven, hanging, drowning, cutting his wrists in the bathtub, and standing at the edge of the roof of a building. Wilbur's determination to commit suicide ends once his love for his brother's wife becomes mutual. This perpetuates the misconception that love conquers mental illness. Equally disturbing is the film's blatant stereotypes of two psychologists leading a group; one smokes cigarettes during sessions and comments that the patients would be better off without group therapy; the other violates boundaries with a patient, licking his ear, going out on a date, engaging in sexual activity in a hospital closet, and violating confidentiality.

Another film about a character repeatedly attempting suicide and failing can be found in *The Face* (1999, South Korea). The protagonist is a diagnostic quandary – she lives a completely isolated life, rarely leaves her house, has no friends, and her only social contact is her younger sister who berates her and abuses her. She is socially inept

Critical Thinking Questions

- Are dysthymic disorders, major depressive episodes, and major depressive disorders qualitatively different phenomena, or are they simply different quantitative expressions of a single disorder?
- If you genuinely believe a friend is suicidal, what are your ethical and moral obligations?
- Do your responsibilities to that person change if you are a therapist rather than a friend?
- Is there a suicide hotline in your community? Do you know how to access it?
- How do you distinguish between idle passing thoughts of suicide and a cry for help?
- The suicide rate for both men and women is much higher in Asian countries and in Sweden, Denmark, and Austria than in the United States. What cultural factors could account for these differences?
- Kathy in *House of Sand and Fog* (2003) does not receive treatment for her depression. What percentage of depressed individuals go untreated? About how long does it take a depressed individual to seek treatment following the onset of their disorder?
- At one point in *Mr. Jones* (1993), a physician compares bipolar disorder to diabetes. In what way is the comparison apt? In what way is it misleading?
- Patty Duke is a well-known personality who has "come out of the closet" and openly shared the story of her mood disorder (see *Call Me Anna*; 1990). Can you think of other celebrities who have been candid about their own struggles with mental illness? Did any of them have bipolar disorder?
- How might you distinguish between someone experiencing a manic episode, someone experiencing the elation and energy associated with amphetamine abuse, and someone with a high level of enthusiasm/vitality?
- Dr. Bowen in *Mr. Jones* (1993) states, "You're not a sick person; you're a person with a sickness!" What is the significance of this semantic distinction?
- Do filmmakers have a responsibility to avoid glamorizing suicide to prevent contagion, or is a director's sole responsibility to make the best possible film without worrying about things like social influence?

and spends her life sewing, until her mother dies suddenly, after which she strangles her younger sister to death. This character seems to lose touch with reality, suggesting a link between dissociation and suicide attempts. The film ends with the protagonist escaping from life by swimming away on an inflatable tube in the ocean; this is simultaneously a suicide attempt (not dissimilar from the protagonist in Kate Chopin's *The Awakening*) and her ultimate dream (to learn to swim). The viewer may also be reminded of another attempted suicide by drowning in *The Piano* (1993).

Further Exploration

If you have time to read only one book relevant to this chapter, make it:

McKeon, R. (2009). *Suicidal behavior*. Cambridge, MA: Hogrefe Publishing.

If you only have time for one article, read:

Picture This: Depression and Suicide Prevention (a Substance Abuse and Mental Health Services Administration publication). Enter the title into a web search engine to download a PDF copy.

Mood Disorders and Suicide

Bipolar Disorder
- *Blue Sky* (1994)
- *Mr. Jones* (1993)
- *Michael Clayton* (2007)

Depression
- *The Visitor* (2007)
- *Scent of a Woman* (1992)
- *American Splendor* (2003)

Suicide
- *House of Sand and Fog* (2003)
- *The Hours* (2002)
- *Dead Poets Society* (1989)
- *Seven Pounds* (2008)

Chapter 6

Personality Disorders

Llewelyn Moss: If I was cuttin' deals, why wouldn't I go deal with this guy Chigurh?
Carson Wells: No, no, no. You don't understand. You can't make a deal with him. Even if you gave him the money he'd still kill you. He's a peculiar man. You could even say that he has principles. Principles that transcend money or drugs or anything like that. He's not like you. He's not even like me.
Dialogue about the psychopath Anton Chigurh in *No Country for Old Men* (2007)

Questions to Consider While Watching *No Country for Old Men*

- Do you think the diagnosis of antisocial personality disorder adequately explains the personality dynamics of Anton Chigurh?
- What advice would you give to a colleague who stated they were treating someone who fit the description of Chigurh given in the epigraph?
- What clues are given in the film that explain why Chigurh acts the way he does?
- Is there a typical childhood for those with antisocial personality? What are some common themes?
- Is it possible for a person to experience absolutely no guilt and remorse for severe wrongdoings?
- Do most people with antisocial personality disorders engage in highly risky behavior?
- Is there any way Chigurh could ever have a positive prognosis? Can someone with a diagnosis of antisocial personality disorder recover?
- Can a person have several different personality disorders at the same time?
- Is antisocial personality disorder more common in men or in women? Why?
- How is a personality disorder qualitatively different from an Axis I *DSM-IV-TR* disorder?

Patient Evaluation

Patient's stated reason for coming: "I am looking for someone. You're not the man I am looking for." He later added, "This guy wanted me to come speak with you," referring to a probation officer who accompanied him. The probation officer stated that this evaluation is "a recommendation of the court."

History of the present illness: Anton Chigurh is a 48-year-old man who has never married, lives alone, and does not appear to have any meaningful relationships. He has had a number of legal problems, most recently for car theft and arson. He has been accused of murder but has been acquitted. The officers at the local jail know Mr. Chigurh well because he is arrested a couple of times each year. He has escaped from his jail cell on two previous occasions.

Past psychiatric illness, treatment, and outcomes: Mr. Chigurh reported a long history of rule-breaking behavior and problems with the legal system. He was raised in foster homes during his childhood and was placed in juvenile detention centers and psychiatric treatment centers for much of his adolescence. As a child, he tortured and killed dogs, cats, and rabbits. He stated he has been given a number of diagnoses over the years; these include schizophrenia, depression, and bipolar disorder. He denied problems controlling his impulses, saying any action he takes is conscious and deliberate, not impulsive. He does not report any pleasure resulting from his acts of arson. He denied feelings of guilt or remorse for his previous illegal activities. He stated he has never backed down from a fight and is often the instigator.

Medical history: Mr. Chigurh denied any significant medical history or use of prescription medications. He reports being physically healthy.

Psychosocial history: Mr. Chigurh says he is self-employed but would not explain his work any further. He noted he has never held a regular job with an employer for longer than one day. He dropped out of high school and did not attend any college class or receive a GED. He has committed a number of felonies and misdemeanors and has spent several months in jail as an adult. He is socially isolated, and he has no interest in making friends or initiating intimate relationships; however, he does state that he "knows" a lot of people who are acquaintances and work contacts.

Drug and alcohol history: Mr. Chigurh reported he used to use hallucinogens and "other stuff" on a daily basis over several years. He noted he has not used a single illegal drug for over 20 years. He has not used alcohol or smoked a cigarette for over 20 years. When asked about the turning point two decades ago, Mr. Chigurh refused to share much, stating: "Sometimes things happen."

Behavioral observations: Mr. Chigurh was very taciturn, and rarely spoke more than a sentence or two at a time; his voice tone was deep and he was very clear and precise in his choice of words. His range of affect was limited – flat with mild agitation. Mr. Chigurh described his mood as "good." His eye contact was direct and penetrating to the point of inappropriate staring at the interviewer; it was uncertain as to whether he was trying to intimidate the interviewer or whether this was his typical style. His appearance was clean and casual. He was particularly insightful and appeared to understand the rationale behind each of the interviewer's questions; however, he refused to offer insights into his own behaviors or personal life.

Mental status examination: Mr. Chigurh was oriented to person, place, time, and situation, and he scored 30 out of 30 on the Mini Mental State Examination. There was no evidence of cognitive difficulty or psychiatric disturbance on the mental status examination. Homicidality was indeterminate; he did not give a yes or no response but also did not reveal any details as to any harm he was intending to inflict. He denied suicidality. Hallucinations, delusions, and paranoia were not exhibited and explicitly denied; however, he did make cryptic comments such as when the interviewer asked about his thoughts about the man who recently turned him to the authorities; Mr. Chigurh replied, "I freed him. Sometimes people get lucky."

Mr. Chigurh stated that since he answered a number of questions and took the mental status exam that the interviewer should play a game with him in return. For rapport building purposes and because it was toward the end of the interview, the interviewer agreed to participate. Mr. Chigurh took out a coin and stated "Heads or tails, call it." He flipped the coin, and the interviewer guessed correctly; Mr. Chigurh then smiled and walked out of the room without saying another word.

Functional assessment: Mr. Chigurh reported he is functioning adequately in all areas of his life. By societal standards, he is not functioning well socially, psychologically, or personally. Mr. Chigurh shows no concern about these areas.

Strengths: Mr. Chigurh is quite intelligent and seems to be very aware of what is going on in his environment and the motives of those around him. He seems to be patient and highly self-controlled. He displayed a dry sense of humor.

Diagnosis: Antisocial personality disorder

Treatment plan: Mr. Chigurh is at high risk of harming again although no specific plan or intention has been shared. His violent and aggressive history, his diagnosis, and his lack of empathy for others support this belief. His enigmatic presentation and unsettling body language do not help his case. A release of information was signed that permits the interviewer to communicate regularly with Mr. Chigurh's probation officer. The interviewer will consult with a forensic psychologist colleague on this case and may contact the American Psychological Association ethics office for consultation on best approaches at present to prevent harm to others and for advice about how to respond to future scenarios that might emerge. The top treatment priority should be ensuring the safety of others who may come into contact with Mr. Chigurh.

Prognosis: Poor. This man shows no remorse, no interest in changing anything about himself, and no awareness that anything that he has done is wrong.

Psychopathy, Antisocial Personality, and *No Country for Old Men*

Javier Bardem's 2007 Academy Award-winning performance as Anton Chigurh is one of the most chilling portrayals of psychopathology and evil in cinema history. It is hard to imagine Chigurh not being named as one of the top 5 villains on the next American Film Institute's list of top heroes and villains in cinema history (see Appendix A). His portrayal is as engaging as it is frightening. On one level, he is a man after money, simply doing a job; on another level, he is a cold-blooded, psychopathic serial killer; on still another, he symbolizes evil itself. It is fair to call him amoral – he is someone totally devoid of a moral code; on the other hand, some might say he is a man of principle, following his belief in one thing – fate. At times, Chigurh uses a coin toss to determine whom he will kill; at other times he simply kills anyone who gets in his way. He does not show a hint of goodness, morality, or care for anyone with whom he comes into contact; meaning and purpose are the furthest thing from his mind. He employs a unique weapon – a penetrating captive bolt pistol that is normally used to stun or kill cattle.

The character of Chigurh is a fascinating film portrayal – he has a deep, harsh voice, penetrating eyes, and a steady, self-assured gait. He is usually fairly taciturn; when he does speak, he chooses his words carefully. His nationality and ethnicity are intentionally left unclear so he could potentially be from anywhere. His behavior is incredibly resourceful with a high level of "negative ingenuity" (creativity in the moment and for malicious purposes). He appears as unstoppable, and he adeptly "uses" everyone he encounters. There are no walls or locked doors that can slow him down or block him; his bolt-gun blows through every lock he encounters. It seems to make no difference where a person goes if Chigurh is waiting there to deliver his or her fate. In one scene he is put on the defensive, yet he finds a way to disappear. This is another critical aspect of his character. Just as one does not necessarily see "pure evil," but perhaps forms of evil, we do not see Chigurh and he does not want to be seen. One character refers to him as a ghost. Indeed, the first shot of him (and several other shots) in the film is a shadow as he sits in the back seat, just before an escape and a brutal killing. He follows his subjects silently and then suddenly is present; just as quickly as he appears, he disappears. When asked if he was going to kill a man, Chigurh responds "That depends, can you see me?"

When reading these descriptions, it is probably clear that Chigurh is not a typical antisocial personality. He not only displays a pervasive pattern of breaking rules, irresponsibility, impulsiveness, and aggressiveness, but he is also a serial killer devoid of any hint of humanity. The diagnosis of psychopathic personality (not a formal *DSM-IV-TR* diagnosis, but something discussed later in this chapter) provides a more accurate and apt description.

No Country for Old Men (2007) won a number of awards, including Academy Awards for Best Director, Best Picture, and Best Adaptive Screenplay. Directed by the Coen Brothers, the film merges a number of genre elements – thriller/suspense, crime drama, and western.

Anton Chigurh's character can be compared with the late Heath Ledger's Academy Award-winning performance as The Joker in *The Dark Knight* (2008). The Joker is an incredibly engaging – and more charismatic – villain who clearly fits the dimensions of the psychopathic personality. He displays no remorse or hint of human goodness and kills at will. Both of these characters would be on the severe end of this personality disorder dimension. Viewers are very curious about each of these characters and eagerly anticipate each scene in which they appear. There are a number of explanations for viewers' fascination with these two characters and those of other psychopaths such as Hannibal Lecter in *The Silence of the Lambs* (1991) and Alex in *A Clockwork Orange* (1971). Curiosity researcher Todd Kashdan offers three explanations (Kashdan, 2009, and personal communication):

1) **Exposure**: Movies are a safe place for the viewer to experience one's greatest fears and this opportunity is often relished since the viewer always knows at some level that what they are seeing is not real. These films combine curiosity and fear, producing a blended emotional state that can be a very pleasurable and positive experience. The viewer's anxiety amplifies the pleasure of the intrigue and the resulting positive experience is more intense and long-lasting.

2) **Thrill seeking**: Some viewers enjoy taking personal and emotional risks for the sake of the experience. Since much of life falls into the neutral category and there are typically few instances in which we can experience intense emotions (e.g., hatred), these movies let us fill out the full spectrum of experiences allowing the viewer to experience intense sensations.

3) **Social scripts**: We know that courage and overcoming fear can lead to positive outcomes. Some viewers get to tap into this positive social script, while for others who don't necessarily enjoy the experience, it is nothing more than a test of courage. There are few occasions in which we get to do this, so the viewer will often seek them out, even if he or she doesn't particularly enjoy the experience. This occurs when a viewer has an emotion profile of high curiosity and low pleasure.

Types of Personality Disorders

All of us have unique personalities and our own individual personality traits. On occasion, these

Table 6.1. Characteristics of personality disorders with examples from contemporary cinema

Disorder Cluster	Personality Disorder	Characteristics	Classic Film Examples	Recent Film Examples
A	Paranoid	Distrust and suspiciousness about the motives of others	Lt. Cmdr. Philip Francis Queeg (Humphrey Bogart) in *The Caine Mutiny* (1954); Fred C. Dobbs (Humphrey Bogart) in *The Treasure of the Sierra Madre* (1948)	Paul (John Diehl) in *Land of Plenty* (2004); Dell Spooner (Will Smith) in *I, Robot* (2004)
	Schizoid	Detachment from social relationships and a restricted range of emotional expression	Will Penny (Charlton Heston) in *Will Penny* (1968)	Bartleby (Crispin Glover) in *Bartleby* (2001); Ed Crane (Billy Bob Thornton) in *The Man Who Wasn't There* (2001)
	Schizotypal	Acute discomfort in close relationships, cognitive or perceptual distortions, and behavioral eccentricities	Jack Arnold Alexander Tancred Gurney (Peter O'Toole) in *The Ruling Class* (1972)	Willy Wonka (Johnny Depp) in *Charlie and the Chocolate Factory* (2005); Charlie Fineman (Adam Sandler) in *Reign Over Me* (2007)
B	Antisocial	Disregard for and violation of the rights of others	Alex (Malcolm McDowell) in *A Clockwork Orange* (1971); Bruno Anthony (Robert Walker) in *Strangers on a Train* (1951)	Chris Wilton (Jonathan Rhys Meyers) in *Match Point* (2005); Andy Hanson (Philip Seymour Hoffman) in *Before the Devil Knows You're Dead* (2007)
	Borderline	Instability in emotions and interpersonal relationships, inadequate self-image, fear of abandonment, and marked impulsiveness	Alex Forrest (Glenn Close) in *Fatal Attraction* (1987)	Barbara Covett (Judi Dench) in *Notes on a Scandal* (2006); Margot (Nicole Kidman) in *Margot at the Wedding* (2007)
	Histrionic	Excessive emotionality and attention seeking	Blanche DuBois (Vivien Leigh) in *A Streetcar Named Desire* (1951)	Carolyn Burnham (Annette Bening) in *American Beauty* (1999)
	Narcissistic	Grandiosity, a need for admiration, and lack of empathy for the problems and needs of others	Norma Desmond (Gloria Swanson) in *Sunset Blvd.* (1950)	Troy Duffy as himself in *Overnight* (2003); Ron Burgundy (Will Ferrell) in *Anchorman: The Legend of Ron Burgundy* (2004)
C	Avoidant	Social inhibition, feelings of inadequacy, and hypersensitivity to criticism or negative evaluation	Laura Wingfield (Jane Wyman) in *The Glass Menagerie* (1950)	Amélie Poulain (Audrey Tautou) in *Amelie* (2001); William Forrester (Sean Connery) in *Finding Forrester* (2000)
	Dependent	Submissive and clinging behavior and fears of separation	Bob "Bobby" Wiley (Bill Murray) in *What About Bob?* (1991)	Claire Richards (Renée Zellweger) in *White Oleander* (2002)
	Obsessive-Compulsive	Preoccupation with orderliness, perfectionism, and control	Felix Ungar (Jack Lemmon) in *The Odd Couple* (1968)	Al Fountain (John Turturro) in *Box of Moonlight* (1996)

personality traits get us in trouble. For some individuals, their personalities result in a persistent pattern of recurring interpersonal difficulties. When there is a persistent pattern of inflexible and maladaptive behavior that *continually* gets an individual in trouble or that causes him or her considerable subjective distress, a diagnosis of personality disorder may be appropriate.

People with personality disorders exhibit enduring, pervasive, and inflexible patterns of behavior that deviate markedly from societal expectations. Their behavior seems odd, unusual, or peculiar to most other people. However, to the individual the experience is so ingrained that it is **ego-syntonic** – it does not bother them, i.e., they have learned to be comfortable with their own pathology.

The list of ten personality disorders in Table 6.1. is not arbitrary but is based on a conceptual model that groups all personality disorders into one of three relatively distinct clusters. **Cluster A** (for *odd or eccentric behavior*) includes the paranoid, schizoid, and schizotypal personality disorders. **Cluster B** (for *dramatic, emotional, or erratic behavior*) includes the antisocial, borderline, histrionic, and narcissistic personality disorders. **Cluster C** (for *anxious or fearful behavior*) includes the remaining personality disorders: avoidant, dependent, and obsessive-compulsive. Just as it is a challenge for clinicians to diagnose a personality disorder in a single meeting with a client, it is challenging to diagnose cinematic characters with personality disorders in films that take place over a short period of time. Films that show the developmental course of a character from childhood to adulthood and that depict the character in a variety of settings leave the viewer in a better position to make the diagnosis (e.g., *Red Dragon* (2002), *The Silence of the Lambs* (1991), *Hannibal* (2001) and *Hannibal Rising* (2007), the four films documenting the life of Hannibal Lecter.

A personality disorder diagnosis is inappropriate in any situation in which aberrant behavior results from transient situational factors (e.g., an individual who repeatedly gets his or her tax returns audited may become paranoid about the government). Finally, it is critical that cultural variables be considered when a diagnosis of personality disorder is being considered. For example, the Italian film *Down and Dirty* (1976) includes a protagonist who appears to have an antisocial personality. However, his behavior must be understood in terms of the culture of southern Italy and the debilitating and corrosive effects of poverty.

Some personality disorders are more common in men (e.g., antisocial and narcissistic personality

disorders), while others are found more often in women (e.g., borderline, histrionic, and dependent personality disorders). This is quite consistent with cinematic portrayals, as we will soon show.

Cluster A Disorders

These "odd and eccentric" disorders are rare and hence their depiction in cinema is uncommon (unlike other disorders such as dissociative identity disorder, which, though rare in reality, are often shown in movies).

Paranoid Personality Disorder

People with a paranoid personality are isolated and suspicious. They are convinced that others are talking about them behind their backs or plotting against them. The behaviors of others are carefully scrutinized for evidence of intent to harm, and overtures of friendship or good will by other people are rejected as manipulative gestures or parts of a plot. Ironically, because paranoid individuals behave in peculiar ways, a self-fulfilling prophecy occurs and people *do* begin to discuss the paranoid individual behind his or her back. Paranoid people tend to have few or no friends. They personalize almost everything and misinterpret casual remarks to make them fit into their belief structure.

Land of Plenty (2004, US/Germany) is a Wim Wenders film about misguided post-9/11 patriotism and paranoia in the US. A young woman, Lana (Michelle Williams) returns to the US from Tel Aviv with a mission to meet her Uncle Paul and deliver a letter to him on behalf of her mother. Paul is a highly suspicious and paranoid man whose life is preoccupied with searching for individuals with bombs or who may be attacking the city of Los Angeles. He has an irritable disposition, often characteristic of those with this personality disorder. When he communicates to others, his verbiage is intense and convincing. Paul lives in a dilapidated van, uses a makeshift camera with a joystick and monitor, and covers the walls of his van with newspaper clippings. Some of these come from the garbage cans he digs in looking for evidence. He racially profiles Arabic men and when he encounters a homeless man wearing a turban, he immediately concludes the man is a terrorist. He later watches a drive-by killing of the man – and since he was taping the man's every move, he is able to keep the tape to re-watch for his own amusement. Paul notes he had been exposed to Agent Orange in Vietnam; therefore, a physical disorder would need to be ruled out before any psychological diagnostic conclusions could be made.

"They're trying to infect our country. They're trying to destroy us. I won't let 'em do that."

Paul revealing his paranoia in
***Land of Plenty* (2004)**

The dangers associated with having a leader with a paranoid personality become clear in *The Last King of Scotland* (2006), in which Academy Award winner Forest Whitaker portrays the leader of Uganda, Idi Amin. On the one hand, Amin is quite charismatic as he tries to convince the people that he is their rightful leader and the "father" of Uganda. He is also often fun-loving, friendly, jovial, and teasing. On the other hand, he is shown to be a ruthless dictator, explosive and unpredictable, who murdered over 300,000 Ugandans during his reign. Paranoia was a significant part of this man's personality, and he used his paranoia to justify his horrendous actions.

"But a man who shows fear. He is weak... and a slave"

Idi Amin's ironic observation in
***The Last King of Scotland* (2006)**

A convincing portrayal of paranoid personality disorder found in Detective Del Spooner (Will Smith) in *I, Robot* (2004). Spooner is a highly suspicious, judgmental, and angry person, particularly around robots, which are a mainstay in this world of 2046. Spooner takes a shower with no curtain and his frustrated mistrust of robots leads him to push away a friendly robot delivering a package. His misperceptions bring him to randomly chase down and tackle a robot running with a purse, which he has assumed is a robbery even though no robots have ever committed a crime at this point in history. Much of the plot transgresses due to Spooner's paranoia, which other characters recognize. One man (Dr. Alfred Lanning, played by James Cromwell) counts on Spooner's paranoia

to save the human race from robots. As with many films depicting a paranoid character (e.g., Jerry Fletcher, played by Mel Gibson, in *Conspiracy Theory*, 1997), the psychopathology is often distorted by the entertainment value of the plot which results in a character's paranoia proving to be accurate and justified in the end.

Ben Stiller's character Chas Tennenbaum in *The Royal Tenenbaums* (2001) displays numerous paranoid characteristics that seem stable over time. He has an underlying anger and rage toward his father, unrealistic fears, and displays excessive concern and hypervigilance regarding his environment and home.

Humphrey Bogart's role as Captain Queeg in *The Caine Mutiny* (1954) is a wonderful illustration of the paranoid personality. Queeg becomes preoccupied with trivial misdemeanors by sailors while he ignores the important parts of his job – such as maintaining the morale of his men. He eventually falls apart under pressure when he is called to the witness stand to testify in a court martial hearing for an insubordinate junior officer. There is a famous scene in which Queeg takes two ball bearings out of his pocket and begins to move them around nervously in his palm, and everyone in the court senses that this man is not well adjusted. Bogart plays another paranoid personality in *The Treasure of the Sierra Madre* (1948) in which he becomes obsessed with the idea that his partners are out to steal the gold all three men have agreed to split between them.

Schizoid Personality Disorder

The individual with a schizoid personality has little interest in and avoids close interpersonal relations. He or she is likely to be described as a loner who lacks meaningful ties to a family, community, or value system. These individuals are unlikely to display strong emotions or tenderness to others; they appear apathetic, diffident, and indifferent. They most often have little or no interest in sexual encounters and few marry.

There are some excellent portrayals of schizoid personality in the cinema. Two examples come from two films named *Bartleby*; both are remakes of a Herman Melville short story, "Bartleby the Scrivener." The 2001 version is a fascinating, cult film about a quiet, passive man named Bartleby (Crispin Glover) hired for a mundane office job. He thoroughly does his job at first but soon begins to refuse doing extra work, repeating the mysterious phrase, "I would prefer not to." This quirky behavior continues as he stares for hours at an air conditioning vent and displays no interest in socializing with his work peers. Schizoid individuals are often isolated from society, and an opening scene symbolizes Bartleby's isolation as he is depicted enclosed and caged on an overpass bridge above a busy, productive society represented by an expressway below. His speech is slow, eye contact is limited, and affect is flat and emotionless throughout the film. At times, he displays an incongruent, distant, random smile or two, but he does not engage others interpersonally with smiles or laughter. Often, there is no understandable reason as to why a person behaves in a schizoid manner, and the film parallels this idea, as no explanation is overtly given for Bartleby's behaviors, lack of emotions, or social apathy. The earlier 1970 version portrays very similar schizoid traits for the lead character and the plot is very similar to the new version. This older film is black and white, dark, slow, and gloomy.

Another classic example of schizoid personality is found in the Coen Brothers' film noir, *The Man Who Wasn't There* (2001), where even the title of the film suggests a schizoid quality. Billy Bob Thornton plays Ed Crane, an aloof, taciturn barber who appears disinterested in life and claims he dislikes most things and that his life has been one of "no excitement." He is unemotional with flat affect and a monotone voice. He moves slowly and stiffly, and even the way he smokes cigarettes is a slow, unconscious, steady ritual. His responses to others are dull with heavy sighs, and he is passive when criticized. He does not seem very bothered by the fact that his wife is cheating on him with his best friend. He allows himself to be exploited by a traveling salesman. The only relationship he seems to invest emotional energy in is with a young girl; he appears committed to helping her pursue her dream of becoming a musician. Also consistent with schizoid characteristics is that no one "really knows him;" this is reinforced by his inability to share himself with others.

Crispin Glover plays another socially awkward, schizoid character in *Willard* (2003). Willard is isolated from others and his only companions are the rats that congregate in his basement. After one rat, whom he names Socrates, saves him from a suicide attempt he distances himself further from people and rallies the rats to help him get revenge.

In the film *Heavy* (1995), the lead character displays a schizoid reaction to his mother's death. He becomes frozen, emotionless, sexually disinterested, and isolated with flattened affect. In order to qualify for a diagnosis of schizoid personality disorder, his bereavement would need to be differentiated and his personality assessed prior to his mother's death. The film offers another interesting schizoid description about the lead character's isolation through his belief that you can be as "big as an ox and no one sees you."

The figure of the loner is a staple in western films, and many of these characters would meet the criteria for schizoid personality disorder. These individuals avoid close relationships, prefer solitary activities, lack close friends and confidants, and appear indifferent to the praise or criticism of others; the title character (Charlton Heston) in *Will Penny* (1968) is one example; the eponymous lead (Robert Redford) in *Jeremiah Johnson* (1972) is another.

Schizotypal Personality Disorder

People with schizotypal personality have "schizophrenia-like" characteristics but do not typically meet the diagnostic criteria for schizophrenia. They hold odd or peculiar beliefs, thoughts, and/or behaviors. They are often very superstitious, have unusual perceptual experiences, and are suspicious and paranoid.

Adam Sandler's portrayal of Charlie Fineman in *Reign Over Me* (2007) is an impressive portrayal of someone with a schizotypal personality disorder. Charlie has lost his whole family – three daughters and his wife – in the 9/11 tragedy, but the viewer sees the character's deterioration and not his immediate reaction to the tragedy. Instead, the story picks up years later and the viewer observes a man who would qualify for the diagnosis of schizotypal personality. Charlie exhibits eccentric and bizarre behavior, is odd in his appearance (e.g., he is unkempt, and he constantly wears headphones while riding around on a motor scooter), and seems childlike. He appears to be clueless socially and interpersonally – brutally cold and inappropriate at times (e.g., eats with his new friend's family but sits on the counter while singing to himself with his headphones on). When he speaks with others it is only to ask random trivia questions. He repeatedly remodels his kitchen and spends his time in one of two activities: death metal drumming or playing solitary video games. The features of personality disorders in each cluster may merge and overlap at times. For example, Charlie appears to have no desire to connect with others (schizoid) and is highly suspicious of others (paranoid). Before making a diagnosis of schizotypal personality disorder, the clinician would need to discern how much of Charlie's personality features are truly a prolonged bereavement, or the extent to which they might be related to severe depression or PTSD, and the therapist would need to know what Charlie's personality was like prior to the tragedy.

An outstanding illustration of a schizotypal personality can be found in Johnny Depp's unique portrayal of Willy Wonka in Tim Burton's *Charlie and the Chocolate Factory* (2005), a portrayal that is much more clear in terms of this diagnosis than the portrayal by Gene Wilder in *Willy Wonka and the Chocolate Factory* (1971). Depp's Wonka has a quality of desperate aloofness in which his isolation, unusual perceptual experiences, and odd thinking are much more apparent. He lives alone and his only friends are a culture of dwarfs (Oompa-Loompas). He is quirky when he does communicate – for example, he exhibits disorganized speech, uses note cards to compensate for his poor social skills, talks to himself in public, and is unable to say the word "parents." His appearance is colorful and eccentric. The film depicts a familial root for Wonka's personality in that he lived alone with his father who was distant and authoritarian, and he showed no concern when his son decided to run away from home.

In *The Royal Tenenbaums* (2001), Owen Wilson plays Eli, a man who wears flamboyant outfits and uses unusual words. He has a quirky tone of voice, exhibits odd and eccentric behavior, and often does not have a firm grasp on reality. His apartment has numerous odd paintings covering the walls. It is uncertain how much these qualities result from his drug abuse; regardless, his behavior and interactions are quite schizotypal.

Denis Leary plays a truly fascinating man who has paranoid schizophrenia in *Final* (2001). He displays some interesting schizotypal traits as well, but to qualify for a diagnosis of schizotypal personality, these traits could not occur exclusively with the schizophrenia episodes.

The character Ernest (Maury Chaykin) in *Bartleby* (2001) displays many schizotypal traits. He has a poor use of logic and when he gets upset, he speaks in a verbal salad, mixes words, and is somewhat nonsensical. His appearance is disheveled. He is easily overwhelmed by stress. His behavior is often inappropriate for the situation, as he never appears to be working when he is at the office, he displays no reaction after spilling water and copier ink, and he is later repeatedly and genuinely scared by a pop-up spin toy. He presents with a constant paranoid, concerned look on his face and has blunted affect throughout the film.

The schizotypal personality is demonstrated in Flannery O'Conner's novel *Wise Blood* (1952) and in the 1979 John Huston film adaptation. The Southern preacher works hard to convince people

---

 Additional Questions for Discussion (Cluster A Disorders)

- Where do you draw the diagnostic line for these disorders, and how can one differentiate them from similar Axis I counterparts (e.g., schizophrenia)?
- What are some etiological components for schizoid personality (such as for the title character in *Bartleby*)?
- Is there any validity to the idea that people who are odd and eccentric, as illustrated by these examples, are simply extremely creative people?
- What is the treatment of choice for someone with a Cluster A diagnosis?
- Do any of the characters in the films discussed above make meaningful changes in their personal, social, or occupational life? Are Cluster A disorders resistant to change?

---

to join his "Church Without Christ." He has numerous peculiar beliefs, odd speech, constricted affect, strange behavior, and few close friends. These five characteristics would be sufficient to justify the diagnosis of schizotypal personality.

Hyler (1988) uses DeNiro's portrayal of Travis Brickle in *Taxi Driver* (1976) to illustrate the schizotypal personality. He feels this film is such a useful tool for teaching medical students about psychopathology that he has incorporated it into a computer program that can be used to teach medical students to perform and record a complete mental status exam (Hyler & Bujold, 1994).

Cluster B Disorders

Each of the personalities in this cluster is often lively and colorful, fitting the description "dramatic, emotional, and erratic." Consequently, individuals with Cluster B disorders are common in movies, as they tend to make fascinating, stimulating cinematic characters. They are often attention grabbing, conflicted, manipulative, charming, and charismatic – many of the qualities the moviegoer typically loves or hates. In addition, they often have troubled pasts, and the viewer gets to observe them escape from present pain or make impressive changes, either way making for good drama.

The Talented Mr. Ripley (1999) is a wonderful example of a film's character (Tom Ripley, played by Matt Damon) who displays characteristics of each of the disorders in this cluster. Even the opening credits get at the complexity of this disorder, listing the following adjectives to replace "talented" in the title: mysterious, yearning, secretive, lonely, troubled, confused, loving, musical, gifted, intelligent, beautiful, tender, secretive, haunted, passionate.

Antisocial Personality Disorder

People with antisocial personality break the law, can be physically aggressive, manipulate others, lie, take senseless risks, and have little or no sense of remorse or guilt about the consequences of their behavior. These individuals violate the rights of others and appear to experience distress only when their behavior results in punishment or incarceration. They are impulsive, thrive on the "pleasure principle," and have a great deal of trouble planning their future behavior or anticipating its consequences. Individuals with antisocial personality disorder have a great deal of trouble learning from their mistakes and find themselves dealing with similar legal and interpersonal problems throughout their lives.

The Assassination of Jesse James by the Coward Robert Ford (2007) portrays the obvious antisocial characteristics of a well-known train robber, Jesse James (Brad Pitt), and it also illustrates James' calm manipulation and defiant recklessness, as well as a high level of paranoia. He becomes suspicious that his followers and fellow criminals are out to get him. His paranoia leads him to become more controlling, impulsive, and unpredictable, especially as the price on his head increases. James would likely be diagnosed with **personality disorder not otherwise specified (NOS)** with antisocial and paranoid traits.

Before the Devil Knows You're Dead (2007) is an intense Sidney Lumet melodrama in which the story defines the characters (in a drama the characters define the story). Two brothers struggling financially and craving a better life plot to rob a "mom and pop" jewelry store; however, the owners are their own mom and pop. After things go wrong with the robbery, the antisocial tendencies of each brother strongly emerge and deceit, impulsivity, and recklessness run rampant. Lumet reveals how each character is ultimately a flawed human being, and each becomes terrible in their revenge, decompensation, or inaction.

People with antisocial personality disorder often have multiple sexual partners and tend to use others for sexual gratification, with little concern for the needs or feelings of their sexual partners. They can be superficially warm and charming but become distant and aloof after their sexual conquest. This is evident in Johnny, the intellectual, philosophical, and antisocial character portrayed

---

Questions to Consider While Watching *Before the Devil Knows You're Dead* **(2007)**

- It seems that each of the characters in the film could change. Why don't they? Is resistance to change common in those with antisocial personality?
- Do the actions and inactions of the characters of Philip Seymour Hoffman, Albert Finney, and Ethan Hawke make them evil? If not, what would a person have to do to be considered simply evil?
- Philip Seymour Hoffman's character abuses drugs as a way of coping with a horrifying set of circumstances. How common is this among people with antisocial personality disorders?
- The film's unique title comes from a famous Irish toast: "May you have food and raiment; a soft pillow for your head; may you be 40 years in heaven; before the devil knows you're dead." What does this mean? Why is the title appropriate for this film?

---

by David Thewlis in *Naked* (1993). Robert Duvall plays a complicated, antisocial minister who philanders, abuses, and projects his problems onto other characters and God in *The Apostle* (1997). Duvall's character, Sonny, is driven but flawed. He is a "spiritual antisocial" in that he passionately preaches and his manipulation and charm often take the form of genuinely wanting to help others have more meaningful lives; however, he externalizes his problems by blaming Satan and not taking responsibility for his life. He abuses alcohol, is unfaithful to his wife, threatens her with a gun, throws an object through a window, and, most seriously, grabs his wife roughly by the hair and attempts to drag her away from the baseball game and then hospitalizes his wife's boyfriend by hitting him on the head with a baseball bat. He lies to others about his past, despite their trust in him as their spiritual leader. Sonny certainly embodies the qualities of narcissism as well, with his grandiose speech and in his preaching, and he feeds off others' admiration and his ability to stake out a position in center stage. This film will remind some of the role of the much more psychopathic "preacher" played by Robert Mitchum in the classic film *The Night of the Hunter* (1955).

The fascinating film *Tape* (2001) takes place in one setting (a motel room) with only three characters (played by Ethan Hawke, Robert Sean Leonard, and Uma Thurman). Despite this simplicity, the film is a complex look at a devious, antisocial personality, Vince (Hawke), and his manipulation of two high school friends. Vince is a 28-year-old without a job who volunteers as a firefighter. He presents as unstable, using drugs, jumping and running around the small motel room, "chugging" beers, and throwing the cans around. He has a history of drug dealing and reports that he has "anger tendencies" and "unresolved issues." At times, he is sweet and soft spoken, but the viewer soon realizes he is purposefully acting this way to manipulate his friends. With extreme craftiness, he secretly "tape records" his friend John (Leonard) revealing some vulnerable information (about a date rape in high school) after Vince interrogates him in cross-examination style; displaying a total lack of empathy, he blackmails John and calls another old friend (Vince's ex-girlfriend and John's date rape victim), Amy (Thurman), with the hopes of continuing his plotted manipulation.

Jonestown: The Life and Death of Peoples Temple (2006) utilizes old footage, tapes, writings, and interviews with several survivors and family members of those involved in what has been called the largest mass suicide in modern history. On November 18, 1978, in Jonestown, Guyana, 909 members of Peoples' Temple killed themselves along with their evangelical leader, Jim Jones. Members of the church adored Jones for his charisma and his messages of integration, hope, equality, and justice. Many embraced him as godlike and considered him a savior. What was missed by those who died and many others was that Jim Jones was a vicious antisocial personality. He abused power and used the congregation to meet his own sexual needs (in one case explaining to a woman shivering while he had sex with her, "I'm doing this for you"). He frequently humiliated, shamed, and manipulated the congregants, finding pleasure in spanking or beating people in front of the congregation as punishment for petty transgressions. Jones once staged a blind woman in a wheelchair and performed a fake healing. He convinced people to sell their homes for the church and in return he promised that the church would take care of elderly family members. He encouraged people to not think for themselves so that he could think for them; he reflected that he was happy to play whatever role the congregant needed – friend, brother, savior, or God. Jones exhibited significant pathological traits as a child; for example, he killed cats so that he could officiate at their funerals.

The true story of Danny Burrows (played by Ryan Gosling) in *The Believer* (2001) speaks to the serious love-hate relationship a young man has with himself as he adopts a dramatically contradictory role as a Jewish Nazi. In the opening sequence, the viewer sees Burrows, who presents as a stereotypic skinhead displaying Nazi symbols, seek out and beat a young Jewish man in the middle of the street. He embraces repugnant Nazi beliefs, ranking races by worthiness in the following order: Whites, Asians, Blacks, and Jews. At the same time, Burrows is highly intelligent and articulate, speaking charismatically to adults many years older than him about Nazi order, discipline, and values, articulating "kill your enemy" and "Judaism is a sickness" messages. His aggressiveness and impulsivity lead him to instigate numerous fights. Burrows displays little remorse for any of his antisocial behaviors until, while ransacking a synagogue with a Fascist group, he begins to show concern for how people treat a scroll containing sacred Jewish writings. He brings the scroll home, takes painstaking care of it, and begins to teach his girlfriend Hebrew. From here, he must face his internal contradiction and deal with the consequences of the lifestyle he has created for himself.

Another film illustrating an antisocial personality that is based on a true story is the film *Shattered Glass* (2003) about Stephen Glass (Hayden Christensen), the *New Republic* magazine writer who went to extensive lengths to fabricate and embellish stories. Both the film and Christensen do a remarkable job of depicting not only the elaborate deceit, fantasy, and double life associated with this personality disorder, but also the neurotic quality of the "antisocial in trouble." The latter phrase refers to anxiety mixed with a façade of change that comes about when a person with an antisocial personality disorder is caught or about to be caught. Glass' response is to become emotional, obsequious, and/or apologetic. His manipulations take many forms, from trying to emphasize his need for the editors' support and how important it is (when he is lying) to trying to play others against one another to incessant repetition of the question "Are you mad at me?" Glass does not see the consequences of his actions as he continues to tell various lies and stories to cover up earlier lies, digging himself deeper into deception with each interaction; we later see the tremendous impact of his behavior on the *New Republic*.

Another "caught" antisocial is Edward Norton's character in *25th Hour* (2002), who has 24 hours before he must serve a prison term for trafficking marijuana. Since he is caught, he is forced to face some of his shame, guilt, and anger. In one unforgettable scene, he externalizes intense anger, blaring out "fuck you" to every race, group, district, and borough in New York City, as well as his father and girlfriend. We can infer he is saying this to himself as well, especially since he is looking at himself in the mirror while talking, but the acceptance of personal responsibility seems to be missed – as it often is in the antisocial personality. This Spike Lee film brings up important issues of regret and choice and brilliantly leaves many questions unanswered.

Catch Me If You Can (2002) is another film about a character with an antisocial personality disorder. The film is based on the true story of Frank Abagnale Jr., a con man who used his charm and good looks to defraud banks of millions of dollars in the 1960s. The role of Abagnale is played by Leonardo DiCaprio, who successfully impersonates a Pan-Am co-pilot, a physician, and an attorney. Abagnale is pursued for six years by FBI agent Carl Hanratty (Tom Hanks) before he is eventually captured, and he winds up consulting with the FBI on fraud crimes.

An interesting contrast of antisocial personalities occurs in *Levity* (2003), a film in which Billy Bob Thornton plays a person with an antisocial personality trying to make amends for his actions (a murder many years ago), and Morgan Freeman plays an antisocial preacher who uses a fake identity to hide from the police. Likewise, Tom Hanks is a charming person with an antisocial personality who cleverly uses sophisticated speech and extensive rationalizations to manipulate an old woman for his own purposes in *The Ladykillers* (2004).

A somewhat less dramatic illustration is found in the callous manipulation of naive home buyers vividly portrayed by Jack Lemmon, who plays a desperate and unhappy real estate salesman in *Glengarry Glen Ross* (1992). The manipulation of others for personal gain without concern for the consequences of one's behavior is a characteristic feature of antisocial personality disorders. Natasha Richardson and Mia Farrow play two consummate con artists in *Widow's Peak* (1994), although the diagnosis of antisocial personality is incompatible with the character portrayed by Farrow for most of the film. Many films appear to depict antisocial behavior, but it is often unclear as to whether these characters would meet all the criteria for the disorder. *Compulsion* (1959) depicts two antisocial fraternity men, Artie and Judd, who are intent that the perfect crime is "the true test of the superior intellect." They believe they should be able to manipulate the system to get away with murder simply because "we can." Each has an antisocial personality disorder, although Artie's case is more

severe. He is cool, smooth, and calculating under pressure, and enjoys listening to the police discuss the murder of which he is the perpetrator, taking pleasure in their confusion and chaos.

Some actors like Kevin Spacey can make a career out of playing antisocial characters. Though Spacey can play a variety of characters with vastly different personalities, he has played an impressive range of roles that illustrate some dimension of the antisocial personality; for example, he portrayed an arrogant writer in *The United States of Leland* (2004), an unhappy man who becomes obsessed with "the pleasure principle" in *American Beauty* (1999), a devious serial killer in *Se7en* (1995), a con man in The *Usual Suspects* (1995), a brutal executive in *Swimming with Sharks* (1994) , and an ineffectual, unethical and depressed therapist in *Shrink* (2009).

While the film *Enron: The Smartest Guys in the Room* (2005) describes the antisocial behavior of various executives in a corrupt organization, the film *The Corporation* (2004) demonstrates that the typical corporation meets the criteria for psychopathy (e.g., callous unconcern for others, failure to conform to social norms).

"The fatal flaw at Enron, if there was one you'd say, it was pride but then it was arrogance, intolerance, greed."

The underlying issues in the executives in *Enron: The Smartest Guys in the Room* (2005)

Antisocial vs. Psychopathic Personality

Though **psychopathic personality disorder** is not an actual diagnosis, it is a commonly used term, and there is often confusion when the labels antisocial personality, sociopath, and psychopath are all lumped together. Robert D. Hare, the world's leading authority on psychopathy, has been doing research on psychopaths for over 40 years. Hare explains that most psychopaths fit the criteria for antisocial personality; however, the reverse is not necessarily true. Hare adds that crosscultural studies have noted that psychopathy is generalizable. He cites a number of criteria for psychopathic personality including shallow emotions, glibness, manipulativeness, a parasitic lifestyle, episodic relationships, persistent violation of social norms, egocentricity, lack of remorse/empathy, low frustration tolerance, and lying (Hare, 2006).

In movies, psychopaths and sociopaths are often described as people who have "no conscience." Consider *Pirates of the Caribbean* (2003; 2006; 2007) and contrast Johnny Depp's character as the antisocial pirate with many of the pirate zombies led by Geoffrey Rush's character. The latter are clearly psychopathic. Table 6.2. uses contemporary films to clarify the difference between antisocial personality disorder and psychopathy.

Two particularly powerful films pose interesting questions relevant to this distinction: *Monster* (2003) and *American Psycho* (1999). *Monster*'s Aileen (Charlize Theron) might be a rare example of a serial killer who seems more antisocial than psychopathic. She is able to express and share love for another (her lover, played by Christina Ricci) and in the film she claims that her killings were in self-defense (as did serial killer Aileen Wuornos

in real life). In *American Psycho*, Patrick Bateman (played by Christian Bale) is shown killing many people throughout the film. If we are to take this literally, then he is clearly a psychopathic personality. Interestingly, the film also suggests that all of the murders depicted in the film are in Bateman's thoughts/fantasies, which is supported by plot elements, by his extensive fantasy doodles, and cinematically at the end through close-up shots of Bateman's head. The viewer is left to believe that Bateman is very narcissistic and has heavy antisocial traits, but is not a psychopath.

The cinema is replete with examples of characters who illustrate the psychopathic personality. Some salient examples include Anthony Hopkins' portrayal of a murdering cannibal, Hannibal Lecter in *The Silence of the Lambs* (1991), *Hannibal* (2001), and *Red Dragon* (2002); Kurt Dussander (Ian McKellen) in *Apt Pupil* (1998), a film that depicts the rekindling of a suppressed psychopath-

Table 6.2. Differentiation of antisocial personality from psychopathic personality through movies

Personality Type	Film	Personality Characteristics
Antisocial	Jack Sparrow (Johnny Depp) in *Pirates of the Caribbean* (2003; 2006; 2007)	Manipulative and devious, though Jack Sparrow does show qualities of trust, care, allegiance, and teamwork
	Monty Brogan (Edward Norton) in *25th Hour* (2002)	History of not conforming to laws/rules, impulsive, irritable, and reckless disregard but shows remorse and care for others
	Johnny (David Thewlis) in *Naked* (1993)	Deceitful, impulsive, self-centered, lacks empathy, irresponsible; also shows fleeting concerns and care for others and for the betterment of society
	Euliss "Sonny" Dewey – The Apostle E.F. (Robert Duvall) in *The Apostle* (1997)	Heavily deceitful, impulsive, and dangerous in words and behaviors; also shows genuine care for others, love for God, and exhibits remorse
Psychopathic/ Sociopathic	Barbossa (Geoffrey Rush) in *Pirates of the Caribbean* (2003; 2007)	Kills at will for own gain, embodies the seven deadly sins, particularly greed
	Vann (Owen Wilson) in *The Minus Man* (1999)	Serial killer with no conscience and no reason or purpose, kills randomly
	Mickey Knox (Woody Harrelson) and (Mallory Knox) Juliette Lewis in *Natural Born Killers* (1994)	Torture and kill anyone who gets in their way or bothers them, without hesitation or regret
	Elijah Price (Samuel L. Jackson) in *Unbreakable* (2000)	Complete disregard for human life as he commits mass murder out of a self-serving need to find his "better half"

ic personality; *In Cold Blood* (1967); *The Boston Strangler* (1968); *Henry: Portrait of a Serial Killer* (1990); Fritz Lang's child serial killer in *M* (1931); and Dennis Hopper as a sociopath in both *Blue Velvet* (1986) and *Speed* (1994). Charles Manson, as portrayed by Steve Railsback in the film *Helter Skelter* (1976), is another example of the indifferent disregard for social values and moral behavior that is found in people with psychopathic personalities. (Manson, responsible for the death of nine people in 1969, has never shown any remorse for his behavior or the deaths of his victims.)

"A door had been opened that couldn't be shut."

Kurt Dussander (Ian McKellen), a reclusive former Nazi henchman in hiding, in *Apt Pupil* (1998)

The legendary director Stanley Kubrick frequently depicted psychopathic personalities in his films. Perhaps his most famous is the street hoodlum, Alex, in *A Clockwork Orange* (1971); other characters in his films with strong psychopathic tendencies include the Senior Drill Instructor (Gunnery Sergeant Hartman) in *Full Metal Jacket* (1987), the deteriorating character of Jack Torrance (Jack Nicholson) in *The Shining* (1980), the deceptive computer, Hal, in *2001: A Space Odyssey* (1968), the obsessed pedophile in *Lolita* (1962), and the generals who confronted Kurt Douglas' character in the anti-war masterpiece *Paths of Glory* (1957).

A classic example of a psychopathic personality is found in Alfred Hitchcock's *Strangers on a Train* (1951). Bruno Anthony (Robert Walker), who repeatedly engages in unlawful behavior (including murder), is deceitful and glib shows impulsivity, and there is never any reason to suspect he feels any remorse for the murder he commits or his plan to have his father murdered.

Borderline Personality Disorder

Borderline personality disorder is characterized by unstable but intense interpersonal relationships, labile mood, impulsive behavior, and erratic emotions. These individuals are easily angered, but their anger may pass as quickly as a summer storm, leaving no sign of its recent presence. Fear of abandonment is a pathognomonic characteristic of

borderline personalities. These individuals become overly attached in almost all of their relationships: When they initially become romantically involved, their partners are apt to feel smothered by the intensity of the relationship and perplexed by the wild swings between affection and anger; when they enter therapy, therapists quickly become concerned about their excessive dependence and inappropriate adulation. These are the patients most likely to call in the middle of the night, insisting on an emergency consultation or late-night office visit. This is most apt to occur when the patient feels isolated or alone (e.g., when the therapist is about to take a vacation). They often vacillate between indiscriminate adulation and active hatred (referred to as "love-hate" or "push-pull"), sometimes within the space of hours.

Suicidal gestures and self-injury are common in people with borderline personality disorders. These gestures cannot be ignored, because completed suicide occurs in about 10% of borderline personality disorder cases. However, it is more common for the patient to behave in ways that are more attention seeking than life threatening, such as swallowing 20 Valium and then calling a crisis center or making superficial cuts on the upper arm before calling a suicide hotline. Self-mutilation is also a common and serious problem with borderline personalities. The symptoms of borderline personality disorder overlap with those of both depression and bipolar disorders, and some borderline personality patients respond to treatment with either antidepressants or mood stabilizers. Women are diagnosed with borderline personality disorder much more often than men.

Glenn Close's character Alex Forrest in *Fatal Attraction* (1987) offers one of the best available depictions of borderline personality disorder. Michael Douglas plays Dan Gallagher, a happily married New York attorney who becomes sexually involved with Alex Forrest, a glamorous and sexually aggressive publishing executive. What starts out as a simple, one-night affair for Dan turns into a nightmare for him and his family as Alex becomes increasingly possessive and manipulative. Dan tries to extricate himself from the affair, but Alex resorts to verbal threats, telephone calls to his wife, a suicide gesture (slashing her wrists after Dan tells her the affair is over), and intimidation of his wife and child. The performance by Close dramatically illustrates many characteristics of patients with a borderline personality disorder: anger, impulsivity, emotional lability, fear of rejection and abandonment, inappropriate behavior, vacillation between adulation and disgust, and self-mutilation. Although people with borderline personality disorder can be dangerous to others (as displayed dramatically in *Fatal Attraction*), this is not typically the case and these individuals are probably more likely to be dangerous to themselves. If the individual has strong antisocial personality characteristics as well (which Alex Forrest does), the risk of danger to others rises.

Nicole Kidman portrays the title character in *Margot at the Wedding* (2007). Margot, a likely borderline personality, has separated from her husband and she and her son are spending time at her sister's home for a wedding. As noted earlier in the chapter, it is difficult to diagnose a personality disorder with only a snapshot of the individual's life (e.g., a period of just a few days). Margot has very loose boundaries, labile affect, is impulsive in her speech, and she shares the confidential news of her sister's pregnancy. Her mannerisms, speech, and behavior frequently reveal tension, anger, impulsivity, and reactivity. It is clear there has been significant tension over the years between the two sisters and a history of abuse which they discuss casually in front of their children. Margot roars with uncontrollable laughter when describing a rape. Margot also displays her fear of abandonment at the end of the film when she goes running uncontrollably after her son on a bus after just having sent him off, leaving her handbag and other items behind her on the ground. Most of her behavior and reactions are at least mildly inappropriate and have a significant impact on her life.

A more intense example of borderline personality disorder can be found in Rae (Christina Ricci) in *Black Snake Moan* (2006), a film that exposes the protagonist's character flaws through a mixture of tragic scenes and beautiful interpersonal scenes. Rae is an unstable young woman whose fear of abandonment intensifies when her boyfriend Ronnie (Justin Timberlake) leaves for war. She covers over her fear with alcohol, drug abuse, and casual sex with multiple men. Sex is the only way she knows to relate to others. She has a history of abuse and allows others to take advantage of her. She displays a high level of explosive behavior and transient dissociative symptoms, both characteristic of people with borderline personality disorders. Also interesting is that over time she reverts back to her same pervasive patterns of seductiveness and explosiveness.

Christina Ricci has become very successful at portraying borderline personality, as demonstrated by two other films. In *Prozac Nation* (2001), her character, Elizabeth Wurtzel, displays an intense fear of abandonment, is emotionally labile,

possesses and then rejects her boyfriend, sabotages her friends, experiences multiple crises, has a deep underlying self-hatred, and reports a history of self-injurious behavior. She also suffers from co-morbid depression. Likewise, her character Amanda Chase in Woody Allen's *Anything Else* (2003) displays borderline personality qualities in her interpersonal relationships and her affective instability. She has some attention-seeking qualities, is dishonest, manipulatively takes advantage of a dependent man, uses drugs, and is defensive and self-righteous in explaining her decisions and behaviors.

Another Woody Allen character – albeit deeper and darker – displaying a borderline personality disorder is Maria Elena, played by Academy Award winner Penelope Cruz in *Vicky Cristina Barcelona* (2008). She is unstable, intense in relationships, sexually impulsive, affectively labile, has rage-like temper and revengefulness, and is briefly suicidal with dissociative symptoms.

A more manipulative illustration of borderline personality can be found in Barbara Covett (Judi Dench), in *Notes on a Scandal* (2006). Barbara, a veteran teacher, discovers a younger teacher, Sheba Hart (Cate Blanchett), having an affair with a 15-year-old student and the two women engage in a battle of manipulation and deceit. Barbara is a lonely woman with no friends or intimate contacts and seems to crave touch and emotional connection; she feels an intense attraction toward Sheba, sexualizes her, and engages her in a touching/stroking game. People with borderline personality disorders often misread and distort the realities of interpersonal situations, particularly those involving intimacy, and Barbara misreads their friendship as evidence of a deeper, more intimate connection. At the same time, she has no qualms about taking advantage of Sheba's trust and loyalty and she betrays Sheba's trust, just as Shakespeare's Iago betrays Othello. Barbara also displays the pathognomonic symptom of fear of abandonment, even with respect to her cat. The viewer peers into Barbara's internal world through voice-over narration associated with her thinking and her journaling. In watching this film, the viewer is reminded that people with personality disorders exhibit repetitive behavioral patterns over time, and we learn that Barbara had often been obsessed with younger teachers and that in the past her behavior had led to a restraining order against her by another teacher; in a concluding scene, the viewer sees Barbara grooming her next victim.

The hospital staff in the film *Girl, Interrupted* (1999) apply the diagnosis of borderline personality disorder to the lead character, Susanna (Winona

Ryder). It is difficult to justify this diagnosis, as Susanna only seems to display two behaviors fitting this diagnosis – a suicide attempt and sexual promiscuity. However, she is clearly depressed and has serious relationship problems. A rare depiction of male borderline personality can be found in Tom Ripley (Matt Damon) in *The Talented Mr. Ripley* (1999). Ripley has a tremendous fear of abandonment and even commits a murder in order to prevent himself from experiencing the pain of abandonment. Other potential examples of borderline personalities include Theresa Dunn (Diane Keaton) in *Looking for Mr. Goodbar* (1977) and several of the female supporting characters in Martin Scorsese's *After Hours* (1985). Catherine Tramell (Sharon Stone) in *Basic Instinct* (1992) and *Basic Instinct 2* (2006) displays a number of borderline characteristics, not all of which are explicit *DSM-IV-TR* criteria; for example, she is interpersonally manipulative, sexually exploitative and impulsive, seductive in therapy sessions (in the latter film), emotionally labile, angry, and vengeful.

Histrionic Personality Disorder

The defining feature of histrionic personality is dramatic attention-seeking behavior. These individuals are self-centered and preoccupied with their appearance. They feel uncomfortable in any situation in which they are not "center stage," and they can quickly turn their emotion on or off and with little provocation. They resent attention directed at others and will often engage in excessive behavior to have the focus of attention redirected to themselves. They initially seem to be spontaneous and interesting people, not unlike Rosalind Russell's portrayal of the title character in the film *Auntie Mame* (1958). However, true histrionic personalities soon find that others quickly tire of their desperate attempts to remain at the center of attention and are angered by their inability to engage in equitable social interaction.

Carolyn Burnham (Annette Bening) in *American Beauty* (1999) is very melodramatic and clearly a character with a histrionic personality. She is unhappy and under-stimulated in her marriage, and she is having an affair with a man whom she admires for superficial reasons – he is rich, successful, charming, and highly narcissistic. She ruins a rare intimate moment with her husband Lester (Kevin Spacey) when she shows obsessive concern that he might spill beer on the couch. She is exact in her appearance, dressing in elegant clothes that make her stand out. At work as a real estate agent, Carolyn attempts to sell a house by exaggerating the house's appearance to unimpressed customers. She shows excessive emotionality and breaks down when faced with the reality that bright smiles and superficiality do not sell houses, and she goes into an emotional fit, crying, slapping herself in the face, stomping on the floor, and yelling, "Shut up! Stop it! You're weak! You baby! Shut up! Shut up! Shut up!" In social situations, Carolyn displays a very loud laugh that can be heard across a crowded room. She is socially inappropriate and highly critical of family members, such as when she greets her daughter after her daughter's dance routine, "I watched you closely. You didn't screw up once" with a big smile on her face as if she has just made an important, helpful observation. Her daughter looks at her in disgust.

In addition, rapid shifting from one extreme emotion to another is common in people with histrionic personality disorders. Carolyn quickly switches from hysterical laughter to blatant seriousness with a man she desires, and later from tearful crying to anger and slapping her daughter's face. Histrionic personalities are often very suggestible as well. Carolyn displays a ridiculous level of awe for another real estate agent's mantra, "You cannot count on anyone except yourself," and she follows and teaches this as the most important lesson to learn in life. In summary, appearance and style are far more important than substance for the person with a histrionic personality disorder.

Another precisely accurate example of a histrionic personality is Katharine Hepburn's portrayal of a dying mother in *Long Day's Journey into Night* (1962). Family life centers around the mother, and her two sons and her husband dote on her. She is extremely concerned with her appearance, openly fishes for compliments, and makes frequent references to her lost beauty. If she were being clinically evaluated, Hepburn's character Mary Tyrone would be diagnosed as having histrionic personality disorder on Axis II and as opioid-dependent (morphine) with physiological dependence on Axis I.

In *White Oleander* (2002), Robin Wright Penn plays Starr (an appropriate name for a histrionic character), the first mother-figure for a young adolescent, Astrid (Alison Lohman), whose biological mother has been incarcerated. Starr is a former stripper, recovering alcoholic, and born-again Christian who encourages Astrid to read the Bible and accept Jesus as her savior. At first, Starr is kind and overly helpful in her care for Astrid; soon the viewer realizes these are superficial overtures that develop into a dangerous murder attempt when Starr becomes threatened as she realizes that Astrid's emerging sexuality appeals to her husband.

Narcissistic Personality Disorder

People with a narcissistic personality have an intense need for admiration, often self-centered, and have an exaggerated sense of their own importance. They may spend a great deal of time fantasizing about success or power. They feel entitled to special treatment and expect that others will automatically comply with their expectations; this often leads to their appearing conceited and pretentious. Their preoccupation with themselves leads them to overlook or devalue the contributions of others. The name of this disorder is taken from the Greek myth of Narcissus, who fell in love with his own reflection. Mirrors are often used in films portraying narcissists to symbolize self-reflection, infatuation with self, and distorted or broken mirrors represent a fractured sense of worth or esteem.

Although presenting as confident and secure, people with narcissistic personality disorder have low self-esteem and harbor unconscious feelings of insecurity, unworthiness, and self-doubt. Consider the film *Phone Booth* (2003), only worthwhile for the ending in which a highly narcissistic New Yorker is stripped of his defenses and completely unravels, admitting to all his deceits, manipulations, and cover ups, from the expensive clothes he wears to his deep relationship fears to keeping a young male sidekick around to feel better about himself. Suddenly, all his grandiosity, entitlement, and conceit are gone. He had never admitted these deeper issues even to himself in a conscious way, and they remained present but deeply embedded. It took an extreme situation to trigger awareness and admission. Of course, most narcissists do not come to such insights about themselves, and when they do, it is not long before they return to their old patterns.

The narcissistic wound is also exhibited in *Overnight* (2003) a docudrama that tells the rags to riches to rags story of Troy Duffy, a bartender offered an attractive deal by Miramax for his screenplay. Nevertheless, it is Duffy's narcissism – his grandiose sense of self-importance, preoccupation with success, entitlement, and interpersonal exploitativeness – that leads to his downfall and the likelihood he will never work in Hollywood again. The film does a good job of depicting a deeply troubled/wounded man who is completely unaware of his shortcomings.

Contemporary cinema is replete with examples of narcissistic personality disorders: Andy Garcia's fascinating character, Byron, in *The Man from Elysian Fields* (2001), is a narcissistic, struggling writer who eventually realizes his narcissism and subsequent self-inflicted destruction and makes a change by facing his pain; Nicholas Cage's corporate character Jack Campbell in *The Family Man* (2000) states his only concerns are for money and power, nothing deeper; Ben Stiller's ridiculous character Derek in *Zoolander* (2001), is too self-absorbed to realize he has been brain-washed; and John Turturro's character Dante Dominio is a narcissistic opera singer and performer in *The Man Who Cried* (2000).

"Underneath all that bravado beats the heart of a guy who's not nearly as cocky as he wants everybody to believe."

Liz (Susan Sarandon) calling out the narcissism of Alfie (Jude Law) in *Alfie* (2004)

In *Roger Dodger* (2002), Roger Swanson (Campbell Scott) is a classic narcissistic personality – a womanizer who is teaching a 16-year-old adolescent about how men think and see the world. He teaches the boy to see, think, and perceive sex everywhere he looks. Roger creates various "opportunities" for the boy to seduce women – at the bar, at a party, and then with prostitutes. He has no qualms about encouraging the boy to take advantage of a drunken woman who has passed out. Roger displays little true empathy for the boy as he thrusts him to manhood. Underneath Roger's inflated self-image and conceit is his rage at being rejected by his attractive boss (Isabella Rosselini) who has put an end to their love affair.

In *Lovelife* (1997), Alan (Jon Tenney) is a minor writer and professor who thinks he is very important. He seems to care only for himself and his work. He treats women poorly and exploits them through seduction, deceit, and manipulation, and he eloquently explains his approach and craft to a barfly. In denying his own arrogance, Alan believes he is compassionate and sensitive because he has to struggle to manage a relationship with two women (the real issue is that one of the women is not as fawning as the other). He believes women should be at his "beck and call" (one character describes him by saying "he says what he wants and everybody jumps").

> "I want somebody to think I'm the greatest thing that ever happened to them and without me they couldn't go on."
>
> A narcissistic writer in *Lovelife* (1997)

The film accurately portrays the underlying sensitivity to criticism and inherent low self-esteem of the narcissist (which frequently results in narcissistic injuries). Alan gets very upset, stubborn, and passive-aggressive when his girlfriend does not come to his lecture; he expresses an intense fear of abandonment as he makes a big production about his girlfriend leaving a party without him, he then grovels on his knees with the girl standing over him, and lays in a girl's lap to receive the motherly nurturance and attention he so deeply craves.

> "Let's hurt someone."
>
> Chad (Aaron Eckhart) in
> *In the Company of Men* (1997)

Director Neil LaBute created unforgettable and cruel narcissists in two of his bitterly satirical movies – *In the Company of Men* (1997) and *The Shape of Things* (2003). Though there are two male narcissists in the former movie, Chad (Aaron Eckhart) is more pathological as he convinces his friend that they should seduce a vulnerable, deaf woman and get her to fall in love with both of them, planning to subsequently dump her. Chad feels entitled to do this, blaming women for being rejecting, controlling, and manipulative, ostensibly believing he and his partner can restore dignity to men through revenge and the pain of the innocent. In *The Shape of Things*, a character named Evelyn (Rachel Weisz) transforms Adam (Paul Rudd), an anxious, insecure, shy person, into a physically attractive, stylish, confident man. Without any qualms, she shocks Adam, the viewer, and the audience to whom she is giving a presentation when she reveals that her relationship with Adam has been a class "project" in which she used a human subject to prove that people are like clay and can easily be molded and manipulated. When talking with Adam afterward, Evelyn has a strongly stubborn, con-

fident, and resentful expression on her face. She believes she has made him a better person and thus should be thanked for her behavior. The characters in each film have strong antisocial qualities evident in their complete disregard for others and social convention and in their pathological manipulation. They are literally predators who consciously seek out their prey – a vulnerable, neurotic individual with poor esteem. The endings of both movies reveal just how pathological both characters are as they reveal their manipulative "game," totally devoid of empathy. A similar plotline depicting extensive female manipulativeness can be found in *My Summer of Love* (2004).

Female narcissists are less common, but also include Madonna portraying a grandiose, striking Eva Peron in *Evita* (1997). Eva emphasizes physical appearance, presentation to others, and her posture as critically important features. She manipulates people throughout the film for her own advantage – to help her rise in her career and look better in front of others. Annette Bening as Julia Lambert in *Being Julia* (2004) is another example of a female narcissist. Julia is a star of the theater who relishes her success and revels in her fame; however, feelings of self-loathing break through whenever she is rejected. She has been addicted

---

 Additional Questions for Discussion (Cluster B Disorders)

- Why are most film examples of borderline personality cases women and most examples of narcissists men? Is this an accurate clinical picture?
- What qualities of the Cluster B disorders make them the most common personality disorders found in jails and prisons?
- Do you agree with the distinction between the Antisocial Personality and Psychopath/ Sociopath? State your case.
- Does society have a role in the creation of serial killers?
- One way of interpreting *Monster* is that Aileen Wuornos is a victim of circumstance. Would Aileen have developed into a murderer if she had not been a prostitute? What would have happened if she had never been abused?
- With which of these disorders is a client most likely to seek treatment? When and why? Who is least likely to ask for help?
- How close does Tom Ripley's character in *The Talented Mr. Ripley* come to meeting the criteria for each of the four disorders in this cluster?

to work most of her career, but taking a break and having an affair revitalize her and her narcissism seems to shift. The character also has some histrionic qualities as throughout the film it is often difficult for the viewer to discern when Julia is acting and when she is feeling/expressing real emotions. In addition, Mena Suvari's adolescent character Angela Hayes in *American Beauty* has narcissistic traits clearly seen in her preoccupation in becoming a model, her lack of empathy for a new student who has been hospitalized, and her strong beliefs that she is somehow special and important.

Other classic narcissistic characters include Norma Desmond (Gloria Swanson) in *Sunset Blvd.* (1950) and an (initially) arrogant and self-serving Whitey Marsh (Mickey Rooney) in *Boys Town* (1938). In *The Doctor* (1991), William Hurt plays Jack MacKee, a self-centered and narcissistic physician who cares little for anything except himself and his career until he develops a tumor in his throat and discovers what it feels like to be a patient. Finally, Warren Beatty plays Bugsy Siegel, a narcissistic and self-centered gangster in the Barry Levinson film *Bugsy* (1991).

Cluster C Disorders

As is true in clinical settings, characters in films will have symptoms and personality characteristics that overlap with more than one disorder in each cluster. For example, it is clear that Robin Williams' milquetoast character in *One Hour Photo* (2002) has a personality disorder, however, he has characteristics of several disorders, most of which are found in cluster C. He lives alone, being too scared to take the risks that relationships require (avoidant); he is obsessed with a pseudo family (dependent); and he is orderly and rigid in handling photos at work and hoarding photos at home (obsessive-compulsive). Add in some depression with psychotic features, a probable history of past sexual abuse, and voyeuristic elements and Williams' character becomes even more complex.

Avoidant Personality Disorder
People with **avoidant personality disorder** have a tremendous fear of being exposed as inadequate and inferior. They are hypersensitive to criticism and shape their lives around fear of rejection and disapproval. They generally avoid intimate relations, convinced that they would be ridiculed as inadequate lovers. They conceptualize the world (and especially interpersonal relationships and interactions) as unsafe and threatening. They have

diminished self-esteem and describe themselves as inept, incompetent, and inferior. They are apt to spend much of their time at home and alone, in large part because of their concern that their personal deficiencies will be revealed if they venture out in public. These pervasive feelings of inferiority typically originate in childhood. In Adlerian terms, the person with an avoidant personality lacks the *courage to be imperfect*. However, it is important for clinicians to be sensitive to cultural differences that may affect a client's behavior. For example, in some Asian cultures, self-deprecation and extreme modesty about one's own achievements are normative behaviors and not indicative of a maladaptive personality trait.

This diagnosis overlaps substantially with the diagnosis of **social phobia, generalized type**. The overlap is so substantial that many clinicians find the distinction between the two diagnoses to be meaningless, and the *DSM-IV-TR* acknowledges that the two diagnoses may be simply different ways of conceptualizing the same (or similar) conditions. Keep this in mind as you read about the characters in the following films.

Avoidant personality can be distinguished from schizoid personality in that although both avoid interpersonal contact, the avoidant person actually craves the intimacy lacking in life. *Finding Forrester* (2000) is about a high school student, Jamal, who befriends a reclusive, retired professor and writer, William Forrester (Sean Connery), who seems to want more intimate connections. This film is about people who are trying to get "unstuck" from their avoidance patterns. In *Finding Forrester*, Connery's character does not leave his apartment and can only be seen by others when he is cleaning his windows. He wrote an award-winning book 50 years ago but has not been published since then. He seems to have given up, perhaps because of fear of rejection. He avoids other people and denies being interested in any life other than his own. When he does eventually go out, he has a panic attack when in a crowd. He is socially inappropriate, such as when he closes the door in the face of Jamal without a "goodbye." There is a fundamental sadness in William's isolation in his apartment; he actually does look for connection as a voyeur, watching others outside with interest and keeping his windows clean so he can continue observing the outside world. The viewer begins to wonder how much of William's isolation is loneliness. The protagonist frequently drinks alcohol alone, often while working. He avoids discussing personal issues such as his family history or his work. Clearly, he is reluctant to risk interpersonal sharing, and although this changes significantly as the friendship with Jamal develops, William keeps the secret of his cancer to himself.

Dependent Personality Disorder

Dependent personalities have extreme difficulty making decisions. They are submissive and look to others for structure, meaning, and direction in their lives. They tend to be passive and clinging. These people lack assertion skills and submit to the will of others. They sometimes submit to verbal, physical, or sexual abuse by their spouses and others. They lack self-confidence and feel they cannot manage on their own. They fear the loss of approval that may occur if they express their own opinions or beliefs. They invest tremendous time and energy in maintaining a relationship with the person upon whom they are dependent. When a close, dependent relationship ends, they almost immediately seek out another relationship that supports their chronic need for succor.

An amusing illustration of a dependent personality occurs in the 1991 film *What About Bob?* Bob, played by Bill Murray, is the patient of a psychiatrist played by Richard Dreyfuss. Bob pursues the beleaguered psychiatrist across the country when the psychiatrist tries to take a short vacation. Almost all therapists have had overly dependent patients, although they are unlikely to have encountered a case as extreme as that of Bob. The film is an interesting starting point for a discussion of transference and countertransference.

"I've been seeing myself through him for years."

Dependent personality in *Lovelife* (1997)

In *Lovelife* (1997), a female bartender, Molly, maintains a high level of obsequiousness toward her narcissistic boyfriend, Alan, doing everything she can for him and losing her own identity in the process. Molly believes Alan can do "no wrong" and that he has no flaws; in addition, she subjects herself to his unrelenting criticism. Like many other dependent personalities, she finds herself rejected by her boyfriend who takes up with another woman; when he loses that other woman, he shows up and Molly takes him back.

In *White Oleander* (2002), Renee Zellweger plays Claire Richards, a foster mother with a dependent personality. Claire's submissiveness to her husband, her inability to confront or challenge his decisions, and her vulnerability to manipulation by others lead her to commit suicide. Jason Biggs' agreeable, people-pleasing character Jerry Falk in *Anything Else* (2003) is so dependent he has to be "tricked" into being alone, into asserting his needs, and into challenging himself.

Obsessive-Compulsive Personality Disorder

A person with obsessive-compulsive personality has enduring, inflexible, and maladaptive personality traits that involve perfectionism, orderliness, and an excessive need for control. They display exacting attention to detail and may devote a great deal of time to making lists and plans. Time is seen not as the fabric of life but rather as an enemy and something to be conquered. All of this psychological energy is expended in a futile attempt to achieve a sense of control over the exigencies of life and the vicissitudes of fortune. Two films that are solid depictions of obsessive-compulsive personality disorder are *The Odd Couple* (1968) and *M*A*S*H* (1970). *The Odd Couple* presents a memorable performance by Jack Lemmon as Felix Unger, the neurotic roommate of Oscar Madison (Walter Matthau), who roams the house with a can of air freshener, determined to eliminate any unpleasant smells. In *M*A*S*H*, Major Frank Burns (Robert Duvall) spends the entire war fretting about the antics of "Hawkeye" Pierce (Donald Sutherland) and "Trapper" John McIntyre (Elliott Gould) and the inability of the system to set limits on their exuberant behavior. He is obsessed with rank and bitterly resents any undue familiarity by enlisted men or junior officers. He also works hard to ensure that the enlisted men do not fraternize with Korean women. He is self-righteous, moralistic, and rigid, despite the fact that he is having an ongoing affair with "Hot Lips" Hoolihan (Sally Kellerman). He becomes furious when he doesn't get his way, and he is totally ineffectual in responding to the cavalier attitudes of his tent mates.

It is important to understand the difference between obsessive-compulsive personality disorder and obsessive-compulsive disorder. The first disorder reflects a maladaptive personality style; the second indicates the presence of a serious mental disorder characterized by recurrent and persistent thoughts, images, or impulses (obsessions) and repetitive behaviors or mental acts (compulsions) that the individual cannot avoid or suppress. For example, an obsessive-compulsive personality may need to be constantly cleaning the house and "picking up." This is maladaptive (when excessive) but may not significantly impair the person's life, and may be mildly adaptive in some roles. However, the patient with an **obsessive-compulsive disorder** – e.g., Nicholas Cage's character Roy Waller in *Matchstick Men* (2003) – spends much of the day focused on their obsession or engaged in compulsive behavior. This individual is significantly distressed by his or her problem, and realizes that the behavior or thoughts are abnormal and out of control. In contrast, people with **obsessive-compulsive personality disorder** are far less likely to be troubled by their condition.

John Turturro plays Al Fountain, a man with obsessive-compulsive personality disorder (OCPD) in *Box of Moonlight* (1996). Turturro's character is a rigid, overly conscientious, rule-driven man in both his work as a manager and in his family life with his wife and children. Al is rigid about the way his child learns using flashcards and obsessively asks about their use; he seems unable to handle joking, and has to rehearse a social situation before its occurrence. He is awkward and rigid at his job, bossing others around, seems robotic and machine-like, and is stiff in behavior (e.g., walking). The depiction of the effect of these OCPD traits on the family and co-workers is very clear: Family members are avoidant, passive, or hesitant around him and his co-workers make fun of him behind his back.

Al takes time off work and family to loosen up as he goes on a journey to search out his past. Along the way, two Jehovah's witnesses quickly and accurately get at his pain and sense of loss over the years (perhaps confronting the etiology of his OCPD), but they soon turn religious and proselytizing, which only alienates him. In a couple of scenes, Al sees things going backwards – e.g., water being poured and a child riding a bike. Does this represent his own life going backwards? It is a fascinating cinematic example of the lack of progress that occurs when one is so stuck in routine that it seems as if one is going backwards. Moreover, it is a metaphor for time, one of the biggest enemies to someone with OCPD.

Films Portraying Various Personality Disorders

Some readers may want to see films that depict several personality disorders in one viewing for educational and clinical purposes. These films present interesting dynamics in their portrayal of interactions between different pathologies. Some examples follow.

Bartleby (2001) displays a classic example of schizoid personality in the lead character, Bartleby, portrayed exquisitely by Crispin Glover. Surrounding Bartleby, amidst a colorful office, are co-workers who are narcissistic (Joe Piscopo as Rocky, a self-inflated womanizer), schizotypal (Ernie, a disheveled man who often speaks in word salad), histrionic (Vivien, seductive and attention seeking), and dependent (the boss, unable to separate himself from a "fired" employee).

In *White Oleander* (2002), we see a young girl under the care of various "mother-figures," each with their own personality flaws. The child goes from her biological mother, Ingrid (an antisocial manipulator), to Starr (a dangerous histrionic), to Claire (a dependent personality with low self-esteem), and eventually to Rena (an antisocial personality who forces her foster children to sell clothes on the street to make money). The eyes of each mother seem to say it all, from the penetrating eyes of Ingrid to the downtrodden eyes of Claire.

The Royal Tenenbaums (2001) portrays the ultimate dysfunctional family, with pathologies that include narcissism, dependency, incest, suicidal behavior, paranoia, addiction, depression, and antisocial behavior, along with a schizotypal friend.

Woody Allen's *Anything Else* (2003) portrays an older man with a narcissistic personality disorder who befriends a young person with a dependent personality disorder in a relationship with someone with a borderline personality.

French director, Jean Pierre-Jeunet purposefully creates films with very interesting and quirky personalities who play their roles on elaborate, often fantastical, set designs. For examples, see

---

 Additional Questions for Discussion (Cluster C Disorders)

- How close does Robin Williams' character in *One Hour Photo* (2002) come to meeting the criteria for each of the disorders in this cluster?
- Since anxiety is a strong component of these disorders, can medication be an important part of treatment?
- Is the treatment the same for a person with OCD as with OCPD?
- What advantages are associated with being OCPD, avoidant, or dependent?

Amelie (2001), *The City of Lost Children* (1995), and *Delicatessen* (1992).

International Films: Personality Disorders

Cluster A

The character Joseph (Dominique Pinon) in *Amelie* (2001) meets the criteria for a paranoid personality, as he is so suspicious of his ex-girlfriend dating and meeting other men that he sits all day in the café where she works and watches her closely. He carries a small tape recorder in his pocket and records her various laughs, comments, and conversations with his own play-by-play and time of day voice-over. The viewer sees this is a pattern (thus providing additional weight for the diagnosis) as he continues similar suspicious behavior with the next woman he begins to go out with and then again with the first girlfriend when the new girlfriend dumps him. Anger and quick defensive reactions are common in the paranoid personality and are clearly part of Joseph's personality.

Cluster B

A classic in film history is *Breathless* (1960, France) by Jean-Luc Godard, one of the leading directors of the French New Wave cinema of the 1960s. This movement involved filmmakers who shifted toward being more abstract and experimental in writing style and narrative structure, and emphasized psychological and social issues such as psychopathology and alienation rather than hard sciences and technology. In *Breathless*, the protagonist, Michel Poiccard (Jean-Paul Belmondo), is a young hoodlum and an anti-hero. He steals, gets in police chases in which he glibly kills one of the officers, and spends his time on the run from the authorities. He becomes truly fascinated by an American girl (Patricia Franchini, played by Jean Seberg) and tries to convince her to escape to Rome with him. This character is devoid of empathy and is characterized by selfishness, rudeness, blaming, and objectification of women.

Polish director Krzysztof Kieslowski created *The Decalogue* (1989) , an extraordinary work composed of ten 1-hour films portraying a variety of tenants in a apartment complex. Each film relates loosely to one of the ten commandments.

There are a number of antisocial characters scattered throughout the films, such as the mother who uses deceit and manipulation in an attempt to keep her daughter's child from her, and the young vagabond who wanders the streets and randomly strangles a taxi cab driver. *Perfume: The Story of a Murderer* (2006, Germany) is an interesting film from independent director Tom Tykwer, about a boy who grows up with a superior olfactory sense. He becomes obsessed with this ability, smelling anything in the environment, near or far. As the character, Jean-Baptiste Grenouille (Ben Whishaw), matures to adulthood, he develops a mission to "preserve scent" and to "keep smell" as he searches for the ultimate perfume. Along this journey, he directly and indirectly begins to cross boundaries (e.g., he inappropriately grabs the arm of a woman on the street without speaking to her and carefully smells her arm) and kill people – in one scene, he obsessively smells a woman after accidentally killing her by covering her mouth to prevent her from screaming; he then strips her naked and smells her whole body carefully. Recklessness, irresponsibility, and lack of remorse are key features of this character.

Tsotsi (2005, South Africa/UK) is a movie about an African gangster who kills others when needed and brutally beats a fellow gang member to a pulp. One day Tsotsi (Presley Chweneyagae) robs a woman and steals her car but discovers there is an infant in the back seat. He reluctantly decides to care for the baby, and this experience slowly transforms his character. Through flashbacks the viewer learns of Tsotsi's painful past – his longing for a connection with his mother, his physically abusive father, his observation of his father abusing animals, and the neglect his father orchestrated in intentionally keeping Tsotsi separate from his mother despite living in the same household. The viewer begins to feel some sympathy for this brutal character and this experience for the viewer intensifies when Tsotsi's caring and nurturing of an infant leads him to make a connection with a caretaking mother in his village, renew a friendship with the man he beat up, and sacrifice his livelihood by returning the infant to its mother.

Another young person with an antisocial personality disorder is portrayed in a film that won the Palm D'or award at Cannes, *The Child* (2005, France). A somewhat endearing, petty street thief, Bruno (Jérémie Renier), becomes much less likeable when he sells his newborn for money. The film shows an interesting depiction of selling a baby: Bruno makes a phone call, goes into a seemingly abandoned house, walks up several flights of stairs, places his baby on his jacket in a room, walks into the next room and closes the door. He makes a call on his cell phone, saying "it's done," waits a short time, and then goes back into the first room and picks up his jacket and money.

The intriguing movie *Swimming Pool* (2003, France/UK) portrays a young woman, Julie (Ludivine Sagnier), who is seductive, provocative, and has a desire for excitement. She presents as nonchalant and laid back, but she is also someone who can be easily hurt or angered. She is sexually impulsive and promiscuous, having sex with a different man each night. She throws herself at older men, even when they express disinterest. One night she appears with a bruise on her face around her eye and the viewer is left to speculate as to what sort of danger she had been involved in while staying out the whole night. She is manipulative and jealous when her roommate begins to dance with a man. Julie acts out in anger when she is rejected. Her instability leads to a dissociative episode where she thinks she sees her mother (who is deceased) and expresses happiness at the prospect of her mother's return, screams when she is told that her mother is not there, and then faints. Julie also experiences a loss of memory, in which she is unable to remember killing her lover.

Zaza (Michel Serrault), the gay transvestite performer in *La cage aux folles* (*Birds of a Feather*, 1978, France), provides a wonderful example of a histrionic personality. She is dramatic and flamboyant, and almost everything she does is exaggerated. When her partner Renato (Ugo Tognazzi) tells her that he plans to invite his ex-wife to an important dinner with his son's future in-laws, Zaza is highly insulted and announces her intention to commit suicide. Neither Renato nor the viewer thinks for a minute that she is serious about her threat.

Cluster C

Sheila McCarthy plays Polly Vandersma, an insecure, socially awkward, temporary worker with avoidant traits in the popular Canadian film, *I've Heard the Mermaids Singing* (1987). She is naïve, socially inhibited, and seems to have a fragile self-esteem and self-concept. The voice-over narration done by McCarthy provides insights into her thinking and feeling when she is interacting with others.

Audrey Tautou's whimsical and endearing title character in *Amelie* (2001, France) has many avoidant personality characteristics. Amelie wants contact with others, especially intimate love,

though she is unable to take the risk. The emphasis in the film is on her thoughts and the challenge involved in meeting a man; the key theme, which the movie cleverly portrays cinematically, is her constant avoidance of actually meeting a man who comes into her life. After doing a good deed, Amelie appears nervous and looks away, ignoring an opportunity for human interaction; she simply does not know how to interact socially. The film is rare in its sophisticated exploration of the causes of Amelie's anxiety and avoidant behavior. It notes that, from birth, she was trapped between a neurotic mother (who had "shaky nerves" and was anxious about everything) and an iceberg father, who avoided all feelings. In addition, she had no playmates or social life and therefore became used to isolation, fantasy, and imagination. Other contributing etiologies are presented when she is tricked by a neighbor into feeling guilty as the "cause" of natural disasters, when her mother is dramatically killed in front of her, and when she has ongoing problems in relating and communicating with her father.

A common pattern for people with avoidant personality is the problem of self-sacrifice – devoting oneself to helping others and losing sight of one's own struggles and self-care. Amelie epitomizes self-sacrifice as she devotes herself to being a regular "do-gooder," helping others find joy and become "unstuck" from their life patterns. Amelie is personally stuck in her avoidant pattern and does not know it. Eventually, she learns to reach out to others for support and develops the courage necessary to face her fears.

Audrey Tautou portrays a cluster C character, Michèle, in another French film, *God is Great and I Am Not* (2002), in which she has a quirky element of dependent personality (but probably not the disorder) insofar as she repeatedly compromises her beliefs by conforming and converting to the religion of her partner at the time. She is shown trying to dedicate herself to Catholicism and Buddhism before finding a Jewish man and converting to Judaism. Her fear of being alone leads her to become suicidal after the end of an intimate relationship.

In the Spanish period film, *Mad Love* (2002), a woman compulsively attaches to her husband despite continuous evidence of his philandering. She becomes preoccupied and worried about his whereabouts, yet she maintains a high level of excitement when he returns from a journey that has obviously involved infidelities. In one scene, he resists a warm embrace despite her clinging and affectionate behavior, and she asks him to lie to her about where he has been. Even when she is rejected by him, she obsessively continues to love him and believe they will be reunited upon her death.

"I want to love you even if you loathe me."

A classic dependent quote from "Joan the Mad" in *Mad Love* (2002)

Critical Thinking Questions

- Why do many of the films portraying personality disorders exhibit some of the most compelling and memorable characters?
- Why is the public so fascinated and drawn to characters who are so diabolically evil (e.g., the Joker, Anton Chigurh, or Hannibal Lecter)? Is it appropriate for these characters to receive so much attention in the media and many of the major movie awards?
- Is it useful to treat life-long personality characteristics as *diseases* (i.e., should personality disorders be included in the *DSM-IV-TR*)?
- It is difficult to treat personality disorders, and treatment may last for several years. Should insurance companies be required to cover the treatment of these conditions?
- Is the concept of *evil* meaningful when discussing people with antisocial personality disorders?
- How does a personality feature (such as suspicion) differ from a personality disorder (such as paranoid personality disorder) or a disease (such as paranoid schizophrenia)? Are the differences qualitative as well as quantitative?
- *Fatal Attraction* (1987) originally ended with a suicide by Alex Forrest, using a knife that had Dan Gallagher's fingerprints on it. However, viewers did not like this ending, and it was replaced with the memorable bathtub scene. Would the original ending have been more consistent with a diagnosis of borderline personality disorder?
- What problems can therapists anticipate when they are treating clients with borderline personality disorders?

Further Exploration

If you have time to read just one book relevant to this chapter, make it:

Yudofsky, S. C. (2005). *Fatal flaws: Navigating destructive relationships with people with disorders of personality and character.* Arlington, VA: American Psychiatric Publishing.

If you only have time for one article, read:

Widiger, T. A., & Trull, T. J. (2007). Plate tectonics in the classification of personality disorder: Shifting to a dimensional model. *American Psychologist, 62,* 71–83.

Personality Disorders

No Country for Old Men (2007)
The Talented Mr. Ripley (1999)
Sunset Blvd. (1950)
The Odd Couple (1968)
Notes on a Scandal (2006)
Fatal Attraction (1987)
American Beauty (1999)
A Clockwork Orange (1971)
Bartleby (2001)
Charlie and the Chocolate Factory (2005)

Chapter 7

Substance Use Disorders

And if you keep usin' that needle they'll take away your music and put you in jail. Is that what you want?
Ray Charles' wife Della Bea Robinson addressing her husband in *Ray* (2004)

Questions to Consider While Watching *Ray*

- How does a heroin addiction differ from an alcohol addiction?
- How is it possible that Ray Charles could function as a performer while he was addicted to heroin?
- What examples of denial are illustrated by the film?
- Does the fact that Ray is blind help or hurt his music? Does it in any way interact with his substance abuse?
- At what point is it clear that Ray has an addiction problem?
- Does Ray Charles have any other addictions?
- What factors contributed to his use of heroin?
- How does Ray Charles' heroin addiction compare with George Jung's cocaine addiction in *Blow* (2001)?
- How common is it for substance abusers to have a double life? Is a double life typical for musicians?

Patient Evaluation[2]

Patient's stated reason for coming: "I have to seek the cure or go to jail."

History of the present illness: Ray is a 34-year-old, African American, married male who began using heroin at age 15. He currently uses both heroin and marijuana. He is seeking detoxification and treatment for heroin addiction. He last used heroin 6 hours ago prior to his arrest.

Past psychiatric illness, treatment, and outcomes: Ray denies any psychiatric treatment. He reports that he has had two or three vivid memories (that may have been flashbacks) of past traumatic events when high on heroin.

Medical history: Ray became blind at age 7 as a result of either childhood glaucoma or untreated infection. No other medical history is known.

Psychosocial history: Ray Charles Robinson was born on September 23, 1930, in Albany, Georgia. He is the older of two siblings. Moving to Florida as an infant, he grew up in poverty in the segregated South during the Great Depression. At age 5, Ray witnessed the drowning of his younger brother in a washtub. Not realizing that his brother was drowning, he stood by helplessly until his mother pulled the child from the water. At age 7, Ray lost his sight. He became self-reliant at a school for the blind and relies on his other highly developed senses to compensate for his loss of sight. Ray barely knew his father, who had two other families and died when Ray was 10 years old. Five years later, his mother died. He left school at age 15 and began working as a musician with various bands. Today, he is on his way to becoming one of the greatest artists in the music industry.
Ray Charles, once divorced, lives a luxurious lifestyle with his current wife Della Bea Robinson in Beverly Hills, California. They have three children. He also has several other children from extramarital relationships. His first sexual encounter occurred when he was 13. He says that he has "rarely gone a day without sex." He reports having no capacity – and little desire – to be faithful to one woman.

---

2 This fictitious interview is based on the character portrayed in the film *Ray*. It is not intended in any way to represent an interview with the real Ray Charles.

Drug and alcohol history: Ray Charles began using heroin approximately 20 years ago at age 15. He regularly "shoots up" and carries drug paraphernalia with him at all times. He reports that he uses heroin because he wants to, not as a reaction to any trauma in his life. He can easily afford to buy the heroin necessary to support his habit, and he has not sought treatment for his heroin addiction. He is seeking treatment now to avoid going to prison. He regularly uses alcohol and marijuana and smokes 2 packs of cigarettes per day.

Behavioral observations: Ray Charles is a pleasant, attractive, well-dressed African American male, who wore sunglasses and quietly answered the assessment questions. He demonstrated continuous, slight involuntary movements of the head and trunk.

Mental status examination: Ray was well oriented to person, time, situation, and place. There is no evidence of memory impairment. Ray has normal cognitive functioning, and there is no evidence of psychosis. He earned a score of 30/30 on the Mini Mental State Examination.

Functional assessment: Ray Charles is a very successful pianist, singer, and song writer who is very capable of supporting himself and his family. He has never used a cane or a guide dog; his other senses are highly developed. His interpersonal relationships seem chaotic, but he does not want to address these issues.

Strengths: Ray Charles recognizes his addiction will interfere with the pursuit of his music career. He is extraordinarily creative and innovative in his work. He is a man with remarkable resiliency considering the hardships he has overcome in his life.

Diagnosis: Opioid dependence, nicotine dependence, rule out cannabis dependence

Treatment plan: (1) detoxification; (2) inpatient treatment; (3) outpatient follow-up with possible methadone treatment.

Prognosis: Given this patient's long history of substance use, availability and access to drugs, and lack of internal motivation to remain abstinent, prognosis is guarded.

Ray and Heroin Addiction

The Academy Award winning film *Ray* is based on the first 35 years of the life of Ray Charles (Jamie Foxx), the legendary musical genius of rhythm and blues who lived until the age of 73. Charles' childhood years are marred with racial discrimination, extreme poverty, an absent father, the traumatic drowning of his younger brother, and the loss of his sight. His early interest in music is fostered by a local café musician. At age 15, following the death of his mother, he leaves school and begins touring the South with a number of dance bands that play black dance halls. Charles' second wife, Della Bea Robinson (Kerry Washington) struggles with his absence, addictions, and extramarital affairs. In the movie, she stays with him, but in reality, Della Bea left the marriage. Throughout the movie, Ray's iconic success in music is contrasted with a struggle for a personal identity, multiple failed and conflicting relationships, a need for constant sexual gratification, and an overall fear of being alone.

Ray Charles begins his 20-year heroin addiction in his teenage years with an injection from an older musician. Ray immediately experiences the surge of pleasure and the "rush" that occurs as heroin crosses the blood-brain barrier, is converted to morphine, and binds rapidly to the brain's opioid receptors. Ray also experiences other heroin effects. Clouded mental functioning is shown in the film, but nausea, vomiting, and suppression of pain (other short-term effects) are not. A user's response to heroin or other opioids will vary depending on

> "It ain't like I'm new at this. If I felt it would jeopardize you, music, or the baby, then I would stop..."
>
> Ray Charles (Jamie Foxx) in *Ray* (2004)

dose level and experience with the drug. During a state of opioid intoxication, the user tends to be euphoric, drowsy, apathetic, and usually indifferent to his or her surroundings. Constipation is common. The user's pupils become markedly constricted, and hallucinations may occur. Judgment is often impaired, although an experienced user may function in routine occupational and social roles.

The long-term effects of heroin are quite devastating and include addiction, infections (from dirty needles), collapsed veins, abscesses, infection of heart lining and valves, and arthritis. The primary long-term effect for Ray is addiction. All opioids produce significant tolerance, and withdrawal symptoms are common when drug use is discontinued. In *Ray*, withdrawal is graphically depicted. As tolerance develops, heroin users frequently require doses in excess of 100 times the amount that was originally necessary to produce a state of euphoria. In *Ray*, viewers can clearly see the tolerance develop. Typical of addictions, Ray Charles becomes more impaired as he continues to use heroin. Unlike most people with heroin addictions, Ray has extensive financial resources and does not have to engage in typical drug-seeking behavior such as theft or prostitution. Eventually, he is arrested by the FBI for possession of heroin. He seeks treatment because it is a better alternative than prison.

Drug Abuse

The use of mind-altering substances appears to have existed almost from the time that humans first became aware of the potent effects plants could have on human perception. Substance use disorders (alcohol or drugs) include substance abuse and substance dependence problems. **Substance abuse** is defined as a *pattern* of use characterized by *recurrent adverse consequences* related to the use of the substance. The diagnosis requires evidence of impairment as evidenced by one of the four following criteria: (1) failure to meet role obligations, (2) recurrent use in situations, such as driving, in which clear hazards are present, (3) recurrent legal problems, and (4) continued use, despite social or interpersonal problems related to the substance. In addition, the symptoms must never have met the criteria associated with the diagnosis of substance dependence.

In addiction or **substance dependence,** tolerance, withdrawal, and compulsive drug-taking behavior are present. The symptoms associated with dependence on different drugs are similar (but not identical) across drug categories. Dependence is diagnosed when clients present with three or more of the seven criteria listed in Table 7.1. at any time during a 12-month period.

Opioids

The opioids, a class of drugs, include opium, morphine, codeine, methadone, Percodan (a combination of aspirin and oxycodone), and heroin. They are highly addictive and lead to severe physical and psychological dependence. These drugs are sometimes lumped together under the general rubric of narcotics. Opium is usually smoked; the

Table 7.1. Criteria for substance dependence

Criteria (adapted from the *DSM-IV-TR*)	Examples from *Ray* (2004)
1. Tolerance, defined by (a) a need for ever increasing amounts of the substance to achieve intoxication or (b) diminished effect with use of a set level of the substance	Throughout the film, Ray continues to use more and more heroin.
2. Withdrawal, defined by (a) specific effects associated with the particular substance being abused or (b) use of a substance to relieve or avoid the withdrawal symptoms	Ray's withdrawal from heroin is life threatening. He refuses to use any medication to ease the physiological and psychological effects of his "cold turkey" withdrawal.
3. Using the substance in larger amounts or over a longer period than was intended	He continues to use heroin more frequently throughout the movie, even when he intends to attend family functions.
4. A persistent desire to cut back or eliminate use of the substance	Ray says he could quit whenever he wants, and he knows he should quit.
5. A great deal of time is devoted to acquiring the substance or recovering from its effects	He is often intoxicated. He seems to have easy access to the drug.
6. Important social, occupational, or recreational activities are ignored because of the preoccupation with use of the substance	He misses important family events when under the influence.
7. The substance use is continued despite recurrent physical or psychological problems resulting from its use.	He continues to use even though he is often scratching, unable to concentrate, and losing balance.

other drugs are most often ingested or injected. In most countries, opioids are controlled substances. If used legally, these drugs are prescribed for pain or diarrhea, with the exception of methadone, which is used to treat opioid addiction. Fentanyl and meperidine are opioid analogs (chemical compounds that are similar to other drugs in their effects, but differ slightly in their chemical structure) that are legally prescribed for pain, but are also illegally sold as recreational drugs. Fentanyl is especially dangerous because it is 50 times more potent than morphine.

In addition to *Ray* (2004), there are other films that depict the use of opioids. Robert De Niro can be seen smoking opium in both the opening and the ending scenes of Sergio Leone's *Once Upon a Time in America* (1984), and opium plays a significant role in both *Indochine* (1992) and Bernardo Bertolucci's *The Last Emperor* (1987).

Katharine Hepburn plays a morphine addict with an alcoholic son (Jason Robards) in the film adaptation of Eugene O'Neill's *Long Day's Journey into Night* (1962). Morphine abuse is also portrayed in the science fiction thriller *Pitch Black* (2000). An example of the ability to function despite being very high on drugs can be found in Quentin Tarantino's *Pulp Fiction* (1994). Vincent (John Travolta) shoots up before going out on a date with his boss' wife, Mia (Uma Thurman), who snorts cocaine before meeting him. The two wind up at "Jack Rabbit Slims" and maintain a coherent – if not stimulating – conversation. They even manage to win a dance contest. Later in the evening, Mia discovers the heroin in Vincent's coat pocket. Believing it to be cocaine, she proceeds to snort a line of the drug and goes into a coma. Vincent eventually manages to save Mia's life by plunging a syringe filled with epinephrine into her heart.

One of the most descriptive, yet disturbing, portrayals of heroin addiction is in the classic film *Requiem for a Dream* (2000). Most of the main characters are substance dependent – prescription diet pills for Sara (Ellen Burstyn) and multiple other substances including heroin for the teenagers Harry (Jared Leto), Marion (Jennifer Connelly), and Tyrone (Marlon Wayans). In this film, Harry's arm is eventually amputated because of drug-related untreated infections that lead to gangrene.

Opioid withdrawal occurs when use of opioid drugs is discontinued or when an opioid antagonist (any drug that blocks the effects of an opioid) is administered. Complete withdrawal usually takes 3–8 days. Opioid withdrawal can lead to the following symptoms: Dysphoric mood, nausea or vomiting, muscle aches, lacrimation (crying) or

rhinorrhea (a "runny nose"), diarrhea, yawning, fever, or insomnia. Examples of opioid withdrawal can be seen in *Ray* and in the Frank Sinatra film *The Man with the Golden Arm* (1955).

The classic film about the heroin trade is William Friedkin's *The French Connection* (1971). Friedman won an Academy Award for his directing, and Gene Hackman won the Academy Award for best actor for his role as police detective Jimmy "Popeye" Doyle. *The Connection* is a 1961 film about a group of junkies waiting for the arrival of a pusher. A more powerful and realistic presentation of teenage addiction and prostitution is *Christiane F.* (1981, Germany) which explores the drug culture of West Berlin. Other film examples of heroin addiction include *High Art* (1998), *Who'll Stop the Rain* (1978), *Mona Lisa* (1986), *Chappaqua* (1966), and *Lady Sings the Blues* (1972).

One of the most powerful drug films ever made is Gus van Sant's 1989 film *Drugstore Cowboy*, starring Matt Dillon as Bob, the leader of a group of four addicts who rob drugstores to maintain their habit. The film is especially memorable because of a very realistic cameo of William Burroughs playing an old, burned out, addicted, and defrocked priest living in a seedy motel. Bob sees in the priest the image of the man he (Bob) will eventually become. His decision to go straight and the dilemmas he faces (including attempts by his friends to seduce him back to the world they formerly shared) seem very realistic.

Alcohol[3]

Oliver Wendell Holmes, Jr. once remarked, "There is in all men a demand for the superlative, so much so that the poor devil who has no other way of reaching it attains it by getting drunk," and the use of alcohol can be traced back at least 5,000 years. The relationship among alcohol, drugs, and mysticism has been explored in books such as William James' *Varieties of Religious Experience* (1902) and Aldous Huxley's *Doors of Perception* (1954).

Alcohol and the Brain
Alcohol is quickly absorbed into the bloodstream and transported to the liver, which is capable of metabolizing about one ounce of 100-proof alcohol

---

3 In this chapter, we use the nonspecific, nondiagnostic term "alcoholism" to refer to both "alcohol dependence" and "alcohol abuse," because in many films the distinction is unclear. When it is clear, we differentiate between the two.

in an hour. If a person consumes only one drink per hour, the liver is able to keep up and alcohol does not affect the brain. However, at consumption rates greater than one drink per hour, the brain is quickly affected, with obvious consequences. In particular, there is rapid uptake of alcohol in the cerebellum, and this results in staggering, diminished coordination, and slower reaction times. Judgment is impaired, and alcohol can trigger aggression in some individuals. Although alcohol may initially facilitate sexuality by reducing inhibitions, at higher levels there is clear impairment of sexual functioning. In the words of Shakespeare, alcohol "provokes and it unprovokes; it provokes the desire, but it takes away the performance." (*Macbeth*, Act II, Scene 3).

The Lost Weekend

Billy Wilder's classic film *The Lost Weekend* (1945) is a powerful portrayal of alcoholism. The protagonist, Don Birnam (Ray Milland), is ready to sacrifice his brother's trust, his career as a writer, and the love of his girlfriend Helen (played by Jane Wyman) for one more drink. Early in the film, we see clear examples of denial, believed by many to be the characteristic defense mechanism of the alcoholic. Don Birnam minimizes the significance of his drinking as long as he can, but eventually he realizes that it is ruining his life. A scene in which Birnam watches an imaginary bat kill and eat a mouse is an effective illustration of the type of hallucinations characteristic of **delirium tremens**. Birnam eventually hocks his girlfriend's coat to get a gun and writes a suicide note. However, Helen arrives before he pulls the trigger, and the film ends with Birnam planning the novel he is going to write and, in a heavily symbolic gesture, dropping a cigarette in a glass of rye.

"One's too many and a hundred's not enough."

A bartender chides Don Birnam in Billy Wilder's *The Lost Weekend* (1945)

Despite an ending that is somewhat too pat for contemporary viewers, the film is still a dramatic illustration of the destructive effects of alcohol. Milland won an Academy Award for best actor for his portrayal of Birnam, and the film earned additional Academy Awards for best picture, best direc-

tor, and best screenplay. Billy Wilder, the film's director, consulted with Alcoholics Anonymous before beginning work on the film.

Patterns of Alcohol Abuse

DSM-IV-TR lists seven characteristic symptoms of dependence and requires that at least three occur at any time in the same 12-month period for the diagnosis of substance dependence. Some of the symptoms that apply to Don Birnam's alcoholism are presented in Table 7.2. The symptoms of dependence are the same for all psychoactive substances (alcohol or drugs).

Epidemiology of Alcoholism

The majority of American adults (about 65%) drink at least occasionally, and 1 in 10 adults consumes more than one ounce of alcohol per day. Males tend to tolerate alcohol more easily than females, in part because they typically weight more, and so the definition of a heavy drinker needs to be adjusted for males and females. However, it is generally accepted that individuals who average more than three drinks per day are heavy drinkers. Many individuals will consume far more than this average: 10% of all drinkers consume more than 50% of all alcohol.

It is estimated that more than 7% of the adult population in the United States – approximately 14 million people – are alcoholics. Alcoholism is one of the most serious public health problems in the United States, costing billions annually in lost productivity, increased healthcare costs, and accidents. Alcohol abuse contributes to about 30% of all motor vehicle accidents, and it is responsible for about half of all traffic fatalities.

About 10% of adults seeking treatment by physicians are dependent on alcohol, and about a third of admissions to general hospitals are for alcohol-related problems. The mortality rate for alcoholics is 2–3 times greater than that of the general population, and the life span of alcoholics is 10–12 years shorter. In addition, the children of alcoholic parents are at increased risk for hyperactivity, low IQ, emotional problems, child abuse, and fetal alcohol syndrome (NIAAA, 2000). Despite the severity of these problems, less than 10% of those addicted to alcohol will receive treatment for their problems.

The Portrayal of Alcoholism in Films

Images of alcohol and drinking are ubiquitous in contemporary films, and one is hard-pressed to name adult films in which alcohol use is not portrayed. This may reflect the fact that alcohol affects everyone directly or indirectly.

Table 7.2. Criteria for alcohol dependence

Criteria	Examples from *The Lost Weekend*
1. Alcohol is consumed in a larger amount or over a longer period than the individual intended.	Birnam is drinking when the film begins, and he drinks throughout the film.
2. People know that their use of alcohol is excessive but fail in their attempts to control their drinking.	Birnam tries repeatedly to go on the wagon and has "taken the cure" at least once without success.
3. A great deal of time is devoted to acquiring alcohol, drinking it, or recovering from its effects. In severe cases, almost all of the individual's waking hours are devoted to the substance.	Birnam is preoccupied with rye and has hidden it throughout his apartment. He thinks about little else, and he steals a purse and robs a liquor store to support his addiction.
4. Intoxication or withdrawal symptoms occur at work or in other inappropriate situations (e.g., while driving a car).	Birnam has quit writing altogether and has pawned his typewriter to buy rye.
5. Important social, occupational, or recreational activities are replaced by alcohol.	Birnam's relationship with his brother is seriously damaged by his drinking, and he avoids spending a weekend in the country with his family. He also comes close to destroying his relationship with his girlfriend.
6. Alcohol use persists, despite increasing awareness of the problems it causes.	Birnam describes himself as a "drunk," and he is acutely aware of his declining prowess as a writer.
7. Tolerance develops, and an increased amount of alcohol is required to produce the same effect. (Tolerance is less marked for alcohol than for some other drugs.)	The film shows Birnam drinking approximately two quarts of rye per day, far more than most people would be able to tolerate.
8. Withdrawal symptoms develop when the individual cuts back on their use of alcohol.	Birnam develops delirium tremens and hallucinates in the film.
9. After experiencing withdrawal symptoms, the individual begins to drink to avoid these unpleasant experiences rather than to produce the pleasant feelings initially associated with alcohol use.	When questioned by a bartender about drinking so early in the morning, Birnam remarks, "At night it's a drink; in the morning it's medicine."

The early success of *The Lost Weekend* (1945) led to other films with alcoholism as a central theme, including *Key Largo* (1948), *Harvey* (1950), *Come Back Little Sheba* (1952), *A Star Is Born* (1954), *Cat on a Hot Tin Roof* (1958), and *Days of Wine and Roses* (1962). Other relevant films include *Who's Afraid of Virginia Woolf?* (1966), *Arthur* (1981), *Barfly* (1981), *Tender Mercies* (1983), *Paris, Texas* (1984), *Under the Volcano* (1984), *Hoosiers* (1986), *Ironweed* (1987), *The Verdict* (1987), and *Clean and Sober* (1988).

In contrast to the sobering representations of alcoholism in films such as *Clean and Sober* (discussed later in the chapter), some films portray the alcoholic as happy and carefree. *Harvey* (1950) and *Arthur* (1981) are the two most obvious examples. Writing about *Arthur*, Vincent Canby (1981, p. 10) noted:

Not since Nick and Nora Charles virtually made the dry martini into the national drink... has there been quite so much boozing in a movie without hidden consequenc-

es. Arthur drinks scotch the way people now drink Perrier... When he goes giggling about town, sloshed to the eyeballs, he's not seen as a case history but as eccentric.

Unfortunately, the film presents an appealing model of Arthur tooling about Long Island in his Rolls-Royce. In the film, he has the good fortune to have a chauffeur; most of the teenage audience emulating his example won't be so lucky.

Movies *reflect* social mores as interpreted by filmmakers, and this certainly applies to the use of alcohol. In the recent film *Revolutionary Road* (2008), alcohol plays an important role in anesthetizing the boredom and rigidity of gender roles of the 1950s. In turn, movies *affect* social mores in a cyclical manner. A film presentation of the ways in which families are affected by alcoholism is found in *When a Man Loves a Woman* (1994). Other powerful films about alcoholism and its treatment include *Leaving Las Vegas* (1995), in which Nicholas Cage willingly drinks through graphically depicted delirium tremens until his death, Steve Buscemi's *Trees Lounge* (1996), and *Drunks* (1997). This last film is an especially helpful introduction to Alcoholics Anonymous (AA) and is highly recommended to anyone who has not had an opportunity to visit an open AA meeting. In addition, anyone interested in the way in which alcoholism is portrayed in films should read an excellent book by Norman Denzin, *Hollywood Shot by Shot: Alcoholism in American Cinema* (1991).

The functional impact of alcoholism is portrayed in the film *The Prize Winner of Defiance, Ohio* (2005), starring Julianne Moore and Woody Harrelson as the parents of 10 children growing up in the 1950s. Harrelson gives a strong performance as Kelly Ryan, an alcoholic who spends his weekly paycheck on alcohol, to the point that the family cannot afford milk and risk foreclosure of their home. Kelly shows a childlike dependency, and he is unable to care for his children or take care of the house. He is enabled by a community that, true to the time and culture, had no diagnosis or solutions for alcoholism; a police officer arrives after a dramatic incident resulting from Kelly's alcohol abuse and simply talks about baseball; a priest takes it a step further in the wrong direction and places blame on Kelly's wife, Evelyn, saying she has to try harder to give him a better home.

"This has been going on for a very long time. Every night he drinks a six pack and a pint of whiskey and by the end of the week there's nothing left of his paycheck. It's all gone to the liquor store."

Evelyn Ryan describing her husband's alcoholism to deaf ears in *The Prize Winner of Defiance, Ohio* (2005)

Following Meg Ryan's outstanding portrayal of a woman with alcoholism in *When a Man Loves a Woman* (1994), several films have portrayed depressed women who are either dependent upon or abuse alcohol; some recent examples include *House of Sand and Fog* (2003), *Monster's Ball* (2001), and *28 Days* (2000). In the latter film, Sandra Bullock portrays Gwen Cummings, a writer who is remanded to a rehabilitation setting by a judge after a drunk driving accident. Bullock's character displays symptoms of intoxication and

tolerance, as evidenced by excessive drinking, blackouts, use of an "eye opener" in the morning, and drinking throughout the day. In addition to extreme denial, she is impulsive and enjoys taking risks. Her out of control behavior includes carrying a drink wherever she goes, creating a spectacle at her sister's wedding, and inadvertently starting a fire while drinking, Her withdrawal symptoms are depicted as shaky hands, cravings, agitation, and a strong desire to immediately replace alcohol with pain medication, nicotine, or any other drug she can get her hands on. A complicating factor not uncommon for alcoholics is a partner who drinks heavily; in this film the boyfriend is an alcoholic and significant enabler who is very rejecting and critical of treatment. Helen Hunt plays an alcoholic working two jobs to pay her bills while secretly drinking in *Pay It Forward* (2000). Even a very small amount of alcohol is associated with violence by Kim Bassinger's character in *Final Analysis* (1992).

Alcohol abuse is evident in several lead characters, such as the title character (Robert Duvall) in *The Apostle* (1997), William Forrester (Sean Connery) in *Finding Forrester* (2000), Willie (Billy Bob Thornton) in *Bad Santa* (2003), and Matt Damon's character, Rannulph Junuh, in *The Legend of Bagger Vance* (2000), who drinks heavily upon returning from war. Alcohol only exacerbates his isolation and loneliness. Alex and his "droogs" use alcohol to "sharpen up" before committing violent acts in *A Clockwork Orange* (1971).

Alcoholism is particularly common in Western films, with saloons, bar fights, whiskey bottles, drunken gunfighters, and town drunks being staples of the genre (Wedding, 2001). *High Noon* (1952), *Stagecoach* (1939), *Shane* (1953), *Rio Bravo* (1959), and *Unforgiven* (1992) are classic examples.

"Now it's thirty days later. I've been to a funeral, been on about nine million job interviews, I'm $52,000 in debt, and I've got this chip. Suddenly I've got this startling belief that I'm an alcoholic and a drug addict."

Daryl Poynter (Michael Keaton) referring to his 30-day sobriety chip from Alcoholics Anonymous in *Clean and Sober* (1988)

Clean and Sober (1988) stars Michael Keaton as Daryl Poynter, an alcoholic and cocaine addict, and Morgan Freeman as an addictions counselor known simply as "Craig.". Some of the most interesting scenes in the film show Poynter at AA meetings and in group therapy. The film ends with Daryl getting his 30-day AA chip, acknowledging to the group that he is both an alcoholic and a drug addict, and realizing that each of us can be responsible only for his or her own behavior.

Sedative-Hypnotics

Sedative drugs produce a calm feeling of well-being in low doses and induce sleep in larger doses. These drugs include barbiturates such as amytal, nembutal, seconal, and phenobarbital, as well as **anxiolytics** (anxiety-reducing drugs) such as the **benzodiazepines** (Valium, Librium, etc.). Xanax, a more recently developed anxiolytic with a short half-life, combines the anxiety-reducing properties of other benzodiazepines with a mild antidepressant effect. It has become one of the most widely prescribed drugs in the United States. Some of the problems associated with Valium addiction are portrayed in the autobiography and film *I'm Dancing as Fast as I Can* (1982).

Barbiturates are muscle relaxants that induce feelings of well-being in small doses; with larger amounts, the user falls into a deep and profound sleep. Although tolerance develops extremely rapidly with barbiturates, the dose that is lethal remains relatively constant. This puts the barbiturate abuser at high risk and is one of the reasons barbiturates are rarely prescribed for anxiety. However, they remain the medication of choice in some cases of epilepsy.

The effects of barbiturates mimic the effects of alcohol and include symptoms such as slurred speech and staggering gait. These effects may be especially pronounced when barbiturates are combined with alcohol, and this combination is likely to be especially lethal. Marilyn Monroe committed suicide using a combination of alcohol and sleeping pills. In addition, barbiturate withdrawal is generally more difficult and more painful than withdrawal from narcotics, and it is more likely to be life threatening.

Benzodiazepines have largely replaced barbiturates for the treatment of insomnia because they are less addictive and not as likely to be successfully used in suicide attempts. Benzodiazepines are especially widely prescribed in the United States, and many people feel they are prescribed too frequently.

Stimulants

Stimulant drugs excite the central nervous system (CNS), fight fatigue, suppress one's appetite, and enhance mood. Cocaine, amphetamines, methamphetamines (meth), MDMA (ecstasy), nicotine, and caffeine are all stimulants with varying consequences of addiction. These substances activate the reward systems of the brain resulting in a pleasurable feeling. Cocaine and methamphetamine effects are highly addictive and can lead to serious consequences such as tremors, psychosis, and convulsions. Lethal overdose generally causes death from respiratory failure. Drug cravings and stress lead to drug seeking behavior. **Methylphenidates** (Ritalin, Concerta, etc.) are also classified as stimulants, but are legally prescribed for attention deficit/hyperactivity disorder.

Cocaine

Cocaine is usually snorted or, more rarely, injected intravenously. Sigmund Freud's recreational and therapeutic use of cocaine has been documented and is described in the film *The Seven Percent Solution* (1976), a historical fantasy in which Freud and Sherlock Holmes share their love of cocaine and pool their deductive talents to solve the puzzle of a missing patient.

The film *Blow* (2001), named for the street name of cocaine and based on the life of a cocaine smuggler, George Jung (Johnny Depp), chronicles the rise and fall of one of America's most powerful drug traffickers. This movie portrays the influence of the seductive forces of money and power on a seemingly typical adolescent of the sixties who would rather smoke marijuana at a California beach rather than work. He discovers that it is easy to make money selling marijuana. While imprisoned for his marijuana dealing, he was introduced to the world of cocaine trafficking. This film shows the social realities of the illegal, but profitable, drug culture. George also displays the physiological and psychological symptoms of addiction and withdrawal.

"The official toxicity limit for humans is between one and one and half grams of cocaine depending on body weight. I was averaging five grams a day, maybe more. I snorted ten grams in ten minutes once. I guess I had a high tolerance."

George Jung in *Blow* (2001)

Other compelling films dealing with cocaine addiction include *The Bad Lieutenant* (1992), starring Harvey Keitel, Martin Scorsese's *Goodfellas* (1990), Brian De Palma's *Scarface* (1983), and Alejandro Gonzalez Inarritu's *21 Grams* (2003), featuring a tormented woman played by Naomi Watts.

Crack cocaine, named after the sound made as the drug is consumed, takes the form of small "rocks" and is smoked. The effects of smoking crack cocaine occur almost immediately, but the high that is produced is relatively brief. Although crack is relatively inexpensive, crack addicts can quickly develop addictions that require hundreds of dollars each day to support. For many people, cocaine addiction leads to prostitution, theft, or violence. The day-to-day life of a crack dealer is portrayed by Djay (Terrence Howard) in *Hustle and Flow* (2005), a man who tries to make money to support his family but begins to question himself as to what kind of life he ultimately wants to be leading. *Half Nelson* (2006) is a well-directed film in which Ryan Gosling portrays a drug addicted teacher/coach of inner city students in a racially diverse neighborhood. He uses cocaine regularly – alone and with strange women – and smokes crack in the girl's locker room after a game. While he is a creative and engaging teacher, his drug addiction leads him to be distant, avoidant, angry, tired in class, and disengaged from his family.

MacArthur Park

The independent film *MacArthur Park* (2001), depicts Cody, a man addicted to crack and struggling to leave both his addiction and the park where he lives with other homeless crack addicts. He has a reason to leave: His son recently found him and his son has a home where Cody could recover. This film depicts the obstacles of crack addiction Cody must overcome in order to leave.

"I'm not homeless I just don't wanna go home."

Cody in *MacArthur Park* (2001)

The film explores a world of crack addiction where extensive drug abuse and dependence – as well as drug selling and producing – are depicted. The film's characters use large amounts of crack to cope with their pain and to avoid withdrawal effects. A variety of characters are depicted, and each has a different relationship with the park's drug world: Some are leaving the lifestyle; others are trying to leave, entering the world, deteriorating in it, or have no interest in leaving; while still others are simply "lost causes."

The screenplay was written by Tyrone Atkins, a man who was homeless in Los Angeles' MacArthur Park and addicted to crack cocaine; he wrote most of the story while in jail; after leaving jail, he returned to the park before entering a rehabilitation program.

Sweet Nothing

Another film illustrating the degradation associated with crack addiction is *Sweet Nothing* (1996), a true story based on a set of diaries discovered in an abandoned apartment in the Bronx. The film demonstrates the corrosive effects of the protagonist's addiction on his marriage, his relationship with his children, his friends, and his job. At one point, Angelo, the lead character, actually misses his father's funeral because he has an opportunity to get high and this need has come to supersede all others. Angelo loses the ability to become aroused by his wife, and we watch him become increasingly paranoid as the film progresses.

Cocaine has affected the lives and careers of numerous actors and directors. For example, Tommy Rettig (best known as Jeff, Lassie's master in the TV series) was sentenced to five years in federal prison for smuggling cocaine; Richard Pryor became badly burned as a result of an explosion related to smoking crack cocaine; and when Rainer Werner Fassbinder, considered by many to be Germany's finest director, died at the age of 37, his death was attributed to heart failure resulting from a combination of barbiturates and cocaine.

Amphetamines

Common amphetamines include **amphetamine** (Benzedrine), **dextroamphetamine** (Dexedrine), and **methamphetamine** (Methedrine). Amphetamines or derivatives are commonly found in nasal decongestants and appetite suppressants. These agents are taken orally. Methamphetamine crystals ("ice"), a highly concentrated form of amphetamine, can also be smoked, injected or taken orally, producing a high that can last as long as 14 hours. Khat, a shrub grown in Africa and the Middle East, produces leaves that can be chewed to produce an amphetamine-like effect. The use of khat is referred to in *Black Hawk Down* (2001). In *Walk the Line* (2005), a drama based on the life of Johnny Cash,

Joaquin Phoenix is masterful in the role of the musician. The film tells the story of Cash's rise in the music business, his history of amphetamine abuse, and his love for singer June Carter (Reese Witherspoon). Cash chronically abused prescription drugs, among other substances, often using them to manage tension and stress. Tolerance and withdrawal (both physiological and psychological) are well-portrayed, as is intoxication as Cash falls over on stage while performing a song. The film parallels *Ray* (2004) in that both depict renowned musicians who overcome trauma, rise to the top of the music business, fall dangerously into drugs, are unfaithful in their marriages, lead a double life, recover from drug dependance, make a comeback in their music, and inspire millions.

Amphetamines are highly addictive, and tolerance for drugs like methamphetamine develops rapidly. There is a characteristic withdrawal syndrome that includes depression, fatigue, nightmares, insomnia or sometimes hypersomnia, increased appetite, and either psychomotor retardation or agitation. This "crashing" effect appears to be the price the user must pay for the euphoria that accompanies the initial drug use. Amphetamine-induced psychoses often produce symptoms that closely resemble those found with serious mental disorders such as schizophrenia.

The film *Dopamine* (2003) features a lead character who engages in heavy use of stimulants. He gets amphetamine pills from a drug dealer and stays up all night working; in one scene, he has lined up seven cups of coffee next to his computer. Two better films that offer more compelling portrayals of stimulant abuse are *Requiem for a Dream* (2000) and *Spun* (2002).

Requiem for a Dream

The unforgettable *Requiem for a Dream* (2000) tells the stories of four lonely, desperate characters, each on the wrong track and each destroying his or her life with drugs. Uppers are not the only drug portrayed in the film, which notably contains one of the most descriptive, yet disturbing, portrayals of heroin addiction; essentially, these characters will take any drug available. Drugs take the place of food, sex, life goals, and just about everything else. The effect of drugs on the body and mind is unrelenting. Sara (Ellen Burstyn) takes drugs to lose weight so that she can appear in a live broadcast of a television show. Her son, Harry (Jared Leto), repeatedly steals Sara's television set (even though it is chained to the wall) and pawns it for drugs.

Director Darren Aronofsky uses extreme close-ups to demonstrate the effects of drugs. He shows characters swallowing pills, injecting substances, and snorting drugs followed by predictable physiological effects (e.g. pupil dilation), all with exaggerated sound effects. Vigorous camera-work, editing, and split-screen techniques allow the viewer to experience the confusion and fast-paced world of addicts abusing "uppers."

In the end, each is alive but destroyed, well past the point of no return, living in a hospital, prison, psychiatric institution or on the streets as a prostitute. In his review, Roger Ebert appropriately labels this film as playing like "a travelogue of hell."

Spun

Spun (2002) is a devastatingly realistic portrayal of several methamphetamine addicts. Virtually every character is a meth addict – Mickey Rourke plays the cook, who sets up meth labs in various shady apartments until they blow up, and John Leguizamo plays Spider Mike, the addicted dealer. Another character dependent on methamphetamine is the cook's girlfriend, Nikki (Brittany Murphy), whose dog has turned green due to the meth lab. The lead character, Ross (Jason Schwartzman), is so preoccupied with using and having meth available at all times that he forgets he had chained a woman to his bed during sex. Ross wants to have another chance at a relationship with a different woman, Amy, who left Ross because of his meth abuse and moved on in her life; she is able to see through Ross's denial so patently evident in one of his comments, "You know what the best part is, Amy? I'm not hooked. I can stop at anytime."

"Spoof, dope, crank, creep, bomb, spank, shit, bang, zip, tweak, chard. Call it what you will, it's all methamphetamine. That's what I'm here for."

An opening quote from an addict in *Spun* (2002)

These characters are depicted doing meth around the clock – off a girl's body, off a urinal, and "doing a round" while driving. Symptoms of intoxication are present in each character: Inappropriate laughter, jerky, quick body language and movement, and completely trashed living quarters; this is a world in which no one sleeps, everyone talks fast, and no one has any real relationships. The post-intoxication impairment following the repeated pattern of getting high on meth and crashing to sleep after several days of being awake is called being "spun." All these characters surround themselves with meth – they all get spun. The consequences depicted are clear: The meth addict will eventually be jailed, hospitalized, blown up, or (if lucky) he or she will find a way to escape the lifestyle.

As in *Requiem for a Dream* (2000), the camera speeds everything up to let the viewer experience in some small way what it is like to take methamphetamines. A character inhales meth, and a close-up shows his eyes bloodshot and wide open; cartoon images accentuate thoughts and drug effects; other close-ups display spinning movements with pupils dilating and contracting.

Hallucinogens

Hallucinogens, sometimes referred to as psychedelics, are drugs that distort the perception of reality. Users report hallucinations involving all senses, **synesthesia** ("crossed" sensations, such as hearing sights and seeing sounds), and depersonalization. These drugs can also have profound effects on mood.

Hallucinogens can occur in the natural environment but are more often produced synthetically. Naturally occurring hallucinogens include **mescaline**, derived from the peyote cactus, and **psilocybin**, which is present in psilocybe mushrooms. Some Native Americans use psilocybe mushrooms in religious ceremonies.

Mescaline can also be produced in a laboratory. However, the best-known and most widely used of all synthetic hallucinogens is **lysergic acid diethylamide** (LSD). It is most often swallowed as a pill, but it can also be mixed with a fluid, licked off of blotter paper, or swallowed in sugar cubes or gelatin sheets. LSD is colorless, tasteless, and extremely potent. It produces varied symptoms and can result in affective changes that range from euphoria to absolute terror. The most dramatic effects are often sensory in nature: When the drug experience is positive, it allows the user "to see a world in a grain of sand / And a heaven in a wild flower, / Hold infinity in the palm of your hand / And eternity in an hour" (William Blake, *Auguries of Innocence*). Unfortunately, the experience is not always this benign, and injury or death can result from bad decisions made while under the influence of the drug. Some users have also reported "flashbacks" in which they re-experience the sensory phenomenon associated with previous trips weeks or years after last using the drug. The drug is not addictive, but tolerance develops rapidly.

In a *Playboy* interview, the renowned director Stanley Kubrick made the following constructive observation about LSD:

> One of the things that's turned me against LSD is that all the people I know who use it have a peculiar inability to distinguish between things that are really interesting and stimulating and things that appear to be so in the state of universal bliss that the drug induces on a 'good' trip. They seem to completely lose their critical faculties and disengage themselves from some of the most stimulating areas of life. Perhaps when everything is beautiful, nothing is beautiful.

In the film *In the Name of the Father* (1993), prisoners cope with the monotony of prison life by licking LSD off the back of a jigsaw puzzle. The puzzle is a large world map, and the prisoners get high "one country at a time." The LSD experience is also portrayed in any number of films from the 1960s that document the youth culture of that period.

Phencyclidine (PCP), also known as angel dust, is another powerful hallucinogen that has been used since the early 1960s. It can be taken in pill form or dusted onto marijuana and smoked. The drug produces symptoms even more marked than those associated with LSD and may result in analgesia, depersonalization, paranoia, rage reactions, or schizophrenia-like psychoses. Hallucinogen use is depicted in *Easy Rider* (1969) and *Fear and Loathing in Las Vegas* (1998).

The stylized, partly computerized characters of *A Scanner Darkly* (2006) portray a science fiction/fantasy world characterized by paranoia, drug abuse, and government control. Richard Linklater directs Keanu Reeves, Robert Downy, Jr., Winona Rider, and Woody Harrelson in this story about a family man who is unhappy so he leaves his life to become a narcotics agent. During his training, he learns that good agents do drugs in moderation. The made-up drug in the film is Substance D (D stands for despair, desolation, and death) to which 40% of the population is addicted. A number of intoxication and withdrawal symptoms are dramatized including tactile hallucinations (e.g., bugs crawling all over the body), shakiness, bloodshot eyes, extreme paranoia, dramatic anger, and a suicide attempt. One character develops an extensive hallucination in which a foreign creature spends eternity reading his life sins without ever pausing.

Inhalants

Common substances that inhalant addicts inhale are glue, gasoline, paint thinners, spray paints, cleaners, and spray-can propellants. Methods used to inhale the vapors include soaking a rag with the substance, placing the substance in a paper or plastic bag, inhaling directly from the container, or spraying the substance into the nose or mouth. The chemicals inhaled reach the lungs and bloodstream very rapidly.

Love Liza

In *Love Liza* (2002), Wilson (masterfully acted by Philip Seymour Hoffman) is a computer technician who becomes addicted to inhaling gasoline following his wife's suicide. This is a fairly bizarre and atypical bereavement reaction. Wilson is an emotional wreck and puts all his energy and concerns into "huffing" gasoline. The method he uses is to soak a rag with gasoline and hold the rag over his face while he inhales. He is frequently shown bending over to smell gasoline at gas station pumps and the opening in his car's tank.

When intoxicated, Wilson's speech becomes slurred, distorted, inappropriate, and at times nonsensical. His interpersonal relationship skills dramatically diminish to a level that appears confusing, rude, and distant to the person speaking with him. Cinematic elements enhance the effects of his blurred vision, and in one scene he experiences hallucinations. Wilson vacillates from complete euphoria from the gasoline highs, which lead to grossly inappropriate behavior such as swimming in a lake while remote-controlled boats are racing and cheerfully attempting to converse with other drivers on a highway, to severe agitation and anger outbursts evident when he is not huffing or is awakening from a blackout. Wilson becomes more isolated as the film progresses and would probably be completely isolated if it were not for people eager to support him. His judgment is impaired in other ways such as when he supplies two young huffing adolescents who have been banned from gas stations with the intoxicant.

The consequences of his huffing include the loss of a new job, damage to important relationships, and his house burning down. Wilson is experiencing so much pain that he can't bring himself to read his wife's suicide note; instead, he carries it around with him as a constant reminder of her death. Upon eventually reading it, he knows exactly what to do. Overall, this portrayal of a serious and severe addiction is realistic, honest, and not melodramatic.

Cannabis

Marijuana is obtained from the hemp plant *Cannabis sativa*. The active ingredient in marijuana is the drug **tetrahydrocannabinol** (THC). The greater the THC content, the more potent the drug. The THC content of marijuana purchased illegally varies widely, but, in general, THC levels have been increasing over the past three decades, and the marijuana used today is approximately five times stronger than that widely available on street corners and on college campuses in the 1960s. The resin of the *Cannabis sativa* plant can be used to produce **hashish**, a stronger form of the drug.

Marijuana has medicinal value, and it can be obtained legally for the treatment of some disorders. The drug enhances appetite and is often helpful in controlling the nausea associated with chemotherapy. Other physical effects include tachycardia, sedation, and psychomotor impairment. Like the hallucinogens, marijuana can produce markedly varied psychological effects, depending on the mood and situation of the user. Most often, the drug produces mild euphoria, giddiness, and a general sense of well-being. However, at a different time and in a different setting the same drug can produce marked apprehension or paranoia.

Examples of marijuana use can be found in countless films. One especially memorable scene involves a group of characters (played by Dennis Hopper, Peter Fonda, and Jack Nicholson) sitting around a campfire and smoking marijuana in *Easy Rider* (1969).

The low-budget, anti-drug exploitation film *Reefer Madness* (1936), formerly titled *Tell Your Children*, became a cult classic among young people who smoked marijuana in the 1960s. Many people believed the film was tongue-in-cheek; however, it was meant to be a serious film. It begins by dramatizing marijuana with introductory text referring to it as "ghastly," a menace to society, a "deadly narcotic," and "public enemy #1," followed by various mock newspaper headlines on the dangers and societal consequences of marijuana use. The film turns to a parent meeting in which an expert speaks of the dangers to concerned parents and the need for a united front against marijuana; the bulk of the film (which runs like a satirical story) revolves around a group of normal-looking drug dealers who get adolescents addicted to marijuana by throwing wild jazz parties. Everyone who uses marijuana has serious deleterious effects – laughing foolishly and uncontrollable, extreme shakiness, intense anger and edgyness, pacing, terror and panic, and paranoia; further effects are sexual abuse, suicide, and murder. Marijuana is clearly portayed as a drug that changes one's character for the worse. The film ends with the same parent meeting noting that these are the dangers and consequences of addiction and concludes with a finger pointing at the camera and an admonition that the viewer's children could be next. Clearly this film does little to educate the viewer about marijuana, its side effects, or consequences; if it was, ever taken at face value misconceptions would widely be perpetrated. The film does document the misconceptions that people have had in the past and the power of group contagion and its ability to produce paranoia and hysteria.

"Your honor, in this case the state waives trial of defendant Ralph Wiley. It is convinced that he is hopelessly and incurably insane, a condition caused by the drug marijuana to which he was addicted. It is our contention, your honor, that the defendant be placed in an institution for the criminally insane for the rest of his natural life."

A psychologist as expert witness reporting to the judge on the condition of a man who has used marijuana in *Reefer Madness* (1936)

The Cheech and Chong movies celebrate marijuana use and ridicule its classification as a narcotic. Other movies emphasizing marijuana include the Coen Brothers' noir *The Big Lebowski* (1998) and the outlandish comedy *Half Baked* (1998).

Polysubstance Dependence

Polysubstance refers to the use of three or more groups of substances (excluding nicotine and caffeine) with no particular substance predominating. *Naked Lunch* (1991), the David Cronenberg film adaptation of the William Burroughs' book, is fascinating albeit not always tightly linked to the novel. William Lee, the protagonist, is a polydrug addict trying to go straight. Unfortunately, both he and his wife are addicted to bug spray, and Bill's job as an exterminator makes it almost impossible

for him to avoid this particular drug. The cinematic representation of visual hallucinations in *Naked Lunch* is especially fascinating.

In the B movie, *Shadow Hours* (2000), a young man working as a gas station attendant is lured back into drug addiction by a wealthy, mysterious writer who advises the young man he must go into the abyss before he can get back to sobriety. The two men visit dance clubs, drug fests, strip clubs, fight clubs, sadomasochistic clubs, and torture events.

Tobacco

The drug most often portrayed on television and in films is tobacco. Epidemiological studies suggest it is also our most lethal drug. The Centers for Disease Control and Prevention (CDC) estimate that tobacco accounts for 440,000 deaths annually in the United States (approximately one out of every five deaths). Although fatality rates are only one index of the severity of a drug problem, it is clear that none of the drugs typically regarded as our most "serious" are ultimately as dangerous as cigarettes.

In part because of the pain of withdrawal, less than 5% of smokers are successful in their attempts to stop smoking, although about 35% try to stop each year (and 80% express the desire to stop). Some of the symptoms associated with nicotine withdrawal include dysphoric or depressed mood, insomnia, irritability/anger, anxiety, difficulty concentrating, restlessness, decreased heart rate, and increased appetite or weight gain.

The morbidity and mortality associated with tobacco use have been underscored by a series of reports issued since 1964 by the Office of the Surgeon General. Partially in response to the massive public education efforts spearheaded by the surgeon general, numerous Americans have stopped smoking. In addition, the American Medical Association and the American Public Health Association have been very vocal in their opposition to tobacco use.

Various films depict people smoking cigarettes, and it is actually difficult to find a standard drama or comedy where smokers are absent. *Coffee and Cigarettes* (2003), directed and written by Jim Jarmusch, explores the use of nicotine and another under-rated addictive substance, caffeine. Several separated vignettes of different characters are connected only by conversation and the use of coffee and cigarettes, some characters using the substances more compulsively than others. There are comical interactions between musicians Iggy Pop and Tom Waits, between actors Alfred Molina and Steve Coogan, between Bill Murray and two members of the Wu-Tang Clan (where Murray drinks coffee straight from the pot), and between Cate Blanchett and herself. Gwyneth Paltrow's character, Margo, is addicted to nicotine and finds creative ways to hide her smoking habits in *The Royal Tenenbaums* (2001). Ironically, the satirical comedy *Thank You for Smoking* (2005), while being about a lobbyist who works for a marketing organization supported by major tobacco companies, does not portray a single character smoking in the film. Aaron Eckhart plays Nick Naylor, a master-of-spin, who is able to argue that cigarettes should be made available for patients with cancer. In one scene, he is abducted and covered with nicotine patches; however, what keeps him alive is the fact that he has a high tolerance from heavy smoking (though he is never shown smoking).

Substances Depicted in Films

Countless films depict characters abusing substances, and at times it is unclear what substance is being abused. Rather than labeling the character as a "drug addict," it is more important to decipher the particular substance being abused as each substance has different characteristics (e.g., tolerance, withdrawal, and intoxication levels). Table 7.3. helps make this clarification with some of the best portrayals of substance abuse in films. The number of psi's (Ψ) provides a rating scale, further emphasizing the importance of each – see Appendix F for details on this scale.

Substance Abuse Recovery

Many films depict characters who are former substance abusers in full recovery (i.e., sustained full remission) and are not depicted as abusing or relapsing in the film. Support groups are a key component for many individuals' recovery from alcohol and drug abuse. The founding of AA, by Bill Wilson and Dr. Bob Smith, which has paved the way for countless support groups over the decades, is portrayed in *My Name is Bill W.* (1986).

Rachel Getting Married (2008) is a Jonathan Demme film that realistically portrays substance abuse recovery, emphasizing some of the family dynamics that can erupt when an addict returns home from rehabilitation. Kym (Anne Hathaway) leaves rehab for a few days to spend time with her family as they prepare for the wedding of her sister, Rachel. The family tries to accept her although they cannot help but be hypervigilant, cautious, and tense at times. Kym displays some explosiveness and many issues emerge from the past (e.g., Kym's tragic incident years ago when she was supposed to be looking after her baby brother, however, she drove off a bridge while high on drugs and he died in the accident) and from the present (e.g., tension with her sister's best friend seemingly competing for Rachel's attention). At times, Kym's sickness emerges, such as when she gives a rehearsal dinner speech that is tangential and self-involved (and embarassing for her family) before taking time to comment on the bride and groom. Remarkably, Kym maintains her sobriety throughout the party-filled weekend and the tensions and issues that come up. However, after a physical and emotional fight with her mother, she drives her car off the road, perhaps as a suicide attempt (symbolically atoning for the egregious behavior years ago that killed her brother). It is never clear what drug(s) Kym is addicted to, but the film alludes to alcohol and other substances. Despite the dreary topic, the film illustrates the importance of humor and hope, two important elements for an addict and a family dealing with an addict. The film is also strong in its portrayal of support group meetings, which are accurately portrayed as real, supportive, and helpful for those who participate. Individuals share their personal stories, recite the 12 steps, and common 12-step adages (e.g., "keep coming back, it works if you work it"), prayers (e.g., the serenity prayer), and themes (e.g., life can feel boring without substances) are shared. Kym is persistent in her life with her family, which is critical for substance abuse recovery, and puts forth good effort; she is difficult yet endearing for both her family and the viewer.

28 Days (2000), discussed earlier in the chapter, also depicts 12-step support groups; in this case, it is AA. In addition to the serenity prayer, inspiring AA adages used include: "It works, if you work it, you're worth it"; "God never gives us more than we can handle"; and "we are better, together." An alcohol/drug counselor (Steve Buscemi) is a recovering addict (also common for alcohol/drug counselors) and shares his story as a source of inspiration.

Another film depicting a character trying to make it outside of an institution (although in this case it is a release from prison) is Sherry Swanson

Table 7.3. Substances abused with accompanying film examples

Abused Substance	Film Example(s)	Comments	Rating
Alcohol	*Leaving Las Vegas* (1995)	Nicholas Cage as an alcoholic giving up	ΨΨΨ
	Born on the Fourth of July (1989)	Tom Cruise as a bitter veteran	ΨΨΨ
	House of Sand and Fog (2003)	Jennifer Connelly relapsing	ΨΨΨΨ
Heroin	*Pulp Fiction* (1994)	Uma Thurman mistakes cocaine for heroin in classic Tarantino scene	ΨΨΨΨ
	Quitting (2001)	Deterioration and withdrawals	ΨΨΨ
Sedatives /Hypnotics	*I'm Dancing as Fast as I Can* (1982)	Valium addiction	ΨΨ
Cocaine	*Traffic* (2000)	Dynamic, integrated drug film	ΨΨΨΨ
	Blow (2001)	Johnny Depp as a famous cocaine importer	ΨΨΨ
Crack Cocaine	*MacArthur Park* (2001)	Gripping realism in LA	ΨΨΨ
Amphetamine	*Walk the Line* (2005)	Johnny Cash mixing uppers & song	ΨΨΨΨ
	Requiem for a Dream (2000)	Ellen Burstyn's role is unforgettable	ΨΨΨ
	Spun (2002)	Methamphetamine addiction and lifestyle	ΨΨΨ
Hallucinogens	*Fear and Loathing in Las Vegas* (1998)	Normalizes drug use	ΨΨ
Inhalants	*Love Liza* (2002)	Philip Seymour Hoffman depicts gasoline huffing	ΨΨΨ
Steroids	*The Wrestler* (2008)	Mickey Rourke pumping for a fight	ΨΨΨ
Marijuana	*The Big Lebowski* (1998)	Jeff Bridges as "The Dude"	ΨΨ
Nicotine	*The Royal Tenenbaums* (2001)	Gwyneth Paltrow's character tries to hide her smoking habits	ΨΨΨΨ
Caffeine	*Coffee and Cigarettes* (2003)	Vignettes with both substances	ΨΨΨ
Combination	*Eyes Wide Shut* (1999)	Speedball (cocaine & heroin)	ΨΨΨΨ
Polysubstance	*Naked Lunch* (1991)	Bug spray and other substances	ΨΨ

(Maggie Gyllenhaal) in *SherryBaby* (2006). Sherry has been clean for two and a half years following a 6-year heroin addiction; however, she has strong urges within four days of her release. She tries to do what is right but she has few coping resources and she still craves heroin. She functions out of a survivor mentality – she is manipulative, lacks empathy, and displays poor social judgment; she has significant inner rage and aggression and frequently slams doors and curses. In one scene, her emotionally aloof father takes advantage of her and fondles her breasts when she is having a vulnerable moment; the stress associated with her father's sexual abuse, triggers an immediate relapse. The opening song of the film repeats the line "there's an angel on my left but the devil's on my right," which describes the inner struggles of the addict, particularly those who are trying hard to maintain sobriety.

Benicio Del Toro plays a recovery alcoholic and ex-con who becomes a born-again Christian

Table 7.4. The 12 steps and 12 traditions[4]

1. We admitted that we were powerless over alcohol – that our lives had become unmanageable.

2. Came to believe that a power greater than ourselves could restore us to sanity.

3. Made a decision to turn our will and our life over to the care of God *as we understood Him*.

4. Made a searching and fearless moral inventory of ourselves.

5. Admitted to God, to ourselves, and to another human being the exact nature of our wrongs.

6. Were entirely ready to have God remove all these defects of character.

7. Humbly asked Him to remove our shortcomings.

8. Made a list of all persons we had harmed, and became willing to make amends to them all.

9. Made direct amends to such people whenever possible, except when to do so would injure them or others.

10. Continued to take personal inventory and, when we were wrong, promptly admitted it.

11. Sought through prayer and meditation to improve our conscious contact with God *as we understood Him*, praying only for knowledge of His will for us and the power to carry that out.

12. Having had a spiritual awakening as the result of these steps, we tried to carry this message to alcoholics, and to practice these principles in all our affairs.

in *21 Grams* (2003). In *A Mighty Wind* (2003), Eugene Levy's folk singing character, Mitch, has flat affect, slowed speech and thought, and presents with wide-eyed expressions, each assumed to relate to significant drug abuse in his past.

The 12 steps are a set of guidelines that have become a tradition for numerous support groups. These important beliefs have revolutionized the conceptualization and treatment of substance abusers and have contributed to saving the lives of countless addicts. Table 7.4. lists the 12-step approach used by Alcoholic's Anonymous; however, the word "alcohol" can be easily replaced by "drugs" (Narcotic's Anonymous), "sex," "gambling," "money," or "food," depending on the person's addiction.

A young man, Hongsheng, at one time a famous actor, is living with his parents to maintain sobriety from heroin addiction. He is bitter and verbally abusive toward them. Through flashbacks, the viewer learns of his deterioration due to heroin dependence and the ramifications of its abuse; he is left with a renowned career in shambles, loss of several friends, a delusional obsession with John Lennon, hallucinations, and significant anger outbursts.

"I was fighting with myself. I didn't know what I was fighting about."

Hongsheng in *Quitting* (2001)

International Films: Substance Use Disorders

The film, *Quitting* (2001, China), by Chinese director Zhang Yang, depicts heroin abuse and withdrawal, intermixing both through flashbacks.

Vodka Lemon (2003, France/Italy/Switzerland/Armenia) is a slow but engaging comedy/drama with an interesting and subtle vibrancy from exiled Iraqi Kurd director, Hiner Saleem. The film takes place in Armenia, post-USSR and depicts the romance of a widowed man and woman after they

---

4 The 12 steps are reprinted with permission of Alcoholics Anonymous World Services, Inc. Permission to reprint the Twelve Steps does not mean that AA has reviewed or approved the contents of this publication, nor that AA agrees with the views expressed herein. AA is a program of recovery from alcoholism only – use of Twelve Steps in connection with programs and activities which are patterned after AA, but which address other problems, or in any other non-AA context, does not imply otherwise.

meet during their daily, separate trips to honor the gravesite of those they've lost. The background of this minimalist film is alcohol. It seems that all of the townspeople drink alcohol as a coping strategy that is accepted as an established part of daily life. Everybody drinks all the time, hence the

Critical Thinking Questions

- Can a case be made for the prohibition of alcohol and tobacco, or is this simply a societal experiment that has already been tried without success? On the other hand, would the legalization of some drugs lead to a decrease in drug addiction?
- What are the advantages and disadvantages of the 12-step approach?
- Compare the number of films depicting a character using only one substance with those using multiple agents. Which substance is most likely to be a solitary addiction?
- Compare the social treatment of persons addicted to legal substances (alcohol, nicotine) with those addicted to illegal agents (cocaine, heroin, marijuana).
- What role, if any, did heroin play in Ray Charles' success? Were there any other addictions evident in the film?
- Should intoxication from alcohol and drugs be a mitigating factor in sentencing prisoners for crimes they committed while high (e.g., murder in *Dead Man Walking* (1995))?
- How important is it for therapists treating alcoholism and drug abuse to have been in treatment for these problems themselves? Can a non-addict ever truly understand the needs and problems of the addict?
- What are the arguments for and against the legalization of drugs in the United States?
- How many places do you suppose there are in the world similar to the park in *MacArthur Park* (2001)? Does every major city have such a place?
- Whom do you find to be the most sympathetic character in *Requiem for a Dream* (2000)? Does your choice change at different points of the film?
- Do most methamphetamine addicts behave in ways similar to the characters in *Spun* (2002)?
- What is the difference between "recovered" and "recovering" in addiction terminology?
- If an individual has one definite addiction, how likely are they to have a second addiction?
- What is the relationship between drugs and violence? Which drugs have the highest incidence of aggressive behavior? Identify films that support your answer.

need for the only store in town – a "vodka lemon" shop where people purchase vodka by the bottle. No unruly behaviors or symptoms result from the extensive alcohol use, barring one exception which may or may not have been alcohol related.

No Such Thing (2001, Iceland/US), a film by independent auteur Hal Hartley, tells the story of a young woman (Sarah Polley) who goes to investigate the story of a "monster" who has killed a film crew (including her cameraman-fiancé) in a remote Icelandic village. She tracks down the monster, who is an isolated, grotesque alcoholic, and befriends it, bringing it home to America despite the fact that the monster breathes fire, kills people at will, and is described as indestructible, beyond science and unable to even commit suicide. It is interesting to reflect on what the monster (and alcohol therein) represents, as well as the dichotomies that arise – hope/fear, good/evil, comedy/tragedy, denial/reality, and humanity/shadow.

16 Years of Alcohol (2003, UK) portrays Frankie, an alcoholic, who as a child of an alcoholic observed his father's infidelity, alcoholism, and violence, and grew up to repeat the same patterns. The film pays homage to another film that mixes violence and substances, *A Clockwork Orange* (1971, US/UK); this film includes a scene in which a gang which has been drinking severely beats up a bartender in a tunnel, very similar to what Alex and his droogs do in an early scene in this classic film. Women with alcoholism are portrayed in *Rain* (2001, New Zealand) and *Walking on Water* (2002, Australia).

Further Exploration

If you have time to read just one book relevant to this chapter, make it:

Earleywine, M. (2009). *Substance use problems.* Cambridge, MA: Hogrefe & Huber Publishers.

If you only have time for one article, read:

Courtney, K. E., & Polich, J. (2009). Binge drinking in young adults: Data, definitions, and determinants. *Psychological Bulletin, 135,* 142–156.

Substance Use Disorders

Stimulants

Spun (2002)
Blow (2001)
Requiem for a Dream (2000)

Alcohol

The Lost Weekend (1945)
Days of Wine and Roses (1962)
Leaving Las Vegas (1995)

Opioids

Ray (2004)
Long Day's Journey into Night (1962)
Pulp Fiction (1994)
Sweet Nothing (1996)

Chapter 8

Sexual and Gender Identity Disorders

I'm not like everybody else. I'm a hermaphrodite.
Teena Brandon's self-diagnosis in *Boys Don't Cry* (1999)

Questions to Consider While Watching *Boys Don't Cry*

- How do films promote gender roles and sexual stereotypes?
- Which actors do you identify as especially masculine or feminine? Why?
- How would you react if you discovered that the person you were flirting with was actually impersonating someone of a different gender?
- Why are John and Tom so angry when they discover that Teena is actually female?
- Can you imagine yourself falling in love with someone who is a transsexual?
- How should parents decide about how to raise a child if the child is born with ambiguous genitalia?
- Freud once wrote: "Anatomy is destiny." What did he mean by this? Do you agree?
- Are gender identity problems like those illustrated in *Boys Don't Cry* common?
- Do gender identity disorders occur more often in (anatomical) males or females?
- What are the features that distinguish tranvestism, transsexualism, and homosexuality?
- Is it accurate to describe Teena Brandon as a lesbian?
- What are the behavioral characteristics that we use to identify whether or not a given individual is male or female?
- Is it more respectful to use masculine or feminine pronouns when referring to someone who is anatomically male but psychologically female?
- Is there any evidence that gender modification surgery contributes to the happiness of transsexuals? If so, should insurance companies be required by law to pay for this surgery if it is desired?
- What is the sexual orientation of a man who has a happy, well-adjusted relationship with a post-surgery male-to-female transsexual?
- Is it likely that someone like Teena Brandon would have been more comfortable and safer living in a large, metropolitan environment like San Francisco or Boston?

Patient Evaluation[3]

Patient's stated reason for coming: "There's something wrong with me. I've got a gender identity disorder."
History of the present illness: Teena Brandon is a 21-year-old female who presents with a self-diagnosed gender identity disorder. She reports feeling "like a boy" since early childhood. Her identity as a psychological male has been strong and persistent. Even as a very young child, Teena expressed little interest in playing with girls' toys. She remembers envying boys both their status and their games. Although she has never seen a psychiatrist or

---

3   This fictitious interview is based on the character portrayed in the film *Boys Don't Cry*. It is not intended in any way to represent an interview with the real Teena Brandon.

psychologist, Teena has read widely about gender identity disorders and she is quite knowledgeable about her current condition. She has told a woman she was dating that she is a hermaphrodite; however, she realizes this is incorrect, and reports she only uses the term because it makes it easier for others to understand her concerns about gender and self-identity. Teena has been – and remains – preoccupied with her wish to be identified as a male and to live as a man.

Past psychiatric illness, treatment, and outcomes: There is no significant history of psychiatric illness. Teena has never been hospitalized or treated by a psychologist or psychiatrist. She has frequently contemplated suicide but has never made a suicide attempt or gesture. She saw a guidance counselor in high school when she believed she was depressed, but she did not share her concerns about gender at that time.

Medical history: The medical history is not significant. According to the patient, she has been examined by several physicians, including gynecologists, all of whom assured her that her genitalia were anatomically and functionally "normal." Menses are regular, although this patient goes to great lengths to hide the fact that she is menstruating. Breast development is normal; Teena binds her breasts so they will not show underneath her clothes.

Psychosocial history: Teena Brandon was put up for adoption shortly after she was born, and she has never met her biological parents. She lived with a variety of foster parents; after turning 18, she moved to a trailer park in Lincoln, Nebraska where she lived with her older brother until approximately six months ago when she moved to Falls City. Teena was socially isolated and ostracized in school, and she reports that other children always regarded her as "peculiar." At the age of 13, Teena began to refer to herself as "Brandon Teena," and this is the name she uses whenever possible. She met normal developmental milestones, but has never had any interest in dating boys. She has been attracted to females since puberty, and typically fantasizes about women. Teena does not identify herself as a lesbian, but all of her sexual experiences to date have been with women. Teena does not allow the woman she dates to touch or view her genitals. There is a history of petty theft and forging checks.

Drug and alcohol history: Teena has been using and abusing both alcohol and drugs since her early teens. The list of abused substances includes marijuana, LSD, and (most frequently) methamphetamine. She has avoided legal difficulties, but acknowledges "blackouts" that have occurred on many occasions. Alcohol use occurs almost daily; recreational drugs are typically used at weekends, in part because Teena cannot afford more frequent use. Teena cannot remember the last time she went 24 hours without drinking beer; however, there is no evidence of withdrawal or other signs of alcoholism.

Behavioral observations: Teena is a slender and attractive young woman who came in for the evaluation dressed in blue jeans and a flannel shirt. Her hair was closely cropped. She asked that she be called Brandon, although she acknowledges that her legal name is Teena Brandon. She was diffident and quiet, but answered all questions that were asked. She was polite and cooperative. She appeared mildly anxious.

Mental status examination: Teena identified the day of the month as the 23rd rather than the 24th. There were no other errors on the Mini Mental State Examination, and this patient earned an overall score of 29/30.

Functional assessment: Teena is intelligent and friendly. She possesses considerable insight into her gender identity concerns, and she has read widely about these issues. Although she has only attained a high school education, it is likely that she could compete successfully in a college setting. Her excellent interpersonal skills and her self-effacing sense of humor will serve her well in a variety of occupational roles.

Strengths: Intelligence, social skills, humor, self-insight.

Diagnosis: Gender identity disorder, sexually attracted to females; alcohol abuse; rule out alcohol dependence.

Treatment plan: Continue to see this patient on a weekly basis to establish rapport and explore her feelings regarding gender. Consult with a specialist in gender identity disorders to see if Teena might be a candidate for hormone therapy or gender reassignment surgery.

Prognosis: Guarded. Teena's intelligence and interpersonal skills make her a good candidate for psychotherapy. She is adamant that she is a male, and no ambivalence is present; however, I continue to be concerned about both her deception involved in her attempts to "pass" as a male, and her misuse of alcohol and drugs.

Gender Identity Disorders

Although the *DSM-IV-TR* refers to gender identity disorders, the term **transsexual** is still widely used in clinical practice. Individuals who have a gender identity disorder are uncomfortable with their anatomic sex and believe they are trapped in the wrong body. There is often a strong desire to replace their genitals with the genitalia of the opposite sex; these urges can be intense enough to lead to self-castration in males. While identity issues usually originate in childhood, the diagnosis is given only after an individual has reached puberty. Those with gender identity disorder often suffer from concomitant depression, and suicide attempts are common (APA, 2000).

Boys Don't Cry and Other Gender Identity Films

Hilary Swank is unforgettable as Teena Brandon in Kimberly Peirce's 1999 film *Boy's Don't Cry*, and she won a Best Actress Academy Award for her role in this film. The film is based on a true story that had earlier been portrayed in a 1998 documentary titled *The Brandon Teena Story*.

Boys Don't Cry vividly portrays Brandon's attempts to pass as a male by using a rolled up sock as an ersatz penis, as well as her dismay when she is menstruating. She develops a loving, sensual, and happy relationship with Lana, portrayed by Chloë Sevigny. The film accurately presents Brandon's story, and it precisely captures the hatred and homophobia displayed by John Lotter and Marvin Nissen, two men who initially befriended Brandon and later raped and killed her after learning that they had been deceived about her gender identity. The interrogation by a prurient, insensitive, and bumbling sheriff is chilling and sadly accurate. The film doesn't glamorize Brandon, and it accurately presents the confusion, dismay, pathos, and despair that frequently accompany those situations in which one's anatomical gender doesn't match one's deepest perception of self. The film is required viewing for anyone interested in understanding more about transsexualism.

"God meant for me to be somebody else."

Roy in *Normal* (2003)

Other films focusing on gender identity disorder include *Normal* (2003) and *Soldier's Girl* (2003). All three of these films show the pain that a person with gender identity disorder faces and the struggles associated with sharing information about sexual identify with loved ones and society. In *Normal*, Roy (Tom Wilkinson) believes he was born in the wrong body and he wants a sex change operation. His wife of 25 years (Jessica Lange) expresses a variety of reactions – denial, shock, anger, rejection, depression, and finally acceptance – as they ultimately work to keep their marriage intact. Roy desires to be accepted by his congregation, co-workers, boss, children, and society, but each presents a different struggle. *Soldier's Girl* is

based on the tragic true story of Barry Winchell, a young man who enters the military and falls in love with a transsexual (a man who dressed as a woman in preparation for gender modification surgery).

Transamerica (2005) is a touching film that stars Felicity Huffman as Bree, a presurgical male to female transsexual who is saving money and seeing a therapist in preparation for her upcoming operation. She receives a phone call from her son, Toby, a son she didn't know she had (he was the byproduct of a casual college affair). Her therapist makes reuniting with her son a prerequisite for surgery, and this leads to a long road trip from New York to Phoenix, where Bree reunites with her dysfunctional family.

"Don't you find it odd that plastic surgery can cure a mental disorder?"

A fascinating comment explored in *Transamerica* (2005)

Interest in the phenomenon of transsexualism burgeoned in the United States and Europe six decades ago after the 1951 gender modification surgery of Christine Jorgensen. (*The Christine Jorgensen Story*, a low-budget and somewhat insipid film, was released in 1970). The mid-1980s witnessed a revival of interest, after widespread publicity and a television movie (*Second Serve*) about the sexual conversion of male surgeon Richard Raskins into a female tennis star, Renee Richards. Other films that have explored transsexualism include *Myra Breckinridge* (1970) (starring film critic Rex Reed), *Dog Day Afternoon* (1975), *The World According to Garp* (1982), and *Come Back to the Five and Dime, Jimmie Dean, Jimmie Dean* (1982). *The Crying Game* (1993) is a rich and nuanced film that explores a complex transsexual relationship.

The surgical treatment of transsexuals remains controversial, although tens of thousands of patients have undergone the procedure. Transsexualism occurs more often in biological males than in biological females, and many more males apply for conversion surgery. Transsexuals can be heterosexual, homosexual, or asexual, both prior to and after their surgery. Many professionals who have worked with these patients have been struck by the fact that sexual behavior per se is often a secondary concern; the core issue is one of sexual *identity*, not sexual behavior.

The Range of Normal Sexual Behavior

Few areas of human behavior are as complex, varied, and interesting as sexual behavior. Both social scientists and the public are fascinated by the multitude of possibilities inherent in our sexuality. It is important to appreciate that the range of normal sexual behavior is exceptionally broad, and many behaviors that seem unusual or disturbing to some people do not qualify for a *DSM-IV-TR* label. As a rule, remember that complex or elaborate sexual fantasies are commonplace and do not suggest that any type of psychological disturbance is present. A psychological problem exists when a person acts on his or her fantasies with unwilling partners or behaves in ways that distress other people.

Filmmakers have been quick to exploit our fascination with sexual behavior, and contemporary cinema is replete with examples of sexual psychopathology. A serious student can learn a great deal about abnormal psychology from selective viewing.

Sexual Dysfunctions

The human **sexual response cycle** includes the following four phases:
(1) *Desire*: fantasies related to sex
(2) *Excitement*: arousal, sense of pleasure with physiological changes
(3) *Orgasm*: peaking of sexual pleasure with release of sexual tension
(4) *Resolution*: sense of muscular relaxation and general well-being
There can be a sexual disorder at any level. For example, **male erectile disorder** (impotence) is an excitement/arousal disorder while a male's **premature ejaculation** is an orgasm disorder. Other dysfunctions include **dyspareunia,** which is recurrent genital pain during sexual intercourse, and **vaginismus,** which is a recurrent involuntary spasm of the outer muscle area of the vagina that interferes with sexual intercourse.

The films *sex, lies, and videotape* (1989), *Boxing Helena* (1993), *Italian for Beginners* (2001), and *Monster's Ball* (2001) each depict at least one scene where a man becomes impotent and has to face the consequences. Warren Beatty plays an impotent Clyde Barker in *Bonnie and Clyde* (1967), and Peter O'Toole is impotent as a result of age and prostate cancer in *Venus* (2006). *Intimacy* (2000) depicts the frustration associated with premature ejaculation.

The Oh in Ohio (2006) depicts a high school teacher who is frustrated by his wife's inability to achieve an orgasm and sexual satisfaction during their ten years of marriage. He eventually has an affair with one of his students. His wife feels abandoned and becomes open to sexual exploration for the first time in her life, eventually having a satisfying sexual experience (an affair) with a character played by Danny DeVito, a swimming pool salesman. During a workshop on orgasm, one woman describes her vagina as a "velvet volcano." *Amy's Orgasm* (2001) is a film in which a confident, self-assured woman who writes self-help books about how women can manage just fine without men falls in love with a "shock jock" radio announcer and finds sexual fulfillment.

Kinsey (2004) is an important film about a college professor, Alfred Kinsey (Liam Neeson), who helped reshape the way people viewed sexuality in the middle of the last century. Kinsey published two landmark books based on interviews with tens of thousands of people across the country: *Sexual Behavior in the Human Male* (1948) and *Sexual Behavior in the Human Female* (1953). Many people criticized Kinsey's methodology and research, but his impact on society is undeniable. Kinsey contributed to normalizing homosexuality, premarital sex, and the use of multiple sexual positions; he also debunked numerous misconceptions (e.g., the belief that masturbation is harmful). The film portrays Kinsey training his team in conducting interviews that are objective and unbiased, reminding them that "maintaining a nonjudgmental attitude is harder than you think." A particularly striking scene occurs during Kinsey's straightforward teaching approach in his course on human sexuality where he displays slides of human genitalia. The film also depicts many of the shortcomings of this famous researcher, including his ritualistic compulsiveness (suggesting an obsessive-compulsive personality), barbiturate abuse, lack of personal sexual boundaries, and his superficiality in his interpersonal relations.

Sexual Addictions

Sexual addiction is increasingly being recognized as a growing problem in contemporary society. Patrick Carnes, one of the world's leading authorities on sexual addiction, has written extensively on the topic, addressing sexual compulsivity (*Don't Call It Love* and *Out of the Shadows*), internet sex addiction (*In the Shadows of the Net*), and each of the paraphilias mentioned later in the chapter. There are movies that represent each of these areas.

I am a Sex Addict (2005) is an autobiographical documentary film that emphasizes the role of compulsivity in sexual addictions – for the director/actor, the acting out was compulsive sex with prostitutes and compulsive masturbation. The important role of 12-step recovery groups (e.g., Sex Addicts Anonymous) is highlighted as are a number of unhealthy and healthy coping strategies. A better movie, *De-Lovely* (2004), documents the numerous compulsive homosexual affairs of Cole Porter and the conflict he felt about reconciling these affairs with his very genuine love for his wife.

Good films on sex addicts will not only reveal the behaviors of the addict but also the consequences and realities of the decisions they make. Characters who are presented as male sex addicts include Joe Taylor (Ewan McGregor) in *Young Adam* (2003), the title characters in *Alfie* (2004) and *Don Juan DeMarco* (1995) (played by Jude Law and Johnny Depp, respectively), and Sammy Horn (Michael Des Barres) in *The Diary of a Sex Addict* (2001).

The classic Luis Buñuel film *Belle de Jour* (1967) portrays a married woman who takes a job as a prostitute. The film illustrates female sexual addiction and depicts the creation of a double life. As the protagonist sinks deeper into her new lifestyle and becomes more comfortable with her lies, she becomes unable to extricate herself. Other female sex addicts are depicted in *Swimming Pool* (2003) and in one segment of *Personal Velocity* (2002), and Juliette Marquis plays the role of a confident, self-assured, and enthusiastic porn star in *This Girl's Life* (2003).

On_Line (2002) examines the serious problem of internet addiction. In the film, a man is abandoned by his fiancée; consequently, he spends countless hours on the internet, partly to help his roommate with a popular pornographic website designed to "link people together with their fantasy." At the end of the film, the viewer learns that the fiancée had been a person online with a webcam whom he watched all day and had never personally met. His compulsive fantasy had become so ingrained that it shaped his personal reality. The film accurately portrays the intense loneliness, isolation, and lack of intimacy or connection that internet addicts and internet sex addicts experience.

An important feature of sex addiction is the secrecy of the behavior. The link between secrecy and sexuality is explored in *Far From Heaven* (2002), *Unfaithful* (2002), and *The Secret Lives of Dentists* (2002). Film directors Pedro Almodóvar, Peter Greenaway, and John Waters are especially known for their creative depiction of sexuality, sexual addiction, and paraphilias.

The Paraphilias

The *DSM-IV-TR* uses the term **paraphilia** as a substitute for antiquated and emotion-laden expressions such as sexual deviation or perversion. These older labels have strong pejorative connotations and carry a bias that is inappropriate in either research or treatment.

The paraphilias include fetishism, transvestic fetishism, pedophilia, exhibitionism, voyeurism, sexual masochism, sexual sadism, frotteurism, and telephone scatalogia. It is important to reiterate that at some time in their lives most people have had fantasies or have engaged in a behavior that may fit one or more of the categories listed above. However, sexual fantasies *per se* are not a psychological problem – and do not warrant a diagnosis – unless a person has acted on his or her fantasies or is significantly distressed by them. The male who has fantasies about peeping through a window and watching his neighbor undress, for example, is not engaging in deviant behavior. In fact, fantasies of this type are common among males. The behavior would be deviant if the man could be aroused *only* by the fantasy, or if he acted out and actually spied on his neighbor.

Transvestism

Unlike transsexuals, **transvestites** are comfortable with their anatomic sex. However, transvestites derive pleasure and satisfaction from cross-dressing and being identified as a female, and cross-dressing and fantasies about cross-dressing play a prominent role in the sexual lives of transvestites. The transsexual male may cross-dress, but this is not done for purposes of sexual arousal but, rather, because female clothes are important in establishing a female identity. In contrast, the transvestite is likely to be a masculine, heterosexual male who becomes sexually excited when he dresses up in women's clothes. The transvestite does not desire to *be* a woman, but merely wants to be admired as one, or to experience the sexual excitement associated with wearing women's clothes. Brown (1994) maintains that the majority of wives who discover their husband's cross-dressing after marriage come to accept the behavior, and suggests there are no ill effects on children from these marriages. The children of transvestites engage in appropriate sex-role behavior as adults and are unlikely to cross-dress themselves.

As with transsexualism, transvestites may be heterosexual or homosexual, although most are clearly heterosexual. Transvestites cannot be asexual, since sexual arousal is part of the definition of the syndrome.

The cross-dressing behavior of the transvestite almost always begins in childhood, although few little boys who dress up in the clothes of their mother or sister will grow up to have sexual identity problems. While transsexualism is found among both males and females, the diagnosis of transvestism is almost inevitably reserved for males, and there are very few case studies of women who become sexually aroused by wearing men's clothes.

Many transvestites cross-dress only on special occasions, and they may attempt to suppress the behavior, yielding to the impulse only when anxious, during periods of stress, or when separated from a sexual partner. The preferred objects of clothing include nightgowns, panties, bras, hose, and high heels. These garments are often the stimuli associated with fetishes, and in the *DSM-IV-TR* transvestism is referred to as **transvestic fetishism**. It is similar to other forms of fetishism in that sexual arousal is associated not with an individual but, rather, with inanimate objects (women's clothing).

The topic of cross-dressing (but not necessarily transvestism) is surprisingly common in films, where it is generally treated with humor and almost never as a serious issue. One comedy that addresses cross-dressing is the popular film *Tootsie* (1982), in which an unemployed actor played by Dustin Hoffman pretends to be a woman in order to get an acting job. The counterpart to this film is Blake Edward's *Victor/Victoria* (1982) in which Julie Andrews portrays a starving cabaret singer who gets her big break when she manages to land a job singing as a male female impersonator. Both films are sensitive analyses of the complex relationships linking gender and role.

Other films that have explored cross-dressing include *Some Like It Hot* (1959) directed by Billy Wilder and starring Marilyn Monroe, Tony Curtis, Jack Lemmon, and George Raft. This is the classic example of this genre. More recently, *Mrs. Doubtfire* (1993) starred Robin Williams as a man who passes himself off as a "nanny" in order to spend more time with his children. The movie *Yentl* (1983) stars Barbra Streisand as a woman who must dress in male clothes and pretend to

be a man in order to achieve an education. *To Wong Foo, Thanks for Everything, Julie Newmar* (1995) is an entertaining film that examines the lives of three transvestites whose car breaks down in a small town filled with bigots. This film stars Wesley Snipes and Patrick Swayze. In Jane Campion's *Holy Smoke* (1999), Harvey Keitel's authoritarian character falls into a sexual obsession and begins to cross dress as he regresses and deteriorates.

"I'm the Latina Marilyn Monroe. I've got more legs than a bucket of chicken!"

Miss Chi-Chi Rodriguez in *To Wong Foo*

Unfortunately, some otherwise good films, such as Brian De Palma's *Dressed to Kill* (1980), starring Michael Caine and Angie Dickinson, link transvestism with violence and sociopathy. There is no evidence that transvestites are more likely than the average individual to be homicidal, although, like others whose sexuality may be viewed as deviant by the majority culture, they are significantly more likely to be victims of crime.

Fetishism

An individual has a **fetish** when an inanimate object habitually arouses him or her. A diagnosis is justified only if the sexual arousal associated with the object or fantasies about it are intense, recurrent, and last for at least six months. Sex often involves masturbation with the fetish, or the fetish may be incorporated into sexual activity with one's partner. The term *fetish* is used to refer to both the object itself and the inordinate attraction to it. However, the true fetish involves inanimate objects such as panties, silk stockings, garter belts, high heel shoes, or rubber items of clothing or body parts not normally associated with sexual activity (e.g., hair, feet, or the stumps of amputated limbs). Normally the link to sexuality can be surmised, but occasionally a patient will report sexual arousal to stimuli as obscure as file cabinets or baby buggies, and it is difficult to determine (a) how arousal initially could have been paired with the stimulus or (b) the potential symbolic value of the fetish. The fetish is often used for masturbation, but it may also be worn, worshipped, put in the rectum, hoarded, fondled, or sucked (Chalkey & Powell, 1983).

Some authorities have speculated that fetishism is related to the same psychological impulses that trigger transvestism and kleptomania (an overwhelming desire to steal, usually trivial or inexpensive objects). The differences among the three conditions seem trivial in comparison with the similarities that link the disorders. The person with a sexual fetish longs to relate to the object sexually, the transvestite longs to wear it, and the kleptomaniac longs to steal it. Anxiety frequently precedes the unusual behavior, and masturbation is common.

A number of films have included either leading or secondary characters with a fetish. One favorite is *Claire's Knee*, a French film directed by Eric Rohmer and released in 1971. This charming movie details the obsession of a soon-to-be-married writer for his friend's daughter – or, more exactly, the daughter's right knee. The erotic elements in the film are handled with delicacy and good taste, and the writer's fixation on the girl's knee soon seems entirely plausible.

Peter Greenaway's *Pillow Book* (1997) portrays a woman with a fetish for calligraphy. She melds calligraphy with sex, and the calligraphic pen symbolizes the instrument of pleasure. She develops a passion for calligraphy and experiences withdrawal without it. She searches for the ideal mate to write on her; she rules out the old for not having enough energy, and the young for their distracted nature. She captures and tests out a graffiti writer and other random people to write on her in her search. "You're not a writer, you're a scribbler," she tells one candidate.

Another not-to-be-missed film demonstrating a sexual fetish is Steven Soderbergh's *sex, lies, and videotape*. This intelligent film, which won the Best Picture and Best Actor award at the 1989 Cannes Film Festival, was written, directed, and edited by Soderbergh. The film describes how the lives of three people (a man, his wife, and her sister, with whom he is having an affair) are changed forever by the arrival of the man's college roommate, Graham Dalton. Dalton is an impotent male who can achieve orgasm only by masturbating while he is watching the videotapes he makes of women discussing the intimate details of their sexual lives. Dalton has decided to live his life with absolute honesty, and he shares the details of his sexual life with Ann, the rejected wife. The two eventually become lovers, and there is a dramatic confrontation between Dalton and his old roommate (Ann's husband). Dalton is transformed through his relationship with Ann, and eventually he is able to move out of his isolation and into an emotionally satisfying and sexually mature relationship.

An equally powerful film is *Equus* (1977). This movie stars Richard Burton as Martin Dysart, a disillusioned psychiatrist who has lost all traces of passion in his life. The film revolves around Dysart's treatment of Alan Strang (Peter Firth), a young man arrested for blinding six horses. This cruel act is linked to Strang's fascination with horses; he finds them both threatening and sexually exciting. The film offers some insight into how an animal fetish might develop.

Some films utilize fetishes solely for comic purposes and offer little insight into the paraphilias, as in *Sex and Zen* (1993) and a woman who proclaims to have a "Santa fetish" in *Bad Santa* (2003).

Crash (1996) is a controversial NC-17 David Cronenberg film about people who have developed fetishes for cars and car wrecks. The film is based on a novel by J. G. Ballard, and the opening scene shows a woman rubbing her breasts against the wing of a plane and then licking metal while an apparently anonymous lover enters her from behind. She later relates this experience to her husband, who in turns shares his day's sexual adventures. The husband later becomes involved in a serious car accident in which the driver of the other car is killed. This man's wife, Helen, survives the accident but is hospitalized and has to walk on crutches while she recovers. Shortly after leaving the hospital, she becomes sexually involved with James, the man who had been driving the car that had killed her husband. Helen arouses James by telling him stories about all the men with whom she has had sex in cars. Both individuals find themselves sexually aroused by crashes and the accouterments of highway deaths (ambulances, flares, fire trucks, etc.). They are increasingly drawn into a deviant subculture that shares their sexual fascination with metal, cars, and crashing. This group is led by an unusual man who amuses himself and others by reenacting the 1955 death of James Dean in his sports car "Little Bastard." In addition to its main theme of fetishism, the film involves exhibitionism, voyeurism, troilism (pleasure in having sex in front of others), and homosexuality. The film ends with a suggestion of necrophilia – James deliberately drives his wife's sports car off the road at high speed, and she is thrown from the car. He determines she is alive, and then embraces her unconscious and injured body while muttering, "Maybe the next one, darling, maybe the next one."

Additional Questions for Discussion

- Are the fetishes described in *Crash* simply too far-fetched to be believed?
- Metal, leather, and plastic are all common fetishes. What is it about these particular materials that make them sexually arousing for some patients with a paraphilia?
- How common is it for a husband and wife to share fantasies about sex with other partners?
- How is it possible for sexual arousal (a positive experience) to so often become linked with pain (a very negative experience for most people)?

Exhibitionism

The exhibitionist's preferred form of sexual gratification is exposing the genitals to unsuspecting strangers. Masturbation often occurs during or after the exposure. The exhibitionist will almost never attempt to have intercourse with the person intimidated and would likely be personally intimidated and frightened by an opportunity for an adult sexual encounter. Although reports of exhibitionism in a neighborhood usually result in increased concern about the possibility of rape, exhibitionism and rape are dramatically different behaviors and are almost never linked.

Exhibitionism can occur at any age, but typically develops in males in their mid-twenties. Despite the popular image of a "dirty old man in a raincoat," the incidence of exhibitionism falls off rapidly after the age of 40 and is rare in older males who are cognitively intact. Many exhibitionists have never had meaningful or satisfying adult sexual relationships; others have normal psychosexual development histories.

Reports of true exhibitionism in females are quite rare, although some women may be aroused by exposing their breasts or legs in public. Exhibitionism in females can also be used as a way of establishing dominance in a nonsexual encounter with males. The potential for psychological manipulation through exposure was dramatically portrayed during Sharon Stone's interrogation scene in *Basic Instinct* (1992). A brief scene of exhibitionistic behavior is depicted in *Natural Born Killers* (1994) and *Morvern Callar* (2002).

The Good Mother (1988) raises interesting questions about the boundaries between healthy sexuality and exhibitionism. Diane Keaton plays Anna Dunlap, the divorced mother of a six-year-old daughter. Anna falls in love with an artist and

starts to live a bohemian life that includes nudity in front of her daughter. Her new lover at one point innocently lets the daughter touch his penis when he is getting out of the tub and she expresses natural childhood curiosity. When the ex-husband learns about this event, he sues for custody, and Anna is forced to renounce her lover in order to maintain visitation rights with her daughter.

Additional Questions for Discussion

- Is it normal for a child to be interested in an adult's genitals?
- If you were the judge in *The Good Mother*, would you have made the same decision?
- Did the bohemian artist in *The Good Mother* make a foolish error of judgment, or was it appropriate to let himself be touched by his lover's daughter?
- How do children who grow up in households where nudity is common adjust sexually and interpersonally?
- What is the link between voyeurism and exhibitionism?
- At what age does it become sexually stimulating and inappropriate for a child to sleep with a parent?

Voyeurism

The **voyeur** is a "peeping Tom" who experiences arousal and derives sexual satisfaction from spying on unsuspecting people, usually strangers, as they are getting undressed, using the toilet, or having sexual relations. Although it is normal to want to look at the bodies of others (e.g., at the beach), the voyeur goes to great lengths to find surreptitious hiding places from which he or she can watch others without being detected. Arousal is always associated with the clandestine aspects of the situation; voyeurs report less interest in watching pornographic films, visiting topless or nude beaches, or attending topless bars – all experiences where public voyeurism has been sanctioned.

As is the case with exhibitionism and obscene phone calls, it is rare for the voyeur to attempt to initiate sexual relationships with the victim. The voyeur will most often masturbate while viewing the arousing scene or later, when replaying the scene in memory. Although it is rare for voyeurs to progress to crimes of sexual violence, more than two thirds of males who commit sex-related murders report early experiences with voyeurism (Ressler, 1986).

An interesting variation of voyeurism is **troilism**, or sexual gratification derived from watching other people have sex (or allowing others to watch oneself engage in sexual activity – behavior more logically linked to exhibitionism than voyeurism). This practice is sometimes referred to as **scoptophilia**. Variations on these themes include the **ménage à trois** ("family of three"), swinging, and couples that have monogamous sex in each other's presence. Swinging or mate swapping is probably widespread, although AIDS and other sexual diseases have presented serious obstacles to this form of sexual expression. A failed attempt at swinging is portrayed in Paul Mazursky's 1969 film *Bob and Carol and Ted and Alice*, starring Robert Culp, Eliot Gould, Dyan Cannon, and Natalie Wood. The film celebrates social permissiveness and the mores of the late sixties more than sexual freedom; in the final scene, Bob, Carol, Ted, and Alice, all in bed together, reaffirm their commitment to monogamy.

Other films depicting voyeurism include *Lovelife* (1997) and the Canadian film *The Adjuster* (1991). Most films that have dealt explicitly with voyeurism have been misleading presentations that perpetuate common myths. For example, *Peeping Tom* (1960) presents the story of a voyeur (raised by a sadistic psychologist) who tortures his victims and then photographs them as they are dying. This is an example of sexual sadism, not voyeurism. The pain of voyeurism is evident in the film *Voyeur Confessions* (2001).

Some films depict a strong voyeuristic component without depicting explicit sexual fantasy or gratification. Christopher Nolan's debut film, *Following* (1998), tells a creative story about a man who enjoys picking out one person in a crowd and then following this individual for a day. The voyeur is a lonely writer who convinces himself he follows people to get character ideas for his stories. His habit has qualities of an addiction insofar as it becomes "irresistible" to him, he is unable to keep it under control, he obsesses about it, and he employs various cognitive justifications for maintaining this inappropriate and disturbing behavior.

Another nonsexual (perhaps impotent) voyeur is displayed in Hitchcock's classic film *Rear Window* (1954). Voyeurism is clearly portrayed; James Stewart's character watches his neighbors incessantly, and he cannot pull away from his window. His whole life revolves around looking into others' lives, and he satisfies his psychological needs in this way. He also resists and rejects a beautiful, caring woman. If the viewer assumes Stewart's character is wrong about the murder and

that all his behavior was pure voyeurism with no positive, beneficial outcome, it is hard to avoid the conclusion that this is a film about voyeurism.

Sexual Masochism

The **sexual masochist** becomes sexually excited when he or she is humiliated, beaten, bound, or made to suffer. It is important to appreciate that the diagnosis of sexual masochism is made only when patients actually engage in these behaviors. As is the case with other paraphilias, masochistic fantasies are both common and harmless, and moderate sadomasochistic behavior (e.g., scratching and biting) can be a rewarding part of normal sex play.

Masochists allow themselves to be abused in a variety of ways, including bondage, whipping, handcuffing, spanking, cutting, and burning. They are often verbally abused as well as physically mistreated. Humiliation may be necessary for arousal to occur – e.g., a masochist may be forced to wear a diaper, or his partner may defecate or urinate upon the masochist. Whips, chains, leather, and rubber accouterments often play an important role in the sexual activity of the masochist, who is happiest with a (mildly) sadistic partner. A woman who caters to the sexual preferences of masochistic men is referred to as a **dominatrix**. Masochists may be gay or straight, although the majority of sadomasochistic encounters are heterosexual. Among homosexuals, masochists appear to outnumber sadists (Innala & Ernulf, 1992).

Secretary (2002) is an intriguing film about a young woman (Maggie Gyllenhael) who is depressed and seriously self-injurious. She takes a job as a secretary working for a successful attorney, Mr. Grey (James Spader). She begins to enjoy his harsh criticism of her mistakes and a sadomasochistic relationship develops. Grey enjoys spanking her, yelling at her, and engaging in other sadistic behavior, but he prohibits her from injuring herself (paradoxically using his sadism to control her masochism). The film opens with her nicely dressed at work, arms tied to a long bar behind her neck. She picks up items with her teeth or by turning her torso horizontally. Through a variety of sadomasochistic behaviors, she matures, stops her self-abuse, and develops a meaningful relationship with her boss, eventually marrying him.

Quills (2000) depicts the last years of the Marquis de Sade (Geoffrey Rush), who spent years in an institution. The protagonist engages in a variety of paraphilias that give his life meaning and pleasure.

The Piano Teacher

In *The Piano Teacher* (2001), Erika Kohut (Isabelle Huppert) is a highbrow, successful pianist. She performs concerts for standing-room-only crowds and gives demanding lessons to her students. Erika clearly presents as a sexually repressed and conservative woman with a stern, controlling presence. The film takes its time in getting to important themes and core issues, allowing the viewer to be gradually introduced to her world and values. The viewer sees her go to a porn shop briefly in which she chastises a young male student before she leaves. In another scene, she goes into a booth in the shop to watch a video. These scenes progress to acting out sexually with a male student in a public restroom; in this scene, she is mildly sadistic and very controlling. A relationship begins, and it is only then that her deepest fantasies (and true diagnosis) are revealed. She is in fact masochistic. In one scene, she sets up a blockade so her nosey, controlling mother is unable to burst into her room. Erika gives her lover a letter revealing her fantasies about sadomasochistic behavior. As he reads the letter he learns about her desires to be reminded of her powerlessness, to be gagged, and to be hit if she disobeys any of his commands or rules. Next, she reveals her stash of ropes and other sadomasochistic toys. He responds by telling her that he feels both love and repulsion, and that she is "sick" and needs treatment.

"The urge to be beaten has been in me for years."

The Piano Teacher (2001)

The film makes inferences about etiology, mostly surrounding a forceful, controlling mother who needs to know every last detail about her adult daughter. The mother is physically controlling, aggressive, and quick to criticize everything from Erika's attire and her piano playing (although Erika is an expert pianist) to a benign conversation she has with a young man. She instructs her daughter, "No one must surpass you, my dear." Erika's father had reportedly died of mental illness in an asylum.

Autoerotic asphyxia, using self-strangulation to produce excitement or to intensify erections or ejaculation, is an unusual but not uncommon paraphilia, often related to masochism. Autoerotic

Questions to Consider While Watching *The Piano Teacher*

- Was Erika's letter to her lover a true expression of love?
- Why is Erika afraid of being seduced?
- How did Erika's mother contribute to her paraphilia?
- Is it typical for masochists to occasionally adopt the role of a sadist?
- How common is it for people to adopt fantasy roles during sex?

asphyxiation results in more than 50 deaths in the United States each year (Centers for Disease Control and Prevention, 2008). Blanchard and Hucker (1991) were able to review the cases of 117 males who died during autoerotic asphyxial activity. Autoerotic asphyxia is especially significant because most of the deaths that result from this practice are assumed to be accidents.

Most of what we know about the practice of autoerotic asphyxia is derived from police reports following death investigations. The victims tend to be young white males. Bondage accouterments are often employed, along with mirrors and cameras. Transvestism is a common practice in these cases. There is often evidence that ejaculation occurred before death.

Sexual Sadism

Sexual sadism presents the mirror image of sexual masochism. The sadist derives sexual pleasure from the suffering and humiliation of his or her victims. Partners may be consenting or nonconsenting. If the partner is consenting, the diagnosis requires that sexual sadism be "repeatedly preferred or exclusive" and that "bodily injury that is extensive, permanent, or possibly mortal is inflicted in order to achieve sexual excitement."

The terms **sadism** and **masochism** were first used by a German sexologist, Richard von Krafft-Ebing, in the nineteenth century. Krafft-Ebing, who wrote *Psychopathia Sexualis*, the first medical school textbook on sexuality (first published in 1886), took the term sadism from the name of the French author Marquis de Sade. De Sade's novels and short stories are replete with abuse, torture, and murder, all of which are linked with sexual gratification. One of his works, *The 120 Days of*

Sodom, was made into the movie *Salo or The 120 Days of Sodom*, (1976), directed by Pier Paolo Pasolini.

Sadomasochistic sex often involves elaborate sex toys such as chains, whips, rubber and leather garments, and spike heels. Flagellation and bondage are common practices.

Although some sadists are also rapists, it is important to understand that rapists do not derive sexual pleasure from the rape itself. Rape is an act of violence in which sexual arousal may play virtually no role. In contrast, the sexual sadist derives intense sexual pleasure from the suffering of the victim.

It is important to distinguish between *minor* sadism and masochism (sex play involving bondage and discipline or dominance and submission) and *major* sadism and masochism involving torture and the risk of death and bodily injury (Arndt, 1991). There is some evidence that at the minor level there are more women who dominate males; at the extreme level, men are more likely to abuse women.

Films depicting sexual sadism are fairly common in the United States, and they play for large audiences in Europe and Asia as well. Many of these films are heavy-handed and crude and have little social value. A salient exception is David Lynch's *Blue Velvet* (1986).

Blue Velvet

Blue Velvet opens with Bobby Vinton's song of the same name and scenes of a bucolic Midwest neighborhood. This idyllic scene is soon interrupted, and the viewer is never really allowed to relax again until the film concludes.

The plot of the story involves a student, Jeffrey Beaumont (Kyle MacLachlan), who is home from college to care for his father who has just had a stroke. While walking in a field near his house, Jeffrey discovers a severed ear. It turns out to be the ear of the husband of a cabaret singer, Dorothy Vallens (Isabella Rossellini). Dorothy's husband and son are being held hostage to force her to comply with the sexual demands of a local gangster, Frank Booth (Dennis Hopper). Dorothy, one of the most complex characters in the film, discovers Jeffrey in her apartment after he goes there in a foolish attempt to solve the crime. In a controversial scene Dorothy discovers Jeffrey and uses a knife to force him to have sex with her. She displays many of the features of masochism previously discussed; these become more prominent later when Frank arrives and proceeds to savagely abuse her. Frank, both obsessed with Dorothy and

fixated on the song "Blue Velvet," has cut off a piece of Dorothy's blue velvet bathrobe. It is a fetish that Frank carries with him and uses during other sexual encounters. Hopper is unforgettable as Frank Booth, who is addicted to inhalants as well as sadistic sex.

"I have a part of you with me. You put your disease in me. It helps me. It makes me strong."

A masochistic and troubled Dorothy in *Blue Velvet* (1986)

One troubling aspect of the film is that both Dorothy and Jeffrey seem attracted to sadomasochistic sex after they have been exposed to it. A subplot involves Jeffrey's involvement with Sandy, the daughter of a corrupt local detective. The relationship with Sandy seems pale and insipid after the intensity of a sexual encounter with Dorothy.

The film won the National Society of Film Critics award for Best Film of 1986, and Lynch was selected as Best Director of the year by the same group. It is a brutally honest film, and not one that will appeal to all viewers. However, it is a film rich in psychopathology and one worth seeing by anyone interested in the complex world of the sexual psychopath.

Frotteurism

The **frotteur** is someone who derives sexual pleasure from brushing or rubbing against others in a seemingly inadvertent but clearly sexual manner. Frotteurs frequent crowded stores, escalators, buses, and subways, where their behavior can be attributed to crowding. The *DSM-IV-TR* lists frotteurism as an independent paraphilia, although many authors view it as a variation of exhibitionism.

The film *Dummy* (2003) portrays an unemployed man who is a frotteur. The man is balding, and wears thick glasses. He is included in the film purely for laughs. Though his behavior is not depicted cinematically, the character clearly meets the *DSM-IV-TR* criteria for frotteurism.

Pedophilia

The **pedophile** is someone who is sexually aroused by children and who has acted on these desires or who is markedly distressed by them. The pedophile can be attracted to girls, boys, or both, although heterosexual pedophilia appears to be somewhat more common than homosexual pedophilia. The *DSM-IV-TR* stipulates that the child be prepubescent (generally age 13 or younger) for a diagnosis of pedophilia to be appropriate. In addition, the diagnosis is not used unless the perpetrator is at least 16 years old and at least five years older than the child involved.

Although not a formal diagnostic label, the term **ephebophilia** is sometimes used to describe a person who is attracted to post-pubescent adolescents; the ephebophile's attraction is exclusive and specific to this age group (ages 14–17). The phrase **Lolita syndrome** is also used to describe men attracted exclusively to female adolescents. Though often illegal, ephebophilia is not seen as pathological and is even normative in some societies in which adolescent girls routinely marry older, adult men. Ephebophilia illustrates the conflict that often exists between biology and societal norms.

Ephebophilia is portrayed in the coming of age film *Towelhead* (aka *Nothing is Private*; 2007), the first film directed by Alan Ball (who also produced and co-wrote *American Beauty* (1999), a film that deals with the emerging sexuality of two young girls). In *Towelhead*, several adults abuse Jasira, a 13-year-old girl, including her mother's boyfriend, who feigns paternal concern while he is shaving Jasira's pubic hair. "Towelhead" is a derisive term for someone of Arab descent; the protagonist's father is a strict Lebanese American who is ill-prepared to deal with his daughter's sexual maturation or the challenges of menstruation.

Venus (2006) stars Peter O'Toole as a septuagenarian actor with prostate cancer who becomes romantically and erotically involved with a woman 53 years younger than he is; the movie makes this relationship seem entirely plausible.

While an adolescent achieves sexual maturation (puberty) around 13, most mental health professionals believe adolescents are not prepared to deal with the demands of sexual intimacy at such an early age and recommend a slow transition to adult sexuality; however, there is wide variation in the ages at which different cultures define the age of consent for sexual intercourse, and the minimum age of consent varies across countries from age 12 to 18.

Hard Candy (2005) illustrates the ways in which the internet has opened new avenues for pedophiles to exploit their victims. The film involves an online relationship between a 14-year-old student and a 32-year-old photographer who is a pedophile. The two eventually meet, and both understand from innuendo that they are meeting to have sex; however, in a curious twist, the precocious 14-year-old winds up in control of the situation and proceeds to castrate the older man (who may have been involved in the disappearance of a child whose photo is included in his files) and the man eventually commits suicide.

While most cases of ephebophilia (and most movies with this theme) involve older men who are attracted to young girls, two films have successfully explored relationships between older women and teenage boys. *Private Lessons* (1981) is a movie about a French maid who seduces a 15-year-old boy; the film depicts grooming, boundary violations, and sexual abuse of a minor. *The Reader* (2008) is a more powerful, engaging and compelling film in which Kate Winslet plays Hanna Schmitz, a 36-year-old woman who becomes involved with a 15-year-old boy. They have an affair one summer and then she drops out of his life, only to reappear 8 years later when she is on trial for war crimes committed as a concentration camp guard. The title of the film comes from the fact that Hanna and her adolescent lover begin each of their trysts with him reading to her. Kate Winslet won an Academy Award for her role in this film.

"She had favorites. Girls, mostly young. We all remarked on it, she gave them food and places to sleep. In the evening, she asked them to join her. We all thought – well, you can imagine what we thought. Then we found out – she was making these women read aloud to her. They were reading to her. At first we thought this guard... this guard is more sensitive... she's more human... she's kinder. Often she chose the weak, the sick, she picked them out, she seemed to be protecting them almost. But then she dispatched them. Is that kinder?"

A witness describes Hanna Schmitz's behavior in *The Reader* (2008)

Another nondiagnostic variation of pedophilia is the rare condition called **infantophilia**; this term is applied to adults with a primary sexual attraction to children from birth to age 5. The movie *Bliss* (1997) includes a scene illustrating infantophilia.

Many pedophiles report being sexually abused as children (Freund, Watson, & Dickey, 1990). Pedophiles who have been attracted to children since adolescence are identified as **fixated pedophiles**. In contrast, if an individual has satisfying adult sexual experiences, but then reverts to a sexual preoccupation with children, the person is classified as a situational or **regressed pedophile**.

There are between 100,000 and 500,000 cases of child sexual abuse in the United States each year, and the number of cases is probably rising (Centers for Disease Control and Prevention, 2008).

Most people consider the practice of pedophilia reprehensible, perhaps because children are among the most vulnerable members of the human family. However, the widespread availability of "kiddie porn," despite the social opprobrium associated with the practice, suggests that sexual interest in children is as common as most of the other paraphilias. Empirical data document the extent of sexual attraction to children by adults. For example, Briere (1989) surveyed undergraduate males and found that 21% acknowledged being sexually attracted to children, 9% had sexual fantasies involving children, and 7% would consider having sex with a child if certain they could avoid being detected or punished.

Pedophiles and ephebophiles seduce their victims using play, food, or gifts, which are followed by appropriate touching eventually leading to inappropriate touching and assault. The seduction of an adolescent is powerfully and realistically portrayed in *Blue Car* (2003), in which a young, vulnerable girl is seduced by her teacher. Most viewers are not aware that the teacher is manipulating the adolescent from the very beginning of the film. The seduction of adolescents is also depicted in *American Beauty* (1999), *Lolita* (1962), *Lolita* (1997), *Y Tu Mama Tambien* (2001), and *Manic* (2003). In *The Magdalene Sisters* (2002), a priest has sex with a vulnerable, emotionally and physically abused adolescent girl.

Child sexual abuse is portrayed in the powerful and riveting documentary, *Capturing the Friedmans* (2003), as well as in the very dark comedy, *Happiness* (1998). In *Capturing the Friedmans*, a father (Arnold) and his son (Jesse) are accused of pedophilia. When their house is searched, child pornography is found hidden throughout the home. The movie does not fully indict or acquit either individual.

Mysterious Skin (2004) tells the story of two boys growing up in a small Kansas town. Both boys are molested by their Little League coach, but they respond in very different ways. Brian repressed the experience and only remembered waking up with a nose bleed; he accounts for the missing five hours in his life by developing a deep conviction that he has been abducted by aliens. Neil responds by becoming a teenage prostitute, working at first in local parks before moving to New York where his clients are mainly older white men. The film presents an even handed and unsensationalized examination of the effects of childhood sexual abuse.

"Little Red Riding Hood! That's it! That's it. The Woodsman,
 he cuts open the wolf's stomach, the girl comes out without a scratch...
[But have you ever seen] a seven-year-old sodomized in half?
She was so small, just broken. I saw 20-year vets on that job.
Hard guys, they just broke down and cried. I was there,
I cried... There ain't no fucking woodsman in this world."

A police sergeant describing the stress involved in working with children victimized by pedophiles in
The Woodsman (2004)

Two films offer especially sensitive portrayals of the problem of pedophilia: *Little Children* (2007) and *The Woodsman* (2004). Director Todd Field's *Little Children* is a powerful film that shows how difficult it is to find and maintain long-term love relationships. Kate Winslet plays Sarah Pierce, a disenchanted stay-at-home mother whose husband is addicted to online pornography. One of the characters in the film, Ronnie, lives with his mother after completing a prison term for exposing himself to a little girl. Ronnie's mother is convinced that he'll become attracted to adult women if he only starts to date one; however, the date she arranges for him turns into a disaster when he asks his date to drive him by a playground so he can masturbate. Before his mother dies from cancer, she writes him a short note, simply asking him to "be a good boy." He responds to his grief by castrating himself, and his life is saved by Sarah, who is able to set aside her previous repugnance and aversion to relate to Ronnie as a genuinely suffering human being. *The Woodsman* stars Kevin Bacon as a pedophile who has just been released from prison after serving a 12-year sentence; the film shows him continuing to struggle with his demons, at the same time he is trying to establish a mature sexual relationship with a woman with whom he works. The movie underscores the complexity of the problem without providing pat solutions or a feel-good ending.

Incest

Incest is treated as a subclass of pedophilia in the *DSM-IV-TR*. The term refers to sexual relations between persons too closely related to marry. Russell (1983, 1984) has reported that the incidence of incest for stepdaughters and stepfathers is as high as 16%, and stepfathers are seven times more likely to abuse their children than biological fathers. Barnard et al. (1989) report that one out of six women who have stepfathers experienced sexual abuse at some point during childhood.

The prevalence of the various paraphilias can be estimated by surveying pornography and looking at what topics are the most popular. For example, Lebegue (1991) reviewed 3,050 magazine and book titles collected by the 1986 Attorney General's Commission on Pornography. He found that sadomasochism was by far the most common paraphilia; however, incest titles (e.g., *Suzie Loves Her Daddy*) comprised more than 21% of 746 titles judged to relate to *DSM-IV-TR* paraphilic diagnoses.

Stanley Kubrick's *Lolita* (1962) is the classic example of incest in a contemporary movie. The film takes liberties with Vladimir Nabokov's novel, but the changes were made with the permission of the great writer, who served as screenwriter for the movie. A psychoanalyst has argued that Nabokov himself was a pedophile as a result of childhood sexual abuse by an uncle (Centerwall, 1992). Considered quite daring when it was released more than four decades ago, the film portrays the love of Humbert (James Mason) for Lolita (Sue Lyon). Shelly Winters plays Lolita's mother and Peter Sellers has two roles in the film. Like many actual incestuous stepfathers, Mason's downfall comes from the restrictions he places on his daughter's emerging sexuality and his paranoia about her sexual experience with anyone but him. *Lolita* was remade in 1997 with Jeremy Irons playing the role of Humbert.

There are vivid scenes of bathroom seduction by a stepfather (Karl Malden) in Barbra Streisand's film *Nuts* (1987). The classic example of the combination of pedophilia and sociopathy is found in the 1931 Fritz Lang film *M*, in which Peter Lorre plays a child molester stalking the streets of Berlin. A riveting presentation of the fate of child molesters when they are caught and incarcerated is found in the 1977 prison drama *Short Eyes*.

AKA (2002) is a creative film that depicts a father who sexually abuses his son. In *Dolores Claiborne* (1995), a father sexually abuses his daughter in various ways; one scene occurs when the father makes his daughter masturbate him while riding on a boat in cold weather, claiming her hands are needed to keep him warm.

The drama in the controversial film *Priest* (1994) in part derives from the fact that a young girl tells her priest that she is being abused by her father (who attends mass every Sunday), and the priest is deeply troubled by his inability to break his vow of confidentiality to protect the child. The plot is complicated further by the fact that this same priest is involved in a sexual relationship with a gay friend, while his superior has broken his vows of celibacy and become sexually involved with the housekeeper.

Other Paraphilias

Telephone Scatologia

Most American women and a considerable number of men have experienced obscene phone calls (although it appears this will be replaced with offences committed on the Internet). *DSM-IV-TR* identifies the practice of making obscene calls for sexual gratification as **telephone scatologia**. Clinical assessment of 19 male adolescent sexual offenders who had committed exhibitionism or telephone scatologia showed that the majority were maladjusted, had committed numerous sexual offenses, and came from multi-problem families. Several of them appeared to be sexually deviant. Antisocial traits, sexual deviance in the family, homosexual conflicts, repressed sexuality, and sexual deviance were considered to be contributing factors (Saunders & Awad, 1991)

People who engage in telephone scatologia are generally males with low self-esteem. They often feel sexually inadequate, and the outrage of their victims gives them a feeling of power. These feelings of power are similar to those that accompany exhibitionism; however, the man making obscene phone calls is far less likely to be apprehended, and the practice provides similar thrills with far fewer risks. Obscene phone callers seldom seek out contact with the individuals they call.

Another variation of telephone scatalogia involves "dial-a-porn" services. These "900" numbers allow one to engage in paraphilic behavior without risk and with a seemingly enthusiastic partner. The lead character in Spike Lee's *Girl 6* (1996) and a woman supporting her family in Robert Altman's *Short Cuts* (1994) work as phone sex operators handling such calls. In the latter film, the woman moans, groans, and sighs at the same time she is changing the diapers on her baby and cooking her family's supper. Adam Sandler's character Barry Egan connects with a phone sex company in *Punch Drunk Love* (2002).

Philip Seymour Hoffman portrays a lonely man who is addicted to telephone scatalogia in *Happiness* (1998). He initiates innocuous phone conversations, and then probes for more intimate details while he masturbates.

Miscellaneous Paraphilias

Other paraphilias include **coprophilia** (feces), **urophilia** (urine), **klismaphilia** (sexual pleasure from enemas), **partialism** (exclusive focus on part of the body), **necrophilia** (sex with corpses), and **zoophilia** (animals). Alfred Kinsey investigated zoophilia (bestiality) and found that in some rural areas up to 65% of boys had experienced sexual contact with animals.

Necrophilia is believed to be extremely rare, although estimating the prevalence of the disorder is difficult for obvious reasons. In *Kill Bill, Vol. 1* (2003) a hospital aide sells the right to have sex with patients in comas; this behavior would probably be considered to be a form of necrophilia. Public interest in necrophilia was heightened by the arrest of Jeffrey Dahmer, someone who murdered his victims, had sex with their corpses, mutilated their bodies, and ate various body parts. Dahmer was tested with the **Minnesota Multiphasic Personality Inventory** (MMPI), a psychological test widely used to assess psychopathology. A computerized assessment of Dahmer's test results reported, "[This patient] is likely to have significant psychological problems... He typically deals with frustration by acting out in an extrapunitive way... [He is] quite conflicted over sexual issues." *Dahmer* (2002), a film based on the life of Jeffrey Dahmer, has little value as either entertainment or pedagogy.

John Waters is a director whose films are often designed to shock the viewer, and he has produced interesting cult films with sexual themes (e.g. *Pink Flamingos*, 1972); his recent film *A Dirty Shame* (2004) about a woman who becomes a sex addict after a head injury portrays a large number of fetishes, but the viewer actually learns little about fetishism from watching this somewhat insipid movie. The film stands in marked contrast to Molly Parker's sensitive portrayal of necrophilia in *Kissed* (1966). Parker's character, Sandra Larson, first becomes fascinated with death observing dead sparrows and chipmunks; she buries the animals but later digs them up and rubs her body with them. Sandra eventually gets a job in a funeral home; she has sex with the corpses but treats the sex act as a quasi-religious ritual. This film makes necrophilia seem more plausible than most of us believe it to be, and perhaps a little less reprehensible.

Necrophilia is sometimes portrayed or alluded to in vampire movies. One of the best of these is *Bram Stoker's Dracula* (1992), directed by Francis Ford Coppola. There are a number of case studies of people who are aroused by the sight of blood; this phenomenon is frequently referred to as **vampirism**.

International Films: Sexual and Gender Identity Disorders

Edouard Molinaro's *La Cage aux Folles* (*Birds of a Feather*, 1978) is a comedy that portrays the relationship between two middle-aged homosexual lovers, Renato and Albin. Renato owns and manages La Cage aux Folles, a nightclub in the south of France in which all the performers are male transvestites who perform as women. Albin, whose stage name is Zaza, is the star performer at La Cage aux Folles, as well as Renato's lover and longtime companion. Albin cross-dresses both on and off stage and has adopted an exclusive feminine identity.

It is important to understand that this film is a farce and not an accurate presentation of either homosexual relationships or transvestites. Albin's role as a drag queen is as exaggerated as his feminine mannerisms, and probably served to perpetuate many of the stereotypes about homosexuality that existed when the film was released in 1978. However, despite reliance on stereotypes, the film can be credited for its presentation of an enduring, loving relationship between its two lead characters. Both men are secure in their sexual identity, even though it does not conform to conventional norms, and they know the life they have made for themselves is the right one for them. At one point Renato remarks, "Yes, I use make-up. Yes, I live with a man. Yes, I'm an old fag. But I know who I am. It's taken twenty years and that deputy isn't going to destroy it."

The film also highlights the sanctimonious hypocrisy of many of those people who are so quick to limit sexual expression in others and illustrates the perils inherent in denial of one's true sexual identity. The film is best viewed as the hilarious farce it is, and one does the film a disservice by insisting that it portray too strong a social message.

Breakfast on Pluto (2005, Ireland/UK), Neal Jordan's adaptation of a novel by Patrick McCabe, is an Irish film that presents the life of "Kitten," an orphan and a transvestite who enjoys dressing up in women's clothes from a very early age. This film is less a gender identity study than the story of societal abuse, ostracization, tragedy, and/or diagnostic pathology. It is about an individual who happens to cross dress and have gender issues and overcomes enormous stressful and tragic experiences, including but not limited to serious life threats, prostitution, homelessness, job loss, and his house being burned down. Kitten perseveres through all of this. Transvestites are portrayed in the award-winning film *All About My Mother* (1999, Spain) and in *House of Fools* (2002, Russia).

Breaking the Waves (1996) is a powerful Danish film that examines troilism in a situation in which a formerly virile man paralyzed from an industrial accident insists that his wife have intercourse with other men so he can derive vicarious satisfaction from her stories. The wife, a devout Catholic, goes along with her husband's demands because she is convinced that these voyeuristic pleasures are the only thing keeping her husband alive.

Korean Director Chan-wook Park's unforgettable film *Old Boy* (2003) presents a man caught up in a terrible situation in which he unwittingly and unavoidably becomes involved in an incestuous relationship with his daughter, someone he has not seen for 15 years. Another film from Korea is the comedy *Sex is Zero* (2002), a cult film in Korea about the sexual energies and promiscuity of adolescents and college students. The film depicts a number of normal and abnormal sexual behaviors, including rubbing against others on a in subway (differentiated from frotteurism), sex with a blow-up doll, men gawking at women doing aerobics and sunbathing, compulsive masturbation, priapism, and young males' obsession with female breasts. The film's director claims that 80% of what happens in the film is based on real experiences.

Pedro Almodóvar's *Tie Me Up! Tie Me Down!* (1990) is a provocative investigation of the relationship between a mildly masochistic woman and the man who kidnaps her and holds her hostage, hoping she will eventually come to love him. The theme is ancient, present in other movies, such as William Wyler's 1965 film *The Collector*. However, few directors have developed the concept with as much skill as Almodóvar, who previously directed another complex psychological investigation of the relationships between men and women, *Women on the Verge of a Nervous Breakdown* (1988). *Tie Me Up! Tie Me Down!* tells the story of Ricky, a young man released from a mental institution, whose only ambition is to find a woman, Marina, he had slept with once when he had escaped from the institution. Marina, an actress and a former drug addict, now stars in pornographic movies and has no memory of her tryst with Ricky. Their interactions after the kidnapping present the viewer with an odd mix of sexual violence and comedy, and the film constantly jumps between the themes of love and control. Love eventually wins out, and Ricky and Marina develop a healthy, satisfying relationship. The movie sounds misogynistic, but Almodóvar very skillfully demonstrates the power Marina maintains throughout her captivity.

Akai hashi no shita no nurui mizu (*Warm Water Under a Red Bridge*, 2001), a Japanese film directed by Shohei Imamura, tells the story of a woman who retains water in her body that she can only release by "doing something wicked" like stealing things or having sexual intercourse. The woman's water is a symbolic life force; fish flourish and plants grow larger when exposed to it. Despite its unusual plot, this is a film well worth seeing.

There is a fascinating portrayal of autoerotic asphyxia in another Japanese film, Nagisa Oshima's *Ai No Corrida* (*In the Realm of the Senses*; 1976). This movie documents the sexual obsessions of two Japanese lovers who are preoccupied with sexual pleasure. The woman increasingly resorts to strangulation to prolong the erections of her lover; eventually and predictably, he dies during one of these episodes. In one graphic scene, the woman severs off the man's penis. The film is based on the true story of a woman who accidentally strangled her lover and then wandered around in a daze, carrying her lover's severed penis with her. Oshima was tried for obscenity in Japan when the film was released, but he was eventually acquitted. His stature as a filmmaker was vindicated by the critical and commercial success of the film in Europe and the United States.

A Short Film About Love (1988), a Polish movie directed by Krzysztof Kieslowski, is about Tomik, a shy and withdrawn 19-year-old voyeur who uses a telescope to spy on an older woman who lives in a nearby apartment. He becomes increasingly obsessed with the woman and eventually confesses that he has been watching her have sex with her numerous lovers. She is at first outraged, then intrigued. She later repositions her bed so he can observe her more easily when she is having sex with one of her lovers. Eventually the teenager has brief physical contact with her, but it is an unsatisfying, humiliating experience, and he flees from her apartment and attempts suicide by slitting his wrists. He survives, and while he is in the hospital recovering, the woman, Magda, becomes increasingly obsessed with him, using binoculars to watch his apartment to see when he will return. The first part of the film is presented from his perspective; the second from hers. The film is reminiscent of Hitchcock's masterpiece *Rear Window* (1954).

Many of the foreign films discussed are classics and highly recommended. The films are engaging and provocative, and they will help viewers understand the complex, complicated, and endlessly fascinating varieties of human sexual experience.

Further Exploration

If you have time to read just one book relevant to this chapter, make it:

Kahr, B. (2008). *Who's been sleeping in your head? The secret world of sexual fantasies*. New York, NY: Basic Books.

If you only have time for one article, read:

Riggle, E. D. B., Whitman, J. S., Olson, A., Rostosky, S. S., & Strong, S. (2008). The positive aspects of being a lesbian or gay man. *Professional Psychology: Research and Practice, 39*, 210–217.

Authors* Picks

Sexual and Gender Identity Disorders

Paraphilias

☐ *Lolita* (1962)
☐ *Secretary* (2002)
☐ *Towelhead* (2007)
☐ *The Reader* (2008)
☐ *The Woodsman* (2004)

Gender Identity Disorders

☐ *Boys Don't Cry* (1999)
☐ *Transamerica* (2005)
☐ *Breakfast on Pluto* (2005)

Sexual Dysfunction

☐ *The Oh in Ohio* (2006)
☐ *Kinsey* (2004)

Critical Thinking Questions

- Do the *DSM-IV-TR* transgender categories transvestic fetishism and gender identity disorder perpetuate social stereotypes and discrimination against gays and lesbians?
- In *La Cage aux Folles* (1978), would there have been deleterious psychological effects if Renato's son had been raised by Renato and Albin? What is your evidence?
- *La Cage aux Folles* suggests that gay men are likely to be especially creative and artistic. Is there any evidence supporting this stereotype? If not, where did it originate?
- The problem of sexual addiction is increasing. What societal factors may contribute to and reinforce this addiction? When is a sex addict most likely to seek treatment? What treatments are available? Are they successful?
- Is pedophilia more common among certain groups, cultures, sexual orientations, or professions? What is the relationship between pedophilia and the priesthood?
- Homosexuality was deleted from the *Diagnostic and Statistical Manual* of the American Psychiatric Association in 1973. What brought about this decision? What have been its effects?
- Body piercing of the genitals and nipples became common in the 1990s, whereas it was quite rare in the 1950s. Would these behaviors have been viewed as sexual deviance in the 1950s? How do culture and context influence the process of labeling pathology?
- Why is it that women's clothes (e.g., dresses and slips) are distinctly feminine, while men's clothes (e.g., pants and belts) are far less likely to be regarded as exclusively male?
- Is it ethical for therapists to work with gays and lesbians to modify their sexual orientation? If so, under what conditions would it be appropriate?
- What psychological theories have been put forward to explain the development of fetishes and other paraphilias?

Chapter 9

Schizophrenia and Delusional Disorders

"My name is John Nash! I'm being held against my will! Someone call the Department of Defense!"
John Nash (Russell Crowe) in *A Beautiful Mind* (2001)

Questions to Consider While Watching *A Beautiful Mind*

- What is paranoid schizophrenia? What evidence of this disorder is depicted with this patient?
- Are auditory hallucinations more or less common than visual hallucinations in people with schizophrenia?
- What is the etiology of John Nash's illness?
- Describe the course and progression of John Nash's illness as depicted in the film.
- Can mental health providers make accurate predictions about the likelihood of violence in people with mental illness?
- Is there any relationship between John Nash's mathematical genius and the course of his illness?
- What elements of anxiety and depression are present in John Nash and at what points in the film are they heightened?
- Can a patient with schizophrenia comprehend the reality of his or her delusions when he or she is confronted with absolute and contradicting truths?
- John Nash is depicted as having aged quite a bit in the film when compared with his wife and other characters. How can the lifestyle of someone with an untreated mental illness contribute to aging?
- How were Nash's delusions of paranoia and conspiracy affected by the realities of his job working for the government?
- What treatments are appropriate in addition to medication?
- What clues does director Ron Howard give in the first half of the film to indicate John Nash is in the early stages of schizophrenia?
- How do the cinematic elements, such as lighting and musical score, enhance the depiction of John Nash's schizophrenia?

Patient Evaluation[4]

Patient's stated reason for coming: "They say I've been diagnosed with schizophrenia. I take medicine for this condition. I don't see why I should be here today to talk about my problems. I can find the solution myself. I only came because I promised my wife I would."

History of the present illness: Professor John Nash is a 38-year-old, Caucasian male who presents to this outpatient clinic with a complex history of visual and auditory hallucinations, intense periods of agitation, confusion, paranoia,

---

4 This fictitious evaluation is written as if John Nash was interviewed shortly after his release from one of his psychiatric hospitalizations.

and delusional thinking. He experiences frequent visual hallucinations that are delusional and usually dangerous, although, on occasion, benign and supportive. The former most commonly take the form of a demanding Department of Defense agent who gives orders. The latter hallucinations are described as a young man and little girl, whom Professor Nash states are an old college roommate and the roommate's niece, respectively. He reported significant delusions of reference and claims he decodes messages from newspapers and magazines as a part of his top-secret work for the Pentagon. Nash eventually became convinced that his psychiatrist, whom he assaulted at one point, was a Russian spy and that his hallucinated friend had betrayed him. Professor Nash believes a radium die containing access codes has been implanted in his arm. There is a history of self-mutilation of his left arm in an apparent attempt to remove this device.

Past psychiatric illness, treatment, and outcomes: Professor Nash's symptoms began during his doctoral studies at Princeton University. He first received inpatient psychiatric treatment at the age of 33. He reports a history of two previous hospitalizations and a past diagnosis of "schizophrenia." His most recent hospitalization was ten months ago with a duration of four months. Records of these hospitalizations will be requested. In both instances, he received insulin-shock therapy five times per week for ten weeks.

Medical history: Professor Nash suffers from impotency as a result of the medication he is taking. There is also a long scar on his left arm, apparently the result of a previous attempt to cut out an imaginary communications device he believed was implanted in his arm. There is no other significant medical history.

Psychosocial history: Professor Nash quotes his first grade teacher who once said he was "born with two helpings of brain and only a half a helping of heart." He added, "my wife is helping me with the latter." He has been married for 8 years. He reports this is a happy marriage and describes his wife as the most beautiful, accepting person he has ever met. They have one child together, a two-and-a-half-year-old son. Professor Nash earned a PhD in Mathematics from Princeton University. He has a history of various academic awards, including the distinguished Carnegie fellowship.

Drug and alcohol history: Professor Nash denied any significant history of alcohol or drug abuse. He stated he has an occasional beer, and there is a history of binge drinking during graduate school.

Behavioral observations: Professor Nash presented as disheveled and unshaven, with clothes that did not match. He entered and left the office with his head down and a shuffling gait. He occasionally talked to himself in the form of "asides." His eye contact was poor, particularly when answering questions. Mood and affect were dysphoric. Speech was coherent but at times tangential. There was a marked tremor present, possibly a symptom of tardive dyskinesia. Professor Nash has some insight into the nature of his condition but refuses to accept its seriousness. He seemed to be preoccupied with objects in the office, such as the reflection of the light shining on a water glass.

Mental status examination: Professor Nash scored 30/30 on the Folstein Mini Mental State Examination. He was fully oriented at the time of the interview. He was particularly strong with the serial sevens as he swiftly counted backwards from 100 down to 23 accurately, despite the interviewer telling him he could "stop" several times.

Functional assessment: Professor Nash graduated with his PhD ten years ago. He worked as a professor at MIT for six years, teaching classes and conducting research. He is currently unemployed. He is a well-known and highly respected scholar in his field. Socially, he is quite withdrawn, has limited social skills, and his current social support consists of two work colleagues and his wife. He states he does not like to socialize but that he enjoys teaching "eager, young minds."

Strengths: This patient is clearly gifted in the areas of science and mathematics. He has conducted seminal work in his field. His love for his wife is strong and apparent. He enjoys star-gazing, going on walks, and spending time with his wife. He is a very creative and curious man who is adept at critical thinking.

Diagnosis: Schizophrenia, paranoid type. There is clear evidence of both visual and auditory hallucinations and paranoid delusions. There is no evidence of medical conditions or a history of substance abuse that could account for these symptoms. He experiences mild depression as a result of the challenges of rehabilitation, though these do not appear to warrant a separate diagnosis.

Treatment plan: Relapse is highly likely if this patient does not follow up with treatment recommendations, particularly his medication regimen. He could be dangerous if he responds to his delusions. He requires outpatient treatment focused on relapse prevention and regular psychiatric visits to provide medication review and monitoring until his condition further stabilizes. He would likely benefit from a psychiatric rehabilitation approach that emphasizes social skills training, peer support, and facilitated occupational integration into the community.

Prognosis: Good, pending adherence to medication regimen and psychiatric rehabilitation.

Schizophrenia and *A Beautiful Mind*: Realities, Misconceptions, and Recovery

A Beautiful Mind (2001) is based on the biography of the same name by Sylvia Nasar, written about the life of John Forbes Nash, Jr., who won the Nobel Prize for Economics in 1994. John and Alicia Nash have noted in interviews that they are satisfied with the final film product. Dr. Nash was often on the set of *A Beautiful Mind* and consulted with Russell Crowe and Ron Howard in the production process. Although the film is true to the "spirit" and major events of John Nash's life, it does leave out some of the less flattering details such as his divorce and remarriage to Alicia and an arrest history.

The film depicts the horrors, traumas, and suffering of schizophrenia, and it illustrates that people with schizophrenia can find a sense of normalcy in life, certainly outside of mental institutions, sometimes functioning as well as anyone in society. The film has educated millions of viewers about the realities and challenges of schizophrenia. However, it has flaws and may mislead viewers in some significant ways. For example, auditory hallucinations are more common and occur far more frequently than visual hallucinations, yet visual hallucinations are portrayed as one of John Nash's most salient symptoms, and the public is left to believe that this is a standard presentation for those with schizophrenia. Director Ron Howard was using the visual medium of film, and therefore he chose to emphasize visual phenomena.

"Often what I feel is obligation... or guilt over wanting to leave, rage against John, against God. But then I look at him and I force myself to see the man that I married and he becomes that man. He's transformed into someone that I love and I'm transformed into someone that loves him. It's not all the time but it's enough."

Alicia Nash in response to a question of how she is coping with her husband's illness in *A Beautiful Mind* (2001)

The film digs deep into the challenges associated with treatment and rehabilitation of a person coping with a severe mental illness. Few films have done as good of a job depicting the impact of severe mental illness upon healthy family members. The latter part of the film depicts John Nash's wife, Alicia, playing an important role in helping him "live with the realities of schizophrenia." She helps him remember to take his medications. She works longer hours, takes a large role in child rearing, and manages household chores, all in addition to helping in her husband's recovery.

Relapse is common in people with schizophrenia due to numerous challenges, such as depression associated with recovery, the reality of remembering to take medications several times per day, and the multiple unpleasant side effects of the medication. This film is an accurate depiction of the difficulty of compliance with medication regimens and it shows the impact of psychotropic medications on John Nash's ability to work, his difficulties in taking care of his son, and his inability to sexually satisfy his wife.

"He's been injected with a serum. I can see him because of the chemicals enlisted in my bloodstream when my implant dissolved. I couldn't tell you, it was for your own protection."

John Nash during a relapse after not taking his medication in *A Beautiful Mind* (2001)

It is a challenge for the person with schizophrenia to adapt and become integrated into the community. The depiction of John Nash's struggle to adapt is another strength of the film. Stress triggers his delusions, he longs to give up and become further isolated, but he also has moments of grace and connection with others.

The film illustrates the fears of the public about schizophrenia, and specifically examines the impact of the illness on Nash's friends. His best friend goes to Nash's house and is visibly nervous, hesitant in his speech, and laughs uncomfortably. Another friend watches Nash closely when Nash enters the office. Other reactions are more negative: Some students at the university make fun of Nash and mimic his awkward gait and posture, while others stare in disbelief at his odd behavior.

A Beautiful Mind can be compared to the more recent film, *Proof* (2005), starring Anthony Hopkins as a world-class mathematician with schizophrenia working at an elite university. *Proof* also depicts the impact of schizophrenia on family members (in *Proof*, it is the father-daughter relationship). Frederick Frese, a psychologist and Professor of Psychology who shares that he has schizophrenia himself, reviewed this film for *PsycCRITIQUES* and made the observation that *Proof* "does an excellent job of capturing what is happening in the mind as it experiences the expanded horizon of meaningfulness that occurs in schizophrenia" (Frese, 2006).

The Diagnosis of Schizophrenia

Schizophrenia usually first occurs during late adolescence or early adulthood, but it can begin in childhood or middle/late adulthood. Even though the frequency of the illness is equal in both genders, symptoms in males often occur earlier than in females.

In order for a person to be diagnosed with schizophrenia, certain symptoms must be present. According to the *DSM-IV-TR*, there must be continuous signs of the disturbance for at least six months and, during one month (the active phase), two or more of the following must be present: Delusions, hallucinations, disorganized speech, grossly disorganized or catatonic behavior, or negative symptoms. The individual's ability to function in work, social relations, and self-care decreases during the active phase and rarely returns to the individual's premorbid level of achievement.

Following the active phase of the illness, the following must be present in order to meet diagnostic criteria: Marked social isolation or withdrawal, and marked impairment of role function.

"The nightmare of schizophrenia is not knowing what's true. Imagine if you had suddenly learned that the people, the places, the moments most important to you were not gone, not dead, but worse... they've never been. What kind of hell would that be?"

Psychiatrist Dr. Rosen educating Alicia Nash about her husband's schizophrenia in *A Beautiful Mind* (2001)

Schizophrenia is categorized into five types: Paranoid, disorganized, catatonic, undifferentiated, and residual.

The **paranoid type** is characterized by systematized delusions or frequent hallucinations related to a single theme (e.g., hearing denigrating voices). These individuals are often extremely anxious, angry, or argumentative, and they may become violent. There is not the strong relationship between violence and schizophrenia that many people expect (and which most movies suggest is common). Among people diagnosed with schizophrenia, paranoid patients are the most likely to commit acts of violence. This is a common subtype portrayed in films; it is popularized in films such as *A Beautiful Mind* (2001), *Donnie Darko* (2001), and *Gothika* (2004). The documentary *People Say I'm Crazy* (2004) is a remarkably honest and real portrayal of the daily life of a courageous man coping with paranoid schizophrenia.

The **disorganized type** presents with a picture of incoherent speech and disorganized behavior. These patients rapidly shift from one idea to another; often these ideas are unrelated. They may also express inappropriate emotion, such as laughing on a sad occasion. They usually have very strange mannerisms and are extremely socially impaired. Robin Williams' character in *The Fisher King* (1991) and Geoffrey Rush's portrayal of David Helfgott in *Shine* (1996) have many attributes of this subtype (in addition to paranoid type). Ralph Fiennes' title character in *Spider* (2002) is one of the best examples of this subtype.

The most salient symptom of the **catatonic type** is psychomotor disturbance. For example, catatonic persons may appear to be in a stupor, completely unaware of their environment. They may maintain one posture for a long time (**waxy flexibility**), crawl into a fetal position, hold an arm in a bizarre position, or sit stiffly in a chair; it may be difficult to move the individual because of the muscle rigidity. At times these individuals become very excited or agitated, but then slip into the previous mannerisms. At times they are mute. This type of schizophrenia is less common than other types. The film *Awakenings* (1990) is a dramatic portrayal of catatonia (although this particular film depicted a neurological rather than psychiatric condition). Many films depicting psychiatric institutions have one or two characters (often in the background) who have catatonic schizophrenia, as in *K-Pax* (2001) and *House of Fools* (2004).

Schizophrenia of the **residual type** is a category for persons who do not exhibit any of the symptoms of the active phase (hallucinations, delusions, etc.) but do have other symptoms such as social withdrawal or eccentric behavior

(APA, 1994). Eugene Levy's character, Mitch, in *A Mighty Wind* (2003) illustrates this subtype. Mitch sits alone and stares for hours in a drab motel room, displays psychomotor retardation, exhibits blank, distant, and quizzical facial expressions, and has inappropriate social skills, yet he does not appear to be in the active phase of schizophrenia. These are residual effects. The viewer learns Mitch had previously been hospitalized for severe depression, anger outbursts, and eccentric behavior, though an actual diagnosis is never given.

The **undifferentiated type** is characterized by psychotic symptoms (delusions, hallucinations, etc.) without salient characteristics of the other types. The undifferentiated type of the illness is frequently found in inpatient settings. Any film with a psychiatric hospital as the setting would have patients on the ward or in the day room that would be diagnosed with schizophrenia, undifferentiated type.

Family Dynamics and Schizophrenia

In the 1960s and 1970s, a popular theory implicated dysfunctional family communication patterns in the etiology of schizophrenia. Communication within the family of a person with schizophrenia was believed to be indirect, unclear, incongruent, and growth impeding. Communication within theses families was thought to be distorted and based on "double messages." The child received two opposing messages from the parent and, thus, was in a **double bind**. For example, a parent might say, "Come here and give me a hug" and, when the child responded, the parent would push the child away. The child then would feel that pleasing the parent was an impossible "no win" situation and would develop schizophrenia in response to this psychological bind. The **schizophrenogenic family** was characterized as being severely fused. Members of these families never adequately separated or developed into individuals; and, thus, the family had no boundaries. This view of distorted family communication has been largely discounted as a cause of schizophrenia.

Despite the fact that no one seriously believes that parents "cause" their children's schizophrenia, this misconception persists in both popular culture and contemporary cinema. Peter Winter's mother in *Clean, Shaven* (1993) is portrayed as cold, aloof, and withdrawn; there is a clear implication that she is at least in part responsible for her

son's illness. Likewise, the movie *Shine* (1996), Scott Hick's fascinating film about the life of child prodigy and pianist David Helfgott, clearly implicates David's father as the root of his son's subsequent mental illness. The father is alternately loving and hateful, telling his son, "No one can love you like me!" while at the same time actively working to limit his son's future and potential. A similar theme can be found in the 1962 film *David and Lisa*, in which David's mother – a woman focused on appearances – makes some efforts to support David but ends up appearing insensitive to her son's abilities and problems. The father is depicted as passive, distant, and unavailable to David in his younger years. Both parents are ineffective in dealing with David's problems, and the film suggests there is a link between the dysfunctional parental communication and David's mental illness.

Misconception: People With Mental Illness are Violent

One of the most profound yet common stereotypes in contemporary cinema is the connection filmmakers draw between mental illness and violence. This misconception is strongest in films that portray schizophrenia and delusional conditions. It is often not directly stated in the film, however, the plotline and ensuing messages are usually clear to the viewer: They see a character being treated for a psychological problem or they see a character begin to deteriorate with mental illness and the next thing the viewer sees is that person perpetrating a violent act. This is unfortunate because the general public is poor at understanding the relationship between violence and mental illness, and many individuals, influenced by media reports, are likely to exaggerate their own personal risk when interacting with someone who has a mental illness. The reality is that people with mental illness are far more likely to be the victim of a violent act than the perpetrator; moreover, research also shows that mental illness is neither a necessary nor a sufficient cause for violence (Stuart, 2003). The data are mixed as to whether people with mental illness are more or less likely to react with violence than the general public. Yet filmmakers use this stereotype as it provides a clear understanding of what is often unspeakable and perplexing; it is a way to clear up ambiguity and to make sense of the human psyche.

"I was Mr. Nobody till I killed the biggest somebody on earth.... I was nothing and [then] I was a big shot."

"There was no emotion in my blood, there was no anger, there was nothing. It was dead silence in my brain, dead cold quiet. He looked at me, he looked past me. Then I heard my head, [it] said do it, do it, do it, over again."

Mark Chapman explaining his murder of John Lennon

Films portraying the assassination of public figures are a clear example of filmmakers leveraging this idea. Two in particular – *The Killing of John Lennon* (2006) and *The Assassination of Richard Nixon* (2004) – portray men who obsess over a public figure and subsequently murder or attempt to murder as a result of a strong delusional process. Both men are scruffy, irritable, quirky, socially awkward, and withdrawn. Each has a deep insecurity and inferiority and an anger toward some aspect of the social system (e.g., consumerism, politics), and each uses violence to deal with these frustrations. Each is a fascinating, accurate portrayal of the internal dialogue and reasoning that fosters a grandiose delusional state. In *The Killing of John Lennon*, Mark Chapman is very grandiose and paranoid, displaying mood changes and delusional explanations for his behavior. He shows no remorse or regret and believes he later

"That little guy can't do it anymore. He just can't do it anymore... because there's a cancer in the system. The whole system has a cancer and I'm being punished because I resist. But somebody has to resist, just somebody has to resist."

"I know what it's like to not be respected, to be lied to, and to be treated like a great big nothing."

Samuel J. Bicke's (Sean Penn) delusions that led to his assassination attempt on Richard Nixon in *The Assassination of Richard Nixon* (2004)

received a message from God to plead guilty. In the end, both films leave the viewer with a strong sense of connection between schizophrenia/delusions and violence/murder.

Another film that makes people fear those with mental illness is *Keane* (2004), a movie in which a man frantically searches for his daughter whom he has lost at a port authority bus terminal in New York City. Damian Lewis as the protagonist, a man with schizophrenia, does a marvelous job portraying how he struggles to hold reality together yet continues to deteriorate. Nevertheless, the aspects of the film that most viewers will remember are the scenes of intense and bizarre behavior. In one particular scene, William Keane chases a man (whom he's never before seen) in a parking garage.

William H. Macy's portrayal of a man losing touch with reality in *Edmond* (2005), written for the screen and the stage by David Mamet, is equally chilling. Edmond breaks up with his wife and slowly deteriorates as he starts to wander the streets of New York City looking for sex. He begins to self-destruct and his loneliness, isolation, instability, and lack of responsibility and empathy become clear. The viewer will easily remember standout scenes of Edmond impulsively screaming at a woman who does not listen to him on the subway and his murder of a waitress after having sex with her. He later rationalizes his killing as the result of too much coffee, and he claims that there are just too many people in the world.

There are literally hundreds of suspense and horror movies about "psychotic killers" who are on a rampage, usually attacking females. While entertaining for some, these films typically have nothing to do with any particular mental disorder, and they perpetuate the stigma associated with mental illness. The term psychotic is used to induce fear and suggest unpredictability. Pictures such as *The Caretaker* (1964), *The Silent Partner* (1979), *Alone in the Dark* (1982), *Angel in Red* (1991), and *Cape Fear* (1991) have contributed to shaping the stigma experienced by people with mental illness.

Two recent horror/thriller films that portray characters deteriorating with mental illness who consequently become violent are *May* (2002) and *Love Object* (2003). *May* is a macabre, well-acted character study of a veterinary technician whose best friend is her doll. As she continues to fail at intimate and social relationships, she begins to become psychotic. She begins to kill in order to get ideal body parts that she combines to form a whole. In *Love Object*, a young man believes his lifelike sex doll is real and comes to believe he is being controlled and attacked by the doll; these delusions deepen and extend to violence in the outside world.

"If you can't find a friend, make one"

An example of psychotic thinking in *May* (2002)

Even the portrayal of schizophrenia in the widely popular *A Beautiful Mind* (2001), albeit helpful in educating the public in a number of ways, also highlights scenes in which John Nash becomes violent or dangerous to his wife and to their newborn baby, particularly when he is in a paranoid state. Other classic examples of this stereotype include Annie Wilkes, the delusional character played by Academy Award winner Kathy Bates, who tortures a writer she is obsessed with in *Misery* (1990), the isolated female protagonist in Roman Polanski's *Repulsion* (1965, UK), and Robert De Niro's classic role of a delusional killer, Travis Bickle, in *Taxi Driver* (1976). Numerous other films portray people with schizophrenia and related disorders who are violent and/or dangerous.

Schizophrenia and Delusional Disorders in Contemporary Films

Schizophrenia

Can films educate students and the general public about the realities of schizophrenia? In one study, a video was constructed with segments from popular movies depicting inaccurate and accurate portrayals of schizophrenia (Owen, 2007). The researchers randomly assigned college students to either a video presentation or a traditional lecture on schizophrenia, and later tested the students' knowledge of schizophrenia. The results showed knowledge improvement following both the movie clips and the lecture; however, the movie clips had a greater corrective effect for female students.

Canvas

This 2006 film from first-time director/writer, Joseph Greco, is an outstanding portrayal of schizophrenia, paranoid type. It is based on some

of Greco's experiences growing up with a parent coping with the symptoms of schizophrenia. Indeed, some individuals in the mental health community believe Marcia Gay Harden's portrayal of schizophrenia is the most accurate in film history. Harden plays Mary Marino who desires to be close to her husband and son, but who finds that her illness is a significant obstacle to achieving this goal. She regularly has auditory hallucinations and tries to drown out the sound, first with running water and later by literally pouring water on her forehead. She displays inappropriate affect (e.g., laughing at the dinner table during conversation about a serious matter), embarrasses her son by running after the bus saying that she was concerned about his safety, and seems to be socially unaware of the discomfort her symptoms cause others with whom she interacts. In a memorable scene, Mary runs around in the rain, fear-struck and paranoid as she wakes up the neighbors searching for a wire tap. The film references the Baker Act (also called the Florida Mental Health Act), a law that can be invoked by judges, police, physicians, or mental health professionals. The Baker Act allows for involuntary examination of individuals who have mental illness and are a harm to themselves or others or who neglect their own basic needs. Mary is routinely picked up by police when her paranoid behavior puts her safety at risk.

Important themes in the film include the loss of a family member (to institutionalization), the struggles associated with coping with mental illness, and the challenge of finding hope at the most trying of times. The realities of severe mental illness are not minimized – Mary is often in and out of the hospital, she frequently stops taking her medication, and her illness has a profound impact on her family. Her husband obsesses about building a boat and her son begins to avoid school. Nevertheless, each of the three taps into an outlet of creativity to cope with the situation – each has a different "canvas," whether it be painting, knitting, or construction/building.

"When you paint, they go away"
"Who?"
"The voices"

Mary Marino interacting with another patient in *Canvas* (2006)

The film is a wonderful portrayal of the impact of mental illness on the family; it is also tender, hopeful, and positive, with an ending that is neither contrived nor forced.

K-Pax

In this 2001 film, Kevin Spacey plays Prot, a man claiming to be from the planet K-Pax who has traveled to Earth by light beams. At the outset, we see Prot appear in a busy train station amongst sparkles of light. Soon he is falsely accused of a crime and admitted to a psychiatric institution. The psychiatrist, Dr. Powell (Jeff Bridges), takes an interest in working with Prot when he learns Prot is unresponsive to conventional psychiatric medications. As their relationship progresses, Dr. Powell learns much about the identity of Prot and the differences between K-Pax and earth. Prot offers extensive (and savant-like) explanations of his planet's rotational patterns, discusses the ways in which men and women procreate on his planet, and gives descriptions of the differences between the planets. Many of Prot's delusions are bizarre, which keeps him from being given a diagnosis of delusional disorder. The viewer essentially has two options at this point: Prot is either a man with schizophrenia or a spiritual guide from another planet. We can view the film accepting the former as true to help us understand the predicament in which a delusional patient finds himself. He is completely trapped by his delusions and does not have a way out; the painful challenge of this is that the patient is not aware he is delusional. Viewers who choose the latter option are choosing a fascinating, inspirational take on the film, while at the same time buying into the myth that the person with mental illness is an "enlightened member of society" (Hyler, Gabbard, & Schneider, 1991).

But it gets more complex. As Dr. Powell questions Prot on where he comes from and where he has visited on this planet, another diagnostic explanation emerges. We learn through flashbacks and hypnotic regression that Prot is Robert Porter, a man who found the bodies of his murdered and raped wife and child, and then experienced the trauma of encountering the killer in his home and breaking the murderer's neck. Prot then washes his bloody hands with a water hose (hence his water phobia) and attempts suicide in a nearby river. The viewer is left to assume Prot was found and taken to the psychiatric hospital. Consequently, additional diagnostic considerations emerge, such as PTSD and dissociative fugue. His sudden travel, assumption of a new identity, and inability to recall his past (other than

Additional Questions for Discussion (K-Pax)

- What diagnoses do you believe are appropriate for Prot's character? Explain.
- How does Prot fit the other patients on the ward into his delusional framework?
- What would be appropriate criteria for releasing Prot from the hospital?
- Compare the portrayal of mental illness depicted in this film and in *A Beautiful Mind* (2001).
- Discuss the differences of the role of the psychiatrist and treatment in this film and in *A Beautiful Mind*. How does the time period each film is set in play a role?

under hypnosis) make a strong case for the diagnosis of dissociative fugue.

In the end, Prot becomes catatonic – unresponsive and rigid as he is pushed around in a wheelchair – providing further evidence to support a diagnosis of schizophrenia.

Spider

The viewer realizes this is a deeply psychological movie as he or she sees the opening credits. Inkblots, similar to those used with the classic psychological assessment tool, the **Rorschach Psychodiagnostik**, are integrated into the opening. The viewer is thus invited to "interpret" and challenge what he or she is seeing from the very start to the ambiguous ending.

Director David Cronenberg sets the tone of this 2002 film in the first scene, which depicts "the flow of humanity" – an arriving train, the hustle of activity, and a multitude of people heading toward their own destinations – contrasted with the lead character, Spider (Ralph Fiennes), slowly stepping off the train, disoriented and isolated from everyone else. This dark and dreary film maps out the psychological terrain of a man with schizophrenia. Spider has minimal dialogue so the viewer learns about his inner world through his facial expressions, body language, and utter isolation.

The adult character Spider, played by Ralph Fiennes, has been discharged from an institution and attempts to integrate into a group home. He has many symptoms of schizophrenia, including delusions, mumbling and disorganized speech, incoherent and grossly disorganized behavior, an unclean and disheveled appearance, and negative symptoms including severely flattened affect and shuffling gait.

Ingeniously, Cronenberg places the present-day Spider character in all of the memory scenes as Spider tries to reassemble his past. The adult Spider is shown observing his parents and himself as a boy interacting with the world. Some of these memories are false and some are accurate, but neither the viewer nor Spider himself knows the truth. To make matters more complicated, Spider fuses identities of his memories as well as his past and present, which results in further confusion and distortion.

This is also a good depiction of **childhood schizophrenia** as we see the young boy distort reality, express paranoia that his father and his father's mistress killed his mother, and the boy's complete isolation from social contact.

"You're by yourself too much. You need some mates. When I was your age I had mates. Every young lad needs... needs some mates."

Bill Cleg (Gabriel Byrne) speaking to his delusional son Spider

---

Throughout the film, several metaphors are used to portray Spider's struggle to recognize real-

 Additional Questions for Discussion (*Spider*)

- What makes this character's portrayal of schizophrenia so provocative and realistic?
- Are some of the behaviors portrayed by Spider (e.g., collecting little objects from the street, lying in a fetal position in the bathtub) common characteristics of schizophrenia?
- What does this film have to say about the etiology of schizophrenia?
- In interviews, director David Cronenberg has spoken to the potential for multiple endings for this film. Reflect on different options and cite which fits best with this portrayal of schizophrenia.
- Cronenberg states he wants the viewer to "become Spider." Why? Does this happen for you?
- This film obviously deals with a person with schizophrenia. Why isn't the word or any other diagnosis ever mentioned in the movie?

ity and the disintegration of reality into psychosis. In one scene, Spider is carefully putting together a very complex puzzle of hundreds of pieces and in a latter scene after putting together some painful memory fragments, he angrily destroys the puzzle, throwing the pieces to the floor in the day room. Broken mirrors, pieces of glass, and twine, used to create what appears to be a spider's web, symbolize his mental state.

Delusional Disorders

Contrary to popular belief, a delusional disorder is not a type of schizophrenia, and hallucinations are not a predominant feature of delusional disorders. The delusions experienced by someone with a delusional disorder are not bizarre; instead, they involve situations of everyday life, such as being poisoned, followed, or loved, when in fact this is not the case in reality. The delusions can be erotomanic, grandiose, jealous, persecutory, somatic, or a combination of these types. A person with delusional disorder can usually function fairly well in his or her daily life.

Lars and the Real Girl (2007) is an exceptional portrayal of delusional disorder. Ryan Gosling portrays Lars, a taciturn, aloof young man who lives in a detached residence near his brother's family. Lars does everything he can to avoid social contact, intimacy, and conversation. One day he purchases a lifelike doll on the Internet, names it Bianca, and comes to believe Bianca is his actual girlfriend. He takes Bianca to parties, to church, to family dinners, and treats her with respect, telling her his innermost secrets and feelings. Interestingly, the small community decides to join Lars' delusion, talking to, spending time with, and even fighting over who will be able to interact with her. It is this community support that fosters Lars' connections with real people until he feels safe enough to let the delusion go.

In *The Truman Show* (1998) no psychotic disorders are portrayed. However, this Peter Weir movie is a useful teaching tool in understanding delusional disorders. It flips the essence of a delusion on its ear. The film is about the unreal life of Truman Burbank. Everything around him has been created for him (or, better stated, for the viewing public of the reality show) – all the people in the city, the buildings, the street lamps, the water, even the sun! It is all an extensive production set for a television show, yet Truman accepts his town of Seahaven as his reality; it is all he has known from birth to young adulthood. His name is appropriate as he is the only "true man" because everyone else, including his wife, best friend, mother, and father, are set actors. Eventually, Truman senses that he is trapped in a "world within a world" and tries to escape this contrived reality.

"We accept the reality with which the world is presented to us."

Christof (Ed Harris) in
The Truman Show (1998)

Imagine that there was no television show and that Seahaven was like any other town; in this scenario, would Truman's behavior be seen as delusional? All of his behaviors would probably be seen as paranoid: His questioning and threatening of his wife with a knife, his suspicious looking around the store, his pausing in the middle of the street and stopping traffic. Most of the world around him would be incorporated into his delusional framework. He would include various environmental elements in his delusions: The camera equipment that suddenly falls from the sky, the rain water that just rains down on him and then follows him when he steps out of it, the observation of inconsistency in his wife's behavior. Further

 Additional Questions for Discussion (*The Truman Show*)

- How can this movie help the therapist or client understand the popular treatment approach of cognitive-behavioral therapy?
- In some ways, this film is a psychological study. What are the moral and ethical drawbacks and possibilities in creating a research case study in a controlled environment as seen in this film? Will this be done in the future? Would it better society in some way?
- In Truman's world, the society revolves around him. Is this belief common for a person who has symptoms of paranoia, delusions, or schizophrenia?
- As Truman is leaving his world, Christof encourages him not to leave saying "I know you better than you." If Truman were to believe this, would this suggest psychosis? Do most people with a psychotic disorder believe some variation of this?

paranoid behaviors are exhibited when he follows his wife and he questions who he can trust. Truman explains that he believes his whole life is "building to something" and that he needs to escape to Fiji for a while. We would probably interpret this as delusional thinking.

Instead, what really happens is Truman does what a person with delusional disorder does not typically do. He challenges his own perception of reality, and this is ultimately what sets him free.

Other Films Portraying Psychotic Disorders

People with schizophrenia often get stereotyped as being the "crazy person on the street" which generalizes to the misconception that all eccentric behavior is "crazy." Films depict such instances with minor characters that may or may not have much impact on the plot, but nevertheless this misconception helps shape the stigma associated with mental illness. In *Cinema Paradiso* (1988), one man who appears to have schizophrenia makes serious claim to a public square at a certain time each evening. Each day, he runs around a small area of the street he believes he owns exclaiming, "The square is mine. It's twelve o'clock, the square is mine!" refusing to allow anyone to step in this area. Later in the film (many years later), he continues the behavior, claiming "It's my square. It's mine. The square is mine." Though not critical scenes to the film, the eccentricity and subsequent label do not go unnoticed by the viewer.

At times, the psychosis depicted in films is a brief break with reality (i.e., a **brief psychotic disorder**), often with an obvious trigger. Consider Bernardo Bertolucci's most recent film, *The Dreamers* (2003), in which a young man triangulates with a pair of enmeshed fraternal twins (male and female). At one point, when the young man and the female twin are about to have sex, she begins to hear her twin brother in the next room with another woman. She breaks with reality screaming to the young man "Who are you? What are you doing in my room? Get out!" while pounding on her brother's wall. The next morning, after a restful sleep, she is coherent and once again oriented to reality. If her symptoms lasted longer than one day, she would be likely to receive a diagnosis of brief psychotic disorder. The experience of the female twin in *The Dreamers* is similar to the experience of a character in *Jesus of Montreal*

(1989, Canada/France) who has a psychotic break in the subway in which he suddenly begins to blurt random, abstract sentences to strangers and then passes out; in such cases, one would immediately wonder if there were an underlying medical cause for the syncopal episode.

Shared psychotic disorder (also called *folie à deux* [French for "a madness shared by two"]), a condition in which an individual develops a delusion in the context of a close relationship with someone who already has a delusion, is seldom depicted in films. The film *Birth* (2004) is an exception. This independent film features Nicole Kidman as Anna, who encounters Sean, a young boy with the delusion that he is the incarnation of Anna's deceased husband. Anna is skeptical at first but as she begins to spend time with Sean she begins to believe him, sharing his delusion. Of course, no other characters believe this could be anything but a delusion, and the boy is later confronted by Anna's husband's mistress who claims the husband would have sought out others first. This breaks the delusional framework – and the boy, who "only feels love" for Anna – disappointedly tells Anna he is not the husband. Her *folie à deux* no longer possible, Anna moves on with her life. To a much lesser extent, *Who's Afraid of Virginia Woolf* (1966) portrays a husband and wife who appear to have characteristics of a shared psychotic disorder involving a son who never existed.

John Cassavetes' *A Woman Under the Influence* (1974) presents some challenging differential diagnosis questions. With Mabel Longhetti (Gena Rowlands), there is some evidence for **schizoaffective disorder,** as she is clearly not in touch with reality and has various mood problems; however, it is unclear whether she experiences her psychosis for two weeks without any mood symptoms. In addition, she has the hallmark borderline personality criterion – an intense fear of abandonment – and she self-mutilates. She is referred to as chronically nervous by others including her own child, and a diagnosis of anxiety disorder would have to be considered as well. More information would be needed to be able to ensure proper differential diagnosis.

Psychotic disorder due to a general medical condition can arguably be seen in *Synecdoche, New York* (2008). Philip Seymour Hoffman portrays Caden Cotard; the name "Cotard" is a direct reference to Cotard's syndrome, a nihilistic or negation delusion. This is a rare neuropsychiatric disorder in which the individual holds a delusional belief that he or she is dead or does not exist. The character Cotard struggles with a number of existential, relationship, and life problems, bordering on the somatic and delusional, with accompanying mood disturbances. The actual diagnosis isn't certain, largely due to the surrealistic filmmaking and complexly layered plot of filmmaker Charlie Kaufman.

Terry Gilliam's 1991 film *The Fisher King*, stars Robin Williams as Parry, an obsessed yet benign street person. Parry believes himself to be a knight whose mission is to save the Holy Grail. Throughout the film, Parry has several hallucinations, including seeing friendly "little people" who communicate with him regularly and give him guidance. The Red Knight is a frightening hallucination that appears at times of extreme stress or when he is reminded of his personal tragedy.

In *Sophie's Choice* (1982), Sophie (Meryl Streep), Nathan, (Kevin Kline), and Stingo (Peter MacNicol) become inseparable friends, with Sophie and Nathan maintaining a turbulent romantic/sexual relationship and Stingo eventually falling deeply in love with Sophie. Sophie and Stingo struggle to understand Nathan's eccentric, erratic behavior, which at different times involves intense love, suspiciousness, anger, hostility, and paranoia. Initially, Nathan merely appears to be an unstable, "moody" person who claims to be a Harvard graduate and an overworked research biologist. As the story unfolds, the audience learns that Nathan has been diagnosed with paranoid schizophrenia and he is only marginally coping with life. His symptoms are exacerbated by the use of amphetamines and cocaine, and his psychotic thinking leads to vicious accusations and unpredictable behavior. His bizarre behavior becomes more pronounced as his interpersonal stress increases and his denial is challenged. It is unclear how much Nathan's drug use influences his symptoms; if it were determined that his symptoms developed during or within a month of his substance intoxication or withdrawal, he would qualify for a **substance-induced psychotic disorder** diagnosis.

One of the most vivid cinematic portrayals of psychiatric decompensation occurs in *The Caine Mutiny* (1954). Humphrey Bogart plays Captain Philip Francis Queeg, the obsessive-compulsive skipper of a World War II destroyer. The ship's crew silently watches the deterioration that occurs as Queeg is put under increasing pressure, and eventually a junior officer, Lieutenant Barney Greenwald, takes command. Greenwald is later court-martialed, and the film's most dramatic moment comes when Queeg cracks under the stress of the courtroom examination while playing with steel ball bearings, as he does when he is anxious.

> "Ah, but the strawberries! That's, that's where I had them. They laughed at me and made jokes, but I proved beyond the shadow of a doubt, and with, with geometric logic, that, that a duplicate key to the wardroom icebox did exist."
>
> Captain Queeg in *The Caine Mutiny*

International Films: Schizophrenia and Other Psychotic Disorders

Two recent films from South Korea are particularly noteworthy for their portrayal of mental illness: *Save the Green Planet* (2003) and *I'm a Cyborg, But That's OK* (2006). In the former, a young man pursues individuals he perceives are aliens that come from Andromeda and he must stop them from destroying the planet. He and his girlfriend capture these individuals and torture them, although he believes he is taking away their powers by going after their "sensitive zones" (eyes, feet, and genitals) and by limiting their telepathy (which aliens do through their hair). He believes he is heroic and saving the human race. He experiences a number of **ideas of influence** as seen in his correspondence with the aliens. In *I'm a Cyborg, But That's OK*, a young woman, Young-goon, is admitted to a psychiatric institution. She embodies a delusion that she is a cyborg and frequently communicates with clocks and vending machines. She refuses to eat, believing she will break down if she eats. She wears her dead grandmother's dentures in order to communicate and feels she has to kill the staff so she imagines shooting the doctors, nurses, and hospital staff with guns that are her fingers.

> "I did as the broadcast told me and they brought me here. I'm a machine, but I didn't come with an instruction manual or a label on me anywhere. I still don't know what my purpose was. What was I made for?"
>
> Young-goon in *I'm a Cyborg, But That's OK* (2006)

In the memorable opening scene, while working on an assembly line, Young-goon matter-of-factly follows what her auditory hallucinations ("a broadcast") say to her – she cuts her arm, put wires in it, and then plugs the wires into the wall. The film also touches on the origins of Young-goon's psychosis: Her grandmother, also treated for schizophrenia, thought she was a mother-mouse caring for a number of baby mice and ate a diet of only radishes.

I'm a Cyborg, But That's OK is a good example of the power of psychotic beliefs and the futility of a helping professional in challenging such beliefs when the professional is contending with the client's psychosis, culture-bound issues (the secrecy and shame of such beliefs thus leading to a lack of disclosure, as evidenced in this film), mutism, and the client's own lack of awareness of her own beliefs and their impact. Interestingly, most of the psychological jargon and diagnoses are accurate in the film. As is the case for most films portraying psychiatric hospital wards, the portrayal of the psychiatric patients suggests that people with mental illness are wild and crazy, with some literally rolling around on the floor. It raises the question, should the emphasis of such films be to educate the viewer or help the viewer to better empathize? This film emphasizes the dramatic, the interesting, and the eccentric, revealing the character's innermost, highly distorted delusional beliefs; this helps the viewer empathize with the character but at the sacrifice of educating the viewer about the realities of mental illness and its treatment.

He Loves Me, He Loves Me Not (2002, France) might be the most effective and clear-cut use of the cinema to depict a delusional disorder. It is the directorial debut of French director Laetitia Colombani. First, the viewer is completely taken in as they see reality from Angelique's (*Amelie*'s Audrey Tautou) perception of her blossoming love relationship with a man named Loic. Midway through, the film literally rewinds, flashes back to the beginning, and then gives us the vantage point of Loic, who is a married doctor who barely knows Angelique exists. It is only as the second half of the film unfolds that the viewer can then back-track in his or her mind to remember how Angelique perceived the relationship and compare it with what Loic sees and experiences. It is the latter that becomes reality. Thus, the viewer eventually realizes everything in the first half of the film is Angelique's delusion. The viewer learns she obsessively calls Loic, leaving 23 messages. Her obsessions with drawings, following him around, and writing notes all reinforce and maintain her delusional framework.

The delusional person can readily function in society as shown with Angelique successfully taking care of her house, working a regular job, wearing appropriate attire, and communicating with others around her. Without knowing her thinking, we would not know she is delusional, particularly with her very sweet, often smiling, and innocent presentation. The film also depicts the risk in breaking the framework of a person's delusional mind-set. It is here we see the stereotype of the violent psychiatric patient, as Angelique takes on the frame of mind "if I can't have him, no one will" and attempts to murder two innocent people.

Most films are sympathetic in their depiction of people with delusional disorder, especially when it is ambiguous as to whether the disorder is real or whether the character is being misjudged for his or her idiosyncrasies. However, *He Loves Me, He Loves Me Not* is not at all ambiguous. The film maintains honesty and clarity about the disorder and its purpose in showing drastically different truths, where one side is actually much "more real" than the other. Angelique's diagnosis of delusional disorder is discussed in the end when she is taken to a psychiatric hospital. The filmmakers knew what they specifically wanted to achieve with this deeply psychological film and they accomplished it.

11'9"01 – September 11 (2002, UK/France/Egypt/Japan/Mexico/US/Iran) is what followed when producer Alain Brigand proposed to 11 renowned directors to "create a film lasting eleven minutes, nine seconds and one frame – September 11 – around the events of September 11 and their consequences." He asked them to look toward their own cultures, memories, stories, and language in constructing their short film. The filmmakers include directors from Bosnia-Herzegovina, India, the United States, Japan, Egypt, Mexico, Iran, the United Kingdom, France, West Africa, and Israel. In one segment, Japanese director Shohei Imamura depicts a man who heads off to war as a soldier and returns home as a snake (in human form). He maintains and embodies this severe, bizarre delusion, slithering around, hissing like a snake, biting the woman who feeds him, and eating a live rat. He is eventually kept in a cage and then forced out of the home. Before slithering into a body of water, he is asked "Does being a man disgust you that much?" In a terrifying and poignant way, this simple question (and the psychosis) speaks to the horror of war.

House of Fools (2002) is a Russian/Chechnyan film based on a true story. Set in 1996, during the first Chechen war, the film depicts a psychiatric hospital located on the border of a war-torn area. The hospital staff flee due to conflict in Chechnya, leaving the patients to fend for themselves. Soldiers find refuge in the hospital and interact with the patients. As with most films depicting psychiatric institutions, there is a hodge-podge of psychopathology depicted. One patient, Jana, has hallucinations (or are they daydreams?) of herself in a video that portrays the famous singer, Bryan Adams, who appears in the film as himself, often singing the lyrics "have you ever really loved a woman?" Jana has a **delusional disorder, erotomanic type**, as she believes Bryan Adams is her fiancé and that he is in love with her. Her room is covered in Bryan Adams posters. In a later scene, she naively believes the mock marriage proposal made to her by a soldier seeking refuge. Soon she finds herself in a bind, struggling to choose between the deceptive solider and the delusion of Bryan Adams. In one scene, Jana is gripping broken glass so hard that her hand becomes cut and bloodied. She uses a fantasy of Bryan Adams to cope with the pain. Jana denies her illness, telling people she was once sick but isn't anymore. Furthermore, she believes she is a teacher for her fellow patients, teaching them yoga and how to play the accordion. Jana tries to help other patients when they make mistakes or need guidance. Cinematically, the viewer sees her reality of bright colors and light where the staff and patients are dancing to her music. This cinematic technique – weaving from patient perception to reality – is used frequently in the film. Other patients include a person with delusions, a psychotic fire starter, a psychotic transvestite, a psychotic midget, and a person who is catatonic.

Something Like Happiness (2005, Czech Republic) portrays the complex dynamics among three adults who are friends from childhood, Tonik, Monika, and Dasha. A single mother of two, Dasha deteriorates into psychosis, neglects her children and is only concerned about having a male companion. She is admitted to a psychiatric ward and becomes determined to become pregnant. In an upsetting scene, Dasha, upon being released from the ward, goes to her friend's home where her children have been properly cared for and interrupts the children's special party, grabbing them, forcing them into her car, and refusing to let them get their belongings.

Werner Herzog's *Aguirre, the Wrath of God* (1972, West Germany/Peru/Mexico) shows the Spanish conquistadors' search for the mythic treasure of El Dorado deep in the Amazon reaches of Peru. Aguirre is a defiant, competitive, power monger who leads a mutiny. During long, fruitless journeys in the jungle, he loses touch with reality and develops a **delusional disorder, grandiose type**. His appearance becomes boggy eyed, shaky, hypervigilant, and preoccupied. Aguirre's grandiosity continues to increase as he speaks of getting larger ships for bigger conquests. He shows a blatant disregard for his men's needs and leads them to suffering and destruction. At one point he exclaims, "I, the wrath of God, will marry my own daughter" and speaks of ruling with her.

"If I, Aguirre, want the birds to drop dead from the trees then the birds will drop dead from the trees. I am the wrath of God. The earth I walk upon sees me and quakes. But whoever follows me and the river will win untold riches."

Aguirre's delusions of grandeur in
Aguirre, the Wrath of God (1972)

As previously noted, filmmakers often link violence and psychosis. *Rampo Noir* (2005, Japan) is a collection of four short, surreal horror films – *Mars's Canal*, *Mirror Hell*, *Caterpillar*, and *Crawling Bugs* – that are adaptations and tributes to the Japanese poet, Rampo. Each gives a different perspective on violence and a disturbing environment or situation relating to hell. Since each has a strong surreal component, each provides a different perspective on mental illness, violence, and psychosis. *Mars's Canal* uses no sound with the exception of static and creates intentional defects in the visual image. The viewer sees surrealist images of a naked man along a landscape, violence with a naked woman, and darkness slowly creeping over a character's face (e.g., to show the slow deterioration that is often associated with mental illness). This segment ends with a quote from Rampo: "Reality is seen in dreams. What you dream at night is real." Another character portraying a link between psychosis and violence is the thief in *The Cook, The Thief, His Wife, and Her Lover* (1989).

An Angel at My Table (1990), Jane Campion's film autobiography of New Zealand writer Janet Frame, is a compelling story of misdiagnosis and malpractice. Frame, an awkward, anxious, and socially inept adolescent, is misdiagnosed as having schizophrenia after an apparent panic attack and winds up receiving shock treatment and being

hospitalized for eight years. She narrowly avoids receiving a frontal lobotomy, a popular treatment at the time.

Crimson Gold (2003, Iran) illustrates themes of classism, highlighting the distance and tension between the wealthy and the poor in modern-day Iran. Hussein is a taciturn pizza delivery man who delivers pizza to both rich and poor; however,

Critical Thinking Questions

- In considering the impact of mental illness on the family and community, what are the most salient themes a film can address? Compare and contrast how *Canvas* (2006), *Spider* (2002), and *Lars and the Real Girl* (2007) treat the impact of illness on families.
- Consider a quote from John Nash in *A Beautiful Mind* (2001): "She never gets old. Marcee can't be real. She never gets old." How common is this kind of insight for a person with schizophrenia or delusional disorder?
- In *A Beautiful Mind*, John Nash explains that he won't talk back to his visual hallucinations so as to not feed them and keep them alive. How effective is this approach for most people with schizophrenia?
- Do familial environment and parental role contribute to development of mental illness in a child? How?
- Do films such as *Clean, Shaven* (1993), *Shine* (1996), and *David and Lisa* (1962) do a disservice to parents by blaming them for what is essentially a biological disorder over which they have no control?
- Films such as *Shine*, *David and Lisa*, and *Benny and Joon* (1993) all suggest that love can at least partially offset the deleterious effects of a disease such as schizophrenia. Is there any evidence suggesting this is true?
- In one memorable scene in the film *Clean, Shaven*, Peter Winter is in the library, hitting his head against the stacks. If you had been present, would you have ignored the behavior or tried to intervene and help in some way?
- John Nash in *A Beautiful Mind* is a genius, Prot in *K-Pax* has many savant-like qualities, and Peter Winter in *Clean, Shaven* graduated "in the top 5 percent of his high school class." Is there any relationship between schizophrenia, psychosis, and intelligence? Are extremely bright people more or less likely to develop such a disorder?
- What other films can you think of that present good and bad portrayals of schizophrenia or delusional disorder?

when he is treated poorly and rejected – both when wearing a suit and tie and dressed more casually – by a jewelry store manager, he explodes. It is interesting to note that the lead actor (in real life) has been diagnosed with paranoid schizophrenia; this is never mentioned or explicitly portrayed in the film, but it helps account for the uncanny accuracy of the character's flat affect and distant behavior.

Further Exploration

If you have time to read just one book relevant to this chapter, make it:
Silverstein, S. M., Spaulding, W. D., & Menditto, A. A. (2006). *Schizophrenia.* Cambridge, MA: Hogrefe & Huber Publishers.

If you only have time for one article, read:
Bellack, A. S. (2004). Skills training for people with severe mental illness. *Psychiatric Rehabilitation Journal, 27*, 375–391.

Schizophrenia and Delusional Disorders

Shine (1996)
Sweetie (1989)
Clean, Shaven (1993)
Birth (2004)
Spider (2002)
A Beautiful Mind (2001)
Canvas (2006)
Lars and the Real Girl (2007)
Through a Glass Darkly (1961)
He Loves Me, He Loves Me Not (2002)

Chapter 10

Neuropsychological Disorders

"I have no short-term memory. I know who I am. I know all about myself. I just – since my injury I can't make new memories. Everything fades. If we talk for too long I'll forget how we started and the next time I see you I'm not gonna remember this conversation. I don't even know if I've met you before. So if I seem strange or rude or something...I've told you this before, haven't I?
Leonard Shelby in *Memento* (2000)

Questions to Consider While Watching *Memento*

- How does Leonard's personality interact with his illness?
- What are the various compensatory strategies Leonard uses throughout the film?
- Even with all the strategies Leonard has developed, is it realistic to believe he could do what he does in this film?
- How does memory for eyewitness testimony relate to Leonard's memory problems?
- How does the filmmaker's depiction of memory speak to more than just those with cognitive disorders?
- What neurological symptoms does this film create for you, the viewer, to experience? Why is this done?
- Leonard exhibits several paranoid traits. Are paranoia and suspicion characteristic of cognitive disorders?
- What clues indicate that Leonard is about to forget something?
- How long could a person with these symptoms survive on his or her own without constant support and monitoring?
- Do the symptoms of anterograde amnesia improve over time?
- What is the difference between anterograde and retrograde amnesia?

Patient Evaluation

Patient's stated reason for coming: "I need you to help me find out who killed my wife. I was told you could help me. Teddy sent me." (Patient stated this as he referred to notes on a crumpled piece of paper taken from his pocket).

History of the present illness: Mr. Leonard Shelby is a 29-year-old Caucasian male who suffered a severe head injury three years ago. He experienced a severe concussion on the left side of his head as he fought with an intruder who broke into his home, raped his wife, and tried to suffocate her. As a result, Mr. Shelby suffers from severe anterograde amnesia, a memory dysfunction that prevents him from converting short-term to long-term memory.

Past psychiatric illness, treatment, and outcomes: According to the available medical records, Mr. Shelby has lived "off and on" at the neuropsychiatric unit of a hospital for the last two years. He has also been placed in group care facilities on two occasions but fled both times within a month. He also escaped from the hospital; each time he has fled, it has been "to find out who killed my wife and get revenge." The year immediately after the injury, this patient lived with his wife as they tried to cope with the wife's rape trauma and adapt to Mr. Shelby's head injury. Records indicate Mr. Shelby has killed at least three people, two of whom he believed had raped his wife.

Medical history: Medical records indicate Mr. Shelby has been prescribed several types of anti-depressant and mood stabilizing medications; however, he is noncompliant with all medications whenever he is away from the hospital.

Psychosocial history: Mr. Shelby had been married for eight years when his wife died. Medical records indicate Mr. Shelby killed his wife by giving her an overdose of insulin. Apparently, his wife was skeptical of his anterograde amnesia diagnosis and decided to "test" his short-term memory loss. She tested his memory by asking him to give her insulin shots repeatedly, thinking this extreme and life-threatening situation would force him to admit he was "faking." However, he was not faking, and his wife went into insulin shock and coma, from which she never recovered.

Mr. Shelby graduated from college with an undergraduate degree in Finance. He does not have any children, and he is not currently in a relationship. He has been unemployed since his injury. For eight years prior to the injury, he worked as an insurance claims investigator. He states he enjoyed this work and found it very fulfilling. He began to tell a story about a client he once worked with named Sammy Jenkins; he told parts of this story on three separate occasions during the interview. It may be significant that he has "Remember Sammy Jenkins" tattooed on his left arm.

Drug and alcohol history: There is no significant history of drug or alcohol abuse.

Behavioral observations: Mr. Shelby was 15 minutes late for the interview. He wore a sport coat and slacks that appeared unwashed. Interestingly, he took a photograph of the interviewer upon walking into the examination room, saying "it's so I can remember you" as he wrote down the interviewer's first name and the words "Teddy recommended: Shrink" on the photograph.

Mr. Shelby used numerous compensatory strategies to assist his memory during this interview, including note cards, handwritten pieces of paper, photographs of people with names and notes written on them, and his own tattoos. The latter, he stated, are for "vital information." He often repeated, "You really do need a system if you're gonna make it work." On two occasions, he began to take off his jacket and shirt to read the tattoos on his chest but the interviewer stopped him and encouraged him to read them later. Frequently, the pieces of paper oriented him to where he was and why he was being examined. He asked himself numerous questions, and he repeated many statements at different points during the interview. This pattern of repetition occurs every 10–15 minutes.

Mental status examination: Mr. Shelby was suspicious and guarded during the evaluation. Mood and affect were labile, quickly shifting from agitation to dysphoria. Anxiety was evident after some questions when the patient appeared to have lost his memory; when this occurred, he would fumble with his photographs and notes, or attempt to read his body tattoos. There was no evidence of flight of ideas, hallucinations, or delusions. There was no significant suicidal or homicidal ideation present, although the latter is a significant concern due to his history. Short-term memory is extremely limited. Anxiety and agitation exacerbate his memory problems.

Mr. Shelby was oriented to person. He was not oriented to place, time, or situation. However, he was able to figure out each with the help of compensatory strategies. He showed the interviewer some of his notes and writings. Many were phrases and random thoughts, tasks to do, and ideas. The purpose of these notes is multi-fold: first, they serve as a compensatory strategy to help him stay "on track" long enough to complete tasks; secondly, they help him remember important past events and people, and third, they coach him along through his difficulties. He forgot my name several times during the interview, but, as we concluded, he quickly referred to his photograph of me, mentioned my name and smiled.

Mr. Shelby was given the Mini Mental State Examination twice, the first time without the use of notes and the second time with notes. He scored a 15/30 and a 23/30, respectively. Without the use of compensatory strategies, Mr. Shelby struggled with orientation, memory recall, and serial sevens. He was able to following simple commands, name objects in the room, write a sentence, and copy a complex drawing. When using compensatory strategies on the second examination, the main benefit came when he was tested for orientation to date and place.

Functional assessment: Mr. Shelby has almost no ability to convert short-term memory to long-term memory. This has a severe and serious impact on every activity in his life. He has difficulty taking care of himself, and he needs to be reminded to eat meals, change his clothes, and perform other activities of daily living. His injury prevents him from working or going to school and limits his ability to maintain new relationships. Mr. Shelby does not have insight into his actions, speech, emotions, or thoughts, as he forgets them within 15 minutes.

Strengths: Mr. Shelby is creative, spontaneous, and intelligent. His personality is energetic, engaged, and interesting. He is disciplined and systematic in the organization of compensatory memory strategies. He is highly motivated, and perhaps this motivation can be channeled in prosocial directions. He is aware of his condition and appears to know that he suffers from a problem with the consolidation of memories.

Diagnosis: Amnestic disorder due to head trauma; antisocial personality disorder.

Treatment plan: Mr. Shelby should be monitored closely on the neuropsychiatric unit. In addition, his notes, writings, and photographs should be closely monitored due to the high homicide risk that appears to rise quickly and for no obvious reason.

A complete neuropsychological evaluation is recommended with periodic follow-up testing to assess changes in functional ability, and especially memory. Occupational therapy should also be consulted so the patient can be trained in additional compensatory strategies, particularly ones involving activities of daily living.

Prognosis: Poor.

Memento, Memory, and Viewer Empathy

Memento (2000) is a psychological thriller that centers on the life of Leonard Shelby (Guy Pearce), a man with anterograde amnesia that makes it impossible for him to transfer new experiences into long-term memory. The movie chronicles the psychological and social complications associated with this memory disorder, as well as this man's efforts to get revenge for past offences against himself and his wife. This is the second film of director Christopher Nolan (see also *Following* (1998) and *Insomnia* (2002), both discussed in this book), who amazingly created this incredibly complex film in 25.5 days.

Memento is a cleverly edited film that begins at the end of the story and works backward: The color portions of the film progress backward in approximately ten-minute segments, and these clips are juxtaposed with black and white clips that move forward in time.

Leonard has lost his wife and is struggling to avenge her loss by finding the killer. He does not remember that he is the person who killed her when she "tested" his amnesia by having him administer repeated doses of insulin until she went into shock and coma, and subsequently died. Leonard actually believes that Sammy Jenkins injected the insulin. Leonard believes that Sammy Jenkins was malingering (with anterograde amnesia) when Leonard was a claims investigator. Leonard fuses his story with Sammy's and distorts reality. The film cleverly gives the viewer clues to the truth that Leonard is both denying and forgetting. For example, in one scene, one frame of Leonard is superimposed on the character of Sammy Jenkins, and it is unclear who is actually in the hospital. Another example involves a flashback at the end of the film (the beginning of the story) of Leonard and his wife lying in bed together; the camera focuses briefly on the words "I've Done It" tattooed on his chest, as if to give the viewer one final piece of direct evidence.

The film does a brilliant job of depicting the suffering of someone with a memory disorder, and illustrates the painstaking discipline and detail-oriented approach necessary for someone to cope with such a disorder using compensatory strategies (e.g., tattoos and Polaroid photographs of people and places). As if Leonard isn't facing enough as a man who has lost the ability to consolidate memories, he must also cope with others determined to take advantage of his illness, manipulating and lying to him. Ultimately, he has no one he can rely on or trust, including himself, as those who appear to help only "use" him (e.g., for drug deals, for

murderous revenge, or to make some extra money, all at his expense). Eventually, he is confronted with a harrowing truth. A corrupt police officer, Teddy, tells him: "you don't want the truth... you create your own truth." The viewer eventually comes to realize that Leonard has not known the truth from the beginning, and he is preparing to kill an innocent man.

Perhaps the most remarkable aspect of this film is its ability to force the viewer to experience the world as someone with anterograde amnesia experiences it. The viewer experiences the protagonist's struggles, distortions, lapses, questions, and emotions as he or she tries to put together the scenes going backward while making sense of the juxtaposed black and white scenes that are going forward. The viewer is constantly re-evaluating and re-thinking what has just been seen. The film demands both strong concentration and memory from the viewer, who almost immediately begins to appreciate the majesty of something most of us take for granted: The ability to convert new information into long-term memory. The viewer experiences the protagonist's confusion, as he or she tries to decide who is manipulating whom, and feels what the amnestic patient feels when trying to sort through conflicting distortions of time, place, person, and situation. The viewer questions his or her own memory, and must also adopt some cognitive strategy in order to keep all the confusing aspects of the film straight. The viewer also begins to lose trust in the film's characters, particularly the "unreliable narrator" (Leonard) who comes by the role honestly due to his anterograde amnesia.

This film's complexity extends further to address existential themes about our search for meaning, the loss of identity, finding and operating out of the "shadow," the role of truth and lies (both to oneself and to others), the problem of coping with a cognitive disorder, and the ubiquitous power of denial.

Neuropsychological Disorders

This chapter describes conditions that result in a significant deficit in cognition or memory and consequently have an impact on the individual's ability to function normally. First, general categories of cognitive disorders are discussed – dementia, delirium, and amnesia. Next, specific conditions are covered – head trauma, brain tumors, stroke, and epilepsy.

Dementia

The term **dementia** refers to a collection of brain disorders characterized by memory disturbance, impaired judgment, and personality change. Insidious onset and gradual deterioration of cognitive abilities characterize the dementias. Although some authorities believe the term should be applied only to those conditions that are nonreversible, the more common practice (and that followed by *DSM-IV-TR*) is to use the term descriptively, without any implications for prognosis. Hence, brain dysfunctions from causes as diverse as nutritional deficiencies and Cushing's syndrome can be diagnosed as dementias.

Dementia can be caused by any number of medical conditions or they can be substance induced. Some of the more commonly known medical causes are cerebrovascular disease, head trauma, Parkinson's disease, HIV, Huntington's disease, Pick's disease, and Creutzfeldt-Jakob disease. *Awakenings* (1990) offers excellent demonstrations of dementia and catatonia due to Parkinson's disease. The film is based on the experience of neurologist Oliver Sacks, best known as the author of *The Man Who Mistook His Wife for a Hat*.

The single leading cause of dementia is **Alzheimer's disease**, responsible for about half of all cases of dementia. Alzheimer's is a public health problem of enormous dimensions, and one that is becoming an increasing problem as the average life span steadily increases.

The brains of patients with Alzheimer's disease are demonstrably different from those of age-matched controls, and they contain **senile plaques** and **neurofibrillary tangles.** Although some neuronal loss is universal with aging, the brain of the Alzheimer's patient shrinks at a more rapid rate. Psychological tests are often the best indicators of the presence of Alzheimer's disease, especially in the early stages, as these patients will often maintain excellent social skills and use these skills to disguise the marked problems they develop with their memory. Other early signs of the insidious onset of Alzheimer's disease include diffuse generalized anxiety and inappropriate social behavior. An official diagnosis of Alzheimer's cannot be made until after the individual has died and an autopsy has been performed.

Iris

Iris Murdoch was one of the greatest writers and thinkers of the 20th century. She wrote 26 novels, six philosophical works, and several plays. The content and purpose of her intricate works can be simplified in one phrase: She wanted to teach humans how to be free and how to be good. Murdoch was a deep, complex, and gifted thinker. It is bitterly ironic to see such a brilliant and well-used brain deteriorate with dementia, as we observe in the film *Iris* (2001).

Some of the early signs of Iris' dementia are indicated in her experiences of memory loss – she would forget what she had just said and frequently repeat herself. She then began to talk to herself, exhibit blank stares and flat affect, display further language disturbance (i.e., babbling), and lose her ability to care for herself. Her writing, which had always flowed easily and extensively, came to be constricted and limited, and she would frequently sit at a table with blank pages in front of her. Her care for her home and house became nonexistent. The film depicts the development of increasingly serious symptoms, and shows Iris (Judi Dench) in serious danger on several occasions – e.g., jumping out of a moving car, trying to control the steering wheel when on the passenger side, and leaving her house to wander in the middle of traffic. The viewer sees Iris slowly retreat into a world of her own; at first, it is for brief periods and she comes back to reality, but she experiences increasingly longer periods of isolation and quiet. She does emerge from her world at times to say "I love you" to her husband in powerful cinematic moments.

The film *Iris* also speaks deeply to the challenges and responses of the caretaker of someone with Alzheimer's. John Bayley (Jim Broadbent), Iris' loving husband, joins Iris in denying her disease at first, saying "she disappears into a mystery world… [but] she always comes back." As he continues to watch his wife display more serious symptoms, his emotions catch up with him and he screams out in anger. Several scenes show John Bayley deep in despair as he sits alone, helpless to do anything to stop the disease. He sadly repeats the phrase: "Love will soon be over." It is fascinating to watch him experience predictable stages of grief: denial, anger, questioning/challenging, sadness, and finally acceptance when he takes Iris to a nursing home.

"She's in her own world now,
perhaps that's what she always wanted."

John Bayley on his wife's illness
in *Iris* (2001)

Love and Dementia

Two other recent films have portrayed husbands coping with their wives' dementia: Sarah Polley's *Away from Her* (2006) and Nick Cassavetes' *The Notebook* (2004). The first film portrays an Ontario couple who have been married for 44 years; the wife, Fiona (Julie Christie), is becoming increasingly forgetful and she and her husband Grant (Gordon Pinsent) are acutely aware that whatever is happening, it is something far more serious than benign senescent forgetfulness. In addition to her forgetfulness, Fiona finds herself engaging in seemingly irrational behavior (e.g., putting a frying pan into the freezer after it is washed, being unable to retrieve the word "wine"). She realizes that she needs nursing home care, and she doesn't want to be a burden on her husband. The husband, a college English professor guilty about his history of infidelity during the marriage, eventually capitulates to this plan, agreeing that his wife needs to be in a setting in which she can confront her illness "with a little bit of grace." When Grant takes Fiona to the nursing home, he accompanies her to her room and they have sex ("I'd like to make love, and then I'd like you to go. Because I need to stay here and if you make it hard for me, I may cry so hard I'll never stop.") No visitors are allowed for the first 30 days of residency in the nursing home, allegedly to facilitate the new resident's adjustment. (Visitor restriction is very unlikely in any nursing home.) During this time Fiona becomes romantically, albeit not sexually, involved with another resident in the facility. Part of the cinematic tension in the film involves the fact that it is never entirely clear whether Fiona's interest in Aubrey, the other resident, is simply due to her lost memories of her marriage and husband or a willful way to get back at Grant because of his history of extramarital affairs with his students. The film is also remarkable for the persistence and unconditional love of Grant – not dissimilar from John Bayley's – in visiting Fiona regularly despite her obvious intimate involvement with another man.

The Notebook (2004) stars Gena Rowlands and James Garner as a married couple coping with the wife's dementia. Allie Calhoun (Gena Rowlands) is in a nursing home; her husband (Duke) has moved in with her and spends each day reading to her out of a notebook. We later learn that she has written the story of their romance and life together so that she can continue to relive it even as her illness progresses. A series of flashbacks is used to tell the story of their initial love affair, separation, and eventual reunion. The film is sentimental and unduly romanticizes Alzheimer's, but at the same time it illustrates the dramatic loss of memory that is one of the defining features of the disease.

The Savages

Laura Linney and Philip Seymour Hoffman play a brother and sister confronting the dilemma of caring for an aging, demented father in *The Savages* (2007). The two siblings have never been close to their father, but when his girlfriend dies, decisions about his care are foisted upon them. They are initially notified of their father's condition when he begins writing on the wall with his own excrement; for many demented individuals, loss of bowel and bladder control become powerful metaphors for the loss of self associated with diseases like Alzheimer's. The movie illustrates how depressing some nursing homes can be – even very expensive ones – and it provides a compelling example of the stress associated with the decisions children often must make when a parent develops dementia.

> "People are dying, Wendy! Right inside that beautiful building right now, it's a fucking horror show! And all this wellness propaganda and the landscaping, it's just there to obscure the miserable fact that people die! And death is gaseous and gruesome and it's filled with shit and piss and rotten stink!"
>
> Jon Savage confronting his sister in *The Savages* (2007)

The tempo of life in a nursing home is captured in *Assisted Living* (2003), a pseudo-documentary filmed with real residents of a real nursing home in Kentucky. In one scene, Todd, an under-equipped, pot-smoking orderly, amuses himself by pretending to be God on phone calls with a resident. Despite Todd's antics, it is also clear that he cares about many of the residents and he goes out of his way to help one of the residents who is quickly deteriorating with Alzheimer's.

Dementia vs. Depression

One of the most important tasks confronting clinicians working with older patients is the often difficult discrimination between dementia and

clinical depression. Appropriate diagnosis is critical in these cases so that a depressed patient will not go untreated because he or she is inappropriately believed to be suffering from Alzheimer's disease. In the majority of cases, the two disorders will present in ways that are different enough for the alert clinician to distinguish between them. For example, Alzheimer's has a more insidious onset, whereas depression may come on more rapidly. The patient with Alzheimer's always will have genuine cognitive deficits and experience difficulty with learning new tasks. The depressed patient will lack motivation and may have trouble concentrating but should be able to learn adequately, although slowly. The depressed patient is also more likely to experience loss of appetite and a fluctuating course, and he or she is far more likely to have a history of affective illness. In addition, depressed patients tend to acknowledge and sometimes even exaggerate their problems. In contrast, patients with Alzheimer's are far more likely to cover up their difficulties, deny that they are having problems, and may be euphoric. Finally, in the later stages of the illness, patients with true dementias will often have abnormal brain images and electroencephalograms.

Another important film portraying Alzheimer's disease is a made-for-TV movie, *Do You Remember Love?* (1985), in which Joanne Woodward plays a college professor who develops the devastating disease. Woodward's portrayal is sensitive and moving. There is also a memorable scene between Jane Fonda's character and her mother in *Agnes of God* (1985). Fonda plays Dr. Martha Livingston, a psychiatrist who goes to visit her mother in a nursing home. The scene opens with the mother watching a children's cartoon program. The disoriented mother gets Martha confused with her younger sister, who had died years earlier in a convent.

Jessica Tandy very convincingly portrays an old woman who eventually develops Alzheimer's disease and is placed in a nursing home in *Driving Miss Daisy* (1989). Tandy won an Academy Award for her performance in this film.

Delirium

Delirium refers to the rapid onset of confusion and disorganized thinking (a "clouding" of cognition) and is often characterized by rambling, incoherent, or inappropriate speech. Emotions are often inappropriate as well; for example, the delirious individual may be extremely anxious or euphoric in situations in which these reactions would be inappropriate. Delirium can also cause illusions, hallucinations, or misinterpretations of sensory stimuli; for example, a doctor's look of concern may be perceived as extreme anger by the delirious patient. Most films depicting dementia will show some examples of delirium as well (e.g., *Iris*).

Delirium most often (but not always) results from a disturbance of the metabolism of the brain, and causes can include infections, insufficient oxygen levels, ionic imbalances, vitamin deficiencies, and kidney disease. One common cause of delirium is either acute intoxication with – or withdrawal from – drugs. **Delirium tremens** is a common problem for alcoholics with a history of problem drinking. Patients experiencing the "DTs" become disoriented, hallucinate, and display marked tremors. Other symptoms may include intense fear, fevers, and sweating. The intensity of delirium tremens is vividly portrayed in Billy Wilder's film, *The Lost Weekend* (1945), and in Nicholas Cage's character in *Leaving Las Vegas* (1995).

Amnesia

Patients with amnesia display marked impairment of short-term memory with relatively intact long-term memory and preserved intellectual functioning. In its extreme form, the disorder results in the total inability to learn new information. A patient with an amnestic syndrome will be unable to recall the doctor's name, no matter how many times it is presented; simple learning tasks such as recalling the names of four objects become virtually impossible. The patient will be able to *repeat* the four items, suggesting intact understanding of the task and good receptive and expressive language skills; however, after dozens of trials the patient will still be unable to recall the four items from memory.

Patients with amnestic syndromes will sometimes **confabulate** and present detailed and plausible explanations for their obvious inability to acquire new information. The patient who can't remember four numbers for more than a few seconds will explain that he was never any good at math, and the patient in a psychiatric hospital may say he is there because of problems with his kidneys. One of our patients with an amnestic syndrome was asked four times during a one-hour, taped interview what he had had for breakfast that morning. The patient responded by supplying four different "menus" during the interview, each equally plausible. On each occasion, he had absolutely no recollection of being asked this question earlier in the interview.

One of the most commonly encountered amnestic syndromes is **Wernicke-Korsakoff syndrome**. Patients with this disorder have great difficulty with new learning, fail to recall recent experiences, exhibit gait disturbances secondary to cerebellar dysfunction, and display a variety of ocular disturbances, including impaired conjugate gaze. This condition is found in older alcoholics after many years of substituting the nutritionally empty calories of alcohol for the protein, carbohydrates, vitamins, and fat found in a normal diet. The disorder is particularly related to deficiencies in thiamin (vitamin B1), and some public health experts have recommended "enriching" spirits with vitamins in the same way we enrich bread. Although this could be done with minimal cost, the distillers have not been enthusiastic about this procedure, despite its potential benefit to alcoholics.

A number of films have portrayed characters with amnesia, including *Spellbound* (1945), *Mirage* (1955), *Anastasia* (1956)*,* and *Desperately Seeking Susan* (1985). The 1983 film *The Return of Martin Guerre* creatively explores the limits of memory and the extent to which it can be influenced by motivation and need. Dissociative amnesia (see Chapter 3) needs to be differentiated from amnesia caused by a substance or general medical condition (including head injuries).

Head Trauma

The link between head injuries, amnesia, and movies is very strong. The cinema can relay countless creative stories (as we will illuminate below) in which someone experiences head trauma and becomes amnestic to the life of their past – they can start over from scratch, they can try to rediscover life with a deeper appreciation, other people can manipulate them, etc.

Although not given a separate rubric in the *DSM-IV-TR* nomenclature, it is common to see references to **dementia pugilistica** (punch-drunk syndrome) in the professional literature and in the medical charts of aging boxers. These patients, after a lifetime of repeated blows to the head (with concomitant brain injuries), often develop difficulty with movement and a tremor similar to that found in **Parkinson's disease**. They develop slurred speech and diminished mental agility, and they become especially sensitive to the effects of alcohol. Dramatic mood swings (referred to as **emotional lability**) are common, and these individuals are quick to become angry, engage in fights, and become paranoid. Many of these symptoms can be seen in Robert De Niro's portrayal of Jake LaMotta in *Raging Bull* (1980).

The repetitive head blows associated with boxing have been shown to cause brain injuries that may not be detected by an MRI. There is evidence that microstructural damage exists in professional boxers when compared to a age- and sex-matched control group (Zhang, et al., 2003).

"You don't understand! I could've had class. I could've been a contender. I could've been somebody, instead of a bum, which is what I am."

Terry Malloy (Marlon Brando) in
On the Waterfront (1954)

This problem is so serious that the American Medical Association and other professional organizations have called for the elimination of professional boxing as an organized sport. Indeed, it is hard to find redeeming social value in a sport in which the express purpose is to damage the brain of an opponent. However, boxing remains a popular American pastime, and this popularity is reflected in films such as *The Great White Hope* (1970), *The Harder They Fall* (1956), *The Joe Louis Story* (1953), *Kid Galahad* (1937/1962), *On the Waterfront* (1954), *Requiem for a Heavyweight* (1962), the ever popular *Rocky* films (1976, 1979, 1982, 1985, 1990, 2006), and many others.

When visualizing brain injuries, it is useful to remember that the cranium is a closed, solid container and the brain is soft and consists of a jelly-like substance that moves inside the skull when the head is struck. The brain is actually quite fragile, albeit well protected by the skull and meninges (the three layers of protective covering that are found between the skull and brain).

Head injuries are usually classified as **concussions, contusions,** or **open-head injuries**. Concussions occur when the brain is jarred, and amnesia and loss of consciousness are common consequences. Impaired memory and concentration, headaches, fatigue, anxiety, dizziness, and irritability characterize the post-concussion syndrome. Contusions occur when the brain is actually bruised, most often because of an impact between the brain and the skull. Contusions produce more serious neurological consequences than concussions and can result in death. Contusions are characterized as **coup injuries** if the damage is at the site of impact (e.g., at the point where a baseball bat hits the skull). **Contrecoup injuries** occur opposite the point of impact. They most often result from acceleration injuries (such as occur when a moving head hits a stationary steering wheel). Open-head injuries occur when the skull is hit with sufficient force to open it and expose the underlying neural tissue. Open-head injuries from missile wounds are common in wartime, and much of what we know about the organization of the brain is the result of examination of soldiers injured in battle.

The effects of head injuries often become apparent only hours or days after the initial injury. This occurred in the case of actress Natasha Richardson, daughter of Vanessa Redgrave and wife of Liam Neeson. Richardson died two days after suffering a head injury as a result of a skiing accident during a Quebec holiday. Paramedics at the scene were turned away because the actress reported that she felt fine and was in no distress.

Raging Bull

Raging Bull (1980) is a Martin Scorsese film starring Robert De Niro (who won an Academy Award as Best Actor for his role in this film), Cathy Moriarty, and Joe Pesci. This engrossing drama portrays the life of Jake LaMotta (De Niro), a prizefighter confronted with the need to find purpose and meaning in life once he leaves the ring. LaMotta's marriage fails, his wife takes their children with her, sexual jealousy drives a wedge between him and his brother, and he ultimately is forced to mutilate and then hock the jewels in the belt he received for winning the world middleweight championship. The viewer is never certain whether LaMotta is a pathetic or a heroic figure, but the film ends with reconciliation between the two brothers and with the protagonist successfully performing a Broadway reading of the works of several notable authors. The recitation of one of Marlon Brando's monologues from *On the Waterfront* (a 1954 Elia Kazan film about the life of a down and out prizefighter) is Scorsese's way of paying homage to another great filmmaker and provides a dramatic conclusion for the film.

Raging Bull is replete with examples of LaMotta's poor judgment. Two especially vivid examples are his failure to defend himself in the final round of a fight with Sugar Ray Robinson (Johnny Barnes) and his decision to let two 14-year-old girls into his nightclub after each girl kisses him. Impaired judgment is common in aging prizefighters. It is also likely that LaMotta's history of repeated blows to the head (concussions)

Additional Questions for Discussion (*Raging Bull*)

- What actually happens to the brain of a fighter when he is "knocked out?"
- The American Academy of Neurology has supported a ban on professional boxing since 1983. Do you agree with this position?
- What are the characteristic features of chronic traumatic encephalopathy? What features of Robert De Niro's portrayal of Jake LaMotta suggest the disorder is present?
- Is the protective headgear used by amateur boxers effective in protecting against head injuries?
- In the film, LaMotta, as an old man, becomes sexually involved with two young girls. Is this an example of impaired judgment?
- LaMotta is incredibly jealous of his second wife, and he becomes convinced she is having multiple affairs. Is this paranoia the result of personality or cerebral impairment?
- What is the "Madonna–Whore" complex? How is it illustrated in the life of Jake LaMotta?

contributed to his sexual jealousy and paranoia and was responsible for the slurred speech he exhibits in the film as he ages.

Other Films Dealing with Head Trauma

In addition to *Memento* (2000), discussed in detail earlier in this chapter, many films display serious neurological symptoms such as the amnesia that can result from a head injury. One of the best is David Lynch's challenging film *Mulholland Drive* (2001), which begins with an automobile accident. The amnestic female survivor, Rita (a name she took from a movie poster) finds refuge in the condominium of an aspiring Hollywood actress, Betty (Naomi Watts). The two women befriend each other and Betty takes a particular interest in helping Rita (Laura Harring) find answers to the questions regarding her identity. The already unique film takes a major surrealistic twist and the viewer is left to either accept the events as they are portrayed or challenge them as illusions. Like Christopher Nolan in *Memento*, Lynch creates a rich atmosphere that allows the viewer to experience the confusion and discomfort of amnesia as he or she increasingly becomes disoriented to person, time, place, and situation. Lynch does not attempt to give answers or insights into amnesia but rather to depict the experience for a character and to give a particular experience to the viewer. It is the viewer who is challenged, like the amnestic character, to accept the film as an experience; this is perhaps more important than a pat explanation for what is happening in the film. This is reinforced at the film's conclusion (and final word) when a character on stage looks at the viewer and with a finger to her lips, says "Silencio."

In contrast to *Memento*'s unforgettable depiction of anterograde amnesia, *The Majestic* (2001) depicts retrograde amnesia. Jim Carrey plays disenfranchised screenwriter Peter Appleton, who, upon being accused of communist ties, goes for a drive away from his Hollywood home. His car topples over a bridge into a river and he subsequently develops retrograde amnesia after he hits his head on a rock in the river and is washed up on the shore of a small town. The townspeople mistake Peter for a former townsperson, Luke Trimble, who had gone to war many years ago and the town proclaims Peter (now Luke) a hero, someone who had been lost for almost a decade after going to war. Not remembering his past, Luke identifies with many of the townspeople and rebuilds the local theater. He does not go through the pain, confusion, mental torture, and frustration that one would expect with retrograde amnesia. Instead, Luke readily accepts his new role and does not seriously challenge himself to figure out where he was over the previous ten years. A theory of "double amnesia" is hypothesized, whereby he could have gone to war, experienced PTSD and memory loss, reestablished his life for years as a writer, and then, upon getting involved in an accident, experienced amnesia a second time.

Two 1991 films address the complexity of amnestic symptoms that result from head injuries, *Regarding Henry* and *Shattered*. *Regarding Henry* is a Mike Nichols film starring Harrison Ford as a high-powered attorney who suffers a major traumatic head injury. After coming out of a coma, he discovers that his life can never be the same. There are interesting scenes in a rehabilitation hospital, and the viewer gets some sense for the sequelae of a head injury. However, the film is flawed by an unrealistic presentation of the deficits following head injury and by the simplistic assumption that someone's personality could be *improved* by a head injury. In *Shattered*, an architect undergoes extensive reconstructive surgery of his face following an automobile accident. Amnesia symptoms mix with his memories (that may or may not be distorted) and the inconsistent stories relayed by various people in his life.

The Lookout (2007) presents the story of a talented and handsome high school hockey player who sustains a serious closed head injury after a car wreck that resulted from a school prank (drunk driving with the lights off on the night of the high school prom). As a result, he winds up as a bank's janitor, the only job he can handle. He displays classic signs of head injury, coping with these problems by repeating a kind of mantra for people with head injuries: "Ritual. Pattern. Repetition." One of the characteristics of head injuries is poor judgment, and the head injured Chris Pratt displays extremely poor judgment as he gets caught up in plans to rob the bank at which he works. We also see his constant reliance on a notebook in which he frequently writes notes to himself, and he has put labels on almost everything in his apartment; these are actually valuable **compensatory strategies** (coping strategies) for people with head injuries. He also has problems with impulse control; for example, when meeting with his case worker, Chris blurts out "I want to fuck you." However, he is clearly acutely aware of his deficits, and at one point he notes "I call tomatoes lemons, [but] I know it's not right."

Brain Tumors

Aberrant behavior and abnormal sensations and perceptions can result from brain tumors (**neoplasms**). The specific behaviors that result will vary across individuals as a function of lesion site, size, type, and rate of growth. Brain tumors often, but not always, result in headaches and seizures. However, less than one out of a thousand people who have headaches will be found to also have a brain tumor.

An individual's premorbid personality will in part determine how he or she reacts to a brain tumor. About half of all patients with brain tumors first complain of psychiatric or behavioral symptoms, especially when the tumor involves the frontal or temporal lobes. Hallucinations, depression, apathy, euphoria, social impropriety, and personality change can all result from brain lesions.

Patients who have **frontal lobe lesions** are likely to display personality changes. They may be passive, apathetic, depressed, and slow to respond. Paradoxically, frontal lobe lesions also may exhibit result in irritability and problems with anger control. **Temporal lobe tumors** are often misdiagnosed as psychiatric disorders, and this is especially likely to occur in those cases that result in **psychomotor seizures**. These tumors can produce hallucinations, stereotyped movements, feelings of unreality, and intense fear. Reports of déjà vu (feeling you are re-experiencing a former experience) and **jamais vu** (feeling that familiar settings and situations are now very strange) are common with temporal lobe tumors. Patients with **parietal lobe lesions** often report abnormal sensory experiences (e.g., smelling burning rubber), may have difficulty with simple copying tasks, and may exhibit **anosognosia** (denial of illness). **Occipital lobe tumors** produce relatively few psychological symptoms, but these lesions may result in visual field defects.

Stroke

A **cerebrovascular accident** (CVA), more commonly known as a stroke, occurs when there is inadequate supply of blood and oxygen to the brain. Strokes are characterized by sudden onset and are often fatal. Cerebrovascular disease is currently the third leading cause of death in the United States, following heart disease and cancer. Twenty individuals will experience cerebrovascular accidents for every one who develops a brain tumor.

Infarctions occur when arterial blood flow is blocked. This can occur when a piece of fat or cholesterol becomes lodged in a vessel. This sudden blockage of blood flow is called an **embolus.** Blood flow can also be impeded by the gradual buildup of **atherosclerotic plaque** along the inside of a vessel, resulting in a **thrombus.** Vessels sometimes burst, and the resulting cerebral hemorrhage can be life-threatening. Only about 20% of patients survive a cerebral hemorrhage. An **aneurysm** occurs when part of a vessel "balloons" and threatens to burst. Signs of a ruptured aneurysm include painful headaches, nausea, and vomiting.

Transient ischemic attacks (TIAs) are "ministrokes" that last for less than 24 hours. Many patients who experience TIAs will go on to have actual strokes. Other risk factors for cerebrovascular accidents include diabetes, heart disease, and the use of oral contraceptives in women who also smoke. The patient experiencing a TIA will become disoriented, confused, and sometimes amnestic.

In John Steinbeck's novel *The Grapes of Wrath,* Grandpa Joad dies from a stroke. We do not actually see the old man die in John Ford's film adaptation, *The Grapes of Wrath* (1940), but there is a memorable scene in which his relatives bury him alongside the road because they are too poor to do anything else. Tom Joad (Henry Fonda) writes a short, poignant note to leave at the grave: "This here is William James Joad, died of a stroke, old, old man. His folks buried him because they got no money to pay for funerals. Nobody kilt him. Just a stroke and he died."

David Lynch's *Blue Velvet* (1986) opens with a man watering his yard. As we watch, he has a stroke and falls to the ground. His dog comes over and proceeds to drink out of the hose, and at this point the viewer becomes aware that this will not be an ordinary movie.

Epilepsy

People with **epilepsy** experience uncontrollable attacks of abnormal neuronal activity. These brain "storms" can result from a variety of causes, and it is critical to remember that epilepsy is a *symptom* of a variety of brain disorders, not a disease in itself.

Head trauma is the most common cause of epilepsy and about half of all penetrating head wounds will result in seizures. Prodromal symptoms and auras often precede seizures. **Prodromal symptoms** are "feelings" that a seizure is about to occur and usually appear several days before the seizure itself. In contrast, an **aura** signals the imminent arrival of a seizure and occurs only minutes before the seizure itself. Auras are often auditory or gustatory sensations.

Jacksonian seizures occur when there is a motoric response, such as twitching or jerking that is confined to one side of the body. A "Jacksonian march" results when minor motor movements in a finger or toe become more exaggerated and spread to other parts of the body on the affected side. If the initially isolated abnormal brain activity spreads to the other hemisphere, the entire body may stiffen or jerk; this attack is referred to as a **grand mal seizure**. Grand mal seizures typically last from 2–5 minutes and are sometimes referred to as **tonic-clonic** seizures because of their alternating periods of rigidity and jerking. In contrast, **petit mal seizures** (absence seizures), which are relatively common in young children, do not result in falling, jerking, or loss of muscle tone. The child experiencing a petit mal seizure will be, for a very brief period (usually 2–10 seconds), very unresponsive to the external environment.

Complex partial seizures (also referred to by the older terms *psychomotor* or *temporal lobe seizures*) are of considerable interest to anyone working in the field of mental health, because these disorders often mimic psychiatric diseases. The patient with complex partial seizures may hallucinate, engage in stereotyped motor behavior, experience feelings of unreality, or become extremely anxious. The sensations of déjà vu and jamais vu are often reported. The EEG is typically found to be normal in these patients, and about one in five will experience auditory or visual hallucinations. Unlike the hallucinations of the patient with schizophrenia, however, auditory hallucinations in the patient with a complex partial seizure will be localized within the head (rather than from an external source); and they will rarely contain bizarre, threatening, or accusatory material.

One of the world's leading experts on epilepsy was fond of relating a story about a patient who had a genuine seizure disorder that could be documented with electroencephalography. However, she only seized when she heard Mahalia Jackson singing "My Heart Has a Life of Its Own." The song could be sung by anyone else, and the patient wouldn't seize. Likewise, she could listen to Mahalia Jackson sing anything else, and she wouldn't experience seizures.

After several weeks in the hospital, someone asked the patient what was so special about Mahalia Jackson singing "My Heart Has a Life of Its Own."

"Didn't you know?" she replied. "That was the song they played at my mother's funeral as her casket was being lowered into her grave."

A character in independent auteur Hal Hartley's *Simple Men* (1992) suffers from epilepsy, and the diagnosis of temporal lobe epilepsy is made in *Happy Accidents* (2001) due to a character's petit mal seizures and heightened sense of emotion. Interestingly, the diagnosis is made by a psychologist who in addition to practicing outside of her competence loses additional credibility by stating that the man is delusional. The made-for-television movie *First Do No Harm* (1997) stars Meryl Streep and depicts a young boy with a type of epilepsy where there is no known cause. The film explores particular types of diet in the treatment of epilepsy. The depiction of seizures in movies is fairly common and is portrayed for a variety of reasons: As a response to insulin-shock treatment in *A Beautiful Mind* (2001), ECT in *One Flew Over the Cuckoo's Nest* (1975), and brain surgery in *Molly* (1999).

International Films: Neuropsychological Disorders

The inspirational Argentinean film *Son of the Bride* (2002), which was nominated for an Academy Award as Best Foreign Film, follows a man too busy for his family until he suffers a heart attack. This brings him to re-evaluate his life and his relationships, one of which is with his mother, who is suffering from Alzheimer's disease. He had always found his mother to be cynical, controlling, and demanding, and he managed this situation by distancing himself from her. He is inspired by his father who ritualistically and lovingly visits his wife every day, showing nothing but faithful love and devotion to her despite her rambling speech, distant stares, and frequent inability to recognize her family. This is a touching, realistic, and emotional portrayal of Alzheimer's disease and the family members' reactions and coping.

In the Finnish film *The Man Without a Past* (2002), a man is robbed and brutally beaten while sleeping outside. He suffers a severe head injury and physicians pronounce him medically dead and walk out of the room; suddenly, the man wakes up, rises, and simply walks out of the hospital beyond the sight of staff. He has retrograde amnesia since the time of the injury and is forced to re-create his life. Although he is an outcast in society, he manages to cope with a greedy landlord, works at the Salvation Army, dates a woman, and finds a trusted companion in a dog and eventually a community. Pieces of memory return to him as he begins to find, reject, and come to terms with his past.

The sequelae of head injury secondary to a motor vehicle accident are portrayed in the French film *The Accidental Hero* (2002).

A Spanish film, *The City of No Limits* (2002), depicts a family patriarch (Max) who is dying of a brain tumor. Max displays paranoia and quirky behaviors. Medical doctors describe his psychological state as "verging on derangement." He stares at objects, carefully touches walls, speaks of video cameras watching him, calls a phone number that does not appear to exist, and tries to escape the hospital. He has a concerned and paranoid expression on his face, does not trust others, is constantly fearful, and is dishonest. Some of his comments appear random: "I'll never tell you where they are," and "Don't speak in front of them." He becomes preoccupied with escaping from the hospital to meet with someone named Rancel, wanting to warn him "before it is too late." He is not compliant with his medications. Though the viewer does not know his psychological condition prior to the brain tumor's onset, it is to be assumed most of these symptoms have emerged because of his tumor. Overall, Max's condition waxes and wanes: At times, Max is coherent and oriented; on other occasions, he confuses novels with reality. Important family secrets are uncovered due to Max's seemingly random and ridiculous comments.

The Belgian film *De Zak Alzheimer* (*The Memory of a Killer,* 2003) portrays a hit man in the early stages of Alzheimer's. He is repelled by his last assignment – he has been told to kill a 12-year-old girl forced into prostitution by her father – and he knows that his increasing forgetfulness puts him at great risk. The protagonist is all too familiar with the progression of Alzheimer's because he regularly visits his older brother who has the same disease.

Bille August, the Danish director of the heart-wrenching *Pelle the Conqueror* (1987), turned to the tragedy of Alzheimer's disease with the film *A Song for Martin* (2002). The film depicts the life story of a composer, Martin, who falls in love with his first violinist. The two divorce their spouses to be together, and the relationship is fairly idyllic until Martin begins to show early signs of forgetfulness and eventually it becomes clear that

he is the victim of a dementing illness. The film provides an excellent illustration of the demands Alzheimer's disease can place on a caregiver. Film critic Shelley Cameron called this film "one of the most moving portraits of human relationships ever chronicled."

A powerful, haunting Japanese film, *Narayama Bushiko* (*The Ballad of Narayama,* 1983), deals with the village practice of taking old people to the top of a mountain on their 70th birthday where they are left to die. As the U.S. population ages, nursing homes are increasingly serving as our own mountain top.

Further Exploration

If you have time to read just one book relevant to this chapter, make it

Sala, S. D. (Ed.) (2007). *Tall tales about the mind & brain: Separating fact from fiction.* New York, NY: Oxford University Press

If you only have time for one article, read:

Green, C. S., & Bavelier, D. (2008). Exercising your brain: A review of human brain plasticity and training-induced learning. *Psychology and Aging, 23,* 692–701.

Neuropsychological Disorders

Head Trauma

- *Memento* (2000)
- *Raging Bull* (1980)
- *On the Waterfront* (1954)
- *The Lookout* (2007)

Dementia

- *Iris* (2001)
- *Away from Her* (2006)
- *The Savages* (2007)
- *A Song for Martin* (2002)
- *The Memory of a Killer* (2003)
- *The Notebook* (2004)

Chapter 11

Disorders of Childhood and Adolescence

"It used to be kind of a hassle to put on underwear in the morning,
Now its kinda easy...ya know."
Justin Cobb in *Thumbsucker* (2005)

Questions to Consider While Watching *Thumbsucker*

- How does Justin's obsession with his thumb influence his psychosocial development?
- There are many self-gratifying habits; why does thumbsucking attract so much attention?
- Is hypnosis, as depicted in the film, a useful treatment for thumbsucking and other childhood habits? Is it helpful to use hypnosis with children?
- How often do children with ADHD abuse stimulants?
- What percentage of children and adolescents are incorrectly diagnosed as having ADHD? What percentage are not diagnosed with ADHD when they should be?
- Describe the relationship between the two brothers. Is it a typical sibling relationship?
- In most U.S. cultures, children do not call their parents by their first name. How do the interaction dynamics change when parents are called by their first names?
- How can a clinician differentiate between normal adolescent development and psychiatric disorders?

Patient Evaluation

Patient's stated reason for coming: "I want to get off of these drugs."

History of the present Illness: Justin is a 17-year-old Caucasian male who has a history of underperforming in school and refusing to participate in the debate club. His high school counselor diagnosed Justin with attention-deficit/hyperactivity disorder and recommended treatment with a commonly prescribed stimulant. Justin was taken to the family health care provider who prescribed the drug at the parents' request. Justin was never thoroughly evaluated for ADHD. Following the initiation of the drug, his behavior and performance in school improved. Within a short period of time, he began abusing the stimulant to enhance his academic performance. His parents were unaware of the extent of drug overuse and are uncertain how Justin obtained illegal amounts of the drug.

Past psychiatric illness, treatment, and outcome: Justin's parents deny any past psychiatric treatment. Justin admits to being hypnotized by the family dentist who was concerned about the effect of thumbsucking on his teeth. He sucks his thumb when stressed and when he needs comforting. He is embarrassed by this infantile habit and is highly motivated to stop. When using the stimulant, he no longer has any desire to suck his thumb, reports feeling confident, and is successful in school. He is concerned that once he stops using stimulants, his compulsive thumbsucking and lack of confidence will return.

Medical history: Justin and his parents stated Justin does not have any significant medical history.

Psychosocial history: Justin is the elder of two boys who address their parents by their first name due to their father's insecurity about aging. His mother, a nurse at an alcohol and drug rehabilitation center, describes Justin as sensitive, shy and awkward around others. His father runs a local store and has high expectations for Justin, but his son rarely meets these expectations. The father and son often argue about Justin's lack of motivation, but are getting along better since Justin has been taking the stimulant. Justin, an underachiever until recently, has few friends and only recently started dating. He has had limited sexual experience.

Drug and alcohol history: Justin denies using substances before the initiation of the prescribed stimulant. Since he began taking the stimulants, he has experimented with alcohol and marijuana. He does not regularly use either and attributes his use to curiosity.

Behavioral observations: Justin is a well dressed, slightly nervous, thin adolescent who shifts in his chair frequently, talks softly, and does not maintain eye contact when discussing difficult topics.

Mental status examination: He is oriented to time, place, situation, and person. He appears to have normal cognitive functioning. He denies psychosis. There is no evidence of delusions.

Functional assessment: Justin has a history of uneven performance in school. He feels uncomfortable in his interpersonal relationships.

Strengths: Justin is a creative and intelligent adolescent. He has an interest in branching out socially and relationally and has recently become interested in debating.

Diagnosis: Stimulant abuse; rule out attention-deficit/hyperactivity disorder

Treatment plan: Gradually withdraw stimulant; refer for a complete psychiatric evaluation, and initiate counseling to improve self-esteem.

Prognosis: Very good.

Thumbsucker and Attention-Deficit/Hyperactivity Disorder

In the award winning "coming of age" film *Thumbsucker* (2005), 17-year-old Justin Cobb (Lou Pucci) comforts himself by sucking his thumb, but is also highly distressed by his infantile habit and his inability to stop the obsessive behavior. As an awkward, self-conscious teenager, his psychological stress leads to failure on a debate team, poor performance in school, and a break-up with his girlfriend. Justin's dentist Perry Lyman (Keanu Reeves) confronts Justin about his thumbsucking and uses hypnosis to make the thumb distasteful. Justin's frustration increases when he is unable to find an adequate substitute for his thumbsucking. A well-meaning, but ill-informed school counselor diagnoses Justin as having attention deficit/hyperactivity disorder (ADHD) and strongly recommends a stimulant (Ritalin) as treatment. After starting the stimulant, Justin's behavior improves and he begins to excel on the debate team. The transition from a shy and socially inept teenager to debate team star is dramatic.

Errors in diagnosing ADHD are common. In order to be diagnosed with ADHD, the patient must be carefully evaluated. If ADHD is present, treatment should include counseling in addition to medication. This film demonstrates the negative outcomes associated with a misdiagnosis and inappropriate medication. It is unlikely that Justin had ADHD, and it is certainly unlikely that he would have had legal access to the amount of Ritalin he eventually wound up taking.

Child Mental Health

Psychiatric problems of children are not as easily diagnosed as those of adults, and the symptoms of mental illness in children are often difficult to distinguish from those changes associated with normal growth and development. For example, an imaginary friend of a 4-year-old is normal, but for an adolescent, an invisible friend would be considered a psychotic hallucination.

Children who receive mental health treatment usually fall in one of the following categories:

1. Children whose behavior is a response to family disruptions, crisis or dysfunction.

2. Children whose behavior does not conform to social norms and is troublesome to others (disruptive behaviors or conduct disorders).

3. Children who experience repeated and excessive depression, anxiety, or states of personal distress.

4. Children whose cognitive or neuromotor development is not proceeding normally (developmental disorders).

Child and Adolescent Behavioral Disorders in Contemporary Films

A child's behavior may appear to be symptomatic of a psychiatric disorder but, in reality, be a response to parental marital discord or family dysfunction. Complex family relationships provide filmmakers opportunities to dramatically portray multiple plots and subplots with relatively few characters. In Noah Baumbach's highly acclaimed film *The Squid and the Whale* (2005), two brothers, 16-year-old Walt (Jesse Eisenberg) and 10-year-old Frank (Owen Kline), are the center of their divorcing parents' feuds. The father, Bernard (Jeff Daniels), is an impossible character – jealous, self-absorbed, condescending, and narcissistic. He is a self-proclaimed novelist who feels victimized by being relegated to a college teaching position. The mother Joan (Laura Linney) is emerging as a legitimate writer whose success only fuels her husband's animosity towards her. When the parents separate, Walt, who idolizes and imitates his father, chooses to live with Bernard. Frank, the more emotional of the two brothers, stays with his mother Joan. Both boys develop abnormal behaviors. Frank drinks alcohol, masturbates, and smears his ejaculate on books and a locker at school. Walt plagiarizes a Pink Floyd song as his own, breaks up with his girlfriend, and refuses to see his mother who has had an affair while still married. Walt is referred to a therapist who helps him increase self-awareness. In isolation, any of these abnormal behaviors could have been symptoms of a mental disorder. Instead, these behaviors are all reactions to the chaotic family crisis.

Another interesting but disturbing film, one which explores a child's attempt to make sense out of chaotic and dysfunctional family interaction, is *Running with Scissors* (2006). This award winning film is based on real life memoirs of Augusten Burroughs who was handed off to his mother's psychiatrist after his parents' divorce. Burroughs is the son of poet and writer Margaret Robison and the late John G. Robison, head of the philosophy department at the University of Massachusetts at Amherst. Augusten Burroughs (Joseph Cross) is a young gay child who is consumed with adoration for his mother Deirdre (Annette Bening), who is attempting to launch her career as a poet. Augusten spends his childhood skipping school and practicing to become a performer. Augusten's father Norman (Alec Baldwin) teaches philosophy and abuses alcohol. The mother and father spend most of their time arguing. When the parents separate, Augusten, aged 12, is given to Deirdre's psychiatrist, Dr. Finch (Brian Cox), who is a very eccentric physician. As Deirdre sinks into her mental illness, Augusten avoids school, keeps a diary, becomes sexually involved with one of Finch's patients, and develops a friendship with Finch's younger daughter. During this time, he perfects his cosmetology skills. In real life, Burroughs dropped out of school after the 6th grade and obtained a GED at age 17.

He became a successful advertising executive, then left the field and became a successful writer.

> "I want rules... and boundaries... because... what I've learned is that... without them...all life is... is a series of surprises...."
>
> Augusten Burroughs in *Running with Scissors* (2006)

The Academy Award-winning satiric comedy *Little Miss Sunshine* (2006) portrays a family in crisis. Olive Hoover (Abigail Breslin) has fantasized about winning a beauty pageant for her entire young life. Although she doesn't fit the stereotypic contestant profile, Olive does manage to become a finalist in the Little Miss Sunshine pageant. Her family takes off in an old Volkswagen bus to attend the pageant. The family characters are unforgettable – her father (Greg Kinnear) is an unsuccessful motivational speaker/author, her brother Dwayne (Paul Dana) is a lost soul who has not spoken for months but has dreams of being an air force pilot, her uncle Steve (Frank Ginsberg) has just been released from a psychiatric facility after a suicide attempt and requires close observation. One of the best performances is that of Olive's grandfather (Alan Arkin), who supports her sense of self-worth. Olive, probably the healthiest member of the family, does not have a mental illness or emotional problem, but she is an example of a child much wiser than her years who helps an unhealthy family grow psychologically.

Attention Deficit/Hyperactivity Disorder

Children and adolescents are frequently diagnosed with attention deficit disorder (ADD) or attention-deficit/hyperactivity disorder (ADHD). Children and adolescents with **ADD** or **ADHD** either have marked disturbances in attention, concentration, following directions, and listening (ADD) or are hyperactive and impulsive (ADHD). The current estimate of prevalence in school-age children is 6%. Boys are more likely to be affected than girls (Scahill, Hamrin, Deering, & Pachlar, 2008). Children are frequently misdiagnosed with ADD or ADHD by school counselors, teachers and general practitioners.

Oppositional Defiant Disorder and Conduct Disorder

The diagnosis of **oppositional defiant disorder** is given to children and adolescents who have a pattern of negativistic, hostile, and defiant behavior, such as losing their temper, being argumentative, and being easily annoyed and resentful. The diagnosis of **conduct disorder**, at times similar in appearance, is given to children and adolescents who violate the basic rights of others or societal norms with aggression to people or animals, destruction of property, theft, deceit, and/or truancy. In many countries, these diagnostic labels are not used. However, behavioral problems are universal, as are the movies that depict them.

Life as a House and My First Mister

Two important films portray highly troubled, isolated, suicidal, and oppositional adolescents – *Life as a House* (2001) with the character of Sam (Hayden Christensen) and *My First Mister* (2001) with Jennifer (Leelee Sobieski) as the protagonists. Each film presents a highly troubled and alienated young person who is transformed through meaningful relationships. The major difference between the lead characters is their gender, and watching both films will help you appreciate the differences in psychosexual development between boys and girls.

In *Life as a House*, we are introduced to Sam, a character with a rebellious, gothic appearance as evidenced by his colored hair, lip ring, eye make-up, and tough exterior. In an early scene, he huffs paint while choking himself (autoerotic asphyxiation) in his closet. He resorts to this practice whenever he needs to escape from people and reality: He locks his door, plays loud music (e.g., Marilyn Manson), uses drugs (pills, pot, and huffing), and masturbates. With his extreme negativism and oppositional personality, it is easy to see how he believes that no one understands him and why he must come up with complicated ways to isolate himself. At one point in the film, he reveals he has been using drugs since the age of 12. He earns money to buy drugs through prostitution, finding this preferable to working hard to earn less money. Sam is able to articulate that he wants to become something he is not and does not know how; this leaves him to feel like "nothing." Beneath his rough exterior is a wounded and isolated adolescent longing for a meaningful connection. He finds the needed friendship and love when he establishes a relationship with his dying father; at that point,

Sam's behaviors, attitude, and appearance are transformed.

"I like how it feels not to feel."

Sam (Hayden Christensen) in
Life as a House (2001)

My First Mister portrays a similarly troubled youth, 17-year-old Jennifer, who is also gothic in appearance. She wears mostly black and has multiple facial piercings. She is very isolated with no real friends and no genuine interest in her needy mother or distant stepfather. She comments that she has never had a boyfriend or, for that matter, any friends. The closest Jennifer can get to people is when she views them through her binoculars. She fantasizes about living with the Partridge family. She has a blunted, sad affect and is highly negativistic and critical about life. She is preoccupied with death and she writes melancholy poetry about death, hopelessness, and "not existing." She likes to lie on gravesites, and exclaims, "I'm gonna go to hell anyway." More serious problems include self-injurious behaviors (cutting her arm) and visual hallucinations of her deceased grandmother. She finds meaning and purpose in a random, healthy relationship that blossoms with a man who she works with in a men's clothing store.

Both films include characters in search of their identities who work through oppositional and conduct problems to find them.

Thirteen

This film depicts a nightmarish reality for some parents; for others, it may serve as a wake-up call. *Thirteen* (2003), directed by Catherine Hardwicke, depicts a rapid transformation from childhood to adolescence and the pervasive influence of peer pressure during the teen years.

Tracy Freeland (Evan Rachel Wood), a 13-year-old 7th grader, is eager to be accepted by the "in group" in her school. She earns acceptance from this group when she rejects her current, less popular friends and spontaneously steals money from a woman on the street. She takes her soon-to-be best friend Evie Zamora (Nikki Reed) on a shopping spree, buying clothing and shoes. A friendship soon develops, and an emotional roller coaster ride begins, characterized by rebellion,

Additional Questions for Discussion
(*Life as a House and My First Mister*)

- Contrast the lead characters and the parental figures in each film.
- How likely is it for a teen to undergo rapid, positive transformation as depicted in these films? What type of transformation is most common (i.e., physical, attitudinal, social or emotional)?
- Is there a connection between music preferences (e.g., rap, grunge or heavy metal) and adolescent behavior?
- Do body piercings provide any evidence of psychopathology or is this simply a manifestation of healthy adolescent rebellion?
- Both characters live in good homes and had opportunities to thrive in those environments. How do you account for the oppositional behavior we see at each film's onset?
- Both characters engage in some severe self-destructive behavior (e.g., prostitution; self-cutting). How common is such self-destructive behavior in adolescents? In children?
- If a troubled adolescent were to watch one of these films, how likely is it he or she would change his or her behavior?

acting out, parental opposition, and misconduct. Tracy gets her tongue and belly button pierced, exhibits self-injurious behavior, abuses substances, tells numerous lies, and lets her grades plummet. She also becomes sexually promiscuous. An opening scene (a flash-forward) depicts Tracy and Evie getting high and amusing themselves by punching one another in the face.

"I'll die for you but I won't leave you alone right now."

Melanie Freeland (Holly Hunter) to her daughter who has been used and betrayed in *Thirteen* (2003)

As these oppositional behaviors escalate, Tracy becomes more and more isolated from her mother (Holly Hunter). Tracy becomes angry with her mother and resists any attempts to set parental limits on her behavior. The mother makes genuine attempts to establish appropriate boundaries, yet frequently falls short because of her own struggles and limitations as a recovering drug addict. The mother and daughter eventually come to know each other better as a result of their frequent fights. Evie's mother, on the other hand, is a self-absorbed abuse victim who allows and even encourages the girls to drink and smoke. The plot culminates in a bitter betrayal by Evie, demonstrating that peer relationships can end as abruptly as they begin.

Elephant

This award-winning (Cannes) 2003 independent film, directed by Gus van Sant, is a realistic and artful portrayal of an American high school and the routine life of students just prior to a massive school shooting, reminding the viewer of Columbine and subsequent tragedies. The film is eerie and foreboding in that it is much more about nonverbal behavior than about dialogue; this heightens the importance of the cinematic craft, a craft van Sant has mastered, particularly in his unique camera work and use of **non-diegetic sound** (i.e., sounds whose source cannot be seen in

 Additional Questions for Discussion
(*Thirteen*)

- Would one of these two teens benefit more than the other in a juvenile detention program?
- How common is it for 7th graders to use drugs and alcohol, become promiscuous, have their bodies pierced, or practice self-injurious behaviors?
- What does current research say about the social influences of peers? At what age does peer influence peak?
- Does Tracy become involved with an African-American athlete primarily to upset her mother?
- Is peer influence more important than parental influence?
- How should parents respond when adolescents refuse to accept parental boundaries?

the film). The viewer is taken along as the camera slowly follows several major characters as they go through their daily routines (e.g., walking down long hallways, greeting fellow students), and going in and out of buildings (into danger or safety zones, unbeknown to them), often with non-diegetic music in the film's background. It is interesting to note the title outside the building reads simply "high school," letting this particular school represent every high school.

Additional Questions for Discussion (*Elephant*)

- Why did van Sant choose this title?
- The film provides considerable latitude for viewers to explain the behaviors of Eric and Alex. Which explanations seem most compelling?
- Did Eric and Alex have a history of violent, delinquent, or deviant behavior?
- What is the purpose of the film? How does the director's style enhance this purpose?
- What warnings signs are presented in the behaviors of these two characters? Could this shooting have been prevented? How?
- Would stricter gun control laws have minimized the likelihood of the Columbine shootings?

Two characters, Eric (Eric Deulen) and Alex (Alex Frost), are depicted playing a video shooting game and looking up information about guns on the internet. They order guns and receive them in the mail in a large package without difficulty. Later, these two teens plot their shooting spree with a map of the school, planning to "pick off" as many classmates as possible in the school's high-traffic areas.

Although the film is realistic, the viewer is left with more questions than answers about causes, prevention, psychopathology, and etiology. At the same time, this is part of the director's craft, and he deliberately lets each member of the audience draw his or her own conclusions.

Kids and *Gummo*

These two movies are listed together because both are extraordinarily disturbing films. Harmony Korine, who wrote the script for *Kids* (1995), was both writer and director for *Gummo* (1997). Both films provide a frightening perspective on the lives of adolescents, the former in an urban setting and the latter in a small town/rural setting.

Kids, directed by Larry Clark, is a fast-paced film that allows the viewer to experience the thoughts, words, and behaviors of young adolescents as they interact with each other. One unforgettable scene depicts 15 or so skateboarding teens who brutalize a man who had the temerity to criticize one of the skateboarders. The plot revolves around the character of Telly (Leo Fitzpatrick), a scrawny but confident adolescent who takes tremendous pride in his ability to seduce virgins. Unbeknown to him, Telly is HIV positive, and he is rapidly spreading the virus to his vulnerable partners, most of whom have never had sex before.

Telly is extremely narcissistic, and the viewer assumes he would not change his behavior even if he knew his diagnosis. One of Telly's victims, a teenage girl, finds out she has been infected by Telly, and much of the film involves her frantic attempts to get him to stop spreading the disease. The HIV virus is a metaphor for the spread of violence amongst inner-city youth.

Gummo is a realistic and poignant film that portrays lower-class, antisocial children and adolescents. The film includes numerous disturbing scenes of animal torture, drug abuse, and bizarre behavior such as that exhibited by one man who has a fight with an inanimate object. The film's two main characters, Solomon (Jacob Reynolds) and Tummler (Nick Sutton), bicycle around shooting stray cats and collecting them in garbage bags to sell them to a storeowner so they can get high on glue or have sex with a mentally retarded girl. At times, these two characters are violent just for the sake of violence; they repeatedly whip a hanging dead cat and later take turns shooting a dead cat in the pouring rain. They break into the home of their competitor (another cat killer), masked with guns and a golf club, and unhook the life support of an infirm elderly woman. Each adolescent is reared by a single parent with limited parenting skills; Solomon's mother threatens to kill him with a toy gun for not smiling, and later washes him in filthy bathwater while serving him spaghetti and milk.

There are many other quirky and disturbed characters in the film, including a boy who dresses like a bunny, urinates on traffic at overpasses, drowns a cat, and fakes his own death, and a developmentally disabled girl who laughs while she shaves her eyebrows and compulsively treats her doll as if it were a real infant. The director, Harmony Korine, has a cameo appearance in the film as a drunken adolescent who randomly pours beer on his head while describing his history of sexual abuse and trying to seduce a gay, African-American midget. Korine's character recollects thowing marbles on his mother's belly when he was a young child – if he hit her navel, he would get five dollars but whenever he hit her arm, he was hit with a rolling pin.

These characters lack insight into their behavior, and they are not able to appreciate the consequences of their acts. Most lack empathy and have little regard for ethical or moral standards; it is reasonable to assume that many will become adults who qualify for a diagnosis of antisocial personality disorder.

Many viewers stay to the end of the credits of *Gummo* to confirm that the animal abuse scenes are simulated, that prosthetic animals are used, and that

Additional Questions for Discussion (*Kids* and *Gummo*)

- Is there any artistic merit in films as shocking as these?
- Compare and contrast potential diagnoses for the main characters in the two films.
- What role does the lack of authority figures play in the lives of these teens?
- What redeeming scenes are included in each film? How do you respond to these?
- What would be appropriate treatment for the characters in these films? Should these children be treated in the juvenile justice system or the mental health system?

the characters and situations are fictitious; despite the assurance of the credits, viewers know that for many children, the scenes portrayed are all too real.

Other Portrayals of Behavioral Disorders in Children and Adolescents

Oppositional defiant disorder in late teens can also be found in *Don't Come Knocking* (2005), in which a young man displays outrage and defiance after his biological father, a washed-up actor, returns to town wanting to see him.

In *American Beauty* (1999), one adolescent secretly smokes marijuana and sells it to his neighbors. In *Manic* (2003), the viewer gets an inside look at the adolescent unit of a psychiatric hospital. This well-acted independent film presents interesting questions about differential diagnosis, demonstrates friction between various adolescents with clashing behavioral problems (e.g., bipolar disorder, impulse control problem, and depression), and offers a good portrayal of group psychotherapy.

My Flesh and Blood (2004) is a documentary about a woman who takes care of special needs children; one child, whose life is explored in detail, has a severe conduct disorder in addition to cystic fibrosis. His anger outbursts and sexual acting out are at times tempered by a needy softness and emotional vulnerability. His behavioral problems are directly related to the loss of his mother as a caretaker (she continues to visit him), the stress of his environment (one caretaker serves 11 special needs children), and the stress of his illness.

Holes (2002), an excellent Disney feature film, depicts various oppositional and rule-breaking youth who are sent to a working camp because of their behavioral problems. One adolescent steals cars and has a tic disorder.

Child and Adolescent Psychopathology: Depression, Anxiety, and Distress in Contemporary Films

Depression in children and adolescents is reaching epidemic proportions, and it is important for all health care providers to screen adolescents for depression. The exact prevalence of depressed children who continue to be depressed into adulthood is unknown. Depression in childhood is sometimes difficult to diagnose because children who are depressed are more likely to withdraw (girls) or act out (boys). In adolescents, the depression is often mistaken for the normal mood lability of teenagers.

In *The Great New Wonderful* (2005), several vignettes interweave around a post-9/11 New York. One vignette depicts an overweight, depressed child who is self-defeating and easily agitated. In addition to a serious case of asthma, he has significant behavioral problems. He sets toys on fire, hits children at school, and viciously attacks an Armenian child, calling him a "sand monkey" while stuffing sand and gravel down his throat. His parents are at a loss for what they can do to help their son and express irritation when the school principal is unable to make meaningful recommendations. Childhood depression, without conduct disturbance, can be found in a young girl in *The Weather Man* (2005).

The United States of Leland

This disturbing 2004 film opens with an adolescent, Leland P. Fitzgerald (Ryan Gosling), reflecting on having killed an autistic boy. Leland does not know why he murdered the boy, and he is beginning to regret his behavior: "I think I made a mistake." His attitudes, the motives for his actions, and his methods for coping are often unclear. Throughout the film, Leland has different insights as he struggles to realize and accept that "nothing can make what happened unhappen."

> "When I say I don't remember that day, I'm not lying. I wish I did but I just don't. Sometimes the most important stuff just goes away. Goes away so bad it's like it was never there to begin with."
>
> Leland P. Fitzgerald

Leland is very insightful and perceptive; he notices small details in his environment and applies these insights in his interactions with others. Yet, as with many depressed individuals and especially depressed teens, he is unable to articulate his feelings. He states he has not cried since he was a little boy; even then, he was very guarded and concerned with what others would think. Leland clearly suppresses his feelings, such as when he refuses to show hurt or anger toward his girlfriend when she admits she broke up with him so she could date a drug dealer. He does not understand his own sadness, he denies anger and displays flat affect throughout the film. He even stabs himself in the hand "because I wanted to know what it felt like."

"There's all this sadness and there's nothing you can do about it, and all I wanted was for it to go away."

Leland explaining his suffering

Leland is very detached, and appears to be uninterested in his own fate. His social behavior is quirky; at times, he says very little and appears to be preoccupied with his environment. There are many scenes indicating that Leland does not know how to connect with others. In short, Leland is a profoundly depressed and troubled adolescent.

Schizophrenia in Children

Schizophrenia is a serious illness that alters thoughts, emotions and behaviors. It is a rare diagnosis in children, and is hard to recognize in its early phases.

 **Additional Questions for Discussion
(The United States of Leland)**

- What diagnosis would you give Leland?
- Do you accept his explanation at the end for why he killed the boy? Is his explanation convincing?
- What is the best treatment approach for a character such as Leland?
- How accurate is memory in recalling traumatic events? Is the depiction in this film accurate?

The features of schizophrenia are fully described in chapter 9. Some of the specific symptoms that one would look for in a child include seeing things and hearing voices that are not real (hallucinations), odd and eccentric behavior and/or speech, unusual or bizarre thoughts and ideas, difficulty separating television and dreams from reality, confusion, extreme moodiness, and paranoid beliefs. In addition, a child may exhibit age-inappropriate behavior (e.g., behaving like a younger child), severe anxiety and fearfulness, difficulty relating to peers and keeping friends, withdrawal and increased isolation, and a decline in personal hygiene (APA, 2000). The movie *Spider* (2002) accurately depicts a child with early symptoms of schizophrenia that follow him into adulthood. The boy, nicknamed "Spider," has delusional and paranoid thinking, eccentric behavior, and severe isolation from peers.

The Butcher Boy

Both Patrick McCabe's 1992 novel and the 1997 Neil Jordan adaptation of the novel offer a chilling introduction to childhood psychopathology. Both works are artistic successes, and Jordan's movie has been compared to classic films in the childhood psychopathology genre, including Stanley Kubrick's *A Clockwork Orange* (1971) and Francois Truffaut's *The 400 Blows* (1959).

The Butcher Boy protagonist, Francie Brady (Eamonn Owens), comes from a highly dysfunctional family. His mother has a long history of mental illness, and periodically experiences "nervous breakdowns." When Francie and his friend Joe (Alan Boyle) try to make sense of her illness, they find some comfort in the metaphor of a car breaking down, and reason that Annie Brady (Aisling O'Sullivan) has simply gone off to a garage to be repaired. The father, Benny Brady (Stephen Rea), is a drunken musician who spends most of his time in a local pub. The father is less than adequate as a role model – e.g., he responds to a faulty television set by kicking in the screen and threatening to beat up the individual who sold it to him. While a dysfunctional family unit is typically not sufficient to *cause* mental illness, it can clearly *exacerbate* any psychiatric symptoms or conditions that may be present.

The book and film take place in the early 1960s, a period of global tension and significant apprehension about the spread of communism. These societal concerns shape Francie's delusions, which focus on global conquest by aliens (a metaphor for communists) and nuclear disaster. Although schizophrenia, Francie's presumed illness, is found across cultures, the specific manifestations of the illness are shaped by cultural experiences and expectations.

In a poignant moment in the film, Francie discovers his mother standing on a table next to a chair, contemplating hanging herself. She eventually commits suicide by drowning in a local lake. Francie, who has run away from home, misses his mother's funeral. Both the townspeople and the father blame Francie for his mother's death, and he blames himself. The incident underscores the penchant children have for attributing misfortune in the family to their own misbehavior, as well as the fact that people who have made previous suicide attempts are at a great risk for actually succeeding in killing themselves in the future.

"Any odd time they'd take me down to the room and hand me bits of paper all blotted with ink. What do you think about that says the doc. You won't be writing any more messages on that paper I says. Why not says the doc lifting the specs. It's destroyed I says, look at it. Hmm hmm. In the school for docs that what they taught them. Lift your specs and repeat after me – hmm hmm!"

From Patrick McCabe's
The Butcher Boy (1992)

Francie is eventually hospitalized, receives electroconvulsive therapy, and is threatened with lobotomy. He escapes from the psychiatric hospital and returns to his village and his job as a butcher boy. He subsequently commits a gratuitous murder, is captured, escapes, sets fire to his former home, prepares to perish in the flames, and is then rescued, treated, and hospitalized. He remains a psychiatric inpatient until he is discharged to a half-way house in midlife. In the final scene of the film, Francie Brady is revisited by the Virgin Mary and the viewer is left wondering about the success of treatment and the long-term prognosis for this fascinating character.

The behavior of children with schizophrenia often changes slowly over time, as we note in the case of Francie Brady. The early problems of children who are subsequently diagnosed with schizophrenia are often first noticed by the child's teachers. Schizophrenia is a life-long disease that

can be controlled but not cured; we see this clearly as a middle-aged Francie Brady prepares to leave the hospital and once again has a conversation with the Virgin Mary.

"Mary had the same face as ma used to have sitting staring into the ashes. It was funny that face it slowly grew over the other one until one day you looked and the person you knew was gone. And instead there was a half-ghost sitting there who had only one thing to say: All the beautiful things of this world are lies. They count for nothing in the end."

From Patrick McCabe's
The Butcher Boy (1992)

An interesting diagnostic dilemma is presented in the classic film *The Exorcist* (1973). A child with truly disturbing psychiatric symptoms is initially diagnosed by a pediatrician as having ADHD and Ritalin is prescribed; when this fails she is referred to a chain-smoking neurologist who diagnoses her with psychomotor seizures, but there is no response to the treatment he initiates; desperate for help, the mother visits a child psychiatrist who is also a Jesuit priest. The priest's talents and training as a psychiatrist don't serve him well; however, as a priest he succeeds in exorcising the demon that has possessed the child. *The Exorcism of Emily Rose* (2005) tells a similar story about a 19-year-old girl who dies during an exorcism ritual conducted by her family priest.

Other Noteworthy Films Portraying Psychopathology in Children and Adolescents

The Magdalene Sisters (2002) is a somber film based on a true story that depicts the verbal, emotional, and physical suffering of young girls who are sent to a boarding home run by nuns. The girls are forced to work long hours; they endure physical, sexual, and verbal abuse, and they are required to turn over all their possessions to the nuns, who seem more concerned about money than character. Many of these girls are sent to the home without legitimate reasons. Humiliation is an institutional norm, and it causes one particularly vulnerable adolescent to have a psychotic break. The girls cope in a variety of ways; one girl takes her revenge on an abusive priest by rubbing an allergy-inducing plant on his underwear when she is doing his washing; the plant results in intense itching that dramatically disrupts a religious service the priest is leading.

Pieces of April (2003) depicts a young woman who has recovered from severe conduct and oppositional behavioral problems as a youth. April (Katie Holmes) is living alone and away from her family and trying to prepare a final Thanksgiving dinner for her mother (Patricia Clarkson) who is dying from breast cancer. April ultimately succeeds in creating a pleasant meal for a critical, ailing, and dysfunctional family.

The exact nature of the illness that causes a teenage boy to blind six horses is never identified in *Equus* (1977), despite the best efforts of a psychiatrist played by Richard Burton, but it is clear that the boy is deeply troubled. His problems seem to relate to his emerging sexuality – in one scene he is impotent when confronted with his first sexual opportunity. Likewise, there is no clear diagnosis for the child in *The Tin Drum* (1979) who, on his third birthday, decides to stop growing, but it is clear that the boy is responding to the madness of the world around him and events over which he has no control (like the suicide of his mother).

A US film that depicts Tourette's disorder is the short documentary *I Have Tourette's but Tourette's Doesn't Have Me* (2005), in which children aged 8–14 share their struggles, symptoms, coping, and triumphs over having Tourette's.

International Films: Child and Adolescent Psychopathology

The French film *The Chorus* (2004) is about life at a boarding school for troubled children. The school is headed by a dictatorial headmaster, M. Rachin (Francois Berléand). The movie depicts defiance, conduct problems, running away, and children who draw obscene pictures of teachers, and set traps for the teaching staff. Indeed, some of the children would qualify for conduct disorder or oppositional defiant disorder. Clément Mathieu (Gérard Jugnot) is hired to teach these rowdy children. With the superintendent's approval, he turns his four o'clock study hall into a chorus class. Pierre Morhange (Jean-Baptiste Maunier), the most problematic student, has a beautiful voice and eventually joins the choir. The choir and Mathieu are able to expose Rachin's cruelty.

A number of short films depicting childhood psychopathology are especially interesting. The award-winning animated Australian film *Harvie Krumpet* (2003) is about the life of Harvek Milos Krumpetzke, born in Poland in 1922. He is raised by an illiterate mother with schizophrenia. When he becomes a refugee during World War II, he changes his name to Harvie Krumpet. He has Tourette's disorder and overcomes numerous challenges, such as frequent trips to the hospital due to brain trauma, being struck by lightning, and testicular cancer. He is incorrectly labeled with mental retardation, which brings consequences of its own. His wife dies suddenly of a blood clot, he grows senile and has strong suicidal intentions and plans. Despite his bad luck and circumstances, he remains quite optimistic.

The short film, *The Antichrist* (2002, Poland) depicts four boys exploring a field in which explosion are occuring because of excavations. One boy, who has a number of defiance and conduct symptoms, calls himself the Antichrist and challenges the other boys engage in dangerous behavior. He catches a fish with his bare hands and then gleefully stabs it. He also buries himself alive, runs barefoot in thistles, and rides down a treacherous rocky hillside on his bicycle. The film suggests this character will likely develop an antisocial personality.

Pan's Labyrinth (2006, Spain/Mexico/U.S.) is an excellent movie portraying a child's reaction to a difficult and traumatic family situation. This is the story of a young, imaginative girl, Ofelia (Ivana Baquero), who travels with her pregnant and sick mother Carmen Vidal (Ariadna Gil) to the country to meet and live with her stepfather, the sadistic and cruel Captain Vidal (Sergi López). In order to survive her abusive world, she creates a fantasy wonderland inhabited by a faun, a man whose eyes are in the palms of his hand, a giant toad, and other creatures. These creatures accept Ofelia as a long-lost princess. Her strong ability to fantasize seems to keep conditions like acute stress disorder at bay.

To Be and To Have (2005, France) is a realistic classroom film that is part-documentary and part-drama about a creative small town teacher who teaches children of different ages, learning levels, and types of problems. While not discussed in the film, some children have symptoms of ADHD, inattentive type, pervasive developmental disorder, and potentially a communication disorder or selective mutism.

The 2003 Brazilian film *City of God* looks at children and adolescents growing up in a poor, gang-infested area of Rio de Janeiro (called the "City of God") who must choose between a life filled with drug dealing, guns, and violence and a life based on the hope that they will be able to escape their circumstances. These young children quickly learn to show no fear, and they do not seem to care if they live or die. The film depicts very young children (referred to as "runts") running around with guns and talking about getting revenge by murdering their enemies. The film is especially disturbing because it is based on a true story (it is estimated that at least 100,000 people are involved in drug dealing in Rio), and conduct disorders are the norm for children and adolescents living in the City of God. The film contrasts two of the younger boys brought up in this culture: One, the protagonist, finds passion and meaning in photography and rejects gang-life; the other, named Li'l Zé, achieves his life goal of rising to power to take over as drug boss in the City of God by killing his competition. The Rio police walk around in fear and largely ignore the drug dealers; before the dealers rose to power, the police would come into homes and pillage.

An interesting and provocative dilemma emerges for the children of the City of God: A child can either choose an honest occupation and live in poverty or become rich by dealing drugs. If these children choose to deal drugs, there is a well-established career trajectory: First, they act as a drug delivery boy, then as a lookout, then dealer, soldier, and eventually manager. For many of these children, the life of a drug dealer is the more appealing option.

One of the most powerful cinematic portrayals of childhood psychopathology is found in the 1994 New Zealand film *Heavenly Creatures*, directed by Peter Jackson and starring Kate Winslet. The film is based on the true story of two teenage girls, aged 15 and 17, who conspire to murder the mother of one of the girls. The older girl went on to develop a significant reputation as an author of murder mysteries, writing under the name of Anne Perry. The girl's confusion and mental illness in *Heavenly Creatures* is artistically captured in film through her interactions with life-size clay figures that inhabit a medieval fantasy land.

Fanny and Alexander, an Academy Award winner for Best Foreign Film, is an excellent 1982 Swedish movie. Touted as one of Ingmar Bergman's finest films, the movie takes place in a Swedish provincial town in the early 1900s and centers on the experiences of two children, Fanny and Alexander, who are growing up within a large, happy extended family. Their father dies and their mother remarries. Their new stepfather is a stern, authoritarian clergyman who is incapable of understanding the feelings of others. Throughout the movie, Alexander has unusual experiences. He periodically has visits from his father' ghost. The viewer is given the impression that his father is watching over him throughout the movie. Alexander's imagination causes a statue to take on a lifelike image and move. He also believes that he has magical powers and, at the end of the movie, Alexander believes that he willed the house fire that caused his stepfather's death.

Several high-quality foreign films portray normal children living in abnormal or compromised circumstances. *Lilja 4-ever* (2002) is a devastating Swedish/Danish film about a 16-year-old girl living in a broken-down tenement "somewhere in the former Soviet Union." She is abandoned by her mother and engages in escapism and fantasy with her only friend, an 11-year-old boy. She is betrayed by a man she loves and sold into prostitution in another country where she experiences one tragedy after another.

The Polish film *Island on Bird Street* (1997) is based on a true story about a boy who creates a secret hideout and learns how to survive under traumatic circumstances while he waits for his father's return during the Nazi occupation of Poland. The New Zealand film *Rain* (2002) is another movie that emphasizes the resiliency and endurance of a young person – in this case, a young girl who faces the drowning of her beloved younger brother and the alcoholism, depression, and infidelity of her mother.

Other films explore the ways in which children are affected by poverty. These include *El Norte* (1983, U.S./UK), a film about two children escaping poverty in Guatemala and exchanging it for poverty in Los Angeles; *Pixote* (1981, Brazil), a film that describes the ways in which street children in Brazil are almost inevitably drawn into a squalid life of crime, drugs, and prostitution; and *Salaam Bombay* (1988, UK/India/France), a movie that follows the lives and misfortunes of children living on the streets of Bombay. *Ratcatcher* (1999, UK/France) is about an adolescent with conduct problems living in Glasgow in an area filled with trash, dead rats, lice, and social decay. A French film fantasy, *The City of Lost Children* (1995), directed by Jean Pierre-Jeunet & Marc Caro, depicts a young girl, Miette, who is forced to steal in order to support two evil Siamese-twin sisters. Miette develops a safe, collaborative relationship with a mentally challenged circus strongman and together they try to stop a mad scientist who kidnaps children and steals their dreams.

The film *Born into Brothels: Calcutta's Red Light Kids* (2004, US) portrays the lives of the children of prostitutes living in Calcutta. This film won an Academy Award for Best Documentary of 2004.

Slumdog Millionaire (2008) is a powerful portrayal of the poverty and squalor associated with life in the slums of Mumbai.

Truffaut's *The Wild. Child* (1970, France) explores the life of a feral child, and Werner Herzog's *Every Man for Himself and God Against All* (1974, West Germany) addresses a similar theme in its exploration of the effects of a childhood filled with almost complete isolation, deprivation, and torture.

In the classic Italian film *Cinema Paradiso* (1988), a young boy becomes enamored with a local cinema and finds a father figure in the projectionist while growing up in a small town just after World War II. The beautifully simple film *Children of Heaven* (1997, Iran) depicts children coping in a poor section of an Iranian city. In the French film, *Monsieur Ibrahim* (2003), an adolescent without a mother resorts to stealing from a local store so he can continue to make meals for his critical father (as well as save up money to purchase the services of a prostitute). The protagonist develops a deep, fatherly friendship with the storeowner and is eventually abandoned by his father.

Further Exploration

If you have time to read just one book relevant to this chapter, make it:

Brown, R. T., Antonuccio, D. O., DuPaul, G. J., Fristad, M. A., King, C. A., Leslie, L. K., et al. (2008). *Childhood mental health disorders: Evidence base and contextual factors for psychosocial, psychopharmacological, and combined interventions.* Washington, DC: American Psychological Association.

If you only have time for one article, read:

Yeates, K. O., Bigler, E. D., Dennis, M., Gerhardt, C. A., Rubin, K. H., Stancin, T., et al. (2007). Social outcomes in childhood brain disorder: A heuristic integration of social neuroscience and developmental psychology. *Psychological Bulletin, 133*, 535–556.

Authors' Picks

Disorders of Childhood and Adolescence

Oppositional Defiant Disorder and Conduct Disorders

- [ ] *Life as a House* (2001)
- [ ] *My First Mister* (2001)
- [ ] *The Chorus* (2004)
- [ ] *Thirteen* (2003)
- [ ] *Kids* (1995)

Attention-Deficit / Hyperactivity Disorder

- [ ] *Thumbsucker* (2005)

Dysfunctional Families

- [ ] *Fanny and Alexander* (1982)
- [ ] *Little Miss Sunshine* (2006)
- [ ] *Pan's Labyrinth* (2006)

Childhood Schizophrenia

- [ ] *The Butcher Boy* (1997)

Critical Thinking Questions

- Many films portray children who are resilient at very difficult times and in challenging environments. How common is this? Is psychopathology the opposite of resilience? Can a child be mentally ill and resilient at the same time?

- Should adolescents who commit serious crimes like rape and murder be tried as adults? At what age should a child be held responsible for committing "adult crimes?"

- Before her death, Francie's mother in *The Butcher Boy* (1997) repeatedly played a song about a woman who committed suicide. Do suicidal individuals typically signal their intent like this?

- In *The Butcher Boy*, Benny Brady attempts to spank Francie after his first incident with Mrs. Nugent. Is spanking ever justified? What alternative means of punishment are most appropriate?

- The film *Kids* (1995) deals with sex, drugs, violence, and AIDS. Is the film accurate in its suggestion that these issues are becoming increasingly salient for very young adolescents?

- William Golding's 1954 novel *Lord of the Flies* and the films based on it (1963, 1990) suggest that without adult supervision young children quickly become savages. Do you find this position plausible? Are the kids in *Gummo* (1997) simply savages?

- Films often portray step-parents as cold and sadistic. Is there any empirical evidence for this or is it a simplistic and misguided stereotype?

- Some groups have criticized director Neil Jordan for Sinead O'Connor's portrayal of the Virgin Mary in *The Butcher Boy*. Did you find the role offensive?

- Francie repeatedly bullies Phillip Nugent in *The Butcher Boy*. Is there a relationship between school bullying and future mental illness or antisocial behavior?

Chapter 12

Mental Retardation and Autism

"Easter's coming. Why do you think the Hulk is so mad? Why is he mad at me. Maybe I did something bad to him... I love you Eugene... Gene tell me about when we were born."
Dominick

"You were born first. And 12 minutes later I was born. You are the big brother. Our mother died when we were born. Our father worked in the steel mill."
Eugene

"And you and me was always together. Our father had to go away. I fell down and hurt my head and that is why I can't remember."
Dominick

Dominick and Eugene (1988)

Questions to consider while watching *Dominick and Eugene* (1988)

- Is *Dominick and Eugene* an accurate picture of mental retardation?
- Is Dominick's gullibility typical for persons with mental retardation? Is it typical for persons with mental disorders?
- What role did Mrs. Gianelli play in raising Dominick and Eugene?
- When Jennifer was introduced to Dominick, was his reaction normal or was it exaggerated because of his dependency on Eugene?
- Is it realistic to think that Dominick can live independently without Eugene?
- How much did Ray's guilt contribute to his constant concern and care for Dominick? If there had been no accident, and the mental retardation had been caused by other factors, do you think that Eugene would have provided care for him?

Patient Evaluation

Patient's stated reason for coming: "I am saving Joey. I don't ever want anyone to hurt him. His brother Michael was hurt."

History of present illness: Dominick "Nicky" Luciano was arrested for kidnapping an infant (Joey) after the infant's sibling died. Mr. Luciano is a 26-year-old Caucasian male with mental retardation who lives with his twin brother, Eugene, a medical student. He reports witnessing the dead child's father throwing the child (Michael) down the stairs, and subsequently the father threatened to harm Dominick if he ever told anyone what he saw. While witnessing the father's abuse, Dominick remembered being abused by his own father.

Past psychiatric illness, treatment, and outcomes: Dominick has no history of psychiatric disorders.

Medical history: Dominick has no known medical disorders or history of medication. He had a head injury at a young age.

Psychosocial history: Dominick has lived with Eugene and been supported by his caretaker, Mrs. Gianelli, since their father left home 20 years earlier. Dominick is very attached to his brother. Dominick's income as a garbage collector helps pay the family's bills. Dominick has an IQ of 65.

Drug and alcohol history: Dominick denies any history of drug or alcohol use. He has had one episode of alcohol intoxication.

Behavioral observations: Dominick is a very engaging 26-year-old man.

Mental status examinations: Dominick was alert and oriented to time, place, and person. He denied hallucinations and delusions. He was unable to complete serial sevens, and had difficulty with memory recall and copying a complex drawing. He had no problems with short-term memory questions. He denied suicidal and homicidal ideation. His thinking is concrete, but judgment appears average. He scored 22 on the Mini Mental State Examination.

Functional assessment: Dominick is employed by the city. He has worked as a trash collector for 5 years and is reported to be a reliable, efficient employee. He lives with his brother Eugene, who is a medical student at a local university. Eugene has taken a position in California and will be leaving Pittsburgh within 2–3 months. Dominick is well supported by his neighbor (Mrs. Gianelli), his employer, Mr. Johnson, and numerous acquaintances in the community. He is well-liked by his peers, but is easily taken advantage of when he attempts to please others. He can live independently with some supervision. His physical growth is normal, but his psychosocial development is delayed. He is not sexually active, and he has not been seeking a partner. His friendships have all been with coworkers and acquaintances.

Strengths: He is an engaging, attractive young man who is steadily employed. He is looking forward to living independently in his current apartment after his brother moves to California. He has community support for independent living. The kidnapping charges have been dropped and he is ready to testify about Michael's death.

Diagnosis: Mild mental retardation; rule out: post-traumatic stress disorder related to childhood abuse.

Treatment plan: 1) With support from functional adults, Dominick can live independently; 2) Dominick should receive short-term counseling or therapy to address separation issues with his brother.

Prognosis: Good.

Dominick and Eugene and Mental Retardation

Dominick and Eugene (1988), directed by Robert M. Young, is a movie about twin brothers Dominick (Tom Hulce) and Eugene Luciao (Ray Liotta), who live together in a low-income Pittsburgh neighborhood. Dominick ("Nicky") experienced brain trauma as a child and is developmentally disabled. He also has a learning disability and memory problems. The story begins as the twins approach their 26th birthday. Dominick is interested in the Hulk; Eugene ("Gino") is completing medical school and has been accepted into a California residency program. Gino, who feels responsible for his brother and who is afraid to tell him about his plans to move, is frequently angry with Nicky. The movie depicts the change in the brotherly relationship as each matures and responds to his respective need to live separately. It also highlights the strength of people with mental retardation.

Movies and Persons with Disabilities

Similar to films portraying people with psychological disorders, films depicting individuals with disabilities are often either shocking or overly sentimental. Writers often base their stories on stereotypes, but often have no personal experience interacting with people with disabilities. Their stories are frequently implausible and sentimental. Disabilities often are used as a plot device, and the character of the person with the disability is not developed fully in the story. For example, *The Other Sister* (1999) is a romantic comedy depicting the intellectual and developmental struggles of Carla Tate (Juliette Lewis) as she works hard to become an independent adult. The reviews were very mixed – some see the movie as a snapshot of many families who are reluctant to admit a child is mentally challenged. Many film critics found the film offensive and argued that mental retardation was being used as a gimmick for the plot. The comedy *The Ringer* (2005) received similar criticism. In this Farrelly brothers' film, Steve Barker (Johnny Knoxville) is desperate for money and decides to enter the Special Olympics in order to beat the reigning champ in the racing event. Special Olympics International supports this film and consequently there are over 150 Special Olympic athletes in the film, with a handful having important supporting. Some stereotyping is present, including the use of the word "retard" and the depiction of a person of normal intelligence faking mental retardation with a fake voice, unlikely behavior, mussed hair, and a contrived laugh. On the other hand, the film normalizes mental retardation by showing that people with mental retardation experience normal emotions and activities – we see them struggling to compete, laughing, and supporting others; in addition, several of the characters with mental retardation use sarcasm and wit to provide clever comic relief.

In *Cinema of Isolation: A History of Physical Disability in Film* (1994), Martin Norden writes about the stereotypes of women with disabilities and develops a four-fold typology: the "sweet innocent" in *Stella Maris* (1918), the "obsessive avenger" in *Freaks* (1932), the "civilian superstar" in *Interrupted Melody* (1955), and the "bitter" in *What Ever Happened to Baby Jane?* (1962). Norden also discusses realistic depictions of women with disabilities as in *The Other Side of the Mountain* (1975), *Gaby* (1987), *Passion Fish* (1992), and *The Theory of Flight* (1998).

Diagnosis of Mental Retardation

Below-average intelligence and impaired adaptive functioning characterize mental retardation. The diagnosis is made through clinical assessment, historical accounts from parents and teachers, and standardized tests. Diagnosis usually occurs during childhood. Because intelligence tests have been standardized at 100 with a standard deviation of 15, the usual threshold for mental retardation is set at two standard deviations below the mean or lower (i.e., an intelligence quotient of 70 or less). Impaired adaptive functioning is primarily a clinical judgment based upon an evaluation of age-appropriate tasks.

The film *I Am Sam* (2001) depicts an adult, Sam (Sean Penn), with mental retardation with some autistic behaviors who lives independently and who has been able to support his 7-year-old daughter Lucy. He thinks very concretely and has difficulty with conceptual thinking. His reading and math ability are very limited. Sam lives in an apartment with his daughter whom he has cared for since birth. Sam has assumed responsibility for raising his daughter with the help of a neighbor. He has not had contact with any family members. He has several friends who also have mental impairments who provide support to Sam and his daughter.

Sam and his daughter have approximately the same intellectual abilities, and they enjoy playing in the park, singing songs, and reading together. When Lucy surpasses her father's intellectual capacity, she is embarrassed by his limited cognitive abilities. She struggles to cope with classmates and friends making fun of Sam, and frequently tells her friends that she is adopted. At a birthday party planned by her father, Lucy becomes distraught over her father's child-like behavior. Child Protective Services eventually takes Lucy away from her father.

"You don't know what it is when you try, and you try, and you try and you never get there!"

Sam expressing the challenges of his life in *I Am Sam* (2001)

According to the *DSM-IV-TR*, mental retardation is identified as a mental disorder and is prevalent in 1% of the population. The range of mental retardation extends from mild to profound (see Table 12.1). Before a child is diagnosed with mental retardation, other deficits or impairments in functioning must be present in addition to low scores on an intelligence test (e.g., the child does not meet the expected standards for his or her age or cultural group in communication does not use community resources, lacks self-direction, has limited academic skills, or has problems with leisure, health, or safety).

Questions to Consider While Watching *I Am Sam*

- Is Sean Penn's portrayal of Sam an accurate picture of mental retardation? Why or why not?
- What specific behaviors lead the protective service worker to conclude that Sam is unable to be an effective parent?
- Is it realistic to think that a man with the intelligence of a 7-year-old could responsibly raise a child?
- What type of social supports would a parent who has mental retardation need in order to be an effective parent?
- What issues will Sam face as a single father raising a daughter through later childhood and early adolescence?
- How was Sam influenced by his own childhood experience in an institution?
- Was Lucy's embarrassment normal behavior for a 7-year-old?

Table 12.1 Levels of mental retardation by IQ range

Category	IQ Level	Approximate % of Persons
Mild	50–55 to 70	85%
Moderate	35–40 to 50–55	10%
Severe	20–25 to 35–40	3–4%
Profound	Below 20–25	1–2%

Even though mental retardation is classified by the *DSM-IV-TR* as a disorder, it is not a disease. The term **mental retardation** denotes the degree to which a person functions below cultural and social norms at a particular time and place. Persons with mental retardation form a heterogeneous group. There are various causes of mental retardation – these include drug or alcohol abuse in the mother, chromosomal or genetic disorders, or lack of oxygen during a difficult delivery (Leonard & Wen, 2002).

Down syndrome, a disorder caused by the individual having three chromosomes 21, has an incidence of 1 per 1,000 live births. These children have distinctive physical characteristics that include hypotonia, hyperflexibility, midface depression, and short ear length. People with Down syndrome are frequently victims of stereotyping and prejudice. In the early 1960s, about 10% of all residents who were institutionalized had Down syndrome. They were institutionalized because it was thought that anyone with Down syndrome needed to live apart from the rest of society. This has been shown to be a very inaccurate stereotype. Families of children with Down syndrome have become pioneers in the understanding of developmental disabilities and vocal critics of social policies that seek to institutionalize people with mental retardation.

Today a child who is diagnosed with mental retardation is usually kept within the family environment, and only those who have profound mental retardation reside in residential care centers. If a child is diagnosed with mental retardation, he or she is best taught in an adaptive learning environment that focuses on discrete skills. The ultimate goal is to help the individual function as independently as possible. With appropriate training, many adults with mental retardation live productive, independent lives.

Ira Wohl's film *Best Boy* (1979) is a documentary that examines the life of Wohl's cousin, Philly, a man with mental retardation who has spent his entire life living with, and being protected by, his parents. The film beautifully documents the concerns of Philly's parents about who will take care of him after their death. Philly's father dies while the film is being made, and his mother reluctantly allows Philly to become involved in an adult day services program. The film is deeply moving and very effective in its examination of mental retardation as a social problem. In addition, the film does a beautiful job portraying the emotional richness of Philly's life and the strong bonds that have been formed between this man and his family.

Best Boy illustrates one of the dilemmas confronting Western society as we grow older. As the population ages, the number of aging individuals with mental retardation is also increasing, although their life expectancy is somewhat lower than that for the population at large. This problem is compounded by the fact that individuals with mental retardation are at greater risk for developing dementia. In the case of Philly, he is forced to leave his parents' home – the only home he has ever known – and learn to cope with the outside world. Older individuals who are **deinstitutionalized** face similar difficulties when they leave the security of large state hospitals, where they have lived for years, and begin to adjust to life in small group homes in community settings.

Ira Wohl produced a moving sequel to *Best Boy* titled *Best Man: "Best Boy" and All of Us Twenty Years Later* (1997). This film brings the viewer up to date on the life of Philly, who now lives in a group home in Queens. He has a full and meaningful life, and he is shown preparing for a significant, albeit delayed, rite of passage – his Bar Mitzvah.

Some films depict a character with a disability who significantly impacts other characters, as in the comedy *There's Something About Mary* (1998). The protagonist's brother Warren (W. Earl Brown) has mental retardation and autistic tendencies. He exhibits **echolalia**, perseverates in his play, displays finger-flicking behavior, and wears earmuffs to block out disturbing sounds. He clearly likes the lead character, Ted (Ben Stiller), but when Ted touches him near his ears, Warren's sensitivity leads to a violent reaction – he picks Ted up and spins him around before throwing him down on the coffee table. It is an upsetting incident, but the whole family realizes that it happened due to a triggering event and was not due to malevolence on Warren's part.

Mary (Cameron Diaz) lives near Warren and remains an active part of his life. She volunteers and spends time with Warren and other people with disabilities. Mary is not simply a "do good" person, she is a good sister. The antagonists in the film attempt to fake being "good," but eventually their manipulations fall short. In addition, although Warren has a significant disability, he does do comical and outrageous things. Since it is a comedy and all the other non-disabled characters do things that are comical, it does not appear that the director has singled out Warren. His behaviors clearly influence the lives of the other characters.

In M. Night Shyamalan's *The Village* (2004), Noah Percy (Adrien Brody) is a highly stereotypic "village idiot" who exhibits goofy and inappropriate laughter, an inability to control his impulses, an obsession with an attractive girl, and mental slowness. While some of these characteristics apply to people with mental retardation, the character in Shyamalan's film is one-dimensional. He eventually attempts to murder the hero and heroine. This perpetuates both the damaging stereotype that people with mental retardation are inferior to those with normal cognitive functioning as well as the misconception that all people with any kind of mental problem are violent.

Films – like real life – often show persons with disabilities, particularly mental retardation, being exploited of by others. In *Amelie* (2001), one character is ridiculed and mistreated by his boss in front of others. Socially, he does not know when to quit and he repeats a particular phrase to the point of screaming laughter. Though he is depicted with borderline intellectual functioning and noted as "slow," his character is more developed as he takes charge of a fruit stand, demonstrates competence in this new role, enjoys painting with a friend, and experiences a deep appreciation of life. In one of the many disturbing scenes in *Gummo* (1997), an adolescent with mental retardation is sold to young boys for sex. A number of other films have poignantly illustrated the difficulties – and sometimes the beauty – in the lives of people who have mental retardation. Three especially memorable films are *Charly* (1968), *A Day in the Death of Joe Egg* (1972), and *Of Mice and Men* (1992). Although the 1992 version of *Of Mice and Men* is memorable, with John Malkovich playing the role of Lennie, the younger brother with mental retardation, we recommend you also watch the 1939 film version in which Lon Chaney Jr. plays Lennie.

Forrest Gump

The now classic film *Forrest Gump* (1994) portrays 40 years in the life of a man who has a marginal IQ of 75 but whose innocence and common sense make him seem wise. Forrest's condition would be classified as **borderline intellectual functioning** today, and he would probably be tested for a learning disability.

This superb film begins with Forrest, played by Tom Hanks, telling his life story. When Forrest is a child, his mother (Sally Fields) believes in him and is determined that he should have a full, complete life. Forrest has a weak spine and needs to wear leg braces. He is forced to run from other children to protect himself, so that even with the leg braces he becomes an outstanding runner. Eventually, a local football coach spots Forrest and signs him to play college football. He begins a brilliant career that eventually leads him to the army and service in Vietnam. He wins a medal and becomes a table-tennis star. After being discharged from the army, Forrest goes into the shrimp business and becomes a millionaire. Forrest has a life-long friend, Jenny Curran (Robin Wright Penn), who often came to his aid as a child. As an adult, he is able to help her as she and her son cope with disability and death resulting from AIDS.

Even with a limited intelligence and modest academic ability, Forrest is able to feel good about himself and who he is – a simple man who leaves his mark on the world. The development of his self-esteem has its roots in his childhood and his mother's confidence in him. The friendship with Jenny encourages him. Because of the support of these two women, Forrest never realizes that he could not succeed.

Drill Sergeant: "Gump! What's your sole purpose in this army?"
Forrest Gump: "To do whatever you tell me, drill sergeant!"
Drill Sergeant: "God damn it, Gump! You're a goddamn genius! This is the most outstanding answer I have ever heard. You must have a goddamn I.Q. of 160. You are goddamn gifted, Private Gump."

Forrest Gump (1994)

Radio

Inspired by a true story, *Radio* (2003) is the story of Coach Harold Jones (Ed Harris) who takes in a young man, Radio (Cuba Gooding, Jr.), and makes him an assistant coach for the football team. Though he is never given a diagnosis in the film (other than as the label "slow"), Radio, like Forrest, would probably be diagnosed with borderline intellectual functioning. At the beginning of the film, Radio barely speaks a word, mostly uttering sounds, is hunched over in posture, and walks around with a shopping cart for several miles to get groceries. He lives alone with his mother and is almost completely isolated. He is never given a chance at life. Early in the film, Radio is cruelly ridiculed and mistreated by several football players. One particular player continues his cruel taunting of Radio, but he accepts the criticism without complaining. Given an opportunity to help out the football team, Radio agrees and begins to talk much more, interacts interpersonally, and helps out the team in significant ways; in fact, he becomes a symbol of inspiration for the players and his life changes significantly.

Coach Jones goes out of his way to help give Radio opportunities; he defends Radio in front of the community, and integrates him into the school system. When the coach is asked why he is helping Radio, he responds: "It's the right thing to do." The story speaks to the courage and sacrifices of two men who influence one another and in turn grow in courage and dedication. Coach Jones admits part of his dedication and care for Radio arises from childhood shame for not taking action to protect a boy with a disability who was being tortured.

Autistic Disorder

An **autistic disorder** is usually diagnosed before the age of three. This condition occurs 4–5 times more frequently in males than in females and is prevalent in 4–5 per 10,000 children under 15 years of age. Approximately 75% of persons with autistic disorder have mental retardation, and about half do not communicate verbally. Autism is a complex problem and requires special treatment and family support.

Problems in social interaction and communication are the primary symptoms of autistic disorder. Many children with autism are not able to maintain eye-to-eye gaze, respond with facial expressions, or use normal body posture and gestures. As children with autism grow older, they do not typically develop peer relationships that are appropriate to their developmental level. They often do not express pleasure in other people's happiness or participate in interpersonal "give or take." These children can be very frustrating to their parents

because of a lack of emotional warmth that is clear and visible.

Children with autism have major problems in communication. There is a delay or sometimes a complete lack of development of spoken language. If there is speech, there is impairment in the ability to initiate or sustain a conversation with others. Their use of language is often repetitive or idiosyncratic. As children, they may not be able to engage in make-believe play or social imitative play appropriate to their developmental level.

Other symptoms of autism are repetitive and stereotyped patterns of behavior, interests, and activities. There is often an encompassing preoccupation with one or more stereotyped and restricted activities; this preoccupation is abnormal in its intensity and focus. In children, preoccupation with moving, circulating objects is common. Stereotyped, repetitive motor mannerisms may also be present. For example, children may rock for hours, twist their fingers, rub their hands on their legs, spin, or repeat complex body movements. People with autism compulsively adhere to specific, often nonfunctional, routines or rituals. The children are frequently preoccupied with objects rather than people. A child with autism may be fascinated with a motor, a piece of equipment, or a model automobile. The child may literally spend hours taking the object apart and putting it together again.

Most adults with autism continue to be inattentive to social convention, lack social skills, have few or no friends, and often do not marry. They may also be troubled by chronic anxiety. Their repetitive behavior and movements usually continue (Micaki, Chakrabarti, & Fombonne, 2004).

In addition to treatment with medication, behavior modification, and individualized educational approaches, the family plays a critical role. Most families need help in order to deal with special children, and need to learn to implement treatment programs conducted within the home in order to help the child generalize from an academic setting to the home. Parents learn how to teach their children appropriate social and communication skills, as well as behavior modification techniques. Family therapy is recommended in order to help the family cope with problems associated with raising a disabled child.

The prognosis for children with autism is mixed. If they begin to acquire language, are socially responsive, and improve their cognitive skills by the age of 5–7, they have a better prognosis than those children who do not. Approximately 25% of children with autism develop seizures, usually in early adolescence. During puberty, they may experience behavioral changes, including a negativism that sometimes leads to aggression. Most do not develop hallucinations or delusions. However, their behavior and thinking may continue to be peculiar and concrete and their affect flat.

Rain Man and Autism

Rain Man (1988) won Academy Awards for Best Actor, Best Director, Best Picture, and Best Original Screenplay. The film stars Dustin Hoffman as Raymond Babbitt and Tom Cruise as Raymond's younger brother, Charlie. The drama opens with Charlie, a cynical hustler in his mid-twenties, unemotionally learning of his father's death. Charlie and his father had been estranged for many years. Charlie's father only left a 1949 Buick to his youngest son, but he left $3 million in a trust fund for a secret beneficiary.

Charlie traces the beneficiary and discovers that he has an older brother, Raymond, who is autistic. Raymond's world is bound by the rituals of watching television programs and eating certain foods on certain days. The books and baseball memorabilia in his room must be in order, or Raymond becomes agitated and begins reciting the Abbot and Costello routine, "Who's on First." When the sanatorium administrator refuses to give Charlie half of the inheritance, Charlie removes his brother.

Charlie wants to return to the coast, but Raymond refuses to fly. The story unfolds as Charlie and Raymond cross the country in their father's Buick. Their adventures include viewing an accident, after which Raymond refuses to travel on interstate highways, and a day in a motel because Raymond refuses to go out in the rain. Raymond has many idiosyncrasies, such as having maple syrup on the table before the pancakes are served, insisting upon snacks of apple juice and cheese balls, imitating any noise he hears, and being preoccupied with television. One of Raymond's most significant symptoms is his tendency to constantly repeat the same word or phrase.

Raymond has **savant** abilities, which occur in about 10% of people with autism. When this occurs, the individual usually scores low on standardized IQ tests but has one or two outstanding talents, such as calculating dates, drawing, or musical performance. Raymond has unusual memory and mathematical skills that Charlie plans to use to recoup his business losses through gambling in Las Vegas. When Raymond inadvertently makes a date with a prostitute, Charlie teaches his brother

how to dance. When the woman fails to show up, Raymond dances with Charlie's girlfriend, Susanna (Valeria Golino), who gives Raymond his first kiss.

Charlie: "He's not crazy, he's not retarded but he's here?"
Dr. Bruner: "He's an autistic savant. People like him used to be called idiot savants. There are certain deficiencies, certain abilities that impair him."
Charlie: "So he's retarded."
Dr. Bruner: "Autistic. There are certain routines, rituals that he follows."
Charlie: "Rituals, I like that."
Dr. Bruner: "The way he eats, sleeps, walks, talks, uses the bathroom. It's all he has to protect himself. Any break from this routine leaves him terrified."

Rain Man (1988)

Charlie develops an appreciation for the complexity of the illness when Raymond becomes upset after being frightened by the noise of a smoke detector. The movie ends when Charlie, who has developed a sensitivity and love for his brother, turns down a $250,000 settlement and lets his brother voluntarily admit himself back into Wallbrook.

Overall, this is a technically correct portrayal of a character with autism – Raymond has all the correct mannerisms, tics, and tendencies of any number of real-life people with autism. The story surrounding the characters is also realistic – many families were separated by institutionalization as people with disabilities were simply erased from family memory. (For example, Charlie had completely forgotten he ever had an older brother).

Rain Man does reinforce the misconception that "it's an institution or nothing" for people with significant disabilities. However, the assumption that someone like Raymond would be happiest in a large institution is questionable. Although the familiarity and smooth routines often occurring in an institutional setting enhance Raymond's comfort and adaptation, people like Raymond can also live quite fully, successfully, and happily in their own homes, with individualized supports as needed and with housemates of their own choosing. Paid relationships need not be their only choices for com-

Additional Questions for Discussion (*Rain Man*)

- Is the scene in which Raymond calculates complex square roots but cannot make change for a dollar realistic?
- Why is Raymond unable to appreciate the humor in Abbott and Costello's "Who's on First" routine?
- Would Raymond realistically be "a voluntary admission free to leave at any time," as Dr. Bruner maintains?
- Identify examples of repetitive behavior in the film. Are these behaviors more likely to occur when Raymond is stressed?
- Why is Raymond's favorite word "definitely"?
- Raymond smiles at one point and appears to appreciate the ironic humor involved in asking for maple syrup when it is already on the table. Is the appreciation of subtle humor like this characteristic for someone with autism?
- How would you rate the quality of care provided for Raymond at Wallbrook?
- Raymond's knowledge of trivia serves him well when watching the quiz show Jeopardy. What sorts of games or activities would Raymond find the most difficult?

panionship. Some states (e.g., Michigan) no longer admit people with developmental disabilities into state hospitals, and only a few hundred people with developmental disabilities remain in this sort of environment. We now know that many individuals with mental retardation and severe autism can be integrated into the community. While this generally means transitioning into group homes, there is a newer movement that helps people with even the most significant disabilities live in their own homes with housemates they choose.

In *Silent Fall* (1994), a retired child psychiatrist (Richard Dreyfuss) works with Tim Warden (Ben Faulkner), an autistic boy who was a witness to his parents' murder. Tim rocks, enjoys spinning and movement, twirls and fidgets with his fingers while watching them in front of his face, and has limited communication through grunting and moaning noises. He displays a distant look in his eyes with flat affect, and maintains certain rules such as never eating anything that is round in shape. He communicates through cards, nonverbals, drawings, and figures. He displays **echolalia**, repeating others' speech at certain times while impersonating them. He bangs his head against the wall when he gets upset or stressed.

The United States of Leland (2003) portrays a boy with autism who fidgets, cries, and has limited eye contact; he spends most of his time staring off into space or keeping his head down. His most notable trait is his frequent repetition of the phrase "sing a song." He has limited communication with everyone, including his sister to whom he is closest. This film was extremely controversial within the autism community. In the film, the lead character, Leland P. Fitzgerald (Ryan Gosling), stabs the autistic brother of his girlfriend without a clear explanation other than cryptic comments, such as "there's all this sadness and there's nothing you can do about it and all I wanted was for it to go away." Many disability activists believe the film promotes themes of mercy killing of people with disabilities, moral euthanasia, and the message that living with a disability is a fate worse than death.

August Rush (2007) is a film about an orphan (Freddie Highmore) in search of his musician parents. It turns out that Freddie, who is mute and has behaviors characteristic of a person with autism (though they would be unlikely to meet to the diagnostic criteria for the disorder), has inherited his parents' musical ability; in fact, he is a savant who teaches himself to play a guitar almost immediately after picking it up. He eventually winds up training at the Juilliard where he astonishes the faculty with his precocious musical ability. Somewhat predictably, he becomes reunited with his parents by the end of the film.

Leonardo DiCaprio plays the protagonist's autistic younger brother in *What's Eating Gilbert Grape?* (1993). This character is not a savant, and he certainly is no saint; however, he is realistically portrayed as a needy, younger sibling growing up in a family that loves him.

In the classic *To Kill a Mockingbird* (1962), a young Robert Duvall makes his film debut as Boo Radley, a neighbor with autism who kills a man to protect two young children. His diagnosis is not mentioned and it probably would not have been recognized as autism at the time the film was made.

Molly (1999) is a disappointing film about a woman with autism. Molly (played by Elisabeth Shue) undergoes experimental surgery that temporarily brings her back to normal functioning; her brain eventually rejects the cells used in the operation and she returns to her pre-surgery levels of functioning. Molly's brother, Buck, initially avoids and fears his sister and agrees to try anything to make her better, but this enthusiasm is followed by disappointment in the surgery's failure. The film ends with a stereotypic "change-of-heart" ending when Buck arranges for Molly to live with him.

The Boy Who Could Fly (1986) tells the story of a young girl, Millie Michaelson (Lucy Deakins), who moves to a new house and neighborhood after the death of her father, who committed suicide after a diagnosis of cancer. She copes with her grief by becoming involved with the boy who lives next door, a boy with autism who spends much of each day on his roof, preparing to fly. His parents were killed in a plane crash, and the boy developed his fixation of the idea of flying immediately after their death.

Asperger's Disorder

Asperger's disorder is a pervasive developmental disorder often referred to as "high functioning autism." It is a subgroup of what are normally called autism spectrum disorders or pervasive developmental disorders. People with Asperger's disorder have very limited social interactions, and restricted, repetitive, and stereotyped patterns of behavior, interests, and activities are present. They are frequently labeled as odd and eccentric. However, language skills are generally intact, and cognitive development is not delayed.

American Splendor (2003) is about Harvey Pekar (Paul Giamatti), a comic book writer whose friend and co-worker is a man (Toby Radloff) with Asperger's. Toby is socially awkward, has a monotone voice, and restricted patterns of interest and behavior. Toby is a self-proclaimed "world-class nerd" who wears a button reading "Genuine Nerd" and proudly recounts once driving over 200 miles to see the movie *Revenge of the Nerds*. Overall, the portrayal is realistic and challenges the viewer's stereotypes about Asperger's.

The movie *Mozart and the Whale* (2005) is based on the real life story of Jerry and Mary Newport who both have Asperger's. Jerry Newport is a savant who has the ability to calculate numbers and dates and who reportedly was unaware that he had a form of autism until he saw *Rain Man*. He subsequently organized support groups around the country. Mary has prodigious artistic talents. The title for the movie is based on a Halloween party where Jerry was dressed as a whale expressing his adoration of *Free Willy*. Mary arrived in the guise of Nannerl Mozart, the brilliant musician whose life was overshadowed by her famous brother. The ups and downs of their relationship and their struggles to live a quality life are documented in their publications, presentations, and various television programs. The film *Mozart and the Whale*

depicts Donald Morton (Josh Hartnett) a taxi driver who organizes an Asperger's support group and Isabelle Sorenson (Radha Mitchell) who joins the group. The two characters clash. The movie deals with the development of a meaningful relationship between Donald and Isabelle in spite of their opposing personalities and the symptoms of their disorders. For example, when Donald nervously brings Isabelle to the cluttered apartment he shares with an array of uncaged birds, she announces in her typically forthright manner, "This is about sex," an approach too direct for Donald. Isabelle is extremely labile and emotionally insecure, creating legitimate doubt as to whether she, more than Donald, can ever handle a permanent relationship. This film received mixed reviews, but has the advantage of having been written by individuals who actually have the disorder.

In *Breaking and Entering* (2006), Will (Jude Law), and his live-in girlfriend, Liv (Robin Wright Penn), raise a young adolescent girl, Beatrice (Poppy Jones), who has an autism spectrum disorder. Beatrice displays behaviors typical of autism spectrum and pervasive developmental disorders, including limited social skills, repetitive behaviors (endlessly watching herself on video), and being upset by changes in her environment or routine. She also demonstrates sensory issues related to music. When stressed, she closes her eyes and repeats words. She thinks concretely and has an unusual collection of batteries. Her behavior places strain on Will and Liv's relationship. Liv becomes closer to Beatrice, while Will avoids the situation by working and distancing himself from the two of them.

Disorders Usually First Diagnosed in Infancy, Childhood, or Adolescence

Two other pervasive developmental disorders include (1) **childhood disintegrative disorder**, in which there is normal development for at least the first two years, then language, social, motor, or play skills are lost, and (2) **Rett's disorder**, which appears primarily in girls who exhibit normal development for at least the first 6 months, but between the ages of 5 and 48 months show a deceleration of head growth and loss of previously acquired purposeful hand movements, with the development of stereotyped hand movements and a loss of social engagement. Other developmental delays include severely impaired expressive and receptive language with severe psychomotor retardation development.

Other disorders evident early in life depicted in films include a learning disorder in *Cinema Paradiso* (1988), a communication disorder (stuttering) in *The Straight Story* (1999) and *Liam* (2000), **Tourette's disorder** in *Niagara, Niagara* (1997), **pica** in *The Princess and the Warrior* (2001), and a rare genetic disorder, **progeria**, in *Jack* (1996). The latter film accurately depicts some of the developmental issues a child with progeria is likely to face; however, the film is not fully accurate in its clinical depiction of the disorder.

International Films: Mental Retardation and Autism

Few films present a character who "happens to have" a disability where the disability is treated as just another aspect of the character's life. An exception are films by French director Jean Pierre-Jeunet, whose *Amelie* (2001) and *The City of Lost Children* (1995) depict such characters and suggest their meaningful contributions far outweigh the significance of their disability.

Pauline and Paulette (2001) is an award-winning Belgian comedy-drama directed and co-written by Lieven Debrauwer. Pauline (Dora vander Groen) is a 66 years old woman with mental retardation who has been cared for by her sister Martha. When Martha dies, her younger sisters Paulette (Ann Petersen) and Cecile (Rosemarie Bergmans) become responsible for Pauline. Both sisters are very busy in their own lives. According to Martha's will, her wealthy estate will only be divided in three equal parts if one of the sisters looks after Pauline. If they decide to place her in an institution, Pauline will be the only heir. This film depicts a family's dilemma and difficulties when faced with making decisions about loved ones. It also highlights the reality of mental retardation and underscores the degree of love and commitment required by family members taking care of another family member who has mental retardation. In contrast to the U.S. film *I Am Sam* (2001), this movie focuses more on character development (e.g., kindness, curiosity, creativity, playfulness and love).

The Dead Mother (1993, Spain) portrays Leire, a mute, young girl with characteristics of mental retardation and autism, who is the only witness to a burglar who breaks into her house and kills her mother. Twenty years later, Leire is in an institution and by chance the criminal sees her and, fearing she might turn him in, kidnaps her and holds her for ransom. Leire displays flat affect and muscle rigidity. She is easily distracted by details (e.g., a crack on a wall, bubbles in a bathtub, her own hands), has poor eye contact, and reacts to loud noises. While living in the institution, Leire displays a traumatic response to blood and shakes

Critical Thinking Questions

- Howard Gardner describes seven kinds of intelligence (verbal, visual, physical, musical, mathematical and logical, introspective, and interpersonal) in his book *Frames of Mind* (1983). How does this model help you understand individuals such as Raymond Babbitt, Sam Dawson, and Forrest Gump?
- Some films, such as *Mozart and the Whale* (2005) and *I Am Sam* (2001), have actors portraying characters with disabilities playing important roles in the film. How much does this enhance the overall film?
- Explain how films that portray autism such as *Molly* (1999) and *Rain Man* (1988) do a disservice to people with autism.
- Is there anything a person with a disability cannot do that a person without a disability can? How about the reverse?
- How are persons with mental retardation and other disabilities stigmatized in today's society? In your town or city?
- If a child without a disability was substituted for the murdered child with autism in *The United States of Leland* (2003), would this change the story and the film's meaning?
- How have the parents of children with autism been stigmatized in the past? Are there comparable examples of inappropriate stigmas today for the parents of children with other conditions?
- Do people with mental retardation experience sexual feelings like everyone else? If so, how can health professionals support natural sexual expression while at the same time avoiding exploitation and abuse?
- Which labels are more useful: Specific terms such as "autism" or more generic labels such as "pervasive developmental disorder"?
- Why does it matter what labels are used to refer to people with disabilities?
- Do people who are at greater genetic risk for having children with severe developmental disorders have a moral obligation not to have children?

and cries when a boy falls and cuts himself. She is not toilet trained and is obsessed with chocolate, which makes her vulnerable to manipulation and exploitation. She rarely, if ever, laughs and is limited in her social responses. She displays some functional difficulties, such as difficulty dressing, and she is unable to bathe herself. Leire is an innocent character whose behavior stands in marked contrast to the pathological criminals around her.

We highly recommend *The Black Balloon* (2008; Australia) as the best available film to help viewers understand and appreciate the stress associated with raising a child with autism. The film accurately depicts the conflicting emotions of love and anger that often characterize family interactions when one member of the family has a significant intellectual deficit. The film's director, Elissa Down, grew up with two autistic brothers, and it is likely that this experience contributed to the film's integrity, honesty and veracity.

Further Exploration

If you have time to read just one book relevant to this chapter, make it:

Jacobson, J. W., Mulick, J. A., & Rojahn, J. (Eds.). (2007). *Handbook of intellectual and developmental disabilities.* New York: Springer.

If you only have time for one article, read:

Seida, J. K., Ospina, M. B., Karkhaneh, M., Hartling, L., Smith, V., & Clark, B. (2009). Systematic reviews of psychosocial interventions for autism: An umbrella review. *Developmental Medicine & Child Neurology, 51,* 95–104.

Authors' Picks

Mental Retardation and Autism

Mental Retardation

- *Forrest Gump* (1994)
- *Dominick and Eugene* (1988)
- *I Am Sam* (2001)
- *Pauline and Paulette* (2001)
- *The Ringer* (2005)
- *Of Mice and Men* (1939; 1992)

Autism

- *Rain Man* (1988)
- *Mozart and the Whale* (2005)
- *Breaking and Entering* (2006)
- *The Black Balloon* (2008)

Chapter 13

Sleep, Eating, Impulse Control, and Adjustment Disorders

"Let me sleep...just let me sleep."
Will Dormer suffering from sleep deprivation in *Insomnia* (2002)

Questions to Consider While Watching *Insomnia*

- How long can a person go without sleep?
- Is insomnia more often a primary condition or it usually secondary to other psychological disorders?
- What are the most common psychological disorders of which insomnia is a symptom?
- How common is the degree of insomnia Will Dormer experiences?
- How does stress contribute to Dormer's insomnia?
- What are the physical and psychological causes of insomnia depicted in the film?
- What is the impact of Dormer's insomnia on his mental status and interpersonal relationships?
- How is the condition of insomnia expressed through the film's landscape and cinematography?
- What coping strategies does Dormer use in attempting to get to sleep? What are some strategies he does not try?
- What is the psychological role of guilt in the film? Who is really guilty? What is guilt's role in Dormer's mental status?
- Is Dormer a "good" cop or a "bad" cop? Is his character redeemed in the end?
- Is it appropriate for nonmedical therapists to prescribe over-the-counter medications like melatonin and Kava Kava?
- Should psychologists be permitted to prescribe sleep medications like Ambien for patients with insomnia?

Patient Evaluation

Patient's stated reason for coming: "I can't sleep. It's too bright in this place. I haven't slept for days. You got any tricks up your sleeve?"

History of the present illness: Detective Will Dormer is a 52-year-old Caucasian male who is self-referred to this clinic because of serious problems with insomnia. Detective Dormer arrived from out-of-town five days ago for a murder investigation he is leading. He has not slept in five and a half days. Prior to this episode of insomnia, he reports some problems sleeping for about a month or two, sleeping an average of five hours per night. He frequently awakens during the night, unable to get back to sleep; overall, his sleep is not restful. As the current insomnia symptoms have worsened, he has experienced concentration problems, forgetfulness, and several visual and auditory hallucinations. He states he has experienced all of these symptoms in the past, but only as a consequence of insomnia. Work performance has been seriously affected, and he believes if he continues without sleep he risks losing his job. He is not interested in social relationships – the insomnia only contributes to this lack of interest. Three days ago, Detective Dormer's partner was murdered while on duty. Detective Dormer feels significant guilt and responsibility, and he believes he should have saved his partner or somehow prevented the murder.

Past psychiatric illness, treatment, and outcomes: Detective Dormer has no previous psychiatric history. He reports he has battled insomnia throughout his adult life with the longest span of no sleep prior to the present episode of insomnia having been three days.

Medical history: Detective Dormer reports he may have sleep apnea, but he has never been formally tested for sleep problems. He reports previously being diagnosed as hypertensive, but this is currently untreated. He has no history of psychiatric treatment, severe medical illness, or diseases. He has been injured twice on the job. On one occasion he was shot in the arm, and on another occasion he was cut on the neck with a knife; the resulting scar was visible during the interview.

Psychosocial history: Detective Dormer has worked as a criminal investigator for the police department for 30 years. He states, "I've always worked in the city so I've seen everything. I've caught a lot of scum." He was married for 10 years but divorced 15 years ago. He maintains occasional, friendly communication with his former wife. He has not remarried. He has no children. He has few meaningful friendships. From time to time, he isolates himself from others; however, this behavior does not appear to be related to depression.

Drug and alcohol history: Detective Dormer denied a history of drug abuse. He drinks alcohol frequently after work. He reports having two drinks each evening to relieve the tension and stress he experiences on his job. He drinks to the point of intoxication about twice per month. He denies significant problems due to his alcohol use.

Behavioral observations: Detective Dormer was appropriately dressed. His overall appearance was unkempt. He appeared exhausted with bags under his eyes, slightly open mouth, and poor eye contact. He intermixed periods of blank stares and periods of frequent blinking as if he was trying to keep his eyes open. At times, his speech was slurred; this appeared to be due to fatigue. Detective Dormer's mood and affect were agitated. He also reported some apathy about the case on which he is currently working.

Mental status examination: Detective Dormer scored a 28/30 on the Mini Mental State Examination. His concentration was appropriate for serial sevens and other tasks. He did not recall all three objects at first but then suddenly exclaimed, "It's all in the details," and he remembered two of the three. He chose not to copy the drawing, stating, "I'm too exhausted to put forth that kind of effort."

Functional assessment: Despite the extreme fatigue and sleeplessness Detective Dormer has recently experienced, he continues to function at work. He reports his concentration and attention have worsened. He continues to drive a vehicle despite his fatigue and difficulty with concentration.

Strengths: Detective Dormer is a very adaptable, strong-willed man. He is an experienced and hard-working police officer.

Diagnosis: Primary insomnia. Detective Dormer reported experiencing symptoms of insomnia over the last one to two months, and these symptoms have exacerbated over the past week.

Treatment plan: (1) Detective Dormer was cautioned about driving anywhere before he gets some sleep, and in fact he was encouraged to take a taxi home. We called a cab from the office. (2) Discussed the principles of stimulus control, with instructions to begin sleep hygiene practices this evening. (3). Suggested Detective Dormer keep a sleep log. (4) Referred Detective Dormer to a local psychiatrist for sleep medication and further assessment. (5) Recommended making an appointment with a university-based sleep lab when he returns home to rule out other sleep-related conditions such as sleep apnea.

Prognosis: Good

Primary Insomnia in *Insomnia*

Sleep disorders are rarely portrayed in films, particularly to the extent they are highlighted in this film. *Insomnia* (2002), a remake of a well-done, 1997 Norwegian film of the same name, is deeply psychological with multiple layers of complexity. One of these layers is the deteriorating mental status of Al Pacino's character, Los Angeles police officer Detective Will Dormer. Director Christopher Nolan accurately depicts this deterioration, documenting both the realities and dangers of the sleep disorder, primary insomnia. This film provides a powerful illustration of the disorder.

Dormer flies to Alaska to lead a murder investigation. He arrives in Alaska, already tired, at a time of year when the sun never sets ("white nights") so it never gets dark outside. (His travel to Alaska from California takes him across just one time zone, so he would not meet the criteria for circadian rhythm sleep disorder, jet lag type.) Throughout the investigation, Dormer lies in bed with his eyes open, struggling to get some sleep. Under internal pressure to sleep, Dormer employs various strategies, such as blocking all light coming into the room, drinking water, hiding the alarm clock, chewing gum, and turning the phone off. As his insomnia worsens, he sees flashes and trickles of light that become associated with flashes of memory. His vision becomes blurry; he nods off during conversation, often has an unkempt appearance, and frequently stares blankly into space. The longer Dormer goes without sleep, the more severe the consequences; his agitation develops into anger outbursts, he nearly runs a woman over with his car, and he begins to hallucinate. Ultimately, Dormer goes six nights without sleep.

Dormer's insomnia symptoms are clearly exacerbated by the psychological pressure he is experiencing. Two major stressors include the pressures of the murder case and his guilt about killing his partner and lying about it to protect himself in the coming Internal Affairs investigation. His current guilt triggers memories of other events in his life about which he feels guilty.

Insomnia is a powerful metaphor in the film. Director Christopher Nolan has discussed the challenges involved in making a film about insomnia that will not tire viewers; to avoid this problem, Nolan utilized various images in the film to symbolize the experience of insomnia. At the film's onset, the viewer is shown miles and miles of Alaskan glaciers – representing something of a dreamscape, followed by endless green trees covered by moving fog. Other examples of sleep-related imagery include empty streets with blinking traffic lights, flashes of light, tunnels and escape hatches, and things as mundane as trance-inducing windshield wipers. These all symbolize haziness, drifting, mental confusion, and disorientation.

"A good cop can't sleep because a piece of the puzzle's missing, and a bad cop can't sleep because his conscience won't let him."

Ellie Burr to Will Dormer in
Insomnia (2002)

Sleep Disorders

Sleep disorders are categorized as either dyssomnias or parasomnias. **Dyssomnias** involve abnormalities in the amount, quality, or timing of sleep. These include insomnia, hypersomnia, and narcolepsy. **Parasomnias** involve abnormal behavioral or physiological events occurring in association with the sleep cycle. These involve problems with nightmares, night terrors, and sleepwalking.

Most sleep researchers recognize five **sleep stages**: stages 1 through 4 and REM (rapid-eye-movement sleep). Each of the first 4 stages of sleep gets progressively deeper and each has distinct differences on an EEG. Stage 1 is a transition stage from wakefulness (light sleep), stage 2 occupies about 50% of the time spent asleep, and stages 3 and 4 (slow-wave sleep) are the deepest levels of sleep. REM is where most dreams are reported; it occurs cyclically throughout the night, and alternates about every hour and a half with non-REM (the first four stages). Individuals with insomnia will typically have increases in stage 1 sleep and decreases in stages 3 and 4. In narcoleptic individuals, the onset of REM sleep is more rapid after sleep onset and there is an increase in REM.

Sleep laboratories are used to conduct sleep studies to ascertain accurate diagnoses. **Polysomnography** (PSG) is the most common sleep test and measures EEG, ECG, respiratory effort, leg movements, and other physiological activities during sleep. The PSG helps to diagnose different forms of **sleep apnea** (most often the cause of the psychological and medical diagnosis, breathing-related sleep disorder). The **Multiple Sleep Latency Test** (MSLT) is used by sleep labs to diagnose narcolepsy. Referrals to sleep labs are usually done through physician prescription, which can often be encouraged by mental health professionals.

Film depictions of sleep disorders are rare. When depicted, they are usually either very brief or flawed. The film *Insomnia* is certainly an exception.

Insomnia

Primary insomnia is characterized by difficulty initiating or maintaining sleep, or nonrestorative sleep for one month which causes significant problems in certain areas of functioning. In any given year, 30–40% of adults will have complaints of insomnia; sometimes this is a symptom of another disorder or a transient reaction to a stress and not "primary" insomnia.

The effects of insomnia are graphically portrayed in *The Machinist* (2004). Christian Bale lost 60 pounds to play the role of the gaunt Trevor Reznik in this film. Trevor is a depressed and lonely man who has been unable to sleep for a significant period of time. He uses stimulants such as caffeine and nicotine, not uncommon among individuals who struggle with insomnia.

Trevor is accused of doing drugs although this is never depicted or indicated. The insomnia clearly affects his daily functioning – he causes an accident, becomes paranoid that his coworkers are plotting against him, and at one point he throws himself in front of a moving car. He displays symptoms of both an amnestic disorder and a psychotic disorder (e.g., hallucinations, paranoia); however, his inability to sleep would need to be treated as the immediate clinical issue. Cinematically, the film's images become less distinct to the viewer as a result of the director's use of muted colors, distorted views through mirrors, and showing Trevor behind and beyond things in his environment.

"I haven't slept in a year."

Trevor Reznik in *The Machinist* (2004)

The symptoms of insomnia are experienced by the two characters in *Lost in Translation* (2003), played by Bill Murray and Scarlett Johansson. Both characters are Americans who have traveled to Japan and experience apathy and loneliness in this unfamiliar setting. Both deal with their insomnia symptoms by going to the hotel bar and watching late-night television. Eventually they meet and build a friendship. One important scene depicts them lying awake in bed together at night; director Sofia Coppola seems to be showing they are facing their symptoms (symbolized by being awake in bed) in a nonsexual, healthy way through communication.

Edward Norton's character in *Fight Club* (1999) suffers from serious insomnia. The insomnia may be a symptom caused by **circadian rhythm sleep disorder, jet lag type**, due to his work which requires frequent travel. He states he feels as though he is never awake or asleep and that he loses weight because he cannot sleep. He exhibits blank stares and his body language suggests that he is exhausted. It may be that jet lag exacerbates a preexisting problem with primary insomnia. His experience of sleeplessness triggers a break with reality leading to the development of dissociative identity disorder. It is important to note that individuals with prolonged severe insomnia may experience dissociative symptoms or psychotic states, but there is no evidence it will cause DID.

"With insomnia, nothing's real. Everything's far away. Everything's a copy of a copy of a copy."

The Narrator in *Fight Club* (1999)

In *Return to Oz* (1985), based on the books *The Marvelous Land of Oz* and *Ozma of Oz* by L. Frank Baum, Fairuza Balk portrays Dorothy who is shown suffering from sleep problems. Aunt Em (Piper Laurie) decides to send Dorothy to a facility for treatment of insomnia where her tendency to repeatedly relate things to Oz is treated as a psychiatric symptom. The psychiatrist explains that ECT will be used to treat her insomnia and her "bad waking dreams" of Oz and its characters. Of course, there's virtually nothing accurate in the depiction of insomnia treatment; however, the film provides an example of how filmmakers can create their own treatments to better fit their plotlines.

Hypersomnia

Primary hypersomnia is excessive sleepiness evidenced in prolonged sleep or daytime sleep episodes for at least one month, which causes significant problems in areas of functioning. Like insomnia, hypersomnia can be a symptom of other disorders (e.g., depression) or a separate entity itself.

In *American Splendor* (2003), Harvey Pekar's girlfriend moves in with him and sleeps all day. She seems to have an agitated depression that manifests itself in irritability and in sleeping on the couch well into the middle of the day. This may reflect hypersomnia; the long periods she spends in bed may also be a symptom of depression.

Narcolepsy

Narcolepsy is a devastating sleep disorder in which the individual experiences uncontrollable and unwanted daily "sleep attacks." People with narcolepsy can fall asleep while talking, eating or walking. The disorder is frequently accompanied by **cataplexy** (sudden loss of muscle tone without loss of consciousness). A rare but accurate portrayal of narcolepsy occurs in Mike Waters (River Phoenix) in *My Own Private Idaho* (1991).

The portrayal of narcolepsy in movies is often brief, unkind, and superficial with the sole purpose of ridiculing the person with narcolepsy. This type of humor is highly predictable as it almost always involves a character falling asleep at an inopportune, unexpected, or embarrassing moment. Though the portrayals are not entirely inaccurate (since sleep attacks in narcolepsy are of rapid onset and can be triggered by intense emotion), they are grossly exaggerated and almost uniformly unflattering. Minor characters in *Moulin Rouge* (2001), *Deuce Bigalow: Male Gigolo* (1999), *Rat Race* (2001), and *Bandits* (2001) have narcolepsy. In *Rat Race*, Enrico Pollini (Rowan Atkinson, best known as Mr. Bean) falls asleep at a critical moment when he is about to win a race, and in *Bandits*, a bank manager falls asleep during a robbery due to the stress of the experience.

Nightmares

Nightmare Disorder is a parasomnia in which an individual repeatedly awakens from sleep recalling a frightening dream. When waking, the individual quickly becomes alert and oriented. Themes of the nightmare usually involve threats to survival, security, or self-esteem. A few films in which nightmares are portrayed include *David and Lisa* (1962), *Mysterious Skin* (2004), *The Pact of Silence* (2003), and Wim Wenders' *Land of Plenty* (2004, U.S./Germany).

Countless movies depict characters experiencing nightmares, yet only a handful would qualify for the diagnosis of nightmare disorder. Many filmmakers enjoy manipulating the plot in such a way that the viewer is never sure whether a film is a dream (or nightmare) or reality. This plot device is used in Cameron Crowe's *Vanilla Sky* (2001). Sometimes the character awakens from a nightmare the viewer may or may not have known was happening; other films leave the viewer confused as to what has actually been experienced or just occurred. David Lynch is famous for the use of this approach; the strategy can be seen in his films *Blue Velvet* (1986), *Lost Highway* (1997), and *Mulholland Drive* (2001). The latter film is very confusing, and its second half is usually assumed to reflect a character's dream/nightmare. In *Wristcutters: A Love Story* (2006), the two lead characters wake up in adjacent beds in a hospital room following suicide attempts, and it is assumed that everything the two had experienced together was only a linked nightmare.

Sleep Terrors

Sleep terror disorder is a parasomnia in which the individual experiences recurrent episodes of abrupt awakening from sleep, often with a panicky scream. The person experiencing sleep terror disorder shows signs of significant distress (e.g., rapid breathing, sweating) and is generally disoriented and unresponsive to attempts to comfort him or her. The individual does not recall the dream itself or the experience of screaming.

Some films illustrate sleep terrors when a character screams in his or her sleep only to wake up unaware of what they were dreaming. This is depicted by an amnestic woman in *Dead Again* (1991), in an adolescent girl screaming during sleep while on an inpatient unit in *Manic* (2003), in a woman on a psychiatric unit of a woman's prison in *Gothika* (2003), and in a young boy who has been cloned partially with cells taken from a murderous child in *Godsend* (2004).

Sleepwalking

Sleepwalking (somnambulism) is a parasomnia involving repeated episodes of rising from bed and walking around during sleep. During these episodes, the person has a blank stare, is unresponsive to others, and can only be awakened with great difficulty. The person does not remember the episode and there is no impairment in mental activity or behavior upon awakening.

In *Secondhand Lions* (2003), Hub (Robert Duvall) sleepwalks each night and goes to stand near a pond; sometimes he acts out an imaginary battle. Garth (Michael Caine) warns others not to awaken the sleepwalker, particularly because Hub will fight in his sleep if he is disturbed. The film suggests that Hub is searching for a love who has died. A young adolescent, played by Haley Joel Osment, enjoys watching Hub but is anxious about his safety.

In *Donnie Darko* (2001), the lead character Donnie (Jake Gyllenhaal) hallucinates and is discovered by his psychiatrist to be a sleepwalker, often following his hallucinations outside when sleeping or napping.

Waking Life (2001) blends animation and drama in a surrealist film with the feel of a lucid dream. The movie addresses existential themes and questions our own wakefulness during the day, utilizing the metaphor of humans as "sleepwalking" through the days often unaware of what is going on around them. The film explores dream states, reality, and the insights that can be reached with each. Many important questions and issues are raised for the viewer to reflect upon, with themes of "creating one's own life," reality vs. illusion, lucid dreaming, free will vs. determinism, mindfulness vs. automatic pilot, destiny, and the experience of suffering in life. Similar themes are explored in the 2004 film *Sleepwalking*.

"The trick is to combine your waking rational abilities with the infinite possibilities of your dreams.
Because, if you can do that, you can do anything."

Guy Forsyth in *Waking Life* (2001)

Eating Disorders

There are two major categories of eating disorder: anorexia and bulimia. Other problems with eating include the diagnosis of **obesity**, which is a general medical condition, and disorders of feeding and eating usually diagnosed in infancy or early childhood such as **rumination disorder** and pica. For a graphic depiction of an adult with **pica**, see the film, *The Princess and the Warrior* (2000), which portrays an adolescent psychiatric patient chewing and swallowing glass.

Anorexia Nervosa

In anorexia, the individual refuses to maintain an appropriate body weight for his or her age and height and has an intense fear of gaining weight or becoming fat even though he or she is underweight. The anorectic patient also has a distorted perception of his or her weight and shape. Many symptoms are similar to those associated with starvation, such as amenorrhea, abdominal pain, and lethargy. Depression and obsessive-compulsive features associated with food are quite common co-occurring disorders. Anorexia presents serious health risks and may lead to death by starvation, suicide, or electrolyte imbalance (more than 10% of anorectics are likely to die, making anorexia one of the most lethal psychological disorders).

Thin (2006) is an HBO documentary that provides an inside look at the lives of women with eating disorders and their residential treatment from intake to discharge. Four women, aged 15–30 and living in South Florida, suffer from anorexia or bulimia. The film depicts the young women in their counseling sessions, weighing in, during group activities, and socializing. Anxieties about weighing in, avoidance of food, medication misuse, and other issues common to those with eating disorders are portrayed. The film illustrates important themes related to the intense challenges of recovery, the significant cost of treatment, noncompliance, the sabotage of a fellow patient's treatment, and the high relapse rate.

Big budget films rarely portray anorexia; however, the disorder is often portrayed accurately in television movies (which sometimes can be rented at video stores). A compelling examination of anorexia and its treatment is found in the film *The Best Little Girl in the World* (1981). Jennifer Jason Leigh dropped down to 90 pounds for the role of Casey Powell in this movie. Other films depicting anorexia include *For the Love of Nancy* (1994), which stars Tracey Gold, *Dying to Be Perfect* (1996), *Dying to Dance* (2001), and *Hunger Point* (2003).

Bulimia Nervosa

Bulimia is characterized by **binges**, which are self-indulgent and unrestrained eating episodes. In addition, some behavior is used to prevent weight gain, such as **purging** (self-induced vomiting), misuse of laxatives, diuretics, enemas, or medications, fasting, and/or excessive exercise. Bulimics are preoccupied with their body weight or shape. Depression, anxiety, substance abuse, and borderline personality are the most common co-occurring diagnoses.

In *Center Stage* (2000), one of the dancers, Maureen, suffers from bulimia. She has a very controlling mother who is trying to relive her life through her daughter. The mother talks about little other than dance opportunities for Maureen. Maureen has been restricted as a child, and she was not allowed to play tennis or similar games with other children. To please a new boyfriend, she eats junk food and later purges to stay fit for the dance competitions. Elements of denial are evident when she is on a boat with her boyfriend who hears her purging; Maureen claims she is simply experiencing motion sickness. Her boyfriend later confronts her about "hurting her body." An element of insight emerges when Maureen sees another dancer fall and hurt herself, thus becoming unable to dance in the competition; she finds herself wishing she'd been the one who was injured because then the intense pressure both externally (her mother) and internally (herself) would be gone.

In *Life is Sweet* (1990), a rebellious adolescent girl, Nicola, is bulimic, binging and purging on chocolate bars hidden in her bedroom. She attempts to include the chocolate into her sex life by rubbing it over her body. It is clear that she lives in a dysfunctional family obsessed with food, cooking, and the restaurant business. In *Girl, Interrupted* (1999), one of the characters hospitalized with Susanna Kaysen (Winona Ryder) has a serious eating disorder and self-mutilates; her rich, co-dependent father supports his daughter's eating disorder by bringing her baked chicken that she hides and hordes under her hospital bed. The film hints at an incestuous relationship between her and her father, and a pivotal moment occurs in the film when she commits suicide by hanging herself in her shower. *Requiem for a Dream* (2000) includes one character who is obsessed with food but needs to lose weight in order to appear on a television game show; her obsession with weight loss leads her to become addicted to diet pills.

In *Elephant* (2003), numerous characters are shown going through a typical day before a school tragedy occurs. Three adolescent girls, Brittany, Jordan, and Kelly, focus on the caloric contents of their lunch food. After eating, they walk into the bathroom together and, each using separate stalls, collectively purge. They do it quickly and without a word about the behavior – acting nonchalantly in the middle of their conversation. They are depicted as attractive with slender bodies, and the three girls obviously want to maintain their appearance. Purging together provides social support for their aberrant behavior.

Although 90% of people with bulimia are females, the prevalence seems to be rising in males. The film *Seabiscuit* (2003) displays a male horse-racing jockey (Tobey Maguire) who forces himself to throw up in order to maintain his low weight so he can ride faster. Ben Stiller's narcissistic, male-model character in *Zoolander* (2001) refers to purging after meals to lose weight, to look better, and keep his job.

Bulimic themes are also evident in *Heathers* (1989), the Korean film *301, 302* (1995), *Angus* (1995), *When Friendship Kills* (1996), and *Drop Dead Gorgeous* (1999).

Binge-eating disorder, while not a formal *DSM-IV-TR* diagnosis, occurs when an individual eats a large amount of food and lacks control over

his or her eating. *I Want Someone to Eat Cheese With* (2007) portrays an overweight man struggling with food; he frequently binges on snacks while sitting alone on the front of his car in an empty parking garage, he routinely breaks his diet, and he attends Overeaters Anonymous support group meetings.

Body Image and Eating Disorders

Body image is one of the most significant problems with regard to both anorexia and bulimia. Many films, however, display characters struggling with their body image though not all of them suffer from formal eating disorders. Often the use of a mirror or reflective surface shows characters viewing and assessing themselves to convey a character's dissatisfaction with his or her body. Many times the image in the reflection is shown as distorted, blurred, formless, or unclear to emphasize self-hate, self-deprecation, or self-distortion.

Soldier's Girl (2003) and *I've Heard the Mermaids Singing* (1987) depict characters with problems with body image who stand in harsh self-judgment in front of a mirror. Toward the end of the acclaimed docudrama, *What the Bleep Do We Know?!* (2004), the lead character (Marlee Matlin) stares in the mirror at her body, wearing only underwear, examining it with distaste, distortion, and rage. *What's Eating Gilbert Grape* (1993) has a key character, Gilbert's mother, who weighs over 500 pounds and is too large to leave the house or even get off the sofa where she lives out her dreary existence. Gilbert (Johnny Depp) gives other children a "leg up" when they come to peer in the window at this morbidly obese woman.

Impulse Control Disorders

Impulse control disorders are categorized into the following categories: Intermittent explosive disorder, kleptomania, pyromania, pathological gambling, and trichotillomania.

Intermittent Explosive Disorder

Anger is a normal emotion all humans experience. At times, it is a healthy indicator of internal stress, a sign that deep emotions are being tapped, or a cue someone has offended us. In many instances, the anger turns from thoughts and feelings into behaviors and is acted out in some form. Anger can be extraordinarily destructive and this destructiveness comes across verbally or physically. Intermittent explosive disorder occurs when there are several discrete episodes of aggressive impulses that result in serious assaults or property destruction. Several good films depict intermittent explosive disorder.

"But you know what scares me the most? When I can't fight it anymore, when it takes over, when I totally lose control... I like it."

Bruce Banner in *Hulk* (2003)

Acclaimed director Ang Lee's *Hulk* (2003) is a commentary on anger and, more specifically, intermittent explosive disorder. The whole film is about raw anger: Anger being unleashed, the dangers and detrimental effects of anger, the build-up and development of anger, and family of origin issues in regard to anger. When Bruce Banner (Eric Bana) transforms into the Hulk, there is enormous destruction of property and this occurs in intermittent episodes of rage as he shifts into the role of Hulk and then back to the scientist role after his anger subsides. If this film is viewed by someone eager to understand the psychological phenomenon of anger better, the film is educational as well as entertaining. A recent remake, *The Incredible Hulk* (2008), starring Edward Norton as Bruce Banner, also provides a useful perspective on this particular impulse control disorder.

In *Punch Drunk Love* (2002), Barry Egan (Adam Sandler) is a quirky, serious character who alternates between extreme passiveness (often to his sisters' requests) and brief explosions of anger. Interestingly, when he is confronted with danger, he either runs away or explodes with rage (illustrating the "fight or flight" response).

In *Manic* (2001), an adolescent Lyle (Joseph Gordon-Levitt) is sent to an inpatient unit for what appears to be intermittent explosive disorder: While angry, he had smashed a peer's head with a baseball bat. Though Lyle does begin to relate and connect with others as well as understand himself in a deeper way, he continues to explode periodically with his rage directed towards others. Lyle is sporadic in his anger management attempts –

sometimes he stops his anger choosing not to fight and other times he provokes fights. Lyle reflects that the cause of his anger is that his father was physically abusive and his peers made fun of him because of this. An authoritative psychologist (Don Cheadle) utilizes an intervention that involves telling Lyle he is "just like dad" with regard to his anger outbursts.

Mateo (Djimon Hounsou), a man dying of AIDS, frequently screams and destroys property in his apartment in *In America* (2003). Another man dying of AIDS, Roy (Keifer Sutherland) in *Behind the Red Door* (2001), has repressed rage from the diagnosis and from a family history of anger and abuse. His outbursts emerge verbally and at seemingly random times (e.g., when his rice is not fully cooked).

The title character in *Antwone Fisher* (2002) exhibits explosive anger, attacking his fellow sailors in response to minor provocation. The viewer later learns that beneath the anger lies intense internal pain and unresolved abuse issues. The classic character of Bluto in *Popeye* (1980) could also be diagnosed with this disorder.

Kleptomania

Kleptomania is the recurrent failure to resist impulses to steal objects that are not needed for personal use or for their monetary value. Feelings of tension precede the theft act, and pleasure or relief occurs at the time of the theft.

The independent film *Klepto* (2003) uses kleptomania as a major plotline. In an opening scene, a young woman, Emily (Meredith Bishop), steals some CDs after eyeing a camera; she runs out of the store and is chased by an employee. Her stealing behavior throughout the film does not occur because she needs the particular items or money, but it is a way to manage stress. It quickly becomes clear that she loves the rush she experiences whenever she steals something. Those with kleptomania feel a sense of increasing tension prior to stealing and pleasure or relief at the time of theft

---

"I have a mental condition and I have to take things. I'm addicted to getting caught."

Emily explaining her kleptomania in *Klepto* (2003)

---

and/or immediately thereafter. After the pleasurable rush, Emily feels worse as she realizes how out of control she is; in turn, this leads her to steal more. She stores boxes of unopened and unused stolen items in her car trunk. Emily realizes she cannot stop herself from stealing, exclaiming "I'm a pill freak with a bad habit," referring to a large collection of bottles of medications. Emily is an interesting contrast with her mother who is a compulsive shopper who accumulates a $100,000 debt but is unable to stop buying things (see the section on impulse control disorder NOS later in this chapter). Emily later finds out that her father was a thief who died in prison. Emily eventually gets treatment for her impulse control disorder – she takes medication and sees a therapist who comes across as supportive and inquisitive.

It is uncertain whether the characters in the following films meet the full *DSM-IV-TR* criteria for kleptomania, but they are at least interesting to consider: *Niagara, Niagara* (1997), *Female Perversions* (1996), and *Mortal Transfer* (2001). In *Mortal Transfer*, one of the psychiatrist's patients is undergoing psychoanalysis and cannot resist her impulses to steal, including taking objects from her psychiatrist's desk. Kleptomania symptoms can also be found in *Virgin* (2003), although the protagonist would undoubtedly carry multiple psychological diagnoses.

"I steal to stop me from killing myself."

Maddie Stevens in
Female Perversions (1996)

Pyromania

Pyromania is deliberate and purposeful fire setting on more than one occasion, in which there is tension prior to the act, pleasure or relief after it, and a fascination and curiosity with fire itself.

In *House of Fools* (2002), one of the patients at a psychiatric hospital, Mamud, is a veteran with pyromania. After burning the curtains down in the hospital, he quickly exclaims, "it wasn't me!" Mamud is restricted from having any fire-setting materials and even the patients are instructed not to give him matches. Francie in *The Butcher Boy* (1997) sets fires, but he would not qualify for this

diagnosis insofar as his aberrant behavior is better explained by other diagnoses.

Pathological Gambling

Pathological gambling is diagnosed when there is persistent, recurrent gambling behavior. The prototypical gambler with this diagnosis has made several unsuccessful attempts to stop gambling, gambles with increased amounts of money, "chases" losses, lies to cover up the problem, and escapes from personal problems or internal pain by gambling.

Gambling is fairly frequent in movies. Although not all of these films depict characters who would meet criteria for a gambling addiction (pathological gambling), one film is a particularly compelling example – *Owning Mahowny* (2002).

Owning Mahowny

This film is based on true events that occurred in Toronto between 1980 and 1982; the movie tells the story of a man who stole $10.2 million from his employer to support his gambling addiction. He eventually served a 6-year prison term for fraud.

Philip Seymour Hoffman stars as Dan Mahowny, a man described at the onset as having three lives: (1) a public life, (2) a private life, and (3) a secret life. Mahowny has a loving, dedicated girlfriend and at work he is the youngest in his position as a loan officer, someone described as having an "impeccable record" and "excellent judgment." His secret life involves his very serious, self-destructive gambling problem.

Psychologist: "How would you rate the thrill you got from gambling, on a scale of one to 100?"
Dan Mahowny: "Um... a hundred."
Psychologist: "And what about the biggest thrill you've ever had outside of gambling?"
Dan Mahowny: "Twenty."

Owning Mahowny (2002)

Mahowny accumulates a debt of $10,300 by placing bets with shady bookies. He decides to write fake loans in order to pay off his debt. He then begins to gamble with this money at casinos to pay off the debt more quickly. He flies to Atlantic City numerous times to gamble. Along the way, he tells various lies to his girlfriend Belinda (Minnie Driver) and his boss in order to keep his secret life hidden. While gambling, Mahowny appears to be in a trance – very focused and absorbed in the experience, losing track of time. His losses progressively increase; he loses $15,000 one night and then $100,000 another night, unsuccessfully attempting to "chase" losses by doubling-up on his bets. His denial is obvious to the viewer such as when he frequently convinces himself that he is "in the zone." Mahowny deteriorates psychologically and behaviorally and his behavior becomes erratic, his appearance disheveled and unkempt, and his self-care poor. At one point, he gives a friend money to hold, making him promise not to give it back to him no matter what; soon Mahowny is screaming at his friend to "give me my money and stay away from me." Scenes like this dramatically display the intensity and power of this addiction. Mahowny is alone and depressed, he does not get enough sleep, and he even falls asleep while driving. The film is a dramatic depiction of the despair of someone caught in the throes of a gambling addiction.

The casino realizes its potential profit and goes to great lengths to keep Mahowny gambling, following him, watching him, trying to entice him, offering him food, drinks, a free hotel stay and women, and even sending him a "friend" to shadow him and keep him there. Mahowny rejects the women and alcohol; he is referred to as a "purist" in his gambling addiction because he does not mix sex, alcohol, or drugs with his gambling.

The addiction worsens when Mahowny takes

Additional Questions for Discussion (*Owning Mahowny*)

- How common is it for someone to have a "secret life"?
- What is the difference between having a debt problem and having a gambling problem? How does each apply to Dan Mahowny?
- What addictions typically co-occur with gambling? What is the percentage of gamblers who are purists?
- At what point does Mahowny's behavior become unmanageable and out of control?
- In what ways does Mahowny lie to himself?
- What treatments and support groups are available for someone like Dan Mahowny?

his girlfriend on a special vacation and then neglects her; when she confronts him about this while he is gambling, he simply begs for a "few more minutes," ultimately choosing gambling over love. This scene illustrates the huge disparity that has developed in their relationship; she continues to be focused on the relationship, while his addiction leaves him too engrossed in gambling to even care what happens to her.

In another movie based on a true story, *Two for the Money* (2005), a young, savvy football expert, Brandon Lang (Matthew McConaughy) is hired by Walter Abrams (Al Pacino) to work in a fast-paced business as a gamblers' advisor (helping gamblers make good bets on football games). Walter is a recovering pathological gambler of 18 years – though he is clearly experiencing similar highs from devoting his life to helping betters. Much of his life relates to gambling – he bets on his salesmen, he watches each football game closely, and his income is based on how successful his clients are. He sees the successes of Brandon, who seems to beat the odds and predict game outcomes at an 80% success rate, becomes attached to his new protégé, and obsesses about building an "empire" around Brandon. Walter is unable to quit, focused on riding the excitement he experiences when working with Brandon. Walter displays typical gambler self-sabotaging behavior, taking increasingly high-risk bets. He continues despite clear evidence of a serious heart condition that he treats with medication. The film depicts a Gamblers Anonymous meeting in which one member speaks honestly of his struggles; however, Walter attempts to take advantage of the man by giving away a business card tempting the man to reclaim his addiction. The deep sense of inherent defectiveness and shame common to this addictive behavior is portrayed in the film.

Oscar and Lucinda (1997), based on the 1988 Booker prize-winning novel by Peter Carey, portrays two outcasts who connect through pathological gambling. Oscar Hopkins (Ralph Fiennes) copes with his anxiety disorder by gambling. He won his first bet on horse racing (this is common for those with the disorder) and is unable to stop gambling. He is quite distressed by his behavior, even breaking his own strict adherence to keeping the Sabbath holy and free of gambling. He rationalizes his gambling, arguing that belief in God is a gamble, so how could gambling not be accepted by God? Another rationalization is that he is not gambling for personal gain because he gives away his winnings. When he has periods of sobriety during which he is able to stay away from gambling, he lives in constant fear that he will revert to his old habits and ways. Lucinda Lepastrier (Cate Blanchett) stays up all night gambling, tries to hide her behavior from others, and uses gambling as a way to cope with loneliness. Oscar and Lucinda make a pact to not gamble or lead one another in that direction, and they attempt to put their energy productively into a floor washing competition. Soon they break the pact and make the ultimate gamble – their inheritance.

In *Dinner Rush* (2001), a cook at an upscale New York City restaurant is unable to control his betting on sports teams. This significantly affects his work performance, interpersonal relationships, and his ability to focus. He exhibits the common gambler's behavior of attempting to "chase" his losses. The impact on his life and functioning is clear: He continues to upset more and more people around him, and eventually he puts his life in danger.

In *21* (2008), an MIT Student is accepted into Harvard medical school but is unable to pay the $300,000 tuition, so he reluctantly takes part in an illegal card counting operation, lead by his teacher (Kevin Spacey). The teacher crosses a number of boundaries as he promotes this illegal activity, manipulates his students, fixes grades in his course, and orchestrates some nasty university politics. While the film is not particularly strong in portraying elements of pathological gambling, it does illustrate a common dynamic gamblers and other addicts experience – a double life. In addition to his normal life as a student, the protagonist creates a gambler's (or card counter's) life in which he spends time in exciting cities, takes on a variety of high-roller personas, and becomes invested in a new peer group. As is the case many of these instances, all is well until the two lives converge. This film is based on a true story of how six MIT students took on Las Vegas and walked away with millions.

Trichotillomania

Trichotillomania refers to pulling out one's hair to such an extent that it results in noticeable hair loss. There is an increase in tension prior to pulling the hair, and pleasure or relief upon pulling the hair out.

Trichotillomania is rarely depicted or even referred to in movies. It is one of the least represented psychological disorders in film. A noteworthy exception is the brief portrayal of the disorder in *Dirty Filthy Love* (2004, UK), a film about a man with obsessive-compulsive disorder (OCD). In attempting to manage his condition through treatment, self-help, and support groups, the protagonist meets a woman who has been diagnosed with OCD but displays behaviors of trichotillomania. The viewer observes her pulling out a couple of hairs. She later gets in a fight and her wig is pulled off exposing the bald patches fairly typical for those suffering from this condition. A clinician would have to decide if the individual's repetitive pulling behaviors are a compulsion in response to an obsession (in which case only the diagnosis of OCD would be given); there is not enough information given in this film to clearly diagnose this character. Interestingly, experts are debating whether trichotillomania is better classified as an impulse control disorder or as an anxiety disorder (a variation of obsessive-compulsive disorder).

An experience with similar dynamics to trichotillomania is compulsive skin picking. The film *Personal Velocity* (2002) depicts an adolescent boy who skin-picks his fingers, arms, and other areas of his body. Many of the areas are infected. The boy appeared to have been severely abused and is running away by hitchhiking; he presents as severely withdrawn.

Impulse Control Disorder NOS

This diagnosis is given to anyone with an impulse control disorder who does not meet criteria for other impulse control disorders, does not qualify for another diagnosis, and has difficulties controlling his or her impulses. Impulse control problems overlap with a number of other diagnoses and problems. Many of these conditions can be better explained by treating them as a natural consequence of a mood disorder, namely bipolar disorder, discussed in Chapter 5. Sexual addictions, sometimes seen as impulse control disorders themselves, are discussed in Chapter 8. Binge-eating, discussed in this chapter, has a strong impulse control component. Impulse control problems play a significant role in drug and alcohol abuse, which is discussed in Chapter 7.

Maxed Out (2006) is a documentary that looks at the impulse control problem of compulsive spending. The film focuses on the problem of credit card debt, the cyclical patterns therein, and the factors that contribute to the development of this disorder. The film notes that a family living in today's world has less money for the essentials than a family living in the 1970s, $9,200 is the average American credit card debt, and 10 million people filed bankruptcy over a recent 10-year period. Some of the consequences of excessive credit card debt include depression and suicide. Problems with impulse control often play a significant role in the development of compulsive spending and the accumulation of massive debt.

Adjustment Disorders

An adjustment disorder is diagnosed when a person develops significant emotional or behavioral symptoms in response to a particular psychosocial stressor; the response exceeds what would typically be expected in such a situation. Social, academic, or occupational functioning may be affected. Adjustment disorders are usually associated with depression, anxiety, disturbance of conduct, or some mixture of each. The adjustment disorder displayed by Terry Ann Wolfmeyer (Joan Allen) in *The Upside of Anger* (2005) includes a mixture of disturbance of conduct and emotions. We see this in her reaction when she learns her husband has been having an affair, and she becomes convinced that he has gone off to Sweden to be with a younger woman. Terry becomes incredibly bitter, irritable, lonely, and explosive. She begins to drink alcohol regularly and becomes more conflictual and cynical, particularly when interacting with her daughters.

It is not difficult to find films portraying adjustment disorders – numerous films exhibit characters facing a stressor, conflict, or challenge and frequently this affects an area of their functioning in a significant way. Many films depicting relationship stress or those addressing problems with work show characters with adjustment disorder symptoms, such as the anxiety displayed by Harry Sanborn (Jack Nicholson) in *Something's Gotta Give* (2003) and the disturbance of conduct exhibited by Tommy Rowland (Matt Dillon) in *Beautiful Girls* (1996). The protagonist in *Meet Bill* (2007), played by Aaron Eckhart, is a man languishing in several areas of his life. He struggles to cope with his wife's infidelity and this leads to numerous changes in his life; while at first it disturbs his functioning, he eventually finds ways to make meaning out of the stress he is experiencing. A similar theme (adjusting to infidelity) can be found in *Tennis, Anyone...?* (2005).

Films that integrate several vignettes or stories are almost certain to have at least one character with an adjustment disorder. Some good examples include *Lantana* (2001), *The Last Kiss* (2006), and *13 Conversations About One Thing* (2001).

It is important to distinguish adjustment disorders from bereavement. **Bereavement** is not a psychological disorder. It is the expected response to the death of a loved one, whereas an adjustment disorder occurs when the reaction to a death is in excess of or more prolonged than what is expected. It is challenging to differentiate between simple bereavement and the diagnosis of adjustment disorder, and it seems inappropriate and inhumane to put an arbitrary time limit or label on how long it should take to recover from a painful loss. Sandy Edwards (Toni Collette) in *Japanese Story* (2003) and a young girl in *Ponette* (1996) both experience protracted bereavement.

In each of the following three films the bereaved character copes by immediately going on a journey in reaction to his or her pain: Jack Nicholson as Warren loses his life-long wife in *About Schmidt* (2002), a young woman loses her beloved father in *Searching for Paradise* (2002), and another young woman loses her boyfriend to suicide in *Movern Callor* (2002).

One example of symptoms in excess of those associated with bereavement and meeting criteria for a diagnosis of at least an adjustment disorder is found in the film *Mother Ghost* (2002). A man begins to have significant conflicts with his wife, ignores his son, numbs his pain by getting drunk, is unable to sleep, and his deceased mother's jewelry begins to appear. The reactions to deaths in both *Truly, Madly, Deeply* (1991) and *In the Bedroom* (2001) seem to go beyond healthy bereavement and consequently would warrant a diagnosis, though by the end of each film, the viewer gets the sense that the characters have found healing and have learned to cope with their losses.

International Films: Sleep, Eating, Impulse Control, and Adjustment Disorders

Sleep Disorders

Control (2003, Hungary) is a comedy/drama filmed in a Budapest subway dealing with fictitious characters reflecting universal themes of good vs. evil and feeling trapped in life. There are various odd characters in the film, one of whom is a worker with narcolepsy who falls asleep on the job when he gets angry or stressed. When conflicts arise between co-workers, he immediately falls asleep and experiences an utter sense of confusion upon awakening.

Nightmares in an adult related to childhood sexual abuse are portrayed in *Don't Tell* (2005, Italy/UK/France/Spain) and *The Celebration* (1998, Denmark/Sweden), and they play an especially important role in the former film. The 7th 1-hour film in renowned Polish director Krzysztof Kieslowski's 10-film series *The Decalogue* (1989, Poland) offers a good portrayal of **sleep terror disorder**. A child in the film has recurrent night terrors in which she screams in her sleep each night, is difficult to awaken, and is unable to recall her troubling dreams after she awakes. In the film, she is described as suffering from nightmares.

Eating Disorders

In the dark psychodrama *Primo Amore* (2004, Italy) a goldsmith, Vittorio, becomes obsessed with molding the perfect female body (paralleling his work of transforming metals into pure forms). He finds an already slender art-school model, Sonia, and rigorously controls her diet to get her to lose more weight. Sonia, desperate to please him, is willing to submit to his delusional plans. His role can be seen as the extreme of a "controlling parent." Self-disgust, exhaustion from starvation, secrecy, and sneaking food are characteristic features found in the characters with eating disorders portrayed in this film. Vittorio's behavior is clearly abusive. While not a pure depiction of an eating disorder nor an accurate portrayal of all the dynamics that surround eating disorders, the film is nevertheless useful as a thematic illustration of this serious clinical problem.

Impulse Control Disorders

Happy-Go-Lucky (2008, UK) is an outstanding film by renowned British director Mike Leigh about a young woman, Poppy (Sally Hawkins), who faces life's stressors with a refreshing yet realistic optimism and humor. A supporting character in the film is Poppy's driving instructor, Scott (Eddie Marsan). On the surface, Scott is a fascinating contrast to Poppy's character as he always has a frown on his face and comes across as very tightly wound, controlling, edgy, and angry. His anger emerges in each driving lesson he gives Poppy, usually taking the form of yelling and threatening.

"The American dream never happened. The American nightmare is already here. I mean, look at the Washington Monument. It is 555 feet above the ground and 111 feet below the ground. 555 plus 111 is 666. 6-6-6, Poppy. 6-6-6"

Scott, the explosive driving instructor, during one of his rants in *Happy-Go-Lucky* (2008)

Critical Thinking Questions

- Consider any category of psychological disorders and discuss the impact of sleep deprivation on the disorder's symptoms. Are any of your examples portrayed in movies?
- What are the ways in which insomnia and hypersomnia can be managed psychologically? Are there any films depicting these techniques?
- The ingenious film *Waking Life* (2001) explores the question (noted on the DVD cover), "Are we sleepwalking through our waking state or wake-walking through our dreams?" What is this question asking and how does one go about answering it? What is the clinical utility of such a question?
- Why are eating disorders so rare in popular mainstream cinema? Can a filmmaker do justice to these conditions without being offensive, heavy-handed, or off-putting?
- What role does society have in causing and maintaining eating disorders (e.g., anorexia and bulimia)? Are there countries where these disorders do not occur?
- Does social class influence bulimia and anorexia?
- What are the similarities and differences between impulse control disorders and addictions? How can movies help in making the distinction?
- Considering how fascinating the impulse control disorders are, why are they not depicted in movies more frequently?
- Is trichotillomania categorized better as an obsessive-compulsive disorder or as an impulse control disorder?
- Can adjustment disorders be more severe than other major psychiatric disorders? At what point should they be treated with medication?
- Can adjustment disorders last for years, or is this contrary to the definition?

His mental illness becomes apparent when the viewer observes his inability to control his impulses when he learns Poppy has a boyfriend. He speeds up the car, endangers himself and Poppy, becomes abnormally demanding, and at one point, grabs Poppy's hair and shakes her repeatedly. He screams at her on a public street, unloading his pain. His anger is palpable and striking. However, Scott is not merely a one-dimensional character; the viewer sees glimpses of his desperate side and senses his profound loneliness.

In a remarkable Norwegian film, *Elling* (2002), the character Kjell, upon being released from a psychiatric hospital, has explosive bouts of anger whenever he is frustrated. His condition would likely be diagnosed as intermittent explosive disorder. *2046* (2004, China) is Kar Wai Wong's portrayal of pathological, or at least excessive, gambling in which the protagonist loses most of his money at the end of each month to card playing. As is typical with many addictions, the gambler in this film is addicted to both card-playing and sex.

Further Exploration

If you have time to read just one book relevant to this chapter, make it:

Touyz, S. W., Polivy, J., & Hay, P. (2008). *Eating disorders*. Cambridge, MA: Hogrefe.

If you only have time for one article, read:

Ohayon, M. M. (2002). Epidemiology of insomnia: What we know and what we still need to learn. *Sleep Medicine Reviews, 6*, 97–111.

Authors' Picks

Sleep, Eating, Impulse Control, and Adjustment Disorders

Sleep Disorders
- *The Machinist* (2004)
- *Insomnia* (2002)

Eating Disorders
- *Primo Amore* (2004)
- *Girl, Interrupted* (1999)

Impulse Control Disorders
- *Owning Mahowny* (2002)
- *Klepto* (2003)
- *Happy-Go-Lucky* (2008)
- *Oscar and Lucinda* (1997)

Adjustment Disorders
- *It's a Wonderful Life* (1946)
- *The Upside of Anger* (2005)

Chapter 14

Violence and Physical and Sexual Abuse

"When I woke up, I went on what the movie advertisements refer to as a roaring rampage of revenge.
I roared and I rampaged and I got bloody satisfaction.
I've killed a hell of a lot of people to get to this point.
But I've only one more... the last one... the one I'm driving to right now.
The only one left. And when I arrive at my destination, I am gonna kill Bill..."
Beatrix Kiddo, "the bride," in *Kill Bill: Vol. 1* (2004)

Questions to Consider While Watching *Kill Bill: Vol. 1* (2003) and *Vol. 2* (2004)

- What is the murder rate in the U.S.? In your hometown?
- Is Beatrix Kiddo's ("the bride's") revenge justified?
- What would you say to someone intent on getting revenge via murder?
- Following a 4-year coma, how long should it typically take to work through muscle atrophy in the legs? Can a person "will" their toes to move as the bride does in *Kill Bill: Vol. 1*?
- What is the role of violence in these two films? Does it change from one film to the next?
- Director Quentin Tarantino works hard to develop characters that are violent and dangerous. What is he trying to express in doing so?
- Tarantino blocks out the bride's real name for much of both films. What is the psychological relevance of this?
- There are several seriously violent characters in this film. How do their motives and world views differ from one another? How are they similar? How is their world view different from a nonviolent person?
- One scene involves a deviant hospital worker prostituting coma patients for money. How frequently does something like this occur?
- Tarantino engages the viewer in feeling compassion for a serial killer. How does he do this? Do you feel manipulated by this?

Patient Evaluation

Patient's stated reason for coming: "I have only one thing on my mind... revenge. As soon as I get out of here, I'm gonna kill Bill!"

History of the present illness: Ms. Beatrix Kiddo is a 34-year-old Caucasian woman being evaluated to assess her mental status and to develop treatment recommendations. She was caught by police three days ago driving a stolen vehicle owned by a man who was murdered in the hospital in which she was staying. She is a suspect in several murder investigations, including a mass murder of over 50 people. She is currently in isolation at the county jail. She did not provide details regarding any homicides; however, she was adamant about her plan to kill 5 people, of which, according to Beatrix, only one remains. The person who remains is her ex-boyfriend and former boss, "Bill."

Past psychiatric illness, treatment, and outcomes: Beatrix does not have a history of psychiatric problems. She denied posttraumatic stress symptoms. She denied depression, anxiety, hallucinations, and delusions.

Medical history: Beatrix was hospitalized in a coma for four years following a severe head injury from a gunshot to her head. She awoke from the coma suddenly, immediately remembering the events that lead her to the hospital. Shortly thereafter she overheard a conversation noting she was raped several times while in the coma by a hospital worker who had been prostituting her to various men. She has been out of the coma for about two weeks. Beatrix has no history of taking psychiatric medication. She denied a history of other injuries, illnesses, or medical disorders, other than "occasional bumps and bruises from kung fu training and fighting."

Psychosocial history: Beatrix would not disclose her complete occupational history; however, she did state she "helped rid the world of scum." Following this job, she worked at a music store and became engaged. On the night of the wedding rehearsal, her fiancé and his family were killed and she states she was beaten and shot by the five people mentioned earlier and she was shot in the head by "Bill." She believes this was revenge taken upon her for leaving her previous job. She was pregnant at the time she was shot. She states this caused her to lose the baby and put her in a coma. This disclosure brought tears to her eyes.

Beatrix has never been married. She graduated from high school and then traveled around the world receiving training in various forms of specialized martial arts. Beatrix states she does not have any friends, but paradoxically also states that she makes friends easily.

Drug and alcohol history: Beatrix denied any significant substance use history. She occasionally drinks alcohol (twice per month) and smokes marijuana (once per month).

Behavioral observations: Beatrix presented as pleasant, charming, and engaging. She was quite relaxed throughout the interview. She expressed considerable intensity when she spoke of the revenge she hoped to achieve. Mood and affect were euthymic. Speech was normal, evenly paced, and coherent. She seemed to be very clear in her choice of words as she frequently placed emphasis on particular words. No tangential or circumstantial speech was noted. No psychotic processes were evident. No dissociative symptoms were observed. She appeared guarded throughout the evaluation, but she cooperated fully, and the results of the examination are believed to be valid. There were no inconsistencies in her story that might indicate dishonesty, malingering, or other form of manipulation.

Mental status examination: Beatrix was oriented to place, person, time, and situation. She appears to be very intelligent, both socially and intellectually. She scored 30 out of a total of 30 possible points on the Mini Mental State Examination. No cognitive, attention, concentration, or memory problems were noted, despite the severe head injury and coma in her fairly recent past.

Functional assessment: Beatrix is very bright and clever. She clearly knows how to take care of herself and get her needs met. She does not appear to experience any after-effects from the head injury and coma, other than an intense anger and preoccupation with revenge. Though she ruminates and plans revenge, this does not get in the way of getting her needs met. She states she lacks "mercy, compassion, and forgiveness," but that she has a high dose of rationality. She does present as rational; however, this rationality is not congruent with the allegations of serial killing and her revenge plans involving murder.

Strengths: Beatrix is direct, assertive, and succinct in her communication. She is talented in martial arts and well-skilled in self-defense.

Diagnosis: Adjustment disorder with disturbance of conduct; antisocial personality disorder.

Treatment plan: (1) It is recommended Beatrix not be released at this time due to her significant threats to harm others. (2) Request personality and projective psychological testing to provide a more complete evaluation (e.g., MMPI-2, Rorschach). (3) Request hospital records from her 4-year hospitalization following her head injury. (4) Offer the option of individual psychotherapy to work with decision-making, provide support, and discuss coping strategies.

Prognosis: Guarded

Violence, Revenge, and *Kill Bill*

Beatrix Kiddo (aka "the bride," played by Uma Thurman) is not a typical prototype of a violent figure. She is a middle-aged female who was in a relationship, does not abuse substances, and does not have a poor socioeconomic background. Research has shown repeatedly that substance abuse increases the likelihood of violent acts; other risk factors for violence include being young, male, single, and of lower socioeconomic status. Nevertheless, Thurman is engaging, fascinating, and compelling in her role as the vengeful character in *Kill Bill: Vol. 1* (2003) and *Kill Bill: Vol. 2* (2004), both of which involve dramatic depictions of violence. Some viewers will argue these are two of the most artistic action films ever made. Others will see the violence as overly graphic and gratuitous. Still others will speak of the role of violence influencing today's culture and today's youth and argue that despite the artistry, the violent imagery that defines these films cannot be beneficial for youth or adults. Others will speak to the glorification of murder and the purposeless nature of revenge. Some will say the violence is justified as it is always either in self-defense or directed solely at those individuals who killed her family and left her for dead. Finally, some will note the film is not to be taken "literally," and that it is to be seen for entertainment, distraction, appreciation, and even inspiration (e.g., the theme of a woman's courage and bravery). Each of the above perceptions is valid and at least partially accurate.

In an interview, David Carradine (who played the character Bill) stated "The essence of a Tarantino movie is not the violence, not the action. It's the inside look at the mind, the heart, of violent people." This insight emphasizes looking more deeply at all cinematic characters and looking beyond violent acts to better understand them. There are a variety of violent characters in the film; each is portrayed as unique, with different backgrounds, motivations, thought processes, and actions. Rather than a one-dimensional "bad guy," Tarantino develops all of his characters, showing their flaws, strengths, nuances, and everyday interactions behind their violent presentation.

Some people will be offended by the frequency and intensity of the violence in these films. This is not unjustified, for in many ways these are quintessential violent movies. Scores of people are killed, arms are chopped off, blood sprays, and eyes are ripped out of their sockets, at times in cartoonish ways. The bride is buried alive, she is raped while in a coma, and other characters are tortured as the killer watches them suffer and die. One of the most violent sequences occurs in *Kill Bill: Vol. 1* and is presented completely in animation; this episode presents the traumatic history of one assassin, who as a girl watched her father and mother brutally murdered in front of her. Tarantino does not do this for gratuitous purposes – there are real depths to these characters, an intricate story to be told, and beautiful cinematic artistry to appreciate. The dramatic mixture of violence and cinematic genius is reminiscent of Stanley Kubrick's classic, *A Clockwork Orange* (1971), which was criticized for being overly violent and degrading women, neither of which was Kubrick's intent.

Many of Tarantino's other films involve similar themes and use violence as a communication medium: examples include *Reservoir Dogs* (1992), *Pulp Fiction* (1994), and *Jackie Brown* (1997). He also wrote the screenplay for *From Dusk Till Dawn* (1995). Most recently, Tarantino (along with Robert Rodriguez) wrote and directed two full-length horror films that were shown together as *Grindhouse* (2007) and were touted as a homage to gory exploitation films. Individually, these violent films are titled *Death Proof* and *Planet Terror*; they portray, respectively, a stunt race car driver (Kurt Russell) who stalks and kills women until he encounters a group of women who turn the tables on him, and an army of flesh-eating zombies created by a bio-weapon mishap.

Most people who read this book will have an interest in films and likely be aware of the death of David Carradine in Bangkok, Thailand, on June 4, 2009. Carradine was found hanging by a rope in his hotel room's closet, and speculation about his death has included suicide, murder by Kung Fu gangs he was investigating, and autoerotic asphyxiation. Two of Carradine's ex-wives have reported that he practiced erotic self-bondage. Whatever the cause of his death, he was a gifted actor who was perfectly cast in the *Kill Bill* films.

Violence and Movies: When is Violence Gratuitous?

In the majority of current action and horror movies, the purpose of the violence is to stimulate, dazzle, and entertain the viewer for a brief period. This helps the viewer escape from their present reality and magically enter a more exciting world. Ultimately, the violence in this type of action film (usually a Hollywood product) is unrealistic, unnecessary, and/or gratuitous. It is merely a means to an end – the overriding purpose is to sell movie tickets, not to enhance the cinematic art, to relay an important message to the viewer, or to engender insights.

We have identified seven exceptions to this type of escapism violence. We have grouped films around these thematic exceptions which at least begin an argument that violence in films can have a meaningful purpose. However, this does not mean that the purpose outweighs the negative effects associated with violence.

Depicting a Particular Reality

Often violence is the most succinct and honest way to portray the reality of a particular situation, problem, or conflict. In *Elephant* (2003), the reality of violence in schools is depicted. Director Gus van Sant portrays the typical everyday life of several students who are unaware of the danger and violence about to take place. *Hotel Rwanda* (2004) depicts another terrible reality: The genocide that took place in Rwanda in which nearly 1 million Rwandans were killed. The film focuses on the heroic behavior of a hotel owner, Paul Rusesabagina, who saved well over 1,000 people's lives, and the multiple threats of violence he had to face in order to do so.

Rendition (2007) attempts to show the realities of politics and "Washington." The film is a depiction of "extraordinary rendition" – the detaining of suspected terrorists with minimal evidence (e.g., a phone record) and interrogating/questioning them on foreign soil without judicial oversight. In this film, an Egyptian man traveling in South Africa to attend a conference is detained without due process of law and is then tortured by means of waterboarding and other methods. The film also portrays Islamic extremists, brainwashing, and the training of suicide bombers.

"Sometimes I wonder will God ever forgive us for what we've done to each other? Then I look around and I realize God left this place a long time ago"

Realistic cynicism portrayed in
Blood Diamond (2006)

Blood Diamond (2006) is an intense action film with a deeper purpose – to depict and raise awareness about "conflict diamonds." The film takes place in Sierra Leone in 1999, where a civil war has ravaged the country, leaving millions of refugees; the irony is they were fighting over diamond fields when most of them had never even seen a diamond. The film notes that whenever something of value is found in Africa, many innocent villagers end up dying – this was the case with ivory, rubber, gold, oil, and diamonds. It is further noted that the Americans who purchase two thirds of the world's diamonds are usually unaware of the violence associated with the diamonds they buy. As one character puts it: "In America, it's bling-bling but out here it's bling-bang." Leonardo DiCaprio gives a standout performance as a diamond smuggler who transforms and sacrifices himself to help the victims of the diamond trade. The film concludes by noting that 40 countries

signed the "Kimberley Process" in January 2003 in an effort to stem the flow of conflict diamonds, and that it is up to the consumer to demand conflict-free diamonds. It also notes there are still 200,000 child soldiers living in Africa, and the viewer gets to see horrifying examples of their training.

Sometimes films portray actual historical events, e.g., *Schindler's List* (1993). War films depict not only historical events, but can be generalized to illustrate the atrocities and violence of present-day wars. For example, *Saving Private Ryan* (1998) reveals the realities of war, deglamorizing it while not denigrating the sacrifices made by the men involved. Antiwar films reveal similar realities emphasizing the futility of war. *No Man's Land* (2001), a film that won an Academy Award for Best Foreign Film, is one good example; likewise, Stanley Kubrick made three excellent, antiwar films: *Paths of Glory* (1957), *Dr. Strangelove: or How I Learned to Stop Worrying and Love the Bomb* (1964), and *Full Metal Jacket* (1987).

Showing the Ridiculous and Futile Nature of Violence

The purpose of the film, *Series 7: The Contenders* (2001) is to demonstrate the futility and folly of violence. The film is a tongue-in-cheek fictional reality television show where six people are randomly chosen from their government issued numbers and forced to hunt and kill the others while cameras film them for the television audience. The narrator excitedly describes "real people, real murders" and states that "the rules are as simple as life and death." Dawn, a pregnant woman, is "the longest running contender;" she continues with each new episode enhancing the theme of "kill or be killed." Her success fails to impress her family, and her sister labels her as an "animal, whore, addict, murderer, and thief."

Revealing the Psyche of Violent People

As discussed earlier in the chapter, most of Quentin Tarantino's films embody this theme. Serial killer movies (discussed in more detail later) sometimes attempt to attain this level, but they rarely succeed. In *American Psycho* (2000), assuming the violence is all in Patrick Bateman's mind, the purpose of the violence is to depict the inner psyche and violent fantasies of a disturbed man. The film illustrates a fundamental contradiction as Bateman spends hours daydreaming about violent acts while his body, attire, job, business cards, selection of social outings, and overall presentation are virtually perfect. Thus, the film gets at what no one else in Bateman's world would be privy to – his mind. *Sweeney Todd: The Demon Barber of Fleet Street* (2007) is in part a musical which allows the music to contain or "hold" the violence, almost sectioning it off from the rest of the film. The barber's (Johnny Depp) revenge and killings seem to reveal more about his psyche and deterioration than anything else.

Showing How Violence Is a Cyclical Trap

In *American History X* (1998), one of the purposes of the violence is to show its cyclical nature. This film relates the following sequence of events: A man gets involved in a violent group, he gets out of the group but not before consequences of his involvement emerge, and he tries to challenge and resolve these new conflicts, but ultimately must face the fact that it is too late and violence ensues, completing the circle. The message: Do not get involved with violence in the first place. Mel Gibson's *Apocalypto* (2006) is graphically violent depicting the self-destruction of the Mayan culture.

"I'm going to peel off his skin and make him watch me wear it."

Comment made by a violent Mayan in *Apocalypto* (2006)

A History of Violence (2005), directed by David Cronenberg, depicts Tom Stall (Viggo Mortensen), an everyday family man who owns a café in a small town. He is involved in a holdup by two criminals; however, he instinctively springs to action, killing both men and saving all his customers and workers. The media proclaim him a hero and this news attracts three thugs from Philadelphia who claim Tom has led a previous life filled with violence and that they have come to take him back. The film reinforces research that suggests a history of violence is the best predictor of future violent behavior. It also emphasizes that one can never fully escape one's past, and that once violence starts, it finds a way to cycle back. One of the comments Tom's wife makes after learning about his history illustrates a common misconception in films. She asks: "What are you, some multiple personality schizoid?!" She is confusing two mental disorders in her statement and she assumes that violence must mean mental illness of some kind (in the case of Tom Stall, it does not).

No one is able to escape the shadow part of his or her character in *Crash* (2004). This Academy Award for Best Picture winner integrates a number of stories in an eclectic mix of races and ethnicities in Los Angeles that provides a meaningful look at the pain of racism, the dangers of discrimination, and the possibility of redemption. Even the Buddhist who practices nonviolence eventually resorts to highly violent and threatening acts. The film depicts the vicissitudes of the human condition, and illustrates that violence leads to more violence, which can be verbal, emotional, or physical.

In Wim Wenders' *The End of Violence* (1997), Bill Pullman plays Mike Max, an action/violence film director who hides out from society and starts a new life after he is almost murdered. While this character promotes violence in his movies, he also fears violence as documented by his high level of paranoia, leading him to believe his enemies can come from anywhere – land, water, and sky. A contrasting character (Ray Bering, played by Gabriel Byrne) tries to prevent violence as a secret government officer working a program that oversees the city with thousands of cameras watching over every interaction. The cyclical nature of violence is evident in both the man who directs violent movies only to become an attacked victim of violence and in the man trying to prevent violence through spying, who is himself killed.

Projecting a Dangerous Future

The message associated with these films is clear: If society keeps heading in a particular direction, a dangerous future is inevitable. *A Clockwork Orange* (1971), in a very artistic way, speaks to this theme with regard to youth violence, the role of the prison system, and the predominant psychological approach at the time, behaviorism. Rather than denigrating such a film and labeling it as offensive, it is more helpful to see the film as a message and motivator to promote change in the present. In *Sin City* (2005), the graphic, stylized violence and surreal settings created with computer animation present a violent and dangerous future. The violence and societal control seen in films such as *Equilibrium* (2002) and *The Island* (2005) clearly depict an unpleasant and dangerous future.

Showing the Potential Danger of Authority Roles and Group Contagion

Group contagion occurs when an individual's identity is merged with that of a group and the individual begins to accept and conform to the values and beliefs of the group. This process of **deindividuation** can be linked with increases in aggressive behavior as people feel more anonymous acting within a group rather than alone. These social psychology themes can clearly be seen in *A Clockwork Orange* (1971), *Fight Club* (1999), *Amores Perros* (2000), and gang-related movies such as *South Central* (1992). It also occurs in larger numbers in the persecution of religious figures, where crowds and major groups of people turn against Gandhi in *Gandhi* (1982) and Jesus in *The Passion of the Christ* (2004).

These themes are also present with gang behavior, which is frequently portrayed in movies. *City of God* (2003), a Brazilian drama/documentary about a poor area of Rio de Janeiro, portrays how gangs can take over much of a major city through group violence, leaving the individual with few options other than joining the drug lords or dying. In *South Central* (1992), the gangs portrayed take over the city at night, implement rules that allow them to keep their power, emphasize controlling the "hood" by killing, and enforce the idea that "nothing goes on without we saying so." The film emphasizes three alternatives to gang-life: (1) Kill the enemy; (2) Turn against oneself and go crazy; or (3) Change. The film also speaks to anger and hate in the lead character, Ali, who must change and influence others to break his own "hate cycle," thus removing his "badge of shame." This theme is also found in a non-gang film, *Antwone Fisher* (2002), in which a young African-American man must face his own anger about abuse that can be traced back to the time of slavery.

Gang-related films often explore issues of racism and the link between racism and violence; this is the case in *South Central* (1992) as well as in *8 Mile* (2002), which stars the rapper Eminem. Gangs of violent skin-heads promoting hate are depicted in four especially powerful films: *American History X* (1998), *The Believer* (2001), *MacArthur Park* (2001), and *Hate* (1995).

In the psychologically complex film *Fight Club* (1999), men gather one-on-one to physically and brutally fight one another until one of the combatants can no longer stand. An entirely underground fight club movement grows and moves from city to city. The violence is depicted as a way of expressing anger and repressed rage, as an alternative to the monotony of everyday life, as an antidote to consumerism and depression, and as a way of feeling "really alive."

Demonstrating Obstacles People Must Face with Courage and Sacrifice

Jesus and Gandhi look directly in the face of violent crowds in *The Passion of the Christ* (2004) and *Gandhi* (1982), respectively. Both show the enormous sacrifice and courage that is often necessary in order to confront oppression and defeat violence.

The Impact of Violence in Films

Contemporary films and television programs are replete with violence, and it is difficult to avoid violence in the media or to briefly catalogue the most egregious examples of violence in recent films. According to the American Academy of Pediatrics, the typical American youngster will have witnessed about 200,000 acts of violence on television by the age of 18, and is likely to have witnessed several thousand additional acts of violence in films such as *Rambo III* (1988) or any of the many *Halloween* films.

Several studies have examined the role of violence in television and movies and explored its impact on aggression, attitudes, and behavior. Likewise, hundreds of articles have emphasized the impact of movie violence on children and adolescents, and authors often attempt to link this violence with violent acts committed by teens. However, while viewing violent movies does appear to contribute to increases in acts of aggression, the degree of influence is unclear as many other factors are involved (e.g., video games, parental upbringing, level of poverty, education level, etc.)

Often the person committing the violent act in movies is mentally ill; some researchers have estimated that as many as 70% of movie characters with mental illness are dangerous. This certainly contributes to the misconception that all people with mental disorders are violent. Some films are able to appropriately make the distinction between violence and mental illness, such as Roman Polanski's *Repulsion* (1965), and Martin Scorsese's *Taxi Driver* (1976) and *Raging Bull* (1980) (Zimmerman, 2003).

Serial Killers

People have been fascinated with the topic of serial killers since Jack the Ripper strangled and cut the throats of five London prostitutes in 1888. More recent serial killers include Albert De Salvo (the Boston Strangler), David Berkowitz (the Son of Sam killer), Henry Lee Lucas, John Wayne Gacy, Ted Bundy ("the Preppie killer"), Wayne Williams, Charles Manson, and Jeffrey Dahmer, a harmless-looking young man who killed dozens of other young men, ate their body parts, and kept other parts in his refrigerator. The FBI defines a serial killer as anyone who has committed three or more separate murders. It seems that if a serial killer is fairly well known, a movie will eventually follow; consider the films *Dahmer* (2002), *Ted Bundy* (2002), *Gacy* (2003), *Monster* (2003), *B. T. K.* (2008), *The Night Stalker* (1987), *Summer of Sam* (1999), and *Zodiac* (2007).

Anthony Hopkins plays one of the most terrifying serial killers ever filmed in *The Silence of the Lambs* (1991), *Hannibal* (2001), and *Red Dragon* (2002). *American Psycho* (2000) is a quality film depicting a serial killer if the film is taken literally by the viewer. Another valid vantage point is to consider all of the murders committed by the fictional character, Patrick Bateman, as fantasies rather than reality; there are numerous cinematic elements to support this hypothesis, although few viewers leave the theater with this impression.

Contrary to media presentations and popular opinion, few if any serial killers are psychotic. (David Berkowitz was a salient exception.) In contrast, many are sexual sadists who derive sexual excitement from the murders they commit; most are sociopaths who experience little remorse or regret for their crimes. Both John Wayne Gacy and Jeffrey Dahmer were homosexual pedophiles.

Some serial killers commit multiple murders for utilitarian reasons – i.e., they are "hit men" who kill for money. This is the kind of serial killer portrayed by Jack Nicholson in *Prizzi's Honor* (1985). Quality documentaries addressing the lives of sociopathic serial killers include *In Cold Blood* (1967) and *Henry: Portrait of a Serial Killer* (1986). The latter is loosely based on the life and confessions (since called into question) of Henry Lee Lucas. Henry (Michael Rooker) shares a cheap room with Otis (Tom Towles), a man he had met in prison in Vandalia. The film is controversial because it presents graphic details of several murders, including one in which Henry and his roommate, Otis, pretend their car isn't running and then kill a man who stops to help.

In a subsequent scene, Henry and Otis videotape the murder of an entire family. The film develops a triangular sexual tension between Henry, Otis, and Becky (Tracy Arnold), Otis' sister, a woman down on her luck who has come to live with her brother. In the final scene of the movie, Henry decapitates Otis. The movie is especially powerful insofar as it seems to trivialize murder, as in the scene in which Henry and Otis murder two prostitutes, then go out and casually share an order of French fries.

A family of serial killers can be seen in Rob Zombie's horror films, *House of 1000 Corpses* (2003) and *The Devil's Rejects* (2005). Serial killers also are depicted in numerous other popular films, such as *Se7en* (1995) and the *Scream* films (1996, 1997, 2000).

Physical and Sexual Abuse in Films

Domestic Violence and Films

Domestic violence is a serious, ubiquitous, and under-reported problem in our society. Violence sufficient to cause death or serious injury will occur in about 1 in 25 families, and hitting, slapping, or punching will occur in approximately one in four families. It is unfortunate that some men feel that marriage gives them special license to hit, hurt, or rape their spouse. (Whether or not a man can be charged with raping his wife is one of the themes explored in the 1959 film *Anatomy of a Murder*.) Two out of three female victims of violence know their attackers; however, they frequently will not report their abuse because they desire to protect their assailants or because they fear reprisals (Abbey, 2005).

The film *Personal Velocity* (2002) studies three very different, vulnerable, and courageous women, each in separate segments. One segment addresses issues of domestic violence; Delia (Kyra Sedgwick) is physically abused by her husband. She is slapped hard in the face at the kitchen table in front of her children for saying the wrong thing, and she is frequently beaten. Delia develops enough motivation to leave when she realizes the pain of what her children are going through; this helps her to "break through the inertia." When speaking to her child, she says she stayed with her husband because he needed her more; this speaks to the irrational self-sacrificing of the victim. In looking back, Delia admits that she and her husband never talked about their problems.

In a later scene, a memory of her husband triggers a catharsis. Delia struggles to create a new life, depending on compassionate people, such as a counselor at a women's shelter and an old acquaintance who houses Delia and her children.

One type of domestic violence that does not get a lot of attention due to its often intangible nature is that of psychological/emotional abuse. Psychological/emotional abuse is a common phenomenon depicted in films that would be too extensive to list here. One poignant example that illustrates emotional abuse occurs in the film *Waitress* (2007). Jeremy Sisko portrays Earl, the husband of Jenna (Keri Russell). Earl is an extraordinarily needy and psychologically abusive husband. He controls her absolutely, does not allow Jenna to have a car, collects her tip money as soon as he sees her, and watches her every action with hypervigilance. He sometimes tells her he will pick her up from work and then decides to simply leave her waiting for hours while at other times he greets her by honking his car's horn, embarrassing her in front of her coworkers. He is fueled by a significant jealousy and becomes upset when she tells him she is pregnant, fearing the baby will take away her attention; he subsequently insists she verbally admit that she will put him ahead of the baby and prioritize taking care of him (he, of course, is fully capable of taking care of himself). He also forces her to repeat verbatim sentences on a number of occasions – usually involving her proclaiming her dedication and allegiance to caring for him – to produce a temporary sense of reassurance. He forces himself upon her sexually but only cares about his personal gratification. Jenna eventually confronts Earl in a classic scene that should not be missed.

Rape and Films

Rape is included in this section rather than in the chapter on sexual and gender identity disorders because rape is an act of violence and an act of sexual abuse, *not* an act of sexual passion. Incest is discussed in the Sexual and Gender Identity Disorders chapter.

The statistics on rape are sobering. The United States has one of the highest rates of rape in the world – four times higher than Germany, 13 times higher than England, and 20 times higher than Japan. It is estimated that one out of three women will be sexually assaulted in her lifetime, and one out of seven will be raped by her husband. Among rape victims, 61% are under the age of 18 and 78% know their attacker. One in four college women have either experienced rape or have been exposed to attempted rape, and the majority of both men and women involved in acquaintance rape had been drinking or using drugs at the time of the rape. About a third of the victims of rape develop a rape-related posttraumatic stress disorder sometime in their lifetime. It is estimated that only about 16% of rapes are reported to the police in the United States, usually because women feel that nothing can be done or because they feel it is a private matter between them and their assailants. When compared with women who have not experienced rape, rape victims are found to be more than nine times more likely to attempt suicide.

Rohypnol (flunitrazepam), a powerful benzodiazepine often referred to as the "date rape drug" is about 10 times more powerful than diazepam (Valium). It is used to treat insomnia and to take the edge off the crash that accompanies withdrawal from binge use of other drugs. Women who have passed out after unwittingly taking Rohypnol have found that the profound sedation and memory impairment that accompany its use have made it very difficult for them to prosecute their assailants. Rohypnol is used to facilitate a rape in the film *Virgin* (2003); the rape has horrific consequences for the woman.

Rape has been a recurrent theme in contemporary American films. There were significant rape scenes in *A Clockwork Orange* (1971), Ken Russell's *The Devils* (1971), and *My Old Man's Place* (1972). Paul (Marlon Brando) rapes a passive and indifferent Jeanne (Maria Schneider) in *Last Tango in Paris* (1973). There is a vicious and unforgettable rape scene in *Blue Velvet* (1986). Farrah Fawcett takes control of the situation and exacts revenge on a rapist in *Extremities* (1986); Dustin Hoffman gets revenge following his wife's graphic rape in Sam Peckinpah's violent film *Straw Dogs* (1971); and two independent women inadvertently kill a man who tries to rape one of them in *Thelma & Louise* (1991). Vietnamese women are raped in several of the Vietnam War films, most notably in *Casualties of War* (1989). Harrison Ford is wrongly accused of rape in *Presumed Innocent* (1990). Date rape occurs in the 1995 film *Higher Learning*; gang rape is portrayed in *Last Exit to Brooklyn* (1989); and there are homosexual rapes in *Deliverance* (1972) and *American History X* (1998). A nun is raped in *Bad Lieutenant* (1992), but the nun forgives her assailant and refuses to press charges against him. Two children play a game of rape in *Welcome to the Dollhouse* (1996).

Ingmar Bergman takes up the theme of the rape of innocence in *The Virgin Spring* (1959), and two rapes occur in the gritty Dutch film *Antonia's Line* (1995), one of which involves a man who rapes his sister who is mentally retarded. *Dead Man Walking* (1995) presents the viewer with difficult choices about the appropriateness of capital punishment in a case of rape and murder, and we are forced to think about whether or not drug intoxication is a mitigating circumstance in this case and others similar to it.

Attempted rape of a man by a woman is discussed extensively in the film adaptation of Michael Crichton's novel *Disclosure* (1994). When Tom Sanders (Michael Douglas) rebuffs Meredith Johnson (Demi Moore), the new female boss, she lies and manipulatively accuses her new subordinate of sexual harassment.

Victims of Physical and Sexual Abuse

Every act of violence or abuse has both a perpetrator and a victim. Both are depicted in films, but for emphasis of story, character development, or artistic integrity, one is often emphasized over the other. The cultural phenomenon *Slumdog Millionaire* (2008), which received eight Academy Awards (including Best Picture, Best Director, and Best Adapted Screenplay), depicts abuse and torture of children and of the protagonist as an adult. This film is a classic underdog story in which the protagonist overcomes a number of adversities in his quest for love.

In the psychological film *Doubt* (2008), Philip Seymour Hoffman portrays Father Brendan Flynn, a priest accused of sexual misbehavior by the school's superior, Sister Aloysius Beauvier (Meryl Streep). As a study of the psychology of doubt, the film is remarkable, as it gives no clear answer as to the priest's innocence or culpability, and the viewer leaves the theater – with doubt. The film is included in this section not for its depiction of abuse, but rather because it illustrates the issues underlying the accusation of abuse.

In the intense, realistic film *Mysterious Skin* (2004), two boys are sexually molested by their coach and their lives go in completely different directions. Brian, as a child, has nightmares, nosebleeds, blackouts, and enuresis, along with nervous, skittish behavior as he enters adolescence. He realizes he has lost time and believes it is linked with a UFO experience. He is described as asexual. Neil, on the other hand, is hypersexual, and likes the attention and grooming of his coach, and he

sets up other children to be groomed by the coach. As an adolescent, he cruises parks, has sex with men for money and takes pride in being written about on dirty bathroom stalls. He has minimal sexual boundaries, uses drugs, gets a sexually transmitted disease, and becomes the victim of severe violence during one of his "tricks."

Antwone Fisher (2002) is based on the true story of a young man, Antwone Fisher (Derek Luke), who enlists in the Navy and begins to have problems with anger and assault. He is sent to a Navy psychiatrist (Denzel Washington) and eventually opens up his traumatic past, which includes a history of significant physical and sexual abuse.

Some films depict entire groups, cultures, or ethnicities that are victims of physical or sexual abuse. *The Magdalene Sisters* (2002), based on a true story, depicts the lives of a large group of young girls sent away for behavior problems who are forced to endure daily physical hardships, abuse, and humiliation. Each adolescent sent to this Catholic workhouse is abused by nuns who seem oblivious to the pain they inflict.

Another type of abuse not often discussed is harassment. Charlize Theron portrays Josey Aimes, a woman who attempts to support her children by working in a blue-collar mining job in *North Country* (2005). She and the other women experience significant harassment (verbal, physical, emotional, and sexual) by the men, including finding semen on her clothes in her locker, confronting words written with feces on the walls in the woman's locker room, and the placement of a vibrator in her lunch pail. Other depictions of violence in the film include rape and physical abuse by one's partner.

Mystic River and Sexual Abuse

In *Mystic River* (2003), director Clint Eastwood depicts three boyhood friends (Sean Penn as Jimmy, Tim Robbins as Dave, and Kevin Bacon as Sean) who reunite following the death of Jimmy's daughter. At the film's onset, the three boys are approached by a man in a car who intimidates them and identifies himself as a cop. Only Dave gets in the car with the man who turns out to be a pedophile. Dave is sexually abused and escapes from his abductor after four days. The story moves ahead about 30 years and the viewer sees the adult Dave, now married with a son. Dave has never fully recovered from the abduction.

Tim Robbins, who won an Academy Award for Best Supporting Actor for his role as Dave, provides a stunning portrayal of a sexual abuse survivor. Dave is passive, timid, unassuming, and unemotional, yet appears to have a happy family life. In what can be viewed as an unfortunate consequence, Dave sees a man abusing a young boy and his own abuse history is triggered; trying to free the boy and (metaphorically) himself, Dave snaps, kills the man and allows the boy to escape. Consequently, Dave is plagued with confusion and pain that he is unable to share with his wife; he tells her a different story, and he becomes a suspect in the murder of Jimmy's daughter who had died the same night. Dave becomes more distant (thus appearing more guilty), increasingly quirky, and begins to talk to himself. In one dramatic scene, he seems to hallucinate, hearing voices in his head.

The Accused and Rape

The Accused (1988) is based on a true story of gang rape on a pool table in a blue-collar bar. The crime was especially despicable insofar as more than a dozen spectators stood by clapping and cheering while a woman was repeatedly raped. No one attempted to stop the rape or assist the victim. The complacency of the bystanders in the film is in part attributed to the fact that Sarah Tobias (Jodi Foster) had been drinking heavily and smoking pot earlier in the evening, had openly flirted with one of the men, was provocatively dressed, and had engaged in a sensuous dance immediately before being raped. Her defense is weakened further by the fact that she had jokingly referred to one of the men earlier in the evening, telling her girlfriend, "I should take him home and fuck his brains out." The attorneys for the defense argue that Tobias is simply "trailer park trash" who was an enthusiastic and willing participant in everything that occurred.

Some of the most vivid scenes in the film occur during an insensitive gynecological examination by a woman doctor who asks detailed questions about Sarah's sexual history ("Have you ever made love to more than one man at a time?") and recent experiences. The insensitivity is compounded by the questions of the assistant district attorney, who wants to know how Sarah was dressed and when was the last time she experienced intercourse before the rape.

Tobias loses the first legal round, when the three rapists are convicted but have their sentences reduced from rape to "reckless endangerment." However, she is eventually successful in convicting several of the men who witnessed the rape and did nothing. The film concludes with two sobering facts: (1) in the United States, a rape is reported every six minutes, and (2) one out of every four rape victims is attacked by two or more assailants.

Neglect and Abandonment

An interesting portrayal of an attempt to resolve neglect can be found in Ben Affleck's directorial debut, *Gone Baby Gone* (2007). In this multilayered, complex film, a young girl, who is the neglected child of a cocaine addict, is missing. As the plot develops, we learn that a retired police captain (Morgan Freeman) has kidnapped the girl, rationalizing he is trying to give her a better life and that she was otherwise destined for a terrible future. We also learn that the captain has a personal agenda in that his only child was murdered years ago. The girl seems to be treated exceptionally well and she has a happy life with her new caretakers. The film concludes with the girl and the protagonist watching television and the camera shifts so that they are then watching the viewer – leaving the viewer with the question of how best to handle a situation in which there are multitudes of parents who neglect their children and potentially high quality parents who would like to have children but cannot.

Questions to Consider While Watching *Gone Baby Gone*

- Should all children who are neglected be taken from their homes? When is "some neglect" too much neglect?
- Where do you believe the child in this film should be placed? Is this where you believe the child will have the best future? Do parental rights override the child's right to a happy, safe, and secure future?
- Whatever you believe, can you make a clear argument and provide a rationale for the other side of the debate?
- What is the role of integrity and psychological courage in this film?
- It has been said that the subtext of this film (and the book) is to raise questions and to document that society does not have any idea how to raise children in a healthy way. Do you agree with this? Why or why not?

International Films: Violence and Physical and Sexual Abuse

Violence

Osama (2003, Afghanistan) is based on a true story, and it is the first movie made in Afghanistan after the fall of the Taliban. It depicts the heavy discrimination, violence, and oppression of women under Taliban rule. Violence is also depicted in the everyday reality of everyone living in a poor section of Rio de Janeiro in *City of God* (2003, Brazil). Gangs and drugs are a normal part of existence for these children. This type of film is often a shock to viewers who live a very different life and are unaware of the daily poverty and dangers other people face.

2LDK (2003, Japan) demonstrates the ridiculous and futile nature of violence. A competition develops between two girls rooming together following an audition for an acting role. Growing anger, resentment, and negative and hateful thoughts develop in each girl. These emotions are artfully shown as the girls speak and act one way with voice-overs revealing their true but opposite thoughts. Eventually they come face-to-face and exchange physical assaults in the forms of electrocution, cleaning fluid, and attacks with a fire extinguisher. Violence is used to reveal the psyche of a violent thief in Peter Greenaway's *The Cook, the Thief, His Wife, and Her Lover* (1989, France/UK). In addition to being intensely controlling, the thief is revealed to be psychotic.

Das Experiment (2001, Germany) illustrates the potential dangers associated with authority roles and group contagion. This film depicts a research study in a prison setting in which subjects are divided into either prisoners who waive their civil rights or guards who are instructed to maintain peace and order. This film bears some initial structural similarity to one of the most well-known psychological experiments ever conducted, Philip Zimbardo's Stanford Prison Experiment. However, the depiction of violence goes well beyond what actually occurred in Zimbardo's study. The violence in this film, though at times exaggerated, is used to show the danger of group contagion and the power of the authority role. Shortly into the study, the guards collude and decide they need to humiliate the prisoners to regain control. Prisoners are stripped, ridiculed, called names, denigrated, urinated on, and even beaten and left to bleed to death. One guard captures and rapes a female psychologist. The prison-

ers experience depression, extreme helplessness, psychosis, and panic attacks. It is difficult for anyone from the U.S. to see this film and not be reminded of the shocking reports of prisoner abuse that occurred at Abu Ghraib prison in Baghdad or at the detention facility at Guantanamo Bay, Cuba.

The Warrior (2001, UK/France/Germany) takes places in feudal India. A warrior, working for a lord as an executioner, destroys entire villages and kills the defenseless and the poor on behalf of the lord. The film illustrates the challenges associated with breaking the vicious cycle of violence.

Abuse

Men who abuse their wives are also likely to abuse their children. Domestic violence can be found in the intriguing film *3-Iron* (2004, South Korea). Alcohol or other drugs are commonly involved in cases of domestic violence, and this relationship is clearly present in *Once Were Warriors* (1994, New Zealand). This remarkable film documents the life of a New Zealand Maori family and the devastating effects of alcoholism and domestic violence on every member of the family, including the husband/father/perpetrator. The film is especially effective in portraying the effects of domestic violence on the children in the family: One son responds by returning to his Maori roots, while a sensitive, poetry-writing daughter responds by committing suicide.

Some of the most troubling portrayals of rape occur in those films in which rape is presented as a woman's fantasy, or in those films in which a woman who is being raped becomes aroused by the experience or attracted to the rapist. These themes

---

 Additional Questions for Discussion (*Once Were Warriors*)

- What role does alcoholism play in the violence we witness in this family?
- To what extent is violence an important part of Maori culture?
- Should a therapist be sensitive to the fact that family violence may believed to be appropriate and justified in some cultures?
- If you were Beth's therapist, would you actively encourage her to leave Jake, or would you leave this decision to Beth (knowing she has always decided to stay with him in the past)?

are found in two otherwise remarkable movies, Pedro Almodóvar's *Tie Me Up! Tie Me Down!* (1990, Spain) and Lina Wertmuller's *Swept Away* (1974, Italy).

If there was ever a character who is a victim of abuse, it would be Lilja in *Lilja 4-Ever* (2002). This poignant Danish/Swedish film develops the character of Lilja, a 16-year-old girl who seems to encounter just about every form of abuse and exploitation a person can experience. She is lied to and abandoned by her mother, rejected by her family, manipulated and sold into prostitution by a man she had hoped to live with, gang raped, physically and sexually abused, and forced to work as an unpaid prostitute. She is completely tossed away by society as the viewer clearly sees at the onset of the film when Lilja is depicted walking the streets, bloodied and beaten up, with no safe place or person to turn to. Nevertheless, Lilja does not take on the victim role of helplessness and fear, but instead pushes forward. Her resiliency is commendable and inspirational, but she eventually reaches a breaking point and begins to contemplate suicide.

The impact of sexual abuse in childhood on adult life is portrayed in two excellent films, *The Celebration* (1998, Denmark/Sweden) and *Don't Tell* (2005, Italy/UK/France/Spain). The former depicts a dramatic announcement and confrontation of the father/perpetrator during his 60th birthday celebration in the presence of a host of extended family members. This film was done according to a film movement and style called **Dogme**, popularized and set forth by Lars von Trier, in which filmmakers abide by certain rules for a more pure film, such as no nondiegetic sound (sound that is added after filming) and no special effects. *Don't Tell* is a powerful depiction of the secrecy and shame surrounding sexual abuse, the role of secrets, and the horror that lies behind facades of normalcy. The film also depicts the enabling role of a spouse: "It's a vice. He doesn't want to hurt you. He's sick" (says the mother as she enables her abusing spouse and rationalizes his behavior).

"I've just never understood why you did it."

"It was all you were good for."

Christian, referring to his father's sexual abuse, and the father's arrogant reaction, in *The Celebration* (1998)

---

5 x 2 (2004, France) explores the relationship of a couple in five stages, beginning at their divorce and flashing backward to when they first met. There are two ambiguous rape scenes in the film; however, most viewers would dismiss the ambiguity and clearly regard the behaviors depicted as rape. One occurs when the couple meets up after having been separated for a year and go to a hotel room to have sex. She is reluctant and passive, and he is animalistic; she wants him to stop after they begin, but he continues and rapes her. In another scene, immediately following his neglect of her on their wedding night, she meets a stranger who after some pleasant dialogue forces himself on her and prevents her from getting away, and she gives in to him.

Many films depict the neglect of children by their parents. One particularly striking film

Critical Thinking Questions

- Some movies (e.g., *Pulp Fiction*, 1994) depict people who commit extremely violent acts but do not suffer the consequences. What kind of meaning and impact does this have on the viewer?
- Do therapists have an obligation to respect cultural values and practices that may be harmful or degrading (e.g., slapping children for misbehaving or female genital mutilation)?
- What is the relationship between pornography and violence against women?
- Should alcohol or drugs be considered mitigating circumstances in cases of rape or murder (e.g., *Dead Man Walking* (1995))?
- Is it possible to develop accurate "psychological profiles" that can help identify serial killers?
- Are there common factors that characterize the childhood experiences of those individuals who grow up to become serial killers?
- How do the media perpetuate violence in American society?
- Should a woman's dress or provocative behavior be treated as extenuating circumstances in a rape case?
- What conformity studies in social psychology can be used to understand the behavior of the bystanders in The Mill bar who do nothing to help Sarah Tobias in *The Accused* (1988)?
- What steps could police officers and hospitals take to ensure rape victims are treated humanely and compassionately?
- In *Mystic River* (2003), how different would Dave (Tim Robbins) be on an emotional and behavioral level if he had not gotten in the car?

in which neglect plays an important role is the Russian film *The Return* (2003). Two boys are abandoned and neglected by their father for 12 years, then suddenly and without warning the father returns. He is quick to leave them again for business, but then changes plans and takes his sons on a trip. The boys are pushed physically and emotionally to survive his challenges (e.g., they are left to do the work of figuring out how to set up a tent, push a car out of the mud, and row a boat in challenging waters) and continued abandonment (e.g., one boy is left in the middle of nowhere in the pouring rain because he asked too many questions about fishing). The father is an enigma throughout the film: Taciturn in speech with comments of "get in" and "get out," cryptic in his behavior, and secretive about his occupation. Among many other themes, one theme is clear: Many issues arise from abandonment and neglect by a parent, and one cannot simply "return" and expect everything to be normal. A mother neglecting her children due to her mental illness and her desperate quest for a man appears in *Something Like Happiness* (2005, Czech Republic).

Nobody Knows (2004, Japan) is based on real events concerning four children (the oldest being 12) who are abandoned by their mother and left to raise themselves. This is one of the most detailed depictions of the realities and struggles of abandonment in cinema history.

Further Exploration

If you have time to read just one book relevant to this chapter, make it:

Wekerle, C., Miller, A. L., Wolfe, D. A., & Spindel, C. B. (2006). *Childhood maltreatment.* Cambridge, MA: Hogrefe & Huber Publishers.

If you only have time for one article, read:

Babcock, J. C., Green, C. E., & Robie, C. (2004). Does batterers' treatment work? A meta-analytic review of domestic violence treatment. *Clinical Psychology Review, 23*, 1023–1053.

Authors* Picks

Violence and Physical and Sexual Abuse

- *Once Were Warriors* (1994)
- *A History of Violence* (2005)
- *A Clockwork Orange* (1971)
- *Hotel Rwanda* (2004)
- *City of God* (2003)
- *Kill Bill: Vol. 1 and Vol. 2* (2003, 2004)
- *Schindler's List* (1993)
- *Mystic River* (2003)
- *The Accused* (1988)
- *Monster* (2003)

Chapter 15

Treatment

"She was fifteen years old, going on thirty-five, Doc, and she told me she was eighteen, she was plenty willing, I practically had to take to sewing my pants shut..., I don't think it's crazy at all and I don't think you do either. No man alive could resist that... and that's why I got into jail to begin with. And now they're telling me I'm crazy over here because I don't sit there like a goddamn vegetable. Don't make a bit of sense to me. If that's what being crazy is, then I'm senseless, out of it, gone-down-the-road, wacko. But no more, no less, that's it."
Randle P. McMurphy responds to a psychiatric interview in *One Flew over the Cuckoo's Nest* (1975)

Questions to Consider While Watching *One Flew over the Cuckoo's Nest*

- Is the stereotype of psychiatric treatment presented in *One Flew over the Cuckoo's Nest* still accurate? Was it at the time?
- Can you identify the theoretical position that links Billy's suicide with an intrusive, overly protective parent?
- How common is it for prisoners to evade punishment in the criminal justice system by entering the mental health system?
- The orderlies and aides in the film appear indifferent and apathetic. What are the entry-level wages for similar positions in your state?
- How would Paul Newman's title character in *Cool Hand Luke* (1967) have fared if he had been transferred to the mental health system?
- Chief Bromden chooses to murder McMurphy rather than have him beaten by the system. Is this a true mercy killing? Is it justified?
- How likely is it that McMurphy's lobotomy would have altered his personality? What is the neurological basis for the personality changes that accompany lobotomy?
- If you were an attendant working at the hospital when the ward psychiatrist recommended a lobotomy, would you have tried to stop it? What political and social tools could you have used?

Patient Evaluation

Patient's stated reason for coming: "I figured the funny farm couldn't be any worse than a chain gang."

History of the present illness: Randle Patrick McMurphy is a 35-year-old Caucasian male, never married, who presents with a long history of minor legal problems dating back to his adolescence. He was awarded a distinguished service cross for leading an escape from a Communist prison camp during the Korean War, but he also received a dishonorable discharge for insubordination, and he has been involved in a series of street brawls and barroom fights since his discharge from the military. He was recently arrested for statutory rape and sentenced to two years of hard labor in the Rivermead Correctional Facility. While at Rivermead, his behavior became increasingly erratic and "goofy," and he was sent to the state hospital for observation, evaluation, and treatment.

Past psychiatric illness, treatment, and outcomes: Mr. McMurphy has been arrested on several occasions for public drunkenness and disturbing the peace. He was typically allowed to "sleep off" these episodes in the county jail; however, because of a conviction of statutory rape of a 15-year-old girl, he was sentenced to two years in prison. He denies any history of psychiatric or psychological treatment, although he was seen sporadically by high school counselors for truancy and problems relating to authority figures, and he has received some counseling by parole officers over the years.

Medical history: Mr. McMurphy had the usual childhood illnesses and met development milestones at the expected times. He broke his arm in a school yard altercation at age 15. He states (proudly) that he has had gonorrhea at least five times. He denies any history of hospitalization or other significant medical treatment.

Psychosocial history: Mr. McMurphy's parents separated shortly after his birth, and he was raised by a widowed aunt (his mother's sister). There were no other children in the home, and the elderly aunt was an ineffectual disciplinarian. Mr. McMurphy made good grades in high school, apparently with little effort; he left high school in the middle of the 11th grade after a high school girlfriend became pregnant. "It was time for Randle Patrick to hit the road," he says. He joined the Navy at age 18 and served for three years; however, he received a dishonorable discharge before completing his last tour of duty due to a history of frequently being absent without leave (AWOL). Since being discharged from the Navy, he has traveled widely and has worked at a series of jobs, including gardener, handyman, bouncer, massage parlor manager, car salesman, apple picker, state fair carney, and mechanic. He has never married, and his relationships with women tend to be short-term and relatively inconsequential.

Drug and alcohol history: Mr. McMurphy is candid about his history of drug use: "I've tried them all at least once." He has experimented with LSD and peyote, has snorted cocaine, and frequently uses amphetamines and barbiturates. However, alcohol remains his drug of choice, and beer and whiskey have been responsible for most of the legal problems Mr. McMurphy has experienced over the past decade. He smokes approximately one pack of unfiltered cigarettes each day.

Behavioral observations: Mr. McMurphy arrived on time for the examination. He was casually dressed. He was cheerful and talkative and seemed proud and happy to have been taken off the prison work detail. He cooperated fully with all tasks and seemed to take pride in his good performance on cognitive tasks.

Mental status examination: Mr. McMurphy's speech was rapid but not pressured. He appears to be quick-witted and mentally agile. Mood was within normal limits. There were no indications of thought disorder present. There is no evidence of suicidal ideation. Mr. McMurphy reports there were several sadistic guards at the prison: "I'll nail their balls to the wall if I ever get the chance." However, this appears to be braggadocio, and McMurphy is not believed to be a danger to self or others.

This patient was fully oriented to time, place ("the looney bin"), and person. He performed all tasks on the Mini Mental State Examination quickly and without difficulty, earning a perfect score of 30. When asked to write a sentence, the patient surprised the examiner by writing a line from Shakespeare: "A man can die but once, and let it go which way it will, he that dies this year is quit for the next." When asked to explain the significance of the line, McMurphy simply remarked, "I read it somewhere and liked it." This does not appear to be evidence of suicidal thinking.

Functional assessment: Although he never finished high school, this patient is believed to have superior intelligence. He is a group leader, and he has quickly become the dominant figure on the ward and the center of most ward activity. He has an exuberant charisma that most of the other patients find very attractive. He has worked in a wide variety of jobs and appears to be a "quick study." There are no significant work limitations, although his history of alcohol abuse may make him a high risk for some jobs (e.g., he would not be a good security guard); he may function best in a highly structured environment. He has limited social support; he is unmarried and is not aware of any living relatives. He has few hobbies and formerly spent most of his leisure time in bars. He is disliked and resented by the ward staff, who regard him as a troublemaker and the instigator of most of the recent disciplinary problems that have occurred on the ward.

Strengths: Mr. McMurphy's engaging personality is his greatest asset. He appears to be a natural leader; both men and women are attracted to his high energy, quick wit, and ebullience.

Diagnosis: 301.7 rule out antisocial personality disorder
302.2 rule out pedophilia
305.00 rule out alcohol abuse

Treatment plan: There is no clear evidence of psychopathology in this individual, and I am unable to ascertain why he was transferred from the state prison to the state hospital. He does not appear to be appropriately placed, and I will investigate other treatment alternatives.

Prognosis: Good.

One Flew Over the Cuckoo's Nest

One of the great joys associated with teaching abnormal psychology courses and using *Movies and Mental Illness* as a text is the opportunity to introduce a new generation of students to films we watched – and loved – as college students. *One Flew over the Cuckoo's Nest* (1975) is one of those films, two others are *Psycho* (1960) and *A Clockwork Orange* (1971).

Films such as *One Flew over the Cuckoo's Nest* attempt to show the human injustices that existed and are occasionally still found in the mental health system. In this classic film, once McMurphy moves from the prison system into the mental health system, he loses almost all civil rights, such as his right to refuse treatment. The issues addressed by the film are not the usual problems of large institutions such as lack of facilities, cleanliness, staff, or organizational communication. Instead, the film addresses fundamental issues of autonomy and paternalism. The treatment team has ultimate control over McMurphy's treatment and discharge. A rigid, controlling nurse, Nurse Ratched, widely regarded as one of the greatest villains in cinema history, engages in an ongoing power struggle with a patient whom she perceives as a threat to her control of the unit. She uses her position and knowledge of the system to gain control over McMurphy. McMurphy's lobotomy is the ultimate abuse of psychiatric power.

Treatment Modalities Portrayed in Films

Individual Psychotherapy

Individual psychotherapy is the most common treatment modality depicted in movies. Sometimes it is quite accurate; at other times, it is preposterous.

The most frequently portrayed theoretical orientation continues to be **psychoanalysis**, though it is also the most stereotyped approach to therapy. Both the frequency of cinematic depictions of psychotherapy and many of the stereotypes can be credited to director Woody Allen, who has portrayed psychoanalysts in his films from the late 1960s through 2003. Interestingly, the psychologist portrayal in the film *Anything Else* (2003) is one of his most stereotypic (e.g., he is a therapist who refuses to respond to important patient questions). One of the least stereotypic portrayals occurred

the previous year when Allen directed *Hollywood Ending* (2002), a film about a man hired to direct a picture being produced by his ex-wife. The protagonist develops a case of psychosomatic blindness, and his therapist is portrayed as someone who accurately diagnoses the conversion disorder and offers helpful suggestions. Other orientations illustrated by films include a humanistic and supportive approach in *Lantana* (2001), and what appears to be **transactional analysis** in *Good Will Hunting* (1997). (Note the titles of the books when Sean Maguire (Robin Williams) pins Will Hunting (Matt Damon) to the wall.) Interestingly, one of the most widely used, popular and empirically validated approaches, **cognitive-behavioral therapy**, is very rarely depicted in films.

"My father was an alcoholic. Mean fuckin' drunk. He'd come home hammered, lookin' to wail on somebody. So, I had to provoke him so he wouldn't go after my mother and little brother."

Will Hunting describing his childhood in a therapy session with Sean Maguire in *Good Will Hunting* (1997)

Antwone Fisher (2002) depicts multiple sessions of individual psychotherapy. Antwone (Derek Luke) and his psychiatrist, Dr. Jerome Davenport (Denzel Washington), slowly work through the topics of anger, physical abuse, sexual abuse, and trauma. The film is framed around the psychotherapy sessions, and the plot deepens whenever Antwone opens up in a deeper way. The sessions can be divided into phases of resistance and exploration: At first Antwone refuses to share anything, later he begins to open up, sharing his physical abuse, next his sexual abuse, and finally his feelings as he witnessed the murder of his best friend. These four therapy phases are appropriately juxtaposed with relevant narrative components.

The psychiatrist is also influenced by the therapy sessions with this patient. Dr. Davenport had not realized the full extent of his isolation, and he was not aware of how he also needed to change. Davenport is humble enough to recognize his own weaknesses as he watched his patient's courage and resilience grow.

In addition to *Antwone Fisher*, other balanced individual psychotherapy portrayals can be seen in *Good Will Hunting* (1997), *K-Pax* (2001), *The Sixth Sense* (1999), *Gothika* (2004), and *Elling* (2002), while unbalanced individual psychotherapy portrayals can be seen in *Normal* (2003), *Lantana* (2001), and *Vanilla Sky* (2001) (Niemiec & Wedding, 2006). A very good albeit brief portrayal of an Asian American therapist whose suggestions are the catalyst for a major turning point in an adolescent's life can be seen in *The Squid and the Whale* (2005).

Successful individual treatment is seen in films such as *Sybil* (1976) and *Ordinary People* (1980). In *Ordinary People*, Conrad Jarrett (Timothy Hutton), following the accidental death of his brother, begins therapy with a psychiatrist (played by Judd Hirsch) who demonstrates warmth and caring and allows his young patient to examine painful family relationships within the safety of individual therapy. In *Equus* (1977), Richard Burton plays a psychiatrist who treats a very disturbed young man played by Peter Firth. During psychotherapy, the true depth of the psychological disturbance is revealed. In some instances, as in *Best Boy* (1979), a rehabilitation program is portrayed.

David and Lisa (1962), a film based on a novel by psychiatrist Theodore Isaac Rubin, is a dated but still sensitive portrayal of a young man with a severe case of what is likely obsessive-compulsive disorder and a phobia about being touched; he becomes curious about Lisa, a young woman who presents as autistic (displaying repetitive behaviors, limited communication, sing-song responses with rhymes). The film presents David's parents in stereotypical roles (e.g., the mother is overly enmeshed in her son's life, while the father is cold and distant), and the ending is trite. These concerns aside, this film is still worth viewing and it portrays mental health professionals, and especially Dr. Swinford (Howard Da Silva), in a sympathetic light.

Films frequently present images of mental health professionals behaving unethically. For example, breaches in confidentiality are evident in *Equus* (1977), and sexual relationships between clients and mental health professionals are depicted in *Prince of Tides* (1991), *Mr. Jones* (1993), *Tin Cup* (1996) and *Bliss* (1997). A psychiatrist rapes his son's best friend in Todd Solondz's *Happiness* (1998).

The relationship between a psychologist and her patient in *Numb* (2007) is especially troubling because the boundary violations are so patently wrong (e.g., the therapist calls her patient at home, meets with him in a restaurant, is inappropriately self-disclosing, and proclaims her love for him in a crowded restaurant).

In *Prime* (2005), Meryl Streep plays Lisa Metzger, a Jewish social worker who discovers that her client Rafi Gardet (Uma Thurman) has taken a younger lover – who is identified later in therapy as Lisa's son, David Bloomberg. Rafi describes her sexual life with David in lurid detail, at one point describing his penis as "beautiful." Streep knows she should reveal this obvious dual relationship, but postpones doing so because she is intrigued and fascinated by what she is learning about her son.

Mumford (1999) is a Lawrence Kasdan film that depicts a man with dubious credentials who sets up shop as a psychologist in a small town – named Mumford. It turns out that Mumford is a former IRS agent and cocaine addict, and he is an imposter pretending to be a psychologist. He commits numerous boundary violations such as going for long walks with a patient whom he finds especially attractive and telling other townspeople intimate details about the lives of his patients; however, the movie also suggests that psychotherapy is primarily "the purchase of friendship," and that credentials and training really aren't all that important as long as one is a sympathetic listener.

"What kind of doctor are you?"
"PhD. Psychologist."
"Oh, not a real doctor."
"That's right. The fake kind."

Mumford responding with sarcasm to a common misconception

Group Psychotherapy

Manic (2003) depicts group psychotherapy on an inpatient unit for adolescents. It is accurate and appropriate as a portrayal of group intervention, perhaps helped by the inclusion of some actual psychiatric patients. The psychiatrist (Don Cheadle) has his hands full with severely depressed individuals, those who are self-injurious, threatening and violent patients, and those with explosive personalities. He attempts to include everyone in group discussions, and he cleverly reframes patient experiences in a positive, balanced way.

In stark contrast, the group therapy sessions portrayed in the film *Wilbur Wants to Kill Himself*

(2002) are disappointing and unrealistic. One of the psychiatrists is overly supportive, obsequious, and flirtatious with patients while the other psychiatrist smokes during sessions, sets himself apart from the group, and makes jokes about not wanting to be there.

Psychiatric Hospitalization

Mental health treatment settings are most often portrayed in films as capacious institutions, and their depiction is almost always negative. Psychiatric hospitals are usually filmed as dark, gloomy, and unwelcoming places with considerable background noise (often screaming), staff nurses dressed in white, and patients with nothing to do other than to walk the halls of the institution acting odd. It is immediately obvious to the viewer when a movie scene takes place in such an institutional setting. From a cinematic perspective, this stereotyped presentation makes sense inasmuch as the viewer is more likely to remember a majestic, foreboding hospital exterior than a simple clinical office. These hospitals typically have stunning architecture, curious corridors, and an interesting dayroom.

Some movies with these dreary though memorable settings include *The Snake Pit* (1948), *One Flew Over the Cuckoo's Nest* (1975), *Don Juan DeMarco* (1994), *Twelve Monkeys* (1995), *Sling Blade* (1996), *Instinct* (1999), *Girl, Interrupted* (1999), *A Beautiful Mind* (2001), *Analyze That* (2002), and *Asylum* (2005).

One Flew over the Cuckoo's Nest (1975) is the classic film that depicts the violation of human rights in mental institutions, but it was certainly not the first. *The Snake Pit* (1948) was one of the earliest films to raise consciousness about the treatment of persons with mental illness. It depicted the institution metaphorically as a zoo in which patients were fenced in, and as a place for visitors to tour, and a place where patients were "herded" into their own cages (rooms). One important difference between the two films is that the character of Virginia in *The Snake Pit* is truly mentally ill, whereas Randle Patrick McMurphy in *One Flew Over the Cuckoo's Nest* is not. *Chattahoochee* (1989) also describes the plight of those who disagree with institutional authority and power, and *Nuts* (1987) portrays a woman's struggle not to be committed to an institution.

The film *K-Pax* (2001) moved away from some of the stereotypes of the psychiatric hospital environment. It depicts an institution in New York

that has adequate light, numerous windows, and meaningful activities for both staff and patients. The patients contact and communicate easily with one other. Although the film loses this focus at times, such as when the patients begin to run about in a frenzy, their excitement is not "crazy" and random but grows out of support for one another. Overall, *K-Pax* portrays a less dehumanizing environment than many older films.

As the closing of psychiatric hospitals continues, there will be fewer institutions to portray in films, and eventually the only portrayals of massive psychiatric institutions in movies will be in period films.

A Clockwork Orange

Stanley Kubrick's *A Clockwork Orange* (1971) does not take place in a psychiatric institution, but instead at a specialized hospital running a research program for the prison system. This film remains a prototype in the cinematic exploration of the ethical issues associated with behavior therapy. In the film, Malcolm McDowell plays Alex, the leader of a vicious gang. Alex and his friends are psychopathic personalities: They thrive on violence and commit both rape and murder without any evidence of remorse. However, at the same time that audiences are repulsed by Alex's violence, they find themselves attracted by his high-spirited personality and his love of classical music.

Alex is captured after being set up by his friends, who have come to resent his authority. He is convicted of murder and sentenced to 14 years in prison; however, he is given the option of early release if he is willing to participate in a conditioning experiment. In scenes almost as horrifying as the earlier rape scenes, Alex is injected with a nausea-inducing drug and repeatedly forced to watch scenes depicting rape and violence while Beethoven symphonies are played in the background.

The conditioning proves to be highly successful, and Alex cannot even think about a violent incident without becoming ill. He is released from prison, but finds himself totally unable to cope with life on the streets. He eventually attempts suicide. While he is recovering in the hospital, a reform movement occurs in the government, and Alex is portrayed as a guinea pig who was abused by the previous administration. The treatment is reversed, and Alex is once again able to fantasize happily about rape and murder. The film dramatically presents the conundrum faced by society as it contemplates treatments that attempt to improve society by limiting personal freedom (e.g., manda-

Additional Questions for Discussion (*A Clockwork Orange*)

- Can Alex accurately be described as evil? Is the concept of evil meaningful for mental health professionals?
- How accurate are the behavior modification practices portrayed in the film? What behavioral treatments most resemble those applied to Alex?
- Are fantasies about rape or murder significant mental health problems? Under what conditions does their presence warrant intervention?
- What diagnostic label in *DSM-IV-TR* would be most appropriate for Alex? For the others in his gang?
- Is Alex treatable? If so, what theoretical orientation, treatment approach, and interventions are likely to be of most help for Alex?
- Can you think of real-life examples of situations in which health professionals have exploited prisoners?

tory injections of drugs such as **Depo-Provera** that reduce testosterone levels and diminish sex drive in men convicted of sexual crimes).

Treatment Interventions

Hypnosis

It is interesting to discuss hypnosis in a book about movies because the film viewer goes in and out of light trance states throughout the movie-viewing experience. However, we have grown so accustomed to the habit of viewing movies and television shows that we rarely realize when we have entered a trance state. Hypnosis has been portrayed in numerous films, but it is rarely given an accurate or realistic portrayal.

Hypnosis has remained a popular intervention for over 100 years and is an empirically validated intervention for many psychological and medical disorders. Hypnosis continues to fight a battle against public misconception, part of which unfortunately is perpetrated by movies (also by stage hypnotists).

The portrayal of hypnosis in films has a history almost as long as movies themselves. The portrayal, however, is predominately a negative, stereotypic one. Barrett (2006) explored the role of hypnosis in over 230 films and found the majority of the portrayals to be negative, with hypnosis being applied to seduce the subject, to bring the

subject to kill, to make the subject harm him- or herself, or to get the subject to commit a crime. She reports there are very few realistic portrayals – exceptions include *Mesmer* (1994, Austria/Canada, directed by Roger Spottiswoode) and *Equus* (1977, UK/US, directed by Sidney Lumet). In the latter film, an accurate explanation of hypnosis by a psychiatrist is depicted.

A common misconception is that hypnosis represents a form of mind control through which a person can be programmed to do things against his or her will. This myth is perpetuated by films like *The Manchurian Candidate* (1952) and its 2004 remake. In the more recent film, a character, upon hearing the designated cue word, immediately comes under the hypnotist's spell (cinematically accompanied by changes in ambient light) and is at once fully controlled by the voice of the hypnotist. Through flashbacks, other characters are shown killing while in a trance. One character is depicted going fully against his own values when he smothers his long-time lover following a trance suggestion. Of course, this is cinematic nonsense.

> "I was a damn good shrink. Nineteen years I worked with a lot of people through a lot of shit. OK, I slept with a patient or two. It's not like I didn't care about them. I loved being a doctor. I used to not charge half my patients. Then the fucking state comes along, they send in some bitch undercover, and I'm fucked. Life isn't fair, is it?"
>
> **Robin Williams reviews his life as a hypnotherapist in *Dead Again* (1991)**

In films like Kenneth Branagh's *Dead Again* (1991) and Woody Allen's *The Curse of the Jade Scorpion* (2001), hypnosis is used as a blatant form of manipulation for malevolent purposes. In the former film, a hypnotist (who is also an antiques dealer) takes advantage of vulnerable people by asking them questions in the trance state about where rare antiques can be found in their home or at their work sites; he then gives the suggestion that the person will have total amnesia for the experience. In the latter film, hypnosis is used to steal jewels; here too, subjects are told they will be totally amnestic for the hypnosis episode. Films like these convince viewers that hypnosis can be used to make people do things that are illegal, unethical, and immoral. Likewise, some films suggest that hypnosis may be painful and destructive. *The Butterfly Effect* (2003) perpetrates this misconception by having a young man replay his past under hypnosis; when he does, we see him squirming in pain, his nose bleeds, and he falls onto the floor only to become amnestic for the experience.

> "Just think of your mind as a movie. You can pause, rewind or slow down any details you want."
>
> A hypnotherapist's advice
> in *The Butterfly Effect* (2003)

Professionals are often depicted as incompetent in their use of hypnosis, such as the psychologist in *Donnie Darko* (2001) who uses hypnosis with a patient who has schizophrenia; this diagnosis would actually be a contraindication for hypnosis. The patient in *Donnie Darko* begins to masturbate while in a trance.

Even when the intent to use hypnosis is justified and well-intentioned, it is most often depicted in an overly dramatic manner; for example, in many films the hypnotic technique of "age regression" is employed and the patient is shown reliving very painful experiences or past traumatic events. The psychiatrist played by Jeff Bridges in *K-Pax* (2001) explains hypnosis, performs an induction, and begins to explore his patient's past. The patient screams in agony and nearly goes into shock. In reality, hypnosis is very rarely this dramatic.

The film *Office Space* (1999) presents an interesting dilemma in which a psychologist induces a trance, deepens the trance – and then has a heart attack and dies before he can bring the patient out of the trance state. In reality, the trance would wear off shortly if not immediately, but since this is a comedy, the character stays in the trance for days.

In each of these films, the subject is depicted as helpless and under the control of the hypnotist. These depictions ignore the well established therapeutic truism that "all hypnosis is self-hypnosis."

Medications

The first genuinely effective antipsychotic medication was **chlorpromazine** (Thorazine), first used as an antihistamine. Several compounds with similar properties were also synthesized. Thorazine was believed to be a miracle drug that would empty all of our mental hospitals. These medications did enable many patients to live once again in the community; unfortunately, they were often indiscriminately prescribed, and dosages were usually excessive. Because of a lack of knowledge about the drug and its consequences, excessive sedation and **extrapyramidal side effects** (muscle cramps of the head and neck, restless pacing or fidgeting, and stiffening of muscular activity in the face, body, arms, and legs) were common. In *One Flew over the Cuckoo's Nest* (1975), the patients receive excessive dosages of medications that sedate them and put them at high risk for debilitating side effects.

Today there are several different classifications of pharmacological agents. **Antipsychotic medications** are given to treat thought disorders, such as schizophrenia, and some mood and anxiety disorders. **Antidepressants** are given for the mood disorders, and **mood stabilizers** such as **Depakote** and **lithium** are common medication choices for bipolar disorders. **Anxiolytic** (antianxiety) medications are carefully prescribed for patients with anxiety disorders. Some of these drugs, such as Xanax, Valium, and Librium, can be addictive. These drugs are also the ones most often used in combination with alcohol and recreational drugs. The 1982 movie *I'm Dancing as Fast as I Can* stars Jill Clayburgh as the award-winning TV producer Barbara Gordon, who becomes addicted to Valium but eventually recovers.

> "You know, our bodies are capable of incredible things when they're subjected to anxiety and stress. I found my ex-best friend's cufflinks in my wife's purse one time. I couldn't get an erection for a year and a half."
>
> Inappropriate self-disclosure by a
> psychiatrist in *Garden State* (2004)

In the film *Garden State* (2004), the overly sedated protagonist, who has been taking various medications for a mood disorder for over a decade, decides on his own to discontinue taking medication after learning of the death of his mother. He prospers without the medication, meets a wonderful woman, learns to be assertive when dealing with his controlling psychiatrist father, and feels genuinely happy for the first time in years. While this film is meant to be inspirational and liberating, it also imparts an inappropriate and confusing message to countless people who are taking similar medications.

Electroconvulsive Therapy (ECT)

In the 1950s, both electroshock and insulin shock became accepted treatment methods to induce seizures, and many psychiatrists were convinced that seizures could be used to protect patients from mental illness. By the 1960s, electrical stimulation, called **electroconvulsive therapy** (ECT), was well established as the safest way to induce seizures.

Originally, ECT was used for many psychiatric illnesses, including schizophrenia. However, more effective pharmacological approaches were ultimately developed for most of these disorders. Today, severe depression, mania, and occasionally some types of thought disorders are treated with ECT, but only when other approaches have failed. The procedure is accompanied by the administration of short-acting general anesthesia and muscle paralytic agents that prevent the muscle contractions associated with seizures. Then a very mild electrical stimulus is passed through the brain, which causes the seizure. A series of 8–10 treatments is usually administered before clinically significant results are obtained.

McDonald & Walter (2001) examined the portrayal of ECT in 22 American movies from the middle of the 20th century to the onset of the 21st century and concluded that ECT was initially portrayed as a severe but helpful treatment, however, progressed to being represented as a negative and cruel treatment. In one study, after viewing ECT portrayed in movies, medical students were more likely to talk friends and family out of receiving ECT and one third reported a decrement in their support for ECT (Walter, et al., 2002).

In the past, ECT was used frequently and indiscriminately, often with excessive voltage. In films such as *One Flew Over the Cuckoo's Nest* (1975) and *An Angel at My Table* (1990), ECT is pictured as a painful, lengthy treatment, with the hapless patient strapped to a table by sadistic attendants. In reality, contemporary use of ECT takes about 5–10 minutes from start to finish and rarely results in a visible seizure. There are also very clear practice guidelines that help physicians identify when ECT is appropriate and when it is not. In *One Flew Over the Cuckoo's Nest,* ECT was used as punishment

for patients who challenged the authority of Nurse Ratched. Its use was just as inappropriate when used to treat New Zealand novelist Janet Frame, as portrayed in *An Angel at My Table*. Another controversial film biography, *Frances* (1982), depicts the 1930s Hollywood actress Frances Farmer and her confinement in mental institutions for rebellious behavior. Frances, played by Jessica Lange, received both shock treatment and a lobotomy.

In *A Beautiful Mind* (2001), John Nash receives **insulin shock therapy** and not ECT, although many viewers don't make this distinction. When insulin shock therapy is used, insulin is injected, the body goes into a state of shock and convulsions ensue. *A Beautiful Mind* shows Nash receiving multiple treatments over several weeks.

Treatment of Different Disorders

Treatment of Anxiety Disorders

There are numerous approaches to the treatment of anxiety, and all of them are at least partially efficacious. Education can be a critical first step in therapy, and it is often tremendously therapeutic for the patient with an anxiety disorder simply to realize that he or she is not going insane and that these disorders are commonplace and often readily respond to treatment. In addition, patients need to realize that their symptoms are not life-threatening, that they will not pass out or fall down no matter how bad they feel, and that many people experience similar symptoms but assign different labels (**attributions**) to these sensations (e.g., a tingling sensation in your stomach before you give a speech can be interpreted as anticipatory excitement and a signal that you're going to do a good job).

It is also critical to carefully assess a patient's prior use of alcohol or drugs as ways of coping with his or her anxiety symptoms. Many of these patients have learned to use substances to modulate their anxiety levels: For example, alcoholism is common in veterans with posttraumatic stress disorders (as portrayed in *Born on the Fourth of July*). In addition, it is necessary to assess the consumption of coffee, soft drinks, and nicotine. All three exacerbate the symptoms of anxiety.

Psychotherapy may be helpful with some patients with anxiety. In particular, behavior therapy appears to be the treatment of choice for many phobic disorders, and some patients have been helped by behavioral methods after years of insight therapy. Almost all behavior therapies will involve exposure to the feared stimulus or situation. *In vivo* **exposure with response prevention** is an empirically-validated approach (and the treatment of choice for OCD and other anxiety disorders) involving a graduated exposure hierarchy of anxiety-arousing stimuli where the patient is prevented from avoiding the stimulus and must use anxiety management coping skills instead. **Flooding** and **implosion** are related techniques that involve massive exposure to the feared stimuli. Mindfulness, relaxation training, and hypnosis may also be used as adjunctive therapies in the treatment of anxiety.

Movies themselves can be powerful stimuli when developing an **exposure hierarchy** for a person with an anxiety disorder. Particular movies can be tailored to the individual's fears, obsessions, and dysfunctional belief patterns. The individual will typically be asked to watch a film or a particular scene (often repeatedly) while practicing anxiety management techniques. For example, a person with a contamination fear of dirt might be asked to watch a war film where dirt, dust, and blood are prominent, such as *Saving Private Ryan* (1998), and the individual will be trained to use coping skills to manage their anxiety as it rises during parts of the film. The individual who is homophobic and afraid of contamination with the AIDS virus might be asked to watch *Kissing Jessica Stein* (2002) and *The Birdcage* (1995), and those afraid of getting in an accident or seeing an accident could watch action films containing multiple crashes such as the *Lethal Weapon* series (1987, 1989, 1992, 1998). Other films that could potentially be used for desensitization purposes include *Cast Away* (2000), *Philadelphia* (1993), and *Super Size Me* (2004) for fear of, respectively, isolation, contamination, and throwing up in public. Children or adolescents afraid of being rejected might be asked to watch *A Bug's Life* (1998), *Shrek* (2001), or *Hercules* (1997), and those afraid of the dark might watch particular scenes from *Harry Potter and the Sorcerer's Stone* (2001) or its sequels. The use of films in therapy is explored further in Wedding and Niemiec (2003).

Cognitive therapy, which includes the practice of **cognitive restructuring**, is often employed in the treatment of anxiety disorders. Cognitive therapy helps patients identify and understand the internal statements and irrational thoughts that may trigger arousal in certain situations and settings (Beck & Emery, 1985). Medication may also be used as a treatment or, more commonly, as an adjunct to therapy. Widely used classes of drugs include **beta-blockers** (often used to treat social phobias) **tricyclic antidepressants**

(often used for panic disorder and agoraphobia) and **selective serotonin reuptake inhibitors** (SSRIs) (for OCD and comorbid depression issues). **Benzodiazepines** are also widely used in the treatment of anxiety symptoms, and include diazepam (Valium), chlordiazepoxide (Librium), and alprazolam (Xanax). In addition, there is growing interest in the use of over-the-counter herbal remedies such as **Kava** (available from health food stores) and **valerian root** in the treatment of mild to moderate anxiety.

Treatment of Mood Disorders

Lithium carbonate is often the treatment of choice for the bipolar disorders. This agent is a naturally occurring element that has been found to be effective in correcting the chemical imbalance associated with this illness. No one is sure how or why lithium works, but it is believed that it either alters the neurotransmitters or inhibits viruses that affect DNA. If lithium carbonate is not effective, other mood stabilizers can be used (**Depakote**).

Cognitive-behavioral therapy (CBT), which addresses a client's defective thinking process, is particularly helpful for patients with depression. This approach to psychotherapy forces the patient to examine the evidence for his or her negative beliefs, and the therapist encourages patients to reframe their beliefs based on the evidence presented in therapy. Once beliefs change, patients begin to perceive the world in a more balanced way, which has an impact on future behaviors. This technique has been very successful and is generally believed to be as efficacious as antidepressants in the treatment of mild to moderate depression.

Treatment of Alcoholism

The first stage of treatment is **detoxification,** or "drying out." This process can vary from several days to a month in duration and is usually extremely unpleasant for the person involved. Vitamins are routinely prescribed in the treatment of addictions. At one time, tranquilizers (primarily Librium and Valium) were often administered to help an individual cope with the physiological distress that accompanies detoxification; however, this approach to treatment has always been controversial and is less common now.

Antabuse (disulfiram) blocks the metabolism of alcohol and may help some alcoholics avoid resumption of drinking after detoxification. An individual taking Antibuse will become violently ill if exposed to even a very small amount of alcohol and will experience nausea, vomiting, sweating, and accelerated respiration and heart rate. Antibuse is most useful in the first months of sobriety, when the craving for alcohol is most intense.

"The last time I seen my father, he was blind and diseased from drinking. And every time he put the bottle to his mouth, he don't suck out of it, it sucks out of him until he shrunk so wrinkled and yellow even the dogs didn't know him."

Chief Bromden describes
his father's alcoholism in
One Flew Over the Cuckoo's Nest (1975)

Alcoholics Anonymous, a self-help fellowship founded in 1935, is widely regarded as an important part of treatment for most alcoholics. More than a million people in the U.S. belong to this self-help group, and there are more than 1.5 million members worldwide. Almost every town of any size has a local chapter of Alcoholics Anonymous, and many large cities have meetings in different chapters every evening of the week. These meetings involve self-disclosure, social support, and a commitment to the disease model of alcoholism. The well-known 12 Steps of Alcoholics Anonymous are presented in Table 7.3 of Chapter 7. The founding of Alcoholics Anonymous is described in the film *My Name Is Bill W.* (1989), and the movie *Drunks* (1995) offers an opportunity to see a realistic presentation of how an AA meeting is conducted.

Al-Anon is a related group for families and friends of alcoholics. The program is modeled on Alcoholics Anonymous and uses a 12-step model. **Alateen** is a similar affiliated group designed to serve teenage children of alcoholic parents.

Although most providers in the substance abuse community are quick to praise the good work done by Alcoholics Anonymous, there is little empirical evidence supporting the program. In addition, some individuals find the quasi-religious philosophy of the organization distasteful.

Treatment of Drug Addiction

Before treatment can begin, **detoxification** must occur. In general, the severity of detoxification from narcotic drugs depends on the health status of the addict and the purity of the drugs he or she has been taking. Withdrawal from barbiturates tends to be more serious than withdrawal from heroin, cocaine, or alcohol. Detoxification is potentially life threatening and should occur in a structured medical setting. The film *Quitting* (2001) depicts the challenges and pain of detoxifying outside of a structured hospital environment. Anxiolytics such as Valium, Librium, and Xanax are sometimes used to reduce the severity of the effects of detoxification.

Methadone is a synthetic narcotic that is taken orally rather than injected. It is administered on a daily basis, usually in an outpatient setting. The drug itself is addicting; however, it is longer lasting, and with daily use the addict is able to avoid the symptoms of withdrawal that typically occur a few hours after use of drugs such as heroin. In addition, the drug blocks the reinforcing effects of other narcotics. With methadone treatment, there is a reduction in intravenous drug use and a concomitant reduction in crime. In addition, the likelihood of needle sharing and AIDS is dramatically reduced. Despite these benefits, methadone maintenance programs remain controversial, and there are some clear disadvantages to methadone maintenance therapy, including the development of a large underground market for methadone, the fact that many people drop out of methadone treatment because of side effects (sweating, impotence, constipation, and insomnia), and the fact that many people are philosophically offended by the idea of giving addicts another addictive drug in the name of treatment.

Some programs have used **narcotic antagonists** such as **naloxone** or **naltrexone** to treat opioid addiction. These drugs block the reinforcing effects of narcotics; in effect, the addict may still take drugs but they no longer produce a "high." However, because of the potential for precipitating withdrawal reactions, these programs are complex and costly and require medical supervision.

Programs such as **Narcotics Anonymous** (NA), modeled after Alcoholics Anonymous, advocate total abstinence from drugs. These programs are often associated with therapeutic communities in which a highly structured program and frequent group therapy are core components of treatment. Former addicts who serve as powerful role models for residents often staff these programs. Therapy is often confrontational and may involve spouses and significant others. The film *Clean and Sober* (1988) presents an excellent example of the kind of treatment that occurs in a **therapeutic community**, with Morgan Freeman in the role of a recovered addict and counselor.

Antidepressant medications are sometimes used to assist in the treatment of amphetamine or cocaine addiction. However, in general, all treatment programs for stimulant addiction have unimpressive success records.

The success of smoking cessation programs has been more notable. Nicotine gum and transdermal nicotine patches hold considerable promise as important aids in comprehensive treatment packages. Behavior modification and hypnosis are two other techniques that have helped many individuals overcome their addiction to nicotine.

Despite the success of some treatment programs, it is clear that the only real solution to the drug problem is prevention. Prevention will involve limiting the flow of drugs to the US and educating the public about the deleterious effects of drug use.

Assisted Suicide

Two very powerful films have addressed the issue of assisted suicide: Clint Eastwood's *Million Dollar Baby* (2004) and Alejandro Amenábar's *The Sea Inside* (2004). We highly recommend both movies.

"I can't be like this, Frankie. Not after what I've done. I've seen the world. People chanted my name. Well, not my name... some damn name you gave me. But they were chanting for me. I was in magazines. You think I ever dreamed that'd happen? I was born two pounds, one-and-a-half ounces. Daddy used to tell me I'd fight my way into this world, and I'd fight my way out. That's all I wanna do, Frankie. I just don't wanna fight you to do it. I got what I needed. I got it all. Don't let 'em keep taking it away from me. Don't let me lie here 'till I can't hear those people chanting no more."

Maggie Fitzgerald in
Million Dollar Baby (2004)

Eastwood's film tells the story of Maggie Fitzgerald (Hillary Swank), a waitress from a poor and dysfunctional family who becomes a champion prize fighter. She is paralyzed after an angry opponent hits her while her back is turned. She subsequently decides that life is not worth living if she is bedridden, and she cajoles her coach (Eastwood) into helping her end her life. In a fascinating critical review of this film in *PsycCRITIQUES: Contemporary Psychology – APA Review of Books*, Kris Hagglund (2005) noted, "individuals who sustain traumatic, body-altering injuries do not want to die. Filmmakers and other artists have historically and irresponsibly perpetuated this myth."

"The person who really loves me will be the one who helps me die. That's love, Rosa. That's love."

Ramón Sampedro in *The Sea Inside* (2004)

The Sea Inside (2004), based on a true story, stars Javier Bardem as Ramón Sampedro, a man who became totally paralyzed after a teenage diving accident. Sampedro wants to die, but the Spanish government and his family won't let him. He spends three decades making his case.

Ethical Issues and the Right to Humane Treatment

As noted earlier, *One Flew Over the Cuckoo's Nest* was not the first movie to portray patients' lack of control over treatment. One of the first movies to address mental illness seriously was *The Snake Pit* (1948), a film directed by Anatole Litvak that stars Olivia de Havilland as Virginia Stuart Cunningham. The movie portrays a woman trying to overcome her illness in a crowded mental institution. The horrifying conditions portrayed in the film actually mobilized state legislators to improve the level of care provided in institutions. This movie was especially effective in portraying the lack of power females have traditionally had in inpatient psychiatric settings. In *The Snake Pit*, Virginia truly has a mental illness and is taken for treatment by a caring husband. However, many women who did not have mental illnesses were placed in psychiatric hospitals and kept there as a convenience for husbands who had grown tired of them (Geller & Harris, 1994).

Another powerful film, *Chattahoochee* (1990), not only depicts the horrible conditions in a Florida state hospital during the 1950s but also one patient's campaign to change these conditions. In this film, Korean War veteran Emmett Foley (played by Gary Oldman) loses many of his rights because of his protests against authority. This film, based on a true story, begins when Emmett Foley becomes depressed by unemployment and tries to provoke the police into killing him after he shoots up the neighborhood. He wants his wife to receive his life insurance (which she would be denied if he committed suicide). Instead, he is sent to Chattahoochee, a prison for people with mental illness. The conditions in Chattahoochee are deplorable. With the support of his friend Walker Benson (Dennis Hopper), he begins a letter-writing campaign to protest against the conditions. His writing privileges are taken away, and he starts writing in a Bible and surreptitiously slipping pages to his sister. A state commission is formed, hearings are held, and conditions improve as a result.

The Jacket (2005) stars Adrien Brody playing the role of Jack Starks, a veteran who sustains a head injury in the Iraq war, enters into a coma, and is taken for dead; however, a hospital attendant notices eye movement, and eventually Brody's character comes out of his coma, although he still has a profound retrograde amnesia. He is wrongly accused of killing a police office, but is found to be not guilty by reason of insanity. He is sent to a psychiatric institute "for the criminally insane" run by Dr. Thomas Becker (Kris Kristofferson), a sadistic psychiatrist. Therapy consists of putting Brody in a wet, hot straitjacket and keeping him in a morgue like room, ostensibly to recreate the sensation of being in the womb. The hospital staff are presented as controlling and abusive, and the film perpetuates the myth that psychiatric hospitals are dangerous places run by inhumane and uncaring staff; in fact, the exact opposite is true, and the individuals who work in these settings include some of the finest people we know.

Ian McKellen is masterful in his role as a sadistic psychiatrist, Dr. Peter Cleave, in *Asylum* (2005). The film is based on a Patrick McGrath novel and takes place in an old, gothic psychiatric hospital. A new psychiatrist, Dr. Max Raphael (Hugh Bonneville), has arrived to take over management of the hospital – the job Peter Cleave

craved – and his wife and young son accompany him. The son befriends a patient, a man who has been institutionalized because he murdered his wife; his diagnosis is "severe personality disorder with features of morbid jealousy." Natasha Richardson plays Stella, the boy's bored mother, and she is soon involved in a torrid affair with the patient. Although we liked the film, we were troubled by the subtext suggesting that psychiatric hospitals are dangerous places staffed by indifferent attendants and cruel professionals.

"I want you to understand what's going to happen next. The shock will wear off, and it will be replaced by a devastating grief. In time, you will come to terms with what you have done and you'll just be very, very sad. And that sadness will stay with you for the rest of your life."

Psychiatrist Max Raphael tells his wife what to expect after the accidental drowning of their son in *Asylum* (2005)

Movies illustrate the ongoing struggles for civil and human rights that have occurred in the mental health system. They also reflect the prevailing stigma affecting persons with mental illness. Our language characterizes individuals with these illnesses as crazy, nuts, or wacky. The people who treat them are called shrinks, do-gooders, or bleeding hearts (Trachtenberg, 1986). The media portray patients as clowns, buffoons, or harmless eccentrics (Hyler, Gabbard, & Schneider, 1991). In *The Dream Team* (1989) and *The Couch Trip* (1988), a little bit of freedom proves adequate to cure mental illness. Other films, such as *Psycho* (1960) and its remakes and sequels, depict individuals with mental illnesses as homicidal maniacs. In John Carpenter's *Halloween* series, an escaped psychiatric patient serially kills teenagers who have engaged in sexual experimentation. When Tommy Lee Wallace directed *Halloween III* (1982), the central villain was portrayed as a madman toy maker who made wicked Halloween masks programmed to harm children. However, the original madman on the loose from a mental hospital returned in *Halloween IV* and *V* (1988, 1989). These films and others have misled the public about the dangerousness of psychiatric patients.

International Films: Treatment

King of Hearts (1966) is a charming French film that has achieved cult status. The movie stars a young Alan Bates as a Scottish soldier sent into a small French village during World War I to disarm a bomb. He discovers that the villagers have all fled, and the inmates of a local psychiatric hospital are running the town. While we enjoyed the film, it does perpetuate the myth that people with mental illness are simply harmless eccentrics.

House of Fools (2002, Russia/France) is a film reminiscent of *King of Hearts* but based on a true story. It takes place in a psychiatric institution in a war-torn country (Chechnya). When the town is about to be taken over by the enemy, the staff evacuate, the patients stay, and the soldiers find refuge in the hospital. The movie raises questions about the insanity of war, and it uses the hospital as a metaphor for the insanity of a world at war.

Intimate Strangers (2004) is a French film built around the idea that accountants and psychotherapists have a lot in common. A woman in a troubled marriage is looking for the office of a psychiatrist she is visiting for the first time when she mistakenly enters the office of a timid accountant just down the hall. She begins to share intimate details about her troubled marriage (e.g., her husband wants her to have sex with other men so he can watch), but the accountant initially does not interrupt – he is in a profession in which people needing tax advice about issues like divorce often reveal very personal facts about their private lives. After some time, it becomes clear that the woman believes she is confiding in a psychiatrist, but by this time the accountant is so intrigued by her story that he is loath to come clean about his own identity. When he does explain the misunderstanding, the patient is upset – but continues to come for therapy sessions because she is benefiting from them and the patient and "therapist" have a good connection with one another. In their review of this film for *PsycCRITIQUES: Contemporary Psychology – APA Review of Books*, John C. Norcross and his son, Jonathan Norcross, remark:

> This film, drawing on the Freudian tradition, can be encountered on a number of levels. As a public portrayal of insight-oriented psychotherapy, the film fails miserably. The film inaccurately depicts psychoanalytic treatment... and reinforces four pervasive stereotypes: That anyone can do psychotherapy; that psychotherapy largely consists of a patient's monologue with occasional open-ended questions from the

Critical Thinking Questions

- Why do films continue to perpetuate psychotherapy misconceptions such as "only psychiatrists practice psychotherapy" and "the most common type of treatment for mental disorders is psychoanalysis?"
- How common is it for a mental health professional to commit a boundary violation? Why is this so frequently depicted in movies?
- What psychotherapy techniques and interventions are rarely portrayed?
- What diagnostic categories are given the most accurate and realistic treatment approach in movies?
- It has been suggested that on a college campus, the only thing separating harmless eccentricity from mental illness is tenure. How does one's environment shape expectations about what is or is not appropriate behavior?
- Vincent van Gogh was a genius, but he was also mentally ill, and his life was tragically cut short by suicide. Would the world be better off if this illness had been diagnosed and treated? Would you take the same position if you knew psychotropic medication would rob van Gogh of his creative spirit and his passion for art?
- Is it ever ethical to treat someone who refuses treatment? If so, who should be empowered to make these decisions?
- There is a clear asymmetry of power and knowledge when doctors meet with family members to discuss treatment options. How does this fact influence the principles of informed consent and patient autonomy?
- Do you think it is ethical to offer early release to prisoners who have committed sexual offenses if they allow themselves to be castrated? What if they simply agree to take medications that eliminate all sexual drive? Are the courts ever justified in mandating treatments of this sort?
- What is the appropriate and ethical response if a therapist discovers a client is dating the therapist's son, as occurs in *Prime* (2005)?
- Movies like *Mumford* (1999) and *Intimate Strangers* (2004) suggest that psychotherapy mainly requires being warm, empathic and caring, and anyone can do it without special training and credentials. Is therapy just "the purchase of friendship"? Is it plausible that a former IRS agent or a tax attorney could impersonate a therapist over many sessions? Why or why not?
- What can mental health professionals (or the public) do to change the stereotypes and misconceptions often perpetuated in films?

psychotherapist; that an erotic transference will inevitably develop between an attractive female patient and a distinguished male therapist; and that… commonsense methods are superior to psychoanalytic treatment in modifying behavior… On the other hand, as a public representation of the intimacy of psychotherapy, the film succeeds admirably. *Intimate Strangers* provides a riveting example of the constructive power of (quasi) psychotherapy and… the centrality of an affirming, empathic relationship to a successful outcome. Love heals both the patient and the psychotherapist. Moreover, the film underscores that therapy can be one rare and privileged place where people can gradually live without secrets and lies.

Treatment

- *K-Pax* (2001)
- *Ordinary People* (1980)
- *Intimate Strangers* (2004)
- *Good Will Hunting* (1997)
- *The Cabinet of Dr. Caligary* (1920)
- *David and Lisa* (1962)
- *One Flew over the Cuckoo's Nest* (1975)
- *The Snake Pit* (1948)
- *Lars and the Real Girl* (2007)
- *Antwone Fisher* (2002)

Further Exploration

If you have time to read just one book relevant to this chapter, make it:

Corrigan, P. W., Mueser, K. T., Bond, G. R., Drake, R. E., & Solomon, P. (2008). *Principles and practices of psychiatric rehabilitation: An empirical approach.* New York: Guilford.

If you only have time for one article, read:

Kazdin, A. E. (2008). Evidence-based treatments and delivery of psychological services: Shifting our emphases to increase impact. *Psychological Services, 5,* 201–215.

Appendix A

The American Film Institute's Top 50 Heroes and Villains[1]

Heroes

1. **Atticus Finch**
   To Kill a Mockingbird
2. **Indiana Jones**
   Raiders of the Lost Ark
3. **James Bond**
   Dr. No
4. **Rick Blaine**
   Casablanca
5. **Will Kane**
   High Noon
6. **Clarice Starling**
   The Silence of the Lambs
7. **Rocky Balboa**
   Rocky
8. **Ellen Ripley**
   Aliens
9. **George Bailey**
   It's a Wonderful Life
10. **T. E. Lawrence**
    Lawrence of Arabia
11. **Jefferson Smith**
    Mr. Smith Goes to Washington
12. **Tom Joad**
    The Grapes of Wrath
13. **Oskar Schindler**
    Schindler's List
14. **Han Solo**
    Star Wars
15. **Norma Rae Webster**
    Norma Rae
16. **Shane**
    Shane
17. **Harry Callahan**
    Dirty Harry
18. **Robin Hood**
    The Adventures of Robin Hood
19. **Virgil Tibbs**
    In The Heat of the Night
20. **Butch Cassidy & the Sundance Kid**
    Butch Cassidy & the Sundance Kid
21. **Mahatma Gandhi**
    Gandhi
22. **Spartacus**
    Spartacus

Villains

1. **Dr. Hannibal Lecter**
   The Silence of the Lambs
2. **Norman Bates**
   Psycho
3. **Darth Vader**
   The Empire Strikes Back
4. **The Wicked Witch of the West**
   The Wizard of Oz
5. **Nurse Ratched**
   One Flew Over the Cuckoo's Nest
6. **Mr. Potter**
   It's a Wonderful Life
7. **Alex Forrest**
   Fatal Attraction
8. **Phyllis Dietrichson**
   Double Indemnity
9. **Regan MacNeil**
   The Exorcist
10. **The Queen**
    Snow White and the Seven Dwarfs
11. **Michael Corleone**
    The Godfather: Part II
12. **Alex De Large**
    Clockwork Orange
13. **HAL 9000**
    2001: A Space Odyssey
14. **The Alien**
    Alien
15. **Amon Goeth**
    Schindler's List
16. **Noah Cross**
    Chinatown
17. **Annie Wilkes**
    Misery
18. **The Shark**
    Jaws
19. **Captain Bligh**
    Mutiny on the Bounty
20. **Man**
    Bambi
21. **Mrs. John Iselin**
    The Manchurian Candidate
22. **Terminator**
    The Terminator

23. **Terry Malloy**
    On the Waterfront
24. **Thelma Dickerson & Louise Sawyer**
    Thelma & Louise
25. **Lou Gehrig**
    The Pride of the Yankees
26. **Superman**
    Superman
27. **Bob Woodward & Carl Bernstein**
    All The President's Men
28. **Juror #8**
    12 Angry Men
29. **General George Patton**
    Patton
30. **Luke Jackson**
    Cool Hand Luke
31. **Erin Brockovich**
    Erin Brockovich
32. **Philip Marlowe**
    The Big Sleep
33. **Marge Gunderson**
    Fargo
34. **Tarzan**
    Tarzan the Ape Man
35. **Alvin York**
    Sergeant York
36. **Rooster Cogburn**
    True Grit
37. **Obi-Wan Kenobi**
    Star Wars
38. **The Tramp**
    City Lights
39. **Lassie**
    Lassie Come Home
40. **Frank Serpico**
    Serpico
41. **Arthur Chipping**
    Goodbye, Mr. Chips
42. **Father Edward**
    Boys Town
43. **Moses**
    The Ten Commandments
44. **Jimmy "Popeye" Doyle**
    The French Connection
45. **Zorro**
    The Mark of Zorro
46. **Batman**
    Batman
47. **Karen Silkwood**
    Silkwood
48. **Terminator**
    Terminator 2: Judgment Day
49. **Andrew Beckett**
    Philadelphia
50. **General Maximus Decimus Meridus**
    Gladiator

23. **Eve Harrington**
    All About Eve
24. **Gordon Gekko**
    Wall Street
25. **Jack Torrance**
    The Shining
26. **Cody Jarrett**
    White Heat
27. **Martians**
    The War of the Worlds
28. **Max Cady**
    Cape Fear
29. **Reverend Harry Powell**
    The Night of the Hunter
30. **Travis Bickle**
    Taxi Driver
31. **Mrs. Danvers**
    Rebecca
32. **Clyde Barrow & Bonnie Parker**
    Bonnie and Clyde
33. **Count Dracula**
    Dracula
34. **Dr. Szell**
    Marathon Man
35. **J.J. Hunsecker**
    Sweet Smell of Success
36. **Frank Booth**
    Blue Velvet
37. **Harry Lime**
    The Third Man
38. **Caesar Enrico Bandello**
    Little Caesar
39. **Cruella De Vil**
    One Hundred and One Dalmatians
40. **Freddy Krueger**
    A Nightmare on Elm Street
41. **Joan Crawford**
    Mommie Dearest
42. **Tom Powers**
    The Public Enemy
43. **Regina Giddens**
    The Little Foxes
44. **Baby Jane Hudson**
    Whatever Happened to Baby Jane
45. **The Joker**
    Batman
46. **Hans Gruber**
    Die Hard
47. **Tony Montana**
    Scarface
48. **Verbal Kint**
    The Usual Suspects
49. **Auric Goldfinger**
    Goldfinger
50. **Alonzo Harris**
    Training Day

1   Reprinted with permission of the American Film Institute. http://www.afi.com/tvevents/100years/handv.aspx

Appendix B

Syllabus for Sample Course that Integrates Films

Movies and Mental Illness: Understanding Psychopathology*

Course Description

This course focuses on the portrayal of mental illness in films. Representations of psychopathological states in films will be examined within the context of contemporary social issues such as stigma and discrimination. Major mental disorders will be highlighted.

Objectives

Upon completion of this course the student will be able to:
1. Discuss the social influence of films.
2. Discuss the significance of film in the public perception of mental illnesses.
3. Compare behavioral symptoms of major mental disorders.
4. Identify discrimination and stigma associated with mental disorders.
5. Analyze the portrayal of various mental illnesses in films.

Required Text

Wedding, D., Boyd, M. A. & Niemiec, R. M. (2010). *Movies and mental illness: Using films to understand psychopathology* (3rd ed.). Cambridge, MA: Hogrefe Publishing.

Learning Experiences

Seminar, dyad presentation, videos, and written papers
    Students should watch the films outside of class, preferably in small groups. All films selected are well known and will be easily available through DVD rental outlets or on the Internet. Please come to class prepared to discuss whether the film presented an accurate portrayal of the condition being discussed for the week.

(a) Tuesdays 10 am – 12)	(b) Thursdays 9–10 am	Topic	Readings
Sep 2	Sep 4	(a) Introduction to the Class (b) Films and Psychopathology	(b) Chapter 1: Films and Psychopathology
Sep 9	Sep 11	(a & b) Anxiety Disorders	(a) Chapter 2: Anxiety Disorders (b) *The Aviator* (2004)
Sep 16	Sep 18	(a & b) Dissociative Disorders and Somatoform Disorders	(a) Chapter 3: Dissociative and Somatoform Disorders (b) *Psycho* (1960)
Sep 23	Sep 25	(a & b) Psychological Stress & Physical Disorders	(a) Chapter 4: Psychological Stress & Physical Disorders (b) *The Wrestler* (2008)
Sep 30	Oct 2	(a & b) Mood Disorders	(a) Chapter 5: Mood Disorders (b) *Seven Pounds* (2008)
Oct 7	Oct 9	(a & b) Personality Disorders	(a) Chapter 6: Personality Disorders (b) *Girl, Interrupted* (1999)
Oct 14	Oct 16	(a & b) Substance Use Disorders	(a) Chapter 7: Substance Use Disorders (b) *Trainspotting* (1996)
Oct 21	Oct 23	(a) Review session (b) Midterm Examination	No readings or film
Oct 28	Oct 30	(a & b) Sexual and Gender Identity Disorders	(a) Chapter 8: Sexual and Gender Identity Disorders (b) *Boys Don't Cry* (1999)
Nov 4	Nov 6	(a & b) Schizophrenia	(a) Chapter 9: Schizophrenia (b) *A Beautiful Mind* (2001)
Nov 11	Nov 13	(a & b) Neuropsychological Disorders	(a) Chapter 10: Neuropsychological Disorders (b) *Iris* (2001)
Nov 18	Nov 20	(a & b) Disorders of Childhood and Adolescence	(a) Chapter 11: Disorders of Childhood and Adolescence (b) *Thumbsucker* (2005)
Nov 25	Nov 27	(a & b) Mental Retardation and Autism	(a) Chapter 12: Mental Retardation and Autism (b) *Rain Man* (1988) or *Dominick and Eugene* (1988)
Dec 2	Dec 4	(a & b) Sleep, Eating, Impulse Control, and Adjustment Disorders	(a) Chapter 13: Sleep, Eating, Impulse Control, and Adjustment Disorders (b) *Owning Mahowny* (2003)
Dec 9	Dec 11	(a & b) Violence and Physical and Sexual Abuse	(a) Chapter 14: Violence and Physical and Sexual Abuse (b) *Kill Bill: Vol. 1* and *Vol. 2* (2003, 2004)
Dec 16	Dec 18	(a) Review Session (b) Final Examination	No readings or film
Dec 23	Dec 25	Winter Break	

*   Adapted from the actual syllabus Danny Wedding used in an abnormal psychology course he taught at Yonsei University in Seoul, Korea where he was the 2008–2009 Fulbright-Yonsei Distinguished Scholar.

Appendix C

Recommended Websites

Movies in General

Movies and Mental Illness – Blog
www.moviesandmentalillness.blogspot.com

Internet Movie Database (the largest movie database)
www.imdb.com

Movie Review Query Engine (over 76,000 movie titles; over 748,000 reviews)
www.mrqe.com

American Film Institute
www.afi.com

Independent Movies
www.indiewire.com

Hogrefe Publishing (contains free movie filmographies, files, and information on *Movies and Mental Illness* and *Positive Psychology at the Movies*; search the site for "movies")
www.hogrefe.com

Voice Awards
http://whatadifference.samhsa.gov/voiceawards/about.html

Other Recommended Movie Databases

Rotten Tomatoes (movie database)
www.rottentomatoes.com

Literature, Arts, and Medicine Database
http://litmed.med.nyu.edu/Annotation?catid=3&action=listcat

AMC Filmsite
www.filmsite.org

Films Dealing with Psychological Issues
www.psychmovies.com

Films Involving Disabilities
http://www.disabilityfilms.co.uk/

Film Review Websites
www.atkinsononfilm.com, www.psychflix.com

Susan Nicosia: Movies and Mental Illness: Psychology, Psychiatry and the Movies
http://www.imagiscape.ca/research/art/Movies%20and%20Mental%20Illness%20Filmography.htm

Hollywood Entertainment Corporation
www.reel.com

Internet Movie Network
www.movieweb.com

Appendix D

12 Misconceptions About Mental Illness and Mental Health Professionals Perpetuated by Movies

Misconception	Film Examples
Love alone conquers mental illness.	*Mozart and the Whale* (2005) *Stateside* (2004) *Wilbur Wants to Kill Himself* (2002) *Matchstick Men* (2003) *Benny & Joon* (1993)
People with mental illness are violent.	*Keane* (2004) *Edmond* (2005) *The Killing of John Lennon* (2006) *The Assassination of Richard Nixon* (2004) *Nightmare on Elm Street* (1984)
People with mental illness are wild and crazy.	*Michael Clayton* (2007) *Mozart and the Whale* (2005) *Black Snake Moan* (2006) *The Big White* (2005) *I'm a Cyborg, But That's OK* (2007)
People referred to as delusional or psychotic are actually telling the truth, mentally healthy, and grounded in reality.	*Flightplan* (2005) *K-Pax* (2001) *Happy Accidents* (2000) *The Jacket* (2005)
Parents cause schizophrenia, autism, etc. (the myth of the schizophrenogenic parent).	*Clean, Shaven* (1993) *Shine* (1996)
All mental illness has a traumatic etiology.	*The Fisher King* (1991) *The Snake Pit* (1948) *The Three Faces of Eve* (1957) *K-Pax* (2001) *Nurse Betty* (2000)
Schizophrenia is the same as dissociative identity disorder, gender identity disorder, etc.	*Me, Myself & Irene* (2000) *Dressed to Kill* (1980)
Psychiatric hospitals are dangerous places, or at the least, unhelpful; the patients are not sick, they are harmlessly eccentric or misdiagnosed.	*One Flew Over the Cuckoo's Nest* (1975) *Asylum* (2005) *The Jacket* (2005) *King of Hearts* (1966) *House of Fools* (2002)
Psychiatric treatment (e.g., ECT, medications) blocks creativity and intelligence.	*A Beautiful Mind* (2001) *A Clockwork Orange* (1971)
It is liberating to discontinue psychiatric treatment on one's own (e.g., medications).	*Garden State* (2004)
The treatment of mental illness involves boundary violations by a therapist (these are usually sexual).	*The Prince of Tides* (1991) *Numb* (2007) *Mr. Jones* (1993) *Final Analysis* (1992)
Psychological diagnoses are routinely made up by psychologists and patients and touted as a standard condition.	*Me, Myself & Irene* (2000): "Advanced delusionary schizophrenia with involuntary narcissistic rage" *Asylum* (2005): "Severe personality disorder with features of morbid jealousy" *Transamerica* (2005): "Gender dysphoria" *The Ringer* (2005): "Highly functioning developmental disability" *Shrink* (2009)

Appendix E

Portrayals of Psychotherapists in Movies

See Niemiec & Wedding (2006) for more details

Balanced Portrayals

Lars and the Real Girl (2007)
The Squid and the Whale (2005)
Transamerica[+] (2005)
The Woodsman (2004)
Stateside (2004)
Intimate Strangers (2004)
Gothika[+] (2004)
Klepto (2003)
Antwone Fisher (2003)
Manic (2003)
Identity (2003)
Elling (2002)
Hollywood Ending (2002)
K-Pax (2001)
The Brothers (2001)
The Sixth Sense (1999)
Girl, Interrupted (1999)
Good Will Hunting (1997)
Don Juan DeMarco (1994)
Ordinary People (1980)
Equus (1977)
David and Lisa (1962)
Psycho (1960)

Unbalanced Portrayals

Numb (2007)
The Departed (2006)
Basic Instinct 2 (2006)
Stay (2005)
Batman Begins (2005)
Prime (2005)
Asylum (2005)
The Great New Wonderful (2005)
The Island (2005)
Dirty Filthy Love (2004)
The Chorus (2004)
Wilbur Wants to Kill Himself (2002)
Normal (2004)
Anything Else (2003)
Vanilla Sky (2001)
I Am Sam (2001)
Happy Accidents (2000)
Analyze This (1998)
Bliss (1997)
Mr. Jones (1993)
Final Analysis (1992)
The Prince of Tides (1991)
The Silence of the Lambs (1991)
What About Bob? (1991)
Jesus of Montreal (1989)
High Anxiety (1977)
One Flew Over the Cuckoo's Nest (1975)
Harvey (1950)

+ Also contains a highly unbalanced portrayal

Films Illustrating Psychopathology

Anxiety Disorders

40 Year Old Virgin, The (2005) Comedy ΨΨ
Screwball comedy depicting issues relevant to those suffering from social phobia, such as fear of embarrassment, dating/sex fears, social inadequacy, and avoidance behavior.

Adaptation (2002) Comedy/Action ΨΨΨΨ
Multi-layered Spike Jonze film in which Nicholas Cage plays twin brothers, one of whom is a neurotic screenwriter struggling to write a story based on a book about orchids.

Analyze That (2002) Comedy/Action ΨΨ
The follow-up film to *Analyze This*, in which a panic-disordered mob boss (Robert De Niro) malingers to get released from prison, tries to maintain an ordinary job, and is convinced to return while stringing along his psychiatrist (Billy Crystal).

Analyze This (1999) Comedy/Action ΨΨ
The original Billy Crystal/Robert De Niro comedy where De Niro plays the lead thug in a New York mafia group who develops panic attacks. De Niro sees a psychiatrist (Billy Crystal) for treatment.

Arachnophobia (1990) Comedy/Horror ΨΨ
A story about a doctor with a paralyzing fear of spiders. (Actually, the spiders in this film are pretty intimidating, and fear appears to be a perfectly reasonable response.)

As Good As It Gets (1997) Romance ΨΨΨΨ
Jack Nicholson won his third Academy Award as Best Actor for this film, in which he portrays a homophobic, racist novelist with an obsessive-compulsive disorder.

Aviator, The (2004) Drama/Biography ΨΨΨΨ
Directed by Martin Scorsese, this film depicts Howard Hughes Jr.'s (Leonardo DiCaprio) early years (1920–1940s) and the progression of his obsessive-compulsive disorder. Winner of five Academy Awards and a Voice Award.

Batman Begins (2005) Action/Drama ΨΨΨΨ
Sophisticated Christopher Nolan film telling the story of Bruce Wayne, a young boy with a phobia who watches his wealthy parents being murdered and subsequently becomes a superhero. Wayne's phobia of bats is conquered through systematic exposure. The movie demonstrates the importance of facing up to what one fears the most.

Big Parade, The (1925) Romance/War ΨΨΨ
This epic film about World War I gives the viewer a sense of the stress of combat and the trauma of returning to civilian life minus a leg or an arm.

Big White, The (2005) Drama/Crime Ψ
Black comedy starring Robin Williams, Holly Hunter, Giovanni Ribisi, and Woody Harrelson. Margaret (Hunter) is diagnosed with Tourette's syndrome, which appears to be adult onset (i.e., it doesn't match *DSM-IV-TR* criteria); she has little self-control over her verbal outbursts.

Black Rain (1989) Drama ΨΨΨ
Black-and-white film by Japanese filmmaker Shohei Imamura about the aftermath of the bomb-

ing of Hiroshima and its long-term psychological effects.

"Who's gonna love me, Dad? Whoever's going to love me?"

Ron Kovic in *Born on the Fourth of July*
(1989)

Born on the Fourth of July (1989)
Drama/War/Biography ΨΨΨΨ
Oliver Stone film about the anger, frustration, rage, and coping of paralyzed Vietnam veteran Ron Kovic (Tom Cruise). Kovic was thrown out of the 1972 Republican convention, but went on to address the Democratic convention in 1976. The film has especially memorable VA hospital scenes.

Brave One, The (2007) Crime/Thriller Ψ
Jodie Foster plays newlywed a radio talk show host. She survives a brutal attack that leaves her fiancé dead. Following the attack, she is extremely anxious, yet she forces herself to get revenge.

Broken English (2007) Comedy/Drama/Romance ΨΨ
Parker Posey portrays an organizer/secretary/event planner who is bored and passes each day searching for a lover on the Internet. She chooses men who are unavailable because of a fear of commitment. When she gets close to a genuine commitment herself, she has panic attacks.

Bubble (2005) Crime/Drama ΨΨ
Minimalist Steven Soderbergh project about three characters in a poor town, working at a factory. One suffers from anxiety and panic attacks.

Cars that Ate Paris, The (1974, Australia) Comedy Ψ
Early Peter Weir film that takes place in a secluded town in rural Paris, Australia, where the main source of income is the revenue from salvaged valuables from carwrecks. Panic attacks and exposure are depicted.

Casualties of War (1989) War ΨΨΨ
Brian De Palma film about five GIs who kidnap, rape, and murder a young Vietnamese girl. The film deals with themes of guilt, stress, violence, and, most of all, the dehumanizing aspects of war.

Coming Home (1978) Drama/War ΨΨΨ
Jon Voigt plays a paraplegic veteran who becomes Jane Fonda's lover in this sensitive antiwar film. Fonda's Marine Corps husband winds up committing suicide. Interesting analysis of the various ways different people respond to the stress of war.

Copycat (1995) Suspense/Thriller ΨΨ
Sigourney Weaver plays a criminal psychologist who struggles with agoraphobia symptoms as she helps police track down a serial killer (Harry Connick, Jr.).

Coyote Ugly (2000) Comedy/Drama ΨΨ
A young woman moves to New York City to try to make it as a songwriter. She takes a job as a "coyote" bartender at a wild, interactive bar and the experience helps her overcome her social anxiety.

Creepshow (1982) Horror ΨΨ
A man with an insect phobia winds up being eaten alive by cockroaches. Directed by George Romero, who also directed the classic film *Night of the Living Dead*. Stephen King wrote the screenplay, and the film is actually better than it sounds.

Da Vinci Code, The (2006) Drama/Mystery ΨΨ
This is a Ron Howard film about a murder inside the Louvre. Clues in Da Vinci's paintings lead to the discovery of a religious mystery protected by a secret society for two thousand years – which could shake the foundations of Christianity. Tom Hanks' character experiences somatic anxiety symptoms including shortness of breath and discomfort in social situations.

Deer Hunter, The (1978) War ΨΨΨΨ
Robert De Niro in an unforgettable film about how Vietnam affects the lives of three high school buddies. The Russian roulette sequences are among the most powerful scenes in film history. Psychopathology themes include drug abuse, PTSD, and depression. The movie won five Academy Awards, including one for Best Picture, and De Niro has described it as his finest film.

Departed, The (2006) Crime/Drama/Mystery ΨΨ
Engaging Martin Scorsese film starring Leonardo DiCaprio, Matt Damon, Jack Nicholson, and Martin Sheen portraying Irish mafia, undercover detectives, and corrupt federal agents. DiCaprio's character experiences panic attacks and anxiolytics are prescribed.

Dirty Filthy Love (2004, UK) Drama/Comedy ΨΨΨ
An outstanding movie about Mark Furness whose life falls apart as a result of his affliction with obsessive compulsive disorder and Tourette's Disorder. Treatment, support groups, and severe symptoms of OCD and Tourette's are shown in the film.

"I'm not sure there is any help for you."

The dummy's comment to his
ventriloquist Steven in *Dummy* (2002)

Dummy (2002) Comedy/Drama ΨΨ
A predictable film starring Adrian Brody as Steven, an aspiring ventriloquist, who is unemployed, naïve, passive, and socially awkward until he finds meaning and social support through his "dummy." Interesting metaphor of the socially phobic person finding his "inner voice." All ventriloquism in the film is actually performed by Adrian Brody. The DVD features interviews and comic classes with champion ventriloquist Jeff Dunham.

Elling (2001) Drama ΨΨΨΨΨ
Norwegian film about two men released from a psychiatric hospital and must prove themselves capable of coping with everyday life. Oscar nominee for Best Foreign Film.

Enduring Love (2004) Drama/Mystery ΨΨΨ
Several men try to save a boy in a hot air balloon that is out of control. All but one let go and the one who hangs on dies; the resulting PTSD and a character with delusional disorder are portrayed.

Everything Is Illuminated (2005) Comedy/Drama ΨΨ
A young Jewish American travels to the Ukraine to find the woman who saved his grandfather from the Nazis. He stores everything in small plastic bags and claims to have a phobia of dogs, but ends up sharing both the backseat of a car and then a bed with a dog.

Feardotcom (2002) Thriller/Horror Ψ
Various characters access a deadly website that makes their deepest fears or phobias come true (e.g., one has a phobia of beetles and soon is covered by them).

Fearless (1993) Drama ΨΨ
Jeff Bridges in an engaging film that portrays some of the symptoms of anxiety in airline crash survivors. Interesting vignettes show group therapy for PTSD victims.

Final Cut, The (2004) Drama/Thriller Ψ
Some PTSD symptoms are displayed in a man (Robin Williams) who creates "rememories" for people at funerals using a microchip implanted in the people's heads while they were living.

Fisher King, The (1991) Drama/Fantasy/Comedy ΨΨΨ
Jeff Bridges plays a former talk show personality who unwittingly encourages a listener to go on a shooting spree. Bridges' withdrawal, cynicism, and substance use can all be interpreted and understood in the context of a post-traumatic stress disorder.

"If you ladies leave my island, if you survive recruit training... you will be a weapon, you will be a minister of death, praying for war. But until that day you are pukes."

Drill instructor Hartman in
Full Metal Jacket (1987)

Full Metal Jacket (1987) War ΨΨΨ
Stanley Kubrick's Vietnam film. The first half of the film is devoted to life in a Marine boot camp, and it is a good illustration of the stress associated with military indoctrination. One of the recruits kills his drill instructor and then commits suicide in response to the pressures of boot camp.

Hamburger Hill (1987) War ΨΨ
A graphic presentation of the stress and horror of war.

High Anxiety (1977) Comedy ΨΨ
Mel Brook's spoof of Hitchcock classics about a psychiatrist who works at "The Psycho-Neurotic Institute for the Very, Very Nervous." The film is better if you've seen the Hitchcock films on which the parody builds.

Home of the Brave (2006) Action/Drama ΨΨ
Soldiers returning from the war in Iraq attempt to reintegrate back home but struggle with the memo-

ries and ramifications of having served in war. Winner of a Voice Award.

House of Games (1987) Crime ΨΨ
Lindsay Crouse plays the lead role as a psychiatrist who has just written an important book on obsessive-compulsive disorders. She becomes obsessed with confidence games and is slowly drawn into the criminal life.

In Country (1989) Drama ΨΨ
Bruce Willis plays a Vietnam veteran with posttraumatic stress disorder who is unable to relate meaningfully to the world around him until he visits the Vietnam memorial.

In the Bedroom (2001) Drama/Suspense ΨΨΨΨ
Introspective film with a talented cast that examines grief, despair, and revenge after the murder of someone deeply loved. Marisa Tomei's character develops an Acute Stress Disorder following the trauma. The film makes good use of silence; these scenes underscore the tension, unspoken feelings, and underlying pain associated with the death of a loved one.

Inside Out (1986) Drama ΨΨ
A little known but interesting film in which Elliott Gould plays a man with agoraphobia. He is able to obtain food, sex, and haircuts in his home, but finds that he cannot meet *all* his needs without leaving his house.

Jacob's Ladder (1990) Drama ΨΨ
Complex film about a Vietnam veteran who has dramatic hallucinations of indeterminate etiology (possibly the result of military exposure to experimental drugs).

"What does your therapist think of all this?"
"Oh, I would never tell my therapist."
"Why not?"
"Because it's private."

Dialogue in *Kissing Jessica Stein* (2002)

Kissing Jessica Stein (2002) Comedy ΨΨΨ
Quality independent film about a neurotic, young woman who in exploring her sexuality and intrapersonal life is able to extend beyond her rigidity and generalized anxiety.

Lady in a Cage (1964) Drama/Suspense ΨΨ
Olivia de Havilland plays an upper class woman trapped inside her home elevator. The film melodramatically portrays claustrophobia and panic.

"Take it all but in the name of humanity, let me out of this cage."

Cornelia Hilyard in *Lady in a Cage* (1964)

Manchurian Candidate, The (2004) Drama/Suspense ΨΨΨ
The new version of this classic film stars Denzel Washington as a Gulf War veteran with PTSD, paranoia, and memories he cannot understand, which lead him to unravel a conspiracy involving brain washing and political maneuvering.

Manchurian Candidate, The (1962) Drama/Suspense ΨΨΨ
Original version stars Frank Sinatra as the veteran who experiences flashbacks and PTSD symptoms.

M*A*S*H (1970) Comedy/War ΨΨΨ
Wonderfully funny Robert Altman film about military surgeons and nurses who use alcohol, sex, and humor to cope with the stress of war. The portrayal of Hawkeye Pierce, half-drunk but always ready for surgery, is troubling for mental health professionals.

Matador, The (2005) Comedy ΨΨ
Pierce Brosnan plays a narcissistic, antisocial "hit man." He suffers from panic attacks (without agoraphobia) that affect his ability to work.

"I've got things a certain way."

Roy Waller in *Matchstick Men* (2003)

Matchstick Men (2003) Comedy ΨΨΨΨ
Nicholas Cage plays Roy Waller, a con man with OCD, agoraphobia with panic, tics, and antisocial personality in this interesting Ridley Scott film. Upon meeting his estranged daughter things begin to change for Waller.

Nothing (2003) Comedy ΨΨΨ
A Vincenzo Natali film about two men who make things disappear by hating and wishing. The film is based on the relationship two good friends, a travel agent who works from home and suffers from severe agoraphobia and a self-absorbed loser who is treated with contempt.

Obsession (1976) Thriller Ψ
Brian De Palma version of Hitchcock's *Vertigo*. The De Palma film doesn't live up to the original.

Open Water (2003) Suspense Ψ
A young couple on a scuba diving trip are left behind to fend for themselves. Sharks circle, distant boats do not see the divers, and fish bite at them. While the film depicts the terror someone would experience if abandoned in the open water, it is not a notable depiction of an anxiety disorder.

Panic Room (2002) Crime/Suspense Ψ
Jodie Foster plays a claustrophobic woman who becomes imprisoned in the panic room of her house when burglars enter.

"Sergeant, I want you to arrange for the immediate transfer of this baby out of my regiment. I won't have any of our brave men contaminated by him."

Paths of Glory (1957)

Paths of Glory (1957) War ΨΨΨΨΨ
Kirk Douglas in an early Stanley Kubrick film about the horrors and stupidity of WWI. There is a memorable scene in which a general repeatedly slaps a soldier, trying without success to bring him out of his shell-shocked state. The scene was repeated in the 1970 film *Patton*.

Pawnbroker, The (1965) Drama ΨΨΨ
Rod Steiger plays a concentration camp survivor who watched his wife being raped and his children being murdered; he copes by becoming numb. Interesting flashback scenes. Steiger lost the 1965 Academy Award for best actor to Lee Marvin in *Cat Ballou*.

Patton (1970) War/Biography ΨΨΨΨ
George C. Scott is perfect in the role of the controversial general who was relieved of his command after slapping a crying soldier who had been hospitalized for combat fatigue, or what would now be called post-traumatic stress disorder. The film won an Academy Award as Best Picture and George C. Scott won the Oscar for Best Actor.

"I want you to remember that no bastard ever won a war by dying for his country. He won it by making the other poor dumb bastard die for his country."

Gen. George S. Patton Jr. in *Patton* (1970)

Phobia (1980) Horror/Mystery Ψ
Canadian film about the systematic murders of phobic psychiatric patients.

Play It Again Sam (1972) Comedy/Romance ΨΨ
Early Woody Allen film depicting social anxiety. A neurotic film critic's wife leaves him and he is crushed. His hero is a tough guy (Humphrey Bogart) whose apparition begins showing up to give him advice. He actually tries dating again and is unsuccessful until he learns to relax.

Princess and the Warrior, The (2000) Drama ΨΨΨΨ
A nurse at a psychiatric hospital is hit by a truck and saved by a crook who cuts a hole in her throat and breathes for her. Upon recovering, the nurse goes on a journey of purpose to find this man. A minor character has PTSD. One intensely graphic and chilling scene depicts a kind-hearted adolescent with **pica**; believing the nurse has rejected him, the teenager eats glass.

Raiders of the Lost Ark (1981) Adventure ΨΨ
Steven Spielberg film with Harrison Ford as anthropologist Indiana Jones, who is forced by the situational demands of heroism to overcome his snake phobia.

Red Eye (2005) Horror/Thriller Ψ
Wes Craven film portraying a character who hates to fly but finds herself on the red eye flight to Miami trapped with a villainous and charming middle-man in a plot to assassinate a Homeland Security official.

San Francisco (1936) Romance/Disaster ΨΨΨ
This is one of the greatest disaster films ever made, and the special effects give the viewer some appreciation for the acute stress one would experience in a real earthquake. Clark Gable and Spencer Tracy have memorable roles in this film.

She's One of Us (2003, France) Drama ΨΨ
A socially awkward and anxious woman struggles in her social interactions. Watch for echoes of Dostoyevsky's "Dream of a Ridiculous Man."

Shoah (1985) Documentary ΨΨΨΨΨ
Widely praised nine-hour documentary about the Holocaust. The film offers some insight into the behavior of both the German officials and their victims and illustrates antisocial personalities and post-traumatic stress disorders.

Something's Gotta Give (2003) Comedy ΨΨ
Jack Nicholson stars as a man who experiences panic attacks as he gradually falls in love with a woman played by Diane Keaton.

Stranger than Fiction (2006) Comedy ΨΨΨ
An IRS auditor (Will Ferrell) suddenly finds himself the subject of a novel being read by the author that only the auditor can hear. The narration affects his entire life – his work, relationships, living situation, and livelihood – including his obsessive behavior (e.g., counting toothbrush strokes and steps).

Twelve O'Clock High (1949) War ΨΨΨ
Gregory Peck in an interesting presentation of the stress of combat and the ways in which leaders can influence the behavior of those they lead.

Unmarried Woman, An (1978) Drama/Comedy ΨΨΨ
Tender, sensitive, and funny film about Jill Clayburgh learning to cope with the stress of being a single parent after her husband abandons her. Her friends, a psychiatrist, and an affair with Alan Bates all help.

"I have this acrophobia. I wake up at night and I see that man falling."

John Ferguson describing his symptoms in
Vertigo (1958)

Vertigo (1958) Thriller ΨΨΨΨΨ
Wonderful Hitchcock film in which James Stewart plays a character whose life is dominated by his fear of heights. He attempts a self created behavior modification program early in the film without success.

Waiting for Ronald (2003) Short Film/Drama ΨΨΨ
This short film about a man who leaves a supervised residence to live with a friend in the community depicts OCD with a hand-washing compulsion.

Walking on Water (2002) Drama ΨΨ
Australian film about a man who becomes haunted by intrusive memories and deteriorates into self-destructive behavior after suffocating a gay friend who was dying of AIDS.

War of the Worlds (2005) Action ΨΨ
Directed by Steven Spielberg and starring Tom Cruise, Dakota Fanning, and Tim Robbins, this film depicts the impact of an alien invasion on a blue-collar father and two children. Cruise's character responds to tragedy with shock; his daughter develops a phobia; and Robbins' character has a psychotic break.

What About Bob? (1991) Comedy ΨΨ
Bill Murray plays an anxious patient who cannot function without his psychiatrist, played by Richard Dreyfuss. Not a great film, but a fun movie that explores the doctor-patient relationship and the obsessive-compulsive personality.

"As a four limb person, I don't feel incomplete. It's more of a feeling that my body doesn't belong to me."
"The relief from the 50 years of torment I had was indescribable."
"I'm complete now."

Comments from individuals who want
or have had healthy limbs removed in
Whole (2003)

Whole (2003) Documentary ΨΨ
Fascinating documentary about individuals who have a strong desire to have one of their limbs amputated, despite being totally healthy. Presents

interesting differential diagnostic questions. Is this OCD, Body Dysmorphic Disorder, an identity disorder, or self-mutilation? One psychiatrist, who interviewed 53 people with this condition, proposed the rubric "Body Integrity Identity Disorder."

Without a Paddle (2004) Drama/Comedy Ψ
Three friends go canoeing after the death of a friend. One is painfully neurotic with numerous phobias including fear of small spaces, the dark, and cellophane wrap. He copes with difficult situations by pretending he is a *Star Wars* character.

Dissociative and Somatoform Disorders

3 Women (1977) Drama ΨΨΨΨ
Strange but engaging Robert Altman film about two California women who seem to exchange personalities.

Agnes of God (1985) Mystery ΨΨΨ
Good performances by Anne Bancroft, Meg Tilly, and Jane Fonda. Fonda plays a court-appointed psychiatrist who must make sense out of pregnancy and apparent infanticide in a local convent. Good examples of *stigmata,* an example of conversion.

Altered States (1980) Science Fiction ΨΨ
Not entirely satisfying film based in part on the sensory deprivation experiments of Dr. John Lilly. The scientist (William Hurt) combines isolation tanks with psychedelic mushrooms to induce altered states of consciousness. Good special effects.

"This is poetry, and don't you deny it. Come back to me when you've written something really perverse, really depraved."

An editor reviews Isabelle's work in *Amateur* (1994)

Amateur (1994) Drama/Comedy ΨΨ
Hal Hartley film in which a man who is amnestic as a result of a traumatic head injury takes up with a nun who has left the convent to write porno-

graphic novels. Almost every character in the film has a complex double identity and is uncertain about who he or she *really* is.

Anastasia (1956) Drama ΨΨΨ
Yul Brynner, Helen Hayes, and Ingrid Bergman star in this film about an amnestic woman who is believed to be the lost princess Anastasia, daughter of the last czar of Russia.

Bandits (2001) Comedy ΨΨ
Loosely based on a true story about two criminals who rob banks in a non-violent way. One of the men (Billy Bob Thornton) is hypochondriacal. In interviews, Thornton stated it was not much of a "stretch" to play this role – has acknowledged phobias for both antique furniture and plastic cutlery.

Black Friday (1940) Horror ΨΨ
Boris Karloff and Bela Lugosi star in this film about transplanting a gangster's brain in a college professor's cranium.

Butterfly Effect, The (2003) Drama/Suspense ΨΨ
A young man (Ashton Kutcher) tries to change his traumatic past with unpredictable and increasingly problematic consequences. When he reflects on blackouts, he enters the memory and is able to change it for the long-term but must face the consequences of the change each time. The film attempts to depict chaos theory, and opens with a famous quotation.

Cyrano de Bergerac (1990, France) Romance ΨΨΨ
Gerard Depardieu stars as the inimitable Cyrano, a man obsessed with the size of his nose and convinced it makes him forever unlovable.

Dark Mirror, The (1946) Thriller Ψ
Olivia De Havilland plays both parts in a story of twin sisters, one of whom is a deranged killer.

Dead Again (1991) Mystery/Romance ΨΨΨ
Emma Thompson costars with her husband, Kenneth Branagh (who also directed the film). The movie illustrates traumatic amnesia and its treatment through hypnosis. The hypnotist, an antique dealer, is not the most professional of therapists!

Despair (1979) Drama ΨΨΨΨ
Fassbinder film based on a novel by Vladimir Nabokov. A Russian Jew émigré in Germany who runs a chocolate factory kills another man who

looks like him, and tries to pass it off as his own suicide. When his plan fails, he becomes psychotic.

Devils, The (1971) Drama/Historical ΨΨΨ
Ken Russell film adapted from Aldous Huxley's book *The Devils of Loundun*. The film traces the lives of seventeenth-century French nuns who ex perienced highly erotic dissociative states attributed to possession by the devil.

Double Life of Veronique, The (1991) Fantasy/Drama ΨΨ
The lives of two women turn out to be linked in complex ways the viewer never fully understands.

Double Life, A (1947) Crime ΨΨ
Ronald Coleman plays an actor who is unable to sort out his theatrical life (in which he plays Othello) and his personal life.

Dr. Jekyll and Mr. Hyde (1932) Horror ΨΨΨΨ
Fredric March in the best adaptation of Robert Louis Stevenson's classic story about the ultimate dissociative disorder. Stevenson was an alcoholic, and the mysterious liquid that dramatically transforms Jekyll's personality may be a metaphor for alcohol.

Exorcist, The (1973) Horror ΨΨ
Linda Blair stars as a 12-year-old girl possessed by the devil in William Friedkin's film based on the William Peter Blatty novel. One of the most suspenseful films ever made.

"It's only after we've lost everything [that] we are free to do anything."

A premise of *Fight Club* (1999)

Fight Club (1999) Drama/Suspense ΨΨΨΨ
A disillusioned, insomniac (Edward Norton) meets a dangerous, malcontent part of himself in the character of Brad Pitt. Norton then establishes "fight clubs" in which men can unload their aggressions onto one another. It is interesting to witness.

Forgotten, The (2004) Drama ΨΨ
A woman grieving over the loss of her nine-year-old son is told by her husband and her therapist that her son never existed, and that all her memories

were created in response to a miscarriage. The mother isn't buying it.

Freud (1962) Biography ΨΨΨ
Montgomery Clift in an interesting account of the early year's of Freud's life. The film illustrates paralysis, false blindness, and a false pregnancy, all examples of somatization disorders.

Great Dictator, The (1940) Comedy ΨΨ
A satire of Adolph Hitler, with Charlie Chaplin in the role of a Jewish barber who suffers amnesia and eventually finds himself assuming the personality of Adenoid Hynkel, the dictator of Tomania.

Hannah and Her Sisters (1986) Comedy/Drama ΨΨΨ
Mickey (Woody Allen) is a hopeless hypochondriac who was formerly married to Hannah (Mia Farrow). Mickey spends his days worrying about brain tumors, cancer, and cardiovascular disease.

"Every husband should go blind for a little while."

Val in *Hollywood Ending* (2002)

Hollywood Ending (2002) Comedy ΨΨΨ
Woody Allen film about a struggling film director (Allen), Val, who develops a conversion disorder (hysterical blindness) and has to direct the film blind.

Home of the Brave (1949) Drama/War ΨΨ
An African American soldier develops a conversion disorder following his return from combat.

Identity (2003) Suspense/Thriller ΨΨΨ
A serial killer with a dissociative identity disorder is at his final hearing before receiving the death penalty. This story juxtaposes with another tale of several people suddenly stuck at an isolated motel and living in terror as they are killed one by one. These two components are cleverly weaved together as the people represent DID alters being killed off.

Last Temptation of Christ, The (1988) Religious ΨΨΨ
Challenging and controversial Martin Scorsese film in which Jesus, while on the cross and in great

pain, has a dissociative episode in which he imagines himself as an ordinary man who married Mary Magdalene and lived a normal life.

Lizzie (1957) Drama ΨΨ
Eleanor Parker, a woman with dissociative identity disorder is treated by psychiatrist Richard Boone.

Loverboy (2004) Drama ΨΨ
An overly protective mother illustrates the rare but fascinating phenomenon of factitious disorder by proxy.

Method (2003) Suspense/Thriller Ψ
An actress studying and playing the role of a past serial killer tries too hard to "feel her character" and she dissociates and takes on her model's past behavior.

Mirage (1965) Drama ΨΨ
A scientist who makes an important discovery develops amnesia after viewing the death of a friend.

My Girl (1991) Drama/Comedy ΨΨ
The film centers on an 11-year-old girl whose mother has just died and whose grandmother has Alzheimer's disease. The child responds by developing a series of imaginary disorders. Strong performances by Dan Aykroyd and Jamie Lee Curtis.

Nurse Betty (2000) Drama/Mystery ΨΨΨΨ
Neil LaBute film about a woman (Renee Zellweger) who witnesses a traumatic event and develops a dissociative fugue. She travels to Los Angeles to find a character in a soap opera. Zellweger's character presents an interesting springboard for a debate about the differences between dissociative fugue and delusional disorder.

Numb (2007) Drama ΨΨ
Matthew Perry portrays a character who develops a depersonalization disorder that he overcomes by falling in love.

Overboard (1987) Comedy ΨΨ
Goldie Hawn plays a haughty millionairess who develops amnesia and is claimed by an Oregon carpenter as his wife and forced to care for his children.

Pact of Silence, The (2003, France) Drama ΨΨ
A Jesuit priest tries to make sense out of a nun's psychosomatic fits that turn out to be related to the experiences of the nun's incarcerated twin sister.

Paris, Texas (1984) Drama ΨΨΨ
Wim Wenders film about a man found wandering in the desert with no personal memory.

Persona (1966) Drama ΨΨΨΨ
Complex, demanding, and absolutely fascinating Bergman film starring Liv Ullmann as an actress who suddenly stops talking after one of her performances. Ullmann is treated by a nurse, and the two women appear to exchange "personas."

"I have not spoken since I was six years old. Nobody knows why, least of all myself."

Ada's thoughts at the beginning of
The Piano (1993)

Piano, The (1993) Drama ΨΨΨΨΨ
Jane Campion film about a woman who had voluntarily stopped speaking as a child. She communicates with written notes and through playing the piano, a pleasure forbidden to her by her New Zealand husband. There are scenes of extraordinary sensuality between Harvey Keitel and Holly Hunter and a dramatic suicide attempt.

Poison Ivy (1992) Drama Ψ
A newcomer into a pathological family plans to take over the role of wife and mother. The father is an alcoholic and the mother is a hypochondriac.

Prelude to a Kiss (1992) Comedy/Romance ΨΨ
The ultimate example of a dissociative disorder. A beautiful young woman and a sad old man kiss on her wedding day and exchange bodies. The film makes this extraordinary event seem almost plausible.

Primal Fear (1996) Drama ΨΨΨ
Richard Gere stars in this suspenseful drama about a man who commits heinous crimes, ostensibly as a result of a dissociative disorder. The film raises useful questions about the problem of malingering and differential diagnosis.

Psycho (1960) Horror/Thriller ΨΨΨΨ
Wonderful Hitchcock film starring Anthony Perkins as Norman Bates, who vacillates between his passive, morbid personality and his alter ego as his dead mother. In the final minutes of the film, a psychiatrist offers a somewhat confused explana-

tion for Bates' behavior. The shower scene is one of the most famous scenes in film history.

"Mother, my mother, uh, what is the phrase? – She isn't qu-quite herself today."

Norman Bates in *Psycho* (1960)

Queen Margot (1994) Drama ΨΨ
Period film set in 1572 France at a time of heavy religious warfare (Catholic vs. Protestant). The king in the film appears to have a somataform disorder.

Raising Cain (1992) Thriller/Drama Ψ
Confusing De Palma film about a child psychologist with multiple personalities who begins to kill women and steal their children for experiments.

Return of Martin Guerre, The (1982) Historical ΨΨΨ
Gerard Depardieu as a sixteenth-century peasant who returns to his wife after a seven-year absence. His true identity is never made clear. This film, the basis for the American movie *Sommersby,* was based on a true story.

Safe (1995) Comedy/Drama ΨΨΨΨ
A rare film almost exclusively focusing on a woman (Julianne Moore) with a somatoform disorder, various treatment approaches, and the effects on her family. This satirical film was cleverly directed by Todd Haynes.

Secret of Dr. Kildare, The (1939) Drama ΨΨΨ
The good Dr. Kildare works hard to cure a patient's conversion disorder (blindness) in this interesting film.

Secret Window (2004) Drama/Suspense ΨΨΨ
Mort Rainey (Johnny Depp) finds his wife cheating on him in a motel; the film jumps forward six months to a scene in which Mort is an isolated writer in a house in the woods and now separated from his wife. He is visited and threatened by an odd psychopath (John Turturro). Based on the Stephen King short story, "Secret Window, Secret Garden." Summary: *Identity* meets *The Sixth Sense.*

Send Me No Flowers (1964) Romance/Comedy Ψ
Rock Hudson plays a hypochondriac convinced he

will die soon. Hudson sets out to find a suitable replacement so his wife will be able to get along without him.

Seventh Veil, The (1945) Drama ΨΨΨ
Psychological drama about a pianist who loses the ability to play. Hypnotherapy makes it possible for Ann Todd to play the piano again and sort out her complex interpersonal relationships.

Sisters (1973) Thriller/Horror ΨΨ
De Palma film about Siamese twins separated as children; one is good, the other quite evil. The use of Siamese twins is a Hitchcock-like twist on the theme of multiple personality.

Something's Gotta Give (2005) Comedy ΨΨ
Jack Nicholson plays a 63-year-old man obsessed with younger women; he has a genuine heart attack that is followed by a series of panic attacks.

Sommersby (1993) Drama ΨΨ
Richard Gere returns to wife Jodie Foster after a six-year absence during the Civil War. Gere is remarkably changed, so much so that it appears he is a different man.

Sorry, Wrong Number (1948) Thriller ΨΨ
Barbara Stanwyck and Burt Lancaster in a murder film. Stanwyck is a rich heiress who is bedridden with psychosomatic heart disease and paralysis.

Spellbound (1945) Thriller ΨΨΨ
Ingrid Bergman and Gregory Peck star in this Hitchcock thriller. Peck is an amnestic patient who believes he has committed a murder; Bergman is the psychiatrist who falls in love with him and helps him recall the childhood trauma responsible for his dissociative state.

Steppenwolf (1974) Drama ΨΨ
Film adaptation of Herman Hesse's remarkable novel about Harry Haller (played by Max von Sydow), a misanthropic protagonist who wrestles with the competing forces of good and evil within himself.

Stigmata (1999) Suspense/Horror Ψ
A beautician begins to have episodes of visions, seizures, and stigmata wounds on her body after her mother sends her a sacred rosary from Brazil.

Suddenly, Last Summer (1959) Drama ΨΨΨ
Adaptation of a Tennessee Williams story about an enmeshed and pathological relationship between a mother (Katharine Hepburn) and her homosexual son and a dissociative amnesia in a cousin who

witnessed the son's death. Among its other virtues, the film includes a fascinating discussion of the benefits of lobotomy.

"He-he was lying naked on the broken stones... It looked as if-as if they had devoured him!... As if they'd torn or cut parts of him away with their hands, or with knives, or those jagged tin cans they made music with. As if they'd torn bits of him away in strips!"

Suddenly, Last Summer (1959)

Sullivan's Travels (1941) Comedy/Drama ΨΨΨΨ
Joel McCrea plays a movie director who goes out to experience life as it is lived outside a Hollywood studio. He winds up getting a head injury, becoming amnestic, and being sentenced to six years on a chain gang.

Sybil (1976) Drama ΨΨΨ
Made-for-TV movie in which Joanne Woodward, the patient in *The Three Faces of Eve,* plays the psychiatrist treating a woman with 16 different personalities.

Thérèse: The Story of Saint Thérèse of Lisieux (2004) Drama ΨΨΨ
The story of Saint Thérèse, the Carmelite nun who wrote *Story of a Soul*, and suffered from various somatic symptoms.

Three Faces of Eve, The (1957) Drama ΨΨΨΨ
Joanne Woodward won an Academy Award for her portrayal of a woman with three personalities (Eve White, Eve Black, and Jane); based on the book by Thigpin and Cleckley.

Twelve O'Clock High (1949) War ΨΨΨΨΨ
Gregory Peck plays the role of General Frank Savage, an effective leader who develops a conversion disorder (psychosomatic paralysis) in response to his role in the death of several of his subordinates. The film is based on a true story.

Unconscious (2004) Drama ΨΨ
A Spanish film that satirizes psychoanalysis; the movie includes examples of hypochondriasis and conversion disorder.

Unknown White Male (2005) Drama ΨΨΨ
An excellent exploration of the fugue state based on a true story about a man who discovers himself on a Coney Island subway with no recollection of who he is or how he got there.

Up in Arms (1944) Musical/Comedy/War Ψ
Danny Kaye plays a hypochondriac in the Army.

Voices Within: The Lives of Truddi Chase (1990) Drama ΨΨ
Made-for-TV movie about a woman with multiple personality disorder; based on the best selling-book *When Rabbit Howls.*

Whatever Happened to Baby Jane? (1962) Drama ΨΨΨ
Bette Davis and Joan Crawford star as two elderly sisters who were formerly movie stars. Jane (Bette Davis) had been a child star, but her fame was eclipsed by the renown of her talented sister, now confined to a wheelchair. Jane torments her sister and experiences a dramatic dissociative episode in the final scene in the movie.

X-Men: The Last Stand (2006) Action/Science Fiction ΨΨ
Superheroine mutant Jean Grey is portrayed as someone with a dissociative identity disorder; the actress playing the role researched DID to make her character more realistic.

Zelig (1983) Comedy ΨΨ
Quasi-documentary about Woody Allen as Zelig, a human chameleon whose personality changes to match that of whomever he is around. He is treated by psychiatrist Mia Farrow, whom Zelig eventually marries. Watch for Susan Sontag, Saul Bellow, and Bruno Bettelheim.

Psychological Stress and Physical Disorders

3 Needles (2005) Drama Ψ
Brutal and disturbing film depicting the transmission of HIV and the misconceptions that arise (e.g., the belief that having sex with a virgin will cure the disease).

12 Angry Men (1957) Drama ΨΨΨΨΨ
Henry Fonda stars in this fascinating courtroom drama that illustrates social pressure, the tendency toward conformity in social settings, and the

stress associated with noncompliance with societal norms.

61 (2001) Biography/Drama Ψ
Billy Crystal film with a subplot focused on the impact of stress on the body of Roger Maris during his quest to beat Babe Ruth's home run record.

Alive (1993) Action/Adventure/Drama ΨΨ
The survivors of a plane crash in the Andes survive for more than 70 days by eating the passengers who died. The film is a vivid portrayal of traumatic stress and its consequences.

All Quiet on the Western Front (1930) Drama ΨΨΨΨΨ
This remarkable film illustrates the horror of war and celebrates pacifism as its only solution. The film poignantly documents that it is young men who fight our wars and shows the folly of jingoism and blind patriotism.

"Oh, God! why did they do this to us? We only wanted to live, you and I. Why should they send us out to fight each other? If they threw away these rifles and these uniforms, you could be my brother, just like Kat and Albert. You'll have to forgive me, comrade. I'll do all I can. I'll write to your parents."

Paul attempts to comfort a man he has killed in *All Quiet on the Western Front* (1930)

Barbarian Invasions, The (2003) Drama/Comedy ΨΨΨΨ
Friends and family gather to support a stubborn, outspoken man suffering from a terminal illness. The film vacillates from light to heavy, from the somber to the humorous. This Canadian film won an Academy Award for Best Foreign Film.

Best Years of Our Lives, The (1946) Drama ΨΨ
Sam Goldwyn film about servicemen adjusting to civilian life after the war. One of the sailors has lost both hands.

Blue (1993) Drama ΨΨΨΨ
British filmmaker Derek Jarman's last film; he died from AIDS shortly after the movie was completed.

Jarman reviews his life and analyzes the ways in which his life has been affected by his disease.

Blue Butterfly (2004) Adventure/Drama ΨΨ
The mother of a terminally ill boy convinces an entomologist to take her son to the Costa Rican rainforest. The boy's brain cancer disappears and both lives are changed forever. The film is based on a true story.

Bone Collector, The (1999) Suspense/Thriller ΨΨ
Denzel Washington is a crime scene specialist with quadriplegia.

Brief History of Time, A (1992) Biography ΨΨΨ
A documentary about the life of Stephen Hawking, a theoretical physicist coping with amyotrophic lateral sclerosis.

Bubble Boy (2001) Comedy Ψ
Outlandish comedy about a boy born without immunity who must live in a bubble.

Bucket List, The (2008) Comedy ΨΨΨ
Jack Nicholson and Morgan Freeman meet as roommates in a hospital. Both are newly diagnosed with cancer and are given less than one year to live. Each makes a list of experiences they want to have before they "kick the bucket". These two very different men spend their last few months together in pursuit of their dreams.

Cactus (1986) Romance ΨΨΨ
Australian film about a woman who loses one eye and considers giving up sight in the other in order to more fully understand the world of her blind lover.

Children of a Lesser God (1986) Romance ΨΨΨ
The film examines the complications involved in a love relationship between William Hurt, a teacher in a school for the deaf, and Marlee Matlin, a young deaf woman who works at the school. Much of the conflict in the film revolves around Matlin's refusal to learn to lip-read. Matlin won an Academy Award as Best Supporting Actress for her role in this film.

Chinese Roulette (1976) Drama ΨΨ
Fassbinder film about a disabled girl and the ways in which she dominates and manipulates her family.

Chrystal (2004) Drama Ψ
Independent film in which one subplot involves a woman suffering from significant chronic pain caused by a motor vehicle accident.

Cinema Paradiso (1988) Drama ΨΨΨΨΨ
A young boy is mesmerized by a movie theater in a small, post-WWII, Italian town, and befriends a crusty yet warm-hearted projectionist who goes blind after a fire accident. Classic Giuseppe Tornatore film.

Common Threads: Stories from the Quilt (1989) Documentary ΨΨΨ
This HBO film examines the lives of five individuals linked by a common illness – AIDS. The movie won the Academy Award for Best Documentary Feature in 1989.

Crash of Silence (1953) Drama ΨΨ
Mother agonizes over whether to keep a hearing impaired daughter at home or send her to a special school.

Crazy Sexy Cancer (2007) Documentary ΨΨ
Young woman faces the stress of her illness by transforming her lifestyle and attitude.

Cure, The (1995) Drama ΨΨ
Two adolescent boys become best friends. One has AIDS from a blood transfusion, leading the boys to set off in search of a miracle cure.

Dance Me to My Song (1998, Australia) Drama ΨΨΨ
A woman with debilitating cerebral palsy competes with her caretaker for a love interest.

Dancer in the Dark (2000, Denmark) Drama ΨΨΨ
Björk portrays Selma, an immigrant, factory worker and single mother with limited intelligence whose vision is deteriorating. Her impending blindness affects her work, her relationships, and her personal life. Her son Gene will probably suffer the same fate unless she can pay for an operation.

Darius Goes West (2007) Documentary ΨΨΨ
Depiction of a man with Duchenne's muscular dystrophy and his journey with friends to get his wheelchair customized by MTV's "Pimp My Ride."

Deaf Smith and Johnnie Ears (1973) Western ΨΨ
A deaf Anthony Quinn teams up with Franco Nero to cope with the challenges of life in rural Texas.

Diving Bell and the Butterfly, The (2007, France) Drama, Biography ΨΨΨΨΨ
Jean-Dominique Bauby, editor of *Elle*, emerges completely paralyzed from a 3-week coma following a stroke. He cannot speak or move his body except for his left eye. Bauby responds to his situation with creativity and bravery. Much of the film is presented in the first person to help the viewer identify with his experience.

Doctor, The (1991) Drama ΨΨΨ
William Hurt plays a cold and indifferent physician whose approach to treatment changes dramatically after he is diagnosed with throat cancer.

Dreamland (2006) Drama Ψ
Coming of age story of a young woman in a remote desert trailer park who makes many sacrifices supporting her family and a friend who has multiple sclerosis and chronic pain.

"Why don't you ask me probing questions about my childhood?"

Stephanie Anderson queries her therapist in *Duet for One* (1986)

Duet for One (1986) Drama ΨΨ
Julie Andrews plays a world class violinist who learns to cope with multiple sclerosis. Good illustration of the effects of chronic illness on psychological health. Max von Sydow plays the role of Andrews' therapist.

Dummy (1979) Drama ΨΨ
Made-for-TV movie about a hearing impaired and mute teenager who is charged with murder and defended by a deaf attorney.

Early Frost, An (1985) Drama ΨΨΨ
Excellent made-for-TV movie (available on video) that explores the pain and anguish involved as a young man explains to his family and friends that he is gay and has AIDS.

Eating (1990) Comedy ΨΨΨ
An extended conversation that examines the relationship among life, love, and food.

Elephant Man, The (1980) Drama ΨΨΨ
David Lynch film about the life of John Merrick, a seriously deformed man who is befriended by a London physician. The film is effective in forcing the viewer to examine his or her prejudices about appearance.

"I am NOT an animal! I am a human being!"

John Merrick in *The Elephant Man* (1980)

Emmanuel's Gift (2005) Documentary ΨΨΨ
Emmanuel was born in Ghana in 1977 with a deformed leg and was destined to become a beggar. However, his mother instilled confidence and hope. This is an inspirational film that challenges negative stereotypes of people with disabilities.

Eye, The (2002) Suspense/Thriller ΨΨΨ
A young, blind woman regains her sight through a cornea transplant. She immediately begins to see ghosts which she identifies as the souls of the dead. Pang Brothers film in the tradition of *The Sixth Sense* and *The Ring*.

Falling Down (1994) Drama ΨΨΨ
Good presentation by Michael Douglas of the cumulative effects of stress on a marginal personality. The film does not give us enough information to clearly diagnose the character played by Douglas, but he does display significant symptoms of paranoia.

Gabby – A True Story (1987) Biography ΨΨΨ
A true story about a woman with cerebral palsy who goes on to become a respected author. Contrast this story with the life of Christy Brown told in *My Left Foot*.

Glengarry Glen Ross (1992) Drama ΨΨΨ
A hard-hitting and powerful presentation of job-related stress and interpersonal conflict in the real estate business. Wonderful cast, with Jack Lemmon playing a figure whose despair over his job is reminiscent of Willy Loman in Arthur Miller's *Death of a Salesman*.

Heart Is a Lonely Hunter, The (1968) Drama ΨΨ
Alan Arkin stars in this adaptation of Carson McCuller's sad, poignant novel about a simple friendship between two men. One of the men is deaf; the other has mental retardation. If you have to choose between the film and the novel, read the novel.

Honkytonk Man (1982) Drama Ψ
Clint Eastwood produced, directed, and starred in this film about a country and western singer with leukemia who hopes to make it to Nashville before he dies.

Hunchback of Notre Dame, The (1939) Horror ΨΨΨΨΨ
Charles Laughton plays Quasimodo in this film adaptation of the Victor Hugo novel. The film is a classic in the genre examining the relationship between body image and self-concept.

Ikiru (*To Live*, 1952, Japan) Drama ΨΨΨΨΨ
A city bureaucrat learns that he is dying of cancer and wants to find some meaning in his life. He becomes assertive in promoting projects for the public good. Until this time, he had lived a very mundane life.

In America (2003) Drama ΨΨΨΨ
Irish family immigrates to the United States to Hell's Kitchen. They befriend a Nigerian painter who is suffering with AIDS.

In for Treatment (1979) Drama ΨΨΨ
Dutch film about the indignities suffered by a cancer patient who has to deal with an impersonal health care system.

I Sent a Letter to My Love (1981) Drama ΨΨΨ
French film about a sister caring for her paralyzed brother. They each seek romance by writing to a newspaper personals column; without realizing what is happening, each winds up corresponding with the other.

Italian for Beginners (2002) Comedy/Drama ΨΨΨ
In a hodge-podge of interrelated stories, one character has pancreatic cancer and suffers extraordinary pain.

It's My Party (1996) Drama ΨΨΨΨ
Sensitive film about a man with AIDS who throws one last party before killing himself. Much of the film centers on the issue of voluntary suicide and the ethics of euthanasia.

Jacquot (1993) Biography ΨΨ
Moving film about the life of French director Jacques Demy, who died from a brain tumor shortly after the film was released.

Johnnie Belinda (1948) Drama ΨΨ
Jane Wyman (who was Ronald Reagan's wife at the time) earned an Academy Award for her performance as a deaf-mute woman who is stigmatized and raped. The film is dated but still offers insights into the ways in which people who are hearing impaired are perceived.

Kurt Cobain About a Son (2006) Documentary ΨΨ
Sensitive portrayal of the infamous grunge rock star using only interviewed audio recordings. Documents Cobain's suffering with severe stomach problems and the stress associated with his illness.

La Symphonie Pastorale (1946) Drama ΨΨΨ
French adaptation of André Gide novel about a Swiss minister who falls in love with his blind protégée and abandons his wife to be with her. When the blind girl later regains her sight, she is tormented by the decisions he has made because of her.

Leap of Faith (1992) Drama ΨΨ
Steve Martin plays itinerant evangelist Jonas Nightengale, whose faith healing stunts require technological support from backstage assistant Debra Winger. Contrast Martin's role with that of Burt Lancaster in *Elmer Gantry* (1960) and the documentary *Marjoe* (1972).

Life on a String (1991) Drama ΨΨΨ
Lyrical movie about a blind Chinese musician who believes his sight will be restored when he breaks his thousandth banjo string. He grows old and wise while he waits.

Light That Failed, The (1939) Drama ΨΨ
Adaptation of Kipling novel about a great artist who goes blind as a result of an injury while in Africa.

Living End, The (1992) Comedy ΨΨ
Two HIV positive men hit the road and explore what it means to live purposively with their disease.

"Let go. It's all right. You can let go now."

Bruce Davison comforts his dying lover in *Longtime Companion* (1990)

Longtime Companion (1990) Drama ΨΨΨ
This film explores the ways in which AIDS has affected a group of gay friends and traces the love and loss that is shared between two men as one of them dies from the disease.

Man Without a Face, The (1993) Drama ΨΨ
Mel Gibson directs and stars in this film about a man whose face becomes terribly disfigured after an automobile accident. He becomes reclusive but finds redemption in his relationship with the 12-year-old boy he tutors.

Marvin's Room (1996) Drama ΨΨΨ
A compelling examination of the way in which chronic illness affects caregivers and families.

Mask (1985) Drama ΨΨ
Cher stars in this film about her character's son, Rocky Dennis, a spunky teenager whose life has been dramatically affected by craniodiaphyseal dysplasia, a disorder that distorts the shape of his skull and face. This is a feel good movie that succeeds. The thwarted love relationship between Rocky and a blind girlfriend underscores our tendency to judge people by their appearance.

Men, The (1950) Drama ΨΨΨ
Marlon Brando in his first film role plays a paralyzed WWII veteran full of rage about his injury and his limitations.

Miracle Worker, The (1962) Biography ΨΨΨ
Patty Duke and Anne Bancroft star in this well-known film about the childhood of Helen Keller and the influence of a gifted teacher.

Motorcycle Diaries (2004, Argentina) Drama ΨΨΨ
Based on the true coming of age story of "Che" Guevara. Two men travel the countryside of South America seeing indigenous cultures while logging observations and experiences in a diary. They help out in communities and at a hospital in Peru with leprosy patients. The struggle with asthma is depicted.

Music Within (2007) Drama/Comedy ΨΨΨ
The true story of Richard Pimentel, a brilliant public speaker, who returned from Vietnam disabled by a severe hearing impairment. He became a passionate advocate for the disabled and is in part responsible for the creation of the 1990 American with Disabilities Act.

My Flesh and Blood (2004) Documentary ΨΨΨ
Moving documentary about Susan Tom, who adopted 11 special needs children and raised them on her own. The children suffer in a variety of ways; their problems include cystic fibrosis, severe burns, developmental disabilities, the absence of legs, and a genetic skin disorder that causes severe pain.

My Left Foot (1989, Ireland/UK)
Drama/Biography ΨΨΨΨ
Based on the true story of Christy Brown, a successful artist/author who triumphed over cerebral
palsy. Brown grew up as part of a large, poor,
working class Irish family. At that time, the world
was ill-equipped to understand or care for people
with cerebral palsy. A prisoner in his own body,
Brown never gave up. He painted and wrote several novels and books of poetry.

My Life (1993) Drama ΨΨΨ
Michael Keaton learns he is dying from cancer and
makes a series of videotapes for his still-unborn
son, including one in which he teaches his son how
to shave.

My Life Without Me (2003) Drama ΨΨΨ
A 23-year-old woman is diagnosed with ovarian
cancer and decides not to tell her family but instead
live her life more fully and prepare them for when
she is gone.

Niagara, Niagara (1998) Drama ΨΨ
Two teenagers on the lam encounter multiple problems en route. Reminiscent of *Bonnie and Clyde*,
the film is chiefly memorable because it is one of
the few films in which Tourette's syndrome is sympathetically and realistically portrayed.

Noise (2007) Comedy ΨΨΨ
Street noise is a stress stimulus for David Owen
(Tim Robbins) who becomes the Rectifier, a
vigilante who takes noise personally. He damages
noisy cars and destroys car alarms. He also seriously damages his relationships and loses his job
and family.

Oasis (2002, Korea) Drama ΨΨΨΨ
A quirky young man is released from prison after
serving 2.5 years for accidentally killing someone
while driving. He becomes curious and interested
in the victim's daughter who has cerebral palsy.
Both individuals are isolated and outcast from their
families, and they find friendship and comfort in
one another.

One Last Thing (2005) Comedy Ψ
A boy with terminal cancer gets a last wish from
the Wish Givers Foundation. He gets to spend a
week alone with a supermodel.

Open Hearts (2003) Drama ΨΨΨ
Danish film about a random car accident that leaves
a man paralyzed from the neck down. He lashes out

in anger unable to accept the reality of his losses.
His girlfriend begins an affair with the driver's
husband.

"My whole life disappeared with you that
morning."

Grieving in *Open Hearts* (2003)

Passion Fish (1992) Drama ΨΨΨΨ
The stress of disability and the demands a disabled
person can make on caregivers are nicely chronicled in this film about a querulous paraplegic
actress and her caretaker/companion.

Patch Adams (1998) Comedy ΨΨ
Robin Williams plays a medical student, nicknamed Patch, who defies the medical institution
and crosses boundaries in using humor and holistic
medical practices with various patients throughout
a hospital. Some humorous and touching scenes
occur on the children's cancer ward and with other
suffering patients.

Phantom of the Opera, The (1925) Horror ΨΨΨ
A disfigured music lover, played by Lon Chaney,
lives in the bowels of the Paris opera house, unable
to achieve romantic love because of his hideous
face. He is eventually hunted down and killed by
an angry mob.

Joe Miller: "What do you love about the
law, Andrew?"
Andrew Beckett: "I... many things... uh...
uh... What I love the most about the law?"
Joe Miller: "Yeah."
Andrew Beckett: "It's that every now and
again – not often, but occasionally – you
get to be a part of justice being done. That
really is quite a thrill when that happens."

Philadelphia (1993)

Philadelphia (1993) Drama ΨΨΨ
Tom Hanks won an Academy Award for his
portrayal of an AIDS-afflicted attorney who is
fired from a prestigious law firm once his illness

becomes known to the partners. There is a particularly moving scene in which Hanks plays an opera and explains to Denzel Washington why he loves the music so passionately.

Pieces of April (2003) Drama/Comedy ΨΨΨ
A young woman, estranged from her family, is determined to impress them with a Thanksgiving dinner. She has a particularly tenuous relationship with her cynical mother who is dying of cancer.

Places in the Heart (1984) Drama ΨΨΨ
Sally Field won an Academy Award for Best Actress for her role in this film about a widowed woman struggling to keep her farm and her family in a small Texas town during the Depression. The film is memorable for bringing together John Malkovich as a blind World War I veteran and Danny Glover as a hapless drifter. The standoff between a blind Malkovich and the local chapter of the Ku Klux Klan is especially memorable.

Promises in the Dark (1979) Drama ΨΨ
Melodrama about a young woman dying from cancer.

Proof (1992) Drama ΨΨΨΨ
Australian drama about a blind man who takes photographs to document his life and its meaning.

Rails and Ties (2007) Drama ΨΨΨ
Engineer Tom Stark (Kevin Bacon) cannot avoid crashing his train into a parked car occupied by a suicidal mother and her 11-year-old son who escapes the car unscathed. Stark's wife Megan (Marcia Gay Harden) is dying of cancer. The film depicts the relationship between the Starks and the young boy who help one another cope with life and death.

Rory O'Shea Was Here (2005) Comedy/Drama ΨΨΨ
Depicts the quest for independence and friendship between two young men, one coping with muscular dystrophy, the other with cerebral palsy.

Savage Nights (1992, France) Drama/Biography ΨΨΨΨ
This controversial film was directed by French filmmaker Cyril Collard, who died from AIDS three days before *Savage Nights* was selected as the best French film of the year. The movie deals with the existential decisions made by a bisexual antihero who continues to have unprotected sex even after learning he has AIDS.

Shadowlands (1993) Biography ΨΨΨ
Wonderful Richard Attenborough film about the late-life romance of C. S. Lewis (Anthony Hopkins) and Joy Gresham (Debra Winger). Lewis must come to grips with the meaning of pain, suffering, and loss when Joy develops cancer.

Shootist, The (1976) Western ΨΨ
John Wayne's last film, about an aging gunfighter dying from cancer. Also stars Jimmy Stewart, Lauren Bacall, Ron Howard, Harry Morgan, John Carradine, Hugh O'Brian, and Richard Boone. John Wayne, a heavy smoker, died from lung cancer after making this film.

> "You aim to do to me what they did with John Wesley Hardin. Lay me out and parade every damn fool in the state past me at a dollar a head, half price for children, and then stuff me in a gunny sack and shovel me under."
>
> John Bernard Books confronts the undertaker in *The Shootist* (1976)

Shop on Main Street, The (1965) Drama ΨΨΨΨ
Czechoslovakian film about a man appointed as the "Aryan controller" of a button shop in World War II. He befriends and hides the Jewish owner of the shop, who does not understand the situation because she is deaf. She assumes the new arrival has been sent as her assistant; when he later hides her to avoid deportation to the death camps, she smothers. Overcome with remorse, he kills himself. Selected as the Best Foreign Film of 1965.

Simple Men (1992) Comedy ΨΨ
Deadpan comedy from auteur director, Hal Hartley, that depicts a character suffering with epilepsy.

Smile (2005) Drama ΨΨ
Well-intentioned film depicting the suffering experienced by those with physical deformities such as cleft palates.

Storytelling (2001) Comedy/Drama ΨΨ
Two separate stories explore issues of race, sex, and exploitation. In the first story, a teenager allows herself to be exploited by her teacher after getting bored with her boyfriend who has cerebral palsy. In the second story, a shoe-store worker dreams of being

a documentary filmmaker and uses a disillusioned teenager and his family as his subjects.

Tell Me That You Love Me, Junie Moon (1970) Comedy ΨΨ
Otto Preminger film in which three unusual roommates come together as a family. Liza Minnelli is disfigured; another has epilepsy; the third is wheelchair-bound.

Terms of Endearment (1983) Comedy ΨΨΨ
Shirley MacLaine, Debra Winger, and Jack Nicholson star in this poignant but funny movie about relationships, caring, and cancer.

Test of Love, A (1984) Drama ΨΨ
An Australian film based on a true story of a teacher's successful attempt to reach out to a disabled girl.

Unbreakable (2000) Drama/Suspense ΨΨΨΨ
Samuel L. Jackson plays Elijah, a comic book collector, who was born with a rare genetic bone disease which makes him highly susceptible to injury. Bruce Willis, on the other hand, plays a security officer who is in a train wreck and is the one survivor and does not have a scratch on him. Second mainstream film by master story-teller, M. Night Shyamalan.

Unfinished Life, An (2005) Drama ΨΨ
A physically abused woman escapes her abuser with her daughter and moves in with her father-in-law (Robert Redford) and a man (Morgan Freeman) he is taking care of. The latter was mauled by a bear, needs daily injections, walks with crutches, and cannot take care of himself.

Vanilla Sky (2001) Drama/Suspense ΨΨΨ
Cameron Crowe film in which Tom Cruise plays a wealthy businessman in NYC who has a car accident and must re-establish his life with a severe facial deformity. This changes his interactions especially with a woman he is falling in love with (Penelope Cruz). He begins to break down further as his dead friend (Cameron Diaz) reappears.

"Got you in a halo, huh. I call that thing a crown of thorns. I thought they was gonna screw it into my brain."

A paralyzed patient describes his rehabilitation in
The Waterdance (1992)

Waterdance, The (1992) Drama ΨΨΨ
Realistic film about the way spinal cord injuries have changed the lives of three men who meet in a rehabilitation hospital.

Whales of August, The (1987) Drama ΨΨ
Vincent Price and Ann Sothern support Lillian Gish and Bette Davis in a remarkable film about what it means to grow old. Davis plays the blind and embittered sister who is still loved by Gish.

Whatever Happened to Baby Jane? (1962) Drama ΨΨ
Bette Davis and Joan Crawford portray two elderly sisters. Crawford is wheelchair-bound as a result of an automobile accident possibly caused by her sister. Davis is obviously demented and terrorizes her younger sister. Surprise ending.

White Heat (1949) Crime ΨΨΨ
James Cagney plays a ruthless gangster who has debilitating migraine headaches that only his mother can cure. The film ties into the psychoanalytic ideas of the day and features a famous ending in which Cagney blows up an oil tank.

"Cody Jarrett. He finally made it to the top of the world. And it blew up in his face."

White Heat (1949)

Wind Will Carry Us, The (1999, France/Iran) Drama ΨΨ
A man and his film crew travel to a remote Iranian village to film the special ceremony that occurs after an old woman dies. Directed by Abbas Kiarostami.

Whose Life Is It Anyway? (1981) Drama ΨΨΨΨ
Richard Dreyfuss plays a sculptor paralyzed from the neck down after a car crash. He argues convincingly for the right to die.

Woman's Tale, A (1991) Drama ΨΨΨ
An Australian film directed by Paul Cox about the final days in the life of a 78-year-old woman dying of cancer.

World's Fastest Indian, The (2005, New Zealand) Drama ΨΨΨ
Heart disease threatens the life of New Zealander

Burt Munro, who spent years building a 1920 Indian motorcycle. Despite the stress of physical illness, Munro pushes forward in an attempt to break a land speed record at the Bonneville Salt Flats.

Wrestler, The (2008) Drama ΨΨΨΨ
Randy "the Ram" is a professional wrestler who is forced to retire due to multiple physical problems following use of steroids and body enhancers. He breaks down (vomits and faints) with a heart attack after a challenging match fighting with glass, a staple gun, and barbs. He attempts a comeback in both his personal life and in wrestling. Directed by Darren Aronofsky.

Yesterday (2004, South Africa) Drama ΨΨΨΨΨ
A woman named Yesterday focuses largely on the present and future as she takes care of her daughter, her dying husband, and her own HIV.

Mood Disorders and Suicide

American Splendor (2003) Comedy/Drama/ Documentary/Animation ΨΨΨΨ
Small time comic book writer and curmudgeon, Harvey Pekar, reaches cult status including several appearances on the David Letterman show. This film integrates a narrative about a depressed couple trying to get along and manage life's stressors, comic book animation, and documentary of the real Harvey Pekar.

"Right now I'd be glad to spare some growth for some happiness."

Harvey Pekar in
American Splendor (2003)

Anna Karenina (1935) Drama ΨΨΨΨ
Greta Garbo leaves her husband (Basil Rathbone) and son to follow a new love (Fredric March); when she sees him kissing another woman, she commits suicide by stepping into the path of an oncoming train. Based on a Tolstoy novel.

Art of Failure: Chuck Connelly, The (2008) Documentary ΨΨ
Quirky, neo-expressionist painter of the 1980s,

inspired by Andy Warhol and Jackson Pollack. The film depicts an agitated depression but it also presents a caricature of the "troubled artist."

Bell Jar, The (1979) Biography Ψ
An unsuccessful attempt to capture the spirit of Sylvia Plath's autobiographical novel *The Bell Jar*. Plath eventually committed suicide by putting her head into an oven and turning on the gas.

Blue Sky (1994) Drama ΨΨΨ
Jessica Lange won an Academy Award for her role as a military wife with a bipolar disorder.

Broken Flowers (2005) Drama ΨΨ
Bill Murray is a depressed Lothario who moves from one casual affair to the next until he gets a letter telling him that he has a 19-year-son and he begins a quest to find the anonymous former girlfriend who wrote the letter.

Cache (2005, France), Mystery/Thriller ΨΨ
A married couple begins to receive videotapes at their doorstep that depict surveillance of their house. The film provides an interesting commentary on the psychology of guilt.

Cooler, The (2003) Drama ΨΨΨ
Unlucky, depressed man (William H. Macy) walks around the casino as "the cooler," someone paid to bring bad luck to successful gamers by appearing near their gambling tables. He is paying off his enormous gambling debts owed to the casino owner Alec Baldwin.

Crossover (1983) Drama Ψ
A male nurse is plagued by self-doubts after one of the psychiatric patients commits suicide.

Devil and Daniel Johnston, The (2005) Documentary/Biography ΨΨΨΨ
Portrait of a musical genius who vacillates between madness and brilliant creativity.

Eye of God (1997) Drama ΨΨ
Some of the scenes in this film address a boy who witnesses his mother's suicide, experiences acute stress disorder, and kills himself at age 14.

Faithless (2000) Drama ΨΨΨΨ
Liv Ullmann directed this film about a woman who has an affair with a deeply depressed man.

Field, The (1990) Drama ΨΨ Ψ
Dramatic presentation of the suicide by drowning

of a young man who finds he cannot live up to his father's expectations.

Flying Scotsman, The (2006, Germany/UK) Drama ΨΨΨ
Champion cyclist who constructed his bike out of pieces of washing machines suffers with depression and suicidal thoughts. This film received an "Honorable Mention" at the Voice Awards.

Fox and His Friends (1975) Drama ΨΨΨ
Werner Fassbinder's scathing indictment of capitalism revolves around the life of a poor gay circus performer who wins money, only to lose it through the exploitation of those he assumes are his friends. He responds by committing suicide.

Garden State (2004) Drama/Comedy ΨΨΨ
A young man flies to his hometown in New Jersey for his mother's funeral. He has been estranged from his family for several years. Without his "bipolar" medication for the first time, he begins to experiment with life and finds love.

Good Morning, Vietnam (1987) Comedy/Drama/War ΨΨ
Robin Williams as an Air Force radio announcer in Vietnam. Williams has a funny, frenetic style that could be described as hypomanic.

Hairdresser's Husband, The (1992) Comedy/Drama ΨΨΨ
A woman chooses to commit suicide rather than face the incremental loss of love that she believes will accompany aging. This is a beautiful movie, despite the somewhat grim ending.

Harold and Maude (1971) Comedy ΨΨΨ
An acting-out teenager and an iconoclastic old woman bond and support one another's eccentricities, including Harold's repeated feigned suicide attempts.

Hitchhiker's Guide to the Galaxy, The (2005) Comedy Ψ
One of the major characters, a robot, exhibits a number of symptoms of depression.

Horse Feathers (1932) Comedy ΨΨ
Groucho Marx plays a manic college president who displays flight of ideation and pressured speech.

Hospital, The (1971) Comedy/Drama ΨΨΨ
George C. Scott is first rate as a disillusioned and suicidal physician despondent in part because

of the ineptitude he sees everywhere about him. There is an especially memorable scene in which Scott is interrupted as he is about to commit suicide by injecting potassium into a vein.

House of Sand and Fog (2003) Drama ΨΨΨΨ
Jennifer Connelly and Sir Ben Kingsley play opposite one another in a gripping and deeply poignant story about two seemingly very different people, each with a legitimate claim to ownership of the same house. The film accurately portrays depression, alcohol abuse, suicide attempts, and suicide.

Hours, The (2002) Drama ΨΨΨΨ
Well-acted and well-crafted tapestry integrating three stories from different times – Nicole Kidman as the renowned novelist, Virginia Woolf, struggling to write her novel *Mrs. Dalloway*; Julianne Moore, who is reading the novel decades later; and Meryl Streep who embodies many of Mrs. Dalloway's characteristics. Each of the four main characters (the three aforementioned and Ed Harris) struggles with some form of mood disorder.

"You cannot find peace by avoiding life."

Virginia Woolf in *The Hours* (2002)

Imaginary Heroes (2004) Drama ΨΨ
A young boy commits suicide by shooting himself, and each member of the family responds to the tragedy in a different way.

Inside Moves (1980) Drama ΨΨ
A man who has failed in a suicide attempt makes new friends in a bar and regains the will to live. Mainly notable as the comeback film for Harold Russell, the double amputee from *The Best Years of Our Lives* (1946).

Into the Wild (2007) Biography ΨΨΨ
Sean Penn directed this film that is based on a true story about an Emory student who graduates, gives away the money he had saved for law school, and moves to Alaska. It is a useful pedagogical exercise to speculate about potential diagnoses for this young man.

It's a Wonderful Life (1946) Drama ΨΨΨ
A Christmas tradition. The film actually presents Jimmy Stewart as a complex character who

responds to the stress of life in Bedford Falls by attempting suicide.

Jellysmoke (2005) Drama/Romance ΨΨΨ
A young man with bipolar disorder is released from a psychiatric institution and struggles to adapt to his new life. Winner of a Voice Award.

> "You see, George, you've really had a wonderful life.
> Don't you see what a mistake it would be to throw it away?"
>
> Clarence in *It's A Wonderful Life* (1946)

Juliet of the Spirits (1965) Drama ΨΨΨ
Frederico Fellini film about a bored, lonely, depressed, and menopausal homemaker who hallucinates about the life of the exotic woman next door.

Last Days (2005) Drama ΨΨΨ
Slow moving Gus van Sant film depicting the final days of Nirvana singer/guitarist, Kurt Cobain. Various manic and depressive symptoms are displayed.

Last Days of Disco, The (1998) Drama Ψ
One of the characters has bipolar disorder and is stereotyped as "looney" and "crazy"; however, he is depicted as compliant with Lithium, and his life is stable and balanced. Interesting contrast to the frequently portrayed stereotypes of bipolar disorder.

Last Picture Show, The (1971) Drama ΨΨΨΨ
Peter Bogdanovich adaptation of Larry McMurtry's novel describing the events – and personalities – involved in the closing of the town's only movie theater. There is a striking presentation of the symptoms of depression in the coach's wife.

Life Upside Down (1964, France) Drama ΨΨΨ
French film about an ordinary young man who becomes increasingly detached from the world. He is eventually hospitalized and treated, but with little success.

Little Miss Sunshine (2006) Comedy ΨΨΨ
Steve Carrell plays a renowned gay Proust scholar who has just been released from the hospital after a suicide attempt.

Lonely Guy, The (1984) Comedy Ψ
Steve Martin plays a depressed and suicidal New Yorker.

Lonesome Jim (2006) Drama ΨΨΨ
Steve Buscemi directed this engaging film about a depressed and discouraged writer who returns to his childhood home in Indiana after failing to make his mark in New York City.

Maborosi (1995, Japan) Drama ΨΨΨΨ
A Japanese film about the effects of a man's seemingly irrational suicide on the wife who is left behind to care for their 3-month-old infant.

Melinda and Melinda (2004) Comedy/Drama ΨΨ
This Woody Allen film alternates between two versions of a story, one tragic, one comic. In the tragic version, we find a depressed and suicidal Melinda.

Michael Clayton (2007) Drama ΨΨΨΨ
Tom Wilkinson plays the role of a brilliant attorney whose bipolar-manic episodes make it almost impossible for him to function as an attorney.

Mind the Gap (2004) Drama ΨΨΨ
The lives of five isolated, lonely and desperate people are intertwined in complex ways: eventually each live intersects with the other four. One poignant segment portrays a suicidal African American man who gets life-saving advice from a priest.

Mishima: A Life in Four Chapters (1985) Biography ΨΨΨ
A fascinating film about one of the most interesting figures in contemporary literature, Yukio Mishima. Mishima, a homosexual, traditionalist, and militarist, committed ritual suicide *(seppuku)* before being beheaded by a companion.

Mommie Dearest (1981) Biography ΨΨ
Biographical film based on the book by Joan Crawford's adopted daughter. Faye Dunaway plays Crawford. The film suggests the great star was tyrannical, narcissistic, and probably bipolar.

Monsieur Ibrahim (2003) Drama/Comedy ΨΨΨ
An elderly widower and troubled teen form a unique friendship while living in Paris in the 1960s. A secondary character, the boy's father, suffers from agitated, masked depression, and eventually abandons his son (who had already been abandoned by his mother) and commits suicide.

Monster's Ball (2002) Drama ΨΨΨ
Emotionally jarring film about two lost, self-hating people who begin to experience emotion and face their pain through their relationship. Stars Billy Bob Thornton and Halle Berry, the latter who won an Academy Award for Best Actress for her role in this film.

"It takes a human being to really see a human being."

Monster's Ball (2002)

Mosquito Coast, The (1986) Adventure ΨΨΨ
Harrison Ford is an eccentric American inventor who flees the U.S. for Central America because of his paranoia. His diagnosis is never clearly stated, but Ford appears to be bipolar (although almost continually manic in the film).

My First Wife (1984) Drama ΨΨ
A moving and well-directed Australian film about a man who falls apart after his wife decides to leave him.

Network (1976) Drama ΨΨΨ
A veteran anchorman who has just been told he is being fired announces on national TV that he will commit suicide on the air in two weeks. Ratings soar. He eventually reneges on his promise but becomes the leader of a national protest movement.

"... I'm as mad as hell, and I'm not going to take this anymore!"

Newscaster Howard Beale in
Network (1976)

Nightmare Alley (1947) Crime ΨΨ
Tyrone Power's favorite film. Power plays a carnival huckster who teams up with an unethical psychologist to dupe the public. Memorable carnival "geek" scenes include biting the heads off chickens.

Nine Lives (2005) Drama ΨΨΨ
This film is directed by Rodrigo Garcia, the son of the novelist Gabriel Garcia Marquez. It consists of nine relatively brief vignettes about the lives of nine women, one of whom is suicidal.

Ordinary People (1980) Drama ΨΨΨ
This film was Robert Redford's debut as a director. It deals with depression, suicide, and family pathology and presents a sympathetic portrayal of a psychiatrist, played by Judd Hirsch. Conrad, the protagonist, would probably meet *DSM-IV-TR* criteria for PTSD as well as depression.

Outcry, The (1957) Drama ΨΨΨ
Antonioni film about a man who becomes depressed and confused when he is rejected by his lover.

Pollock (2000) Drama ΨΨΨ
Ed Harris portrays the troubled painter, Jackson Pollack, who struggles with alcoholism and bipolar disorder.

Prozac Nation (2001) Drama ΨΨΨ
A dramatic and realistic portrayal of depression and borderline personality disorder in a Harvard undergraduate.

Rain (2001) Drama ΨΨ
Coming-of-age New Zealand film about a young girl whose mother is a depressed alcoholic.

Respiro (2002) Drama ΨΨΨ
An Italian film about a woman with a serious bipolar disorder who has to flee and hide in a cave to avoid coerced psychiatric treatment.

Running with Scissors (2006) Biography ΨΨ
Annette Bening plays the role of a bipolar mother who turns over her son's life to her psychiatrist.

Scent of a Woman (1992) Drama ΨΨΨ
Al Pacino plays Colonel Slade, a depressed blind veteran who seems to have lost all meaning in his life until he is challenged by a younger man.

September (1987) Drama ΨΨ
A Woody Allen film in which Mia Farrow plays a depressed woman recovering from a suicide attempt.

Seven Pounds (2008) Drama ΨΨΨΨ
Will Smith plays a character who attempts to use his suicide to gain redemption for an accident he caused that resulted in the deaths of seven people.

Seventh Veil, The (1945) Drama ΨΨ
Psychological drama about a gifted musician who loses the ability to play the piano and becomes

depressed and suicidal. Hypnotherapy makes it possible for Ann Todd to play again, as well as to sort out her complex interpersonal relationships.

Shawshank Redemption, The (1994) Drama ΨΨΨΨ
An outstanding film, memorable in part because of the suicide of one character who finds himself unable to adjust to life outside an institution.

Shopgirl (2005) Drama ΨΨ
A depressed salesgirl learns about the meaning of love through an affair with a much older man (played by Steve Martin, who also wrote the screenplay and the novella upon which the film was based).

Spanglish (2004) Comedy Ψ
An offbeat comedy about a talented cook and his manic wife who hires a Latina housekeeper.

Station Agent, The (2003) Drama/Comedy ΨΨΨΨ
Heartwarming, honest story of three lonely and disparate characters who form a unique friendship with one another. The three characters are a schizoid dwarf whose only desire is isolation, a woman who has repeated conflicts with her husband and attempts suicide, and a talkative man from New Jersey. Good mix of both healthy and unhealthy coping approaches to loneliness and depression.

Suicide Club (2002) Drama/Suspense ΨΨΨ
Fifty-four young girls collectively jump in front of an oncoming subway train, which triggers individual and group suicides around the country. This mysterious Japanese film raises questions of cause, documenting links between suicide and adolescence, violence, and consumerism.

Summer Wishes, Winter Dreams (1973) Drama Ψ
Joanne Woodward is a bored, depressed housewife searching for meaning and purpose in her life. The film includes dreams that may be hallucinations, and a possible somatoform disorder.

Sylvia (2003) Drama ΨΨ
Gwenyth Paltrow portrays the life of respected American poet, Sylvia Plath, who committed suicide in 1963.

Taste of Cherry (1997) Drama ΨΨΨΨ
An Iranian film about a man who wants to commit suicide but who can't find anyone to help him.

Tenant, The (1976) Horror ΨΨΨΨ
Roman Polanski film in which a man rents an apart-

ment previously owned by a woman who committed suicide. The man begins to assume the personality of the woman and becomes suicidal himself.

Tout de Suite, À (2004) Drama ΨΨ
A naive teenager runs away from home with her Moroccan boyfriend who has just killed a man in a bank robbery. She winds up abandoned in Morocco, depressed and exploited.

Umberto D. (1952) Drama ΨΨΨΨ
Classic Vittorio De Sica film about an indigent old man in Rome who is being evicted and must face the prospects of homelessness and isolation. The old man fails a suicide attempt and finds a reason for living through his devotion to his dog.

Vincent (1987) Biography/Documentary ΨΨΨ
An interesting examination of the life of Vincent van Gogh. The focus is on the artist's work rather than his mental illness.

Vincent & Theo (1990) Biography ΨΨΨ
This Robert Altman film deals sensitively with van Gogh's troubled relationships with Gauguin and Theo, the incident with the prostitute and his ear, van Gogh's hospitalization, and finally his suicide.

Virgin Suicides, The (1999) Drama ΨΨ
Sofia Coppola's directorial debut about a repressed family with five daughters, who in response to their mother's control, repression, and forced isolation, decide to commit suicide.

Visitor, The (2007) Drama ΨΨΨ
This film illustrates the apathy and indifference that can sometimes accompany depression. Richard Jenkins plays the role of Professor Walter Vale, a man coping unsuccessfully with the death of his wife.

War Within, The (2005) Drama ΨΨ
An examination of the motives behind the behavior of a suicide bomber.

Wilbur Wants to Kill Himself (2002) Drama/Comedy ΨΨ
Disappointing and highly stereotypic movie of both suicide and boundary-crossing psychotherapists. Perpetrates the misconception that love can conquer mental illness (in this case, multiple, severe suicide attempts).

Winter Passing (2005) Drama ΨΨ
A depressed young woman living in New York

City uses alcohol, drugs and casual sex to cope. She travels to the upper peninsula of Michigan to visit her father, an alcoholic novelist, to see if she can obtain copies of the letters he wrote to her recently deceased mother years earlier.

Woman Under the Influence, A (1974) Drama ΨΨΨ
A John Cassavetes film in which Gena Rowlands plays a homemaker who has to be hospitalized because of a mental illness that appears to be bipolar disorder. Peter Falk plays her mystified husband.

Wristcutters: A Love Story (2006) Fantasy ΨΨ
A young man commits suicide and then finds himself in purgatory, surrounded by other individuals who have all committed suicide in one way or another.

Wrong Man, The (1956) Crime ΨΨ
Hitchcock film in which a man and his wife (Henry Fonda and Vera Miles) become depressed in response to an unjust accusation of murder.

Personality Disorders

25th Hour (2002) Drama ΨΨΨΨ
A Spike Lee film about a young man (Edward Norton) about to go away to prison for 7 years for marijuana trafficking. In making the most of his final hours, he meets with his "recovering alcoholic" father, girlfriend, friends, and an "underground" boss and his henchmen. Look for tributes to 9/11 throughout the film (it was the first film to use Ground Zero as a film scene).

Accidental Tourist, The (1988) Comedy ΨΨΨ
William Hurt plays a withdrawn, unemotional writer whose isolation is compounded when his 12-year-son is senselessly murdered in a fast-food restaurant.

Alfie (2004) Comedy ΨΨΨ
Jude Law stars as a man with a narcissistic personality who prides himself in being a womanizer and not committing in relationships. Law's asides to the audience provide insight into his narcissistic thinking. By the end of the film, Alfie begins to face the impact of his behavior on others.

Amelie (2001, France) Comedy/Romance ΨΨΨΨ
Audrey Tautou stars as Amelie, an avoidant woman who wants an intimate relationship with others but is unable to be direct. Upon deciding to change her life by making a difference in others' lives, she adopts extreme and creative measures to bring joy to others and make connections. Brilliantly directed by Jean Pierre-Jeunet.

American Beauty (1999) Comedy/Drama ΨΨΨΨ
Kevin Spacey has the lead role in this remarkable film about a very dysfunctional family and the ennui that accompanies life in suburbia. Annette Bening plays a woman with a classic Histrionic Personality Disorder. Almost every character ex-hibits some degree of psychopathology. The film is a compelling examination of what Freud called the psychopathology of everyday life.

American Gangster (2007) Crime/Drama ΨΨΨ
An honest detective (Russell Crowe) tries to bring down a heroin kingpin (Denzel Washington) in this Ridley Scott film.

American History X (1998) Drama/Suspense ΨΨΨ
Edward Norton plays an antisocial, white supremacist who decides to change his life when he sees his younger brother is following his example.

American Psycho (1999) Drama/Suspense ΨΨΨ
Christian Bale is Patrick Bateman, a narcissistic Wall Street executive, who emphasizes excess and style over substance in everything from business cards and facial cleansers to restaurant selection and conversation. He is depicted as a serial killer who saves the victim's heads in his refrigerator. However, there is enough cinematic evidence to suggest that there were no murders at all, and everything in the film simply reflects the fantasies of an antisocial mind.

Anatomy of a Murder (1959) Drama ΨΨΨΨ
Jimmy Stewart as an attorney defending a man accused of murder. His case rests on the contention that the defendant could not help behaving as he did because the man he murdered had allegedly raped his wife. The film raises interesting questions about the irresistible impulse defense.

Anchorman: The Legend of Ron Burgundy (2004) Comedy Ψ
A narcissistic anchorman (Will Ferrell) competes with an ambitious female journalist.

Anything Else (2003) Comedy ΨΨ
Woody Allen film about a young man with dependent personality who falls for an erratic young woman (Christina Ricci).

"See where I'm standing? That's where I'm from."

Sonny in *The Apostle* (1997)

Apostle, The (1997) Drama ΨΨΨΨ
Robert Duvall directs, writes, and stars as a philandering but dedicated minister who flees his hometown after committing a violent act. His redemptive journey takes him to a small town where he builds a ministry until his past catches up with him.

Apt Pupil (1998) Drama/Suspense ΨΨΨ
A high school student becomes fascinated with his discovery of a man (Ian McKellen) who was formerly a Nazi henchman. Kurt Dussander is living (and hiding out) in a local town. The student manipulates him to tell him detailed stories of his previous work.

"To the whole world I am a monster."

An escaped Nazi in *Apt Pupil* (1998)

Arsenic and Old Lace (1944) Comedy ΨΨ
Frank Capra film about Cary Grant's two aunts who practice mercy killing by giving their gentlemen guests poisoned elderberry wine. Grant worries about the fact that mental illness not only runs in his family, it gallops!

Assassination of Jesse James by the Coward Robert Ford, The (2007) Crime ΨΨΨ
The humanization and glorification of infamous outlaw, Jesse James (Brad Pitt) is depicted, along with the young, timid Robert Ford who shot him. James was an antisocial personality who was (understandably) paranoid.

Bad Santa (2003) Comedy Ψ
This Terry Zwigoff film stars Billy Bob Thornton

as a rule breaking, crass alcoholic who works as Santa Claus at a department store. The female co-star has a "Santa fetish."

Bad Seed, The (1956) Drama Ψ
Interesting examination of whether or not evil is congenital.

Bartleby (2001) Comedy ΨΨΨΨ
This dark comedy brilliantly casts Crispin Glover as the aloof, quirky clerk, Bartleby, who repeats the same phrase, "I would prefer not to," when asked to work. Ironically colorful set design and a hodge-podge of quirky personalities as supporting cast. This is clearly a "love it or hate it" film, based on a short story by Herman Melville. Bartleby's character is a classic depiction of a person with a schizoid personality.

Bartleby (1970) Comedy ΨΨΨ
Original, black and white, version of the Herman Melville short story, Bartleby the Scrivener. More slow, dark, and dreary than its recent counterpart, yet still an excellent depiction of schizoid personality.

Basic Instinct (1992; 2006) Thriller/Drama Ψ
Sharon Stone as Catherine Tramell, a seductive and manipulative woman with many borderline traits.

Before the Devil Knows You're Dead (2007) Drama/Crime ΨΨΨ
Sidney Lumet directs Philip Seymour Hoffman, Ethan Hawke, Marisa Tomei, and Albert Finney in a film about a heist (of one's own family) gone terribly wrong.

Being Julia (2004) Drama/Comedy ΨΨΨ
Annette Bening portrays an actress with qualities of each of the Cluster B personality disorders, in addition to a work addiction.

Believer, The (2001) Drama ΨΨΨ
Fascinating character study of Danny Burrows who is living his life in an impossible contradiction as a Jewish Nazi. As he faces his true self, his ruthless antisocial characteristics begin to crumble. Based on a true story of events that occurred in Burrows' life in the Fall of 1965.

Bitter Moon (1992) Drama ΨΨΨΨ
Roman Polanski film in which a couple becomes entangled with a woman who meets several criteria for borderline personality.

Black Snake Moan (2006) Drama ΨΨΨ
Samuel L. Jackson plays a broken man who rescues a promiscuous, erratic woman (Christina Ricci) left for dead on the road. Both characters face and share their dark sides.

Box of Moonlight (1996) Drama ΨΨΨ
A rigid, orderly, rule-obsessed man, played by John Turturro, takes extra time off from his job and family to re-discover his lost adolescence. The title becomes a beautiful, transformational metaphor in the film.

Breach (2007) Thriller/Drama ΨΨΨ
A pathological, manipulative CIA official (Chris Cooper) leads a double life in this intriguing thriller. Based on the true story of the worst FBI spy in U.S. history, someone who eventually cost the U.S. government billions of dollars.

Breathless (1960, France) Drama/Crime ΨΨΨΨΨ
Classic antisocial hoodlum in a classic film by French New Wave director, Jean-Luc Godard. The pacing of the film justifies the title, as does the lead performance of the anti-hero.

Bruce Almighty (2002) Comedy Ψ
Whimsical comedy about a man (Jim Carrey) given the opportunity to "be God" for a day.

Butley (1974) Drama ΨΨΨΨ
Alan Bates in a Harold Pinter film adaptation of a London play about the life of a British university professor. Bates' wife and lover are both leaving him, and his colleagues are estranged. Bates seems to fail in every interpersonal encounter.

Caine Mutiny, The (1954) Drama ΨΨΨ
Humphrey Bogart is the ship's paranoid captain, who decompensates under the pressure of testimony when he is called to the witness stand. Humphrey Bogart plays the role of Captain Queeg.

Catch Me If You Can (2002) Drama ΨΨΨ
Steven Spielberg directs Leonardo DiCaprio who plays the role of a manipulative con man with an antisocial personality. He repeatedly changes his identity while defrauding banks and keeping FBI agent (Tom Hanks) one step behind him. Based on the true story of Frank Abagnal, Jr.

Character (1997, The Netherlands) Drama ΨΨΨ
Best Foreign Film winner (Dutch) about a young man's personal and financial struggle to be free of his antisocial father. His mother appears to have a schizoid personality disorder.

> "That boy, I'll strangle him for nine tenths and the last tenth will make him strong."
>
> Dreverhaven describing his son in
> *Character* (1998)

Charlie and the Chocolate Factory (2005) Drama/Comedy ΨΨΨΨΨ
Tim Burton remake of the classic story is well-casted with beautiful set designs. Johnny Depp's portrayal of an eccentric, isolated, and perceptually disturbed Willy Wonka is one of the best depictions of schizotypal personality captured on film.

Child, The (2005, France) Drama/Crime ΨΨΨ
Bruno, who leads a gang of petty thieves, decides to sell his newborn for money.

Come Back to the Five and Dime, Jimmy Dean, Jimmy Dean (1982) Drama ΨΨ
A Robert Altman film in which Sandy Dennis plays a local woman in a small Texas town who is convinced she bore a son by James Dean when he was in town filming *Giant*.

Compulsion (1959) Drama/Crime ΨΨΨ
Two young fraternity brothers believe their perfect crime of murder is "the true test of the superior intellect." Their defense attorney (Orson Welles) gives a memorable speech in an attempt to save their lives.

Conspiracy Theory (1997) Drama ΨΨ
Mel Gibson plays a cab driver with virtually no personal life, who is obsessed with a woman, and who writes a newsletter on conspiracies. His paranoia takes him to every possible place and situation, including one conspiracy that turns out true.

Conversation, The (1974) Drama ΨΨΨ
A Francis Ford Coppola film in which Gene Hackman plays a surveillance expert with a paranoid personality.

Corporation, The (2004) Documentary ΨΨ
Interesting, albeit one-sided, review of corporations that documents the similarities between them

and the characteristics of a psychopathic personality disorder.

Criminal (2004) Drama/Crime Ψ
John C. Reilly portrays an antisocial con-artist who takes an apprentice. The film suffers from a contrived ending, standard fare for "con" films.

Crush, The (1993) Drama/Suspense Ψ
Alicia Silverstone plays a 14-year-old temptress who is obsessed with a 28-year-old man who is simply not interested in her. This is an interesting portrayal of a character who is likely to qualify for a diagnosis of Antisocial Personality Disorder (as soon as she turns 18).

Dark Knight, The (2008) Action/Crime ΨΨΨΨ
Christopher Nolan's follow-up to *Batman Begins* stars Heath Ledger in incredible form as "the Joker," a clever and fearless psychopath who battles Batman (Christian Bale).

Decalogue, The (1989, Poland) Drama ΨΨΨΨΨ
Ten, 1-hour films loosely based on the ten commandments, originally made for Polish television by director Krzysztof Kieslowski. This set of films was hailed as one of the most significant productions in recent history, and the late Stanley Kubrick once said it is the only film masterpiece he knows. Multiple psychological disorders are portrayed in various characters living in an apartment complex.

Dementia 13 (1963) Horror Ψ
Third rate film about an ax murderer; interesting primarily because it is Francis Ford Coppola's first "serious" film.

Divine Secrets of the Ya-Ya Sisterhood (2002) Drama/Comedy ΨΨ
A group of friends teach a young woman (Sandra Bullock) about her troubled mother. Ellen Burstyn and Ashley Judd play the erratic, labile, and abusive mother.

Dogville (2003) Drama ΨΨΨ
Nicole Kidman stars as a woman on the run who finds refuge in a small, isolated town. If a town could be diagnosed, this one would clearly be "antisocial" as group contagion results in manipulation, deceit, and abuse. Unique set design of a town without any houses or doors and is set as if on a theater stage.

Dot the I (2003, UK/Spain/US) Drama/Romance Ψ
A love triangle set in London with various twists of deceit and sabotage that leave the viewer wondering who is manipulating whom.

Dream Lover (1994) Drama Ψ
A sociopathic woman plots to marry a man and then have him committed to an insane asylum.

Employee of the Month (2004) Comedy/Drama Ψ
Dark comedy with Matt Dillon experiencing a day when everything in his "perfect" life goes wrong. Watch for numerous Buddhist references to the fact that "everything is an illusion."

End of Violence, The (1997) Drama ΨΨΨ
Wim Wenders film about a paranoid personality played by Bill Pullman.

Enron: The Smartest Guys in the Room (2005) Documentary ΨΨ
Depicts the antisocial personalities of the Enron corporation leaders and the back-story of their rise to power and eventual downfall.

Equilibrium (2002) Action ΨΨ
This film depicts a futuristic society in which everyone must take a drug to block the disease called "human emotion."

Eulogy (2003) Comedy Ψ
Dark comedy about a dysfunctional family of self-serving, self-absorbed, hypocrites.

Evita (1997) Drama/Musical ΨΨ
Madonna portrays Argentina's first lady, Eva Peron, and depicts her rise from poverty and scandal to fame, fortune, and the adulation of a nation. Eva (Evita) does what it takes to climb the ladder of success, eventually marrying military leader Juan Peron. She speaks out on his behalf, mobilizes the people of Argentina, frees him from jail, and helps him get elected. Antonio Banderas plays her alter ego with running commentary, warnings, criticism, and song.

Family Man, The (2000) Family/Comedy ΨΨ
Corporate executive (Nicholas Cage) obsessed with money, fame, and power gets an opportunity to see how his life would have turned out if he had married his college sweetheart. The film includes obvious parallels with *It's a Wonderful Life*.

Fatal Attraction (1987) Thriller/Romance ΨΨΨ
Glenn Close displays classic characteristics of borderline personality disorder, including fears of abandonment, unstable interpersonal relationships, impulsivity, suicidal gestures, inappropriate and intense

anger, and affective instability. This remarkable film is flawed by a contrived and artificial ending.

Fargo (1996) Comedy ΨΨΨΨΨ
Dark comedy from the Coen brothers about a car salesman (William H. Macy) whose plot to kidnap his wife has gone horribly awry. Frances McDormand has a memorable role as police chief Marge Gunderson.

Finding Forrester (2000) Drama ΨΨ
A high school student befriends an aloof, retired professor and writer who has avoided people for years. Their relationship is "rocky," taking many turns, yet each individual has a profound impact on the other.

Five Easy Pieces (1970) Drama ΨΨΨ
Jack Nicholson, raised in an upper class and gifted family, is a talented pianist who left his affluent life to work in the oil fields. The plot is thin, but the character Nicholson plays is complex and fascinating.

Fracture (2007) Thriller/Drama Ψ
Anthony Hopkins and Ryan Gosling star in this courtroom suspense film in which Hopkins kills his wife and gets away with it.

Freaks (1932) Horror ΨΨΨΨ
Fascinating film about a "normal" trapeze artist who marries a midget and then tries to poison him. When his friends find out, they kill her strong-man lover and turn her into one of them.

From Dusk Till Dawn (1995) Horror Ψ
Quentin Tarantino and George Clooney portray psychopaths who rendezvous at a biker bar that turns out to be run by vampires. The film presents as two very different movies combined – the first is Tarantino-like in character interaction and dialogue, and the second half is a horror show. Robert Rodriguez directs the film.

From the Life of the Marionettes (1980) Drama ΨΨΨ
Bergman film in which an executive rapes and kills a prostitute.

Ghost Dog: The Way of the Samurai (1999) Crime/Drama ΨΨΨ
Jim Jarmusch film about a reclusive man who lives with pigeons and believes he is indebted to a mob boss who once saved his life.

Girl, Interrupted (1999) Drama ΨΨ
A depressed, young woman (Winona Ryder), sent to a psychiatric hospital and labeled with Borderline Personality Disorder, encounters a dangerous patient (Angelina Jolie) with an Antisocial Personality Disorder.

Godfather, The (1972; 1974; 1990) Crime/Drama ΨΨΨΨ
The classic trilogy directed by Francis Ford Coppola about a New York Mafia family who are kind and generous to those who support the family and ruthless to those who oppose it.

God Is Great and I Am Not (2003) Comedy ΨΨ
Audrey Tautou plays a dependent woman who obsessively conforms to the religion of any man she is dating.

Gone with the Wind (1939) Romance/Drama ΨΨΨΨ
In the classic love story, Scarlett O'Hara meets full criteria for histrionic personality disorder; however, some have argued that these surface features are the result of the social forces of her culture & time and that her deeper character structure would not be considered histrionic.

Grey Gardens (2009) Drama/Biography ΨΨΨ
Drew Barrymore and Jessica Lange portray the infamous mother and daughter, Edie and Edith Beales. Lange's character was a first cousin to Jackie Onassis-Kennedy, and displays dependent personality and extreme symptoms of what might be agoraphobia. The extreme avoidance and pathology of the characters results in a deteriorating mansion that is nothing but a dilapidated cesspool of filth and cat urine.

Grifters, The (1990) Crime ΨΨΨ
Anjelica Huston stars in this fascinating introduction to the world of the con. Contrast this film with a movie almost as good, David Mamet's *House of Games* (see Treatment section).

Guy (1997) Drama ΨΨ
Fascinating story about a documentary filmmaker (Hope Davis) who chooses one person (Vincent D'Onofrio) at random and relentlessly follows him, filming his daily life for several days despite the victim's resistance and threats. Her obsession of filming him becomes his obsession with being filmed. The movie addresses narcissism and suggests that obsessions are a core part of human nature.

Heavy (1995) Drama ΨΨΨ
An obese, schizoid man loses his mother (with whom he has lived) and becomes even more withdrawn as he grieves.

I, Robot (2004) Action/Suspense ΨΨ
Surprisingly high quality action film about an agent who battles robots threatening to take over the world. Will Smith's role illustrates paranoid personality traits.

"I did it because I could."

In the Company of Men (1997)

In the Company of Men (1997) Comedy ΨΨΨ
Misogynistic satire of two men (with varying levels of narcissism) who deliberately seduce the same vulnerable girl, lead her on, and then abandon her. Directed by Neil LaBute.

Jonestown: The Life and Death of Peoples Temple (2006) Documentary/Biography ΨΨ
Discussion and explanation of the events that led up to the largest mass suicide in modern history, brought about by the manipulative tactics of the antisocial preacher Jim Jones.

Kalifornia (1993) Thriller ΨΨ
Early Brad Pitt performance as a quirky, ruthless, psychopathic killer who teams up with his naïve sweetheart (Juliette Lewis), a woman with a borderline IQ. There is not a hint of remorse or empathy in Pitt's character.

Knife in the Water (1962) Drama ΨΨΨΨ
One of Roman Polanski's earliest films. A man and his wife on a sailing holiday pick up a hitchhiker. There is mounting sexual tension between the older man and his younger rival. The younger man eventually makes love to the wife after a complex turn of events that occur when the couple becomes convinced the young man has drowned.

La Cage aux Folles (1978) Comedy ΨΨΨ
Zaza (Albin), a transvestite nightclub performer, is a wonderful example of a histrionic personality. He is dramatic and flamboyant and threatens suicide when things do not go his way.

Ladies Man, The (2000) Comedy Ψ
Tim Meadows plays a narcissistic talk-show host and "player." Spin-off of a successful Saturday Night Live skit.

Ladykillers, The (2004) Comedy ΨΨ
Tom Hanks leads a group of thieves in a caper to steal money from a casino by digging underground from an oblivious, good-hearted, elderly woman. Good portrayal of how people with antisocial personalities can use language to manipulate. Directed by the Coen Brothers.

Land of Plenty (2004, US/Germany) Drama ΨΨΨΨ
Wim Wenders film about misguided patriotism and paranoia in post-911 times in America; the protagonist is a classic paranoid personality disorder; this condition has rarely been portrayed so well.

Last King of Scotland, The (2006) Drama/Documentary/Biography ΨΨΨ
Forest Whitaker in an unforgettable, terrifying role as Idi Amin, the charming, charismatic, and paranoid ruler of Uganda who killed over 300,000 people during his reign.

Last Supper, The (1996) Comedy Ψ
Dark comedy of five liberal graduate students seeking revenge against reactionary and conservative dinner guests. The film depicts elements of antisocial and compulsive behavior.

Le Boucher (1969) Thriller ΨΨΨ
Claude Chabrol film in which a butcher who is also a murderer commits suicide when the woman he loves realizes he is a criminal.

Leave Her to Heaven (1945) Romance/Crime ΨΨ
Protagonist commits multiple murders, watches her brother-in-law drown, and terminates her pregnancy by throwing herself down a flight of stairs with no sense of shame or remorse. Dated but interesting portrayal of an antisocial personality.

Lemony Snicket's A Series of Unfortunate Events (2004) Comedy/Drama ΨΨΨ
Jim Carrey plays a comical psychopath who adopts multiple disguises in an attempt to inherit a family fortune that rightfully belongs to three orphans whose parents have died in a fire.

Levity (2003) Drama ΨΨΨ
Billy Bob Thornton plays a "recovered antisocial," who, after his release from prison, tries

to make amends with a family member (Holly Hunter) of a boy he killed decades ago. Morgan Freeman plays an antisocial preacher.

Lord of War (2005) Action/Drama Ψ
Nicholas Cage portrays Uri, an antisocial man who sells illegal arms to various countries. Based on actual events.

Lovelife (1997) Comedy ΨΨ
Film about a group of friends and their struggles in relationships, many with symptoms of disorders that prevent them from connecting – the depressed intellectual, the dependant woman, and the neurotic voyeur – but the standout is the narcissist professor.

Mad Love (2002, Spain) ΨΨ
Spanish film about a princess who marries and later becomes queen and is nicknamed "Joan the Mad" because of her worries about her philandering husband.

Man from Elysian Fields, The (2001) Drama ΨΨΨΨ
A married man (Andy Garcia) becomes an escort and his life falls apart as a result of this decision.

Man Who Cried, The (2000) Drama ΨΨ
Slow-moving film of a young woman (Christina Ricci) who left a very poor Russian family years ago to make it as a dancer in the theater. Sub-par film with an all-star cast including Johnny Depp (in another vagrant role), Cate Blanchett, and John Turturro as a grandiose opera singer.

Man Who Wasn't There, The (2001) Drama ΨΨΨΨ
This Coen Brothers' film noir is a fascinating character analysis of Ed Crane (Billy Bob Thornton) who is an aloof, taciturn, and unemotional barber struggling to find purpose.

Margot at the Wedding (2007) Comedy/Drama ΨΨΨ
Nicole Kidman portrays Margot, a woman with a borderline personality disorder who displays loose boundaries, lability, anger, impulsivity, inappropriate affect, and fears of abandonment during a short visit to her sister's house.

Marriage of Maria Braun, The (1978) Drama/War ΨΨΨ
This Fassbinder film, an allegory about postwar Germany, portrays the dehumanizing effects of war

and its aftermath as we watch the commercial success and personal failures of Maria Braun. There is an explosive finale.

Match Point (2005) Drama/Crime ΨΨΨ
Very engaging and dark Woody Allen film about a young man who inadvertently murders someone and then demonstrates significant antisocial traits that keep him from getting caught.

Me and You and Everyone We Know (2005) Comedy Ψ
A number of odd and quirky characters exhibit subclinical syndromes and features of personality disorders.

Minus Man (1999) Drama ΨΨ
Owen Wilson stars as a charming, kind, drifting serial killer. The film does not explain his behavior, which he claims is spontaneous.

Monster (2004) Docudrama ΨΨΨ
Graphic, disturbing film based on the life of Aileen Wuornos, a prostitute and drifter turned serial killer. Charlize Theron won an Oscar for her powerful performance as Wuornos.

My Summer of Love (2004) Drama/Romance Ψ
Coming-of-age tale of a girl who falls in love with a girl her age who turns out to be a burgeoning case of antisocial personality disorder (compare this film with Neil Labute's *The Shape of Things*).

My Super Ex-Girlfriend (2006) Comedy/Romance Ψ
Uma Thurman portrays G-Girl, a superheroine with great powers but one who also exhibits borderline traits, fear of abandonment, hostility, all-or-none thinking, and revengeful behavior.

Naked (1993) Drama ΨΨΨΨ
Fascinating story about an "existential antisocial," Johnny, wandering the streets of London exchanging philosophical beliefs with various quirky characters. Comedy, love, drama, and violence flow throughout this film. Written and directed by renowned British director Mike Leigh.

No Country For Old Men (2007) Drama/Crime ΨΨΨΨ
Javier Bardem gives one of the most chilling portrayals of psychopathology in cinema history in the role of Anton Chigurh, an evil man who plays with the destiny of everyone he encounters.

Notes on a Scandal (2006) Drama ΨΨΨ
Judi Dench and Cate Blanchett engage in a battle of manipulation and deceit in a movie that depicts ephebophilia, emptiness, objectification, obsession, and borderline traits.

Odd Couple, The (1968) Comedy ΨΨΨ
Jack Lemmon is magnificent as the obsessive-compulsive Felix Unger, who uses air freshener and leaves notes on the pillow of housemate Walter Matthau.

One Hour Photo (2002) ΨΨΨ
Robin Williams in a quirky, dramatic, and disturbing role as the personality disordered, Sy the Photo Guy. Sy collects photographs from a customer's family and finds meaning through their lives until he discovers they are not the perfect family.

"The things we fear the most have already happened to us."

Sy, the Photo Guy, in *One Hour Photo* (2002)

Overnight (2003) Documentary/Drama ΨΨ
A rags to riches to rags story about a narcissistic bartender, Troy Duffy, who is offered an attractive deal by Miramax for his screenplay only to have his pathology eventually sabotage this opportunity.

Paper Moon (1973) Comedy/Drama ΨΨ
Fun Peter Bogdanovich film, with Ryan O'Neal and daughter Tatum working together as a pair of con artists in the early 1930s.

Pacific Heights (1990) Drama/Suspense ΨΨΨ
Michael Keaton plays a classic antisocial personality who becomes a tenant of a Victorian home and refuses to leave or pay rent, reaping significant havoc.

Perfume: The Story of a Murderer (2006, Germany) Drama/Crime ΨΨΨΨ
A young man with a phenomenal sense of smell becomes obsessed with capturing the perfect scent, but he takes his obsession too far. Directed by Tom Tykwer.

Phone Booth (2003) Action/Suspense Ψ
A one-dimensional, narcissistic New Yorker begins to unravel as he is manipulated and forced to stay on the phone on the busy streets of Manhattan with a serial killer (Kiefer Sutherland). Worth seeing for the ending that cinematically shows the deep wounds underlying many narcissistic personality disorders.

Plumber, The (1979, Australia) Mystery/Drama ΨΨ
In this early Peter Weir film, a strange and mysterious plumber seems to be manipulating a woman as he repeatedly returns to her house to check pipes and fix the plumbing. The film raises important questions about trust and class.

Pumpkin Eater, The (1964) Drama ΨΨ
Most memorable for the scene in which Anne Bancroft, responding to the stress of eight children and an unfaithful husband, breaks down in Harrods.

Rampage (1992) Drama/Thriller ΨΨΨ
A film that explores the insanity defense, sociopathy, and mass murder. Directed by William Friedkin, who was also the director for *The Exorcist*.

Reign Over Me (2007) Drama ΨΨΨΨ
Adam Sandler portrays a man with a schizotypal personality who is lost in pathological grief. An old friend (Don Cheadle) works hard to re-orient him back to the world around him. Winner of a Voice Award.

Remains of the Day (1994) Romance/Drama ΨΨΨΨ
Anthony Hopkins plays a butler whose rigid personality will not allow him to experience intimacy or genuine love. Few films have been more effective in presenting this reserved, over-controlled, and limiting personality type.

Rick (2003) Comedy/Drama ΨΨΨ
Satirical comedy starring Bill Pullman as Rick, a narcissistic corporate executive who is self-serving, misanthropic, and cruel. The film has strong independent cinema elements.

Roger Dodger (2002) Comedy ΨΨΨ
Manhattan executive teaches his 16-year-old nephew about women in one night by taking him to the streets of New York. Great portrayal of narcissism.

Royal Tenenbaums, The (2001) Comedy ΨΨΨΨ
Dark comedy classic about the highly dysfunctional Tenenbaum family. The parents (Gene Hackman and Angelica Huston) raise three genius children

(Ben Stiller, Gwenyth Paltrow, and Luke Wilson) who develop significant problems including paranoia, depression, incest, and suicidal thoughts. The family is reunited when the narcissistic father returns home claiming he is dying of stomach cancer. We are left to see the dysfunctional dynamics of the family take place in comical form. A schizotypal personality is also portrayed (Owen Wilson) – a cinematic rarity.

Saw (2004) Horror Ψ
Jigsaw, a serial killer and torturer, manipulates people whom he believes are ungrateful to test how far they will go to save themselves, such as cutting through one's own foot with a rickety saw in order to set oneself free.

Séance on a Wet Afternoon (1964) Crime ΨΨΨ
A British film in which Kim Stanley plays a medium who persuades her husband (Richard Attenborough) to kidnap a child so they can then use her power of clairvoyance to "find" the missing child.

Servant, The (1963) Drama ΨΨΨ
Joseph Losey film in which a wealthy British gentleman and his manservant wind up switching roles. There are strong homosexual overtones in the relationship between the two men, and a complex relationship develops with two women. The film is an interesting examination of dominance and submission.

Sexy Beast (2001) Drama ΨΨΨ
Ben Kingsley portrays a brutal antisocial personality who is anything but sexy.

Shadow of Fear (2004) Drama/Suspense Ψ
Disappointing film about a young businessman who is blackmailed after he accidentally kills a man with his car and tries to cover it up. James Spader's character displays strong antisocial characteristics.

Shape of Things, The (2003) Comedy ΨΨΨ
Disturbing comedy of a woman who helps transform an anxious, insecure man through physical alteration and love only to later reveal it was all a manipulative, self-serving project. Another film by director Neil LaBute who has been appropriately nicknamed by some film critics as Neil La-Brute because of his often brutal character portrayal of people and society.

Shattered Glass (2003) Drama ΨΨΨ
Based on a true story of a young journalist for the popular New Republic magazine, Stephen Glass (well acted by Hayden Christensen), who in 1998 made up several of his published stories. He was fraudulent with people, places, and events, making up fake business cards, notes, websites, numbers, and voice mails. Great depiction of "the antisocial in trouble," where the person becomes neurotic and remorseful. The "real" Glass, a self-proclaimed "pathological liar" in reference to the events in the film, admits that 27 of his 41 published magazine stories were partially or completely made up.

"I wanted every story to be a home run."

The real Stephen Glass in a *60 Minutes* interview, speaking of being out of control and doing anything to please his readers

---

Silence of the Lambs, The (1991) Personality Disorders ΨΨΨΨ
Anthony Hopkins plays one of film history's greatest antisocial personalities, psychiatrist and cannibal Hannibal Lector. Jodi Foster is the FBI agent.

"A census taker once tried to test me. I ate his liver with some fava beans and a nice Chianti."

The Silence of the Lambs (1991)

Sleeping with the Enemy (1991) Suspense ΨΨ
Julia Roberts plays the battered wife of a possessive and sadistic husband played by Patrick Bergin. Roberts fakes her death and assumes a new identity in a desperate attempt to escape.

Small Time Crooks (2000) Comedy Ψ
Woody Allen plays a "foolish antisocial" who devises a plan to rob a bank with his not-so-bright pals. Hugh Grant plays a manipulative, charming, self-serving narcissist.

Sneakers (1992) Drama/Comedy ΨΨ
This film has a star cast that includes Dan Akroyd, who plays an ex-convict with paranoid traits who sees conspiracy in almost every situation.

Speed (1994) Drama ΨΨ
Dennis Hopper plays a deranged sociopath who programs a bomb to explode if a city bus slows to less than 50 miles per hour.

Stagecoach (1939) Western ΨΨΨ
Classic John Ford movie, with Thomas Mitchell playing a drunken physician. Mitchell won an Academy Award for Best Supporting Actor for his role.

Strangers on a Train (1951) Thriller ΨΨΨΨ
Classic Hitchcock film in which Farley Granger is unable to extricate himself from his involvement with sociopath Robert Walker.

Streetcar Named Desire, A (1951) Drama ΨΨΨΨ
Elia Kazan film starring Marlon Brando and Vivian Leigh. Blanche DuBois offers a striking example of a histrionic personality. Brando is unforgettable in the role of Stanley Kowalski.

"They're dead, they're finished! There was a time in this business when they had the eyes of the whole wide world. But that wasn't good enough for them. Oh, no. They had to have the ears of the world, too. So they opened their big mouths, and out came talk. Talk! Talk!"

Sunset Blvd. (1950)

Sunset Blvd. (1950) Drama ΨΨΨΨ
Billy Wilder film in which a narcissistic, histrionic, and delusional Gloria Swanson clings to the memories of her former greatness as a silent screen star. William Holden plays a young man who exchanges attention and sexual favors for security.

Suspect Zero (2004) Thriller/Crime ΨΨ
Ben Kingsley plays a serial killer who tries to catch a serial killer by attempting to tune into the killer's thoughts, intentions, and feelings.

Swimfan (2002) Drama/Suspense Ψ
Girl's one-night-stand with a fellow classmate shifts from infatuation to the conviction "If I can't have you, no one will."

Swimming With Sharks (1994) Comedy ΨΨ
Dark comedy with Kevin Spacey as a nasty, heart-

less, business executive who is held hostage and tortured by an employee he has verbally abused over the years.

Swimming Pool (2002) Drama/Mystery ΨΨΨ
Mystery writer leaves London to find peace, quiet, and inspiration at her publisher's secluded home in a French village. She overcomes her writer's block by writing about the adventures of a seductive, provocative young woman, the publisher's daughter, who has spontaneously moved in.

"I always thought it would be better to be a fake somebody than a real nobody."

Tom Ripley describing his secretive double life in
The Talented Mr. Ripley (1999)

The Talented Mr. Ripley (1999) Drama ΨΨΨΨ
Matt Damon is the deceitful, charming, clever impersonator, Tom Ripley, who manipulates anyone in his path until he can no longer get away with his deceit. Breakthrough film for supporting actor Jude Law.

Tao of Steve, The (2000) Comedy Ψ
Self-serving, amateur philosopher uses some ideas from Buddhist philosophy to pursue and sleep with women.

Tape (2001) Drama ΨΨΨ
Creative, engaging, and honest story of how people manipulate one another to meet their own desires and how they react when their secrets are exposed. It also shows what can happen when someone has unresolved psychological issues. The entire film takes place in one motel room with only three characters – all young veterans – Ethan Hawke, Robert Sean Leonard, and Uma Thurman.

"You talkin' to me? [slower] You talking to me? You talking to me? Well, then, who the hell else are you talking – you talking to me? Well, I'm the only one here."

Travis Bickle rehearsing in *Taxi Driver* (1976)

Taxi Driver (1976) Drama ΨΨΨΨ
The premorbid personality of Travis Bickle illustrates delusional paranoid thinking. Bickle would probably meet the criteria for a diagnosis of schizotypal personality disorder.

Thin Blue Line, The (1988) Documentary ΨΨΨ
Gripping documentary examining the unjust incarceration of a man accused of the murder of a Texas policeman.

Toto le Heros (1991) Drama/Comedy ΨΨΨΨ
An old man in a nursing home reviews his life and his lifelong hatred for his next-door neighbor, who appeared to have every advantage. Wonderful example of a paranoid personality disorder.

Tsotsi (2005, UK, South Africa) Crime/Drama ΨΨΨΨ
An African gangster accidentally kidnaps an infant and in learning to care for the child makes some changes in himself.

Unfaithful (2002) Drama/Suspense Ψ
A married man (Richard Gere) finds out his wife (Diane Lane) is having an affair and he seeks revenge.

Very Bad Things (1999) Comedy Ψ
Dark comedy about a bachelor party gone horribly wrong. As the five men try to cover up an accidental murder, more problems arise.

Vicky Cristina Barcelona (2008) Drama ΨΨΨ
High quality, Woody Allen film about two young women touring Barcelona for the summer who encounter a handsome man and his erratic, labile ex-wife (Penelope Cruz).

Violette Noziere (1978) Biography/Crime ΨΨ
Claude Chabrol film based on the true story about a teenage girl who poisoned her parents, eventually killing her father, whom she claimed had raped and abused her.

Wannsee Conference, The (1984) Historical/War ΨΨΨ
Recreation of the Berlin meeting in which Nazi officers first outlined the "final solution" for dealing with the "Jewish problem."

Whisperers, The (1966) Drama Ψ
Dame Edith Evans stars as a lonely old woman, divorced from her husband and estranged from her son, who devotes her days to worry and paranoid ramblings.

White Oleander (2002) Drama ΨΨΨ
Young girl is tossed around from home to home when her mother is incarcerated. The mother figures include characters played by Michelle Pfeiffer (antisocial), Renee Zellweger (dependent), and Robin Wright-Penn (histrionic). Fascinating dynamics of a young girl's resilience with each personality disordered mother-figure.

"Loneliness is the human condition. Love humiliates you. Hatred cradles you."

A mother teaching her philosophy to her teenage daughter in *White Oleander* (2002)

Wild at Heart (1990) Comedy/Drama/Romance ΨΨΨ
David Lynch film with ex-con Nicolas Cage and his lover, Laura Dern, as two antisocial personalities (despite their apparent commitment to each other). Won the Palme d'Or at Cannes, but not all critics were impressed. Too violent for some tastes.

Willard (2003) Drama ΨΨ
Crispin Glover plays a schizoid man whose only contact is his critical mother and numerous rats living in his basement. He uses the rats for revenge until they turn on him.

Wise Blood (1979) Drama ΨΨΨ
John Huston's adaptation of Flannery O'Connor's gothic Southern novel about an obsessed preacher.

Zoolander (2001) Comedy Ψ
Absurd, over-the-top depiction of a narcissistic model who is brainwashed to become an assassin. Ben Stiller directed, co-wrote, and starred in this film.

Substance Use Disorders

Alcoholism

16 Blocks (2006) Drama ΨΨΨ
A corrupt, burnt out, alcoholic cop risks his job and life by confronting authority in order to save a criminal from being killed. He drinks on the job,

is unshaven, overly fatigued, has poor stamina, slowed movement, and colleagues repeatedly comment about his alcohol abuse.

16 Years of Alcohol (2003, UK) Drama ΨΨ
The impact of parental alcoholism on a boy who eventually becomes an alcoholic. A transformation occurs when he becomes a member of AA and works at letting go of his anger and violent patterns.

28 Days (2000) Drama ΨΨΨ
A writer (Sandra Bullock) is court-ordered into a drug/alcohol rehabilitation center after a drinking and driving accident. The film depicts symptoms of alcoholism and its impact on a family.

Arthur (1981) Comedy Ψ
Dudley Moore as a drunken millionaire who falls in love with Liza Minnelli. A genuinely funny film, but upsetting in its cavalier approach to alcoholism and drunk driving.

Susan: "A real woman could stop you from drinking."
Arthur: "It'd have to be a real BIG woman."

Arthur (1981)

Bad News Bears (2005) Comedy Ψ
Richard Linklater remake portraying a despicable alcoholic (Billy Bob Thornton) who attempts to coach a little league baseball team that has minimal talent.

Barfly (1987) Comedy/Romance/Drama ΨΨΨΨ
Faye Dunaway and Mickey Rourke play two alcoholics whose lives briefly touch. Good examination of skid row alcoholism; based on a story by cult poet Charles Bukowski.

Basketball Diaries, The (1995) Drama ΨΨΨ
Adolescent basketball stars succumb to drug abuse in this film that stars Leonardo DiCaprio and Mark Wahlberg. Adapted from a Jim Carroll novel.

Beloved Infidel (1959) Biography Ψ
Gregory Peck plays F. Scott Fitzgerald and Deborah Kerr is columnist Sheila Graham, who tries to save Fitzgerald from his alcoholism.

Born on the Fourth of July (1989) Drama/War/Biography ΨΨΨ
Tom Cruise plays paralyzed and alcoholic Vietnam veteran Ron Kovic in Oliver Stone's film. Stone won an Oscar as best director for this film.

"You're a T6 – paralyzed from the mid-chest down... you'll be in a wheelchair for the rest of your life."

Ron Kovic's grim prognosis in
Born on the Fourth of July (1989)

Capote (2005) Drama/Biography ΨΨΨ
Philip Seymour Hoffman portrays the writer Truman Capote, and a segment of his life in which Capote gets material from a man who killed a family of four in Kansas for a new non-fiction book. Capote becomes depressed when he is unable to prevent the man from being hanged. He abuses alcohol and never writes again.

Cat Ballou (1965) Comedy/Western Ψ
Light-hearted film, with Jane Fonda playing a schoolteacher turned outlaw. Lee Marvin got an Oscar for his role as an alcoholic gunman. The film perpetuates the myth of the down-and-out drunk whose shooting skills return after he has had a few drinks. Marvin won an Oscar as Best Actor for his role in this film.

"Big Daddy! Now what makes him so big? His big heart? His big belly? Or his big money?"

Cat on a Hot Tin Roof (1958)

Cat on a Hot Tin Roof (1958) Drama ΨΨΨ
Paul Newman, Elizabeth Taylor, and Burl Ives in a subdued adaptation of Tennessee Williams' play about "mendacity." Alcohol plays a prominent role in the life of almost all the characters' lives.

Changing Lanes (2002) Drama ΨΨ
A successful lawyer from a corrupt firm collides with an alcoholic insurance salesman who is on his way to court for a custody hearing and miss-

es the court appearance. The role of Alcoholics Anonymous and the ongoing struggle associated with recovery are depicted.

Charlie Wilson's War (2007) Drama/Biography ΨΨ
Mike Nichols film about a legendary congressman who's also an alcoholic.

Children of Men (2006) Thriller/Drama Ψ
Alcohol abuse and marijuana abuse are depicted in this film about saving the human race.

Come Back, Little Sheba (1952) Drama ΨΨΨ
Burt Lancaster and Shirley Booth in a film about alcoholism and marriage. Booth won an Academy Award for Best Actress for her role.

Come Fill the Cup (1951) Drama ΨΨ
James Cagney and Jackie Gleason star in this serious examination of the problems of alcoholism in an ex-newspaperman.

Dark Obsession (1989) Drama/Mystery ΨΨ
Five drunken British military officers are involved in a hit-and-run accident in which the victim dies. The five men take a vow of silence; one is troubled by the decision. Interesting analysis of responsibility for one's behavior while intoxicated.

Days of Wine and Roses (1962) Drama ΨΨΨΨ
Blake Edwards film starring Jack Lemmon and Lee Remick. Lemmon teaches Remick how to drink. Lemmon is saved by AA; Remick is unable to stop drinking, despite the consequences.

> "You see, the world looks so dirty to me when I'm not drinking. Joe, remember Fisherman's Wharf? The water when you looked too close? That's the way the world looks to me when I'm not drinking."
>
> Kristen describes why she continues to drink in *Days of Wine and Roses* (1962)

Drunks (1995) Drama ΨΨΨΨ
This film is the best available introduction to Alcoholics Anonymous. It is highly recommended for any student who will be working with substance abuse issues.

Educating Rita (1983) Drama ΨΨ
Michael Caine as an alcoholic college professor who takes on the task of educating a working-class woman.

Factotum (2005) Comedy ΨΨ
A struggling writer works multiple odd jobs and sleeps with multiple partners. He consistently drinks on the job and while writing. He loses several jobs, but is unable to stop drinking. The film accurately portrays alcohol dependence.

Fire Within, The (1963, France) Drama ΨΨΨΨ
French filmmaker Louis Malle's remarkable account of alcoholism, suicide, and the existential choices that confront us all.

For One More Day (2007) Drama ΨΨ
A child of divorced parents grows up feeling guilty about his mother's death. As an adult, he becomes depressed and an alcoholic. His suicide attempt is interrupted by his deceased mother who gives him one last day to spend with her. Based on Mitch Album's novel.

Gervaise (1956, France) Drama ΨΨΨ
French film based on Emile Zola's story about a young Parisian woman with an alcoholic husband.

> "Mrs. Robinson, you're trying to seduce me. Aren't you?"
>
> *The Graduate* (1967)

Graduate, The (1967) Drama/Comedy ΨΨΨ
A telling indictment of the shallow values of the time (e.g., "plastics"). Mrs. Robinson's alcoholism impairs her judgment and ruins her life.

Great Man Votes, The (1939) Drama ΨΨ
John Barrymore plays an alcoholic college professor fighting to maintain custody of his children.

Harvey (1950) Comedy/Drama ΨΨΨΨ
Elwood P. Dowd's (Jimmy Stewart) imaginary friend is a six foot white rabbit named Harvey with whom he has a good relationship. Dowd drinks daily, goes to taverns, and has hidden bottles behind books. He always gets two drinks, one for himself and one for Harvey, and therefore has two drinks at a time.

Henry Fool (1997) Comedy/Drama ΨΨ
Hal Hartley film about a taciturn garbage man who befriends a roguish alcoholic.

Iceman Cometh, The (1973) Drama ΨΨ
Lee Marvin in an adaptation of Eugene O'Neill's play about alcoholism and the pathos of dreams unfulfilled.

I'll Cry Tomorrow (1955) Biography ΨΨΨ
Singer Lillian Roth (Susan Hayward) attempts suicide as a way of coping with her alcoholism before AA support helps her find her way.

Ironman (2008) Action/Adventure Ψ
Robert Downey, Jr. portrays a weapon-specialist and superhero who's also an alcoholic.

Ironweed (1987) Drama ΨΨΨ
Jack Nicholson and Meryl Streep in compelling roles as homeless alcoholics. The film, a very realistic portrayal of life on skid row, should be contrasted with another excellent film made the same year, *Barfly*.

Key Largo (1948) Crime ΨΨΨ
Claire Trevor won Best Supporting Actress for her role as an alcoholic singer forced to beg gangster Edward G. Robinson for a drink during a hurricane in Key West.

Last Night at the Alamo (1983) Drama ΨΨΨ
Fascinating examination of bar culture in a small Texas town. Unforgettable characters, most of whom are coping with alcoholism and adultery.

Leaving Las Vegas (1995) Drama ΨΨΨ
Nicholas Cage delivers a stunning performance as an alcoholic who has no interest in quitting. He develops a relationship with a prostitute (Elisabeth Shue) who is the first to truly understand him. Gripping alcohol dependence portrayal with painful delirium tremens on screen.

Legend of Bagger Vance, The (2000) Drama/Inspiration ΨΨΨ
Matt Damon plays Rannulph Junuh, a talented golfer whose game has deteriorated because of his war experiences. He isolates himself, drinks heavily, and plays cards all night. He returns to golf in a promotional event against the top two golfers in the game with the help of an inspirational caddy and mentor, Bagger Vance (Will Smith).

Libertine, The (2004) Drama ΨΨ
John Wilmot, the second Earl of Rochester in 17th century Europe, a poet and author and close friends of Charles II (John Malkovich), desperately uses alcohol to cope with banishment. He drinks constantly for 5 years and the long-term consequences of alcohol use are shown.

Lonely Passion of Judith Hearne, The (1987) Romance ΨΨ
Maggie Smith plays a lonely alcoholic who mistakenly believes she has a last chance to find love and meaning in her life.

Long Day's Journey into Night (1962) Drama ΨΨΨΨΨ
Alcohol is a part of daily life for this deeply troubled family. Numerous examples of family pathology, conflict between father and sons, and denial.

Lost Weekend, The (1945) Drama ΨΨΨΨ
Billy Wilder classic starring Ray Milland as a writer struggling to overcome his alcoholism. Some scenes were filmed at Bellevue Hospital in New York City, and the examples of delirium tremens are very convincing. Polanski borrowed scenes from *The Lost Weekend* as models for his film *Repulsion*.

"It shrinks my liver, doesn't it, Nat? It pickles my kidneys, yeah. But what it does to the mind? It tosses the sandbags overboard so the balloon can soar. Suddenly I'm above the ordinary. I'm competent. I'm walking a tightrope over Niagara Falls. I'm one of the great ones."

Don Birnam talking to his bartender about what it feels like to be drunk in *The Lost Weekend* (1945)

Love Song for Bobby Long, A (2004) Drama ΨΨ
A young woman returns to her hometown, New Orleans, for a funeral and finds two drunken dwellers living in her deceased mother's home. Bobby Long (John Travolta), an English professor, and his former assistant have no intentions of moving.

My Favorite Year (1982) Comedy ΨΨΨ
A great actor (modeled after John Barrymore and Errol Flynn) who has become a pathetic drunk

must confront one of the greatest challenges of his career – a live television performance.

My Name Is Bill W. (1989) ΨΨΨ
Made-for-TV movie about the founding of Alcoholics Anonymous.

National Lampoon's Animal House (1978) Comedy ΨΨ
One of the best of a hundred or so college films that portray fraternity life as a series of beer busts interspersed with an occasional class. At one point, John Belushi, not the brightest of the fraternity brothers, chugs a fifth of Jack Daniels.

Night of the Iguana, The (1964) Drama ΨΨ
Richard Burton and Ava Gardner star in John Huston's adaptation of Tennessee Williams' play. Burton plays a very convincing alcoholic and erstwhile clergyman.

No Such Thing (2001, Iceland/US) Ψ
Hal Hartley film about a belligerent, foul-mouthed monster who is also an alcoholic.

"Think of an idea to change our world... and put it into action."

A student assignment in *Pay It Forward* (2000)

Pay It Forward (2000) Drama/Inspiration ΨΨ
Haley Joel Osment plays a seventh grader implementing a class assignment that has profound effects on the people around him. His mother (Helen Hunt) is a struggling alcoholic.

Prize Winner of Defiance, Ohio, The (2005) Drama ΨΨΨΨ
A stay-at-home mother (Julianne Moore) in the 1950-60s, confronts her alcoholic and dependent husband (Woody Harrelson) with unswerving optimism. The film shows the social expectations of women who stay in relationships with abusive husbands.

Proud and the Beautiful, The (1953) Romance ΨΨ
A film about a woman who helps an alcoholic physician overcome his problems and regain some sense of dignity. Filmed in France and Mexico.

Sideways (2004) Comedy ΨΨΨ
Two men tour California's wine country. One is a depressed alcoholic craving a relationship; the other is going to be married later that week, but he begins an affair with a woman he meets on the trip.

Skin Deep (1989) Comedy ΨΨ
A funny Blake Edwards film about an alcoholic writer who continues to deny his alcoholism long after it has become apparent to everyone else.

Smash-Up, the Story of a Woman (1947) Drama ΨΨ
Melodramatic Susan Hayward film about a movie star who must come to grips with her alcoholism.

Some Like It Hot (1959) Crime/Comedy ΨΨ
Marilyn Monroe portrays a performer constantly sneaking drinks; she is nearly fired for alcohol abuse.

Streamers (1983) Drama ΨΨΨ
Robert Altman film about three soldiers waiting to go to Vietnam. The film deals with themes of homosexuality, violence, and racism, but also illustrates the alcohol abuse that is pervasive in military life.

Sweet Bird of Youth (1962) Drama ΨΨ
Paul Newman in an adaptation of Tennessee Williams' play about a has-been actress (played by Geraldine Page) addicted to alcohol and drugs who takes up with a young, vital Newman.

Taxi Blues (1990, Soviet Union) Drama ΨΨΨ
Alcoholic jazz musician becomes friends with an anti-Semitic taxi driver. This Russian film won the prize for Best Director at Cannes. Fascinating examination of the role of alcohol in the daily lives of the protagonists in Moscow society.

Tender Mercies (1983) Drama ΨΨΨΨΨ
Sensitive and optimistic film in which Robert Duvall plays a successfully recovering alcoholic songwriter. Duvall won an Oscar for this almost perfect performance.

Trees Lounge (1996) Comedy ΨΨΨΨ
Steve Buscemi wrote and directed this compelling film, and he plays the lead character, a 31-year-old unemployed auto mechanic. Few contemporary films present a more vivid picture of the problems associated with alcoholism.

Under Capricorn (1949) Drama Ψ
A little-known Hitchcock film starring Joseph

Cotton and Ingrid Bergman. Bergman is a wealthy socialite whose life is ruined by her alcoholism.

Under the Volcano (1984) Drama ΨΨΨΨ
John Huston directing Albert Finney; excellent portrayal of chronic alcoholism.

Verdict, The (1982) Drama ΨΨΨΨ
Paul Newman in a wonderful role as a disillusioned alcoholic lawyer who becomes genuinely involved with a brain-injured client who is the victim of medical malpractice. He wins the case but continues to drink. Interesting analysis of codependency.

Edward J. Concannon: "Why wasn't she getting oxygen...?"
Dr. Robert Towler: "Well, many reasons, actually..."
Edward J. Concannon: "Tell me one?"
Dr. Robert Towler: "She'd aspirated vomitus into her mask..."
Edward J. Concannon: "She threw up in her mask. Let's cut the bullshit. Say it: She threw up in her mask."

The Verdict (1982)

Vital Signs (1986) Drama ΨΨ
Ed Asner in a surpassingly good made-for-TV movie about a father and son, both surgeons, fighting the twin problems of alcoholism and drug abuse.

Vodka Lemon (2003, France/Armenia) Comedy ΨΨΨ
Minimalist film about grieving widows who befriend one another in a culture where everyone seems to drinks vodka.

What Price Hollywood? (1932) Drama ΨΨ
Alcoholic director helps Hollywood waitress become a star. The figure of the alcoholic director may have been modeled after John Barrymore.

When a Man Loves a Woman (1994) Drama ΨΨ
Meg Ryan as a middle-class alcoholic. This is a melodramatic and somewhat predictable film, but an interesting introduction to AA and Al-Anon. The film explores the role of codependency and a husband's role in his wife's alcoholism.

Drug Abuse

21 Grams (2003) Drama/Mystery ΨΨΨ
Complicated, well-integrated stories of an ex-con and recovering alcoholic (Benicio Del Toro), a cocaine addict (Naomi Watts), and a terminal man awaiting a transplant (Sean Penn), all brought together by an accidental death.

"They say we all lose 21 grams at the exact moment of death... everyone. The weight of a stack of nickels. The weight of a chocolate bar. The weight of a hummingbird."

21 Grams (2003)

Bad Lieutenant (1992) Drama ΨΨΨ
Harvey Keitel stars in one of his most powerful roles as a police lieutenant addicted to cocaine, alcohol, and prostitutes. The film illustrates stark abuse of power and the deterioration of family life that accompanies addiction. Keitel's character has a hallucination in which Jesus Christ comes to him.

Big Lebowski, The (1998) Comedy ΨΨ
Coen Brothers film portraying The Dude (Jeff Bridges), a cannabis-smoking, unemployed drifter in this entertaining, film noir comedy.

Bird (1988) Biography ΨΨ
Clint Eastwood directed this biographical film of the life of jazz great and drug addict Charlie "Bird" Parker. Parker was an addict for all of his adult life, and his addiction killed him at the age of 34.

Blow (2001) Drama ΨΨΨ
Johnny Depp stars as George Jung, a man who claimed to have imported about 85% of all cocaine in America in the late 1970s.

Chappaqua (1966) Drama Ψ
Heroin addict checks in for treatment. The film is most notable for short roles by William Burroughs, Ravi Shankar, and Allen Ginsburg.

Christiane F. (1981) Drama ΨΨΨ
Powerful and frightening examination of the life of a teenage drug addict in West Berlin. Based on a true story, the film is still gripping almost three decades after it was made.

Clean and Sober (1988) Drama ΨΨΨ
Good portrayal of AA, cocaine addiction, and alcoholism.

> "The best way to break old habits is to make new ones."
>
> *Clean and Sober* (1988)

Cocaine Fiends, The (1936) Drama Ψ
Another "word of warning" film that portrays the dangers of cocaine. Made in the same year as *Reefer Madness*. The message in this film is exaggerated and histrionic but somewhat more realistic in its estimate of the dangers of the drug.

Coffee and Cigarettes (2003) Comedy ΨΨΨ
Various conversational skits (starring a variety of talents, including Bill Murray, Roberto Benigni, Cate Blanchett, Iggy Pop, and Steve Buscemi) linked through the characters' use of coffee, tea and smoking. Portrayals of compulsive use of each, side effects, and the desire to quit or avoid the substance.

Connection, The (1961) Drama ΨΨΨ
Heroin addicts in New York wait for their pusher.

Dopamine (2003) Drama/Comedy ΨΨ
Independent film explores the chemistry behind male-female relationships. One character uses amphetamine pills and large quantities of caffeine. Interesting debate on how physical attraction emerges.

> "Most people don't know how they're gonna feel from one moment to the next. But a dope fiend has a pretty good idea. All you gotta do is look at the labels on the little bottles."
>
> Addict reflecting on the pleasures of drugs in *Drugstore Cowboy* (1989)

Drugstore Cowboy (1989) Drama ΨΨΨΨ
Matt Dillon leads a group of junkies who rob pharmacies to support their habit. William Burroughs plays a junkie priest.

> "The governor of Louisiana gave me this. Madame Tinkertoy's House of Blue Lights, corner of Bourbon and Toulouse, New Orleans, Louisiana. Now, this is supposed to be the finest whorehouse in the south. These ain't no pork chops! These are U.S. Prime!"
>
> Jack Nicholson plans for his trip to New Orleans in *Easy Rider* (1969)

Easy Rider (1969) Drama ΨΨΨ
Classic film of the late 1960s with Jack Nicholson as an alcoholic lawyer and Peter Fonda and Dennis Hopper as marijuana-smoking, LSD-using free spirits. The film is dated but still worth seeing.

Fear and Loathing in Las Vegas (1998) Drama/Fantasy ΨΨ
Terry Gilliam's adaptation of Hunter S. Thompson's Gonzo journalism classic. The book is better than the film; although the movie does not glorify drug use, it clearly models the behavior and tacitly condones the practice of driving while intoxicated.

Half Baked (1998) Comedy Ψ
Exaggerated comedy about smoking "weed." Interesting for its classification of different types of marijuana smokers: "you should have been there smoker," the "scavenger," the "enhancer," the "medicinal," the "after school special," the "father, I'm 40 and still cool," the "MacGyver smoker," the "straight-up potheads," and the "I'm only creative if I smoke" smoker.

Half Nelson (2006) Drama ΨΨΨ
A drug-addicted teacher/coach (Ryan Gosling) at an inner city school uses cocaine regularly and smokes crack in the girl's locker room after a game. He has a history of failed rehabilitation, and tries to rebuild relations but struggles with anger and is disengaged from his family.

Hatful of Rain, A (1957) Drama ΨΨ
Melodramatic film about the life and problems of a drug addict. This was one of the earliest films to honestly examine the problem of drug addiction.

High Art (1998) Drama/Comedy ΨΨ
Realistic, well-acted independent film about several people whose lives intersect for drugs, support, and conversation in a New York City apartment.

Hustle and Flow (2005) Drama ΨΨΨΨ
In this Sundance Audience Choice Award film, an aspiring Memphis disc jockey works to get his first record made as he approaches mid-life. He is a pimp, drug user, and dealer who questions his life's purpose and the decisions he has made along the way.

I Don't Buy Kisses Anymore (1992) Comedy/ Romance Ψ
Lightweight but entertaining film about an obese male who falls in love with a woman using him as a subject for her master's thesis.

I'm Dancing as Fast as I Can (1982) Drama ΨΨ
Jill Clayburgh plays the role of a high-powered documentary filmmaker who becomes addicted to Valium and requires hospitalization in a special program for addicts. Based on a true story.

Jungle Fever (1991) Drama/Romance ΨΨΨ
Interesting film about race relations and sexual stereotypes, with a subplot involving Gator, the crack-head brother of the protagonist, who is destroying his middle-class family.

La Femme Nikita (1990) Action/Drama ΨΨ
Sociopathic and drug-addicted woman is sentenced to die for murder and then is transformed into a government agent. Most memorable for the drug-store robbery that opens the film.

Lady Sings the Blues (1972) Biography/Musical ΨΨ
Diana Ross plays heroin addict Billie Holiday.

Long Day's Journey into Night (1962) Drama ΨΨΨΨΨ
Katharine Hepburn plays a morphine-addicted, histrionic mother with an alcoholic son (Jason Robards). One of O'Neill's greatest plays; one of Hepburn's greatest roles. Hepburn's character is a good illustration of a histrionic personality disorder.

Love and Diane (2002) Documentary ΨΨ
A mother recovers from an addiction to crack as she attempts to start a new life and connect with the children she had abandoned.

Love Liza (2002) Drama/Comedy ΨΨΨ
Philip Seymour Hoffman skillfully plays a man who huffs gasoline in response to his wife's suicide. A rare and illuminating depiction of inhalant abuse and intoxication.

Luna (1979) Drama Ψ
Disappointing Bernardo Bertolucci film, with Jill Clayburgh playing the mother of a drug addict son. The film hints at an incestuous relationship between mother and son.

> "What the fuck do I need to be sober for so I can see how fucked up shit really is, please. High is how I am gonna be. I'm high till I die"
>
> A crack addict in *MacArthur Park* (2001)

MacArthur Park (2001) Drama ΨΨΨ
A crack addict struggles to leave drug dependence and his home in the park to live with his estranged son. A quality independent film.

Man with the Golden Arm, The (1955) Drama ΨΨ
Frank Sinatra and Kim Novak in a dated but interesting portrayal of drug addiction. Good example of the challenge of "cold turkey" withdrawal.

Maria, Full of Grace (2004) Drama ΨΨΨ
Fascinating, independent film depicting the realities and dangers young girls from Colombia face as they take jobs as "mules," smuggling drugs into the United States by swallowing them in large latex packages. While this film is not directly about substance abuse, it depicts the drug trade and problems related to ingesting drugs for illegal purposes.

Mask (1985) Biography ΨΨΨ
Bogdanovich film with Cher as the mother of deformed but spunky teenager Rocky Dennis. Sympathetic portrayal of motorcycle gangs. Cher struggles with her angry father and her compulsive use of alcohol and drugs as she works hard to be a good mother.

Mighty Wind, A (2003) Comedy ΨΨ
Hilarious Christopher Guest parody of folk music. One character displays significant remnants of years of drug abuse.

Naked Lunch (1991) Drama/Science Fiction/ Fantasy ΨΨ
This film is based on the novel by William Burroughs and deals with drug abuse, paranoia, and homicide.

New Jack City (1991) Action/Crime ΨΨ
Wesley Snipes and Ice-T in a realistic movie about the business of drugs. Good introduction to cocaine addiction and Narcotics Anonymous.

"If the First Amendment will protect a scumbag like me, it will protect all of you."

Larry Flint on free speech
in *The People vs. Larry Flint* (1996)

People vs. Larry Flynt, The (1996) Biography/ Drama ΨΨΨ
A good movie about a controversial figure, the film forces the viewer to examine his or her views on pornography and free speech. The film is included in this section because of the effects of drugs on the lives of Flynt and his wife, Althea (Courtney Love), after he is shot and becomes addicted to narcotics.

Platoon (1986) War ΨΨΨΨ
Vietnam veteran Oliver Stone directed *Platoon,* one of the most realistic of dozens of war movies. There is an interesting juxtaposition of "boozers" (those who use alcohol to escape) and "heads" (those who take refuge in marijuana and other illegal drugs).

Postcards from the Edge (1990) Comedy/Drama ΨΨΨ
Mike Nichols' adaptation of a Carrie Fisher story about life as the daughter of a famous actress. The mother is alcoholic; the daughter abuses multiple drugs, including cocaine and sedatives. There are brief scenes of therapy and a terrific cast.

Pulp Fiction (1994) Drama ΨΨΨΨ
Quentin Tarantino film about drugs, crime, depravity, the underworld, and life in urban America. One especially memorable scene involves Vincent Vega (John Travolta) smashing an adrenaline-filled needle into Mia Wallace's (Uma Thurman) chest to revive her after she inadvertently overdoses on heroin.

Quitting (2001) Drama ΨΨΨΨ
Slow-moving but interesting Chinese film about a one-time famous actor who deteriorates due to a heroin addiction. The emotional and psychological withdrawals depicted are memorable. This is an important film on addiction and withdrawal.

"What now? Let me tell you what now. I'ma call a coupla hard, pipe-hittin' niggers, who'll go to work on this soon-to-be-dead hillbilly rapist here with a pair of pliers and a blow torch. You hear me talkin', hillbilly boy? I ain't through with you by a damn sight. I'ma get medieval on your ass."

Planning revenge in *Pulp Fiction* (1994)

Ray (2004) Drama ΨΨΨΨ
This award winning film depicts 20 years in the life of Ray Charles when he was addicted to heroin. Physical disability (blindness) and childhood psychological traumas shape the personal life of this renowned artist.

Reefer Madness (1936) Drama Ψ
Campy film depicting the dangers of marijuana. Ironically, several thousand college students have gone to see this film high on the very drug the film condemns.

Requiem for a Dream (2000) Drama ΨΨΨ
Greatly disturbing film about four drug addicts whose lives deteriorate. Unforgettable performances and critically acclaimed. Excellent direction by Darren Aronofsky.

"I'm somebody now, everybody likes me."

Requiem for a Dream (2000)

Rose, The (1979) Musical ΨΨ
Bette Midler portrays Janis Joplin and her problems with Southern Comfort and drugs.

Rush (1991) Crime/Drama ΨΨΨ
Two undercover narcotics agents find addiction to be an occupational hazard.

Scarface (1983) Crime ΨΨΨ
Brian De Palma movie starring Al Pacino as a Cuban immigrant mobster who becomes addicted to the cocaine he is marketing. This long film, which tends to be loved or hated, is based on a 1932 Howard Hawks classic with the same name.

Seven Percent Solution, The (1976) Mystery ΨΨ
Sigmund Freud treats Sherlock Holmes' cocaine addiction. Creative idea and historically accurate in documenting Freud's early enthusiasm for cocaine.

Shadow Hours (2000) Drama Ψ
A wealthy man manipulates a young gas station attendant into drug relapse and fraternizing with three types of "night owls": (1) those who find their prince charming or princess and end at midnight, (2) vampires – prostitutes, drug dealers, and (3) Mr. Hydes – those that can't sleep.

SherryBaby (2006) Drama ΨΨΨ
A woman leaves prison following a 6 year history of heroin addiction and neglect of her daughter; despite the history of abuse, she eagerly wants to re-unite with her daughter and attempt to start anew.

Sid and Nancy (1986) Biography ΨΨΨΨ
Compelling biography of Sid Vicious of the Sex Pistols; offers insight into the worlds of drugs and rock and roll.

> "Dog had a litter of about 8, and my Mother was bending over killing each one of these little puppies in the bathtub. I remember I said 'why?'... She said 'I'm just killing what I can't take care of.' Then my momma said to me, she looked at me and she said, 'I wish I could do that to you.'"
>
> A recollection by the cook in *Spun* (2002)

Spun (2002) Drama/Comedy ΨΨΨ
A well-done, intense film about methamphetamine addiction.

Stardust (1975) Drama Ψ
British film about a rock star whose success is tarnished by drug addiction and mental illness.

Sweet Nothing (1996) Drama ΨΨΨ
An effective examination of the futility, desperation, and violence associated with crack addiction. This is a true story based on diaries found in a Bronx apartment in March of 1991.

Synanon (1965) Drama ΨΨ
Interesting only insofar as the film documents the treatment methods practiced in this highly praised treatment program.

Traffic (2000) Drama ΨΨΨΨ
This Steven Soderbergh film thematically intersects the lives of a newly hired government drug czar (Michael Douglas), his daughter who experiments with crack, police officers struggling with drug cartels, and a suburban wife of a drug lord.

> "I've been known to sniff it, smoke it, swallow it, stick it up my arse and inject it into my veins. I've been trying to combat this addiction, but unless you count social security scams and shoplifting, I haven't had a regular job in years."
>
> *Trainspotting* (1996)

Trainspotting (1996) Drama/Comedy ΨΨΨ
A realistic and disturbing film about the heroin scene in Edinburgh. The film presents accurate depictions of cold turkey withdrawal. There is one memorable scene in which a young mother's baby dies while she is high, and she immediately needs a fix to cope with her grief. Several scatological scenes seem gratuitous and unnecessary.

Veronika Voss (1982) Drama ΨΨ
Rainer Werner Fassbinder film about a German movie star who becomes addicted to morphine. Fassbinder himself died from abuse of alcohol and heroin.

Wasted (2002) Drama ΨΨ
Teens, covering up inner pain, fear, and loneliness, battle their heroin addiction.

What's Love Got to Do with It? (1993) Musical/Biography ΨΨ
Excellent film biography of singer Tina Turner includes some memorable scenes of husband Ike strung out on cocaine.

Who'll Stop the Rain? (1978) Crime/Drama ΨΨ
Also known as *Dog Soldiers,* this film explores the world of drug smuggling and addiction.

Sexual and Gender Identity Disorders

8mm (1999) Mystery/Thriller ΨΨ
Joel Schumacher film about the underground world of "snuff" films. Depicts the worst kind of sadism.

Adjuster, The (1991) Drama ΨΨΨ
This interesting Canadian film explores voyeurism and exhibitionism.

"Being a man one day and a woman the next isn't an easy thing."

Bernadette complaining about life as a transsexual in *Adventures of Priscilla, Queen of the Desert* (1994)

Adventures of Priscilla, Queen of the Desert (1994) Comedy ΨΨ
Terence Stamp plays an aging transsexual who joins with two friends to travel from Sidney to Alice Springs in the Australian outback to perform a lip-synching routine. Much of the film revolves around the prejudice and homophobic hostility the three transsexuals encounter.

AKA (2002) Drama ΨΨΨ
Fascinating artistry where most of the screen is split into three sections where the viewer is simultaneously shown past & present, different character reactions, different camera angles, and even the internal thoughts & behaviors of a character. The lead character, sexually abused by his father, escapes on a journey exploring his sexual and psychological identity. As in *Memento*, the viewer must pay close attention throughout the film.

All About My Mother (1999, Spain) Drama/Comedy ΨΨ
Pedro Almodovar film about a nurse who tragically loses her beloved son and in her grief and travels meets a transvestite prostitute and a pregnant nun (Penelope Cruz). Winner of an Academy Award for Best Foreign Language Film.

Angels and Insects (1995) Drama ΨΨΨ
Complex drama about social class, passion, incest, and hidden sexual secrets in a wealthy Victorian household.

Another Time, Another Place (1983) Drama ΨΨΨ
Sensitive film in which a Scottish woman in an unhappy marriage has a brief affair with an Italian prisoner of war working as a laborer on the farm. The man is accused of a rape he did not commit; his lover can save him, but only at the cost of revealing her adultery.

Bad Timing: A Sensual Obsession (1980) Drama ΨΨ
Art Garfunkel (playing a psychology professor), Harvey Keitel, and Theresa Russell star in a provocative and explicit film about a psychiatrist who becomes sexually obsessed with a young woman after she makes a suicide attempt.

Basic Instinct (1992) Suspense/Thriller ΨΨ
Psychological thriller about a novelist (Sharon Stone) who is a sex addict that entangles an investigator (Michael Douglas) into a complex mystery of murder, sex, and fascination.

Beautiful Boxer (2003, Thailand) Action/Drama ΨΨ
Male to female transsexual makes use of kickboxing skills to pay for a sex change operation.

Psychologist: "Nick, when you recollect your childhood, are your recollections pleasing to you?"
Nick: "Number 1, I don't remember how often I used to jerk off, but it was a lot. Number 2, I wasn't pissed off at my dad, even when I was old enough to know what he and mom were doing in the bedroom. Number 3, I don't look in the toilet before I flush it. Number 4, I haven't wet my bed for a long time. Number 5, why don't the two of you go fuck yourselves; I'm outta here."

Nick feels threatened by a psychological interview in *Basic Instinct* (1992)

Beginner's Luck (1983) Comedy ΨΨ
Lightweight comedy about a law student who becomes involved in a *ménage à trois*.

Belle de Jour (1967) Drama ΨΨΨΨΨ
Luis Buñuel film with Catherine Deneuve playing a bored housewife who amuses herself by working

in a brothel from two until five every afternoon, at least until her sexual obsessions begin to complicate her life. Buñuel may be filming what is just an erotic dream.

Birdcage, The (1996) Comedy ΨΨΨ
Mike Nichols and Elaine May's remake of *La Cage aux Folles*. This film is almost as good as the original, thanks to strong performances by Robin Williams and Gene Hackman.

"Al, you old son of a bitch! How ya doin'? How do you feel about that call today? I mean the Dolphins! Fourth-and-three play on their 30 yard line with only 34 seconds to go!"

A transvestite trying to act masculine in *The Birdcage* (1996)

Breakfast on Pluto (2005) Comedy ΨΨΨ
Neil Jordan's film about an Irish Catholic abandoned child who is raised by a parish priest but later becomes a flamboyant transsexual.

Blame It on Rio (1984) Comedy ΨΨ
Two men take their teenage daughters to Rio's topless beaches, and one of the men, 43 years old, has an affair with the 15-year-old daughter of the other. The film has a vaguely incestuous theme and is modeled after the French film *One Wild Moment*.

Bliss (1997) Drama Ψ
Very fragile woman with a borderline personality disorder goes to a charming sex therapist who sleeps with his patients. The husband finds out; when he confronts the therapist, the husband converts and becomes his disciple. The film illustrates numerous ethical violations, and it demeans sacred Hindu tantric practices.

Blue Angel, The (1930) Drama ΨΨΨΨΨ
Classic film about a phlegmatic professor who loses everything because of his obsession with a cabaret singer.

Blue Car (2002) Drama ΨΨΨ
Independent film about an adolescent girl who is seduced by her teacher. Good depiction of the disturbing, subtle aspects of seduction and sexual exploitation.

Blue Velvet (1986) Mystery ΨΨΨ
A powerful and engrossing David Lynch film about drugs, sexual violence, and sadomasochism. Dennis Hopper portrays Frank Booth, one of the most sociopathic and sadistic villains in film history.

Bound (1996) Suspense/Drama ΨΨ
A tough female ex-con and her new female lover concoct a scheme to steal mob money. This film noir is The Wachowski Brothers' directorial debut.

Boys Don't Cry (1999) Drama ΨΨΨΨ
One of the best films to ever depict the pain and problems that can emerge from gender identity disorder. A brutal, powerful film.

Breaking the Waves (1996, Denmark) Drama ΨΨΨ
A Danish film in which a devout Catholic wife submits to sexual degradation to satisfy the voyeuristic demands of her paralyzed husband.

"Are you sleeping with other men just to feed his sick fantasies?"

A question put to Bess in *Breaking the Waves* (1996)

Burn After Reading (2008) Comedy Ψ
Clever, dark comedy by the Coen brothers in which George Clooney's character has a sexual addiction.

Cabaret (1972) Musical/Drama/Dance ΨΨΨΨ
Liza Minnelli in a film about sadomasochism, bisexuality, and the relationship between sex and power. *Cabaret* won Oscars for Best Actor, Best Actress, and Best Director. One scene in the film is as unforgettable as the classic confession of incest in *Chinatown*.

Caesar and Rosalie (1972) Comedy/Romance ΨΨ
Lighthearted and amusing examination of a *ménage à trois*.

Capturing the Friedmans (2003) Documentary ΨΨΨΨ
Extraordinarily disturbing and emotional documentary about a father and son accused of pedophilia. Important film to see regarding sex addic-

tion, pedophilia, and the importance of not casting judgment too quickly.

> "Don't worry, you've got everything under control."
>
> A therapist's comments to a pedophile who was worried he might molest his own children; he later molests numerous children in a class he teaches out of his home in *Capturing the Friedmans* (2003)

Carnal Knowledge (1971) Drama ΨΨ
This Mike Nichols film traces the sexual lives of two college roommates, played by Jack Nicholson and Art Garfunkel, as they age and become increasingly disenchanted with sex, love, and the possibilities inherent in relationships.

Chinatown (1974) Mystery ΨΨΨΨ
A film about power, incest, and the complexity of human relationships. Actors includes Jack Nicholson, Faye Dunaway and John Huston.

> "You see, Mr. Gettes, most people never have to face the fact that, at the right time and in the right place, they are capable of anything."
>
> *Chinatown* (1974)

Claire's Knee (1971) Drama ΨΨΨ
An intelligent film in which a middle-aged man becomes obsessed with a young girl's knee.

Close My Eyes (1991) Drama ΨΨ
A British film about brother-sister incest.

Closer (2004) Comedy/Drama ΨΨΨ
A quality film with good dialogue and superb acting by Jude Law, Natalie Portman, Julia Roberts, and Clive Owen. Important issues related to sexuality are portrayed, including deceit, infidelity, the failure to self-disclose, dependency, the impact of guilt and shame, and relationship testing. One scene depicts an amusing online con-

versation between two men sending erotic instant messages.

Collector, The (1965) Drama ΨΨΨ
Terence Stamp stars as a young man who collects butterflies. He becomes obsessed with Samantha Eggar, kidnaps her, and winds up inadvertently killing her.

Comfort of Strangers, The (1990) Drama ΨΨ
Sexual conflict and disorders abound as two couples find themselves entangled with one another in Venice.

Crash (1996) Drama ΨΨΨ
A David Cronenberg film about people who become sexually aroused by automobile accidents. The film presents a plausible hypothesis: people have developed fetishes for stranger things, and there are erotic overtones to both cars and speed.

> "You couldn't wait for me? You did the Jane Mansfield crash without me!"
>
> One of many strange interactions in David Cronenberg's *Crash* (1996)

Crime of Father Amaro, The (2002, Mexico) Drama ΨΨΨ
A young priest, newly ordained, goes to a small, Mexican town to serve a parish. He witnesses his pastor having sex with women and he falls for a woman whom he secretively uses for sex until she becomes pregnant.

Cruising (1980) Crime Ψ
Controversial William Friedkin film starring Al Pacino as an undercover police officer who infiltrates gay bars and bathhouses. Gay activists condemned the film because it perpetuates stigma and stereotypes.

Crying Game, The (1992) Drama ΨΨΨΨ
This Neil Jordan film explores homosexuality, transsexualism, interracial sexuality, and the ability of two human beings to love one another deeply in an asexual relationship. Too complex to explain simply, the film must be seen to be fully appreciated.

Damage (1992) Drama ΨΨΨ
A Louis Malle film starring Jeremy Irons as a man who develops a sexual obsession for his son's fiancée. Both the father and the son's girlfriend seem powerless to control their erotic attachment despite its inevitable consequences.

Day in the Country, A (1936) Romance ΨΨΨΨ
Jean Renoir's adaptation of a short story by Guy de Maupassant that describes the seductions of a man's wife and daughter.

De-Lovely (2004) Musical/Comedy/Biography ΨΨ
The story of the life of Cole Porter and his sexual addiction.

Diary of a Sex Addict, The (2001) Drama ΨΨ
Depiction of a classic sex addict who denies, rationalizes and continues a series of affairs until he finally can deceive no longer. He continues his compulsive behavior, even after the consequences of this behavior are almost fatal. The film offers a realistic portrayal of a sex addict.

Therapist: "Which one is really you? The family man or the other guy?"
Patient: "Both"

The Diary of a Sex Addict (2001)

Dirty Shame, A (2004) Comedy Ψ
A woman becomes promiscuous after a head injury.

Door in the Floor, The (2003) Drama ΨΨ
A couple separates after the death of their twin sons. The catalyst for the breakup is Eddie, a 16 year old who takes a job as Jeff Bridges' assistant. Eddie is infatuated by Kim Bassinger's character and masturbates using her photos and undergarments to become aroused. Bassinger eventually seduces Eddie, who reminds her of her dead sons. Based on a novel by John Irving.

Dreamers, The (2003) Drama ΨΨΨ
Fraternal twins take in a roommate in this Bernardo Bertolucci exploration of politics, cinema, and sexuality. The dynamics become complicated when the new roommate falls in love with the female twin, taking her virginity and challenging her enmeshment with her brother.

"A filmmaker is like a peeping Tom, a voyeur. It's as if the camera is the key to your parent's bedroom and you spy on them and you're disgusted and you feel guilty but you can't... you can't look away."

The Dreamers (2003)

Eros (2004) Drama ΨΨΨ
Three noted directors (Michelangelo Antonioni, Steven Soderbergh and Wong Kar Wai) each contribute a short film dealing with some aspect of sexuality (e.g., a *menage-a-trois*, voyeurism, and prostitution).

Everything You Always Wanted to Know About Sex *But Were Afraid to Ask (1972) Comedy ΨΨΨ
Woody Allen classic includes vignettes on crossing-dressing, bestiality, sex in public, and the inner workings of the brain during sexual excitement.

Evil Alien Conquerors (2002) Comedy Ψ
Painfully bad film in which Saturday Night Live star, Chris Parnell, has a foot fetish.

Eyes Wide Shut (1999) Drama ΨΨΨΨΨ
The final Stanley Kubrick film about a man (Tom Cruise) who discovers a sexual underworld after his wife (Nicole Kidman) tells him of her fantasies and previous sexual encounters. Depiction of ephebophilia (sexual attraction of adults to adolescents), orgies, sexual rituals, exhibitionism, prostitution, infidelity, sexual fantasy, seduction, and betrayal. Mythological and Jungian psychology themes are omnipresent.

Far From Heaven (2002) Drama ΨΨΨ
Julianne Moore, living in a conservative area in a conservative time, finds out her husband is a homosexual. Interesting film that explores racism, stereotypes, and secrets.

Fellini Satyricon (1970) Historical ΨΨΨΨ
Controversial Fellini film about the decadence of ancient Rome. The film is visually stunning and explores human vices ranging from homosexual pedophilia to cannibalism. The film can be a springboard for a discussion of hedonism.

Female Perversions (1996) Drama ΨΨΨ
Confused and often confusing examination of the

relationship between women, power, sexuality, and psychopathology. Based on a scholarly book with the same title by psychoanalyst Louise J. Kaplan.

Fetishes (1996) Documentary ΨΨΨ
True examination of the clients of Pandora's Box, an elite club catering to the sexual fetishes of New York City.

Fist in His Pocket (1966) Drama ΨΨΨ
Italian film about a dysfunctional family with multiple examples of psychopathology including epilepsy, murder, and incest.

Flawless (1999) Drama/Comedy ΨΨ
Philip Seymour Hoffman plays a drag queen named Rusty who is saving money for a gender modification operation; Robert De Niro is the homophobic neighbor who takes voice lessons from Rusty following a stroke.

Fried Green Tomatoes (1991) Comedy/Drama ΨΨΨ
Presents a positive, healthy, loving view of an (assumed) lesbian relationship. We are quickly caught up in the complex and intertwined story of these two women.

Girl 6 (1996) Drama/Comedy Ψ
Spike Lee film about a woman who takes a job as a phone sex operator for the money.

God's Little Acre (1958) Drama Ψ
Buddy Hackett and Michael Landon star in this adaptation of Erskine Caldwell's tale of depravity and Georgia farm life.

Good Mother, The (1988) Drama ΨΨΨ
A provocative film in which Diane Keaton plays the divorced mother of a six-year-old daughter. Keaton falls in love with an iconoclastic artist, who allows the daughter to touch his penis when she sees him in the bath and expresses normal childhood curiosity. Keaton is eventually forced to denounce her new lover in order to maintain a relationship with her daughter.

Happiness (1998) Comedy/Drama ΨΨΨ
Disturbing dark comedy portraying a variety of quirky characters. The most striking are the pedophiliac psychiatrist who drugs and rapes his son's best friend and Philip Seymour Hoffman as a man who is obsessed with telephone scatalogia. Director Todd Solondz has a cameo as a doorman.

Joe: "What do you think would happen if I got him a professional... you know..."
Bill: "A professional?"
Joe: "Hooker. You know, the kind that can teach things... first-timers, you know... break him in."
Bill: "But Joe, he's 11."
Joe: "You're right, you're right. It's too late."

Cultures clash in *Happiness* (1998)

Hard Candy (2005) Drama ΨΨ
A pedophile arranges to meet a 14-year-old girl who turns things around and winds up being the aggressor.

Harold and Maude (1972) Comedy ΨΨΨ
A cult film that examines sexual and romantic attraction across generations; this movie will force you to reexamine your feelings about age and death.

Henry & June (1990) Drama ΨΨ
Adaptation of Anais Nin diary detailing her *ménage à trois* with novelist Henry Miller and his wife June.

Holy Smoke (1999) Drama ΨΨΨ
Jane Campion film about a family who believes their daughter (Kate Winslet) is under the power of a cult leader. They hire a renowned "cult exiter" (Harvey Keitel) whose role is to isolate the subject, provoke them, and then reintegrate them into the family. After an interessting role reversal, he finds himself developing a sexual obsession.

Human Nature (2001) Comedy ΨΨ
Fascinating study on instinct and desire about a man raised in the wild and the scientists he encounters.

I am a Sex Addict (2005) Biography/Comedy Ψ
A recovering sex addict describes how his life and marriages have been changed by his addiction to prostitutes.

In the Realm of the Senses (1977, Japan) Drama ΨΨΨ
A sadomasochistic relationship intensifies into highly graphic and unforgettable scenes of autoerotic asphyxiation and the severing of an adult penis.

Intimacy (2000) Drama ΨΨ
Depressed man and woman meet for anonymous sex in a dilapidated apartment once a week. The man becomes curious about the woman and follows her to learn more about her. Slow, dark film that depicts the double life of the addict.

Ju Dou (1990, China) Drama/Historical/Romance ΨΨΨΨ
Wonderful, visually stunning film examining the complex links that bind a husband, his wife, her lover, and the son of the illicit union. Good illustrations of sexual passion and sexual torment.

Jules and Jim (1962, France) Drama ΨΨΨΨ
Beautiful and engaging Truffaut film about a complex *ménage à trois* and an ultimate suicide. The film deals with far more than sexuality; it explores fundamental dimensions of human relationships and the boundaries of friendship and love.

"Love is the answer, isn't it?
But, sex raises a lot of very interesting questions."

Kinsey (2004)

Kinsey (2004) Drama/Biography ΨΨΨΨ
Examination of the life of Alfred Kinsey, a sex researcher who revolutionized the way Americans viewed sexuality. The film depicts Kinsey's obsessive-compulsive personality, his inability to connect in a deep way, and the failure to set boundaries for his own (and his research team's) sexual practices.

Kiss of the Spider Woman (1985) Prison ΨΨΨΨ
A homosexual and a political activist share a prison cell and grow to understand and appreciate each other. William Hurt won an Academy Award for his performance.

Kissed (1996) Drama ΨΨΨ
A controversial but sensitive film dealing seriously with necrophilia. Molly Parker is the protagonist, a young woman obsessed from childhood with death. She gets a job in a mortuary and has ritualistic sex ("crossing over") with the bodies she embalms. Her boyfriend commits suicide in an attempt to compete for her affection and attention.

"I told them my father was a Cultural attaché.
What will they think when they find out he lives with a drag queen?"

Renato's son in *La Cage aux Folles* (1978)

La Cage aux Folles (1978, France) Comedy ΨΨΨ
A gay man and his transvestite lover manage a popular St. Tropez nightclub. Much of the humor revolves around sex roles and the folly of trying very hard to be something you're not.

Last Exit to Brooklyn (1989) Drama ΨΨ
A film based on a controversial book about life in a sordid Brooklyn neighborhood. The film deals with rape, prostitution, homosexuality, and transvestism, but mostly with the sad and bleak reality of the lives of its characters.

Last Tango in Paris (1973) Drama ΨΨΨΨ
Marlon Brando stars in a classic Bernardo Bertolucci film about a man who begins a casual sexual liaison on the day his wife commits suicide. The two lovers never exchange names. The film includes themes of depression, sexuality, loneliness, and cynicism.

Lianna (1983) Drama ΨΨΨ
Sensitive film portraying the emotional life of a woman who leaves her husband and two children after she becomes romantically involved with a lesbian professor teaching a night course in child psychology.

Little Children (2007) Drama ΨΨΨΨ
This film portrays a number of sexually troubled characters, but is especially memorable for the roles of Jackie Earle Haley playing a pedophile and Kate Winslet playing the role of a parent who overcomes her repugnance to befriend him.

"What drives me insane is the twofold nature of this nymphet... this mixture in my Lolita of tender, dreamy childishness and a kind of eerie vulgarity."

Humbert Humbert in *Lolita* (1962)

Lolita (1962) Drama ΨΨΨΨ
James Mason and Sue Lyons star in a loose adaptation of Vladimir Nabokov's novel about pedophilia and murder. Laurence Olivier turned down the role of Humbert Humbert. Directed by Stanley Kubrick; watch for Peter Sellers as Dr. Zempf, the Beardsley High School psychologist.

Luna (1979) Drama ΨΨ
A Bertolucci film that explores mother-son incest and addiction. The film is not Bertolucci's best effort.

Magenta (1996) Drama Ψ
Happily married physician crosses boundaries sexually with his sister-in-law, creating havoc in his family.

Manhattan (1979) Comedy/Romance ΨΨΨΨ
Classic Woody Allen film in which his former wife, played by Meryl Streep, has taken a lover, found happiness, and written a book to tell the world about Allen's kinky habits. Allen's character (in an example of art imitating life) is consumed with guilt over the fact that he is living with a teenage girl.

Marie Antoinette (2006) Drama/Biography Ψ
The Queen finds herself in a loveless and asexual relationship with her husband, Louis XVI.

Mark, The (1961) Drama ΨΨΨΨ
A British film about a pedophile who serves his sentence and is released, supposedly cured. However, a journalist who reveals the man's past hampers his rehabilitation. Interesting film in light of recent court decisions about sex offenders.

Matador (1986) Comedy/Drama ΨΨ
Almodovar film about a bullfighter who acts in snuff films.

Menage (1986, France) Comedy ΨΨ
A French film that examines sex roles, sexual stereotypes, and the need for novelty and excitement in sexual relationships.

> "Well, I'll tell you the truth now.
> I ain't a real cowboy, but I am one helluva stud."
>
> Joe Buck in *Midnight Cowboy* (1969)

Midnight Cowboy (1969) Drama ΨΨΨΨΨ
Jon Voight leaves Texas to make his fortune in New York City working as a stud; instead, he winds up hanging out with Ratso Rizzo, who dies before the two can escape to Florida. This film is a fascinating and complex character study.

Midsummer Night's Sex Comedy, A (1982) ΨΨ
Excellent Woody Allen film about friends and acquaintances who gather at a country house in the woods at the turn of the century. Sexual boundaries blur in this homage to Shakespeare, Renoir, and others.

Mona Lisa (1986) Crime ΨΨΨ
Interesting Neil Jordan film about prostitution, exploitation, drug addiction, and love. Filmed in Soho, the film gives some insight into the two different worlds of prostitution: that of the call girl and that of the streetwalker.

Montenegro (1981) Drama ΨΨ
A Dusan Makavejev film about a bored housewife slowly becoming psychotic. She becomes sexually liberated and then murders her lover. Despite its psychopathological theme, the film is really about politics and social class.

Mrs. Doubtfire (1994) Comedy ΨΨ
Robin Williams cross-dresses as an English nanny to have time with his children.

> "Well, I hope you're up for a little competition. She's got a power tool in the bedroom, dear. It's her own personal jackhammer. She could break sidewalks with that thing. She uses it and the lights dim, it's like a prison movie. Amazed she hasn't chipped her teeth."
>
> Daniel Hillard, disguised as Mrs. Doubfire, tries to discourage Stu, his ex-wife's new lover, in *Mrs. Doubtfire* (1994)

Murmur of the Heart (1971) Comedy ΨΨ
A sensitive, intelligent, and funny French film about an incestuous relationship between a young mother and her adolescent son.

My Beautiful Laundrette (1985) Drama ΨΨ
The two lead characters are homosexuals, although

this fact is almost incidental to the story about alcoholism, street gangs, race relations, and social class.

My Favorite Season (1993, France) Drama ΨΨΨ
A French film dealing with adolescent sexuality, family dynamics, and love between a brother and sister.

My Life to Live (1962, France) ΨΨΨ
Jean-Luc Godard's 12-part examination of the life of a prostitute, starring Anna Karina.

My Own Private Idaho (1991) Drama ΨΨ
River Phoenix, who subsequently died of a drug overdose, plays a homosexual prostitute.

Mystery of Alexina, The (1985) Drama ΨΨ
A story about the psychological sequelae of the decision to raise a male child as a female.

Nine ½ Weeks (1986) Drama/Suspense ΨΨ
Excellent character portrayals by Mickey Rourke and Kim Basinger who meet at a grocery store and later engage in sensual sexual exploration and mild sadomasochism.

Normal (2003) Drama ΨΨΨ
A man (Tom Wilkinson) after 25 years of marriage tells his wife (Jessica Lange) he is a woman trapped in a man's body and he wants gender modification surgery.

Of Human Bondage (1934) Drama ΨΨ
Bette Davis stars in this film about the sexual obsession of a club-footed physician for a cruel, vulgar, and manipulative waitress. Based on a novel by Somerset Maugham. This film is far superior to the two adaptations that followed it.

> "You dirty swine! I never cared for you... It made me sick when you kissed me. I only did it because you drove me crazy. And after you kissed me I always used to wipe my mouth – wipe my mouth!"
>
> *Of Human Bondage* (1934)

Oh in Ohio, The (2006) Comedy ΨΨΨ
A married couple becomes open to new sexual experiences with different partners after a decade

of insipid sex. Sexual desire and sexual disorders are depicted.

Old Boy (2003) Drama ΨΨΨΨ
This is an unforgettable Korean film directed by Chan-Wook Park about a man kidnapped and imprisoned for 15 years who becomes involved in an unwitting incestuous relationship with the daughter he had not seen for 15 years.

On_Line (2002) Drama ΨΨΨ
A film about internet addiction. Emphasis on the lack of connection and relational intimacy of the addict. Depicts an obsession with fantasy that becomes confused as reality.

Oscar Wilde (1960) Biography Ψ
Robert Morley plays Oscar Wilde, the playwright who was convicted of sodomy.

Peeping Tom (1960) Thriller ΨΨΨ
Controversial film about a sexual psychopath who photographs his victims as they are dying. Look for the full-length version of the film, which was released in 1979.

Personal Best (1982) Sports ΨΨΨ
Fascinating film that explores the sexual relationship that develops between two women competing for a position on an Olympic team.

> "It's being aware of what it means to lose oneself before being completely abandoned."
>
> *The Piano Teacher* (2001)

Piano Teacher, The (2001) Drama ΨΨΨΨ
This is a powerful French film about a prominent, masochistic piano teacher who becomes sexually involved with one of her pupils. The film makes sexual obsession understandable and plausible.

Pillow Book (1997) Drama ΨΨΨΨ
Complex Peter Greenaway film about a woman who becomes sexually obsessed with calligraphy. This film is a meditation on love, art and imagination, eroticism, order, and decay.

Pretty Baby (1978) Drama ΨΨ
This Louis Malle film about pedophilia introduces

Brooke Shields as a 12-year-old New Orleans prostitute.

Pretty When You Cry (2001) Drama/Suspense Ψ
Mostly flashbacks as detectives follow up a murder investigation with a young man who tells the story of his infatuation and love for a beautiful woman who was in an abusive relationship. The masochistic-sadistic relationship is portrayed, as well as physical, verbal and emotional abuse.

Princesa (2001) Drama Ψ
Brazilian transvestite moves to Italy and works as a prostitute in order to earn money for his sex change operation.

Priest (1994) Drama ΨΨ
A priest struggles to deal with the sanctity of confession after a young girl tells him she is being molested by her father.

Private Lessons (1981) "Drama Ψ
A French maid seduces a 15-year-old boy and betrays his trust.

Private Parts (1997) Comedy Ψ
Inside look at radio personality Howard Stern and his obsession with sex and outlandish comedy.

Psychopathia Sexualis (2006) Drama Ψ
Based directly on the classic Krafft-Ebing text, the film depicts a variety of fetishes and other paraphilias.

> "Look, maybe your method of massage differs from mine, but touchin' his lady's feet, and stickin' your tongue in her holiest of holies, ain't the same ballpark, ain't the same league, ain't even the same fuckin' sport. Foot massages don't mean shit."
>
> A discussion of foot massage in
> *Pulp Fiction* (1994)

Pulp Fiction (1994) Drama ΨΨΨΨΨ
Quentin Tarantino film depicts an underworld sadomasochistic den of iniquity run by two sexual sadists in the basement of an Army surplus store. A masochistic slave dressed totally in leather lives in a box in the back of the room.

Quills (2000) Drama ΨΨΨ
Depiction of the last years of the Marquis de Sade (well played by Geoffrey Rush) who was sent to the Charenton Asylum for the Insane as punishment for his erotic writings. Interesting portrayal of various paraphilias.

Reader, The (2008) Drama ΨΨΨΨ
Kate Winslet plays Hanna Schmitz, a Nazi concentration camp guard who seduces a young boy who later grows up and becomes a prominent attorney.

Reflections in a Golden Eye (1967) Drama ΨΨ
A John Huston film in which Richard Burton plays the role of a repressed homosexual Army officer serving on a small Georgia military base. Elizabeth Taylor is his sadistic and sexually liberated wife. The film was banned by the Catholic Film Board.

Rita, Sue and Bob Too (1986) Comedy ΨΨΨ
British film about a married man who winds up in a sexual relationship with the two working-class teenage girls who babysit for his children. Interesting examination of the appropriate age for consent and issues of sexual exploitation.

Rocky Horror Picture Show, The (1975) Comedy/Horror/Musical/Dance Ψ
A fun film about a Transylvanian transsexual. From a psychological perspective, the film is not nearly as interesting as those fans who have turned it into a cult classic.

Sailor Who Fell from Grace with the Sea, The (1976) Drama ΨΨΨΨ
Interesting story of adult romance and child psychopathology; based on a novel by Yukio Mishima.

Salo or **The 120 Days of Sodom** (1975) Horror Ψ
Pasolini's adaptation of de Sade's famous novel. Set in the fascist Italy of World War II, this violent film is an interesting introduction to the practice of sadism.

Secretary (2002) Drama ΨΨΨ
A self-injurious, depressed woman is hired as a secretary after leaving a mental hospital; she takes a new job and begins to enjoy the criticism and punishment of her boss. They develop a sadomasochistic relationship in the work setting and eventually fall in love and marry.

Sergeant, The (1968) Drama ΨΨ
Rod Steiger plays an Army sergeant sexually

obsessed with a young private in his outfit. Filmed in France.

"In one way or another I've always suffered. I didn't know why exactly. But I do know that I'm not so scared of suffering now. I feel more than I've ever felt and I've found someone to feel with. To play with. To love in a way that feels right for me."

Reflections on masochism in *Secretary* (2002)

Sex and Zen (1993) Comedy Ψ
Second rate film about a Buddhist who leaves his master and new wife to seek out a life of debauchery and erotic pleasures.

Sex is Zero (2002) Comedy Ψ
A Korean *Animal House*, but not as clever. The film involves lots of teens sexually acting out in a variety of ways.

sex, lies, and videotape (1989) Drama ΨΨΨ
The film revolves around an impotent young man who can achieve orgasm only when masturbating while watching videotapes of women whom he has persuaded to share the most intimate details of their sexual lives. This film won the top award at the Cannes Film Festival.

Short Cuts (1993) Drama ΨΨ
Most memorable for a scene in which a bored woman talks dirty on the phone to earn a few dollars while she changes her baby's diapers. Her husband wonders why she never talks to *him* like that.

Short Eyes (1977) Prison ΨΨΨΨ
A powerful film about life in "The Tombs," New York City's Men's House of Detention. Short Eyes is prison slang for a child molester.

Short Film About Love, A (1988, Poland) Drama ΨΨΨ
This Krzysztof Kieslowski film deals with themes of voyeurism, exhibitionism, humiliation and suicide.

Sliver (1993) Drama Ψ
William Baldwin plays a voyeur who is the landlord of an apartment complex with high tech cameras set up in the tenants' rooms.

Soldier's Girl (2003) Drama/Biography ΨΨΨ
Based on the true story of Barry Winchell who entered the military and fell in love with a transsexual dancer at a club. Military peers find out about the secret relationship and the situation ends tragically.

"The imagination is the most powerful force known to mankind. And it is my imagined self, the one who is beautiful and loving and worthy of being loved, that has been my guiding force. My inspiration. I can only hope to become the person Barry imagined me to be. I pray for the courage it will take to become a real, live soldier's girl."

Soldier's Girl (2003)

Something About Amelia (1984) Drama ΨΨ
Popular made-for-TV movie about father-daughter incest.

Southern Comfort (2001) Documentary ΨΨ
Female to male transgender faces hate and prejudice in this award-winning film.

Strange One, The (1957) Drama ΨΨ
Ben Gazzara stars in this film about homosexuality and sadism in a Southern military academy.

Swept Away (1975) Drama/Comedy ΨΨΨ
Lina Wertmuller's examination of sex roles. A rich woman and a poor deckhand are marooned on an island and find sexual excitement and satisfaction in the new roles each assumes.

That Obscure Object of Desire (1977) Drama ΨΨΨΨΨ
Surrealistic film by Luis Buñuel about violence, love, and sexual obsession in a middle-aged man. The film is complex, intriguing, and full of symbolism, including two actresses playing the same character.

This Girl's Life (2003) Drama Ψ
A female porn star starts a business by getting women concerned about their husbands' fidelity to pay her to attempt to seduce them.

This World, Then the Fireworks (1997) Drama ΨΨ
This film traces the development of incestuous twins who eventually become con artists.

Tie Me Up! Tie Me Down! (1990, Spain) Comedy/Romance ΨΨΨ
A Pedro Almodovar film about a former mental patient, kidnapping, masochism, and sex roles. Some critics have maintained that the film trivializes the problem of sexual violence and denigrates women.

To Our Loves (1983, France) Drama ΨΨΨ
A French film exploring the sexuality of a 15-year-old girl and the way it affects her family.

> Director: "I'd like to make her look a little more attractive. How far can you pull back?"
> Cameraman: "How do you feel about Cleveland?"
>
> *Tootsie* (1982)

Tootsie (1982) Comedy/Romance ΨΨΨΨ
Funny Dustin Hoffman film in which an unsuccessful actor finds success when he impersonates a woman. He learns from the process, and the audience learns some important lessons about gender, sex roles, and human relationships.

Torch Song Trilogy (1988) Drama ΨΨΨ
Anne Bancroft and Matthew Broderick in a film adaptation of Harvey Fierstein's play about a homosexual drag queen and his lovers, enemies, and mother.

Towelhead (2007) Drama ΨΨΨ
A naïve, 13-year-old, Arab-American girl moves from Syracuse to Houston and encounters a number of challenges associated with her emerging sexuality, including being the victim of ephebophilia.

Transamerica (2005) Comedy ΨΨΨΨ
A presurgical male to female transsexual takes a cross country journey with the son she just met for the first time.

Two Women (1960, Italy) Drama/War ΨΨΨ
Classic Vittorio De Sica film starring Sophia Loren. The film is about love, war, rape, and a mother's love for her teenage daughter.

Unbearable Lightness of Being, The (1988) Romance ΨΨΨ
A highly sensual film about a Prague neurosurgeon and his inability to separate sex and love. The film is based on the novel of the same name by Milan Kundera.

Unfaithful (2002) Drama/Suspense ΨΨ
Richard Gere finds his wife (Diane Lane) is cheating on him and plots revenge.

Venus (2006) Drama ΨΨΨ
Peter O'Toole plays an aging actor with prostate cancer who falls in love with a teenage girl.

Victor/Victoria (1982) Musical/Comedy ΨΨ
Blake Edwards film with Julie Andrews as a down-on-her-luck singer who becomes a sensation when she pretends to be a male-female impersonator.

Viridiana (1961, Spain) Drama ΨΨΨΨ
This complex Luis Buñuel film tells the story of a young woman who returns home to visit her uncle just before taking vows as a nun. She resembles her dead aunt, and her uncle drugs her while she is wearing her aunt's wedding dress. He plans to rape her but is unable to commit the act. He commits suicide; she inherits his estate and devotes her life to serving the poor.

Visiting Desire (1996) Documentary ΨΨ
Twelve strangers are brought together to act out their sexual fantasies.

> "Stealing images from life is my life."
>
> A voyeur describes himself in *Voyeur Confessions* (2001)

Voyeur Confessions (2001) Drama ΨΨ
This film captures the pain associated with the life of the voyeur. The movie touches on the etiology of voyeurism, and helps serious students better understand the paraphilias.

Warm Water Under a Red Bridge (2001, Japan) Drama ΨΨΨ
Shohei Imamura film about a businessman who

encounters a woman with a peculiar problem – fluids build up in her and she can only release them by stealing or having an orgasm.

We Don't Live Here Anymore (2004) Drama ΨΨΨ
Two couples (played by Peter Krause, Naomi Watts, Mark Ruffalo, and Laura Dern) find both their marriages failing, in part due to adultery. The movie includes themes of deceit, manipulation, lack of integrity, and the excitement of secrecy. Each couple battles against boredom and idleness, using sex to escape the emptiness of their lives.

Wild Orchid 2: Two Shades of Blue (1991) Drama Ψ
Disappointing film about the daughter of a heroin addict who becomes a prostitute to support her father's habit while maintaining a double identity.

Woodsman, The (2004) Drama ΨΨΨ
Kevin Bacon plays a pedophile recently released from prison struggling to establish a satisfying sexual relationship with a mature coworker.

World According to Garp, The (1982) Comedy/Drama ΨΨ
John Lithgow plays transsexual Roberta Muldoon in a film in which troubled sexuality is commonplace.

Yentl (1983) Musical ΨΨ
Barbra Streisand directed and produced this film, and she has the lead role as a young woman in Eastern Europe who has to pass herself off as a man in order to get an education. Interesting examination of sex roles; terrific performance by Streisand.

Young Adam (2003) Drama ΨΨ
Ewan Macgregor as a sexual addict who becomes intimately involved with his boss' wife, her sister, and a woman he meets at a ship's port.

Zerophilia (2005) Comedy/Romance Ψ
A young man discovers that he has "zerophilia," which means he can switch sexual identities and experience pleasure as either a man or a woman. The film is a less than satisfying exploration of sex roles.

Schizophrenia and Other Psychotic Disorders

11'09"01 – September 11 (2002) Drama ΨΨ
Eleven renowned directors from around the world look to their own cultures to create a short film in tribute to the tragedy of September 11, 2001. This fascinating collection of films includes an allegory from Japan's Shohei Imamura about a man who returns from war believing he is a snake.

13 Moons (2002) Drama ΨΨ
Three priests, a bail bondsman, a musician, and two clowns cross paths on night-time city streets. One character, a drug addict needing an organ transplant, is blatantly psychotic throughout the film.

Aguirre, the Wrath of God (1972, West Germany/Peru/Mexico) Adventure ΨΨΨΨ
Werner Herzog film about Spanish conquistadors searching for the mythic treasure of El Dorado deep into the Amazon of Peru. The narcissistic leader deteriorates into psychosis.

Alone in the Dark (1982) Suspense Ψ
A psychiatrist's family is besieged by a psychotic patient during a citywide blackout.

Amadeus (1984) Biography/Musical ΨΨΨ
The film opens with the court composer Salieri, now old, mad, and suicidal, wondering if he murdered Mozart. Salieri is obsessed with the genius of Mozart and can never forgive his rival for his talent or himself for his mediocrity.

Angel at My Table, An (1990) Biography/Drama ΨΨΨΨΨ
Jean Campion's biography of New Zealand novelist Janet Frame, who was misdiagnosed with schizophrenia and mistreated with electroconvulsive therapy.

Angel Baby (1995) Drama ΨΨΨ
Australian film about two mentally ill people who meet in an outpatient clinic, fall in love, and try to face life together. Unfortunately, their lives fall apart as a consequence of an ill-fated decision to mutually discontinue their medication.

Angel in Red (1991) Suspense Ψ
A psychotic pimp goes gunning for his former employee after she turns to a rival pimp for protection.

Assassination of Richard Nixon, The (2004) Biography/Drama ΨΨΨ
Sean Penn portrays Sam Bicke, an aloof, taciturn, delusional furniture salesman who attempted to kill President Nixon. The film promotes the misconception that people with mental illness are always violent.

Asylum (2005) Thriller/Drama ΨΨ
A husband takes a job at a psychiatric institution and his wife begins to have an affair with a dangerous patient. The film perpetrates the misconception that patients in psychiatric hospitals are violent and dangerous.

Bee Season (2005) Drama Ψ
A father (Richard Gere) becomes over involved in his daughter's spelling bee competitions and looks to Jewish mysticism for support.

Benny & Joon (1993) Comedy ΨΨΨ
A generally sympathetic portrayal of schizophrenia, with a vivid example of decompensation on a city bus; the film trivializes the problem of schizophrenia by suggesting love alone is enough to conquer the problem.

Berlin Alexanderplatz (1980) Drama ΨΨΨΨΨ
This film, a 15-hour Fassbinder masterpiece, traces the gradual moral and mental disintegration of a man who leaves prison resolved to live a good life. The film explores exploitation of women, violence, homosexuality, and mental illness.

Betrayed (1988) Political/Thriller Ψ
Debra Winger plays an undercover agent who falls in love with a seemingly simple farmer, actually a right-wing, paranoid fanatic.

Betty Blue (1986) Drama ΨΨΨ
Artistic, erotic French film about two young lovers and their passions that lead from poverty to violence and destruction. One particularly shocking scene depicts self-mutilation resulting from psychosis.

Bill of Divorcement, A (1932) Comedy ΨΨ
A mentally ill man is discharged from a psychiatric hospital and returns home to his wife and daughter. Katharine Hepburn's debut as a film actress.

Birdy (1984) Drama/War ΨΨΨΨ
Nicolas Cage tries to help his friend, Matthew Modine, who is a catatonic inpatient in a military hospital. Both men are Vietnam veterans, but Modine's problems seem to predate the war.

Birth (2004) Drama/Mystery ΨΨΨ
A rare depiction of shared psychotic disorder (*folie a deux*) featuring Nicole Kidman.

Boxing Helena (1994) Drama ΨΨ
Eminent surgeon is rebuffed by a beautiful woman. His obsessions of her turn delusional as he captures her and eventually amputates her arms and legs while paradoxically fawning over her. Interesting dynamic of his forcing the woman to be physically dependent upon him emerging from his psychological dependence on her. Directorial debut of Jennifer Chambers Lynch, daughter of distinguished filmmaker David Lynch.

"I am still haunted by my love for her... those dreams."

A character in *Boxing Helena* (1994) leaves the viewer to ponder how much of the film is delusion, reality, or a dream

---

Bubba Ho-tep (2002) Comedy/Thriller Ψ
Two rest home residents who believe they are Elvis Presley and John F. Kennedy team up to fight evil.

Camille Claudel (1988) Biography ΨΨΨ
Biographical film of the mistress of Rodin, who spent the last 30 years of her life in an asylum.

Canvas (2006) Drama ΨΨΨΨ
A remarkable portrayal of schizophrenia and its impact on the family, starring Marcia Gay Harden. Winner of a Voice Award for its outstanding depiction of mental illness.

Caveman's Valentine, The (2001) Crime/Drama ΨΨ
Depicts a homeless composer with schizophrenia living in a cave in New York City.

Crimson Gold (2003, Iran) Crime/Drama ΨΨ
A taciturn pizza delivery man becomes explosive after being mistreated.

Dead Man on Campus (1998) Comedy Ψ
Two roommates try to find a roommate who is likely to commit suicide so that they can have their flailing grades excused. The film perpetrates misconceptions that people with mental illness are

violent, that people with mental illness are always psychotic, and that those who are paranoid are the most likely to commit suicide.

Dead of Night (1945) Horror ΨΨΨΨ
Five short episodes loosely linked together. The last of these, "The Ventriloquist's Dummy," stars Michael Redgrave, who has to be hospitalized after he becomes convinced that he and his dummy are exchanging personalities (in fact, they are).

Delusions of Grandeur (1973) Comedy Ψ
In seventeenth-century Spain, a wily servant saves his king from the intrigues of a tax collector.

Derailroaded (2005) Documentary/Biography ΨΨΨ
Portrays the music and life of cult-rock icon "Wild Man Fischer," a man with schizophrenia; the film is both funny and informative, and it is not exploitative.

Don Juan DeMarco (1995) Drama ΨΨΨ
Marlon Brando plays a compassionate psychiatrist to Johnny Depp' character who thinks he is the legendary Don Juan.

"I am the world's greatest lover!"

Don Juan DeMarco (1995)

Donnie Darko (2001) Drama ΨΨΨ
Although this film is about a delusional high school student who frequently hallucinates a "demon bunny" instructing him that the end of the world is near, the film is fairly complex with important comments on fear, the pain of mental illness, and the nature of reality.

Don't Say A Word (2001) Suspense/Mystery ΨΨ
Michael Douglas plays a psychiatrist whose daughter is kidnapped for the ransom of a 6-digit code locked in the brain of a very disturbed psychiatric patient (Brittany Murphy).

Dressed to Kill (1980) Thriller Ψ
Popular film in which Michael Caine plays Angie Dickinson's psychiatrist. The film confuses transsexuality and schizophrenia, but it is exciting, if not always accurate.

Edmond (2005) Thriller ΨΨ
Interesting and memorable story about a man (William H. Macy) who slowly loses touch with reality and never fully returns.

Entertainer, The (1960) Drama Ψ
This film, starring Laurence Olivier and Albert Finney, portrays Olivier as a third-rate vaudevillian whose delusions of grandeur alienate people around him.

Fan, The (1982) Horror Ψ
A Broadway star played by Lauren Bacall is terrorized by an embittered fan.

Fan, The (1996) Drama Ψ
Robert De Niro and Wesley Snipes are wasted in this tired film about a baseball fan who is obsessed with a Giants center fielder.

Final (2001) Drama ΨΨΨ
Well-acted performance by Denis Leary who plays "Bill" in this Campbell Scott film. Bill awakens from a coma in an isolated, bright room of a psychiatric hospital. He has frequent paranoid delusions, anger outbursts, and hallucinations as his therapist helps him remember flashbacks of his car accident and his father's death. Interesting portrayal of the "doctor-patient" relationship, presenting many questions about boundaries, ethics, and relational dynamics.

Fisher King, The (1991) Drama/Fantasy/Comedy ΨΨΨ
Terry Gilliam film in which Robin Williams plays a homeless, mentally ill man who is befriended by a disillusioned former disc jockey. The movie is funny but confusing, and it misleads the public with its suggestion of a traumatic etiology for schizophrenia.

Flightplan (2005) Suspense/Drama ΨΨ
While on a long flight, a woman (Jodie Foster) frantically claims she has lost her child, however, other passengers do not remember a child traveling with her. For much of the film, the viewer is left questioning whether Jodie Foster has a psychotic disorder. The film suggests that individuals referred to as delusional or psychotic are actually telling the truth and their delusions may well be reality-based.

Frailty (2001) Drama/Suspense ΨΨΨ
Bill Paxton plays a serial killing, religious zealot with a delusional disorder who believes he's on a

mission from God to fight off demons (his human victims).

"Now you stay down here until you see the truth. Pray to god, Fenton. Pray for a vision. Only he can help you now!"

Frailty (2001)

Gothika (2004) Suspense ΨΨ
Halle Berry plays Dr. Miranda Grey who works to unravel the mystery of her patient's (Penelope Cruz) psychopathology and is confronted by disturbing secrets and the supernatural.

Goya in Bordeaux (1999) Drama/Biography ΨΨΨ
Spanish film, depicting the famous painter, Francisco de Goya on his deathbed, who recalls major events of his life, hallucinates, and experiences severe migraines. Addresses themes of psychosis and creativity, integrity vs. despair, and the interrelationship of life and death.

Grizzly Man (2005) Documentary ΨΨΨ
Werner Herzog film about Timothy Treadwell, a well-known naturalist who lived with grizzly bears for 13 summers. The viewer wonders if Treadwell had a psychotic or bipolar disorder as he became increasingly wild, and his behavior increasingly bizarre.

Happy Accidents (2001) Romance/Sci-Fi Ψ
A man states he is from the future – the year 2470.

He Loves Me, He Loves Me Not (2002) Drama ΨΨΨΨ
A must-see film for depiction of delusional disorders that is so unique that it could only be done cinematically. First, the viewer sees reality from the young woman's perception and flashes back to the beginning giving the viewer the vantage point of the man she loves. This French film stars *Amelie*'s Audrey Tautou.

House of Fools (2002) Drama ΨΨΨΨ
Based on a true story: the staff in a mental institution flee due to conflicts in Chechnya, leaving the patients to fend for themselves. Soon soldiers occupy the hospital and the viewer is left with various questions of war, politics, mental health treat-

ment and which one is really "crazy." Loaded with psychopathology examples, including a fire-starter, all the schizophrenia subtypes, and a woman who believes she is the fiancé of singer, Bryan Adams (who appears in the film).

Housekeeping (1987) Drama ΨΨΨ
An eccentric aunt comes to care for two sisters in the Pacific Northwest after the suicide of their mother. The girls can't decide if their aunt is simply odd or seriously mentally ill. The viewer confronts a similar dilemma.

I'm a Cyborg, But That's OK (2006, South Korea) Drama/Romance ΨΨΨ
Despite the odd title, this is a fascinating film about a psychotic woman who believes she is a cyborg and is admitted to psychiatric institution.

I Never Promised You a Rose Garden (1977) Drama ΨΨΨΨ
Accurate rendition of the popular book by the same name. The patient has command hallucinations that tell her to kill herself. There is a sympathetic portrayal of psychiatry and treatment; a breakthrough occurs when the protagonist first realizes she is able to feel pain.

Images (1972) Drama ΨΨΨ
Robert Altman's examination of the confused life of a woman with schizophrenia. A difficult film, but interesting, with a heuristic presentation of hallucinations.

Julien Donkey-Boy (1999) Drama ΨΨ
Director Harmony Korine breaks the narrative flow in this film about the horrors of schizophrenia, based on and dedicated to his uncle whom he wanted to take out of a psychiatric institution to be in the film. The film is sometimes shocking and insightful and at other times comedic.

Keane (2004) Mystery/Thriller ΨΨΨ
An engaging depiction of a man who begins to mentally deteriorate because he believes his daughter is missing. The film leaves the viewer wondering what is real and what is psychosis. Unfortunately, a powerful scene in which the protagonist randomly chases and attacks another man will stick out in the viewer's mind as a terrifying link between violence and mental illness.

Killing of John Lennon, The (2006, UK) Biography/Drama ΨΨΨ
Inside-look within the delusional Mark Chapman

leading up to the day he murdered John Lennon. Chapman was obsessed with Holden Caulfield from *The Catcher in the Rye* and believed he was the protagonist; he read from the book at the murder scene and trial. Promotes the misconception that people with mental illness are violent and that Salinger's classic work somehow had something to do with Lennon's murder.

K-Pax (2001) Drama ΨΨΨΨ
Multi-layered film in which Kevin Spacey plays Prot, a man claiming he's from a far away planet who is able to give convincing evidence for his case to astrophysicists. The viewer is left to hypothesize whether the character has schizophrenia, dissociative fugue, or is an enlightened spiritual being; whichever the case, the portrayal and diagnostic criteria are convincing for each.

La Dolce Vita (1960, Italy) Drama ΨΨΨ
Vintage Fellini film with an interesting vignette in which hundreds of Roman citizens develop a mass delusion following reports of a sighting of the Virgin Mary.

Lars and the Real Girl (2007) Drama/Romance/Comedy ΨΨΨΨ
A man's (Ryan Gosling) delusional disorder becomes apparent when he purchases an internet-doll that he believes to be his girlfriend. Sensitive, meaningful film with a quality portrayal of a physician acting as a psychotherapist implementing exposure therapy.

Love Object (2004) Thriller Ψ
A young man dealing with work stress copes by purchasing a $10,600 lifelike, silicone doll that he begins to believe is subtly torturing him as he deteriorates into psychosis.

Lunatics: A Love Story (1992) Comedy ΨΨΨ
A former mental patient spends six months hidden away in his apartment. The lead character has been described in reviews as agoraphobic, but a more serious diagnosis seems appropriate, especially in light of the patient's delusions and hallucinations.

Lust for Life (1956) Biography ΨΨΨΨ
Kirk Douglas as Vincent van Gogh and Anthony Quinn as Paul Gauguin. The film portrays the stormy relationship of the two men and van Gogh's hospitalization and eventual suicide. Contrast with *Vincent* (1987) and Robert Altman's *Vincent and Theo* (1990).

Madness of King George, The (1994)
Historical Biography ΨΨΨ
Nigel Hawthorne as King George III in an adaptation of a stage play examining the reactions of the court and family as the king becomes increasingly demented (due to porphyria, a genetic metabolic disorder).

"One may produce a copious, regular evacuation every day of the week and still be a stranger to reason."

An observation by a court doctor in *The Madness of King George* (1994)

Magic (1978) Thriller ΨΨ
Anthony Hopkins' talents are largely wasted in this Richard Attenborough film about a ventriloquist obsessed with his dummy. Not nearly as good a film as the 1945 movie *Dead of Night*.

Man From Earth, The (2007) Drama/Sci-Fi Ψ
A mysterious, successful professor attempts to convince his friends he can live forever and that he has met a variety of historical figures (e.g., Buddha).

May (2002) Thriller Ψ
Macabre psychological study of an isolated, socially awkward girl who sinks into psychosis as she tries to make a "best friend" by assembling the best parts of other people's bodies. Promotes the misconception that people with mental illness are violent.

Misery (1990) Horror ΨΨ
Kathy Bates plays an apparently delusional woman who becomes convinced she is justified in capturing a novelist and forcing him to rewrite his latest novel to meet her tastes.

Out of the Shadow (2004) Documentary ΨΨΨΨ
Realistic and moving depiction of schizophrenia and its impact on the family.

Outrageous! (1977) Comedy ΨΨ
Canadian film about a gay hairdresser and a woman with schizophrenia who is pregnant.

People Say I'm Crazy (2003) Documentary ΨΨΨ
Cinema verite styled documentary of the daily life of a man with paranoid schizophrenia. Interesting

for discussions on differentiation of schizophrenia, schizoaffective disorder, and mood disorders. Deeply honest, enlightening, and inspiring.

"I cannot trust my own perceptions."

John Cadigan, who directs and plays himself in *People Say I'm Crazy* (2003)

Perfect Strangers (2003) Drama/Suspense ΨΨ
A mysterious man (Sam Neill) invites a woman he has just met to his private island home and then kidnaps her. The two become romantically involved, and she nurses him back to health after he is injured. His obsessions transfer to the woman who frequently hallucinates after her lover dies.

Possessed (1947) Drama ΨΨΨ
Joan Crawford stars in a suspenseful film depicting catatonic schizophrenia with examples of waxy flexibility and numerous other symptoms of severe mental illness.

Promise (1986) Drama ΨΨ
A made-for-TV movie, starring James Garner, about a man who honors a commitment made to his mother to care for his brother with schizophrenia. Excellent illustrations of the symptoms of schizophrenia.

Proof (2005) Drama ΨΨΨ
Gwyneth Paltrow portrays the daughter of a famous mathematician (Anthony Hopkins). She begins to develop similar symptoms of schizophrenia similar to those shown by her father as she attempts to solve a rare proof that has baffled other mathematicians.

Rampo Noir (2005, Japan) Horror Ψ
Four short, surreal horror films that are adaptations and tributes to the Japanese poet, Rampo. Portrayals of hell, mental illness, and psychosis.

Red Dragon (2002) Thriller/Drama Ψ
Ralph Fiennes, as the serial killer in this prequel to *Silence of the Lambs*, deepens in his delusional framework as he becomes convinces he is a dragon. In one scene, he eats a painting of a dragon in order to internalize it.

Repulsion (1965) Horror ΨΨΨΨΨ
Powerful film about sexual repression and psychotic decompensation. Memorable examples of hallucinations (e.g., arms reaching out from walls); the film culminates in an unforgettable murder scene. This was Roman Polanski's first English language film.

Ruling Class, The (1972) Comedy ΨΨΨ
Brilliant British black comedy in which a member of the House of Lords inadvertently commits suicide and leaves his fortune and title to his son who is delusional and has schizophrenia (Peter O'Toole). The son at first believes he is Jesus and later Jack the Ripper.

Saint of Fort Washington, The (1993) Drama ΨΨΨ
A man with schizophrenia is evicted from his home winds up in a shelter, where he is befriended by a street-wise Vietnam veteran. Good portrayal of the life of people who are both mentally ill and homeless.

Santa Sangre (1989) Horror/Thriller ΨΨΨΨ
A disturbing film about a young man forced to witness the mutilation of his mother and the suicide of his father. We never know if these events are real or simply delusions of a patient. The film is complex and visually stunning.

Save the Green Planet (2003, Korea) Drama/Thriller ΨΨ
A young man pursues individuals he perceives are aliens from Andromeda to keep them from destroying the planet.

Scissors (1991) Suspense Ψ
The paranoid delusions of a traumatized young woman take on a frightening reality when she finds her assailant dead.

Scotland, PA (2001) Comedy ΨΨ
Dark comedy that's a subtle parody of Macbeth, about greed, power, love, and "going crazy." A young couple who take over the work at a restaurant after killing the owner, begin to deteriorate with rumination, guilt, and poor coping as police detective (Christopher Walken) investigates the murder case.

Shine (1996) Biography/Drama ΨΨΨΨΨ
True story of David Helfgott, an Australian prodigy whose brilliant career is interrupted by the development of an unspecified mental illness that is probably schizophrenia. The film not so subtly suggests that David's domineering father was directly responsible for his mental illness and

conveys the misleading but endearing message that love and hope can conquer mental illness.

> "David, if you go you will never come back to this house again. You will never be anybody's son. The girls will lose their brother. Is that what you want?... You want to destroy the family... if you love me you will stop this nonsense."
>
> David Helfgott's father admonishes him about leaving home in *Shine* (1996)

Shock Corridor (1963) Drama ΨΨ
Journalist feigns insanity in order to get a story from a man admitted to a psychiatric hospital; later the journalist begins to lose touch with reality.

Snake Pit, The (1948) Drama ΨΨΨ
One of the first films to document the treatment of patients in a mental hospital.

Soloist, The (2009) Drama/Biography ΨΨΨΨΨ
Outstanding portrayal of schizophrenia in which Jamie Foxx portrays a brilliant, isolated musician, Nathaniel Ayers and the development of his friendship with an L.A. Times reporter (Robert Downey, Jr.).

Something Like Happiness (2005, Czech Republic) Comedy/Drama ΨΨ
Three adult friends from childhood support one another as they try to find happiness along different paths; one is admitted to a psychiatric hospital.

Sophie's Choice (1982) Drama ΨΨΨ
Meryl Streep won an Academy Award for her portrayal of a concentration camp survivor infatuated with Nathan, who is described as having paranoid schizophrenia but who may suffer from a bipolar disorder. Based on William Styron's novel.

Special (2006) Drama/Mystery ΨΨΨ
A man obsessed with comic books decides to take an experimental drug. The medication suppresses self-doubt and the man quickly believes he has superpowers – including telepathy, the ability to go through walls, and superhuman crime fighting.

Spider (2002) Drama ΨΨΨΨ
Ralph Fiennes, a patient with schizophrenia, disor-

ganized type, is released from the hospital to a group home. It's a dark, bleak, psychologically complex film and a brilliant portrayal of the isolation and inner world of schizophrenia. Directed by David Cronenberg. The DVD cover reads: "The only thing worse than losing your mind, is finding it again."

Spiderman (2002) Fantasy/Drama ΨΨ
Sam Raimi classic based on the Marvel comic book series. The Green Goblin (Willem Dafoe) hears voices and seems to be mentally ill. The film perpetuates the myth that people who are mentally ill are also violent.

Stateside (2004) Drama ΨΨ
A young, spoiled, rich man turns his life around after he joins the Marines and falls in love with a woman with schizophrenia. Winner of a Voice Award.

Stay (2005) Mystery/Suspense Ψ
Ewan McGregor portrays a psychiatrist who tries to prevent one of his patients (Ryan Gosling) from committing suicide.

Story of Adèle H., The (1975, France) Biography ΨΨ
François Truffaut story about the sexual obsession of the daughter of Victor Hugo for a young soldier she can never marry.

Stroszek (1977, West Germany) Comedy ΨΨ
Offbeat Werner Herzog comedy about three Germans who come to America in search of the American dream. They fail to find it in Railroad Flats, Wisconsin. One of the three has schizophrenia.

Summer of Sam (1999) Drama/Documentary ΨΨΨ
This Spike Lee film succeeds artistically and presents interesting insights into ethnic dynamics and the process of scapegoating; however, it provides little insight into the motives or the mental illness that drove serial killer David Berkowitz, the highly publicized "Son of Sam," to commit multiple murders. The emphasis is on the fear and psychological trauma of people living in New York City who know a serial killer is still loose.

Sweetie (1989) Comedy ΨΨΨΨ
Director Jane Campion paints a memorable and realistic picture of a woman with schizophrenia and the difficulties her illness presents for her and her family.

Sylvia and the Phantom (1945) Drama ΨΨ
French film about a young woman who must distinguish between reality and fantasy, hallucination and phantom, love and illusion. Her many seducers include a narcissist, a lover, a criminal, and a phantom.

Synecdoche, New York (2008) Comedy/Drama ΨΨΨ
Interesting mix of delusion, physical illness, and existential angst in Charlie Kaufman's surrealistic film starring Philip Seymour Hoffman.

Tarnation (2003) Documentary ΨΨΨΨ
Poignant, disturbing, dramatic, and realistic film chronicles the life of a family plagued by mental illness. *Tarnation* illustrates schizophrenia and depersonalization disorder as well as the effects of brain damage and traumatic abuse. The film integrates home movies, photographs, short videos, diaries, and pop culture artifacts into a striking visceral experience. If you can find this independent film, you should watch it.

Taxi Driver (1976) Drama ΨΨΨΨΨ
Robert De Niro becomes obsessed with Jodi Foster and determines to rescue her from prostitution.

Tenant, The (1976) Horror ΨΨΨ
Roman Polanski film about an ordinary clerk who moves into an apartment in which the previous owner committed suicide. The new owner assumes the personality of the old owner, becomes paranoid, and commits suicide in the same way as the previous owner.

"Someday a real rain will come and wash all the scum off the streets."

Taxi Driver (1976)

Through a Glass Darkly (1962) Drama ΨΨΨΨΨ
Powerful and memorable Bergman film about a recently released mental patient who spends the summer on an island with her husband, father, and younger brother.

Truman Show, The (1998) Drama ΨΨΨΨΨ
This Peter Weir film stars Jim Carrey as Truman Burbank, who unbeknownst to him, has had his entire life broadcasted on a popular television show where all the people in his life are actors and his home and town are part of an elaborate production studio. This film provides a fascinating setup for a discussion of delusional disorders.

Virgin (2003) Drama Ψ
A 17-year-old is raped by a man she is infatuated with and subsequently is ostracized, engages in kleptomania, and experiences delusions.

Who's Afraid of Virginia Woolf? (1966) Drama ΨΨΨΨ
A Mike Nichols film, with Elizabeth Taylor and Richard Burton, who appear to have a shared psychotic disorder involving a son who never really existed; the film also portrays alcoholism and interpersonal cruelty. Elizabeth Taylor and Sandy Dennis both won Academy Awards for their performances in this film.

World Traveler (2001) Drama ΨΨ
Julianne Moore has a supporting role as an alcoholic with a delusional disorder.

"Now that we're through with Humiliate the Host... and we don't want to play Hump the Hostess yet... how about a little round of Get the Guests?"

Who's Afraid of Virginia Woolf? (1966)

Zebraman (2004, Japan) Drama/Crime ΨΨ
A passive teaching supervisor becomes the superhero, Zebraman, to escape his miserable, mundane life. The more he accepts his character, the stronger his powers become.

Neuropsychological Disorders

50 First Dates (2004) Comedy Ψ
Adam Sandler plays a veterinarian and womanizer who falls in love with a woman (Drew Barrymore) with a fictional cognitive disorder in that she has no long-term memory as she awakens each morning forgetting everything from the day before (so she repeats the same activities each day, enabled by her family). A flawed *Memento*.

Accidental Hero, The (2002, France) Drama ΨΨ
A boy comes to more fully appreciate his mother after she is involved in a serious car accident and experiences a profound retrograde amnesia.

Alzheimer's Project, The (The Memory Loss Tapes) (2009) Documentary ΨΨΨΨ
Poignant and important HBO series integrated into a deeply meaningful film revealing seven vignettes of individuals at various stages of Alzheimer's Disease and their families. The film addresses both the suffering caused by the disease and the challenges of the caregiver, such as themes of the adult-child role reversal, wandering, loss of independence, and the emotional grieving process. To watch the film online, see http://www.hbo.com/alzheimers/memory-loss-tapes.html

Assisted Living (2003) Comedy/Drama ΨΨ
This movie was filmed in an actual nursing home. A pot-smoking janitor interacts with the residents and slowly learns to care.

Awakenings (1990) Drama ΨΨΨ
Robin Williams as neurologist Oliver Sacks treats patient Robert De Niro in a Bronx hospital. The film documents the use of L-Dopa in the treatment of patients with advanced Parkinson's disease. Good portrayal of the daily life of a mental hospital.

Away from Her (2006, Canada) Drama ΨΨΨΨ
Sarah Polley's directorial debut about a woman (Julie Christie) who realizes she has Alzheimer's disease and convinces her husband (Gordon Pinsent) to take her to a care facility. He visits her regularly despite discovering that she has fallen in love with another man.

Ballad of Narayama, The (1983) Drama ΨΨΨ
This Japanese film tells the story of a small village where by tradition all old people are taken up to the top of a mountain and left to die.

"This is not a hospital. They are not doctors or nurses.
Didn't they tell you? They all believe that the city has got no limits."

A dying character's confusion and paranoia in *The City of No Limits* (2002)

City of No Limits, The (2002) Drama ΨΨ
A family patriarch becomes paranoid and delusional because of a brain tumor; as a result, he shares long hidden family secrets.

Dark Victory (1939) Drama ΨΨΨ
Bette Davis, George Brent, and Humphrey Bogart star, but watch for Ronald Reagan. Davis has a fatal brain tumor. She spends what little time she has left with her brain surgeon husband. The "dark victory" refers to living life well, even when facing death. Remade (not very effectively) with Susan Hayward in *Stolen Hours* (1963).

Death Be Not Proud (1975) Biography ΨΨ
A made-for-TV film based on John Gunther's moving account of his son's struggle with a brain tumor, which killed the boy at the age of 17. The book provides considerable insight into the neurology of brain lesions.

Do You Remember Love? (1985) Drama ΨΨ
Joanne Woodward won an Emmy for her portrayal of a middle-aged college professor who develops Alzheimer's Disease.

Harder They Fall, The (1956) Sports ΨΨΨΨ
Humphrey Bogart in his last film, made the year before his death. The movie is very critical of the sport of boxing and the exploitation of fighters by promoters. A slow-witted boxer has a brain clot and is almost killed in his last fight.

Iris (2001) Drama/Biography ΨΨΨΨ
Based on the life of the famous British novelist and philosophical writer, Iris Murdoch (played by Judi Dench), who deteriorates because of her Alzheimer's Disease. Oscar-winner, Jim Broadbent plays John Bayley, Iris' extraordinarily loving husband. A powerfully realistic and emotional film.

Jacket, The (2005) Drama/Thriller ΨΨ
Adrien Brody portrays a man with retrograde amnesia who is mistreated in a psychiatric hospital in this avant-garde film.

Lookout, The (2007) Drama ΨΨΨ
A high school student suffers a brain injury, and his life is changed forever. The film is a good introduction to many of the symptoms experienced by someone with a traumatic brain injury.

Lorenzo's Oil (1992) Drama ΨΨΨ
True story of the Odone family and their desperate

struggle to save their son's life. The boy has a rare neurological disease that they are told is ultimately fatal. Good illustration of the effects of chronic illness on family functioning.

Majestic, The (2001) Drama ΨΨ
Jim Carrey plays a disenfranchised screenwriter who develops amnesia after his car topples over a bridge. He washes on the shore of a small town whose citizens take him in as a lost war hero.

Man Without a Past, The (2002) Drama ΨΨΨ
A man is severely beaten while sleeping outside and is proclaimed dead. He awakens with amnesia and begins to create a new life for himself before eventually discovering parts of his old life.

Memento (2001) Suspense/Mystery ΨΨΨΨΨ
Christopher Nolan directs this one-of-a-kind, exquisitely crafted masterpiece about a man suffering from anterograde amnesia. The film demands the viewer have very good short-term memory as the major plot progresses backwards scene by scene while juxtaposing past events (going forward) in black-and-white. This is a film not to be missed.

"How am I supposed to heal if I can't feel time?"

Memento (2001)

Memories of Me (1988) Comedy ΨΨ
Henry Winkler directs Billy Crystal, a high-powered surgeon who has just had a heart attack, and Alan King, his actor father who may have Alzheimer's. It turns out that an aneurysm is present, and father and son eventually learn to care for one another.

Memory of a Killer, The (2003) Drama ΨΨ
A hit man in the early stages of dementia attempts to do one last job before retiring.

Mercy or Murder? (1987) Drama ΨΨ
Made-for-TV movie about a Florida man who went to prison after killing his wife because she had advanced Alzheimer's Disease. The film raises interesting questions that society will increasingly be forced to confront.

Million Dollar Baby (2004) Drama ΨΨΨ
A female prize fighter (Hilary Swank) is paralyzed from the neck down after being sucker punched by an angry opponent between rounds; she pleads with her trainer (Clint Eastwood) to end her life before she loses the memory of the crowd's applause.

Mulholland Drive (2001)
Mystery/Drama/Suspense ΨΨΨ
David Lynch film about a woman who experiences a head injury from a car accident, becomes amnestic, and finds refuge in an aspiring Hollywood actress' condominium. This is characteristic Lynch in its non-linearity and themes of reality vs. illusion, identity confusion, and nightmarish dream sequences.

My Girl (1991) Comedy ΨΨ
Eleven-year-old girl is a hypochondriac with a mortician for a father and a grandmother who has Alzheimer's disease.

Notebook, The (2004) Drama ΨΨΨ
Gena Rowlands and James Garner play a couple coping with her ever worsening Alzheimer's disease. Based on the best-selling novel by Nicholas Sparks.

On Golden Pond (1981) Drama ΨΨΨ
Sensitive portrayal of an aging couple (Henry Fonda and Katharine Hepburn) cherishing and struggling with his increasingly apparent dementia.

On the Waterfront (1954) Drama ΨΨΨΨ
Classic Elia Kazan film starring Marlon Brando as Terry Malloy, a prizefighter of limited intelligence who is exploited by almost everyone around him. Brando won an Oscar as Best Actor for his performance as Terry Malloy, who took a dive and spent the rest of his life regretting it.

"You was my brother, Charley, you should've looked out for me just a little bit so I wouldn't have to take them dives for the short-end money."

On the Waterfront (1954)

Pride of the Yankees, The (1942) Biography ΨΨΨ
Gary Cooper stars in this Samuel Goldwyn film

about legendary Yankees' first baseman Lou Gehrig, who had to give up baseball due to amyotrophic lateral sclerosis, which came to be known more widely by the eponym "Lou Gehrig's disease."

> "Some people say I've had a bad break, but I consider myself to be the luckiest man on the face of the earth."
>
> Lou Gehrig giving up baseball in
> *The Pride of the Yankees* (1942)

Private Matter, A (1992) Biography ΨΨ
Provocative made-for-TV movie starring Sissy Spacek as a TV personality who gets national attention after her decision to abort a child likely to be affected by the drug thalidomide.

Raging Bull (1980) Biography/Sports ΨΨΨΨΨ
Powerful film depicting the psychological, moral, and mental decline of a prizefighter. Robert De Niro won an Oscar for his portrayal of Jake LaMotta.

Regarding Henry (1993) Drama ΨΨ
Attorney has his life permanently altered following a head injury; his values change as well as his personality.

Safe House (1998) Thriller ΨΨ
An ex-intelligence operative begins to develop Alzheimer's Disease.

Savages, The (2007) Drama ΨΨΨ
A brother and sister find themselves becoming closer as they attempt to cope with the challenges associated with caring for their father who is suffering from Alzheimer's disease.

Sea Inside, The (2004) Biography/Drama ΨΨΨΨΨ
A sensitive and moving story about a Spanish citizen's quest to end his life.

Shattered (1991) Mystery/Suspense ΨΨ
A man in a near-fatal car accident experiences amnesia and undergoes reconstructive facial surgery. He begins to find inconsistencies in stories from loved ones about his past and his own memories, only to face a shocking truth.

Song for Martin, A (2002) Drama ΨΨΨ
An interesting portrayal of the ways in which a married couple deeply in love is affected by his Alzheimer's disease.

Son of the Bride (2002) Drama/Comedy/Romance ΨΨΨΨ
Moving drama from Argentina with many inspirational and comic moments about a man too busy for his family until he reevaluates his life following a heart attack. A major sub-story is the man's aging father, who steadfastly expresses unconditional love to his wife who is deteriorating with Alzheimer's Disease.

Tuesdays with Morrie (1999) Drama/Inspiration ΨΨ
Made-for-TV movie based on the best-selling Mitch Albom book about a journalist who befriends and finds inspiration from a man dying of ALS.

Waltz with Bashir (2008, Israel) Animation/Biography ΨΨΨΨ
An exploration on the construction and shifting nature of memory. Ari Folman served in the Israeli army during the Lebanon War of 1982 but has no recollection of the events and he attempts to reconstruct them in this film.

Disorders of Childhood and Adolescence

Ali Zaoua: Prince of the Streets (2000) Drama ΨΨΨ
Four young homeless boys, living in poverty on the streets of Morocco, rebel against their gang leader's oppressive rule.

Beautiful Ohio (2006) Drama Ψ
Independent film about two brothers growing up in the Midwest, one is gifted but also has severe oppositional tendencies.

Butcher Boy, The (1997) Comedy ΨΨΨΨ
Dark comedy about a boy with schizophrenia, Francie Brady, living in Ireland in the 1960s. Francie's behavior ranges from absurd and humorous to delusional and dangerous.

Carrie (1976) Horror ΨΨ
This Brian De Palma film is based on a Stephen King novel and depicts the cruelty of adolescents and some of the stresses associated with caring for

a mentally ill mother. Sissy Spacek's performance is remarkable.

"He took me, with the stink of filthy roadhouse whiskey on his breath, and I liked it. I liked it! With all that dirty touching of his hands all over me. I should've given you to God when you were born, but I was weak and backsliding, and now the devil has come home."

A psychotic Francie Brady in
The Butcher Boy (1997)

Chorus, The (2004, France) Drama ΨΨΨΨ
A newly hired boarding school teacher tries to transform troubled kids into positive problem solvers through music and positive rewards. The headmaster, who believes in restriction and punishment, reluctantly agrees to let the new teacher try more positive approaches.

City of God (2003, Brazil) Drama/Foreign ΨΨΨΨ
Painful, sobering and graphic examination of the violence associated with gang-life, drug trafficking, and poverty in Rio de Janeiro. This film depicts young children and adolescents who grow up in an environment in which guns and murder are commonplace.

City of Lost Children, The (1995, France) Fantasy/Comedy ΨΨΨΨ
A mad scientist is aging prematurely so he tries to capture children to steal their dreams. Implicit in the film is the use and abuse of children; film critics have commented that this kind of film could not have been made in the United States. The movie is a black comedy that has been praised for its cinematic craft, creative set design, and the use of quirky, unique characters.

Dangerous Lives of Altar Boys, The (2002) Drama/Comedy ΨΨ
High school outcasts express rebellion in a variety of ways, including abuse of an authoritarian nun (played by Jodie Foster).

Don't Come Knocking (2005) Drama ΨΨΨ
A former Western movie star drowns his sorrow in alcohol and self-pity until he discovers he has a son

and sets out to find him. The son is oppositional-defiant.

Elephant (2003) Drama ΨΨΨΨ
Well-crafted, foreboding, eerie Gus van Sant film addressing the tragedy of recent school shootings. Powerful parallels with the Columbine tragedy. Winner of the Palm award at Cannes for Best Picture and Best Director.

Equus (1977) Drama ΨΨΨ
Richard Burton examines the meaning and purpose of his own life as he attempts to unravel the psychosexual roots that led an adolescent to blind six horses. Wonderful soliloquies by Burton.

"And most importantly, have fun, man!"

Final words of an adolescent to his co-assassin preparing to enter a school building in *Elephant* (2003)

Every Man for Himself and God Against All (1975) Biography ΨΨΨΨΨ
Werner Herzog film based on a true story about a man who spent an isolated childhood virtually devoid of stimulation. This movie should be contrasted with Truffaut's film *The Wild Child* and the more recent film *Nell*.

Face to Face (1976, Sweden) Drama ΨΨ
Bergman film in which Liv Ullmann plays a suicidal psychiatrist estranged from her husband and 14-year-old daughter. During a coma that results from an overdose of sleeping pills, Ullmann dreams about a childhood experience in which she was punished by being locked in a closet.

Fanny and Alexander (1983, Sweden) Drama ΨΨΨΨΨ
Bergman film about two young children and the ways in which their lives change when their father dies and their mother remarries. The film is sensitive, tender, and haunting and shows how the world looks through the eyes of a 10-year-old.

Firestarter (1984) Drama/Suspense Ψ
Early Stephen King film in which Drew Barrymore portrays a young girl with pyrokinetic, telekinetic, and telepathic powers. Barrymore is able to set fires simply by staring at whatever she wants to set on fire.

Forbidden Games (1951) War/Drama ΨΨΨΨ
This beautiful French film is about two children who create and share a private fantasy world. The movie juxtaposes the innocence of childhood with the horror of war.

Four Hundred Blows, The (1959, France) Drama ΨΨΨΨΨ
Semiautobiographical film by François Truffaut about a 13-year-old boy who is caught up in a life of truancy and petty crime. His mother sleeps around; his father is preoccupied and distant. *Four Hundred Blows* is reported to be Truffaut's favorite film.

Psychiatrist: "Your parents say you're always lying."
Antoine Doinel: "Oh, I lie now and then, I suppose. Sometimes I'd tell them the truth, and they still wouldn't believe me, so I prefer to lie."

Strange behavior explained in *The Four Hundred Blows* (1959)

Great New Wonderful, The (2005) Drama ΨΨ
Several stories of New Yorkers converge, including one depicting a child with a serious behavior disorder.

Gummo (1997) Independent ΨΨΨ
This extremely disturbing and unforgettable film directed by Harmony Korine depicts life in a small, rural town after its destruction by a tornado. Despite the lack of a coherent plot, the film gets high marks for its honesty and realism. Various types of psychopathology are presented with an emphasis on conduct disorders.

Harvie Krumpet (2003) Animation/Comedy ΨΨΨ
Short film about a character who faces innumerous tragedies and challenges, including Tourette's disorder.

Hate (1995, France) ΨΨ
Conduct disorders abound among adolescent gangs in a French suburban ghetto in this film about racism and oppression.

Holes (2002) Family ΨΨΨ
One of the better non-animated Disney films about

troubled youth who are sent to a work camp to dig deep holes in the middle of the desert to help three criminals find a lost treasure. Sigourney Weaver has a memorable role in this film.

Innocents, The (1961) Horror ΨΨΨ
Deborah Kerr plays a governess hired to care for two precocious children. Is she hallucinating or delusional, or are there really ghosts in the house? Interesting sexual tension develops between Kerr and the boy. Based on the Henry James novella *Turn of the Screw*.

Island on Bird Street (2000) Drama ΨΨΨ
Polish film about an adventurous, high-spirited boy who escapes from Nazi control; inspired by Robinson Crusoe, he creates a hide-out and waits for his father's return.

"If you deflower a girl... you're the man. No one can ever do that again. You're the only one. No one, no one, has the power to do that again."

Telly describes his fascination with virgins in *Kids* (1995)

Kids (1995) Drama ΨΨΨ
Gritty and disturbing film about urban adolescents, sex, drugs, and violence. The main character is a teenager with AIDS who preys on young adolescent girls, taking particular pride in seducing virgins.

Leolo (1992, France/Canada) Comedy ΨΨΨΨ
Leo, an adolescent boy growing up in a very dysfunctional family in Montreal, is unable to accept the reality of his genetic heritage and concocts a fantasy in which he was accidentally conceived by sperm that crossed the Atlantic in a Sicilian tomato. (The film is better than this brief synopsis suggests.)

Life as a House (2001) Drama ΨΨΨ
Touching film about the transformation of the relationship between a rebellious, addicted adolescent (Hayden Christensen) and his terminally ill father (Kevin Kline).

Lilja 4-ever (2002, Sweden/Denmark) Drama ΨΨΨ
Heartbreaking film about a girl, rejected by her

family and society, who seems to meet with tragedy just when it appears she is headed in the right direction. Lilja is physically, emotionally, and sexually abused in the film.

Little Man Tate (1991) Drama ΨΨΨ
Jodi Foster directed this film about a child prodigy and the tensions that arise between his mother and the psychologist to whom the child's education is entrusted. Foster acknowledged that the film is partly autobiographical.

Lord of the Flies (1963) Drama ΨΨ
Film adaptation of William Goldman's novel about a group of schoolchildren who quickly shed the thin veneer of civilization and become savages. Both the film and book raise interesting questions about nature and nurture. Remade in 1990.

Los Olvidados/The Young and the Damned (1950, Mexico) Drama ΨΨΨ
Luis Buñuel film about juvenile delinquency in the squalid slums of Mexico City.

Magdalene Sisters, The (2002) Docudrama ΨΨΨ
Troubled adolescent girls are sent to a dehumanizing boarding home where they are abused, mistreated and exploited by the nuns who run the home. One particularly abused adolescent sexually acts out with a priest and later becomes psychotic.

Manic (2001) Drama ΨΨΨ
A psychologist played by Don Cheadle tries to help an angry adolescent. Interesting group therapy sessions and inpatient hospital scenes with adolescents who have bipolar disorder, intermittent explosive disorder, major depression, self-injurious behavior, and night terrors.

> "What are wire hangers doing in this closet? Answer me! I buy you beautiful dresses, and you treat them like they were some dishrag. You do! Three hundred dollar dress on a wire hanger!"
>
> Joan Crawford in a manic state berates her daughter in *Mommie Dearest* (1981)

Mommie Dearest (1981) Biography ΨΨ
A film about the pathological relationship between Joan Crawford and her adopted daughter. The movie suggests that Crawford suffered from bipolar disorder.

Monsieur Ibrahim (2003) Drama ΨΨΨ
Heart-warming French film about an adolescent boy raised by a critical, neglecting father; he develops a meaningful friendship with a local store-owner.

My First Mister (2001) Drama ΨΨ
Adolescent girl struggles with severe isolation, depression, self-injurious behavior, and other acting out behaviors until she befriends a 49-year-old man. The teen has a host of behavioral problems including "huffing," autoerotic asphyxiation, isolation from her family, and prostitution.

My Flesh and Blood (2004) Documentary ΨΨΨ
Moving story of Susan Tom, who adopted 11 special needs children and raised them on her own. One has cystic fibrosis and severe anger and oppositional behaviors directed at most people around him.

Nell (1994) Drama ΨΨΨ
Jodi Foster plays a feral child raised in isolation in the North Carolina woods. She is terrified of the doctor who discovers her and eventually learns her own odd language. The doctor consults an expert on child psychology. Interesting examination of Rousseau's concept of the "natural savage."

Noi the Albino (2003) Drama ΨΨΨ
A film about a troubled but gifted teen who struggles with conduct problems in Iceland. The movie provides a realistic evaluation of a gifted adolescent who is out of place in both school and life.

Pelle the Conqueror (1986) Drama ΨΨΨΨ
Moving film about lust, passion, dreams, aging, hope, pragmatic romance, and, most of all, the love between a father and his son. The film won the Grand Prix at the Cannes Film Festival and an Academy Award as Best Foreign Film.

Pieces of April (2003) Comedy ΨΨΨ
Previously troubled adolescent estranged from her family tries to create a pleasant, memorable experience for her dysfunctional family's Thanksgiving dinner. Well-acted by Katie Holmes and Patricia Clarkson.

Pixote (1981) Drama ΨΨΨΨ
A powerful film about the squalid, depressing lives of street children in Sao Paulo. In the film, the

child, Pixote, commits his first murder at the age of 10. Ironically, the child star actually was shot and killed by the police five years after the film was released.

Ratcatcher, The (1999) Drama ΨΨΨ
Young adolescent living in Glasgow has to cope with trash-covered streets, lice, and dead rats. He acts out as he tries to cope with poverty.

Rebel Without a Cause (1955) Drama ΨΨΨ
Dated but still interesting examination of teenage alienation, violence, and family pathology. James Dean is the rebellious protagonist. All three stars (Dean, Natalie Wood, and Sal Mineo) met violent deaths (a car wreck, a drowning, and a murder).

"Boy, if, if I had one day when I didn't have to be all confused, and didn't have to feel that I was ashamed of everything"

Rebel Without a Cause (1955)

Salaam Bombay! (1988) Drama ΨΨΨ
Remarkable story about the way indigent children manage to survive to adulthood on the mean streets of Bombay.

Sixth Sense, The (1999) Drama ΨΨΨ
Bruce Willis plays a Philadelphia child psychologist treating a child who sees himself surrounded by dead people. If this child were seen at a clinic, he would probably be diagnosed with childhood schizophrenia. The film has a surprise ending and offers some insight into a troubled marriage, but it offers little to help us understand child psychopathology.

Splendor in the Grass (1961) Drama ΨΨ
A teenage girl unable to come to grips with adolescent sexuality winds up in a psychiatric hospital.

Squid and the Whale, The (2005) Drama ΨΨΨΨ
This excellent film depicts a family of four going through a divorce. The two children act out in significant ways.

Thirteen (2003) Drama ΨΨΨΨ
Important film about the rise and fall of teen friendships, sexual promiscuity, self-hate, rebellion, and the intense need adolescents fill to fit in

and be accepted. Holly Hunter plays the recovered alcoholic mother struggling with the delicate balance between giving her daughter appropriate levels of freedom and setting limits.

Cole Sear: "We were supposed to draw a picture, anything we wanted. I drew a man who got hurt in the neck by another man with a screwdriver."
Malcolm Crowe: "You saw that on TV, Cole?"
Cole Sear: "Everyone got upset. They had a meeting. Mom started crying. I don't draw like that any more."
Malcolm Crowe: "How do you draw now?"
Cole Sear: "Draw... people smiling, dogs running, rainbows. They don't have meetings about rainbows."

A child figures out how to play the system in *The Sixth Sense* (1999)

Thumbsucker (2005) Comedy/Drama ΨΨΨΨ
An adolescent boy self-soothes by secretly sucking his thumb. He is unable to stop and is diagnosed with Attention Deficit Disorder. His life is transformed after he begins treatment with stimulant medication.

Tin Drum, The (1979) Drama/War ΨΨΨΨ
Political allegory about a child who decides to stop growing. Based on a Gunter Grass novel, the film won an Academy Award as Best Foreign Film. The film recently received considerable attention because a scene in which the child has oral sex with an adult was judged to be obscene under Oklahoma law.

To Be and To Have (2002, France) Documentary/Drama ΨΨΨΨ
A creative teacher finds ways to managing children with a variety of behavioral problems.

To Kill a Mockingbird (1962) Drama ΨΨ
Robert Duvall makes his film debut as Boo Radley, a man with mental retardation who kills another man in order to protect two children.

Tree Grows in Brooklyn, A (1945) Drama ΨΨΨ
Elia Kazan film about a poor Irish family living in

Brooklyn at the turn of the century. The family's problems are complicated by the father's alcoholism.

> "She did something that in our society is unspeakable. She kissed a black man. Not an old uncle, but a strong, young Negro man. No code mattered to her before she broke it, but it came crashing down on her afterwards."
>
> *To Kill a Mockingbird* (1962)

United States of Leland, The (2004) Drama ΨΨΨ
Interesting story about Leland P. Fitzgerald (Ryan Gosling), an adolescent who kills an autistic boy but can't explain why. His emotions are blunted, his social behavior is quirky, yet his thoughts are often insightful and perceptive. Kevin Spacey co-stars.

Weather Man, The (2005) Drama ΨΨ
A meteorologist struggles in his personal life which includes supporting his depressed daughter.

Welcome to the Dollhouse (1996) Comedy ΨΨΨ
Interesting examination of families, emerging sexuality, and the cruelty of adolescents.

Wild Child, The (1969, France) Drama ΨΨΨΨ
François Truffaut's engaging film about the life of a feral child, the "Wild Boy of Aveyron." Based on a true story and the journal of Jean Itard, the doctor who set out to educate the child. Truffaut himself plays the role of Itard.

Willy Wonka and the Chocolate Factory (1971) Family ΨΨ
Five lucky children win a free tour of a wonderful chocolate factory. Four of the five children (excluding the hero, Charlie) are either oppositional, obsessed, or enormously selfish.

Wish You Were Here (1987) Drama ΨΨ
A teenage girl coming of age in Great Britain in the early 1950s must come to grips with her emerging sexuality.

Mental Retardation and Autism

Antonia's Line (1995) Comedy ΨΨΨ
A film with unforgettable characters, including Loony Lips and Dede, two mentally challenged people who fall in love and get married. The film is a joyful celebration of life and family.

Being There (1979) Comedy ΨΨ
Peter Sellers plays the role of a gardener with what appears to be borderline IQ who finds himself caught up in a comedy of errors in which his simple platitudes are mistaken for wisdom. This film is a precursor to *Forrest Gump*.

Best Boy (1979) Documentary ΨΨΨ
Ira Wohl's moving tribute to his cousin (who has mental retardation) examines the options facing the young man when his father dies and his aging mother is no longer able to care for him. This film won an Academy Award as Best Documentary film.

Best Man: "Best Boy" and All of Us Twenty Years Later (1997) Documentary ΨΨΨ
A sequel to the 1979 film documenting that director Ira Wohl's cousin has a rich, full and meaningful life, despite his cognitive limitations.

Bill (1981) Biography ΨΨ
Mickey Rooney won an Emmy for playing a man with mental retardation who was forced to leave an institution after 46 years in this made-for-TV movie.

Boy Who Could Fly, The (1986) Fantasy ΨΨ
Love story about the affection that develops between a teenage girl whose father has just committed suicide and a new neighbor who is autistic.

Breaking and Entering (2006) Drama ΨΨΨ
A Bosnian boy robs an architect who secretly follows the young thief home and eventually becomes involved with the boy's mother. The architect and his live-in girlfriend are raising her adolescent daughter who has a pervasive developmental disorder, but the stress of caring for the child interferes with the adults' relationship. The film also depicts Seasonal Affective Disorder.

Charly (1968) Drama ΨΨ
Cliff Robertson won an Oscar for his role as man with mental retardation who is transformed into a genius, only to find himself reverting to a state of mental retardation. (Compare this film with *Molly* [1999].)

"Why is that people who would never dream of making fun of a blind man or a cripple will make fun of a retard?"

Charly wonders about the cruelty of people in *Charly* (1968)

Child Is Waiting, A (1963) Drama ΨΨ
Burt Lancaster and Judy Garland star in this film about the treatment of children with mental retardation living in institutions.

City of Lost Children, The (1995, France) Fantasy/Drama ΨΨΨΨ
A mad scientist is aging prematurely so he tries to capture children to steal their dreams. The circus strongman named One, who has a developmental disability, teams up with a bold, bright young girl to save the children.

Dangerous Woman, A (1993) Drama ΨΨ
Debra Winger plays a woman with mild mental retardation who becomes involved with an itinerant alcoholic.

Day in the Death of Joe Egg, A (1972) Comedy ΨΨ
British black comedy that examines the issue of mercy killing.

Dead Mother, The (1993, Spain) Drama/Thriller ΨΨΨ
Child with characteristics of autism and a developmental disability witnesses her mother's murder by a petty thief who kidnaps the child, now a man, two decades later.

Dodes'ka-den (Clickety-Clack) (1970, Japan) Drama ΨΨΨ
Akira Kurosawa film about a boy with mental retardation living in the slums of Tokyo. This was Kurosawa's first color film. Although now regarded as a classic, this film was not well received by the public or by critics when it was released, and it's failure led to Kurosawa's attempt to commit suicide by slashing his wrists in 1971. Kurosawa died in 1998 in Tokyo.

Dominick and Eugene (1988) Drama ΨΨΨΨ
This is a coming-of-age film about two brothers. Eugene, who is finishing medical school, is the primary caregiver for his brother Dominick who has mental retardation and works as a Pittsburgh

trash collector. Dominick's income supports the brothers but Eugene wants to move to California for his residency.

Forrest Gump (1994) Fantasy ΨΨΨΨ
Traces the life of Forrest Gump, who triumphs in life despite an IQ of 75 and a deformed spine. The film will make you examine your stereotypes about mental retardation.

Forrest Gump: "Lieutenant Dan, what are you doing here?"
Lieutenant Daniel Taylor: "I'm here to try out my sea legs."
Forrest Gump: "But you ain't got no legs, Lieutenant Dan."

Forrest Gump (1994)

House of Cards (1993) Drama Ψ
Tommy Lee Jones is wasted in an insipid movie about a young girl who becomes autistic and withdrawn.

I Am Sam (2001) Drama ΨΨΨ
Sean Penn portrays a man with mild mental retardation who fights for custody rights for his daughter.

Junebug (2005) Comedy/Drama Ψ
An autistic painter has a minor but highly stereotypic role in an otherwise good film.

Larry (1974) Biography ΨΨ
Dated but still interesting film about a man discharged from a psychiatric hospital and forced to cope with the outside world. The film suggests the patient himself isn't really ill but still acts strange because he has grown up in a world where everyone acts a little odd.

Mozart and the Whale (2005) Comedy/Drama ΨΨ
Based on a true story, two people with Asperger's meet and develop a life long relationship.

Molly (1999) Drama Ψ
This film tries hard to be *Rain Man* with a female autistic character (Elisabeth Shue) but ends up being highly stereotypic, unrealistic, and unhelpful in educating the public about autism.

Of Mice and Men (1992) Drama ΨΨΨ
John Malkovich as Lenny, a farmhand with mental retardation. This is a wonderful film, but see the 1939 original as well.

"He's a nice fella. Guy don't need no sense to be a nice fella."

A comment on Lenny's personality in
Of Mice and Men (1992)

Other Sister, The (1999) Comedy ΨΨ
This film portrays a young woman's struggles to be an independent adult and to distance herself from an overly protective family. She is successful in her special school, enters the local community college against her father's wishes, and develops friendships.

Pauline and Paulette (2001, Belgium) ΨΨΨΨ
Following the death of their older sister Martha, two sisters unwillingly become responsible for their sister Pauline who is developmentally disabled.

Radio (2003) Drama ΨΨΨ
Cuba Gooding Jr. plays a mentally challenged man who when given a chance by the coach (Ed Harris) of the local football team, inspires and influences many lives. With regard to the portrayal of disabilities, the pros outweigh the cons in this heartwarming, true story.

"I know you're in there somewhere."

Charlie Babbitt responds to his brother
Raymond in *Rain Man* (1993)

Rain Man (1993) Drama ΨΨΨΨ
Dustin Hoffman plays an autistic man who is also a savant, initially exploited by an older brother. Hoffman read widely about autism and worked with autistic people when preparing for this role.

Ringer, The (2005) Comedy ΨΨ
A man desperate for money decides to fix the Special Olympics by entering to beat the reigning champion.

Silent Fall (1994) Drama ΨΨΨ
A retired child psychiatrist works with a boy with autism who witnessed his parent's murder.

Sling Blade (1996) Drama ΨΨΨΨΨ
Billy Bob Thornton wrote the screenplay, directed the film, and played the lead in this remarkable film, which examines the life of a 37-year-old man with mental retardation who has been incarcerated in a mental hospital for the past 25 years after killing his mother and her lover. The fact that the protagonist winds up committing a third murder after being released perpetuates the myth that people who have mental retardation are potentially dangerous.

"I reckon I got no reason to kill no one.
Uh, huh."

Karl Childers in *Sling Blade* (1996)

Snow Cake (2006) Drama ΨΨ
Sigourney Weaver portrays a woman with high functioning autism. This film received an "honorable mention" at the Voice Awards.

There's Something About Mary (1998) Comedy ΨΨ
Ted (Ben Stiller) tries to track down and rekindle love with Mary (Cameron Diaz). Mary has a brother with a developmental disability who plays a significant role in the story.

Tim (1979) Drama ΨΨ
In this Australian film, an older woman has an affair with a man with mild mental retardation.

Unforgotten: 25 Years After Willowbrook (1996) Documentary ΨΨΨΨ
Geraldo Rivera follows up on the original Willowbrook State School expose and contrasts the grim reality of institutional life with the current success of some survivors, including Bernard Carabello, a man abandoned by his parents at age three because he had cerebral palsy, who spent 18 years at Willowbrook.

Village, The (2004) Drama/Suspense ΨΨ
Director M. Night Shyamalan's latest "surprise-genre" film about a village surrounded by forest containing the highly feared "those we don't speak

of." Adrian Brody's character is a purposefully stereotypic portrayal of a developmental disability – the "village idiot."

What's Eating Gilbert Grape (1993) Drama ΨΨΨ

Johnny Depp stars in this interesting portrayal of the dynamics of a rural Iowa family and small town America. Depp's life revolves around the care of his brother (who has mental retardation) and his morbidly obese mother.

Sleep, Eating, Impulse Control, and Adjustment Disorders

12 Monkeys (1995) Science Fiction/Suspense ΨΨ

Terry Gilliam film about a time traveler (Bruce Willis) trying to save the world from a deadly plague. Brad Pitt co-stars as a character with paranoid schizophrenia. At times, the film seems to take on a cinematic representation of a nightmare.

21 (2008) Drama ΨΨ

A young man is accepted into Harvard medical school but in order to afford the tuition joins a group of card counters led by their teacher. Kevin Spacey plays the ringleader.

2046 (2004, China/Hong Kong) Fantasy/Drama ΨΨ

One character has a compulsive gambling problem in this film that blends present and future; the movie is directed by War Kar Wai, who films without a script. "Love is all a matter of timing – it's no good meeting the right person too soon or too late."

Behind the Red Door (2001) Drama ΨΨ

Keifer Sutherland plays a man dying of AIDS who exhibits explosive anger.

Best Little Girl in the World, The (1981) Drama ΨΨ

Good made-for-television movie in which a psychiatrist treats a girl who is suffering from anorexia nervosa.

Best in Show (2000) Comedy ΨΨ

A couple entering their beloved dog in a competitive dog show continuously fight; their fights escalate in response to the tension and anxiety associated with the show. They later cure themselves of their "adjustment" problem by blaming their dog

for being self-deprecating and purchase a new dog who does not mind watching them have sex.

Bookies (2003) Drama ΨΨ

Three college roommates, obsessed with gambling, secretly launch a "bookie" operation.

California Split (1974) Comedy ΨΨ

Robert Altman movie starring George Segal and Elliott Gould as two compulsive gamblers. Not as strong a film as *The Gambler*.

Casino (1995) Drama ΨΨ

Martin Scorsese film explores the mafia's relationship to Las Vegas and gives an inside look at casinos and some gambling addiction. A strong cast includes Robert De Niro, Joe Pesci, Sharon Stone, and James Woods.

Center Stage (2000) Drama ΨΨ

A woman fights her way to the top role as a dancer and performs well despite encouragement to drop out. One dancer has bulimia and the portrayal is accurate and well-done; however, the film is clichéd and predictable.

Control (2003, Hungary) Crime/Mystery/Comedy ΨΨ

Themes of good vs. evil come to life in this farcical film depicting a variety of odd characters interacting in the vast, underground Budapest subway system. One character has narcolepsy.

Cooler, The (2003) Drama ΨΨΨ

Unlucky, depressed man (William H. Macy) walks around the casino as "the cooler" carrying bad luck to successful gamblers by appearing near their gambling tables. He is paying off his own enormous gambling debts and appears to have given up the behavior.

Deuce Bigalow: Male Gigolo (1999) Comedy Ψ

Rob Schneider takes a job as a male escort – one of his "calls" is for a woman with Tourette's Disorder and the other is a woman with narcolepsy. The latter falls asleep in the middle of her bowling stride.

Dinner Rush (2001) Drama/Comedy ΨΨ

In New York City sits an upscale restaurant frequented by high brow customers, self-centered art critics, hoodlums from Queens, and casual customers. One of the cooks has a gambling problem.

Elling (2001) Drama ΨΨΨΨ

Norwegian film about two men released from a

psychiatric hospital who must prove themselves capable of coping with everyday life. One man suffers from intermittent anger episodes. Oscar nominee for Best Foreign Film.

Fever Pitch (2005) Comedy Ψ
Jimmy Fallon's character has an obsession with the Boston Red Sox and struggles to adjust to a new relationship that impacts his passion. American remake of the 1997 UK film of the same title, based on the Nick Hornby novel, in which the main character's (Colin Firth) obsession is with the Arsenal soccer team.

Gambler, The (1974) Drama ΨΨΨΨ
James Caan plays a university professor of literature who can't control his compulsive gambling. One of the best film portrayals of pathological gambling.

Godsend (2004) Suspense/Thriller Ψ
Highly disappointing film starring Robert De Niro as a genetics researcher cloning human beings. He clones a child who begins to experience night terrors, hallucinations, delusions, and murderous behavior.

Good Thief, The (2002) Drama ΨΨ
Nick Nolte plays a junkie gambler.

Happy-Go-Lucky (2008, UK) Comedy ΨΨΨΨ
Poppy, an optimistic realist, interacts with a driver education instructor with intermittent explosive disorder in this Mike Leigh film.

House of Games (1987) Drama ΨΨ
A psychiatrist specializes in the treatment of gambling addiction. Fascinating introduction to the world of the con.

Hulk (2003) Action/Drama ΨΨΨ
Ang Lee converts the famous "Incredible Hulk" comic series to film and in doing so creates a wonderful representation of anger and intermittent explosiveness.

"Guess I'm a little cranky, lack of sleep, ya know."

Insomnia (2002)

Insomnia (2002) Drama/Mystery ΨΨΨΨ
Al Pacino stars as Will Dormer, a cop tracking

down a minor writer (Robin Williams) in a murder investigation. Dormer deteriorates with insomnia as he battles guilt, stress, and an Alaskan environment where the sun doesn't set. Directed by Christopher Nolan.

I Want Someone to Eat Cheese With (2007) Comedy Ψ
Portrayal of binge-eating disorder, the challenges of keeping a diet, and Overeaters Anonymous support group meetings.

Klepto (2003) Drama/Comedy ΨΨΨ
Rare film in which the struggles associated with kleptomania are depicted.

Last Kiss, The (2006) Drama ΨΨΨ
Cautionary tale, particularly for those around age 30 about midlife issues, falling in love, rites of passage, fear of commitment, and the importance of honesty. The film also portrays adjustment disorder.

Life is Sweet (1990) Drama ΨΨΨ
Mike Leigh film about a dysfunctional British family. One of the twin girls binges and purges on chocolate bars.

Lost in Translation (2003) Drama ΨΨΨ
Two Americans (Bill Murray and Scarlett Johansson) "stuck" in Japan find solace, excitement, and friendship in one another. Both characters suffer with severe insomnia symptoms.

Machinist, The (2004, Spain) Mystery/Drama ΨΨΨΨ
Christian Bale lost 80 pounds to play the gaunt Trevor Reznik who suffers from severe insomnia that causes what appear to be symptoms of psychosis (one year later Bale gained the weight back to play the muscular Batman in *Batman Begins*).

"I'll be rejected if I meet a good person."

Lyle, defending his façade of anger in
Manic (2003)

Manic (2003) Drama/Action ΨΨΨ
Adolescent inpatient unit has patients with intermittent explosive disorder, bipolar disorder, major depression, self-injurious behavior, and night terrors.

Marnie (1964) Thriller/Romance ΨΨ
Hitchcock film about a sexually frigid kleptomaniac who dominates her new husband. As in other Hitchcock films, the protagonist's problems are found to be rooted in childhood trauma. Watch for the use of a word association test.

Matrix Reloaded, The (2003) Action ΨΨΨ
Keanu Reeves is Neo in this first sequel of the daring Trilogy by the Wachowski Brothers. Neo suffers from insomnia though on a more important level, his insomnia functions as a metaphor for being "awake" and "alive." He also experiences nightmares and frequently worries at night about decisions he needs to make the next day.

Maverick (1994) Western/Drama ΨΨ
Mel Gibson and Jodi Foster star as charming gamblers and cons in a game of high stakes poker.

Maxed Out (2006) Documentary ΨΨ
Interesting statistics and depiction of the struggles and realities of American credit card debt. The film depicts the consequences of "spending" addictions and impulse control disorders.

Meet Bill (2007) Comedy/Drama ΨΨ
Aaron Eckhart portrays a man whose depression worsens when he discovers his wife is having an affair.

Melvin Goes to Dinner (2003) Comedy ΨΨΨ
Interesting dialogue film about an unplanned get-together between four people. They discuss religion, God, faith, ghosts, affairs, and sex. The character Melvin probably has an adjustment disorder.

Mortal Transfer (2001) Mystery/Drama ΨΨΨΨ
French film depicting one of a psychoanalyst's patients undergoing psychoanalysis and struggling with her kleptomania.

Mother Ghost (2002) Drama ΨΨΨ
A man (Mark Thompson) begins to have significant adjustment problems after his mother's death (she died a year ago) resulting in marital conflict, increased alcohol use, and other personal problems. Interesting interaction and therapy with a radio psychologist (Kevin Pollack) on the air.

My Own Private Idaho (1991) Drama ΨΨ
River Phoenix stars as a young male prostitute who has narcolepsy. He is befriended by Keanu Reeves,

and the two leave Portland and travel together. Interesting presentations of dreams that occur during narcoleptic episodes.

Oscar and Lucinda (1997) Drama/Romance ΨΨΨΨ
Pathological gambling and anxiety disorders are well-depicted in this film set in mid-1800s England, starring Ralph Fiennes and Cate Blanchett

Owning Mahowny (2003) Drama ΨΨΨ
Philip Seymour Hoffman, one of today's finest character actors, plays a pathological gambler. Great portrayal of the addictive cycle and elements of denial, deterioration, and self-destruction. The film is based on a true story.

Popeye (1980) Drama ΨΨ
The archetypal Bluto, a character with an intermittent explosive disorder, is foiled by the heroic Popeye, played by Robin Williams.

Primo Amore (2004, Italy) Drama/Romance ΨΨΨ
A goldsmith falls for an art-school model and becomes obsessed with controlling her diet and appearance. This film provides an interesting examination of eating disorders, and it can be viewed as a metaphorical commentary on society's beliefs about the female body.

Punch Drunk Love (2002) Drama/Comedy ΨΨΨ
Adam Sandler in a serious role about a man who alternates from an awkward passivity to explosive anger. Falling in love changes him. Quirky cinematic elements are added by director Paul Thomas Anderson.

Pushing Tin (1999) Drama/Comedy ΨΨ
John Cusack portrays an air traffic controller with Adult-ADD.

Rat Race (2001) Comedy Ψ
Several characters travel long distances in a competition for monetary reward. One character, played by Rowan Atkinson, has narcolepsy.

Return to Oz (1985) Adventure/Family Ψ
A follow up to the classic story, this film depicts Dorothy returning for more adventures in Oz after evading ECT and "dangerous psychiatric treatment" and struggling with a sleep disorder.

Rounders (1998) Drama ΨΨ
Matt Damon stars as a poker player who has gambled away his life savings to a Russian mobster,

gives up gambling, and is lured back into the game by his friend (Edward Norton).

Seabiscuit (2003) Drama ΨΨ
Tobey Maguire plays a disc jockey with bulimic symptoms in order to keep his weight down and compete in horse-racing championships. Bulimic symptoms are fairly common among jockeys, though this is not an emphasis in the film.

Secondhand Lions (2003) Family ΨΨ
A young adolescent (Haley Joel Osment) is forced to live with his two rich uncles (Robert Duvall and Michael Caine), one of whom often sleepwalks.

Secret Lives of Dentists, The (2002) Drama ΨΨ
A married couple, both dentists, is unable to adjust to both living and working together. One begins an affair while the other stews in anger.

Story of Us, The (1999) Comedy/Drama ΨΨ
Bruce Willis and Michelle Pfeiffer star as a couple on the brink of separation after 15 years of marriage. Directed by Rob Reiner.

Tennis, Anyone…? (2005) Comedy ΨΨ
Two small time actors cope with life and find meaning despite the significant stressors in their lives.

Thin (2006) Documentary ΨΨΨ
Four women with anorexia or bulimia allow their treatment experiences – the struggles, progress, relapse, and symptoms – to be documented on film.

To Live (1994) Drama ΨΨΨΨΨ
This epic film by Zhang Yimou follows a Chinese family through tragic and wonderful times. One of the early struggles of the lead character, Fugui, is gambling, he loses his family home and his fortune gambling with dice.

Two for the Money (2005) Drama ΨΨΨ
A young, savvy, football game predictor (Matthew McConaughey) gets hired by a pathological gambler (Al Pacino) to work in a fast-paced business as a gambler's advisor to gamblers betting on football games. Based on a true story.

Upside of Anger, The (2005) Comedy/Drama ΨΨΨ
Joan Allen portrays a woman with an adjustment disorder who discovers her husband has gone off to Sweden with another woman leaving his home and family. She befriends a jovial alcoholic to cope with her anger and the family disruption.

Waking Life (2001) Drama/Animation ΨΨΨ
This unique, creative film follows a character searching for answers to life's most important questions in a world that seems surreal and dream-like. The film is a surrealistic blend of animation and drama with a heavy philosophical and existential bent. The film questions whether we are sleepwalking through our days and our lives, and whether we are more awake when we interact with others or when we dream.

Wrong Man, The (1956) Drama/Crime ΨΨ
Hitchcock film in which a man and his wife (Henry Fonda and Vera Miles) become depressed in response to an unjust accusation of murder.

Violence and Physical and Sexual Abuse

2LDK (2002) Drama/Action ΨΨΨ
A little known but striking independent film about two girls rooming together temporarily as they compete in an acting audition. A simple argument turns into an outrageously violent battle between the two roommates. The methods of violence are unique and extraordinary, despite being contained in one apartment.

3-Iron (2004, South Korea) ΨΨΨ
A man breaks into houses when people are away for vacation and engages in mundane activities while living there temporarily. He encounters a mute woman who is the victim of domestic violence and they continue his activities together.

5 x 2 (2004, France) Drama ΨΨΨ
Five stages of a couple's romance are portrayed backwards from their divorce; the film depicts conflict, rape, emotional stonewalling, poor decisions-making, and relationship neglect.

8 Mile (2002) Drama ΨΨ
Director Curtis Hanson depicts the struggles, racism, and abuse of rapper, Eminem. "8 mile" is a road in Detroit that represents several cinematic themes: it is the borderline and boundary between black and white, city and suburbia, and the authentic and non-authentic.

300 (2006) Action/History ΨΨΨ
Leonidas, the fearless leader of Sparta, leads 300 men against the vast Persian army of well over 100,000 in the infamous 480 B.C. Battle of Thermopylae.

Accused, The (1988) Drama ΨΨΨ
Jodi Foster won an Academy Award for Best Actress for her role as a woman who is gang raped in a bar. Her character chooses to prosecute for rape rather than aggravated assault; and the film examines the legal relevance of lifestyle (alcohol, drugs, and promiscuity) to the event and the complicity of bystanders. Based on a true story.

Aileen: Life and Death of a Serial Killer (2003) Documentary ΨΨΨ
Nick Broomfield directed this documentary about serial killer Aileen Carol Wuornos, a highway prostitute who was executed in Florida in 2002 for killing seven men. The film includes the filmmaker's testimony at Wuornos' trial. (See also *Monster*.)

Air I Breathe, The (2007) Crime/Drama ΨΨ
Violent, action-filled gangster movie that takes interesting themes – happiness, pleasure, sorrow, and love – yet falls short in delivering something meaningful.

American History X (1998) Drama/Suspense ΨΨΨ
Edward Norton plays a former skinhead who has decided to leave gang-life but must also convince his younger brother.

American Psycho (1999) Drama/Suspense ΨΨΨ
Christian Bale plays Patrick Bateman, a narcissistic Wall Street executive, who emphasizes excess and style over substance in everything from business cards and facial cleansers to restaurant selection and conversation. He also has a pathologically violent mind.

Amores Perros (2000) Action/Suspense ΨΨΨ
Mexican film with a non-linear plot with various hit men, murderers, and other perpetrators of highly graphic violence. Abuse and senseless killing of humans and animals are depicted.

Anatomy of a Murder (1959) Drama ΨΨΨΨ
Classic courtroom drama in which Jimmy Stewart plays a prosecuting attorney in a case involving rape and promiscuity. The film presents an interesting analysis of the "irresistible impulse" defense.

Antonia's Line (1995) Comedy ΨΨΨΨ
Remarkable film about the resiliency of the human spirit, the power of love, and the importance of families. It is included here because of its treatment of a rapist, but also because of its treatment of people with mental retardation, the suicide of a major character, the film's open acceptance of sexual differences, and its healthy attitudes about aging and death.

"Every man has got a breaking point. You and I have.
Walter Kurtz has reached his. And, very obviously, he has gone insane."

An Army general tries to describe the aberrant behavior of Colonel Kurtz in *Apocalypse Now* (1979)

Apocalypse Now (1979) War ΨΨΨΨΨ
Francis Ford Coppola produced and directed this classic war film, which stars Marlon Brando, Robert Duvall, and Martin Sheen. The film is loosely based on Joseph Conrad's *Heart of Darkness* and was designed to drive home the madness of war, as well as its folly. Perhaps the best-known line in the film is "I love the smell of Napalm in the morning."

Apocalypto (2006) Thriller/Drama ΨΨ
Exceedingly violent Mel Gibson film depicting the collapse of the Mayan civilization.

Babel (2006) Drama ΨΨΨΨΨ
Stories from a variety of cultures (Morocco, Mexico, Japan) interweave around themes of communication and the tragic consequences of violence and miscommunication.

Bad Lieutenant (1992) Drama ΨΨΨ
Cocaine-addicted, alcoholic police officer who abuses his position and his family reexamines his life and values after investigating the case of a nun who refuses to identify the man who has raped her.

Badlands (1973) Crime/Drama ΨΨΨ
Film based on a true story about a sociopathic young man who takes up with a 15-year-old girl and goes on a killing spree. The film effectively portrays the lack of guilt and remorse that in part defines the antisocial personality.

Blood Diamond (2006) Action/Drama ΨΨΨΨ
Leonardo DiCaprio portrays a rough, mercenary, diamond smuggler who grapples with an American journalist (Jennifer Connelly) and must decide

between money and assisting a fisherman (Djimon Hounsou) whose child has been kidnapped and turned into a terrorist. The film is a wake-up call on the topic of conflict diamonds.

Blue Velvet (1986) Mystery ΨΨΨ
A powerful and engrossing film about drugs, sexual violence, and sadomasochism. Dennis Hopper plays Frank Booth, a sociopathic and sadistic drug addict who appears to be evil personified.

"He kidnapped them to control her, to make her do things. Then she wanted to commit suicide so he started cutting off ears as a warning to her to stay alive. I'm not kidding. Frank loved blue. Blue velvet."

Blue Velvet (1986)

Bonnie and Clyde (1967) Crime ΨΨΨΨΨ
Perhaps the best of its genre, this landmark film examines the lives of five of the most fascinating characters in the history of crime.

Boston Strangler, The (1968) Crime ΨΨ
Tony Curtis, George Kennedy, and Henry Fonda in a film that attempts to portray the inner life of a serial killer.

"I ain't much of a lover boy. But that don't mean nothin' personal about you. I never saw no percentage in it. Ain't nothin' wrong with me. I don't like boys..."

Clyde Barrow to Bonnie Parker in *Bonnie and Clyde* (1967)

Bridge on the River Kwai, The (1957) Drama ΨΨΨΨ
Alec Guinness plays an Academy Award-winning role as a British colonel who becomes so obsessed with building a bridge that he loses sight of his loyalty and allegiance to the allied forces.

Cape Fear (1991) Thriller ΨΨΨΨ
Interesting Scorsese remake of a 1962 classic. This

version includes Nick Nolte playing a sleazy attorney and Robert De Niro is a sociopathic ex-con out to get revenge by hurting Nolte and his family and seducing his teenage daughter.

"Do not speak to me of rules. This is war. This is not a game of cricket. He's mad, your Colonel. Quite mad."

The Bridge on the River Kwai (1957)

Casualties of War (1989) Drama ΨΨ
Sean Penn leads a group of five soldiers who kidnap and rape a Vietnamese girl and subsequently kill her. Michael J. Fox subsequently shows the moral courage to confront the four rapists and murderers. Based on a true story.

Celebration, The (1998, Denmark/Sweden) Drama ΨΨΨ
A man confronts his sexually abusive father during a family gathering celebrating his father's 60th birthday. Film attempts to depict a realistic approach to abuse confrontation and its effect on a family.

City of God (2003) Drama ΨΨΨ
Painfully sobering and graphic look at violence associated with child and adolescent gang-life, drug trafficking, and poverty in a section of Rio de Janeiro, Brazil. Depiction of young children and adolescents walking around with no fear, guns, and only revenge on their minds.

Clockwork Orange, A (1971) Science Fiction ΨΨΨΨ
Stanley Kubrick's masterpiece about "ultraviolence," stereotypes, Beethoven, pathological youth, the future of society, the evils of aversion therapy, good vs. evil, the rehabilitation of prisoners, and free will vs. determinism. It is regarded by many film experts as one of the greatest films ever made.

Cold Mountain (2003) Drama/Romance ΨΨ
Amidst a dramatic love story (between characters played by Jude Law and Nicole Kidman) is a lot of antisocial behavior, violence, immoral behavior, attempted rape, and senseless tortures and killings.

Compulsion (1959) Crime ΨΨΨ
Two homosexual law students kidnap and kill a

young boy. Based on the Leopold-Loeb case, the film examines the morality of capital punishment and features Orson Wells in the role played by Clarence Darrow in the actual case.

Cook, the Thief, His Wife & Her Lover, The (1989) Drama ΨΨΨΨ
Peter Greenaway film far too complex to capture in a sentence or two. Full of psychopathology, the film deals with passion, deceit, gluttony, murder, cannibalism, and man's inhumanity to man.

Copycat (1995) Drama ΨΨΨ
Sigourney Weaver plays a forensic psychologist trying to understand the psyche of a serial killer who models his murders after those committed by infamous murderers, such as Son of Sam and the Boston Strangler.

Crash (2004) Drama ΨΨΨΨ
Director Paul Haggis blends several stories in this eclectic mix of races and ethnicities in Los Angeles that takes a meaningful look at racism, discrimination, corruption, and the possibility of redemption.

Das Experiment (2001) Drama/Suspense ΨΨΨ
Depiction of psychological research experiment in a prison setting where subjects are divided into prisoners who waive their civil rights and guards who are to maintain peace and order. While this film bears some initial structural similarity to the famous Zimbardo Prison Experiment, it in no way portrays it accurately as the film's violence goes well beyond actual events.

"They got me on a greased rail to the Death House here."

Dead Man Walking (1995)

Dead Man Walking (1995) Drama ΨΨΨΨ
Susan Sarandon and Sean Penn star in this dramatic examination of a nun's need to understand and help a man sentenced to die for the rape and murder of two teenagers. The film skillfully examines the death penalty, family dynamics, themes of redemption, and the mitigating role of drugs without ever providing easy answers. Sarandon won an Academy Award for her performance in this film.

Deliberate Stranger, The (1986) Drama Ψ
Made-for-TV movie about serial killer Ted Bundy.

"Lewis, don't play games with these people."

Deliverance (1972)

Deliverance (1972) Adventure ΨΨΨΨ
Jon Voight, Ned Beatty, and Burt Reynolds on a white water rafting trip in Appalachia. Beatty winds up being sodomized, and Reynolds kills the rapist, using a bow and arrow. Based on a James Dickey novel, the film raises interesting questions about personal responsibility and social justice.

Disclosure (1994) Drama ΨΨ
A less-than-illuminating film about reverse sexual discrimination. Stars include Demi Moore and Michael Douglas; based on a novel by Michael Crichton.

Dog Day Afternoon (1975) Crime ΨΨΨ
Al Pacino holds up a bank to get enough money to fund a sex-change operation for his homosexual lover. Good illustration of a basically good person caught up in an stressful situation.

Domino (2005) Action Ψ
A tough, rebellious, female bounty hunter tries to fight fair.

Don't Tell (2005, Italy/UK/France/Spain) Drama ΨΨΨΨ
A young adult woman realizes she has repressed nearly all of her childhood, and following the death of her parents, begins to have nightmares of her father sexually abusing her as a young girl. She consults with her brother to put the pieces together.

Down and Dirty (1976) Drama ΨΨ
An interesting examination of the effects of poverty, squalor, and alcoholism on an Italian family.

Dressed to Kill (1980) Thriller Ψ
The film confuses transsexualism and schizophrenia but offers good suspense. Mimics Hitchcock.

Eastern Promises (2007) Thriller/Drama ΨΨΨ
David Cronenberg film about Russian gangsters.

The film features an unforgettable, intense battle scene in steam room.

Elephant (2003) Drama ΨΨΨΨΨ
Well-crafted, foreboding, eerie Gus van Sant film that attempts to explain a tragic school shooting. Powerful parallels with Columbine. Winner of the Palm award at Cannes for Best Picture and Director.

End of Violence, The (1997) Drama/Suspense ΨΨΨ
Bill Pullman plays an action/violence film director who is almost murdered so he hides out from society and starts a new life. While his character both promotes and greatly fears violence, a secret government worker (Gabriel Byrne) tries to prevent violence by watching over the city with thousands of cameras.

Executioner's Song, The (1982) Made for TV Drama ΨΨ
Tommy Lee Jones plays serial killer Gary Gilmore. Based on a story by Norman Mailer.

Extremities (1986) Drama Ψ
Farrah Fawcett plays a victimized woman who gets revenge on the man who rapes her.

Fight Club (1999) Drama/Suspense ΨΨΨΨ
A disillusioned, insomniac (Edward Norton) meets a dangerous, malcontent part of himself in the character of Brad Pitt. Norton then establishes "fight clubs" where men can violently release their aggressions by fighting one another.

"The great war is a spiritual war; the great depression is our lives."

Fight Club (1999)

Freedomland (2006) Mystery/Drama Ψ
Julianne Moore portrays a neglectful mother; her character stands in marked contrast to Samuel L. Jackson's character who is attempting to redeem himself by caring for his adult son who is in prison.

Gangs of New York (2002) Crime/Drama ΨΨΨ
Martin Scorsese film about the revenge perpetrated upon a gang kingpin named Bill "the Butcher" Cutting (Daniel Day-Lewis).

Godfather, The (1972), **The Godfather, Part II** (1974), and **The Godfather, Part III** (1990) Drama ΨΨΨΨΨ
The three-part gangster trilogy, directed by Francis Ford Coppola, examines violence, corruption, and crime in America.

"We'll make him an offer he can't refuse."

The Godfather (1972)

Gone Baby Gone (2007) Crime/Drama ΨΨΨΨ
An interesting and complex film, and Ben Affleck's directorial debut. The film is about a young girl who has been neglected by her drug-dependent mother and has gone missing. The movie raises fascinating questions about how to raise children and the role of society.

Grindhouse: Death Proof (2007) and **Grindhouse: Planet Terror** (2007) Thriller ΨΨΨ
Two feature lengths films often shown together that pay homage to gory exploitation films. Both feature significant violence – the first involves a gang of women who face off with a murderous racecar driver and the second features an army of flesh-eating zombies. Not surprisingly, the Tarantino-directed film (the first one) is more engaging and interesting than the second one (directed by Robert Rodriguez).

Halloween and its sequels (1978, 1981, 1982, 1988, 1998, 2002, 2006, 2007, 2009) Horror Ψ
Infamous mass murderer depicted as an escaped mental patient and a deranged toy maker. These films have contributed significantly to the negative stereotypes of mental illness.

Hand That Rocks the Cradle, The (1992) Thriller/Drama Ψ
Sociopathic woman seeks revenge for the suicide of her husband by moving in and taking over the family of the woman she holds responsible for her husband's death. Predictable performances, but still an engrossing film.

Heavenly Creatures (1994) Drama ΨΨΨΨ
A New Zealand film directed by Peter Jackson and based on the true story of two adolescent girls who grow up sharing a fantasy world. When the mother of one of the girls decides to separate the children,

they murder her. One of the girls, Ann Perry, now lives in England and writes mystery novels.

Henry: Portrait of a Serial Killer (1990) Crime/Horror ΨΨΨΨ

A violent, controversial film about mass murderer and sociopath Henry Lee Lucas. A scene in which Lucas and his roommate videotape one of their murders is especially unnerving.

"She'd make me watch it... She'd beat me when I wouldn't watch her... She'd make me wear a dress and they would laugh."

Henry Lee Lucas describing abuse by his prostitute mother in *Henry: Portrait of a Serial Killer* (1990)

History of Violence, A (2005) Drama/Mystery ΨΨΨΨ

David Cronenberg film about a quiet, unassuming family man who springs to action when the workers and customers of his café are threatened by thugs. His fighting prowess causes his family to question his past and who he really is.

Honeymoon Killers, The (1970) Crime Ψ

A very realistic black-and-white film based on the true story of a couple who lured, exploited, and then killed lonely women. Both the man and the woman were executed at Sing-Sing Prison.

Hotel Rwanda (2004) Drama/Documentary ΨΨΨΨΨ

Depicts the genocide of the Hutus upon the Tutsis in Rwanda and the courageous efforts of Paul Rusesabagina, a hotel manager who saved over 1200 refugees. The film illustrates courage and persistence; it also shows how one ordinary man can be extraordinary and triumph over evil.

House of 1000 Corpses (2003) Horror Ψ

Musician Rob Zombie directed this film about a family of eerie serial killers that contains some comic relief.

I Spit on Your Grave (1980) Horror Ψ

A terrible film in which a woman systematically gets revenge on the four men who raped her.

"They all felt physically inferior or sexually inadequate. Their childhood was violent... They couldn't distinguish between fantasy and reality. They didn't hate their victims, they didn't even know them."

A doctor describes serial killers in *In Cold Blood* (1967)

In Cold Blood (1967) Biography/Crime ΨΨΨ

This film is based on a Truman Capote biographical novel about two sociopaths who kill a Kansas family. The film explores the family dynamics that in part lead to the senseless murders.

"I've kept you alive for two reasons. First reason is information... But I am gonna ask you questions and every time you don't give me answers, I'm gonna cut something off. And I promise you they will be things you will miss!"

The Bride in *Kill Bill: Vol. 1* (2003)

Kill Bill: Vol. 1 (2003) Action/Suspense ΨΨΨΨΨ

Dynamic Tarantino story of a samurai bride (Uma Thurman) betrayed by her ex-lover and boss. This first film sets up the mythology and the world of the characters. It has more extensive graphic violence than Vol. 2 and an "eastern" martial arts emphasis.

Kill Bill: Vol. 2 (2004) Action/Suspense ΨΨΨΨΨ

Tarantino's conclusion to the revenge story of The Bride. This part emphasizes the unfolding of the stories and further deepening of characters amongst a more "western" style.

"I'm a killer. I'm a murdering bastard and there are consequences for breaking the heart of a murdering bastard."

Bill in *Kill Bill: Vol. 2* (2004)

Killing Fields, The (1984) Drama ΨΨΨΨ
Gripping film about the horrors of war and the particularly gruesome and cruel practices of the Khmer Rouge in Cambodia following the evacuation of American soldiers from Vietnam in 1975.

Lilja 4-Ever (2002) Drama ΨΨΨ
A powerful depiction of the cruelty of violence. An adolescent girl experiences neglect, abandonment, rejection, physical and sexual abuse, gang rape, exploitation, and forced prostitution, all by the age of 16.

Looking for Mr. Goodbar (1977) Drama ΨΨ
Diane Keaton plays a special education teacher with a compulsive need to pick up men in bars and engage in sadomasochistic sex. There are numerous examples of family pathology in the film, and it is interesting to remember how casual sexuality was in a time before AIDS.

M (1931) Crime/Drama/Horror ΨΨΨΨΨ
A must-see Fritz Lang film (his first "talkie") starring Peter Lorre as a sexual psychopath who molests and murders little girls. When tried by a vigilante jury, he pleads irresistible impulse, but the jury is not impressed.

Magdalene Sisters, The (2002) Docudrama ΨΨΨ
Troubled adolescent girls are sent to a dehumanizing, boarding home where they are treated by nuns who run the home with abuse, neglect, and humiliation. The film follows four girls in particular as they experience and respond differently to the highly abusive situation.

Metallica: Some Kind of Monster (2004) Documentary ΨΨΨ
Inside look at the heavy metal band, Metallica, and their personal and interpersonal struggles. The handling of anger is a key theme in the film. The honest expression of emotions by these "stars" is likely to have a positive impact on many fans.

Midnight Express (1978) Biography ΨΨΨ
True story about an American college student who is busted for trying to smuggle two kilograms of hashish out of Turkey and is treated brutally in Turkish prisons before eventually escaping.

Monster (2003) Drama ΨΨΨΨ
A powerful film based on the life of Aileen Carol Wuornos, a highway prostitute who was executed for killing seven men in the state of Florida during the 1980s. (See also *Aileen: Life and Death of a Serial Killer.*)

Murder in the First (1995) Drama ΨΨ
A man imprisoned in Alcatraz for petty theft in the 1930s is put in solitary confinement for three years, becomes deranged, and then kills a guard. The film suggests the system is to blame for the crime. Based on a true story.

Mysterious Skin (2004) Drama ΨΨΨ
Two boys are sexually molested by their coach and their lives go in completely different directions. Intense, realistic portrayal of the ways sexual abuse affects children when they become adolescents and adults.

"Insane, no. Psychotic, yes. A menace to living creatures, yes. But to suggest that they're insane gives the impression that they don't know right from wrong. Mickey and Mallory know the difference between right and wrong. They just don't give a damn."

A psychiatric opinion in
Natural Born Killers (1994)

Natural Born Killers (1994) Crime/Drama ΨΨΨ
A violent Oliver Stone film based on a story written by Quentin Tarantino and starring Woody Harrelson and Juliette Lewis. The film depicts a couple who celebrate their roles as mass murderers and find their new status as cult figures a welcome reprieve from the dreariness of the life they left behind.

Night Porter, The (1974) Drama/War ΨΨ
A former Nazi officer who sexually abused a 14-year-old girl in a concentration camp has the tables turned on him when she shows up at the hotel in which he works. This is one of several films linking Nazi practices with sadomasochistic sex.

No Man's Land (2001) Drama/Suspense ΨΨΨΨ
A Bosnian escapes a firing attack and finds himself in "No Man's Land" between enemy lines. A Serb goes to ensure there were no survivors and finds himself in a standoff with the Bosnian. Another Bosnian survivor, barely alive, awakes

on top of a land mine that will explode if he rises. Heated debates, murder attempts, threats, desperation, and hopelessness characterize each of the three men.

North Country (2005) Drama ΨΨΨ
Charlize Theron transforms herself again (following up her role as a serial killer in *Monster*), this time to play a woman who goes to great lengths to support her children by working in a blue-collar mine where she experiences significant sexual harassment.

"It's the same old story. I've got to learn to keep my mouth shut."

Beth blaming herself for the beating she has received from her husband in
Once Were Warriors (1994)

Once Were Warriors (1994) Drama ΨΨΨΨ
Important New Zealand film about substance abuse and domestic violence among urban Maori tribal people. The film will help you understand a different culture, as well as the ways in which alcoholism interacts with spousal and child abuse in almost every society.

Osama (2003, Afghanistan) Drama ΨΨΨ
Based on a true story of the heavy discrimination, abuse, and oppression of women under Taliban rule.

Passion of the Christ, The (2004)
Drama/Biography ΨΨΨΨΨ
Mel Gibson film depicting the violent torture and suffering of the final hours of Jesus Christ. This highly controversial film is intensely graphic and visual in its portrayal of violence. It is interesting to note that it is Mel Gibson's hand that nails Jesus to the cross.

Peeping Tom (1960) Thriller ΨΨΨ
Controversial film about a psychopathic murderer who photographs his victims as they die.

Personal Velocity (2002) Drama ΨΨΨ
Independent film about three strong women divided into three segments. One segment addresses issues of domestic violence.

"She imagined going back to him like she had done so many times before but this time her body wouldn't follow."

Narration on the escape from
an abusive husband in
Personal Velocity (2002)

Play Misty for Me (1971) Thriller ΨΨΨ
The first film directed by Clint Eastwood. A California disc jockey becomes involved with a listener who is clinging, dependent, fanatical, and ultimately homicidal. Interesting portrayal of sexual obsession.

Prick Up Your Ears (1987) Biography ΨΨΨΨ
A film showing the homosexual relationship and eventual murder/suicide of playwright Joe Orton and his lover.

Rampage (1992) Thriller ΨΨΨ
This movie, directed by William Friedkin, challenges many of the assumptions educated people are likely to hold about the insanity defense.

Rashomon (1950) Drama ΨΨΨΨΨ
Classic Akira Kurosawa film in which a rape-murder is described from four different perspectives by the four people involved. The film makes the point that reality is subjective and that truth, like beauty, is truly in the eye of the beholder.

Rendition (2007) Drama/Thriller ΨΨΨ
An Egyptian man traveling in South Africa at a conference is detained without due process. The film addresses "extraordinary rendition" – detaining suspected terrorists and interrogating them on foreign soil without judicial process – and depicts torture (e.g., water-boarding), brainwashing/training of suicide bombers, and the various realities politicians face.

Reservoir Dogs (1992) Drama ΨΨΨ
Extremely violent but powerful Tarantino film with a graphic and realistic torture scene in which a sociopathic sadist derives great pleasure from using a razor to slowly torment a bound and gagged undercover police officer.

River's Edge (1986) Drama ΨΨΨΨ
A riveting film based on a true-life incident in which a young man kills his girlfriend and then

shows the decomposing body to a series of friends. It takes days before one of his friends finally notifies authorities about the murder.

"Now I'm not gonna bullshit you. I don't really care about what you know or don't know. I'm gonna torture you for a while regardless. Not to get information, but because torturing a cop amuses me. There's nothing you can say, there's nothing you can do. Except pray for death."

The sadistic Mr. Blonde in
Reservoir Dogs (1992)

Rope (1948) ΨΨ
Experimental Hitchcock film about two young homosexual men who kill a friend for sport and then hide the body in a room in which they are hosting a cocktail party. Based on the Leopold-Loeb case.

Santa Sangre (1989) Horror ΨΨΨΨ
A controversial but unquestionably powerful Jodorowsky film about a boy growing up in bizarre circumstances. There are strong themes of violence and incest. Roger Ebert called this film "a collision between Freud and Fellini."

Saving Private Ryan (1998) War/Action ΨΨΨ
Steven Spielberg World War II film regarded by some as the most realistic and powerful war film ever made.

Se7en (1995) Drama ΨΨΨ
Morgan Freeman and Brad Pitt star in this engrossing film about a serial killer (Kevin Spacey) who is obsessed with the seven deadly sins (pride, envy, gluttony, lust, anger, covetousness, and sloth) and who kills his victims accordingly (e.g., a man who is gluttonous is forced to eat until he dies from overeating).

Series 7: The Contenders (2001) Suspense/Comedy ΨΨΨ
Highly violent, tongue-in-cheek film about a reality television show where the contestants must seek out and kill one another.

Seven Beauties (1976) Comedy/Drama ΨΨΨ
Lina Wertmuller film in which the protagonist (the brother of the seven sisters alluded to in the title) must perform degrading sexual acts for the female commandant of a German prison camp to survive the war.

Shelter Island (2003) Drama/Suspense Ψ
A lesbian couple goes to get away at an island house to relax. A stranger (Stephen Baldwin) appears on their doorstep during a storm and things are not what they seem. Simplistic psychology that is not well-applied or developed.

Sin City (2005) Action/Noir ΨΨΨ
Stylized graphic violence tempered by computerized graphics, based on Frank Miller's comic books, with an all-star cast.

Sleepers (1996) Drama ΨΨΨ
Guards at a reform school physically and sexually abuse young boys. After the boys grow up, they avenge their abuse and attempt to manipulate the courts to avoid sentencing. Many stellar actors including Robert De Niro, Dustin Hoffman, Brad Pitt, and Kevin Bacon.

Slumdog Millionaire (2008) Drama ΨΨΨΨ
The Academy Award winning rags to riches story about a young man's destiny that intersperses his performance on "Who Wants to Be a Millionaire" with flashbacks showing significant life experiences that include poverty, abuse, and torture. The film is a classic underdog story with poignant themes of persistence, integrity/honesty, and self-confidence.

South Central (1992) Action/Suspense ΨΨ
A man is released from prison and tries to lead a "clean," gang-free life.

Stone Boy, The (1984) Drama ΨΨ
Robert Duvall and Glenn Close star in this slow-moving but intelligent film about a young man who accidentally shoots his brother and the effect the shooting has on the entire family.

Straw Dogs (1971) Crime ΨΨΨ
Provocative and violent Sam Peckinpah film, with Dustin Hoffman as a peace-loving mathematician who resorts to violence after his wife is raped.

Sweeney Todd: The Demon Barber of Fleet Street (2007) Musical/Thriller ΨΨΨ
Extensive violence tuned to music and dance in Tim Burton's story of revenge starring Johnny Depp and Helena Bonham Carter.

Tattoo (1981) Drama Ψ
Mentally ill tattoo artist kidnaps a model and uses her body as a canvas for his art. This is the type of movie that perpetuates stigma and prejudice about mental illness.

Thelma & Louise (1991) Drama/Comedy ΨΨΨ
Two women friends on the road for a weekend lark wind up fleeing from the law and end their lives in a defiant suicidal act. Powerful feminist film.

There Will Be Blood (2007) Drama/Thriller ΨΨΨ
Daniel Day-Lewis portrays a charismatic, ruthless oil prospector in this story of greed, religion, and family.

Time to Kill, A (1996) Drama ΨΨΨ
Samuel Jackson plays an angry father who murders two white men who have raped his daughter. The film explores themes of racial and social injustice, temporary insanity, and justifiable homicide.

Treasure of the Sierra Madre, The (1948) Drama ΨΨΨ
Tremendous John Huston film starring Humphrey Bogart. The movie explores obsessive greed, the folly of avarice, and the ways in which love of money can come to be the dominant force in one's life. Bogart's character is an example of a paranoid personality disorder.

"Badges? We ain't got no badges! We don't need no badges. I don't have to show you any stinkin' badges!"

The Treasure of the Sierra Madre
(1948)

Triumph of the Spirit (1989) Biography ΨΨΨ
Story of Auschwitz concentration camp during World War II. Good introduction to the horrors and stress of concentration camp life.

Twist of Faith (2004) Documentary ΨΨ
A firefighter faces the trauma of childhood sexual abuse by a priest, speaking to the shame, horror, anger, and dissociation that occurs. He discusses the significant impact of abuse on his life.

Two Women (1961) War/Drama Ψ
This Vittorio de Sica film starring Sophia Loren

examines war, rape, coming of age, and mother-daughter relations. Loren won an Academy Award as Best Actress for this film.

Virgin Spring, The (1959) Drama ΨΨΨ
An Ingmar Bergman film examining the rape and murder of a young girl by three bandits.

Vulgar (2002) Drama ΨΨ
A man working as a clown for children decides he can make more money working as a clown at bachelor parties. He is tortured, gang raped, and blackmailed by a psychopath and his two sons. The film graphically depicts trauma and violence, but there are also comic moments.

Waitress (2007) Comedy/Drama ΨΨΨΨΨ
Inspirational story of a young, pregnant waitress (Keri Russell) who is not enthusiastic about her pregnancy because the child's father is her psychologically abusive and controlling husband (Jeremy Sisko). Sadly, the film's director, Adrienne Shelly, was murdered before the film was widely released to critical acclaim (Shelly's young daughter appears in the final scene).

War of the Roses, The (1989) Drama/Thriller ΨΨ
Marital conflict slowly progresses into an incredible, destructive battle between Oliver and Barbara Rose (Michael Douglas and Kathleen Turner).

Warrior, The (2001, UK/France/Germany) Drama/Adventure ΨΨΨ
A warrior, working for a cruel lord as an executioner in feudal India, takes up the practice of nonviolence. His new mission becomes particularly challenging when his son is kidnapped and killed in front of him.

Zodiac (2007) Crime/Biography ΨΨ
Jake Gyllenhaal portrays an amateur detective in San Francisco who becomes obsessed with tracking down a serial killer in this David Fincher film.

Treatment

Antwone Fisher (2003) Drama/Biography ΨΨΨ
Troubled and angry sailor gets in fights and is referred to a psychiatrist (Denzel Washington). Their relationship develops and he becomes comfortable sharing his history of childhood abuse

and trauma; he makes amends with his past and healing begins. Fair and balanced portrayal of a psychiatrist.

Article 99 (1992) Comedy Ψ
Unsuccessful M*A*S*H*-like attempt to ridicule the quality of care provided in Veterans Administration medical centers.

Bad Timing: A Sensual Obsession (1980) Drama ΨΨ
Interesting and provocative film in which a psychiatrist becomes sexually involved with a troubled and self-destructive woman.

Badlands (1973) Crime/Drama ΨΨΨ
This film is based on a true story about a sociopathic young man who takes up with a 15-year-old girl and goes on a killing spree. The film effectively portrays the lack of guilt and remorse that in part defines the antisocial personality.

"Without treatment, John, the fantasies may take over entirely."

Dr. Rosen attempting to educate John Nash on the importance of continuing his treatment regimen in *A Beautiful Mind* (2001)

Beautiful Mind, A (2001) Drama ΨΨΨΨ
Based on Sylvia Nasar's biography with the same name. Russell Crowe portrays John Forbes Nash, a mathematical genius and Nobel Prize laureate in Economics, who battles schizophrenia and is treated with antipsychotics and insulin-shock therapy.

Beautiful Dreamers (1992) Drama/Biography ΨΨΨ
True story about poet Walt Whitman's visit to an asylum in London, Ontario. Whitman is shocked by what he sees and persuades the hospital director to offer humane treatment. Eventually, the patients wind up playing the townspeople in a game of cricket.

Beyond Therapy (1987) Comedy Ψ
Disappointing Robert Altman film about New York yuppies and their psychiatrists.

Butcher's Wife, The (1991) Romance/Fantasy ΨΨ
Greenwich Village psychiatrist Jeff Daniels finds Demi Moore, the butcher's wife, is giving advice at least as good as his own.

Cabinet of Dr. Caligari, The (1919) Horror ΨΨΨΨ
German expressionistic film about hypnosis and the power of a hypnotist to induce others to do his bidding. One of the earliest stereotypic presentations of the madman who runs a psychiatric hospital.

Captain Newman, M.D. (1963) Comedy/Drama ΨΨΨ
Sympathetic story about an Army psychiatrist (Gregory Peck) taking on the military bureaucracy to provide effective treatment for Bobby Darin. Darin is clearly manic and ultimately commits suicide.

Carefree (1938) Musical/Dance ΨΨ
Fred Astaire is a psychiatrist who was talked out of being a dancer. Ginger Rogers is referred to him for treatment (hypnosis) so she can learn to love one of Astair's friends; he complies with her request, but predictably falls in love with her himself.

Caretakers, The (1963) Drama Ψ
Second-rate film that documents life in a West Coast psychiatric hospital and portrays some of the problems associated with introducing innovations in hospital settings.

Changeling (2008) Drama ΨΨΨ
Based on a true story, Angelina Jolie portrays a desperate but persistent mother whose son is kidnapped by a serial child murderer. She battles with a corrupt Los Angeles police force and a manipulative psychiatrist who twists her words, attempts to blackmail her, uses ECT to punish his patients, and holds innocent women captive in the hospital to protect the police department.

Chattahoochee (1990) Drama ΨΨΨ
Korean War veteran with a post-traumatic stress disorder is hospitalized and treated. Dennis Hopper has a major role as a fellow patient.

Clockwork Orange, A (1971) Science Fiction ΨΨΨΨ
Fascinating interpretation of Anthony Burgess' novel. The portrayal of aversion therapy is somewhat heavy-handed but raises legitimate questions

about the appropriate limits of behavior modification.

Color of Night (1994) Drama Ψ
Bruce Willis plays a disillusioned psychologist who gives up his practice after a patient commits suicide. Willis discovers he is no longer able to perceive the color red. Much of the plot revolves around a patient with multiple personalities who is simultaneously a group therapy patient (as a male) and, unknown to Willis, his lover (in a core personality named Rose).

"There was me, that is Alex, and my three droogs, that is Pete, Georgie, and Dim. . . and we sat in the Korova Milkbar trying to make up our rassoodocks what to do with the evening."

Alex in *A Clockwork Orange* (1971)

Couch Trip, The (1988) Comedy Ψ
Dan Aykroyd plays the role of a psychiatric patient who escapes from an institution and then passes himself off as a Beverly Hills psychiatrist. The film reinforces the notion that psychiatry is mainly pretentious language and social manipulation.

Dark Past, The (1948) Crime ΨΨΨ
A psychologist who is taken prisoner tries to use his training to help his captor. Remake of the film *Blind Alley*.

David and Lisa (1962) Drama ΨΨΨΨ
A dated but still sensitive portrayal of life in a psychiatric institution. Perpetuates the myth that love will conquer mental illness. Strong and balanced portrayal of a compassionate psychiatrist.

Dead Man Out (1989) Drama ΨΨ
Superior and timely made-for-TV movie about a psychiatrist treating a convict so the man will be sane enough to be executed. The film raises meaningful questions about ethical issues and the appropriate limits of professional practice.

Dream Team, The (1989) Comedy ΨΨ
Four psychiatric patients are being taken to a game in Yankee Stadium when their doctor/escort is knocked unconscious and hospitalized. The entire film appears to be based on the well-known (and

better done) shipboard outing by Jack Nicholson and his friends in *One Flew Over the Cuckoo's Nest*.

Jack McDermott: "What about dinner? Who's gonna get us our dinner?"
Billy: "... aren't you the same guy who changed water into wine? Huh? J.C.? Ain't the son of God good for a burger in his town? You get us something!"

The Dream Team (1989)

Face to Face (1976) Drama ΨΨΨ
Liv Ullmann plays a psychiatrist whose life is falling apart. She attempts suicide by taking an overdose and winds up in a coma. Interesting dream sequences with Bergman's usual presumption of childhood trauma as the trigger for adult unhappiness.

Fear Strikes Out (1957) Biography/Sports ΨΨΨ
Anthony Perkins as baseball player Jimmy Piersall, who suffers a mental breakdown as a result of his inability to please a domineering, demanding father. Piersall was successfully treated with psychotherapy and ECT and eventually staged a comeback.

Final Analysis (1992) Thriller/Drama ΨΨ
A complex film that pays homage to Hitchcock; interesting issues of childhood sexual abuse, repressed memories, professional responsibility, and the doctor-patient relationship.

"Just repeat the last two words they say and phrase it like a question."

A psychiatrist joking about his profession in *Final Analysis* (1992)

Fine Madness, A (1966) Drama ΨΨΨ
Sean Connery plays Samson Shillitoe, an eccentric and unconventional poet who is hospitalized and lobotomized because of his sexual peccadilloes and the fact that he can't conform to societal expectations. The film was ahead of its time in

raising important issues about the rights of people with mental illness.

Flame Within, The (1935) Drama Ψ
Dated and insipid film about a psychiatrist who falls in love with a patient.

Frances (1982) Biography ΨΨΨΨΨ
A vivid portrayal of the life of actress Frances Farmer, including her institutionalization, lobotomy, and alcoholism.

Good Will Hunting (1997) Drama ΨΨΨΨ
Robin Williams won an Academy Award as Best Supporting Actor for his role as a counseling psychologist teaching at a community college and treating a troubled young man who is extraordinarily gifted mathematically.

High Anxiety (1977) Comedy ΨΨ
Mel Brooks spoofs Hitchcock films and introduces The Psycho-Neurotic Institute for the Very, Very Nervous.

Home of the Brave (1949) Drama/War ΨΨΨ
Black soldier suffers a mental breakdown and is treated by a sympathetic psychiatrist. One of the first films to deal honestly with racism and bigotry.

House of Games (1987) Crime ΨΨ
A David Mamet film about a psychiatrist specializing in the treatment of gambling addiction. Fascinating introduction to the world of the con.

House of Fools (2002) Drama ΨΨΨΨ
Based on a true story: the chief psychiatrist and treatment staff of a mental institution flee due to conflicts in Chechnya, leaving the patients to fend for themselves. Soon soldiers occupy the hospital and the viewer is left with various questions of war, politics, mental health treatment and which is more crazy – the mentally ill or the politics of war. The film is loaded with examples of psychopathology.

I Heart Huckabees (2005) Comedy/Mystery ΨΨΨ
Dustin Hoffman and Lilly Tomlin play existential psychologists in this quirky, offbeat comedy. Although there is no formal therapy, there are plenty of therapeutic moments.

Inside/Out (1997) Drama ΨΨΨ
A Rob Tregenza film about life in a psychiatric hospital that was well received at the 1998 Sundance Film Festival. The film documents that both patients and staff find it hard to cope with the difficult demands of life.

Intimate Strangers (2004, France) Drama ΨΨΨ
A woman mistakenly receives psychotherapy from an accountant in this thoughtful film.

King of Hearts (1966) Comedy/Drama/War ΨΨΨΨ
A Scotsman separated from his unit wanders into town, abandoned by all except the inmates of the local insane asylum. Must-see film for those interested in public attitudes about mental illness.

Ladybird, Ladybird (1993) Drama ΨΨΨΨ
Dramatic presentation of the clash between the rights of a parent and society's need to protect children.

Lilith (1964) Drama ΨΨ
Strong cast (Peter Fonda, Gene Hackman, Warren Beatty, and Kim Hunter) supports a weak script about a psychiatric inpatient who seduces a neophyte therapist.

Lost Angels (1989) Drama ΨΨ
Donald Sutherland plays a psychiatrist treating a Los Angeles adolescent who is angry and troubled but probably not mentally ill.

"When insurance paid for a year in a place like this, we said it took a year to help a kid. Now insurance pays for three months, and, presto, it takes three months to turn a kid around."

Dr. Charles Loftis complaining about the system in *Lost Angels* (1989)

Ludwig (1973) Biography Ψ
Long and somewhat tedious film about the mad King Ludwig of Bavaria. Good costumes and scenery, but the film teaches us little about mental illness or Ludwig himself.

Macbeth (1971) Drama ΨΨΨ
Powerful Roman Polanski adaptation of Shakespeare's play. It is interesting to speculate about the obsessions of Lady Macbeth and to compare Polanski's version with the earlier Orson Welles' adaptation.

Man Facing Southeast (1986) Drama ΨΨΨΨ
Fascinating Argentine film about a man without identity who shows up at a psychiatric hospital claiming to be from another planet. It seems that this is not just another patient, and neither the hospital staff nor the film's audience ever figures out exactly what is happening. (In a line that is meaningful to one viewer in a thousand, Bill Murray's character in *What About Bob?* pays homage to this film by asking if he can arrange his bed so it faces southeast.)

Man Who Loved Women, The (1983) Comedy Ψ
A remake of the François Truffaut film of the same name. This film involves long sequences in which Burt Reynolds unburdens himself to his psychiatrist.

Marat/Sade (1966) Drama ΨΨΨΨ
In the early 1800s, the inmates of a French asylum put on a play directed by the Marquis de Sade (a patient) based on the bathtub assassination of Jean Paul Marat. The play incites the patients to riot.

Mine Own Executioner (1947) Drama ΨΨ
Confused and troubled psychoanalyst tries to help out a schizophrenic veteran.

Mr. Deeds Goes to Town (1936) Comedy ΨΨΨ
Frank Capra film in which Gary Cooper inherits $20 million and is judged insane when he decides to give it all away to needy farmers.

Mr. Jones (1993) Drama/Comedy ΨΨΨ
Richard Gere portrays a bipolar patient treated by a psychiatrist who falls in love with him. This film raises interesting questions about the therapeutic relationship and boundary issues in psychotherapy.

Mumford (1999) Drama ΨΨΨ
A man named Mumford pretending to be a psychologist sets up shop in a small town named Mumford and begins to help the townspeople.

No Time for Sergeants (1958) Comedy Ψ
Andy Griffith stars; Don Knotts plays an Army psychiatrist.

No Way Out (1950) Drama ΨΨΨ
This was Sidney Poitier's first film. Poitier plays a black physician treating two racist hoodlums. When one dies, his brother (Richard Widmark) incites a race riot. The film was one of the earliest serious examinations of racism in postwar America.

Nobody's Child (1986) Biography ΨΨ
Marlo Thomas won an Emmy for her role as a woman who experiences tremendous personal and professional success when she is released after spending 20 years in a mental hospital.

"Oh Jerry, don't let's ask for the moon. We have the stars."

Charlotte Vale addressing her married lover in *Now, Voyager* (1942)

Now, Voyager (1942) Drama ΨΨΨ
Her psychiatrist and inpatient treatment help sexually repressed Bette Davis find meaning and purpose in her life by serving as a surrogate mother for the daughter of a man she loves. The title comes from Walt Whitman's *Leaves of Grass* ("The untold want by life and land ne'er granted / Now voyager sail thou forth to seek and find.")

Nuts (1987) Drama ΨΨΨ
Barbra Streisand plays a prostitute who has killed a patron. She is resisting an insanity defense, and through flashbacks we learn that she was sexually abused as a child. Interesting examination of civil liberties and forensic psychiatry.

"They was giving me ten thousand watts a day, you know, and I'm hot to trot! The next woman takes me on's gonna light up like a pinball machine and pay off in silver dollars!"

Randle P. McMurphy commenting on ECT in *One Flew Over the Cuckoo's Nest* (1975)

Office Space (1999) Comedy Ψ
A hypnotherapist induces a trance in a patient but suffers a heart attack before the patient comes out of the trance.

One Flew Over the Cuckoo's Nest (1975) Drama ΨΨΨΨΨ
Classic film with Jack Nicholson as Randle P. McMurphy, who takes on Nurse Ratched and the psychiatric establishment. The film offers good insight into life on an inpatient ward, although the portrayal of ECT is stereotyped and inaccurate;

in addition, the suicide of Billy seems to be simplistically linked to his domineering mother. This film took all five of the top Oscars in 1975: Best Picture, Best Actor, Best Actress, Best Director, and Best Screenplay.

Passion of Joan of Arc, The (1928) Historical ΨΨΨ
Historically important silent film that portrays the burning of Joan of Arc as a heretic. The mental status of Joan of Arc remains a controversial subject for historians interested in psychopathology.

President's Analyst, The (1967) Spy/Comedy ΨΨ
James Coburn plays a psychoanalyst working for the President of the United States.

Pressure Point (1962) Drama ΨΨΨ
A black psychiatrist (Sidney Poitier) treats a racist patient (Bobby Darin). Based on a case from Linder's *The Fifty-Minute Hour*.

Prime (2005) Drama ΨΨ
A therapist discovers that her patient is having an affair with the therapist's son and fails to disclose this dual relationship.

Prince of Tides, The (1991) Drama/Romance ΨΨΨ
Barbra Streisand plays a psychiatrist who becomes sexually involved with the brother of one of her patients (Nick Nolte). The film raises interesting questions about the proper limits of the doctor-patient relationship.

Quills (2000) Drama ΨΨΨ
Geoffrey Rush stars in this Philip Kaufman film about the notorious French author who is responsible for the word sadism. The film depicts the abuses that occurred in the eighteenth century in the Charenton Insane Asylum, a mental hospital located in the suburbs of Paris. The Marquis de Sade died at Charenton in 1814.

> "I write of the great, eternal truths that bind together all mankind. The whole world over, we eat, we shit, we fuck, we kill and we die."
>
> The Marquis de Sade describes his views on literature in *Quills* (2000)

Rampage (1992) Drama/Thriller ΨΨΨ
William Friedkin film about a sociopath who is arrested and tried for murder. The film raises important questions about capital punishment, the not guilty by reason of insanity (NGRI) plea, and the role of the expert witness in the courtroom.

See You in the Morning (1989) Drama ΨΨ
A film about a Manhattan psychiatrist with multiple problems, including a failed first marriage. Interesting group therapy sequences and lots of speculation about motivation and purpose.

Shock Corridor (1963) Drama ΨΨ
Samuel Fuller film in which a journalist has himself admitted to an insane asylum in order to get an inside story on a murder but soon becomes psychotic himself. The film is better than it sounds.

Shrink (2009) Drama ΨΨΨ
Kevin Spacey plays a burned out therapist who writes popular self-help books and provides therapy for movie stars; however he is depressed after his wife's suicide and increasingly believes that his profession and his life are futile and pointless.

> "Good night and sweet dreams... which we'll analyze in the morning."
>
> *Spellbound* (1945)

Spellbound (1945) Thriller ΨΨΨΨ
Ingrid Bergman plays a psychiatrist treating Gregory Peck's amnesia. Salvador Dali helped design the film's dream sequence. Producer David Selznick wanted the film to be based on his own experiences with psychotherapy and he used his own analyst as a technical advisor. Watch for the Hitchcock cameo.

Still of the Night (1982) Thriller Ψ
A psychiatrist becomes romantically involved with a woman who may have murdered one of his patients.

Teresa (1951) Drama Ψ
Notable only because it stars Rod Steiger in his first role. Steiger plays a psychiatrist in the film.

Through a Glass Darkly (1962) Drama ΨΨΨΨΨ
Classic Bergman film that follows the life of a mentally ill woman after she is treated with ECT and released from a mental hospital.

Tin Cup (1996) Comedy Ψ Ψ
A promiscuous Texas real estate sales person becomes a psychologist and trades off psychotherapy for golf lessons, eventually winding up in bed with the golf pro.

Touched (1983) Romance Ψ
Two patients on a psychiatric ward fall in love and try to set up a life together after they escape.

What About Bob? (1991) Comedy Ψ
Bill Murray plays Bob Wiley, a patient who becomes overly dependent on his therapist, Leo Marvin, played by Bill Murray. The film is very funny, and it raises interesting questions about transference and countertransference. Note the inane discussion of potential psychotropic medications.

"I'm not a shmuck Bob, and I'm not going to let you breeze into town and steal my family away just because you're crazy enough to be fun."

Dr. Leo Marvin to patient Bob Wiley
in *What About Bob?* (1991)

Whispers in the Dark (1992) Thriller/Drama Ψ Ψ
This murder mystery revolves around a psychiatrist who becomes overly involved in the lives of her patients. Mainly useful as a vehicle for discussion of professional issues and lessons on how *not* to behave in therapy.

References

Abbey, A. (2005). Lessons learned and unanswered questions about sexual assault perpetration. *Journal of Interpersonal Violence, 20*(1), 39–42.

Alper, G. (2004). *Like a movie: Contemporary relationships without the popcorn*. St. Paul, MN: Paragon House.

American Psychiatric Association (APA). (1994). *Diagnostic and statistical manual of mental disorders* (4th ed.). Washington, DC: Author.

American Psychiatric Association. (2000). *Diagnostic and statistical manual of mental disorders* (4th ed., text revision). Washington, DC: Author.

Arndt, W. B., Jr. (1991). *Gender disorders and the paraphilias*. Madison, CT: International Universities Press.

Banks, G. (1990). *Kubrick's psychopaths: Society and human nature in the films of Stanely Kubrick*. Found at www.gordonbanks.com/gordon/pubs/kubricks.html, accessed on December 29, 2004.

Barrett, D. (2006). Hypnosis in film and television. *American Journal of Clinical Hypnosis, 49*, 13–30.

Beck, A. (1976). *Cognitive therapy and the emotional disorders*. New York: Meridian.

Beck, A., Steer, R., Beck, J., & Newman, C. (1993). Hopelessness, depression, suicidal ideation, and clinical diagnosis of depression. *Suicide and Life–Threatening Behavior, 23,* 139–145.

Blanchard, R., & Hucker, S. J. (1991). Age, transvestism, bondage, and concurrent paraphilic activities in 117 fatal cases of autoerotic asphyxia. *British Journal of Psychiatry, 159,* 371–377.

Bordwell, D., & Thompson, K. (1993). *Film art: An introduction*. New York: McGraw-Hill.

Briere, J. (1989). University males' sexual interest in children: Predicting potential indices of "pedophilia" in a non-forensic sample. *Child Abuse and Neglect, 13,* 65–75.

Brown, G. R. (1994). Women in relationships with cross-dressing men: A descriptive study from a nonclinical setting. *Archives of Sexual Behavior, 23*(5), 515–30.

Butler, L. D., & Palesh, O. (2004). Spellbound: Dissociation in the movies. *Journal of Trauma & Dissociation, 5*, 61–87.

Canby, V. (1981). Review of *Arthur. New York Times* (July 17, p. 10).

Cape, G. S. (2003). Addiction, stigma and movies. *Acta Psychiatrica Scandinavica, 107*(3), 163–169.

Casson, I. R., Siegel, O., Sham, R., Campbell, E. A., Tarlau, M., & DiDomenico, A. (1984). Brain damage in modern boxers. *The Journal of the American Medical Association, 251,* 2663–2667.

Centers for Disease Control and Prevention (2008). *Morbidity and Morality Weekly Report, 57*(SS–3), 18.

Centers for Disease Control and Prevention (2008). *Morbidity and Morality Weekly Report, 57*(6), 141–144.

Classen, C., Koopman, C., & Spiegel, D. (1993). Trauma and dissociation. *Bulletin of the Menninger Clinic, 57,* 178–194.

de Leo, D., & Heller, T. (2008). Social modeling in the transmission of suicidality. *Crisis: The Journal of Crisis Intervention and Suicide Prevention, 29,* 11–19.

Denzin, N. K. (1991). *Hollywood shot by shot: Alcoholism in American cinema*. New York: Aldine De Gruyter.

Dick, B. F. (2004). *Anatomy of film* (5th ed). Boston: Bedford/St. Martin's.

Dietz, P. E. , & Evans, B. (1982). Pornographic imagery and prevalence of paraphilia. *American Journal of Psychiatry, 139,* 1493–1495.

Fleming, M., & Manvell, R. (1985). *Images of madness: The portrayal of insanity in the feature film*. Rutherford, NJ: Fairleigh Dickinson University Press.

Frese, F. J. (2006). Another beautiful mind – with daughters. [Review of the film *Proof*]. *PsycCRITIQUES: Contemporary Psychology – APA Review of Books*, 51(33). Retrieved from the *PsycCRITIQUES* database (www.apa.org/psyccritiques/) December 1, 2008.

Fullerton, C. S., Ursano, R. J., & Wang, L. (2004). Acute stress disorder, posttraumatic stress disorder, and depression in disaster or rescue workers. *American Journal of Psychiatry, 161*(8), 1370–1376.

Gabbard, K., & Gabbard, G. (1999). *Psychiatry and the cinema*. Washington, DC: American Psychiatric Press.

Geller, J., & Harris, M. (Eds.). (1994*). Women of the asylum: Voices from behind the walls, 1840–1945*. New York: Doubleday.

Giannetti, L. (1993). *Understanding movies*. Englewood Cliffs, NJ: Prentice Hall.

Goffman, E. (1986). *Frame analysis: An essay on the organization of experience*. Boston: Northeastern University Press.

Goldstein, A. (1996). *Violence in America*. Palo Alto, CA: Davies-Black Publishing.

Hacker, K., Collins, J., Gross-Young, L., Almeida, S., & Burke, N. (2008). Coping with youth suicide and overdose: One community's efforts to investigate, intervene, and prevent suicide contagion. *Crisis: The Journal of Crisis Intervention and Suicide Prevention, 29*, 86–95.

Hagglund, K. J. (2005, September 7). Million dollar baby: An Oscar's worth of grit. [Review of the motion picture *Million Dollar Baby*]. *PsycCRITIQUES: Contemporary Psychology – APA Review of Books, 50*(36). Retrieved from the *PsycCRITIQUES* database (www.apa.org/psyccritiques/) April 21, 2009.

Hare, R. D. (2006). Psychopathy: A clinical and forensic overview. *Psychiatric Clinics of North America, 29*, 709–724.

Hiller, W., & Fichter, M. M. (2004). High utilizers of medical care: A crucial subgroup among somatizing patients. *Journal of Psychosomatic Research, 56*(4), 437–443.

Hyler, S. E. (1988). DSM–III at the cinema: Madness in the movies. *Comprehensive Psychiatry, 29*, 195–206.

Hyler, S. E., Gabbard, G. O., & Schneider, I. (1991). Homicidal maniacs and narcissistic parasites: Stigmatization of mentally ill persons in the movies. *Hospital and Community Psychiatry, 42*, 1044–1048.

Jamison, K.R. (1993). *Touched with fire: Manic–depressive illness and the artistic temperament.* New York: Free Press.

Kashdan, T.B. (2009). *Curious? Discover the missing ingredient to a fulfilling life.* New York: William Morrow.

Kieseppa, T., Partonen, T., Haukka, J., Kaprio, J., & Lonnqvist, J. (2004). High concordance of bipolar I disorder in a nationwide sample of twins. *American Journal of Psychiatry, 161*(10), 1814–1821.

Konigsberg, I. (1987). *The complete film dictionary.* New York: Meridian.

Kuo, W. H., Gallo. J. J., & Eaton, W. W. (2004). Hopelessness, depression, substance disorder, and suicidality: A 3-year community-based study. *Social Psychiatry Psychiatric Epidemiology, 39*(6), 497–501.

Lazarus, R. S. (1999). *Stress and emotion: A new synthesis.* New York: Springer.

Lazarus, R. S. (2000). Toward better research on stress and coping. *American Psychologist, 55*(6), 665–673.

Lazarus, R. S. (2001). Relational meaning and discrete emotions. In K. R. Schere, A. Schorr, & T. Johnstone (Eds.), *Appraisal processes in emotion: Theory, methods, research* (pp. 37–67). New York: Oxford University Press.

Ludwig, A. M. (1998). Method and madness in the arts and sciences. *Creativity Research Journal, 11*, 93–101.

Mann, C. E., & Himelein, M. J. (2004). *Psychiatric Services, 55*(2), 185–187.

McCabe, P. (1992). *The butcher boy.* London: Picador.

McDonald, A., & Walter, G. (2001). The portrayal of ECT in American movies. *The Journal of ECT, 17*, 264–274.

McEwen, B. S. (2005). Stessed or stressed out: What is the difference? *Journal of Psychiatry Neuroscience, 30*, 315–318.

Mehlum, L. (2000). The Internet, suicide, and suicide prevention. *Crisis: The Journal of Crisis Intervention and Suicide Prevention, 21*, 186–188.

Micali, N., Chakrabarti, S., & Fombonne, E. (2004). The broad autism phenotype: Findings from an epidemiological survey. *Autism, 8*(1), 21–37.

Mueser, K. T., Salyers, M. P., Rosenberg, S. D., Goodman, L. A., Essock, S. M., Osher, F. C., & Swartz, M. S. (2004). Interpersonal trauma and posttraumatic stress disorder in patients with severe mental illness: Demographic, clinical, and health correlates. *Schizophrenia Bulletin, 30*(1), 45–57.

National Institute of Mental Health. (January, 2001; revised May, 2003). *In harm's way: Suicide in America* (NIH Publication Number 03–4594). Retrieved on December 29, 2004, from the National Institute of Alcohol Abuse and Alcoholism: http://www.nimh.nih.gov/publicat/NIMHharmsway.pdf.

National Institute on Alcohol Abuse and Alcoholism. (July, 1990; revised October 2000). Alcohol Alert. *Children of alcoholics: Are they different?* (NIH Publication Number 09–PH 288). Retrieved on December 29, 2004 from the National Institute of Alcohol Abuse and Alcoholism: http://www.niaaa.nih.gov/publications/aa09.htm.

Niemiec, R. M., & Wedding, D. (2006). The role of the psychotherapist in movies. *Advances in Medical Psychotherapy and Psychodiagnosis, 12*, 73–83.

Niemiec, R. M., & Wedding, D. (2008). *Positive psychology at the movies: Using films to build virtues and character strengths.* Cambridge, MA: Hogrefe & Huber Publishers.

Norcross, J. C., & Norcross, J. (2005, October 2). A distant look at psychotherapeutic intimacy [Review of the motion picture *Intimate Strangers*]. *PsycCRITIQUES: Contemporary Psychology – APA Review of Books, 50*(41). Retrieved from the *PsycCRITIQUES* database (www.apa.org/psyccritiques/) April 21, 2009.

Norcross, J. C., & Norcross, J. (2006, May 24). Psychotherapist conundrum: My son is sleeping with my patient [Review of the motion picture *Prime*]. *PsycCRITIQUES: Contemporary Psychology – APA Review of Books, 51*(21). Retrieved from the *PsycCRITIQUES* database (www.apa.org/psyccritiques/) April 21, 2009.

Norcross, J. C., & Norcross, J. (2007, July 11). The Ubiquitous Number 23 [Review of the motion picture *The Number 23*]. *PsycCRITIQUES: Contemporary Psychology – APA Review of Books, 52*(28). Retrieved from the *PsycCRITIQUES* database (www.apa.org/psyccritiques/) April 21, 2009.

Norden, M. (1994). *The cinema of isolation*. New Brunswick, NJ: Rutgers University Press.

North, C., & Smith, E. (1992). Posttraumatic stress disorder among homeless men and women. *Hospital and Community Psychiatry, 43,* 1010–1016.

Orchowski, L. M., Spickard, B. A., & McNamara, J. R. (2006). Cinema and the valuing of psychotherapy: Implication for clinical practice. *Professional Psychology: Research and Practice, 37,* 506–514.

Owen, P. (2007). Dispelling myths about schizophrenia using film. *Journal of Applied Social Psychology, 37,* 60–75.

Peake, T. H. (2004). *Cinema and life development: Healing lives and training therapists*. Westport, CT: Praeger

Peterson, C., & Seligman, M. E. P. (2004). *Character strengths and virtues: A handbook and classification*. Washington, D.C./New York: American Psychological Association/Oxford University Press.

Piper, A., & Merskey, H. (2004). The persistence of folly: A critical examination of dissociative identity disorder. Part I. The excesses of an improbable concept. *Canadian Journal of Psychiatry, 49*(9), 592–600.

Putnam, F. (1985). Multiple personality disorder. *Medical Aspects of Human Sexuality, 19,* 59–74.

Saunders, E. B., & Awad, G. A. (1991). Male adolescent sexual offenders: Exhibitionism and obscene phone calls. *Child Psychiatry and Human Development, 21*(3), 169–178.

Scahill, L., Hamrin, V., Deering, C., & Pachlar, M. (2008). Psychiatric disorders diagnosed in childhood and adolescence. In M. Boyd (Ed.), *Psychiatric nursing: Contemporary practice* (pp. 633–672). Philadelphia: Lippincott, Williams, & Wilkins.

Seyle, H. (1956). *The stress of life*. New York: McGraw-Hill.

Seyle, H. (1974). *Stress without distress*. Philadelphia: J. B. Lippincott.

Sieff, E. M. (2003). Media frames of mental illnesses: The potential impact of negative frames. *Journal of Mental Health, 12,* 259–269.

Simonton, D. K. (in press). So you *want* to become a creative genius? You *must* be crazy! In D. Cropley, J. Kaufmann, A. Cropley, & M. Runco (Eds.), *The dark side of creativity*. New York: Cambridge University Press.

Steinberg, M. (1991). The spectrum of depersonalization: Assessment and treatment. In A. Tasman & S. Goldfinger (Eds.), *Review of psychiatry, volume 10* (pp. 223–247). Washington, DC: American Psychiatric Press.

Stuart, H. (2003). Violence and mental illness: An overview. *World Psychiatry, 2,* 121–124.

Szymanski, L. S., & Crocker, A. C. (1989). In B. J. Sadock (Ed.), *Comprehensive textbook of psychiatry* (5th ed.). Baltimore, MD: Williams & Wilkins.

Szasz, T. S. (1974). *The myth of mental Illness: Foundations of a theory of personal conduct*, Revised Edition. New York: Harper Row.

Szasz, T. S. (1977). *Psychiatric slavery: When confinement and coercion masquerade as cure*. New York: Free Press.

Taylor, T., & Hsu, M. (2003). *Digital cinema: The Hollywood insider's guide to the evolution of storytelling*. Studio City, CA: Michael Wiese Productions.

Trachtenberg, R. (1986). Destigmatizing mental illness. *The Psychiatric Hospital, 17,* 111–114.

Uhde, T., Tancer, M., Black, B., & Brown, T. (1991). Phenomenology and neurobiology of social phobia: Comparison with panic disorder. *Journal of Clinical Psychiatry, 52,* 31–40.

Van Ameringen, M., Allgulander, C., Bandelow, B., Greist, J. H., Hollander, E., Montgomery, S. A., Nutt, D. J., Okasha, A., Pollack, M. H., Stein, D. J., & Swinson, R. P. (2003). World Council Association recommendations for the long-term treatment of social phobia. *CNS Spectrums, 8*(8 Suppl 1), 40–52.

Veitia, M. C., & McGahee, C. L. (2001). Nicotine and alcohol addiction. In D. Wedding (Ed.) *Behavior and medicine* (3rd Ed.) (pp. 247–261). Göttingen, Germany: Hogrefe & Huber.

Wahl, O., & Lefkowits, J. (1989). Impact of a television film on attitudes toward mental illness. *American Journal of Community Psychology 17 (4)*, 521–528.

Wahl, O. (1995). *Media madness: Public images of mental illness*. New Brunswick, NJ: Rutgers University Press.

Walter, G., McDonald, A., Rey, J., & Rosen, A. (2002). Medical student knowledge and attitudes regarding ECT prior to and after viewing ECT scenes from movies. *Journal of ECT, 18*(1), 43-46.

Wedding, D. (2000). Cognitive distortions in the poetry of Anne Sexton. *Suicide & Life-Threatening Behavior, 30,* 150–154.

Wedding, D. (2001). The portrayal of alcohol and alcoholism in the western genre. *Journal of Alcohol & Drug Education 46*, 3–11.

Wedding, D., & Niemiec, R. (2003). The clinical use of films in psychotherapy. *Journal of Clinical Psychology 59 (2)*, 207–215.

Zhang, L., Ravdin, L. D., Relkin, N., Zimmerman, R. D., Jordan, B., Lathan, W. E., & Ulug, A. M. (2003). Increased diffusion in the brain of professional boxers: A preclinical sign of traumatic brain injury. *American Journal of Neuroradiololgy, 24*(1), 52–57.

Zimmerman, J. N. (2003). *People like ourselves: Portrayals of mental illness in the movies.* Lanham, MD: Scarecrow Press, Inc.

Film Index

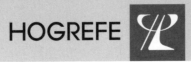